Mini
Service and Repair Manual

John S. Mead MISTC

Models covered

(0646 - 368 - 10AF20)

Mini Saloon, Estate, Van & Pick-up models, including special & limited editions;
848 cc, 998 cc, 1098 cc & 1275 cc
Mini Clubman Saloon & Estate models; 998 cc & 1098 cc
Mini Cooper S Mk III, 1275 GT, 1.3i & Mini Cooper; 1275 cc

Covers mechanical features of Cabriolet
Does not fully cover models fitted with John Cooper performance conversion kits
Does not cover ERA Mini Turbo

© Haynes Publishing 2003

A book in the **Haynes Service and Repair Manual Series**

ABCDE
FGHIJ
KLMN

4

ISBN 1 85960 923 6

British Library Cataloguing in Publication Data
A catalogue record for this book is available from the British Library.

Printed in the USA

Haynes Publishing
Sparkford, Yeovil, Somerset BA22 7JJ, England

Haynes North America, Inc
861 Lawrence Drive, Newbury Park, California 91320, USA

Editions Haynes
4, Rue de l'Abreuvoir,
92415 COURBEVOIE CEDEX, France

Haynes Publishing Nordiska AB
Box 1504, 751 45 UPPSALA, Sverige

Contents

LIVING WITH YOUR MINI

Safety First!   Page   0•5
Introduction to the Mini   Page   0•6

Roadside repairs

If your car won't start   Page   0•7
Jump starting   Page   0•8
Wheel changing   Page   0•9
Identifying leaks   Page   0•10
Towing   Page   0•10

Weekly checks

Introduction   Page   0•11
Underbonnet check points   Page   0•11
Engine oil level   Page   0•12
Coolant level   Page   0•13
Brake fluid level   Page   0•14
Clutch fluid level   Page   0•14
Battery   Page   0•15
Screen washer fluid level   Page   0•15
Wiper blades   Page   0•16
Electrical systems   Page   0•16
Tyre condition and pressure   Page   0•17

Lubricants and fluids

Page   0•18

Tyre pressures

Page   0•18

MAINTENANCE

Routine Maintenance and Servicing

Servicing specifications   Page   1•2
Maintenance schedule   Page   1•3
Maintenance procedures   Page   1•7

Contents

REPAIRS AND OVERHAUL

Engine and Associated Systems

Engine in-car repair procedures – pre-October 1996 models	Page **2A•1**
Engine in-car repair procedures – October 1996 models onward	Page **2B•1**
Engine removal and overhaul procedures	Page **2C•1**
Cooling, heating and ventilation systems	Page **3•1**
Fuel system – carburettor engines	Page **4A•1**
Fuel system – single-point fuel injection engines	Page **4B•1**
Fuel system – multi-point fuel injection engines	Page **4C•1**
Exhaust and emission control systems	Page **4D•1**
Starting and charging systems	Page **5A•1**
Distributor ignition system	Page **5B•1**
Distributorless ignition system	Page **5C•1**

Transmission

Clutch	Page **6•1**
Manual transmission	Page **7A•1**
Automatic transmission	Page **7B•1**
Driveshafts	Page **8•1**

Brakes and Suspension

Braking system	Page **9•1**
Suspension and steering	Page **10•1**

Body Equipment

Bodywork and fittings – pre-October 1996 models	Page **11A•1**
Bodywork and fittings – October 1996 models onward	Page **11B•1**
Body electrical system – pre-October 1996 models	Page **12A•1**
Body electrical system – October 1996 models onward	Page **12B•1**

Wiring Diagrams

Pre-October 1996 models	Page **12A•17**
October 1996 models onwards	Page **12B•12**

REFERENCE

Dimensions and weights	Page **REF•1**
Conversion factors	Page **REF•2**
Buying spare parts	Page **REF•3**
Vehicle identification	Page **REF•3**
General repair procedures	Page **REF•4**
Jacking and vehicle support	Page **REF•5**
Disconnecting the battery	Page **REF•5**
Tools and working facilities	Page **REF•6**
MOT test checks	Page **REF•8**
Fault finding	Page **REF•12**
Glossary of technical terms	Page **REF•21**

Index

Index	Page **REF•26**

Advanced driving

Many people see the words 'advanced driving' and believe that it won't interest them or that it is a style of driving beyond their own abilities. Nothing could be further from the truth. Advanced driving is straightforward safe, sensible driving - the sort of driving we should all do every time we get behind the wheel.

An average of 10 people are killed every day on UK roads and 870 more are injured, some seriously. Lives are ruined daily, usually because somebody did something stupid. Something like 95% of all accidents are due to human error, mostly driver failure. Sometimes we make genuine mistakes - everyone does. Sometimes we have lapses of concentration. Sometimes we deliberately take risks.

For many people, the process of 'learning to drive' doesn't go much further than learning how to pass the driving test because of a common belief that good drivers are made by 'experience'.

Learning to drive by 'experience' teaches three driving skills:

☐ Quick reactions. (Whoops, that was close!)
☐ Good handling skills. (Horn, swerve, brake, horn).
☐ Reliance on vehicle technology. (Great stuff this ABS, stop in no distance even in the wet...)

Drivers whose skills are 'experience based' generally have a lot of near misses and the odd accident. The results can be seen every day in our courts and our hospital casualty departments.

Advanced drivers have learnt to control the risks by controlling the position and speed of their vehicle. They avoid accidents and near misses, even if the drivers around them make mistakes.

The key skills of advanced driving are **concentration,** effective all-round **observation, anticipation** and **planning.** When **good vehicle handling** is added to these skills, all driving situations can be approached and negotiated in a safe, methodical way, leaving nothing to chance.

Concentration means applying your mind to safe driving, completely excluding anything that's not relevant. Driving is usually the most dangerous activity that most of us undertake in our daily routines. It deserves our full attention.

Observation means not just looking, but seeing and seeking out the information found in the driving environment.

Anticipation means asking yourself what is happening, what you can reasonably expect to happen and what could happen unexpectedly. (One of the commonest words used in compiling accident reports is 'suddenly'.)

Planning is the link between seeing something and taking the appropriate action. For many drivers, planning is the missing link.

If you want to become a safer and more skilful driver and you want to enjoy your driving more, contact the Institute of Advanced Motorists at www.iam.org.uk, phone 0208 996 9600, or write to IAM House, 510 Chiswick High Road, London W4 5RG for an information pack.

Working on your car can be dangerous. This page shows just some of the potential risks and hazards, with the aim of creating a safety-conscious attitude.

General hazards

Scalding

• Don't remove the radiator or expansion tank cap while the engine is hot.
• Engine oil, automatic transmission fluid or power steering fluid may also be dangerously hot if the engine has recently been running.

Burning

• Beware of burns from the exhaust system and from any part of the engine. Brake discs and drums can also be extremely hot immediately after use.

Crushing

• When working under or near a raised vehicle, always supplement the jack with axle stands, or use drive-on ramps. *Never venture under a car which is only supported by a jack.*

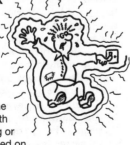

• Take care if loosening or tightening high-torque nuts when the vehicle is on stands. Initial loosening and final tightening should be done with the wheels on the ground.

Fire

• Fuel is highly flammable; fuel vapour is explosive.
• Don't let fuel spill onto a hot engine.
• Do not smoke or allow naked lights (including pilot lights) anywhere near a vehicle being worked on. Also beware of creating sparks (electrically or by use of tools).
• Fuel vapour is heavier than air, so don't work on the fuel system with the vehicle over an inspection pit.
• Another cause of fire is an electrical overload or short-circuit. Take care when repairing or modifying the vehicle wiring.
• Keep a fire extinguisher handy, of a type suitable for use on fuel and electrical fires.

Electric shock

• Ignition HT voltage can be dangerous, especially to people with heart problems or a pacemaker. Don't work on or near the ignition system with the engine running or the ignition switched on.

• Mains voltage is also dangerous. Make sure that any mains-operated equipment is correctly earthed. Mains power points should be protected by a residual current device (RCD) circuit breaker.

Fume or gas intoxication

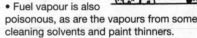

• Exhaust fumes are poisonous; they often contain carbon monoxide, which is rapidly fatal if inhaled. Never run the engine in a confined space such as a garage with the doors shut.
• Fuel vapour is also poisonous, as are the vapours from some cleaning solvents and paint thinners.

Poisonous or irritant substances

• Avoid skin contact with battery acid and with any fuel, fluid or lubricant, especially antifreeze, brake hydraulic fluid and Diesel fuel. Don't syphon them by mouth. If such a substance is swallowed or gets into the eyes, seek medical advice.
• Prolonged contact with used engine oil can cause skin cancer. Wear gloves or use a barrier cream if necessary. Change out of oil-soaked clothes and do not keep oily rags in your pocket.
• Air conditioning refrigerant forms a poisonous gas if exposed to a naked flame (including a cigarette). It can also cause skin burns on contact.

Asbestos

• Asbestos dust can cause cancer if inhaled or swallowed. Asbestos may be found in gaskets and in brake and clutch linings. When dealing with such components it is safest to assume that they contain asbestos.

Special hazards

Hydrofluoric acid

• This extremely corrosive acid is formed when certain types of synthetic rubber, found in some O-rings, oil seals, fuel hoses etc, are exposed to temperatures above 400ºC. The rubber changes into a charred or sticky substance containing the acid. *Once formed, the acid remains dangerous for years. If it gets onto the skin, it may be necessary to amputate the limb concerned.*
• When dealing with a vehicle which has suffered a fire, or with components salvaged from such a vehicle, wear protective gloves and discard them after use.

The battery

• Batteries contain sulphuric acid, which attacks clothing, eyes and skin. Take care when topping-up or carrying the battery.
• The hydrogen gas given off by the battery is highly explosive. Never cause a spark or allow a naked light nearby. Be careful when connecting and disconnecting battery chargers or jump leads.

Air bags

• Air bags can cause injury if they go off accidentally. Take care when removing the steering wheel and/or facia. Special storage instructions may apply.

Diesel injection equipment

• Diesel injection pumps supply fuel at very high pressure. Take care when working on the fuel injectors and fuel pipes.

⚠ *Warning: Never expose the hands, face or any other part of the body to injector spray; the fuel can penetrate the skin with potentially fatal results.*

Remember...

DO

• Do use eye protection when using power tools, and when working under the vehicle.

• Do wear gloves or use barrier cream to protect your hands when necessary.

• Do get someone to check periodically that all is well when working alone on the vehicle.

• Do keep loose clothing and long hair well out of the way of moving mechanical parts.

• Do remove rings, wristwatch etc, before working on the vehicle – especially the electrical system.

• Do ensure that any lifting or jacking equipment has a safe working load rating adequate for the job.

DON'T

• Don't attempt to lift a heavy component which may be beyond your capability – get assistance.

• Don't rush to finish a job, or take unverified short cuts.

• Don't use ill-fitting tools which may slip and cause injury.

• Don't leave tools or parts lying around where someone can trip over them. Mop up oil and fuel spills at once.

• Don't allow children or pets to play in or near a vehicle being worked on.

Mini 850 Saloon

Introduction to the Mini

The brainchild of Sir Alec Issigonis, the Mini was first sold in Britain in August 1959. With its transverse engine and front-wheel drive, it represented a radical departure from the traditional range of domestically produced small cars. The fact that it is still selling well, forty-odd years after its introduction is a tribute to the fundamental soundness of what appeared, at first, to be a somewhat unorthodox design.

Mini models covered by this manual are powered by the well-proven A-series engine in 848 cc, 998 cc, 1098 cc and 1275 cc forms.

The engine crankcase is bolted directly to the transmission casing, which also serves as the sump since the two units share the same oil supply. The manual transmission is of the four-speed all synchromesh type, with a four-speed automatic version being available as an option.

Power to the driveshafts is transmitted via the differential, which is also housed in the transmission casing. The driveshafts have a universal joint at each end, the outer joints being of the Birfield constant velocity type, while at the inner end either a Hooke type or constant velocity type joint may be fitted.

The hydraulic braking system utilises drum brakes on all wheels, with the exception of the high performance Cooper S and 1275 GT versions and 1984-on models, which are equipped with disc brakes at the front. A dual circuit hydraulic system is used on all later models.

The rack-and-pinion steering gear and fully independent suspension provide the Mini with the safe, positive handling characteristics which have endeared this car to so many people since the first models were produced.

Your Mini Manual

The aim of this manual is to help you get the best value from your vehicle. It can do so in several ways. It can help you decide what work must be done (even should you choose to get it done by a garage), provide information on routine maintenance and servicing, and give a logical course of action and diagnosis when random faults occur. However, it is hoped that you will use the manual by tackling the work yourself. On simpler jobs it may even be quicker than booking the car into a garage and going there twice, to leave and collect it. Perhaps most important, a lot of money can be saved by avoiding the costs a garage must charge to cover its labour and overheads.

The manual has drawings and descriptions to show the function of the various components so that their layout can be understood. Tasks are described and photographed in a clear step-by-step sequence.

References to the 'left' or 'right' of the vehicle are in the sense of a person in the driving seat, facing forwards.

Acknowledgements

Thanks are also due to Draper Tools Limited, who provided some of the workshop tools, and to all those people at Sparkford who helped in the production of this manual.

We take great pride in the accuracy of information given in this manual, but vehicle manufacturers make alterations and design changes during the production run of a particular vehicle of which they do not inform us. No liability can be accepted by the authors or publishers for loss, damage or injury caused by any errors in, or omissions from the information given.

Mini Clubman Estate

The following pages are intended to help in dealing with common roadside emergencies and breakdowns. You will find more detailed fault finding information at the back of the manual, and repair information in the main chapters.

If your car won't start and the starter motor doesn't turn

☐ If it's a model with automatic transmission, make sure the selector is in P or N.
☐ Make sure that the battery terminals are clean and tight.
☐ Switch on the headlights and try to start the engine. If the headlights go very dim when you're trying to start, the battery is probably flat. Try jump starting (see next page) using a another car.

If your car won't start even though the starter motor turns as normal

☐ Is there fuel in the tank?
☐ Is there moisture on electrical components under the bonnet? Switch off the ignition, then wipe off any obvious dampness with a dry cloth. Spray a water-repellent aerosol product (WD-40 or equivalent) on ignition and fuel system electrical connectors like those shown in the photos. Pay special attention to the ignition coil wiring connector and HT leads.

A Check that the spark plug HT leads are securely connected to the spark plugs.

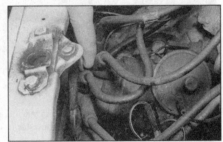

B Also check that the leads are secure in the distributor cap or DIS ignition module.

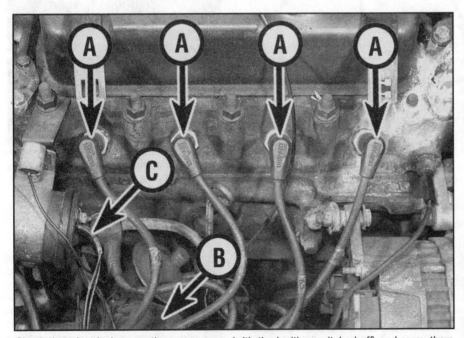

Check that electrical connections are secure (with the ignition switched off) and spray them with a water dispersant if you suspect a problem due to damp

C Check that all ignition wiring connectors such as this at the ignition coil are securely connected.

D Check the security and condition of the battery terminals.

HAYNES HiNT

Jump starting will get you out of trouble, but you must correct whatever made the battery go flat in the first place. There are three possibilities:

1 *The battery has been drained by repeated attempts to start, or by leaving the lights on.*

2 *The charging system is not working properly (alternator drivebelt slack or broken, alternator wiring fault or alternator itself faulty).*

3 *The battery itself is at fault (electrolyte low, or battery worn out).*

When jump-starting a car using a booster battery, observe the following precautions:

✔ Before connecting the booster battery, make sure that the ignition is switched off.

✔ Ensure that all electrical equipment (lights, heater, wipers, etc) is switched off.

✔ Take note of any special precautions printed on the battery case.

Jump starting

✔ Make sure that the booster battery is the same voltage as the discharged one in the vehicle.

✔ If the battery is being jump-started from the battery in another vehicle, the two vehicles MUST NOT TOUCH each other.

✔ Make sure that the transmission is in neutral (or PARK, in the case of automatic transmission).

1 Connect one end of the red jump lead to the positive (+) terminal of the flat battery

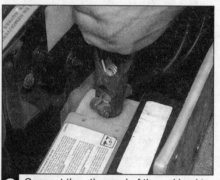

2 Connect the other end of the red lead to the positive (+) terminal of the booster battery.

3 Connect one end of the black jump lead to the negative (-) terminal of the booster battery

4 Connect the other end of the black jump lead to a bolt or bracket on the engine block, well away from the battery, on the vehicle to be started.

5 Make sure that the jump leads will not come into contact with the fan, drive-belts or other moving parts of the engine.

6 Start the engine using the booster battery and run it at idle speed. Switch on the lights, rear window demister and heater blower motor, then disconnect the jump leads in the reverse order of connection. Turn off the lights etc.

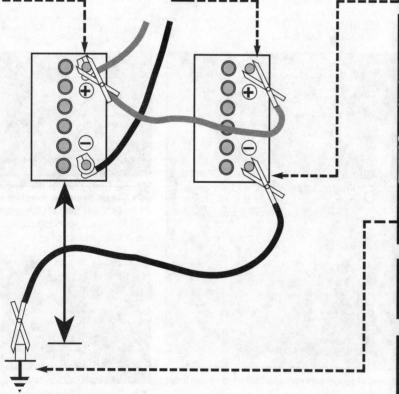

Wheel changing

Some of the details shown here will vary according to model. For instance, the location of the spare wheel and jack is not the same on all cars. However, the basic principles apply to all vehicles.

 Warning: Do not change a wheel in a situation where you risk being hit by other traffic. On busy roads, try to stop in a lay-by or a gateway. Be wary of passing traffic while changing the wheel - it is easy to become distracted by the job in hand.

Preparation

- ☐ When a puncture occurs, stop as soon as it is safe to do so.
- ☐ Park on firm level ground, if possible, and well out of the way of other traffic.
- ☐ Use hazard warning lights if necessary.

- ☐ If you have one, use a warning triangle to alert other drivers of your presence.
- ☐ Apply the handbrake and engage first or reverse gear (or Park on models with automatic transmission).

- ☐ Chock the wheel diagonally opposite the one being removed – a couple of large stones will do for this.
- ☐ If the ground is soft, use a flat piece of wood to spread the load under the jack.

Changing the wheel

1 Lift up the luggage compartment trim (where necessary) and remove the spare wheel and tools from their location (Saloon model shown).

2 Remove the wheel centre trim (where fitted), either by pulling it straight off (plastic trim) or by prising off the steel trim.

3 Slacken each wheel nut by half a turn using the wheel brace in the tool kit. On later models you will need to use the special adapter in the tool kit to slacken the locking wheel nuts.

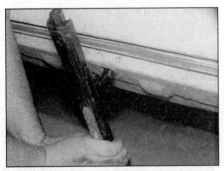

4 Position the jack head under the reinforced jacking point on the sill nearest the wheel to be removed. Note that the jack supplied with Estate, Van and Pick-Up models is designed to bear on the subframe. With the base of the jack on firm ground, turn the jack handle clockwise until the wheel is raised clear of the ground. Unscrew the wheel nuts and remove the wheel.

5 Fit the spare wheel, and screw in the nuts. Lightly tighten the nuts with the wheelbrace then lower the vehicle to the ground.

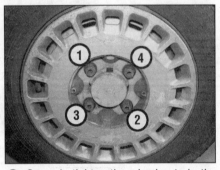

6 Securely tighten the wheel nuts in the sequence shown then refit the wheel trim cap. Stow the punctured wheel and tools back in the luggage compartment and secure them in position. Note that the wheel nuts should be slackened and then retightened to the specified torque at the earliest opportunity (see Chapter 1).

Finally...

- ☐ Remove the wheel chocks.

- ☐ Check the tyre pressure on the wheel just fitted. If it is low, or if you don't have a pressure gauge with you, drive slowly to the nearest garage and inflate the tyre to the right pressure.

- ☐ Have the damaged tyre or wheel repaired as soon as possible.

Identifying leaks

Puddles on the garage floor or drive, or obvious wetness under the bonnet or underneath the car, suggest a leak that needs investigating. It can sometimes be difficult to decide where the leak is coming from, especially if the engine bay is very dirty already. Leaking oil or fluid can also be blown rearwards by the passage of air under the car, giving a false impression of where the problem lies.

 Warning: Most automotive oils and fluids are poisonous. Wash them off skin, and change out of contaminated clothing, without delay.

 The smell of a fluid leaking from the car may provide a clue to what's leaking. Some fluids are distinctively coloured. It may help to clean the car carefully and to park it over some clean paper overnight as an aid to locating the source of the leak. Remember that some leaks may only occur while the engine is running.

Engine/transmission plug

Engine/transmission oil may leak from the drain plug . . .

Driveshaft flange

. . . from a faulty driveshaft flange oil seal . . .

Selector shaft

. . . or from a faulty selector shaft oil seal.

Antifreeze

Leaking antifreeze often leaves a crystalline deposit like this.

Brake fluid

A leak occurring at a wheel is almost certainly brake fluid.

Towing

When all else fails, you may find yourself having to get a tow home – or of course you may be helping somebody else. Long-distance recovery should only be done by a garage or breakdown service. For shorter distances, DIY towing using another car is easy enough, but observe the following points:

☐ Use a proper tow-rope – they are not expensive. The vehicle being towed must display an ON TOW sign in its rear window.

☐ Always turn the ignition key to the 'on' position when the vehicle is being towed, so that the steering lock is released, and that the direction indicator and brake lights will work.

☐ Only attach the tow-rope to the towing eyes provided.

☐ Before being towed, release the handbrake and select neutral on the transmission. **Note:** *On models with automatic transmission, only a suspended tow, with the front wheels clear of the ground is permitted. Due to lack of lubrication without the engine running, transmission damage will result if the car is towed with all four wheels on the ground*

☐ Note that on later models, greater-than-usual pedal pressure will be required to operate the brakes, since the vacuum servo unit is only operational with the engine running.

☐ The driver of the car being towed must keep the tow-rope taut at all times to avoid snatching.

☐ Make sure that both drivers know the route before setting off.

☐ Only drive at moderate speeds and keep the distance towed to a minimum. Drive smoothly and allow plenty of time for slowing down at junctions.

Introduction

There are some very simple checks which need only take a few minutes to carry out, but which could save you a lot of inconvenience and expense.

These *Weekly checks* require no great skill or special tools, and the small amount of time they take to perform could prove to be very well spent, for example;

☐ Keeping an eye on tyre condition and pressures, will not only help to stop them wearing out prematurely, but could also save your life.

☐ Many breakdowns are caused by electrical problems. Battery-related faults are particularly common, and a quick check on a regular basis will often prevent the majority of these.

☐ If your car develops a brake fluid leak, the first time you might know about it is when your brakes don't work properly. Checking the level regularly will give advance warning of this kind of problem.

☐ If the oil or coolant levels run low, the cost of repairing any engine damage will be far greater than fixing the leak, for example.

Underbonnet check points

◀ **998 cc carburettor engine**

A *Engine/transmission oil level dipstick*

B *Engine/transmission oil filler cap*

C *Radiator pressure cap*

D *Brake fluid reservoir*

E *Clutch fluid reservoir*

F *Screen washer fluid reservoir*

Engine oil level

Before you start
✔ Make sure that your car is on level ground.
✔ Check the oil level before the car is driven, or at least 5 minutes after the engine has been switched off.

HAYNES HINT *If the oil is checked immediately after driving the vehicle, some of the oil will remain in the upper engine components, resulting in an inaccurate reading on the dipstick.*

The correct oil
Modern engines place great demands on their oil. It is very important that the correct oil for your car is used (See 'Lubricants, fluids and tyre pressures' on page 0•18).

Car Care
● If you have to add oil frequently, you should check whether you have any oil leaks. Place some clean paper under the car overnight, and check for stains in the morning. If there are no leaks, the engine may be burning oil.

● Always maintain the level between the upper and lower dipstick marks (see photo 3). If the level is too low severe engine damage may occur. Oil seal failure may result if the engine is overfilled by adding too much oil.

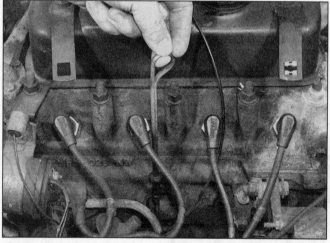

1 The dipstick is located at the front of the engine (see *Underbonnet check points* for exact location). Withdraw the dipstick.

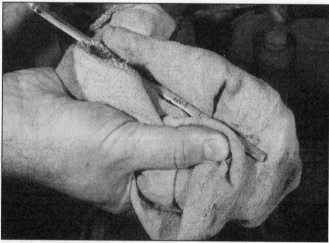

2 Using a clean rag or paper towel remove all oil from the dipstick. Insert the clean dipstick back into the engine as far as it will go, then withdraw it again.

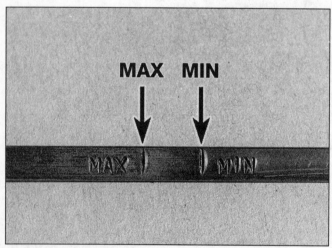

MAX   MIN

3 Note the oil level on the end of the dipstick which should be between the upper (MAX) mark and lower (MIN) mark. Approximately 0.5 litres of oil will raise the level from the lower to the upper marks.

4 Oil is added through the filler on the rocker cover. Unscrew the filler cap and top-up the level; a funnel may help to reduce spillage. Add the oil slowly, checking the level on the dipstick frequently. Avoid overfilling (see *Car Care*).

Coolant level

 Warning: DO NOT attempt to remove the radiator or expansion tank pressure cap when the engine is hot, as there is a very great risk of scalding. Do not leave open containers of coolant about, as it is poisonous.

Car Care

● Adding coolant should not be necessary on a regular basis. If frequent topping-up is required, it is likely there is a leak. Check the radiator, all hoses and joint faces for signs of staining or wetness, and rectify as necessary.

● It is important that antifreeze is used in the cooling system all year round, not just during the winter months. This is due to its cooling and anti-corrosion properties. Do not top-up with water alone, as the antifreeze will become too diluted.

1 To check the coolant level, **wait until the engine is cold.** Turn the radiator pressure cap slowly anti-clockwise and wait until any pressure in the system is released. Once any pressure is released, unscrew it fully and lift it off.

2 Later models are fitted with an expansion tank located separately from the radiator. Unscrew the expansion tank cap in the same way as the radiator pressure cap.

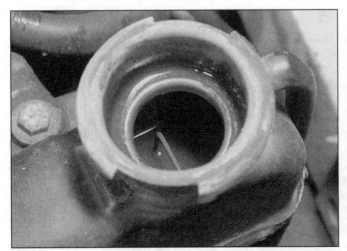

3 The coolant level varies with engine temperature. When cold, the coolant should just cover the wire bridge inside the radiator. When hot, the level may rise slightly above the bridge. On later models with an expansion tank, the coolant level should be up to the horizontal seam half way up the side of the tank, when the engine is cold.

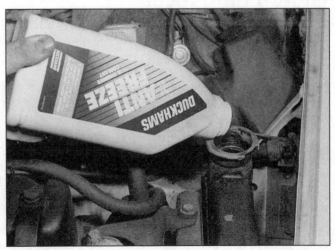

4 If topping-up is necessary, add a mixture of water and antifreeze through the radiator or expansion tank filler neck until the coolant is at the correct level. Refit the cap, turning it clockwise as far as it will go to secure.

Brake fluid level

Warning:
● Brake fluid can harm your eyes and damage painted surfaces, so use extreme caution when handling and pouring it.

● Do not use fluid that has been standing open for some time, as it absorbs moisture from the air, which can cause a dangerous loss of braking effectiveness.

HAYNES HINT
• Make sure that your car is on level ground.
• The fluid level in the reservoir will drop slightly as the brake pads wear down, but the fluid level must never be allowed to drop below the MIN mark.

Safety First!

● If the reservoir requires repeated topping-up this is an indication of a fluid leak somewhere in the system, which should be investigated immediately.

● If a leak is suspected, the car should not be driven until the braking system has been checked. Never take any risks where brakes are concerned.

1 On early models the level can be checked by unscrewing the filler cap and looking into the reservoir; the level should be up to the filler neck. On later models, MAX and MIN marks are indicated on the side of the reservoir. The fluid level must be kept between the marks.

3 Unscrew the reservoir cap and carefully lift it out of position. Where a level indicator is fitted, it will be easier if the two wires on the cap are first disconnected. Inspect the reservoir, if the fluid is dirty, the hydraulic system should be drained and refilled (see Chapter 1).

2 If topping-up is necessary, first wipe the area around the filler cap with a clean rag before removing the cap. This will prevent dirt entering the system.

4 Carefully add fluid, taking care not to spill it on surrounding components. Use only the specified hydraulic fluid; mixing different types of fluid can cause damage to the system. After topping-up to the correct level, refit the cap securely and wipe off any spilt fluid. Reconnect the level indicator wires if they were disconnected.

Clutch fluid level

Before you start

✔ Park the vehicle on level ground.
✔ The engine should be turned off.

Safety First!

● The need for frequent topping-up indicates a leak, which should be investigated immediately.

Warning: Brake/clutch hydraulic fluid can harm your eyes and damage painted surfaces, so use extreme caution when handling and pouring it.

1 The clutch master cylinder and reservoir is located on the engine compartment bulkhead. Wipe the area around the filler cap with a clean rag then unscrew the cap. The level can be checked by looking into the reservoir; the fluid should be up to the filler neck.

2 Later models have a transparent reservoir with MAX and MIN markings on the side. The fluid level should be maintained between these marks.

3 If topping-up is necessary, carefully add fluid, taking care not to spill it on surrounding components. Using a funnel makes this much easier. Use only the specified hydraulic fluid; mixing different types of fluid can cause damage to the system. After topping-up to the correct level, refit the cap securely and wipe off any spilt fluid.

Battery

Caution: Before carrying out any work on the vehicle battery, read the precautions given in 'Safety first' at the start of this manual.

✔ Make sure that the battery tray is in good condition, and that the clamp is tight. Corrosion on the tray, retaining clamp and the battery itself can be removed with a solution of water and baking soda. Thoroughly rinse all cleaned areas with water. Any metal parts damaged by corrosion should be covered with a zinc-based primer, then painted.

✔ Periodically (approximately every three months), check the charge condition of the battery as described in Chapter 5A.

✔ If the battery is flat, and you need to jump start your vehicle, see *Roadside Repairs*.

1 The battery is located in the boot on Saloon models, beneath the rear seat on Estate models or behind the passenger seat on Van and Pick-up models. Release the strap and lift off the cover to gain access. The exterior of the battery should be inspected periodically for damage such as a cracked case or cover.

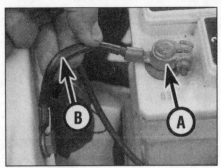

2 Check the tightness of battery clamps (A) to ensure good electrical connections. You should not be able to move them. Also check each cable (B) for cracks and frayed conductors.

HAYNES HINT

Battery corrosion can be kept to a minimum by applying a layer of petroleum jelly to the clamps and terminals after they are reconnected.

3 If corrosion (white, fluffy deposits) is evident, remove the cables from the battery terminals, clean them with a small wire brush, then refit them. Automotive stores sell a tool for cleaning the battery post . . .

4 . . . as well as the battery cable clamps

Screen washer fluid level

Screenwash additives not only keep the winscreen clean during foul weather, they also prevent the washer system freezing in cold weather - which is when you are likely to need it most. Don't top up using plain water as the screenwash will become too diluted, and will freeze during cold weather. *On no account use coolant antifreeze in the washer system - this could discolour or damage paintwork.*

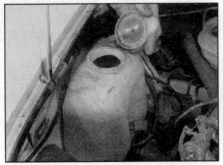

1 The washer fluid reservoir is located at the rear or front right-hand side of the engine compartment, or in the boot. Release the cap and observe the level in the reservoir by looking down the filler neck.

2 When topping-up the reservoir, a screen-wash additive should be added in the quantities recommended on the bottle.

Wiper blades

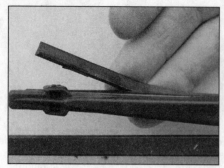

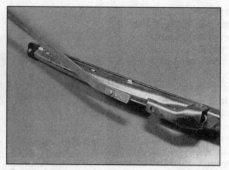

1 Check the condition of the wiper blades; if they are cracked or show any signs of deterioration, or if the glass swept area is smeared, renew them. Wiper blades should be renewed annually.

2 To remove a windscreen wiper blade, pull the arm fully away from the glass until it locks. On early models, ease back the small metal clip that secures the blade to the arm and slide the blade off the arm. On later models, swivel the blade through 90º, press the locking tab with your fingers and slide the blade out of the arm's hooked end.

Electrical systems

✔ Check all external lights and the horn. Refer to the appropriate Parts of Chapter 12 for details if any of the circuits are found to be inoperative.

✔ Visually check all accessible wiring connectors, harnesses and retaining clips for security, and for signs of chafing or damage.

 If you need to check your brake lights and indicators unaided, back up to a wall or garage door and operate the lights. The reflected light should show if they are working properly.

1 If a single indicator light, stop-light or headlight has failed it is likely that a bulb has blown and will need to be replaced. Refer to the relevant Part of Chapter 12 for details. If both stop-lights have failed, it is possible that the stop-light switch is faulty or needs adjusting (see the appropriate part of Chapter 12).

2 If more than one indicator light or headlight has failed it is likely that either a fuse has blown or that there is a fault in the circuit (see the appropriate part of Chapter 12). The fuses on most models are located in the fuseblock situated in the engine compartment. Lift off the cover to inspect the fuses.

3 On later models the fuseblock is located inside the car under the facia on the driver's side. Use a coin to turn the cover retaining screw a quarter turn left or right and lift off the cover.

4 To replace a blown fuse, simply pull it out from its contacts in the fuseblock. Fit a new fuse of the same rating (see the appropriate part of Chapter 12). If the fuse blows again, it is important that you find out why – a complete checking procedure is given in the appropriate part of Chapter 12.

Tyre condition and pressure

It is very important that tyres are in good condition, and at the correct pressure - having a tyre failure at any speed is highly dangerous. Tyre wear is influenced by driving style - harsh braking and acceleration, or fast cornering, will all produce more rapid tyre wear. As a general rule, the front tyres wear out faster than the rears. Interchanging the tyres from front to rear ("rotating" the tyres) may result in more even wear. However, if this is completely effective, you may have the expense of replacing all four tyres at once! Remove any nails or stones embedded in the tread before they penetrate the tyre to cause deflation. If removal of a nail does reveal that

the tyre has been punctured, refit the nail so that its point of penetration is marked. Then immediately change the wheel, and have the tyre repaired by a tyre dealer.

Regularly check the tyres for damage in the form of cuts or bulges, especially in the sidewalls. Periodically remove the wheels, and clean any dirt or mud from the inside and outside surfaces. Examine the wheel rims for signs of rusting, corrosion or other damage. Light alloy wheels are easily damaged by "kerbing" whilst parking; steel wheels may also become dented or buckled. A new wheel is very often the only way to overcome severe damage.

New tyres should be balanced when they are fitted, but it may become necessary to re-balance them as they wear, or if the balance weights fitted to the wheel rim should fall off. Unbalanced tyres will wear more quickly, as will the steering and suspension components. Wheel imbalance is normally signified by vibration, particularly at a certain speed (typically around 50 mph). If this vibration is felt only through the steering, then it is likely that just the front wheels need balancing. If, however, the vibration is felt through the whole car, the rear wheels could be out of balance. Wheel balancing should be carried out by a tyre dealer or garage.

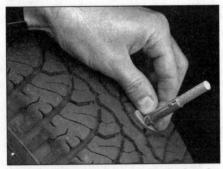

1 Tread Depth - visual check
The original tyres have tread wear safety bands (B), which will appear when the tread depth reaches approximately 1.6 mm. The band positions are indicated by a triangular mark on the tyre sidewall (A).

2 Tread Depth - manual check
Alternatively, tread wear can be monitored with a simple, inexpensive device known as a tread depth indicator gauge.

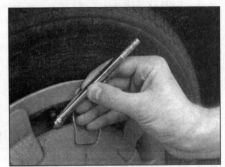

3 Tyre Pressure Check
Check the tyre pressures regularly with the tyres cold. Do not adjust the tyre pressures immediately after the vehicle has been used, or an inaccurate setting will result. Tyre pressures are shown on page 0•18.

Tyre tread wear patterns

Shoulder Wear

Underinflation (wear on both sides)
Under-inflation will cause overheating of the tyre, because the tyre will flex too much, and the tread will not sit correctly on the road surface. This will cause a loss of grip and excessive wear, not to mention the danger of sudden tyre failure due to heat build-up.
Check and adjust pressures
Incorrect wheel camber (wear on one side)
Repair or renew suspension parts
Hard cornering
Reduce speed!

Centre Wear

Overinflation
Over-inflation will cause rapid wear of the centre part of the tyre tread, coupled with reduced grip, harsher ride, and the danger of shock damage occurring in the tyre casing.
Check and adjust pressures

If you sometimes have to inflate your car's tyres to the higher pressures specified for maximum load or sustained high speed, don't forget to reduce the pressures to normal afterwards.

Uneven Wear

Front tyres may wear unevenly as a result of wheel misalignment. Most tyre dealers and garages can check and adjust the wheel alignment (or "tracking") for a modest charge.
Incorrect camber or castor
Repair or renew suspension parts
Malfunctioning suspension
Repair or renew suspension parts
Unbalanced wheel
Balance tyres
Incorrect toe setting
Adjust front wheel alignment
Note: *The feathered edge of the tread which typifies toe wear is best checked by feel.*

Lubricants and fluids

Engine/transmission	Multigrade engine oil, viscosity SAE 10W/40 to API SH and ACEA-A2.96
Cooling system*	Ethylene glycol-based antifreeze and soft water
Carburettor dashpot	Multigrade engine oil, viscosity SAE 10W/40 to API SH and ACEA-A2.96
Clutch system	Brake and clutch fluid to DOT 4+ or DOT 4
Braking system	Brake and clutch fluid to DOT 4+ or DOT 4
Suspension and steering lubrication points	General-purpose lithium-based grease
Handbrake cable guides, sectors and linkage	General-purpose lithium-based grease
Hub bearings	General-purpose lithium-based grease

Later models (from the end of 1999 approximately) use a new orange-coloured long-life antifreeze of a different formula to the blue-green type previously specified. The antifreeze types must not be mixed; seek the advice of a Rover dealer if in any doubt as to the type of antifreeze to obtain.

Choosing your engine oil

Engines need oil, not only to lubricate moving parts and minimise wear, but also to maximise power output and to improve fuel economy.

HOW ENGINE OIL WORKS

• Beating friction

Without oil, the moving surfaces inside your engine will rub together, heat up and melt, quickly causing the engine to seize. Engine oil creates a film which separates these moving parts, preventing wear and heat build-up.

• Cooling hot-spots

Temperatures inside the engine can exceed 1000° C. The engine oil circulates and acts as a coolant, transferring heat from the hot-spots to the sump.

• Cleaning the engine internally

Good quality engine oils clean the inside of your engine, collecting and dispersing combustion deposits and controlling them until they are trapped by the oil filter or flushed out at oil change.

OIL CARE - FOLLOW THE CODE

To handle and dispose of used engine oil safely, always:

- **Avoid skin contact with used engine oil. Repeated or prolonged contact can be harmful.**
- **Dispose of used oil and empty packs in a responsible manner in an authorised disposal site. Call 0800 663366 to find the one nearest to you. Never tip oil down drains or onto the ground.**

Tyre pressures (tyres cold)

	Front	Rear
Crossply tyres:		
Normal use	1.7 bar	1.6 bar
Fully laden	1.7 bar	1.7 bar
Radial tyres:		
145 SR x 10	1.9 bar	1.8 bar
145/70 SR x 12	2.0 bar	2.0 bar
165/60 R x 12	2.0 bar	2.1 bar
165/70 HR x 10	1.7 bar	1.7 bar
175/50 VR x 13	2.0 bar	1.8 bar

Note: *Pressures apply only to original-equipment tyres, and may vary if other makes or types are fitted; check with the tyre manufacturer or supplier for correct pressures if necessary.*

Chapter 1
Routine maintenance and servicing

Contents

Air cleaner element renewal 30
Air pump drivebelt check and renewal 9
Auxiliary drivebelt check and renewal 8
Bodywork, paint and exterior trim check 28
Brake fluid renewal 36
Carburettor idle speed and mixture adjustment 26
Clutch hydraulic check 10
Clutch return stop adjustment 22
Contact breaker points check and adjustment 20
Control box cleaning and inspection 24
Coolant renewal 35
Distributor cap, rotor arm and HT lead check 32
Distributor lubrication 21
Door, boot and bonnet check and lubrication 27
Driveshaft gaiter check 15
Drum brake adjustment 3
Dynamo check and lubrication 23
Emission control equipment check 34
Engine/transmission oil and filter renewal 13

Exhaust system check 7
Front brake wear check 14
Fuel filter renewal (fuel injection models) 37
Fuel system components, checks and lubrication 19
General information 1
Handbrake check and adjustment 4
Headlight beam alignment check 12
Ignition timing check and adjustment 25
Rear brake wear check 17
Regular maintenance 2
Road test 29
Seats and seat belt check 11
Spark plug renewal 33
Steering and suspension check 5
Steering and suspension lubrication 16
Underbody and fuel/brake line check 6
Underbonnet check for fluid leaks and hose condition 18
Valve clearance adjustment 31

Degrees of difficulty

Easy, suitable for novice with little experience	**Fairly easy,** suitable for beginner with some experience	**Fairly difficult,** suitable for competent DIY mechanic	**Difficult,** suitable for experienced DIY mechanic	**Very difficult,** suitable for expert DIY or professional

Lubricants and fluids .... Refer to end of *Weekly Checks* on page 0•18

Capacities

Engine oil with filter change
Manual transmission .... 4.8 litres
Automatic transmission .... 5.0 litres

Engine oil without filter change (approximate)
Manual transmission .... 4.2 litres
Automatic transmission .... 4.4 litres

Cooling system
With side-mounted radiator .... 3.5 litres
With front-mounted radiator .... 4.0 litres

Fuel tank
Saloon and Clubman (approximate):
    Early models .... 25 litres
    Later models .... 33 litres
Estate, Van and Pick-up .... 27 litres
1275 GT .... 33 litres
Cooper S Mk III .... 50 litres

Engine

Auxiliary drivebelt adjustment:
    Engines without tensioner pulley .... 13.0 mm deflection of belt between crankshaft and dynamo/alternator pulleys
    Engines with tensioner pulley .... 6.0 to 8.0 mm deflection of belt between tensioner and alternator pulleys

Cooling system

Specified antifreeze mixture:
    Models with side-mounted radiator .... 30% to 50% antifreeze
    Models with front-mounted radiator .... 50% to 60% antifreeze
Note: *Refer to Chapter 3 for further details.*

Exhaust and emission control systems

Air pump drivebelt adjustment .... 13.0 mm deflection of belt between pulleys

Ignition system

Spark plugs:
    Bosch recommendations:
        All models up to August 1988 .... Bosch WR 8 D+
        All models from September 1988 .... Bosch WR 7 D+
    Manufacturer's recommendations:
        All models up to 1986 .... NGK BPR6E
        998 cc engine models, 1987 to 1989 .... NGK BP4EY
        998 cc engine models, 1989 onwards .... NGK BPR4ES
        1275 cc engine models, 1991 onwards .... NGK BPR6E
    Electrode gap .... 0.8 mm

Clutch

Clutch return stop clearance .... 0.50 mm

Brakes

Minimum brake shoe lining thickness .... 3.0 mm
Minimum brake pad thickness .... 3.0 mm
Handbrake lever travel .... 3 clicks of ratchet

Tyres

Tyre pressures .... Refer to end of *Weekly checks* on page 0•18

Torque wrench settings

	Nm	lbf ft
Auxiliary drivebelt tensioner pulley	25	18
Engine/transmission oil drain plug	35	26
Roadwheel nuts	60	44
Spark plugs	25	18

The maintenance intervals in this manual are provided with the assumption that you, not the dealer, will be carrying out the work. These are the maintenance intervals recommended by the manufacturer for vehicles driven daily under normal conditions. The service interval for many of the operations listed was extended from the 1994 model year and, on later vehicles, you may wish to perform some of these procedures less often. However, we encourage frequent maintenance because it enhances the efficiency, performance and resale value of your vehicle, so the original manufacturer's schedule is the one shown below.

Every 250 miles (400 km) or weekly

☐ Refer to *Weekly checks*

Every 3000 miles (5000 km) or 3 months, whichever comes first

☐ Adjust the drum brakes (Section 3)
☐ Check the operation of the handbrake and adjust if necessary (Section 4)
☐ Check the condition and security of the steering and suspension components (Section 5)
☐ Inspect the underbody and the brake hydraulic pipes and hoses (Section 6)
☐ Check the condition of the fuel lines (Section 6)
☐ Check the condition and security of the exhaust system (Section 7)
☐ Check the condition of the auxiliary drivebelt and renew if necessary (Section 8)
☐ Check the condition of the air pump drivebelt (where applicable) and renew if necessary (Section 9)
☐ Inspect the clutch hydraulic components (Section 10)
☐ Check the condition of the seats and seat belts (Section 11)
☐ Check the headlight beam alignment (Section 12)

Every 6000 miles (10 000 km) or 6 months, whichever comes first

In addition to the items listed above, carry out the following:
☐ Renew the engine/transmission oil and filter (Section 13)*
☐ Check the condition of the front brake shoes/pads, and renew if necessary (Section 14)
☐ Check the condition of the driveshaft gaiters (Section 15)
☐ Lubricate the suspension and steering grease points (Section 16)
☐ Check the condition of the rear brake shoes and renew if necessary (Section 17)
☐ Check all underbonnet components and hoses for fluid leaks (Section 18)
☐ Check and if necessary top up the carburettor piston dashpot and check the linkages (Section 19)

Every 6000 miles (10 000 km) or 6 months, whichever comes first (continued)

☐ Check the condition of the contact breaker points and adjust or renew (Section 20)
☐ Lubricate the distributor (Section 21)
☐ Check and if necessary adjust the clutch return stop (Section 22)
☐ Lubricate the dynamo bearing – early models (Section 23)
☐ Clean and inspect the dynamo charging system control box (Section 24)
☐ Check and if necessary adjust the ignition timing (Section 25)
☐ Check and if necessary adjust the carburettor idle speed and mixture settings (Section 26)
☐ Lubricate the locks and hinges (Section 27)
☐ Check the condition of the exterior trim and paintwork (Section 28)
☐ Road test (Section 29)

* Note: *Frequent oil and filter changes are good for the engine. We recommend changing the oil at the mileage specified here, or at least twice a year if the mileage covered is a less.*

Every 12 000 miles (20 000 km) or 12 months, whichever comes first

In addition to the items listed above, carry out the following:
☐ Renew the air cleaner element (Section 30)
☐ Check and if necessary adjust the valve clearances (Section 31)
☐ Inspect the distributor cap, rotor arm and HT leads (Section 32)
☐ Renew the spark plugs (Section 33)
☐ Check the emission control equipment (Section 34)

Every 24 000 miles (40 000 km) or 24 months, whichever comes first

In addition to the items listed above, carry out the following:
☐ Renew the coolant (Section 35)
☐ Renew the brake fluid (Section 36)
☐ Renew the fuel filter – fuel injection models (Section 37)

Underbonnet view of a Mini 1000 Saloon

1 Brake master cylinder reservoir
2 Clutch master cylinder reservoir
3 Fuseblock
4 Carburettor piston damper
5 Air cleaner
6 Windscreen wiper motor
7 Radiator pressure cap
8 Engine/transmission oil filler cap
9 Alternator
10 Engine/transmission oil dipstick
11 Distributor
12 Ignition coil
13 Vehicle identification plate
14 Clutch slave cylinder
15 Windscreen washer reservoir

Underbonnet view of a pre-October 1996 Mini Cooper

(air cleaner removed for clarity)

1 Alternator
2 Ignition coil
3 Engine/transmission oil dipstick
4 Engine management (fuel injection/ignition) ECU
5 Radiator pressure cap
6 Brake fluid reservoir cap
7 Brake system vacuum servo unit
8 Relay module
9 Fuel cut-off inertia switch
10 Manifold absolute pressure (MAP) sensor fuel trap
11 Fuel return pipe
12 Fuel feed pipe
13 Accelerator cable
14 Throttle body assembly
15 Heater coolant valve
16 Charcoal canister purge valve

Underbonnet view of an October 1996 onward Mini Cooper

1 Alternator
2 DIS ignition module
3 Engine/transmission oil dipstick
4 Engine compartment fusebox
5 Engine management (fuel injection/ignition) ECU
6 Brake fluid reservoir cap
7 Brake system vacuum servo unit
8 Relay module
9 Clutch master cylinder
10 Air cleaner
11 Fuel cut-off inertia switch
12 Expansion tank pressure cap
13 Thermostat housing
14 Engine/transmission oil filler cap

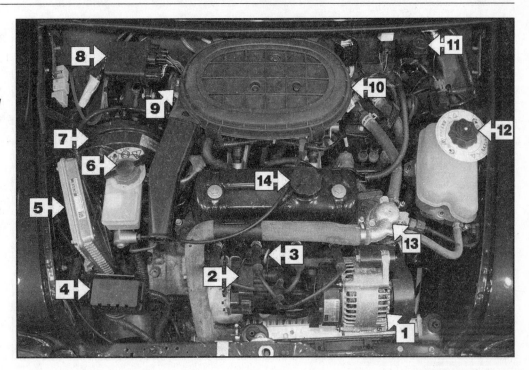

Front underside view of a Mini 1000 Saloon

1 Engine/transmission oil drain plug
2 Oil filter
3 Front suspension tie-bar
4 Disc brake caliper
5 Driveshaft outer CV joint
6 Front subframe
7 Subframe rear mounting
8 Offset sphere type inner CV joint
9 Gearchange extension rod
10 Battery positive cable
11 Steering tie-rod outer balljoint
12 Lower suspension arm
13 Exhaust bracket

Rear underside view of a Mini 1000 Saloon

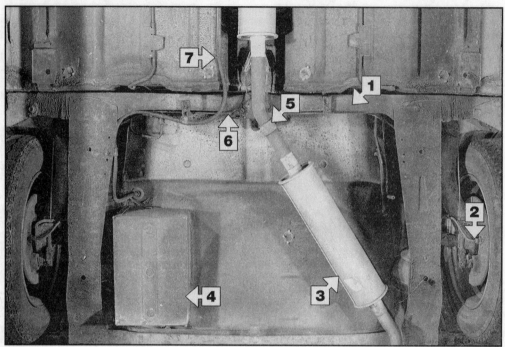

1 Rear subframe
2 Rear brake wheel cylinder attachment
3 Exhaust tailpipe rear silencer
4 Battery box
5 Exhaust mounting
6 Handbrake cable guide
7 Battery positive cable

Rear underside view of an October 1996 onward Mini Cooper

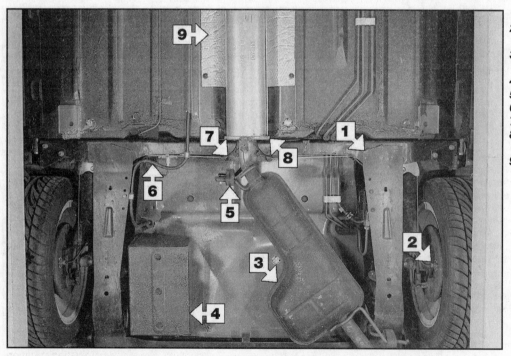

1 Rear subframe
2 Rear brake wheel cylinder attachment
3 Exhaust tailpipe rear silencer
4 Battery box
5 Exhaust mounting
6 Battery positive cable
7 Handbrake cable guide
8 Exhaust tailpipe intermediate silencer
9 Heat shield

1 General information

This Chapter is designed to help the home mechanic maintain his/her vehicle for safety, economy, long life and peak performance.

The Chapter contains a master maintenance schedule, followed by Sections dealing specifically with each task in the schedule. Visual checks, adjustments, component renewal and other helpful items are included. Refer to the accompanying illustrations of the engine compartment and the underside of the vehicle for the locations of the various components.

Servicing your vehicle in accordance with the mileage/time maintenance schedule and the following Sections will provide a planned maintenance programme, which should result in a long and reliable service life. This is a comprehensive plan, so maintaining some items but not others at the specified service intervals will not produce the same results.

As you service your vehicle, you will discover that many of the procedures can – and should – be grouped together, because of the particular procedure being performed, or because of the proximity of two otherwise-unrelated components to one another. For example, if the vehicle is raised for any reason, the exhaust can be inspected at the same time as the suspension and steering components.

The first step of this maintenance programme is to prepare yourself before the actual work begins. Read through all the Sections relevant to the work to be carried out, then make a list and gather all the parts and tools required. If a problem is encountered, seek advice from a parts specialist or a dealer service department.

2 Regular maintenance

1 If, from the time the vehicle is new, the routine maintenance schedule is followed closely, and frequent checks are made of fluid levels and high-wear items, as suggested throughout this manual, the engine will be kept in relatively good running condition, and the need for additional work will be minimised.

2 It is possible that there will be times when the engine is running poorly due to the lack of regular maintenance. This is even more likely if a used vehicle, which has not received regular and frequent maintenance checks, is purchased. In such cases, additional work may need to be carried out, outside of the regular maintenance intervals.

3 If engine wear is suspected, a compression test (refer to Chapter 2A or 2B) will provide valuable information regarding the overall performance of the main internal components. Such a test can be used as a basis to decide on the extent of the work to be carried out. If, for example, a compression test indicates serious internal engine wear, conventional maintenance as described in this Chapter will not greatly improve the performance of the engine, and may prove a waste of time and money, unless extensive overhaul work is carried out first.

4 The following series of operations are those often required to improve the performance of a generally poor-running engine:

Primary operations

a) Clean, inspect and test the battery (See 'Weekly checks').

b) Check all the engine-related fluids (See 'Weekly checks').
c) Check and if necessary adjust the valve clearances (Section 31).
d) Check the condition of the auxiliary drivebelt (Section 8).
e) Top up the carburettor piston damper (Section 19).
f) Check the condition and adjustment of the contact breaker points (Section 20).
g) Inspect the distributor cap, rotor arm and HT leads (Section 32).
h) Renew the spark plugs (Section 33).
i) Check and if necessary adjust the ignition timing (Section 25).
j) Check the condition of the air cleaner filter element and renew if necessary (Section 30).
k) Check and if necessary adjust the carburettor idle speed and mixture settings (Section 26).
l) Renew the fuel filter – fuel injection models (Section 37).
m) Check the condition of all hoses, and check for fluid leaks (Section 18).

5 If the above operations do not prove fully effective, carry out the following secondary operations:

Secondary operations

All the items listed under Primary operations, plus the following:

a) Check the charging system (Chapter 5A).
b) Check the ignition system (Chapter 5B or 5C).
c) Check the fuel system (Chapter 4A, 4B or 4C).
d) Renew the distributor cap and rotor arm (Section 32).
e) Renew the ignition HT leads (Section 32).

Every 3000 miles or 3 months

3 Drum brake adjustment

1 As wear takes place on the brake shoe friction material, the clearance between the friction material and the inner circumference of the brake drum will increase, resulting in excessive brake pedal travel before the brakes are applied. To compensate for this, adjusters are provided at the rear of each brake backplate, enabling the clearance between the brake shoe and drum to be kept to a minimum.

2 At the front, two adjusters are fitted to each brake backplate. At the rear a single adjuster is located at the top of each brake backplate.

Front brakes

3 Firmly apply the handbrake, then jack up the front of the car and support it securely on axle stands (see Jacking and vehicle support).

4 Each front brake has two adjusters of the eccentric cam type, accessible from the rear of each brake backplate. One of these adjusters is located behind the steering arm and insufficient clearance exists to enable an ordinary brake adjusting spanner to be used. Providing the adjuster is not excessively tight or partially seized in the backplate, a 5/16 in AF open-ended spanner can be used quite successfully to turn the adjuster.

5 Begin by turning one of the adjusters in the forward direction of wheel rotation until the wheel is locked **(see illustration)**. Now back it off slightly, until the wheel turns freely. The brake drum may rub slightly in one or two places as the wheel is turned. This is acceptable providing the wheel does not bind. *Caution: If, when attempting to adjust the brakes, the square-headed adjuster is reluctant to turn, it is quite likely that it has become seized in its housing. If this is the* *case do not force it, or you will probably break off the square head, necessitating renewal of the complete backplate assembly. Apply liberal amounts of penetrating oil to the rear of the adjuster and allow it to soak in. Now turn the*

3.5 Adjusting one of the front brake adjusters with a brake adjusting spanner

3.9 Adjusting the rear brakes

adjuster back-and-forth slightly, using gentle force if necessary, increasing the movement each time. When the adjuster turns easily apply a multipurpose grease to the exposed portion of the adjuster at the rear of the backplate and then turn it through its entire travel. Preferably do this with the brake drum removed.

6 Turn the second adjuster also in the direction of forward wheel rotation until the drum locks again. Now back the adjuster off until the wheel turns freely once more.

7 Repeat this procedure for the other front wheel and then lower the car to the ground.

Rear brakes

8 Chock the front wheels then jack up the rear of the car and support it securely on axle stands (see *Jacking and vehicle support*). Ensure that the handbrake is off.

9 Using a brake adjusting spanner, turn the square-headed adjuster in a clockwise direction (viewed from the rear of the backplate) until the wheel is locked **(see illustration)**. The adjusters on the rear brakes are even more prone to seizure than those at the front. If the adjuster is reluctant to turn attempt to free it off as described above. If this fails, remove the rear brake drums and brake shoes as described in Chapter 9, and

clean and lubricate the adjuster thoroughly. When all is well, refit the brake assemblies and start the adjustment procedure again.

10 Now turn the adjuster back a quarter of a turn at a time until the wheel turns freely without binding. A slight rubbing may be felt when the wheel is turned slowly, indicating a high spot on the drum or dust on the linings. This is acceptable providing the drum does not bind.

11 Repeat this procedure for the other rear brake then, before lowering the car to the ground, check the handbrake adjustment as described in the following Section.

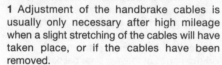

4 Handbrake check and adjustment

1 Adjustment of the handbrake cables is usually only necessary after high mileage when a slight stretching of the cables will have taken place, or if the cables have been removed.

2 Before adjusting the handbrake, check that the footbrake is correctly adjusted as described in Section 3.

3 Chock the front wheels then jack up the rear of the car and support it securely on axle stands (see *Jacking and vehicle support*).

4 Apply the handbrake lever to the third notch of the ratchet and check that the rear wheels are locked. If not, adjust the handbrake as follows.

5 With the handbrake still applied to the third click of the ratchet, tilt the front seats forward, and on models having twin cables, tighten the cable adjusting nuts at the base of the lever until the rear wheels can only just be turned by heavy hand pressure. On models having a single front cable, slacken the locknut and rotate the cable adjusting nut. When the wheels can only just be turned by heavy hand pressure, tighten the locknut **(see illustrations)**.

6 Release the handbrake lever and ensure that the wheels rotate freely. If satisfactory lower the car to the ground.

5 Steering and suspension check

Steering

1 First check for wear in the steering tie-rod outer balljoints. Turn the steering to left or right lock sufficiently to allow the joints to be observed. Now have an assistant turn the steering wheel back-and-forth slightly. If there is any side movement in the balljoint it must be renewed. Similarly place your hand over the rubber gaiter at the end of the rack housing and feel for any excess free play of the inner balljoint. If the condition of this joint is suspect, a further investigation should be carried out with the gaiter removed as described in Chapter 10.

2 Check the tightness of the steering column clamp bolt at the base of the column. Any slackness at this joint can also show up as free play at the steering wheel.

Front suspension

3 To inspect the front suspension, firmly apply the handbrake, then jack up the front of the car and support it securely on axle stands (see *Jacking and vehicle support*).

4 Visually inspect the balljoint dust covers and the steering gear gaiters for splits, chafing or deterioration. Any wear of these components will cause loss of lubricant, together with dirt and water entry, resulting in rapid deterioration of the balljoints or steering gear.

5 Grasp the roadwheel at the 12 o'clock and 6 o'clock positions and try to rock it. If any movement is felt it is likely to be in one or more of the following areas:

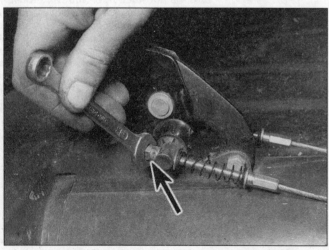

4.5a Handbrake adjustment on models with twin cables

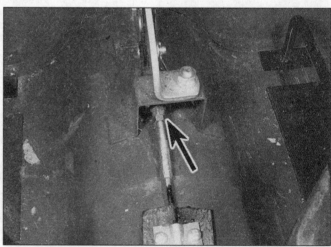

4.5b Handbrake cable adjusting nut on models with a single front cable

Hub bearings

6 Continue rocking the wheel while your assistant depresses the footbrake. If the movement disappears or becomes less severe, then the wheel hub bearings in the swivel hub are at fault. Any perceptible movement at all indicates wear in the hub bearings, and they should be renewed as described in Chapter 10.

Swivel hub balljoints

7 Wear of the swivel hub balljoints is fairly common on Minis and will be quite obvious on inspection because the whole swivel hub will appear to move in relation to the suspension arms as the wheel is rocked. If this is the case, the balljoints should be adjusted, or if badly worn, renewed; these procedures are contained in Chapter 10.

Suspension arm mountings

8 Check for wear of the lower arm inner mounting bushes where the arm is bolted to the subframe. If the bushes are worn, the arm will appear to move in and out as the wheel is rocked.

9 The upper arm inner roller bearings cannot be inspected without partially dismantling the suspension because the rubber cone spring or displacer unit holds the arm in tension and any wear will not be evident. It can be removed for closer inspection if required as described in Chapter 10; however, wear of the upper arm and its bearings is uncommon.

10 With the brakes still firmly applied, try to rotate the wheel back-and-forth. If any movement is now felt, examine the tie-bar between the lower suspension arm and subframe for wear or deterioration of the rubber bushes.

Rear suspension

11 To check the rear suspension for wear, chock the front wheels then jack up the rear of the car and support it securely on axle stands (see *Jacking and vehicle support*).

12 Wear of the rear suspension components can often be felt when driving the car as a tendency for the rear of the vehicle to wander over uneven road surfaces or when cornering. To isolate the worn components, grasp the roadwheel at the 12 o'clock and 6 o'clock positions and try to rock it. If any movement is felt, it is likely to be in one of the following areas:

Hub bearings

13 Continue rocking the wheel while an assistant depresses the footbrake. If the movement disappears or becomes less pronounced, then the bearings in the rear hub are at fault. The bearings should be renewed if there is any appreciable movement whatsoever.

> **HAYNES HINT** *Wear in the rear hub bearings can often be confirmed by slowly turning the wheel with your hand on the tyre. Worn bearings usually exhibit a roughness which can be felt as the wheel is turned.*

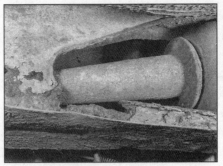

6.3 Advanced state of corrosion on rear subframe side-member

Radius arm bearings

14 With the footbrake still applied, continue rocking the wheel and observe the front of the radius arm. If it can be seen to move appreciably up and down, then wear has taken place in the roller or plain bearing in the radius arm, or on the pivot shaft. If this is the case, the radius arm should be removed for overhaul as described in Chapter 10.

6 Underbody and fuel/brake line check

1 With the vehicle raised and supported on axle stands (see *Jacking and vehicle support*), or over an inspection pit, thoroughly inspect the underbody and wheelarches for signs of damage and corrosion. In particular, examine the bottom of the side sills, and any concealed areas where mud can collect. Where corrosion and rust is evident, press and tap firmly on the panel with a screwdriver, and check for any serious corrosion which would necessitate repairs. If the panel is not seriously corroded, clean away the rust, and apply a new coating of underseal. Refer to Chapter 11 for more details of body repairs.

2 At the same time, inspect the treated lower body panels for stone damage and general condition.

3 Examine the subframes carefully, particularly the side-members of the rear subframe. Corrosion here is a common occurrence on Minis, particularly older

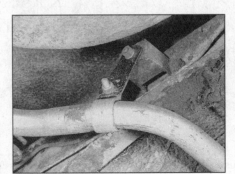

7.2a Exhaust front mounting block . . .

6.5 Inspect the flexible brake hoses in the vicinity of the backplates

models, and is one of the main causes of MOT test failure on these cars **(see illustration)**. Where corrosion has reached an advanced stage, renewal of the subframe is the only satisfactory cure.

4 Inspect all of the fuel and brake lines on the underbody for damage, rust, corrosion and leakage. Also make sure that they are correctly supported in their clips. The battery positive cable which runs under the car from front to rear is a common problem area as it is prone to damage or chafing if not properly routed or secured.

5 Inspect the flexible brake hoses in the vicinity of the backplates or front calipers, where they are subjected to most movement **(see illustration)**. Bend them between the fingers (but do not actually bend them double, or the casing may be damaged) and check that this does not reveal previously hidden cracks, cuts or splits.

7 Exhaust system check

1 With the engine cold (at least three hours after the vehicle has been driven), check the complete exhaust system, from its starting point at the engine to the end of the tailpipe. Ideally, this should be done on a hoist, where unrestricted access is available; if a hoist is not available, raise and support the vehicle on axle stands (see *Jacking and vehicle support*).

2 Check the pipes and connections for evidence of leaks, severe corrosion, or damage. Make sure that all brackets and rubber mountings are in good condition, and tight; if any of the mountings are to be renewed, ensure that the replacements are of the correct type. Failure of the rear mounting rubber blocks on the rear subframe is a common problem – check these carefully **(see illustrations)**. Leakage at any of the joints or in other parts of the system will usually show up as a black sooty stain in the vicinity of the leak.

3 At the same time, inspect the underside of the body for holes, corrosion, open seams, etc, which may allow exhaust gases to enter the passenger compartment. Seal all body openings with silicone or body putty.

7.2b ... and exhaust rear mounting block on rear subframe – pre-October 1996 models shown

4 Rattles and other noises can often be traced to the exhaust system, especially the rubber mountings. Try to move the system, silencer(s) and catalytic converter. If any components can touch the body or suspension parts, secure the exhaust system with new mountings.

 When checking the exhaust, pay particular attention to the mounting on the transmission. Movement of the engine causes this mounting to work loose, causing an annoying squeak or rattle when accelerating and decelerating.

8 Auxiliary drivebelt check and renewal

Note: *If the car is fitted with exhaust emission control equipment it will first be necessary to remove the air pump drivebelt as described in Section 9 to allow access to the auxiliary drivebelt.*

8.6 Dynamo adjusting arm nut located below the water pump

Pre-October 1996 models

Check and adjustment

1 Release the three retaining lugs and remove the engine ignition shield, if fitted. Rotate the crankshaft so that the entire length of the drivebelt can be examined. On manual transmission models, the engine can be rotated quite easily by engaging top gear and moving the car backwards or forwards to allow the belt to be inspected. This should only be done on level ground; and make sure that the car cannot run away. An alternative method, and the method that should be used on automatic transmission models, is to press the drivebelt midway between the water pump pulley and dynamo or alternator pulley and then turn the fan blades.

 Turning the engine will be easier if the spark plugs are removed first – see Section 33.

2 Examine the belt for cracks, splitting, fraying or damage. Check also for signs of

glazing (shiny patches) and for separation of the belt plies. Renew the drivebelt if worn or damaged.

3 If the condition of the belt is satisfactory, check the adjustment as follows.

4 It is most important to keep the drivebelt correctly adjusted; If the belt is too loose it will slip and wear rapidly, resulting in inefficient operation of the water pump and dynamo or alternator. If it is too tight, it will impose excessive strain on the bearings of the water pump, dynamo or alternator causing premature failure of these components.

5 The drivebelt tension is correct when there is 13.0 mm of belt deflection, using light finger pressure, at a point midway between the crankshaft and dynamo or alternator pulleys.

6 To adjust the drivebelt, slacken the mounting bolts of the dynamo or alternator, and also the nut on the adjusting arm located below the water pump **(see illustration)**. Now move the unit either in or out until the correct tension is obtained. It is easier if the adjusting arm nut is only slackened a little so it requires some force to move the dynamo or alternator. In this way the tension of the belt can be arrived at more quickly than by making frequent adjustments. If difficulty is experienced in moving the dynamo or alternator away from the engine, a long spanner or bar placed behind the unit and resting against the block serves as a very good lever and can be held in position while the adjusting and mounting bolts are fully tightened. When levering on an alternator, only lever on the drive end or damage may occur.

7 When the tension is correct, tighten the adjusting arm nut first, followed by the mounting bolts.

Renewal

8 To remove the drivebelt, slacken the two

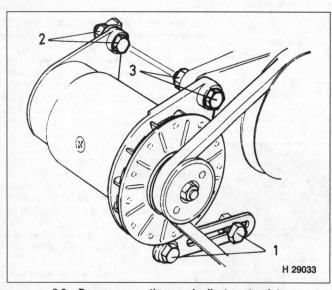

8.8a Dynamo mountings and adjustment points

1 *Adjustment arm retaining nuts*
2 *Securing nut and bolt (rear)*
3 *Securing nut and bolt (front)*

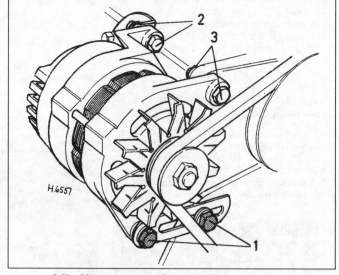

8.8b Alternator mounting and adjustment points

1 *Adjustment arm fixings*
2 *Securing nut and bolt (rear)*
3 *Securing nut and bolt (front)*

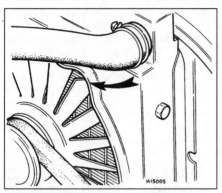

8.9 The gap in the radiator shroud of early models (arrowed) to allow removal and refitting of the auxiliary drivebelt

dynamo or alternator upper mountings and the nut on the adjusting arm below the water pump **(see illustrations)**.

9 Push the dynamo or alternator toward the engine and lift the old belt off the three pulleys. Feed the belt over each fan blade in turn and withdraw it from behind the fan cowling at the special gap just below the top radiator hose **(see illustration)**.

10 Fit the new belt over the fan blades in the same way and then place it in position on the three pulleys.

11 Adjust the belt tension as described previously then refit the air pump drivebelt, where applicable, as described in the following Section. **Note:** *After fitting a new drivebelt, check and if necessary readjust the tension after 250 miles (400 km).*

October 1996 models onward

Check and adjustment

12 Undo the two retaining nuts and withdraw the drivebelt cover from the front of the alternator **(see illustration)**. Rotate the crankshaft so that the entire length of the drivebelt can be examined. The engine can be rotated quite easily by engaging top gear and moving the car backwards or forwards to allow the belt to be inspected. This should only be done on level ground; and make sure that the car cannot run away.

 HAYNES HINT *Turning the engine will be easier if the spark plugs are removed first – see Section 33.*

13 Examine the belt for cracks, splitting, fraying or damage. Check also for signs of glazing (shiny patches) and for separation of the belt plies. Renew the drivebelt if worn or damaged.

14 If the condition of the belt is satisfactory, check the adjustment as follows.

15 It is most important to keep the drivebelt correctly adjusted; If the belt is too loose it will slip and wear rapidly, resulting in inefficient operation of the water pump and alternator. If it is too tight, it will impose excessive strain on

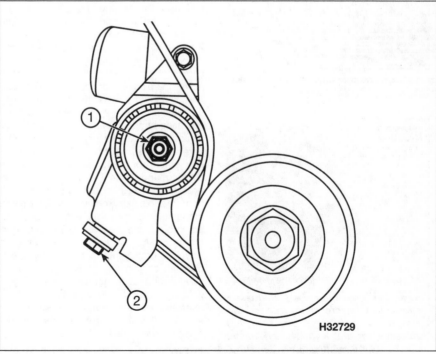

8.12 Undo the two retaining nuts and withdraw the drivebelt cover from the front of the alternator

the bearings of the water pump or alternator causing premature failure of these components.

16 The drivebelt tension is correct when there is 6.0 to 8.0 mm of belt deflection, using light finger pressure, at a point midway between the drivebelt tensioner pulley and the alternator pulley.

17 To adjust the drivebelt, slacken the nut in the centre of the auxiliary drivebelt tensioner pulley **(see illustration)**. Using a suitable spanner, turn the adjusting bolt at the base of the tensioner assembly clockwise to increase the belt tension and anti-clockwise to decrease it. Note that the adjusting bolt is very prone to seizure – if it is stiff to turn, apply liberal amounts of penetrating oil and allow it to soak in fully before proceeding.

18 When the tension is correct, tighten the drivebelt tensioner pulley retaining nut to the

specified torque, then refit the cover to the alternator.

Renewal

19 To remove the drivebelt, remove the alternator cover and slacken the drivebelt tensioner pulley nut.

20 Turn the tensioner adjusting bolt anti-clockwise to release all tension from the belt, then lift the old belt off the three pulleys.

21 Fit the new belt over the crankshaft, water pump and alternator pulleys and against the tensioner pulley, ensuring that it is correctly seated

22 Adjust the drivebelt tension as described previously.

---

9 Air pump drivebelt check and renewal

Check and adjustment

1 The checks and adjustment procedure for the air pump drivebelt are basically the same as described in Section 9 for the auxiliary drivebelt on pre-October 1996 models. Adjust the tension of the drivebelt so that there is 13.0 mm deflection of the belt, using thumb pressure, at a point midway between the two pulleys.

Renewal

2 Release the three retaining lugs and remove the engine ignition shield, if fitted.

8.17 Auxiliary drivebelt tensioner details – October 1996 models onward

1 Tensioner pulley retaining nut   *2 Tensioner adjusting bolt*

3 Undo and remove the two bolts securing the radiator upper mounting bracket to the radiator.

4 Unscrew the radiator filler cap and slacken the top hose securing clips. Carefully ease the radiator as far as possible toward the wing valance. Place a container beneath the engine to catch the small quantity of coolant that will be lost as the top hose is released.

⚠️ *Warning: If the engine is hot, take precautions against scalding.*

5 Slacken the air pump pivot and adjusting link bolts, push the pump in toward the engine, and slip the drivebelt off the two pulleys.

6 Feed the belt between the fan blades and the radiator cowling at the top as the blades are rotated. Now pull the belt out from between the fan and radiator.

7 Refitting the drivebelt is the reverse sequence to removal, adjusting the tension as described previously. Top-up the cooling system as described in *Weekly Checks* on completion.

10 Clutch hydraulic check

1 Check that the clutch pedal moves smoothly and easily through its full travel, and that the clutch itself functions correctly, with no trace of slip or drag.

2 Apply a few drops of light oil to the clutch pedal pivot.

3 From within the engine compartment check the condition of the fluid pipes and hoses. Check for signs of fluid leaks around the slave cylinder rubber boot or from the feed pipe and hose. Apply a few drops of oil to the clutch release lever clevis pin and the pivot on the flywheel housing.

11 Seats and seat belt check

1 Check that the seats are securely attached to the floor crossmember and that there is no sign of corrosion anywhere near the mountings. Check that the seats release and then lock in place when the release mechanism is operated.

2 Check the seat belts for satisfactory operation and condition. Inspect the webbing for fraying and cuts. Check that they retract smoothly and without binding into their reels.

3 Check the seat belt mountings, ensuring that all the bolts are securely tightened.

12 Headlight beam alignment check

Accurate adjustment of the headlight beam is only possible using optical beam-setting equipment, and this work should therefore be carried out by a Rover dealer or service station with the necessary facilities.

Basic adjustments can be carried out in an emergency, and further details are given in the relevant Part of Chapter 12.

Every 6000 miles or 6 months

13.3 Engine/transmission oil drain plug (arrowed)

Keep the drain plug pressed into the sump while unscrewing it by hand the last couple of turns. As the plug releases, move it away sharply so the stream of oil issuing from the sump runs into the container, not up your sleeve.

13 Engine/transmission oil and filter renewal

1 Frequent oil changes are the best preventive maintenance the home mechanic can give the engine, because ageing oil becomes diluted and contaminated, which leads to premature engine wear.

2 Make sure that you have all the necessary tools before you begin this procedure. You should also have plenty of rags or newspapers handy, for mopping-up any spills. The oil should preferably be changed when the engine is still fully warmed-up to normal operating temperature, just after a run; warm oil and sludge will flow out more easily. Take care, however, not to touch the exhaust or any other hot parts of the engine when working under the vehicle. To avoid any possibility of scalding, and to protect yourself from possible skin irritants and other harmful contaminants in used engine oils, it is advisable to wear gloves when carrying out this work. Access to the underside of the vehicle is greatly improved if the vehicle can be lifted on a hoist, driven onto ramps, or supported by axle stands. (see *Jacking and vehicle support*). Whichever method is chosen, make sure that the vehicle remains level, or if it is at an angle, that the drain point is at the lowest point.

Oil draining

3 Position the draining container under the drain plug on the side of the transmission casing, and unscrew the plug **(see illustration)**. If possible, try to keep the plug pressed into the sump while unscrewing it by hand the last couple of turns.

4 Allow the oil to drain into the container **(see Haynes Hint)**, and check the condition of the plug's sealing washer; renew it if worn or damaged. Also wipe off any metal particles that may have accumulated on the magnet.

5 Allow some time for the old oil to drain, noting that it may be necessary to reposition the container as the oil flow slows to a trickle; when the oil has completely drained, wipe clean the drain plug and its threads in the transmission and refit the plug, tightening it to the specified torque.

Oil filter renewal

6 The oil filter is located below the dynamo or alternator on the forward-facing side of the engine on pre-October 1996 models, or on the forward-facing side of the cylinder block, below the DIS ignition model on October 1996 models onward. On early manual transmission models the filter is of the disposable cartridge type contained within an aluminium bowl. On later models a throwaway canister is used. All automatic transmission models utilise the cartridge type filter. To renew the filter proceed as follows.

Cartridge type

7 Reposition the draining container under the oil filter then undo and remove the long centre bolt securing the bowl to the housing **(see illustration)**. On some models it may be advantageous to remove the grille panel, as space is rather limited.

13.7 Cartridge type oil filter and retaining bolt as seen from below

13.9 Components of the cartridge type oil filter

13.12 Fitting a new cartridge type oil filter sealing ring

8 With the bolts released, carefully lift away the filter bowl, which contains the filter and will also be full of oil.

9 Discard the old filter element but first make sure that the metal pressure plate has not stuck to the bottom of it. Now thoroughly clean out the filter bowl, the bolt, and the parts associated with it, using paraffin or a suitable solvent **(see illustration)**. Dry with a lint-free cloth

10 A rubber sealing ring is located in a groove round the head of the filter housing and forms an effective leak-proof joint between the housing and the filter bowl. A new rubber sealing ring is supplied with each new filter element.

11 Carefully prise out the old sealing ring from the locating groove. If the ring has become hard and is difficult to move take great care not to damage the sides of the sealing ring groove.

12 With the old ring removed, fit the new ring in the groove at four equidistant points and press it home a segment at a time. Do not insert the ring at just one point and work round the groove pressing it home as, using this method, it is easy to stretch the ring and

be left with a small loop of rubber which will not fit into the locating groove **(see illustration)**.

13 Reassemble the oil filter assembly by first passing up the bolt through the hole in the bottom of the bowl, with a steel washer under the bolt's head and a rubber or felt washer on top of the steel washer and next to the filter bowl.

14 Slide the spring over the bolt followed by the other steel washer, the remaining rubber washer and finally the filter pressure plate concave face downwards.

15 After fitting the new element to the bowl, position the bowl on the rubber sealing ring then insert and hand tighten the bolt. Before finally tightening the centre bolt, ensure that the lip of the filter bowl is resting squarely on the rubber sealing ring and is not offset or seated off the ring. If the bowl is not seating properly, rotate it until it is. Run the engine and check the bowl for leaks.

Canister type

16 Reposition the draining container under the oil filter then, using a suitable filter removal tool if necessary, slacken the canister initially, then unscrew it by hand the rest of the way; be prepared for some oil spillage **(see illustrations)**. Empty the oil in the old canister into the container.

17 Using a clean, lint-free rag, wipe clean the cylinder block around the filter housing. Check the old canister to make sure that the rubber sealing ring hasn't stuck to the filter housing; if it has, carefully remove it.

18 Apply a light coating of clean engine oil to

the sealing ring on the new canister **(see illustration)**. Screw the canister into position on the housing until it seats, then tighten it firmly by hand only – **do not** use any tools.

19 Remove the old oil and all tools from under the vehicle, then lower the vehicle to the ground.

Oil filling

20 Remove the dipstick and the oil filler cap from the engine. Fill the engine with oil, using the correct grade and type of oil (*see Weekly checks*). Pour in half the specified quantity of oil first, then wait a few minutes for the oil to drain to the transmission casing. Take care during this operation, particularly in cold weather as it is all too easy to fill up the rocker cover before the oil drains down into the engine, with very messy results as it overflows out of the filler neck. Continue adding oil a small quantity at a time, until the level is up to the lower mark on the dipstick. Adding approximately 0.5 litres will raise the level to the upper mark on the dipstick.

21 Start the engine. The oil pressure warning light will take a few seconds to go out while the new filter fills with oil; do not race the engine while the light is on. Run the engine for a few minutes, while checking for leaks around the oil filter seal and the drain plug.

22 Switch off the engine, and wait a few minutes for the oil to settle in the transmission once more. With the new oil circulated and the filter now completely full, recheck the level on the dipstick, and add more oil as necessary.

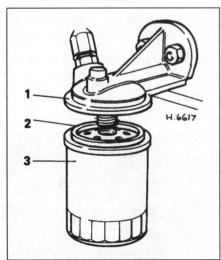

13.16a Canister type oil filter – pre-October 1996 models

1 Housing   3 Filter
2 Sealing ring

13.16b Removing the canister type oil filter on October 1996 models onward

13.18 Apply a light coating of engine oil to the sealing ring on the new oil filter

23 Dispose of the used engine oil and filter safely, with reference to *General repair procedures* at the rear of this manual. Do not discard the old filter with domestic household waste. The facility for waste oil disposal provided by many local council refuse tips generally has a filter receptacle alongside.

14 Front brake wear check

⚠️ *Warning: The dust created by wear of the shoes/pads may contain asbestos, which is a health hazard. Never blow it out with compressed air, and don't inhale any of it. An approved filtering mask should be worn when working on the brakes. DO NOT use petrol or petroleum-based solvents to clean brake parts; use brake cleaner or methylated spirit only.*

Drum brake models

1 After high mileage the friction linings on the brake shoes will have worn, and it will therefore be necessary to fit replacement shoes with new linings.
2 Firmly apply the handbrake, then jack up the front of the car and support it securely on axle stands (see *Jacking and vehicle support*). Remove the front roadwheels.
3 Slacken off the brake shoe adjuster(s) from behind the backplate, and then undo and remove the two brake drum retaining screws.
4 Remove the brake drum from the wheel hub. If the drum is tight, gently tap its circumference with a soft-faced mallet.
5 Brush and wipe away all traces of asbestos dust from the brake shoes, wheel cylinders and backplate, and also from the inner circumference of the brake drum.
6 Inspect the friction material and renew the brake shoes as described in Chapter 9 if they have worn down to less than the specified minimum thickness.
7 The brake shoes must also be renewed if there is any sign of hydraulic fluid contamination of the linings due to a leaking brake wheel cylinder. If this is the case, the cause of the leak must be traced and rectified before fitting new brake shoes.

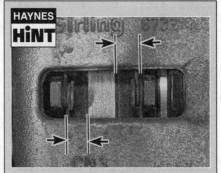
Look through the opening in the caliper and check the thickness of the friction lining material on the brake pads.

8 Brake shoes should always be renewed as complete sets (four shoes to a set), otherwise uneven braking and pulling to one side may occur.
9 It is advisable to check that the brake wheel cylinders are operating correctly before proceeding further. To do this hold the brake shoes in position using two screwdrivers while an assistant very slowly depresses the brake pedal slightly. Check that the wheel cylinder pistons move out as the pedal is depressed, and return when the pedal is released. If this is not the case, it is quite likely that one of the wheel cylinder pistons is seized and the cylinder should therefore be renewed (Chapter 9).
10 Also check the condition of the brake drum, If it is deeply scored on its inner circumference it may be possible to have it skimmed at an engineering works. If the scoring is severe, renewal will be necessary

Disc brake models

11 Jack up the front or rear of the vehicle in turn, and support it on axle stands (see *Jacking and vehicle support*).
12 For better access to the brake calipers, remove the roadwheels.
13 Look through the opening in the front of the caliper, and check that the thickness of the friction lining material on each of the pads is not less than the recommended minimum thickness given in the Specifications **(see Haynes Hint)**. If any one of the brake pads has worn down to, or below, the specified

limit, *all four* pads must be renewed as a set (ie, all the front pads).
14 For a comprehensive check, the brake pads should be removed and cleaned. The operation of the brake calipers can then be checked, and the brake discs can be fully examined. Refer to Chapter 9 for details.

15 Driveshaft gaiter check

With the vehicle raised and securely supported on stands (see *Jacking and vehicle support*), turn the steering onto full lock, then slowly rotate the roadwheel. Inspect the condition of the outer constant velocity (CV) joint rubber gaiters, squeezing the gaiters to open out the folds. Check for signs of cracking, splits or deterioration of the rubber, which may allow the grease to escape, and lead to water and grit entry into the joint. Also check the security and condition of the retaining clips. Repeat these checks on the inner CV joints where offset sphere type joints are fitted. If any damage or deterioration is found, the gaiters should be renewed as described in Chapter 8.

At the same time, check the general condition of the CV joints themselves by first holding the driveshaft and attempting to rotate the wheel. Repeat this check by holding the inner joint and attempting to rotate the driveshaft. Any appreciable movement indicates wear in the joints, wear in the driveshaft splines, or a loose driveshaft retaining nut.

16 Steering and suspension lubrication

1 Unlike most modern cars, there are a number of steering and suspension joints on the Mini which require regular attention. Provision for lubrication of these joints is by means of a grease nipple, to which a grease gun can be engaged. The grease nipples are located in the following areas **(see illustrations):**

16.1a Lubricating the swivel hub upper grease nipple . . .

16.1b . . . the upper suspension arm inner pivot grease nipple . . .

16.1c . . . and the rear radius arm pivot grease nipple

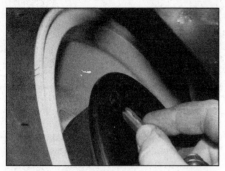

17.1 On later models, extract the blanking plug and look through the hole in the backplate to check the brake lining thickness

a) *Steering swivel hub; two nipples, one upper and one lower on each side.*
b) *Upper suspension arm inner pivot; one nipple on each arm.*
c) *Rear radius arm pivot; one nipple on each pivot. Remove the rubber blanking plug to expose the nipple on early models.*

2 When lubricating the front grease nipples it is preferable to raise the front of the car and support it on axle stands (see *Jacking and vehicle support*) so that the load is taken off the suspension. This will allow the grease to penetrate into the joints more effectively. The rear radius arm pivots can be lubricated with the car on its roadwheels if wished.

3 With the car raised and suitably supported, wipe clean the area all round the grease nipple and the nipple itself. Engage the head of a grease gun, filled with the specified grease, squarely onto the nipple, keeping it pushed fully home. Operate the gun until grease can be seen to appear from under the dust cover over the joint or from around the side of the pivot bushes.

4 When lubricating the rear radius arm pivots, a generous amount of grease will be needed each side, quite a bit more than was required for the front suspension joints. It probably won't be possible to tell when sufficient has been applied, unless you look underneath at the inner attachment on the subframe, it may be possible to see it appear around the inner

HAYNES HiNT

A leak in the cooling system will usually show up as white or rust coloured deposits on the area adjoining the leak

pivot; add a bit more if in doubt! This is a vitally important area on the Mini and it must be well-lubricated.

5 Although not part of the steering and suspension, the handbrake cable guides and the moving sectors on the rear subframe should be lubricated at this time to ensure smooth operation. There are no grease nipples, so the grease should be applied with a wooden spatula or similar tool to lubricate these areas thoroughly.

17 Rear brake wear check

1 The procedure for checking the rear brake components is the same as described in Section 14 for models with drum brakes. Note however, that on later models there is an inspection hole in the brake backplate, through which the thickness of the linings can be observed. To check the lining thickness without removing the brake drum, extract the blanking plug and look through the hole, using a mirror if necessary **(see illustration)**.

18 Underbonnet check for fluid leaks and hose condition

General

1 High temperatures in the engine compartment can cause the deterioration of the rubber and plastic hoses used for engine, accessory and emission systems operation. Periodic inspection should be made for cracks, loose clamps, material hardening and leaks.

2 Carefully check the large top and bottom radiator hoses, along with the other smaller-diameter cooling system hoses and metal pipes; do not forget the heater hoses/pipes which run from the engine to the bulkhead. Inspect each hose along its entire length, replacing any that are cracked, swollen or shows signs of deterioration. Cracks may become more apparent if the hose is squeezed **(see Haynes Hint)**.

3 Make sure that all hose connections are tight. If the spring clamps that are used to secure some of the hoses appear to be slackening, they should be renewed to prevent the possibility of leaks.

4 Some other hoses are secured to their fittings with screw-type clips. Where screw-type clips are used, check to be sure they haven't slackened, allowing the hose to leak. If clamps or screw-type clips aren't used, make sure the hose has not expanded and/or hardened where it slips over the fitting, allowing it to leak.

5 Check all fluid reservoirs, filler caps, drain plugs and fittings, etc, looking for any signs of leakage of oil, transmission and/or brake hydraulic fluid or coolant. If the vehicle is

regularly parked in the same place, close inspection of the ground underneath it will soon show any leaks. As soon as a leak is detected, its source must be traced and rectified. Where oil has been leaking for some time, it is usually necessary to use a steam cleaner, pressure washer or similar to clean away the accumulated dirt, so that the exact source of the leak can be identified.

Vacuum hoses

6 It's quite common for vacuum hoses, especially those in the emissions system, to be numbered or colour-coded, or to be identified by coloured stripes moulded into them. Various systems require hoses with different wall thicknesses, collapse resistance and temperature resistance. When renewing hoses, be sure the new ones are made of the same material.

7 Often the only effective way to check a hose is to remove it completely from the vehicle. If more than one hose is removed, be sure to label the hoses and fittings to ensure correct installation.

8 When checking vacuum hoses, be sure to include any plastic T-fittings in the check. Inspect the fittings for cracks, and check the hose where it fits over the fitting for distortion, which could cause leakage.

9 A small piece of vacuum hose can be used as a stethoscope to detect vacuum leaks. Hold one end of the hose to your ear, and probe around vacuum hoses and fittings, listening for the 'hissing' sound characteristic of a vacuum leak.

⚠ *Warning: When probing with the vacuum hose stethoscope, be very careful not to come into contact with moving engine components such as the fan or drivebelt.*

Fuel hoses

⚠ *Warning: Before carrying out the following operation, refer to the precautions given in 'Safety first!' at the beginning of this manual, and follow them implicitly. Petrol is a highly dangerous and volatile liquid, and the precautions necessary when handling it cannot be overstressed.*

10 Check all fuel hoses for deterioration and chafing. Check especially for cracks in areas where the hose bends, and also just before fittings, such as where a hose attaches to the carburettor.

11 Spring-type clamps are commonly used on fuel lines. These clamps often lose their tension over a period of time, and can be 'sprung' during removal. Replace all spring-type clamps with screw clips whenever a hose is replaced.

Metal lines

12 Sections of metal piping are often used for fuel line between the fuel tank, filter and the engine. Check carefully to be sure the piping has not been bent or crimped, and that cracks have not started in the line.

19.4 Top-up the piston damper on carburettor models

13 If a section of metal fuel line must be renewed, only seamless steel piping should be used, since copper and aluminium piping don't have the strength necessary to withstand normal engine vibration.

14 Check the metal brake lines where they enter the master cylinder for cracks in the lines or loose fittings. Any sign of brake fluid leakage calls for an immediate and thorough inspection of the brake system.

19 Fuel system components, checks and lubrication

1 Sparingly apply a few drops of light oil to the throttle spindles, accelerator cable and the pedal pivot. Similarly lubricate the exposed ends of the choke cable (where fitted).

2 Check that there is a small amount of slackness in the cable so that the throttle linkage closes fully with the accelerator pedal released. Also check that full throttle can be obtained with the accelerator pedal fully depressed.

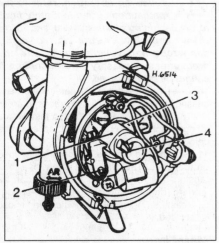

21.4 Distributor lubrication points

1 Contact breaker cam
2 Contact breaker pivot post
3 Centrifugal weights lubrication point
4 Cam spindle

3 If there is any doubt about the cable adjustment, refer to the relevant Parts of Chapter 4 for the full adjustment procedure.

4 On carburettor models, unscrew the piston damper cap from the top of the carburettor dashpot **(see illustration)**. Top up the damper with engine oil until the level is 13.0 mm above the top of the hollow piston rod.

5 Slowly push the damper back into the piston and screw on the cap taking care not to cross-thread it.

20 Contact breaker points check and adjustment

Refer to Chapter 5B.

21 Distributor lubrication

1 It is important that the distributor cam is lightly lubricated with general purpose grease, and that the contact breaker arm, centrifugal advance weights and cam spindle are also very lightly lubricated.

2 Great care should be taken not to use too much lubricant, as any excess that might find its way onto the contact breaker points could cause burning and misfiring.

3 If an ignition shield is fitted over the front of the engine, release the three plastic retaining lugs and lift away the shield. Detach the two spring clips or undo the two screws securing the distributor cap to the distributor body and lift off the cap.

4 To gain access to the cam spindle, lift away the rotor arm. Drop no more than two drops of engine oil onto the felt pad or screw head **(see illustration)**. This will run down the spindle when the engine is hot and lubricate the bearings. The centrifugal advance weights can be lubricated by dropping two or three drops of engine oil through one of the holes or slots in the distributor baseplate. No more than one drop of oil should be applied to the contact breaker arm pivot post.

5 Refit the rotor arm, distributor cap and ignition shield on completion.

22 Clutch return stop adjustment

Note: *As the friction linings of the clutch disc wear, the distance between the clutch release bearing and the clutch thrust plate will decrease. The pressure plate will then move in closer to the clutch disc to compensate for wear. Unless the wear is taken up by adjustment of the stop located between the flywheel housing and the release lever, the clutch will start to slip. On later models fitted*

with the Verto type clutch, the assembly is self-adjusting and the following procedure will not be necessary.

1 To carry out the adjustment, first disconnect the clutch operating lever return spring.

2 Pull the operating lever away from the engine until all the free play is eliminated.

3 Hold the lever in this position and measure the gap between the lever and the head of the stop using feeler blades **(see illustration)**.

4 If necessary, slacken the locknut and adjust the stop bolt until the specified gap is achieved. Then tighten the locknut.

23 Dynamo check and lubrication

Dynamo checks and lubrication consist simply of checking the auxiliary drivebelt condition and tension (Section 8) and adding a few drops of engine oil to the dynamo rear bearing lubricating hole.

24 Control box cleaning and inspection

On dynamo-equipped models, remove the control box cover and check the cut-out and regulator contacts. If they are dirty or rough or burnt, place a piece of fine glass paper (do not use emery paper or carborundum paper) between the cut-out contacts, close them manually, and draw the glass paper through several times.

Clean the regulator contacts in exactly the same way, but use emery or carborundum paper and not glass paper. Carefully clean both sets of contacts from all traces of dust with a rag moistened in methylated spirit. Refit the cover on completion.

25 Ignition timing check and adjustment

Refer to Chapter 5B or 5C.

22.3 Using feeler blades to measure the clutch return stop clearance

26 Carburettor idle speed and mixture adjustment

Refer to Chapter 4A.

27 Door, boot and bonnet check and lubrication

1 Check that the doors, bonnet and boot lid close securely. Check that the bonnet safety catch operates correctly. Check the operation of the door check straps.
2 Lubricate the hinges, door check straps, the striker plates and the bonnet catch sparingly with a little oil or grease.
3 If any of the doors, bonnet or boot lid do not close effectively or appear not to be flush with the surrounding panels, carry out the adjustment procedures contained in the appropriate part of Chapter 11.

28 Bodywork, paint and exterior trim check

1 The best time to carry out this check is after the car has been washed so that any surface blemish or scratch will be clearly evident and not hidden by a film of dirt.
2 Starting at one front corner check the paintwork all around the car, looking for minor scratches or more serious dents. Check all the trim and make sure that it is securely attached over its entire length.
3 Check the security of all door locks, door mirrors, badges, bumpers, front grille and wheel trim. Anything found loose, or in need of further attention should be done with reference to the relevant Chapters of this manual.

4 Rectify any problems noticed with the paintwork or body panels (see the appropriate part of Chapter 11).

29 Road test

Braking system

1 Make sure that the vehicle does not pull to one side when braking, and that the wheels do not lock when braking hard.
2 Check that there is no vibration through the steering when braking.
3 Check that the handbrake operates correctly, without excessive movement of the lever, and that it holds the vehicle stationary on a slope.
4 With the engine switched off, test the operation of the brake servo unit (where fitted) as follows. Depress the footbrake four or five times to exhaust the vacuum, then start the engine. As the engine starts, there should be a noticeable 'give' in the brake pedal as vacuum builds-up. Allow the engine to run for at least two minutes, and then switch it off. If the brake pedal is now depressed again, it should be possible to detect a hiss from the servo as the pedal is depressed. After about four or five applications, no further hissing should be heard, and the pedal should feel considerably harder.

Steering and suspension

5 Check for any abnormalities in the steering, suspension, handling or road 'feel'.
6 Drive the vehicle, and check that there are no unusual vibrations or noises.
7 Check that the steering feels positive, with no excessive sloppiness or roughness, and check for any suspension noises when cornering and driving over bumps.

Drivetrain

8 Check the performance of the engine, transmission and driveline.
9 Check that the engine starts correctly, both when cold and when hot.
10 Listen for any unusual noises from the engine and transmission.
11 Make sure that the engine runs smoothly when idling, and that there is no hesitation when accelerating.
12 On manual transmission models, check that all gears can be engaged smoothly without noise, and that the gear lever action is smooth and not abnormally vague or 'notchy'.
13 On automatic transmission models, make sure that the drive seems smooth without jerks or engine speed 'flare-ups'. Check that all the gear positions can be selected with the vehicle at rest.

Clutch

14 Check that the clutch pedal moves smoothly and easily through its full travel, and that the clutch itself functions correctly, with no trace of slip or drag. If the movement is uneven or stiff in places, check the system components with reference to Chapter 6.

Electrical equipment

15 Check the operation of all instruments and electrical equipment.
16 Make sure that all instruments read correctly, and switch on all electrical equipment in turn, to check that it functions properly.
17 Test the operation of the brake failure warning system (where fitted) by pressing the test switch located next to the heated rear window switch. When pressed, the switch should light and go out when released.
18 If the light should come on when driving, the brake fluid level should be checked (and topped-up, if necessary), as soon as possible.

Every 12 000 miles or 12 months

30 Air cleaner element renewal

Carburettor models

Except Cooper S

1 On models with an air intake duct over the top of the engine, unscrew the two nuts securing the duct to the rocker cover studs.

Release the clip and disconnect the duct from the air cleaner body.
2 Undo and remove the single wing nut and washer on early models, or the twin wing bolts and washers on later models, securing the air cleaner to the carburettor
3 If the air cleaner is retained by a single wing nut lift off the air cleaner top cover. Detach the rocker cover hose, then lift the air cleaner body off the carburettor, tip it up at the front and slide it sideways until it is clear of the long

retaining stud and can be lifted away. Recover the sealing ring.
4 If the air cleaner is retained by two wing nuts, detach the hot air duct (where fitted) and then lift the air cleaner body off the carburettor.
5 With the air cleaner removed from the engine, recover the rubber sealing ring if it stayed behind on the carburettor flange.
6 Lift off the air cleaner cover and withdraw the paper element. On the later type moulded

30.6a Prise off the later type air cleaner moulded plastic cover . . .

30.6b . . . and lift out the element

30.8 Make sure the alignment arrow is toward the lug on the air cleaner body

plastic air cleaners the cover is removed by prising it off with a screwdriver inserted in the slots on the periphery of the cover (see illustrations).

7 Thoroughly clean the inside of the air cleaner body.

8 Refit the air cleaner and element using a reverse of the removal procedure. Make sure that where an alignment arrow is stamped on the top cover, it is pointing toward the location lug on the air cleaner body (see illustration). Ensure also that the rubber sealing ring is in position before refitting the air cleaner.

9 If the air cleaner body incorporates an adjustable air intake spout, this should be positioned adjacent to the exhaust manifold in winter and away from it in summer.

Cooper S

10 Undo and remove the two wing bolts and washers and lift off the air cleaner top cover. Lift out the paper elements and thoroughly clean the inside of the air cleaner body.

11 The air cleaner body may be removed if necessary after disconnecting the engine breather pipe and the throttle return spring. Take care not to lose the two rubber sealing washers from the carburettor flanges.

12 Refitting the air cleaner and elements is the reverse of the removal procedure.

Fuel injection models

13 Release the four retaining clips, then slacken and remove the three screws

securing the air cleaner assembly to the throttle body, and lift off the air cleaner lid. Remove the filter element (see illustrations).

14 Wipe the body of the air cleaner clean, then fit the new element, ensuring that it is correctly seated.

15 Refit the air cleaner lid, and secure it in position with the retaining screws (tightening them securely) and clips.

31 Valve clearance adjustment

Refer to Chapter 2A or 2B.

32 Distributor cap, rotor arm and HT lead check

⚠ **Warning: Voltages produced by an electronic ignition system are considerably higher than those produced by conventional ignition systems. Extreme care must be taken when working on the system if the ignition is switched on. Persons with surgically-implanted cardiac pacemaker devices should keep well clear of the ignition circuits, components and test equipment.**

1 The spark plug (HT) leads should be inspected one at a time, to prevent mixing up the firing order, which is essential for proper

engine operation. Gain access to the leads and disconnect them as described for the spark plug check and renewal.

2 Check inside the boot for corrosion, which will look like a white crusty powder. Clean this off as much as possible; if it is excessive, or if cleaning leaves the metal connector too badly corroded to be fit for further use, the lead must be renewed. Push the lead and boot back onto the end of the spark plug. The boot should fit tightly onto the end of the plug – if it doesn't, remove the lead and use pliers carefully to crimp the metal connector inside the boot until the fit is snug.

3 Using a clean rag, wipe the entire length of the lead to remove built-up dirt and grease. Once the lead is clean, check for burns, cracks and other damage. Do not bend the lead sharply, because the conductor might break.

4 Inspect the remaining spark plug (HT) leads, ensuring that each is securely fastened at the distributor cap or DIS ignition module, and spark plug when the check is complete. If any sign of arcing, severe connector corrosion, burns, cracks or other damage is noticed, obtain new spark plug (HT) leads, renewing them as a set.

> **HAYNES HiNT** *If new spark plug leads are to be fitted, remove the leads one at a time and fit each new lead in exactly the same position as the old one.*

5 Spring back the retaining clips or undo the two screws and remove the distributor cap. Thoroughly clean it inside and out with a dry lint-free rag.

6 Examine the HT lead segments inside the cap. If they appear badly burned or pitted renew the cap. Also check the carbon brush in the centre of the cap, ensuring that it is free to move and stands proud of its holder. Make sure that there are no signs of cracks or black 'tracking' lines running down the inside of the cap, which will also mean renewal if evident.

7 Inspect the rotor arm checking it for security and also for signs of deterioration as described above.

8 Refit the distributor cap on completion.

30.13a On fuel injection models, release the clips (three arrowed) and remove the screws

30.13b Lift off the lid and remove the element

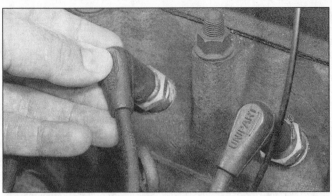

33.5 Pull the leads off the spark plugs by gripping the rubber boot

33.11 Adjusting a spark plug electrode gap

33 Spark plug renewal

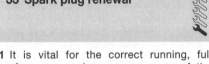

1 It is vital for the correct running, full performance and proper economy of the engine that the spark plugs perform with maximum efficiency. The most important factor in ensuring this, is that the plugs fitted are appropriate for the engine (a suitable type is listed in the Specifications). If this type is used and the engine is in good condition, the spark plugs should not need attention between scheduled renewal intervals. Spark plug cleaning is rarely necessary, and should not be attempted unless specialised equipment is available, as damage can easily be caused to the firing ends.

2 Spark plug removal and refitting requires a spark plug socket, with an extension which can be turned by a ratchet handle or similar. This socket is lined with a rubber sleeve, to protect the porcelain insulator of the spark plug, and to hold the plug while you insert it into the spark plug hole. You will also need a wire-type feeler gauge, to check and adjust the spark plug electrode gap, and a torque wrench to tighten the new plugs to the specified torque.

3 To remove the spark plugs, open the bonnet and, where fitted, release the three plastic retaining lugs and lift the ignition shield off the front of the engine

4 If the marks on the original-equipment HT leads cannot be seen, mark the leads 1 to 4, to correspond to the cylinder the lead serves.

5 Pull the leads from the plugs by gripping the rubber boot, not the lead, otherwise the lead connection may be fractured (see illustration).

6 Unscrew the spark plugs, ensuring that the socket is kept in alignment with each plug – if the socket is forcibly moved to either side, the porcelain top of the plug may be broken off. If any undue difficulty is encountered when unscrewing any of the spark plugs, carefully check the cylinder head threads and sealing surfaces for signs of wear, excessive corrosion or damage; if any of these conditions is found, seek the advice of a dealer as to the best method of repair.

7 As each plug is removed, examine it as follows – this will give a good indication of the condition of the engine. If the insulator nose of the spark plug is clean and white, with no deposits, this is indicative of a weak mixture.

8 If the tip and insulator nose are covered with hard black-looking deposits, then this is indicative that the mixture is too rich. Should the plug be black and oily, then it is likely that the engine is fairly worn, as well as the mixture being too rich.

9 If the insulator nose is covered with light tan to greyish-brown deposits, then the mixture is correct, and it is likely that the engine is in good condition.

10 The spark plug electrode gap is of considerable importance as, if it is too large or too small, the size of the spark and its efficiency will be seriously impaired. The gap should be set to the value given in the Specifications.

11 To set the electrode gap, measure the gap with a feeler blade or adjusting tool, and then bend open, or closed, the outer plug electrode until the correct gap is achieved (see illustration). The centre electrode should never be bent, as this may crack the insulation and cause plug failure, if nothing worse. If the outer electrode is not exactly over the centre electrode, bend it gently to align them.

12 Before fitting the spark plugs, check that the threaded connector sleeves at the top of the plugs are tight, and that the plug exterior surfaces and threads are clean.

13 On installing the spark plugs, first check that the cylinder head thread and sealing surface are as clean as possible; use a clean rag wrapped around a paintbrush to wipe clean the sealing surface. Ensure that the spark plug threads are clean and dry then screw them in by hand where possible. Take extra care to enter the plug threads correctly.

14 When each spark plug is started correctly on its threads, screw it down until it just seats lightly, then tighten it to the specified torque setting (see Haynes Hint).

15 Reconnect the HT leads in their correct order, using a twisting motion on the boot until it is firmly seated. Finally, refit the ignition shield, where applicable.

34 Emission control equipment check

1 Of the emission control systems that may be fitted, only the air pump drivebelt (where applicable), the crankcase ventilation system and the evaporative emission control systems require regular checking, and even then, the components of these systems require minimal attention.

2 Checks and adjustment of the air pump drivebelt are contained in Section 9.

3 The crankcase ventilation system filter in the oil filler cap should be renewed by simply renewing the cap (the new cap is supplied with filter inside). Checks of the other system components are contained in Chapter 4D.

4 Should it be felt that the other systems are not functioning correctly, the advice of a dealer should be sought.

HAYNES HiNT

It is very often difficult to insert spark plugs into their holes without cross-threading them. To avoid this possibility, fit a short length of 5/16 inch internal diameter rubber hose over the end of the spark plug. The flexible hose acts as a universal joint to help align the plug with the plug hole. Should the plug begin to cross-thread, the hose will slip on the spark plug, preventing thread damage to the aluminium cylinder head.

Every 24 000 miles or 24 months

35 Coolant renewal

⚠️ **Warning: Wait until the engine is cold before starting this procedure. Do not allow antifreeze to come into contact with your skin, or with painted surfaces of the vehicle. Rinse off spills immediately with plenty of water. Never leave antifreeze lying around in an open container, or in a puddle in the driveway or on the garage floor. Children and pets are attracted by its sweet smell, but antifreeze can be fatal if ingested.**

Cooling system draining

1 To drain the system, first remove the radiator or expansion tank filler cap (see *Weekly checks*). Move the heater temperature control to the hot position.

2 If the coolant is to be re-used, place clean bowls beneath the radiator and at the rear of the engine to collect the coolant for re-use.

3 Undo and remove the radiator drain plug and cylinder block drain plug, and allow the coolant to drain. If fitted, the radiator drain plug is located at the bottom of the radiator nearest the grille, and the cylinder block drain plug (if fitted) can be found at the rear of the block, beneath the engine tie-bar **(see illustration)**. Note that these fittings are only applicable to early models.

4 On later models the radiator does not incorporate a drain plug, and it is therefore necessary to detach the bottom hose to drain the coolant. To do this slacken the bottom hose retaining clip and pull the hose off the radiator outlet. On side-mounted radiators, the hose clip is very inaccessible and a long thin screwdriver is quite useful here. If the hose proves difficult to remove from the

radiator outlet, it is possible to gently push it off from the access hole under the wheelarch.

5 When the coolant has stopped running, probe the orifices, particularly the cylinder block orifice, with a short piece of wire to dislodge any particles of rust or sediment which may be preventing the coolant from completely draining out.

Cooling system flushing

6 With time, the cooling system may gradually lose its efficiency if the radiator core becomes choked with rust, scale deposits from the water, and other sediment. This is especially likely if an inferior grade of antifreeze has been used that has not been regularly renewed. To minimise this, as well as using only the specified type of antifreeze and clean soft water, the system should be flushed as follows whenever any part of it is disturbed, and/or when the coolant is renewed.

7 With the coolant drained, close the drain taps and refill the system with fresh water. Refit the radiator cap, start the engine and warm it up to normal operating temperature, then stop it and (after allowing it to cool down completely) drain the system again. Repeat as necessary until only clean water can be seen to emerge, then refill finally with the specified coolant mixture.

8 If only clean, soft water and good-quality antifreeze has been used, and the coolant has been renewed at the specified intervals, the above procedure will be sufficient to keep the system clean for a considerable length of time. If, however, the system has been neglected, a more thorough operation will be required, as follows.

9 To flush the system first drain the coolant as described previously. Place a garden hose in the radiator or expansion tank filler cap neck and allow water to slowly run through the system for ten to fifteen minutes.

10 To flush the engine, remove the thermostat (see Chapter 3), insert the garden hose into the thermostat housing, and allow water to circulate until it runs clear from the bottom hose. If, after a reasonable period, the water still does not run clear, the radiator should be flushed with a good proprietary cleaning agent.

11 In severe cases of contamination, reverse-flushing of the radiator may be necessary. To do this, remove the radiator (see Chapter 3), invert it, and insert the garden hose into the bottom outlet. Continue flushing until clear water runs from the top hose outlet. A similar procedure can be used to flush the heater matrix.

12 The use of chemical cleaners should be necessary only as a last resort. Normally, regular renewal of the coolant will prevent excessive contamination of the system.

Cooling system filling

13 Refit the cylinder block and radiator drain plugs or bottom hose connection as applicable.

14 Prepare a sufficient quantity of coolant mixture (water and antifreeze), in the specified concentration, to allow for a surplus, so as to have a reserve supply for topping-up. **Note:** *On models with no cylinder block drain plug, it is not possible to fully drain the coolant. To establish a suitable antifreeze concentration it will be necessary to pour adequate antifreeze directly into the radiator or expansion tank and then top-up with water. Subsequent topping-up should be done with an antifreeze/water mixture.*

15 Set the heater control knob to the maximum heat position and then fill the cooling system slowly. Slow filling reduces the possibility of air being trapped and forming air-locks. It helps also, if the large radiator hoses are gently squeezed during the filling procedure.

16 Do not fill the system higher than within 12 mm of the filler orifice, or maximum mark on the expansion tank. Overfilling will merely result in coolant loss down the overflow pipe due to expansion.

17 When the system is full, refit the filler cap and turn it firmly clockwise to lock it in position. Start the engine and run it at idle speed, until it has warmed-up to normal operating temperature.

18 Stop the engine, allow it to cool down *completely* (overnight, if possible), then remove the filler cap and top-up if necessary. Refit the filler cap, tightening it securely, and wash off any spilt coolant from the engine compartment and bodywork.

19 After refilling, always check carefully all components of the system (but especially any unions disturbed during draining and flushing) for signs of coolant leaks. Fresh antifreeze has a searching action, which will rapidly expose any weak points in the system.

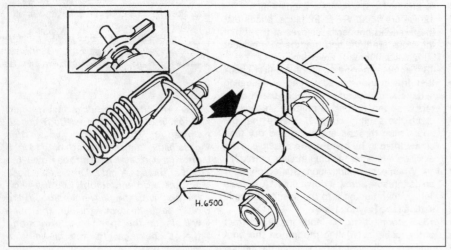

H.6500

35.3 Cylinder block coolant drain tap or plug location (arrowed)

37.5a Fuel filter inlet union (A), outlet union (B) and mounting bracket retaining bolts (C)

37.5b Slacken the union nuts whilst retaining the union adapter/filter with an open-ended spanner

36 Brake fluid renewal

⚠ **Warning: Brake hydraulic fluid can harm your eyes and damage painted surfaces, so use extreme caution when handling and pouring it. Do not use fluid that has been standing open for some time as it absorbs moisture from the air. Excess moisture can cause a dangerous loss of braking effectiveness.**

The procedure is similar to that for the bleeding of the hydraulic system as described in Chapter 9, except that the brake fluid reservoir should be emptied by syphoning, and allowance should be made for the old fluid to be removed from the circuit when bleeding a section of the circuit.

 HAYNES HiNT *Old hydraulic fluid is invariably much darker in colour than the new, making it easy to distinguish between the two.*

37 Fuel filter renewal (fuel injection models)

⚠ **Warning: Before carrying out the following operation, refer to the precautions given in 'Safety first!' at the beginning of this manual, and follow them implicitly. Petrol is a highly dangerous and volatile liquid, and the precautions necessary when handling it cannot be overstressed.**

1 Disconnect the battery negative terminal (refer to *Disconnecting the battery* in the Reference Chapter).
2 Chock the front wheels then jack up the rear of the car and support it securely on axle stands (see *Jacking and vehicle support*).
3 To minimise fuel loss during the following operation, working inside the luggage compartment, remove the top stud, then pivot the fuel tank trim panel downwards and fit a hose clamp to the fuel tank feed hose.
4 Refer to the information on fuel system depressurisation contained in the relevant part of Chapter 4.
5 From underneath the vehicle, slacken the union nuts and disconnect the inlet and outlet pipes from the fuel filter, whilst retaining the union adapter/filter with an open-ended spanner (**see illustrations**).
6 Remove the two bolts securing the filter mounting bracket to the subframe, and remove the filter assembly from the car.
7 Slacken and remove the outlet pipe adapter and O-ring from the filter, then slacken the clamp bolt and slide the filter out of the mounting bracket, noting which way the arrow stamped on the filter is pointing.
8 Remove the plugs from the filter, then fit the outlet pipe adapter (using a new O-ring), and tighten it securely. Ensuring that the arrow is pointing in the direction of the flow of fuel, slide the filter into position in the mounting bracket, and securely tighten the clamp bolt.
9 Refit the filter assembly to the car, tightening its mounting bolts securely.
10 Refit the inlet and outlet pipes to the filter, and securely tighten their union nuts.
11 Lower the car to the ground, then remove the clamp from the fuel tank feed hose, and secure the trim panel in position with its retaining stud. Reconnect the battery, then start the engine and check the filter unions for leakage.

⚠ **Warning: Dispose of the old filter safely; it will be highly flammable and may explode if thrown on a fire.**

Chapter 2 Part A:
Engine in-car repair procedures – pre-October 1996 models

Contents

Compression test – description and interpretation 2
Crankshaft oil seals – renewal 11
Crankshaft pulley – removal and refitting 6
Cylinder head (carburettor engines) – removal and refitting 9
Cylinder head (fuel injection engines) – removal and refitting 10
Distributor driveshaft – removal and refitting 15
Engine oil and filter renewal . . . . See Chapter 1
Engine oil level check . . . . See *Weekly checks*
Engine/transmission mountings – renewal 14
Flywheel (manual transmission models) – removal and refitting 12
General information 1

Oil cooler – removal and refitting 18
Oil filter housing and delivery pipe – removal and refitting 17
Oil pressure relief valve – removal, inspection and refitting 16
Rocker cover – removal and refitting 3
Rocker shaft assembly – removal, inspection and refitting 8
Timing chain, tensioner and sprockets – removal, inspection and
 refitting 7
Top Dead Centre (TDC) for number one piston – locating 4
Torque converter (automatic transmission models) – removal and
 refitting 13
Valve clearances – adjustment 5

Degrees of difficulty

Easy, suitable for novice with little experience	**Fairly easy,** suitable for beginner with some experience	**Fairly difficult,** suitable for competent DIY mechanic	**Difficult,** suitable for experienced DIY mechanic	**Very difficult,** suitable for expert DIY or professional

Specifications

Engine general

Code:	Capacity	Bore	Stroke
85H	848 cc	62.94 mm	68.25 mm
99H	998 cc	64.59 mm	76.20 mm
10H	1098 cc	64.59 mm	83.72 mm
12H	1275 cc	70.61 mm	81.28 mm
12A	1275 cc	70.61 mm	81.28 mm

Compression ratio:
85H 8.3:1
99H:
  Pre-1983 manual transmission models 8.3:1
  1983 to 1987 manual transmission models 10.3:1
  Pre-1987 automatic transmission models 8.9:1
  1988-on (category C) models 9.6:1
  1989-on (low compression) models 8.3:1
  1989-on (high compression) models 9.6:1
10H 8.5:1
12H:
  1275 GT models 8.8:1
  Cooper S Mk III models 9.75:1
12A:
  Cooper models 10.0:1
  All other models 9.4:1
Direction of crankshaft rotation . . . . Clockwise (viewed from timing chain end of engine)
Firing order . . . . 1-3-4-2 (No 1 cylinder at timing chain end of engine)

Lubrication system

Oil pump type . . . . Eccentric rotor type directly driven off camshaft
Oil pressure:
  Running . . . . 4.2 bars
  Idling . . . . 1.0 bar
Oil pressure relief valve spring minimum length . . . . 72.5 mm

Valve clearances

Inlet and exhaust (engine cold):

All engine types except 12A	0.30 mm
12A engines	0.27 to 0.33 mm

Torque wrench settings

	Nm	lbf ft
Automatic transmission input gear retaining nut	95	70
Camshaft retaining plate bolts	11	8
Camshaft sprocket nut	90	66
Connecting rod big-end:		
Bolts	50	37
Nuts	45	33
Converter housing nuts and bolts	25	18
Crankshaft pulley bolt	102	75
Cylinder head nuts:		
Stage 1	34	25
Stage 2	68	50
Engine left-hand plate:		
1/4 in UNF bolts	7	5
5/16 in UNF bolts	16	12
Engine mountings:		
Left-hand engine mounting bracket to transmission	25	18
Left-hand engine mounting to mounting bracket	22	16
Left-hand engine mounting to subframe	22	16
Right-hand engine mounting to flywheel housing cover	18	13
Right-hand engine mounting to subframe	22	16
Engine lower tie-bar to subframe	40	30
Engine lower tie-bar to transmission bracket	40	30
Engine upper tie-bar to bulkhead	22	16
Engine upper tie-bar to cylinder head	22	16
Flywheel centre bolt*	150	111
Flywheel housing nuts and bolts:		
3/8 in UNF	35	26
5/16 in UNC/UNF	25	18
Flywheel housing cover bolts	10	7
Gudgeon pin clamp bolt	32	24
Main bearing bolts	85	63
Oil filter housing nuts	19	14
Oil pipe banjo union	52	38
Oil pressure relief valve nut	60	44
Oil pump bolts	11	8
Rocker cover bolts	5	4
Rocker shaft pedestal nuts	32	24
Tappet side covers	5	4
Timing chain tensioner bolts	22	16
Timing cover:		
1/4 in UNF bolts	7	5
5/16 in UNF bolts	16	12
Torque converter centre bolt	152	112
Torque converter (six central bolts)	29	21
Transmission casing to engine	8	6
Water pump pulley bolts	10	7

*Use a new bolt

1 General information

Using this Chapter

This Part of Chapter 2 is devoted to in-car engine repair procedures for pre-October 1996 models. Similar information covering models from October 1996 onward will be found in Chapter 2B. All procedures concerning engine removal and refitting, and engine block/cylinder head overhaul for all engines can be found in Chapter 2C.

Refer to Vehicle identification in the Reference Section of this manual for details of engine code locations.

Most of the operations included in Chapter 2A are based on the assumption that the engine is still installed in the car. Therefore, if this information is being used during a complete engine overhaul, with the engine already removed, many of the steps included here will not apply.

Engine description

The Mini engine is a four-cylinder, water-cooled, overhead valve type of 848, 998, 1098, or 1275 cc displacement, depending on model and year of manufacture. The engine is bolted to the transmission assembly, which also forms the engine sump, and the complete power unit is supported, via rubber mountings, in the front subframe.

The cast iron cylinder head contains two valves per cylinder, mounted vertically and running in pressed-in valve guides. The valves are operated by rocker arms and pushrods via tubular cam followers from the camshaft, located in the left-hand side of the cylinder block.

The inlet and exhaust manifolds are attached to the rear side of the cylinder head and are linked to the valves via five inlet and exhaust ports of siamese configuration.

The pistons are of anodised aluminium alloy with three compression rings and an oil control ring on all engines except later 1275 cc units. These engines only have two compression rings. The gudgeon pin is retained in the small-end of the connecting rod by a pinch-bolt on 848 cc engines, by circlips on 1098 cc and early 998 cc engines and by an interference fit in the connecting rod small-end bore on 1275 cc and later 998 cc engines. At the other end of the connecting rod, renewable big-end shell bearings are fitted.

On all except 1275 cc Cooper S engines, a single row chain at the left-hand end of the engine drives the camshaft via the camshaft and crankshaft sprockets. On 1275 cc Cooper S models a duplex (twin row) timing chain is fitted. On the 848 cc engine, the camshaft is supported by three bearings, two being bored directly in the cylinder block while a white metal bearing (which is renewable) is fitted at the timing chain end. On the 998 cc, 1098 cc and 1275 cc units three steel-backed metal camshaft bearings are fitted.

The statically and dynamically balanced forged steel crankshaft is supported by three renewable shell-type main bearings. Crankshaft endfloat is controlled by four semi-circular thrustwashers located in pairs on either side of the centre main bearing.

A forced feed system of lubrication is used, with oil circulated round the engine from the transmission casing/sump. The level of engine oil in the sump is indicated on the dipstick, which is fitted on the front facing side of the engine. The oil in the transmission casing/sump is also used to lubricate the transmission and differential.

Oil is drawn from the sump through a gauze screen in the oil strainer and is sucked up the pick-up pipe and drawn into the oil pump. From the oil pump it is forced under pressure along a gallery in the cylinder block and through drillings to the big-end, main and camshaft bearings. A small hole in each connecting rod allows a jet of oil to lubricate the cylinder wall with each revolution.

From the camshaft left-hand bearing, oil is fed through drilled passages in the cylinder block and head to the left-hand rocker pedestal where it enters the hollow rocker shaft. Holes drilled in the shaft allow for the lubrication of the rocker arms, and the valve stems and pushrod ends. This oil is at a reduced pressure to the oil delivered to the crankshaft bearings. Oil from the left-hand

camshaft bearing also lubricates the timing chain. Oil returns to the sump by various passages; the tappets (cam followers) being lubricated by oil returning via the pushrod drillings in the block.

On all models a full-flow oil filter is fitted, and all oil passes through this filter before it reaches the main oil gallery. The oil is passed directly from the oil pump across the block to an external pipe on the right-hand side of the engine which feeds into the filter head. Cooper S and certain later 1275 cc models are fitted with an oil cooler.

The water pump and fan are driven, together with the dynamo or alternator, by an auxiliary drivebelt from the crankshaft pulley.

Both the distributor and oil pump are driven off the camshaft: the distributor via skew gears, and the oil pump via a slotted drive or splined coupling at the flywheel end of the shaft.

Repair operations possible with the engine in the car

The following work can be carried out with the engine in the car:

a) Compression pressure – testing.
b) Crankshaft pulley – removal and refitting.
b) Valve clearances – adjustment.
c) Timing chain, tensioner and sprockets – removal and refitting.
d) Rocker shaft assembly – removal and refitting
e) Cylinder head and valve gear – removal and refitting.
f) Cylinder head and pistons – decarbonising.
g) Crankshaft oil seals – renewal.
h) Flywheel/torque converter – removal and refitting.
i) Engine mountings – renewal.
j) Oil pressure relief valve – removal, inspection and refitting.
k) Oil filter housing and delivery pipe – removal and refitting.
l) Oil cooler – removal and refitting

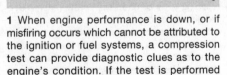

2 **Compression test –**
description and interpretation

1 When engine performance is down, or if misfiring occurs which cannot be attributed to the ignition or fuel systems, a compression test can provide diagnostic clues as to the engine's condition. If the test is performed regularly, it can give warning of trouble before any other symptoms become apparent.
2 The engine must be fully warmed-up to normal operating temperature, the battery must be fully charged, and the aid of an assistant will also be required.
3 On fuel injection models, disable and depressurise the fuel system by removing the fuel pump fuse, then start the engine and run

it until it cuts out. The fuse locations are as follows (see Chapter 12A for additional information):

a) Models with four-fuse fuseblock – remove line fuse 4 located in the line fuse cluster on the engine compartment bulkhead.
b) Models with twenty four-fuse fuseblock – remove fuse 11 located in the engine compartment fuseblock.

4 Disable the ignition system by disconnecting the ignition coil HT lead from the distributor cap and earthing it on the cylinder block. Use a jumper lead or similar wire to make a good connection.
5 Remove all four spark plugs (see Chapter 1) and fit a compression tester to the No 1 cylinder spark plug hole – the type of tester which screws into the plug thread is to be preferred.
6 Have the assistant hold the throttle wide open, and crank the engine on the starter motor; after one or two revolutions, the compression pressure should build-up to a maximum figure, and then stabilise. Record the highest reading obtained.
7 Repeat the test on the remaining cylinders, recording the pressure in each.
8 All cylinders should produce very similar pressures; a difference of more than 2 bars between any two cylinders indicates a fault. Note that the compression should build-up quickly in a healthy engine; low compression on the first stroke, followed by gradually-increasing pressure on successive strokes, indicates worn piston rings. A low compression reading on the first stroke, which does not build-up during successive strokes, indicates leaking valves or a blown head gasket (a cracked head could also be the cause). Deposits on the undersides of the valve heads can also cause low compression.
9 If the pressure in any cylinder is low, carry out the following test to isolate the cause. Introduce a teaspoonful of clean oil into that cylinder through its spark plug hole, and repeat the test.
10 If the addition of oil temporarily improves the compression pressure, this indicates that bore or piston wear is responsible for the pressure loss. No improvement suggests that leaking or burnt valves, or a blown head gasket, may be to blame.
11 A low reading from two adjacent cylinders is almost certainly due to the head gasket having blown between them; the presence of coolant in the engine oil will confirm this.
12 If one cylinder is about 20 percent lower than the others and the engine has a slightly rough idle, a worn camshaft lobe could be the cause.
13 If the compression reading is unusually high, the combustion chambers are probably coated with carbon deposits. If this is the case, the cylinder head should be removed and decarbonised.
14 On completion of the test, refit the spark plugs, reconnect the ignition coil HT lead and, where applicable, refit the fuel pump fuse.

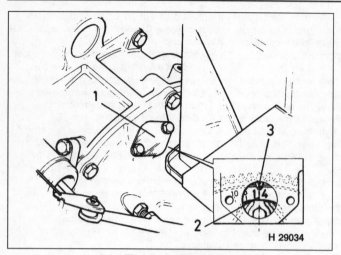

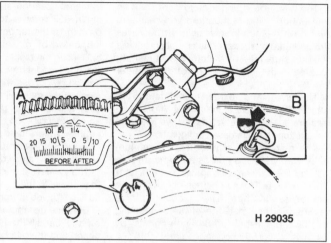

4.4a Timing mark locations – early manual transmission models

1 Inspection cover   2 Timing marks   3 Pointer

4.4b Timing mark locations – automatic transmission models

A Detail showing alternative timing marks   B Insert screwdriver to turn torque converter

3 Rocker cover – removal and refitting

Removal

1 Refer to the relevant part of Chapter 4 and remove the air cleaner assembly.
2 Remove the ignition shield (where fitted) from the front facing side of the engine.
3 Undo the two rocker cover retaining bolts and lift out the bolts and washers along with the ignition shield brackets. On later models, release the heater valve control cable from the clip on the relevant ignition shield bracket.
4 Collect the rocker cover retaining bolt dished washers from the top of the two rubber seals, then withdraw the seals from the rocker cover.
5 Lift off the rocker cover and gasket, then remove the gasket from the cover.
6 Check the condition of the two retaining bolt rubber seals and, if necessary, obtain new seals for refitting, together with the new gasket.

Refitting

7 Prior to refitting, scrape away all traces of old gasket from the rocker cover, then thoroughly clean the cover and the cylinder head mating face.
8 Apply gasket sealant or a suitable adhesive to the gasket locating surface in the rocker cover to retain the gasket in place. Locate the new gasket in position in the cover, ensuring that it seats correctly in the flange around the edge of the cover.
9 Place the cover in position on the cylinder head and fit the two retaining bolt rubber seals.
10 Locate the dished washers over the rubber seals, then refit the retaining bolts, washers and ignition shield brackets. Tighten the two bolts progressively to the specified

torque. Re-attach the heater valve control cable to the clip on the ignition shield bracket.
11 On completion, refit the ignition shield (where applicable) then refit the air cleaner assembly as described the relevant part of in Chapter 4.

4 Top Dead Centre (TDC) for number one piston – locating

1 Top dead centre (TDC) is the highest point in the cylinder that each piston reaches as the crankshaft turns. Each piston reaches its TDC position at the end of its compression stroke and then again at the end of its exhaust stroke. For the purpose of engine timing, TDC refers to the position of No 1 piston at the end of its compression stroke. On the engines covered by this manual, No 1 piston is at the timing chain end of the engine. It is necessary to set the engine in this position when carrying out many of the operations in this Chapter. To do so, proceed as follows.
2 Where fitted, release the three plastic retaining lugs and lift the ignition shield off the front of the engine.
3 Spring back the two distributor cap retaining clips or undo the screws then place the distributor cap to one side.
4 Gain access to the ignition timing marks by undoing the two bolts securing the inspection plate to the top of the flywheel housing and lifting off the plate. On automatic transmission models, withdraw the rubber grommet from the top of the converter housing **(see illustrations)**. On later models there is a timing scale on the timing cover, together with a notch or pointer on the crankshaft pulley **(see illustration)**.
5 Turn the engine over until No 1 piston is approaching TDC on the compression stroke. This can be checked by removing No 1 spark

plug and feeling the pressure being developed in the cylinder as the piston rises, or by removing the rocker cover and noting when the valves of No 4 cylinder are rocking, ie, the inlet valve just opening and the exhaust valve just closing. On manual transmission models, the engine can be turned over quite easily by engaging top gear and moving the car forwards. This should only be done on level ground; and make sure that the car cannot run away. An alternative method, and the method that should be used on automatic transmission models, is to press the auxiliary belt midway between the water pump pulley and dynamo or alternator pulley and then turn the fan blades. Fine positioning of the torque converter can be done by inserting a screwdriver through the access hole and turning the ring gear.

> **HAYNES HINT** *Turning the engine will be easier if the spark plugs are removed first – see Chapter 1.*

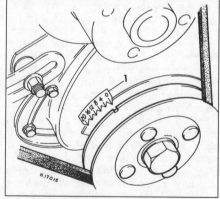

4.4c Timing scale (1) on timing cover of later manual transmission models

6 Continue turning the engine, in the correct direction of rotation, until No 1 piston is at TDC on the compression stroke. Verify this by checking that the timing marks are aligned. The timing marks on the flywheel (or torque converter), and the pointer on the housing, can be viewed through the inspection aperture using a small mirror. The 1/4 mark on the flywheel or torque converter indicates TDC and should be aligned with the pointer in the housing. On later models with a timing scale on the timing cover, the notch in the crankshaft pulley should be aligned with the 0 pointer on the timing cover scale.

7 The distributor rotor arm should now be pointing towards the No 1 spark plug HT lead segment in the distributor cap indicating that the crankshaft is correctly positioned with number 1 cylinder at TDC on its compression stroke. Temporarily place the cap in position to verify this if necessary. If the rotor arm is pointing at the No 4 HT lead segment in the cap, rotate the crankshaft one full turn (360º) until the TDC timing marks are realigned and the rotor arm is pointing at the No 1 segment.

5 Valve clearances – adjustment

1 The valve clearance adjustments should be made with the engine cold. The importance of correct rocker arm/valve stem clearances cannot be overstressed as they vitally affect the performance of the engine. If the clearances are set too wide, the efficiency of the engine is reduced as the valves open later and close earlier than was intended. If, on the other hand the clearances are set too close there is danger that the stems will expand upon heating and not allow the valves to close properly, which will cause burning of the valve head and seat, and possible warping.

2 To gain access to the rocker arms, remove the rocker cover as described in Section 3.

3 It is important that the clearance is set when the tappet of the valve being adjusted is on the heel of the cam (ie, opposite the peak). Turn the engine until valve No 8 (nearest the flywheel end of the engine) is fully open. With the engine in this position, valve No 1 will be fully closed and ready to be checked. On manual transmission models, the engine can be turned over quite easily by engaging top gear and moving the car forwards. This should only be done on level ground; and make sure that the car cannot run away. An alternative method, and the method that should be used on automatic transmission models, is to press the auxiliary belt midway between the water pump pulley and dynamo or alternator pulley and then turn the fan blades.

HAYNES HiNT *Turning the engine will be easier if the spark plugs are removed first – see Chapter 1.*

4 A feeler blade of the correct thickness should now be inserted between the valve stem and rocker arm. When the clearance is correct the feeler blade should be a smooth stiff sliding fit between the valve stem and rocker arm. The correct valve clearances are given in the Specifications at the start of this Chapter.

5 If the feeler blade is a tight or loose fit then the clearance must be adjusted. To do this, loosen the locknut of the adjustment stud and screw the adjuster stud in or out until the feeler blade can be felt to drag slightly when drawn from the gap **(see illustration)**.

6 Hold the adjuster firmly in this position and tighten the locknut. Recheck the gap on completion to ensure that it has not altered when locking the nut and stud.

7 Check each valve clearance in turn in the following sequence (which also avoids turning the crankshaft more than necessary). The valves are numbered from the timing chain end of the engine.

Valve fully open	Check and adjust
Valve No 8	Valve No 1
Valve No 6	Valve No 3
Valve No 4	Valve No 5
Valve No 7	Valve No 2
Valve No 1	Valve No 8
Valve No 3	Valve No 6
Valve No 5	Valve No 4
Valve No 2	Valve No 7

8 When all the valves have been checked and adjusted, refit the rocker cover as described in Section 3. Where removed, refit the spark plugs and HT leads (see Chapter 1).

6 Crankshaft pulley – removal and refitting

Removal

Note: *A new crankshaft pulley bolt locking washer will be required for refitting.*

1 Disconnect the battery negative terminal (refer to *Disconnecting the battery* in the Reference Chapter).

2 Refer to Chapter 1 and remove the auxiliary drivebelt.

3 Refer to Chapter 3 and remove the radiator.

4 Undo the bolts securing the fan to the water pump spindle, and remove the fan.

5 On later models, it may be necessary to remove the lower radiator mounting bracket to gain the necessary clearance to allow removal of the crankshaft pulley. To do this, undo the two nuts and bolts, accessed from underneath the wheelarch, securing the left-hand engine mounting to the subframe. Position a jack with interposed block of wood beneath the engine/transmission and carefully lift the jack until the engine/transmission is raised slightly. Undo the nuts and through-bolts securing the mounting bracket to transmission, and remove the bracket assembly from the vehicle **(see illustration)**.

5.5 Adjusting the valve clearances

6 Bend back the locking tab of the crankshaft pulley bolt locking washer, prising it back with a cold chisel or screwdriver through the radiator grille in the wing. Using a suitable socket or spanner, unscrew and remove the bolt and locking washer. This bolt is sometimes very difficult to release, and hitting the free end of the spanner with a heavy hammer is often the only way to start it. Engage top gear and apply the handbrake hard to prevent the engine from turning. Alternatively, and on automatic transmission models, remove the starter motor (Chapter 5A) and lock the flywheel with a screwdriver or similar tool engaged with the ring gear teeth.

7 Once the bolt has been slackened, set the engine at TDC for No 1 piston as described in Section 2.

8 Placing two large screwdrivers behind the crankshaft pulley at 180º to each other, carefully lever the pulley off. It is preferable to use a proper pulley extractor if this is available, but large screwdrivers or tyre levers are quite suitable, providing care is taken not to damage the pulley flange or timing cover.

Refitting

9 Thoroughly clean the crankshaft pulley then lubricate the oil seal contact surface with clean engine oil. Fit the pulley to the crankshaft, ensuring that the keyway engages with the Woodruff key.

10 Fit the new crankshaft pulley bolt locking washer and screw in the crankshaft pulley bolt. Tighten the bolt to the specified torque while using the same method to prevent crankshaft rotation as was used for removal.

6.5 Left-hand mounting bracket attachment bolts (arrowed) on later manual transmission models

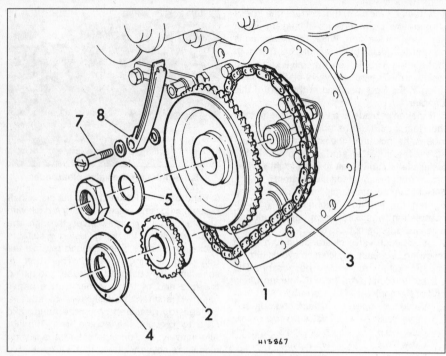

**7.7 Timing sprocket and chain assembly –
later type with tensioner arm**

1 Camshaft sprocket	4 Oil thrower	7 Tensioner retaining
2 Crankshaft sprocket	5 Locking washer	bolt
3 Timing chain	6 Nut	8 Tensioner

11 Bend up the tab of the locking washer to secure the crankshaft pulley bolt.

12 Where removed, refit the radiator lower mounting bracket and secure the bracket to the engine/transmission and subframe. Remove the jack under the engine.

13 Refit the fan to the water pump spindle and secure with the four bolts.

14 Refit the radiator as described in Chapter 3 and the auxiliary belt as described in Chapter 1.

15 Refit the components removed when setting the engine at TDC, then reconnect the battery.

---

7 Timing chain, tensioner and sprockets – removal, inspection and refitting

Removal

1 Set the engine at TDC for No 1 piston as described in Section 4.

2 Remove the crankshaft pulley as described in Section 6, but check that the engine is still set at TDC for No 1 piston before the pulley is withdrawn from the crankshaft.

3 Where applicable, disconnect the breather hose from the oil separator on the timing cover.

4 Unscrew the bolts holding the timing cover to the engine plate and cylinder block. **Note:** *Some of the bolts are larger than the others*

and, on earlier engines, each bolt makes use of a large flat washer as well as a spring washer.

5 Take off the timing cover and gasket.

6 With the timing cover removed, slide off the oil thrower.

7 Bend back the locking tab on the washer under the camshaft sprocket retaining nut and unscrew the nut, noting how the locking washer locating tag fits in the camshaft sprocket keyway **(see illustration)**. Prevent the camshaft sprocket from turning as the nut is slackened using a suitable forked tool engaged with the holes in the sprocket.

8 On later models, unscrew the timing chain tensioner retaining bolt and remove the bolt and tensioner. Note that there is a washer on each side of the tensioner arm.

7.14 Fitting a new tensioning ring to the camshaft sprocket

9 To remove the camshaft and crankshaft sprockets complete with chain, ease each sprocket forward a little at a time, levering behind each one in turn with two large screwdrivers at 180° to each other. If the sprockets are locked solid, it will be necessary to use a suitable puller.

10 With both sprockets removed, extract the Woodruff key from the crankshaft by tapping it out with a small chisel. Note that there may be a number of very thin packing washers behind the crankshaft sprocket; if so carefully remove them.

Inspection

11 Thoroughly clean all the components with paraffin or a suitable solvent and dry thoroughly. Pay particular attention to the timing cover and the mating face on the engine plate, ensuring that all traces of old gasket are removed.

12 Examine the teeth on both the crankshaft and camshaft sprockets for wear. Each tooth forms an inverted V with the sprocket periphery and, if worn, the side of each tooth under tension will be slightly concave in shape when compared with the other side of the tooth. If any sign of wear is present the sprockets must be renewed.

13 Examine the links of the chain for side slackness and renew the chain if any slackness is noticeable when compared with a new chain. It is a sensible precaution to renew the chain at about 60 000 miles, and at a lesser mileage if the engine is dismantled for a major overhaul. The rollers on a very badly worn chain may be slightly grooved. **Note:** *Cooper S type engines use duplex chains.*

14 Also check the rubber tension rings in the camshaft sprocket, where fitted. It is quite likely that the rubber will have become hard due to heat and oil contamination and it is advisable to renew them as a matter of course. The rings are simply prised out with a screwdriver and new rings stretched over the sprocket flanges and into the grooves **(see illustration)**. A spring-loaded rubber tensioner may be fitted on Cooper S type and later engines in place of the tensioning rings. If the rubber pad is grooved where it bears against the chain, it should also be renewed.

15 It is advisable to renew the timing cover oil seal at this stage, referring to the procedures contained in Section 11.

Refitting

16 If new sprockets are being fitted, the alignment between the two sprockets must be checked as follows.

17 Temporarily place the camshaft and crankshaft sprockets in position and place the straight-edge cf a steel ruler from the side of the camshaft sprocket teeth to the crankshaft sprocket. Using feeler blades, measure the gap between the steel rule and the crankshaft sprocket **(see illustration)**. If a gap exists, a suitable number of packing washers (available from Rover dealers) must be placed on the crankshaft nose, behind the crankshaft sprocket, to bring it onto the same plane as the camshaft sprocket. Use the existing packing washers (if fitted) and supplement these with additional washers if necessary. Remove both sprockets once the alignment has been checked and, if necessary, corrected.

18 With the packing washers (where necessary) in position on the crankshaft, refit the Woodruff key to the crankshaft slot. Make sure that the upper surface of the key is parallel with the crankshaft and ensure that it is fully seated by gently tapping it into place. It is advisable at this stage to check that the crankshaft sprocket will slide onto the crankshaft without binding as it is very easy to have the key positioned slightly high at one end. If the sprocket binds, remove the Woodruff key and refit it again. If the edges of the key are burred they must be cleaned with a fine file.

19 Lay the two sprockets on a clean surface so that the timing dots are adjacent to each other. Slip the timing chain over them and pull the sprockets back into mesh with the chain so that the timing dots, although further apart are still adjacent to each other **(see illustration)**.

20 Check that the engine is still positioned at TDC for No 1 piston (Section 4). In this position the crankshaft Woodruff key should be at the 12 o'clock position and the camshaft Woodruff key should be at the 2 o'clock position **(see illustration)**.

21 Fit the timing chain and sprocket assembly onto the camshaft and crankshaft, keeping the timing marks adjacent. If the camshaft and crankshaft have been positioned accurately, it will be found that the keyways on the sprockets will match the position of the keys, although it may be necessary to rotate the camshaft a fraction to ensure accurate lining-up of the camshaft sprocket.

22 Fit the locking washer to the camshaft sprocket with its locating tab in the sprocket keyway.

23 Screw on the camshaft sprocket retaining nut and tighten the nut to the specified torque. Prevent the camshaft sprocket from rotating as the nut is tightened using the same method as was used for removal.

24 Bend up the locking tab of the locking washer to hold the camshaft retaining nut securely.

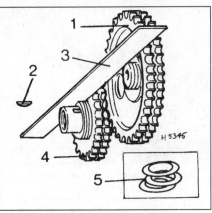

7.17 Camshaft and crankshaft sprocket alignment – double row type shown

1 Camshaft sprocket　*4 Crankshaft*
2 Woodruff key　　　　 *sprocket*
3 Straight-edge　　　 *5 Packing washers*

Note that with single row type sprockets, it is important to align the sides of the teeth and not the raised hub of the sprocket

25 On engines with a separate timing chain tensioner, refit the tensioner and retaining bolt ensuring that there is a washer on each side of the tensioner arm.

26 Fit the oil thrower to the crankshaft with the F mark facing outwards (away from the chain).

27 Lubricate the timing chain, sprockets and the inner lip of the timing cover oil seal with clean engine oil.

28 Position a new gasket on the timing cover and insert two of the larger retaining bolts to locate the gasket in position. Where a large flat washer is used on the retaining bolts, ensure that the flat washer is positioned next

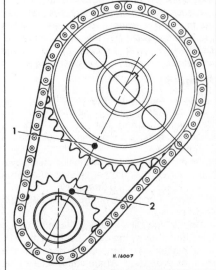

7.20 Timing mark locations relative to keyways

1 Timing dot on camshaft sprocket
2 Timing dot on crankshaft sprocket

to the cover flange and under the spring washer.

29 Hold the two bolts in place and fit the timing cover to the engine plate. Screw in the two bolts finger tight only to retain the cover and gasket. Refit the remaining bolts in their correct locations and also tighten them finger tight only at this stage.

30 Lubricate the oil seal contact surface on the crankshaft pulley, and temporarily locate the pulley on the crankshaft. With the pulley in place to centralise the timing cover, tighten the accessible bolts sufficiently to hold the timing cover in place.

31 Remove the crankshaft pulley and tighten all the timing cover retaining bolts to the specified torque.

32 Where applicable, reconnect the breather hose to the oil separator on the timing cover.

33 Refit the crankshaft pulley as described in Section 6.

---

8 Rocker shaft assembly –
removal, inspection and refitting

General information

1 The rocker shaft assembly is secured to the top of the cylinder head by the cylinder head inner studs and nuts. Although in theory it is possible to undo the head nuts and remove the rocker shaft assembly without removing the head, in practice, this is not recommended. Once the nuts have been removed, the head gasket will be disturbed, and the gasket will almost certainly leak or blow after refitting. For this reason, removal of the rocker shaft assembly cannot be done without removing the cylinder head and renewing the head gasket.

Removal

2 Remove the cylinder head as described in Section 9 or 10 as applicable.

3 To dismantle the rocker shaft assembly, release the rocker shaft locating screw, remove the split pins, flat washers, and spring washers from each end of the shaft and slide from the shaft the pedestals, rocker arms, and rocker spacing springs **(see illustration)**.

7.19 Timing dots on sprockets aligned with chain fitted

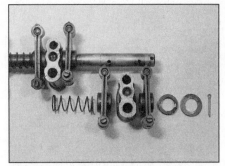

8.3 Rocker shaft components dismantled for inspection

9.15a Recover the pedestal plate (where fitted) . . .

9.15b . . . then lift off the rocker shaft assembly

Keep all the components in order and make a note of each component's correct fitted position and orientation as it is removed, to ensure it is fitted correctly on reassembly.

Inspection

4 Check the rocker arms for wear of the rocker bushes, for wear at the rocker arm face which bears on the valve stem, and for wear of the adjusting ball-ended screws. Wear in the rocker arm bush can be checked by gripping the rocker arm tip and holding the rocker arm in place on the shaft, noting if there is any lateral rocker arm shake. If shake is present, and the arm is very loose on the shaft, remedial action must be taken. Pressed steel valve rockers cannot be renovated by renewal of the rocker arm bush. It is necessary to fit new rocker arms. Forged rocker arms which have worn bushes may be taken to a Rover dealer or engine reconditioning specialist to have the old bush drawn out and a new bush fitted. Forged rockers and pressed steel rockers are interchangeable in sets of eight, but, where one or two pressed steel rockers only require renewal, it is not advised to replace them with the forged type.

5 Check the tip of the rocker arm where it bears on the valve head for cracking or serious wear on the case hardening. If none is present re-use the rocker arm. Check the lower half of the ball on the end of the rocker arm adjusting screw. On high performance Mini engines, wear on the ball and top of the pushrod is easily noted by the unworn 'pip' which fits in the small central oil hole on the

9.16 Remove the pushrods, keeping them in order

ball. The larger this 'pip' the more wear has taken place to both the ball and the pushrod. Check the pushrods for straightness by rolling them on the bench. Renew any that are bent.

Refitting

6 To reassemble the rocker shaft fit the split pin, flat washer and spring washer at the right-hand end of the shaft and then slide on the rocker arms, rocker shaft pedestals, and spacing springs in the same order in which they were removed.

7 Screw in the rocker shaft locating screw and slip the locating plate into position. Finally, fit to the end of the shaft the spring washer, plain washer, and split pin, in that order.

8 Refit the cylinder head as described in Section 9 or 10, as applicable.

9 Cylinder head (carburettor engines) – removal and refitting

Note: *If working on a pre-1990 engine fitted with emission control equipment, it will be necessary to first remove the diverter valve, air pump and associated hoses before proceeding with the removal sequence. Detailed removal procedures for these components will be found in Chapter 4D.*

Removal

1 Disconnect the battery negative terminal (refer to *Disconnecting the battery* in the Reference Chapter). For improved working clearance, remove the bonnet as described in Chapter 11A.

2 On models fitted with an ignition shield over the front of the engine, release the three retaining lugs and lift off the shield.

3 Drain the cooling system as described in Chapter 1.

4 Slacken the clips securing the radiator top hose and remove the hose. On later models, also disconnect the heater hose at the thermostat housing. Where fitted, slacken the water pump-to-cylinder head bypass hose retaining clips.

5 Make a note of the electrical connections at the ignition coil and disconnect them. Now undo and remove the nut securing the coil

bracket to the cylinder head and lift away the coil.

6 Undo and remove the nuts or bolts securing the radiator upper support bracket to the thermostat housing and radiator. Remove the bracket. On later models, disconnect the two vacuum hoses, noting their fitted positions, from the vacuum switch in the thermostat housing.

7 Refer to Chapter 4A and remove the air cleaner assembly and carburettor(s).

8 Undo and remove the retaining nuts and bolts, and lift off the clamps securing the exhaust front pipe to the manifold. On Cooper S models, undo and remove the nuts and flat washers securing the inlet and exhaust manifolds to the cylinder head. Lift off the inlet manifold, ease the exhaust manifold back off the cylinder head studs and tie it securely in this position.

9 On later models, undo the union bolt securing the brake servo vacuum hose to the inlet manifold, and recover the hose union sealing washers.

10 Where applicable, slacken the securing clip and remove the heater hose from the heater valve on the cylinder head. Now disconnect the control cable from the valve.

11 Make a note of their positions and then remove the HT leads from the spark plugs.

12 Detach the temperature gauge wiring connector from the sender unit.

13 Remove the rocker cover as described in Section 3.

14 Slacken the four rocker pedestal nuts and the nine main cylinder head nuts, half a turn at a time, in the reverse sequence to that shown **(see illustration 9.29)**. On some 1275 cc engines an additional nut and bolt are located at each end of the cylinder head, and these must be released first. When the tension is released from all the nuts, they may then be removed, one at a time, from their studs.

15 Recover the pedestal plate (where fitted) then lift off the rocker shaft assembly complete and place it to one side **(see illustrations)**.

16 Lift out the pushrods, keeping them in order according to their respective valves **(see illustration)**.

> **HAYNES HINT** *The easiest way to keep the pushrods in order is to push them through a sheet of thick paper or thin card, in the correct sequence, then number them 1 to 8.*

17 The cylinder head can now be removed by lifting upwards. If the head is jammed, try to rock it to break the seal. Under no circumstances try to prise it apart from the block with a screwdriver or cold chisel, as damage may be done to the faces of the head or block. If other methods fail to work, strike the head sharply with a soft-headed mallet, or with a metal hammer with an interposed piece of wood to cushion the blows. Do not hit the head directly with a metal hammer, as this may cause the casting to fracture. Several sharp taps with the mallet, at the same time pulling upwards, should free the head. Once free, lift the head up and off the studs, then recover the gasket.

18 If the cylinder head is to be dismantled for overhaul, refer to Part C of this Chapter. Refer to Section 8 if the rocker shaft assembly is to be dismantled.

Preparation for refitting

19 The mating faces of the cylinder head and cylinder block must be perfectly clean before refitting the head. Use a metal or hard plastic scraper to remove all traces of gasket and carbon; also clean the piston crowns. Take particular care during the cleaning operations, as the mating faces and piston crowns can be easily scored. Also, make sure that the carbon is not allowed to enter the oil and water passages – this is particularly important for the lubrication system, as carbon could block the oil supply to the engine's components. Using adhesive tape and paper, seal the water and oil holes in the cylinder block. To prevent carbon entering the gap between the pistons and bores, smear a little grease in the gap. After cleaning each piston, use a small brush to remove all traces of grease and carbon from the gap, then wipe away the remainder with a clean rag. Clean all the pistons in the same way.

20 Check the mating surfaces of the cylinder block and the cylinder head for nicks, deep scratches and other damage. If slight, they may be removed carefully with a file, but if excessive, machining may be the only alternative to renewal.

21 If warpage of the cylinder head gasket surface is suspected, use a straight-edge to check it for distortion. Refer to Part C of this Chapter if necessary.

22 Check the condition of the cylinder head studs and nuts, and particularly their threads. Wash the nuts in a suitable solvent and wipe clean the studs. Check each for any sign of visible wear or damage, renewing any if necessary.

Refitting

23 Wipe clean the mating surfaces of the cylinder head and cylinder block, then place the new cylinder head gasket on the block. The gasket is marked FRONT and TOP and should be fitted in position according to these markings (see illustrations). It is also easier at this stage to connect the lower end of the small bypass hose from the water pump to the cylinder block.

24 With the gasket in position carefully lower the cylinder head onto the cylinder block. Make sure that the bypass hose engages with the pipe stub on the cylinder head as the head is lowered into place.

25 Fit the cylinder head nuts and washers finger tight to the five cylinder head holding-down studs, which remain outside the rocker cover.

9.23a The cylinder head gasket is marked FRONT . . .

9.23b . . . and TOP

26 Fit the pushrods in the same order in which they were removed. Lubricate the pushrod ends before fitting, and ensure that they locate properly in the stems of the tappets.

27 The rocker shaft assembly can now be lowered over its eight locating studs. Take care that the rocker arms are the right way round. Lubricate the ball-ends of the valve adjusting screws and insert them in the pushrod cups. **Note:** *Failure to place the ball-ends in the cups can result in them seating on the edge of a pushrod or outside it when the head and rocker assembly is pulled down tight.*

28 Fit the pedestal plate then the four rocker pedestal nuts and washers, and the four cylinder head stud nuts and washers, which also serve to secure the rocker pedestals. Tighten all the nuts lightly at this time.

29 Working in the sequence shown, tighten the nine cylinder head nuts to the specified Stage 1 torque setting, and then to the Stage 2 setting (see illustration). **Note:** *On 1275 cc engines having an additional nut and bolt, these should be tightened last.* When the cylinder head nuts have been fully tightened, tighten the four smaller rocker pedestal nuts to the specified torque.

30 Reconnect the wire to the temperature gauge sender unit.

31 Where applicable, refit the heater hose to the heater valve then tighten the heater hose and the bypass hose retaining clips. On later models, refit the heater hose to the thermostat housing.

32 Refer to Chapter 4D and reconnect the exhaust front pipe and, on Cooper S models, the inlet and exhaust manifolds.

33 Where applicable, position a new sealing washer on either side of the brake servo vacuum hose union, and tighten the union bolt securely.

34 On later models, reconnect the two vacuum hoses to the vacuum switch in the thermostat housing.

35 Refit the radiator upper support bracket.

36 Refit the ignition coil and bracket and reconnect the wiring.

37 Refit and secure the radiator top hose.

38 Refer to Chapter 4A and refit the carburettor(s).

39 Refer to Section 5 and adjust the valve clearances.

40 Refit the rocker cover as described in Section 3, then refit the HT leads and associated components.

41 Reconnect the battery then refill the cooling system as described in Chapter 1. If removed, refit the bonnet, referring to Chapter 11A if necessary.

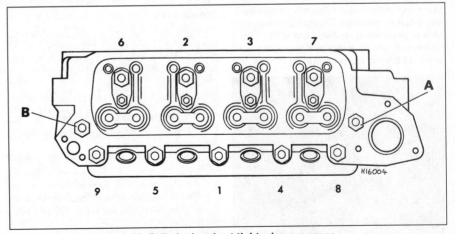

9.29 Cylinder head nut tightening sequence

A and B indicate additional bolt and nut on some 1275 cc engines

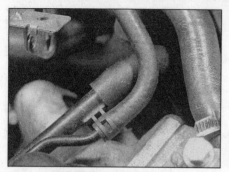

10.19a Disconnect the two vacuum/breather hoses from the left-hand end of the cylinder head . . .

10.19b . . . and the single hose from the right-hand end

10 Cylinder head (fuel injection engines) – removal and refitting

Note: *Observe the precautions in Section 1 of Chapter 4B before working on any component in the fuel system.*

Removal

1 Disconnect the battery negative terminal (refer to *Disconnecting the battery* in the Reference Chapter). For improved working clearance, remove the bonnet as described in Chapter 11A.

2 Release the fasteners and remove the ignition cover from the front of the engine.

3 Drain the cooling system as described in Chapter 1.

4 Refer to Chapter 4B and remove the air cleaner assembly.

5 Firmly apply the handbrake, then jack up the front of the car and support it securely on axle stands (see *Jacking and vehicle support*).

6 Working under the car, slacken and remove the single bolt securing the exhaust front pipe to its mounting bracket on the transmission. Undo the three nuts securing the front pipe to the manifold, then disconnect it and recover the gasket.

7 Trace the wiring back from the exhaust system lambda sensor (which is screwed into the exhaust manifold), releasing it from any relevant cable-ties, and disconnect its wiring connector from the main harness.

8 Lower the car to the ground.

10.20 Remove the nut and release the ignition coil bracket

9 Undo the bolt and remove the retaining clip securing the injector housing fuel pipes to the bulkhead.

10 Bearing in mind the information contained in Chapter 4B, concerning fuel system depressurisation, place absorbent rags around the fuel feed and return hose unions on the throttle body. Remove the fuel tank filler cap to release any pressure in the tank. Using an open-ended spanner to retain each adapter, slacken the union nuts and disconnect the feed and return pipes from the throttle body assembly. Plug each pipe and adapter, to minimise the loss of fuel and prevent the entry of dirt into the system.

11 Release the retaining clips and disconnect the wiring connectors from the injector housing, the throttle potentiometer and the stepper motor. Free the wiring from any relevant retaining clips, and position it clear of the throttle body assembly.

12 Slacken the accelerator cable locknuts, and free the outer cable from its mounting bracket. Release the inner cable from the throttle cam, and position the cable clear of the throttle body.

13 On automatic transmission models, disconnect the governor control rod from the throttle body linkage.

14 Disconnect the two vacuum hoses from the rear of the inlet manifold, noting their correct fitted positions; note that the hoses are colour-coded for identification purposes.

15 Undo the union bolt securing the brake servo vacuum hose to the inlet manifold, and recover the hose union sealing washers.

16 Slacken the retaining clips and disconnect the coolant hoses from the left-hand side of the inlet manifold.

17 Slacken the clips securing the radiator top hose to the thermostat housing and radiator, and remove the hose.

18 Undo the radiator upper mounting bracket retaining bolts, and remove the bracket from the side of the cylinder head and radiator.

19 Release the retaining clip(s), and disconnect the two vacuum/breather hoses from the left-hand end of the cylinder head, and the single hose from the right-hand end of the head (see illustrations).

20 Undo the nut securing the ignition coil to

the front of the cylinder head, then release the coil from its mounting stud and position it clear of the cylinder head (see illustration).

21 Make a note of the correct fitted positions of the HT leads, and disconnect them from the spark plugs.

22 Remove the cylinder head assembly as described in paragraphs 13 to 18 of Section 9, noting that it will be necessary to disconnect the wiring connectors from the PTC heater and coolant temperature sensor (situated on the underside of the inlet manifold) as they become accessible.

Preparation for refitting

23 Refer to Section 9, paragraphs 19 to 22.

Refitting

24 Wipe clean the mating surfaces of the cylinder head and cylinder block, then place the new cylinder head gasket on the block. The gasket is marked FRONT and TOP and should be fitted in position according to these markings (see illustrations 9.23a and 9.23b).

25 With the gasket in position, locate the cylinder head on the holding-down studs and reconnect the PTC heater and coolant temperature sensor wiring connectors.

26 Lower the cylinder head onto the cylinder block and fit the cylinder head nuts and washers finger tight to the five holding-down studs, which remain outside the rocker cover.

27 Fit the pushrods in the same order in which they were removed. Lubricate the pushrod ends before fitting, and ensure that they locate properly in the stems of the tappets.

28 The rocker shaft assembly can now be lowered over its eight locating studs. Take care that the rocker arms are the right way round. Lubricate the ball-ends of the valve adjusting screws and insert them in the pushrod cups. **Note:** *Failure to place the ball-ends in the cups can result in them seating on the edge of a pushrod or outside it when the head and rocker assembly is pulled down tight.*

29 Fit the pedestal plate then the four rocker pedestal nuts and washers, and the four cylinder head stud nuts and washers, which also serve to secure the rocker pedestals. Tighten all the nuts lightly at this time.

30 Working in the sequence shown, tighten the nine cylinder head nuts to the specified Stage 1 torque setting, and then to the Stage 2 setting (see illustration 9.29). When the cylinder head nuts have been fully tightened, tighten the four smaller rocker pedestal nuts to the specified torque.

31 Adjust the valve clearances as described in Section 5.

32 The remainder of the refitting process is a direct reversal of the removal procedure, noting the following points:

a) Ensure that all pipes/hoses are correctly reconnected, and (where necessary) are securely held in position by their retaining clips.

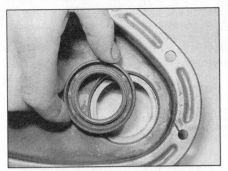

11.3 Timing cover oil seal must be fitted with the open side towards the chain

11.7a Where fitted, remove the primary gear dust shield . . .

11.7b . . . then lift off the C-shaped washer . . .

b) Tighten all nuts and bolts to the specified torque setting (where given).
c) Position a new sealing washer on either side of the brake servo vacuum hose union, and tighten the union bolt securely.
d) Refit the rocker cover as described in Section 3.
e) Ensure that the mating faces of the exhaust manifold and front pipe are clean, and use a new gasket when connecting the front pipe flange.
f) Adjust the accelerator cable and refit the air cleaner as described in Chapter 4B.
g) Refill the cooling system as described in Chapter 1.
h) Refit the bonnet as described in Chapter 11A.

11.7c . . . and backing ring

11.8 Engage the flange of the primary gear removal tool with the primary gear groove

11 Crankshaft oil seals – renewal

Timing cover oil seal

1 Remove the timing cover as described in Section 7, paragraphs 1 to 5.
2 Thoroughly clean the timing cover with paraffin or a suitable solvent and dry thoroughly. Pay particular attention to the mating faces of the cover and the engine plate, ensuring that all traces of old gasket are removed.
3 Drive out the old seal and thoroughly clean the recess in the timing cover. Apply a smear of multipurpose grease to the outer edge of the new seal then, with the timing cover supported, tap the seal into place using a wooden block or the old seal to spread the load. Ensure that the open side of the seal faces inward, towards the chain **(see illustration)**.
4 Refit the timing cover as described in Section 7, paragraphs 27 to 33.

Primary gear oil seal

Manual transmission models

Note 1: *The majority of clutch faults experienced on Mini power units are caused by oil contamination of the clutch friction linings due to the failure of the primary gear oil seal. It is therefore recommended that the seal*

is renewed whenever problems of this nature are encountered.
Note 2: *Rover special tools 18G 1068B and 18G 1043 (or suitable alternatives) will be required for this operation. The accompanying photos in this Section depict the use of a typical alternative to the Rover special tools.*
5 Remove the flywheel and clutch assembly as described in Chapter 6.
6 The primary gear complete with oil seal can now be withdrawn from the crankshaft and flywheel housing as described below.
7 Remove the dust shield (where fitted) then lift off the C-shaped thrustwasher and backing ring that retain the primary gear in position **(see illustrations)**.
8 Now screw in the threaded centre bolt of special tool 18G 1068B until the base of the tool abuts the oil seal. Pull the primary gear outwards as far as it will go and slide the two collets of 18G 1068B between the groove at

the rear of the primary gear splines and the base of the tool body. If an alternative tool is being used, engage the flange of the tool body with the primary gear groove **(see illustration)**.
9 Slowly unscrew the wing nut on tool 18G 1068B while holding the tool body. This will cause the primary gear to be withdrawn from the flywheel housing, bringing the oil seal with it. If an alternative tool is being used, position a suitable thrust pad on the end of the crankshaft and tighten the tool centre bolt against the thrust pad to draw off the primary gear and oil seal **(see illustration)**.
10 When the primary gear and oil seal are clear of the housing, lift them off the end of the crankshaft, remove the tool and slide the oil seal off the primary gear **(see illustration)**.
11 To fit a new oil seal, first slide the primary gear onto the crankshaft and secure with the C-shaped washer and backing ring.

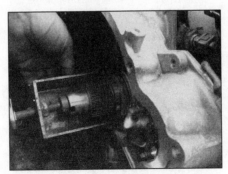

11.9 Tighten the tool centre bolt to draw off the primary gear and oil seal

11.10 Remove the tool and slide the primary gear and oil seal off the end of the crankshaft

11.12 Place a protective sleeve over the primary gear splines . . .

12 To avoid damage to the oil seal as it is fitted, place the protective sleeve, special tool 18G 1043, over the primary gear, or if this tool is not available cover the primary gear splines and the stepped shoulder with masking tape **(see illustration)**.

13 Lubricate the lip of the oil seal, and very carefully slide it over the primary gear and into position against the flywheel housing **(see illustration)**. The open part of the seal must be facing towards the engine.

14 Screw on the threaded centre bolt of special tool 18G 1068B (or similar alternative) and, when the body of the tool contacts the seal, fully tighten the centre bolt, thus forcing the seal squarely into the housing **(see illustration)**. Remove the tool when the face of the seal is flush with the housing.

15 Where applicable, refit the dust shield to the primary gear with the stepped face of the shield (marked FLYWHEEL SIDE) facing away from the engine **(see illustration)**.

16 The flywheel and clutch assembly can now be refitted as described in Chapter 6.

Automatic transmission models

Note: *Rover special tools 18G 1068B, 18G 1087 and 18G 1098 should ideally be obtained for this operation.*

17 Remove the torque converter as described in Section 13.

18 Note the fitted depth of the oil seal in the converter housing so that the new seal may be fitted in the same position.

19 Using a hooked instrument, or alternatively Rover special tool 18G 1087, extract the oil seal from the converter housing.

11.14 Use a suitable fitting tool to press the oil seal fully into the flywheel housing

11.13 . . . then slide the new oil seal over the sleeve onto the primary gear

20 To protect the lips of the new seal as it is fitted, wrap adhesive tape around the converter output gear splines or preferably use Rover special tool 18G 1098.

21 Using a suitable length of tubing or preferably Rover special tool 18G 1068B, install the oil seal into the housing to the same position as noted during removal. Note that if the seal is not positioned correctly it may cover an important oil drain hole in the housing.

22 The torque converter can now be refitted as described in Section 13.

12 Flywheel (manual transmission models) – removal and refitting

The flywheel on all manual transmission models is removed complete with the clutch assembly, the components then being separated after removal. Full details of clutch and flywheel removal and refitting are contained in Chapter 6.

13 Torque converter (automatic transmission models) – removal and refitting

Removal

Note: *Rover special tool 18G 1086 will be required to release the torque converter from the crankshaft.*

1 Firmly apply the handbrake, then jack up

11.15 Refit the primary gear dust shield with the stepped face marked FLYWHEEL SIDE (arrowed) facing away from the engine

the front of the car and support it securely on axle stands (see *Jacking and vehicle support*).

2 Disconnect the battery negative terminal (refer to *Disconnecting the battery* in the Reference Chapter). If greater working clearance is required, remove the bonnet as described in Chapter 11A.

3 Remove the front grille as described in Chapter 11A.

4 Detach the heater air duct from the air inlet under the right-hand front wing. Remove the air inlet from the inner wing panel.

5 Remove the starter motor as described in Chapter 5A.

6 On fuel injection models carry out the following:

a) Remove the air cleaner assembly, the engine management ECU and the crankshaft position sensor as described in Chapter 4B and Chapter 5A or 5B.

b) Disconnect the oil separator breather hose from the right-hand end of the cylinder head, then undo the two bolts securing the separator to the torque converter housing. Remove the separator and hose assembly from the engine, along with its gasket.

c) Slacken and remove the screw, situated just to the right of the brake servo unit, securing the earth leads to the bulkhead.

d) Undo the bolts securing the wiring harness retaining clip and starter motor lead brackets to the converter housing, then position the wiring clear of the engine.

7 On early models, undo and remove the screws securing the starter solenoid to the inner wing panel. Lift off the solenoid and position it out of the way.

8 If the ignition coil is mounted on the flywheel housing, or on a bracket secured to one of the cylinder head studs, remove the coil and mounting bracket and position it well clear.

9 On later Mini 850 and 1000 models, remove the horn and place it to one side.

10 Undo and remove the two bolts securing the engine upper tie-bar and bracket to the side of the cylinder block. Note that on later models one of the bolts also retains the engine earth strap.

11 Undo and remove the nuts and/or bolts securing the radiator upper support bracket to the radiator and thermostat housing. Withdraw the bracket. **Note:** *It is not necessary to remove the support bracket if a large clearance exists between the radiator and left-hand inner wing panel, as is the case on later Mini 850 and 1000 models.*

12 Place a jack beneath the torque converter housing end of the transmission casing and just take the weight of the power unit. Use a block of wood interposed between the casing and the jack to spread the load.

13 From under the car undo and remove the two nuts and bolts securing the right-hand engine mounting to the subframe side-members. The best way to do this is to engage the help of an assistant to hold the bolts from above while the nuts are undone from below. The bolt heads are tucked away beneath the converter housing and can only be reached with a small open-ended spanner.

14 Having released the mounting, jack up the power unit sufficiently to enable the nine bolts securing the converter housing cover to be removed. Note that on early models one of the front bolts also retains the engine earth strap. On all models the rear bolts are nearly inaccessible, requiring a good deal of patience and a short spanner.

15 When all the bolts are undone, lift off the converter housing cover.

16 Knock back the locktabs, and undo and remove three equally-spaced bolts from the centre of the converter. Leave the other three bolts in position.

17 Knock back the lockwasher securing the large converter centre retaining bolt. Using a large socket and bar, undo and remove the torque converter centre bolt and withdraw the driving collar. Use a screwdriver inserted through the hole in the top of the converter housing and engaged with the ring gear teeth to prevent the torque converter from turning.

18 Rotate the crankshaft until the timing marks on the converter periphery are at approximately the 3 o'clock position.

19 The torque converter is a taper fit on the end of the crankshaft and it will be necessary to obtain Rover special tool 18G 1086 (or a suitable alternative) to remove it. The tool is bolted to the torque converter through the holes of the three previously-removed converter retaining bolts. With the adapter in position on the end of the crankshaft, tighten the tool centre bolt until the torque converter breaks free of the taper, and then lift it off the crankshaft.

Refitting

20 Set the engine with No 1 piston at TDC on compression as described in Section 3.

21 Before fitting the torque converter, it will be first necessary to refit the three central bolts, removed to allow the special converter removal tool to be used during dismantling. Then remove each pair of bolts in turn from the converter centre and fit new locking plates. Tighten the six bolts to the specified

14.15 Right-hand engine mounting-to-subframe retaining nuts

torque wrench setting and bend over the lock tabs. *On no account remove all six bolts at any one time.*

22 Slide the torque converter onto the end of the crankshaft, with the timing marks uppermost. Refit the driving collar, a new lockwasher and the retaining bolt. Tighten the retaining bolt to the specified torque then knock back the lockwasher.

23 The remainder of refitting is the reverse sequence to removal.

14 Engine/transmission mountings – renewal

General information

1 The engine/transmission is supported on two rubber mountings which are in turn bolted to the sides of the front subframe. One mounting is located under the radiator (left-hand mounting), and the other at the base of the flywheel or torque converter housing cover, to which it is attached (right-hand mounting). Fore-and-aft movement of the power unit is controlled by a tie-bar, one end of which is attached to the engine, and the other to a bracket on the bulkhead. Rubber bushes are used at each end to absorb vibration. On later models an additional lower tie-bar is used, one end of which is bolted to the subframe and the other to a bracket on the transmission. A point worth noting is that the tie-bar rubber bushes are prone to wear and this is usually noticed as severe judder as the clutch is engaged on manual transmission models, or excessive movement of the complete power unit when accelerating and decelerating.

Right-hand mounting

2 Firmly apply the handbrake, then jack up the front of the car and support it securely on axle stands (see *Jacking and vehicle support*).

3 Disconnect the battery negative terminal (refer to *Disconnecting the battery* in the Reference Chapter). If greater working clearance is required, remove the bonnet as described in Chapter 11A.

4 Remove the front grille, referring to Chapter 11A if necessary.

5 Detach the heater air duct from the air inlet under the right-hand front wing. Remove the air inlet from the inner wing panel.

6 Remove the starter motor as described in Chapter 5A.

7 On fuel injection models carry out the following:

a) *Remove the air cleaner assembly, the engine management ECU and the crankshaft position sensor as described in Chapter 4B and Chapter 5A or 5B.*

b) *Disconnect the oil separator breather hose from the right-hand end of the cylinder head, then undo the two bolts securing the separator to the flywheel/torque converter housing.*

Remove the separator and hose assembly from the engine, along with its gasket.

c) *Slacken and remove the screw, situated just to the right of the brake servo unit, securing the earth leads to the bulkhead.*

d) *Undo the bolts securing the wiring harness retaining clip and starter motor lead brackets to the flywheel/converter housing, then position the wiring clear of the engine.*

8 On early models, undo and remove the screws securing the starter solenoid to the inner wing panel. Lift off the solenoid and position it out of the way.

9 If the ignition coil is mounted on the flywheel/converter housing, or on a bracket secured to one of the cylinder head studs, remove the coil and mounting bracket and position it well clear.

10 On manual transmission models, detach the clutch slave cylinder mounting plate from the flywheel housing, taking care to retain the spacer. Withdraw the cylinder from the pushrod and place the cylinder and mounting plate to one side.

11 On later Mini 850 and 1000 models, remove the horn and place it to one side.

12 Undo and remove the two bolts securing the engine upper tie-bar and bracket to the side of the cylinder block. Note that on later models one of the bolts also retains the engine earth strap.

13 Undo and remove the nuts and/or bolts securing the radiator upper support bracket to the radiator and thermostat housing. Withdraw the bracket. **Note:** *It is not necessary to remove the support bracket if a large clearance exists between the radiator and left-hand inner wing panel, as is the case on later Mini 850 and 1000 models.*

14 Place a jack beneath the flywheel/torque converter housing end of the transmission casing and just take the weight of the power unit. Use a block of wood interposed between the casing and the jack to spread the load.

15 From under the car undo and remove the two nuts and bolts securing the right-hand engine mounting to the subframe side-members **(see illustration)**. The best way to do this is to engage the help of an assistant to hold the bolts from above while the nuts are undone from below. The bolt heads are tucked away and can only be reached with a small open-ended spanner.

16 Having released the mounting, jack up the power unit sufficiently to enable the nine bolts securing the flywheel/converter housing cover to be removed. Note that on early models one of the front bolts also retains the engine earth strap. On all models the rear bolts are nearly inaccessible, requiring a good deal of patience and a short spanner.

17 When all the bolts are undone, lift off the flywheel/converter housing cover.

18 With the cover removed, undo the bolts securing the engine mounting and lift off the mounting.

19 Refitting is the reverse sequence to removal.

14.25 Removing the engine upper tie-bar from the cylinder block

14.30 Lower engine tie-bar attachments

Left-hand mounting

20 Remove the radiator as described in Chapter 3.

21 Position a jack beneath the left-hand side of the transmission casing, and, using a block of wood to spread the load, *just* take the weight of the power unit.

22 Undo and remove the two nuts, bolts and spring washers securing the mounting to the subframe.

23 Raise the jack slightly and remove the bolts securing the mounting to the bracket on the transmission casing. The engine mounting can now be withdrawn.

24 Refitting is the reverse sequence to removal.

Upper tie-bar and bushes

25 Undo and remove the two bolts securing the tie-bar and mounting bracket to the right-hand side of the engine **(see illustration)**. Move the tie-bar sideways and recover any spacing washers that may be fitted.

26 If the tie-bar is secured to its mounting bracket on the bulkhead by a through-bolt and locknut, remove the locknut and bolt and lift away the tie-bar.

27 If the tie-bar is secured by a stud with nuts and spring washers at each end, undo and remove the nuts and spring washers, then slacken the four nuts securing the clutch and brake master cylinders to the bulkhead. When sufficient clearance exists, lift up the tie-bar

upper mounting bracket over the tie-bar stud, and withdraw the tie-bar.

28 With the tie-bar removed, slide out the rubber bushes and spacers and, if there is any sign of swelling or deterioration of the rubber whatsoever, renew the bushes.

29 Refitting is the reverse sequence to removal.

Lower tie-bar and bushes

30 The lower tie-bar fitted to later models may be mounted in one of two positions; either bolted to a bracket on the left-hand side of the transmission at one end and to the rear of the subframe at the other, or bolted to a bracket on the right-hand side of the transmission at one end and to the front of the subframe at the other. The renewal procedure is the same for both types **(see illustration)**.

31 Firmly apply the handbrake, then jack up the front of the car and support it securely on axle stands (see *Jacking and vehicle support*).

32 Undo and remove the bolts securing the tie-bar to the transmission bracket and subframe, and withdraw the tie-bar.

33 To remove the bushes it will be necessary to draw them out using a tube of suitable diameter, a long bolt and nut, and packing washers. The new bushes are refitted in the same way but lubricate them with liquid detergent before fitting.

34 Refitting is the reverse sequence to removal.

15 Distributor driveshaft – removal and refitting

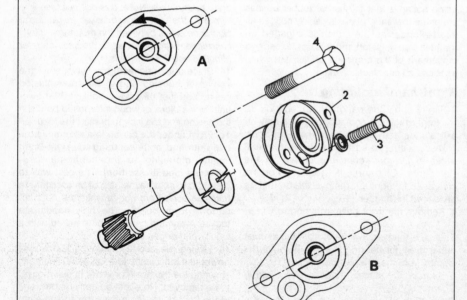

15.4a Distributor driveshaft components and fitting details – carburettor engines

Inset A shows the position of the slot ready for fitting
Inset B shows the shaft correctly installed

1 Driveshaft
2 Housing
3 Retaining screw

4 5/16 in UNF bolt (for removal and refitting of driveshaft)

Removal

1 Set the engine with No 1 cylinder at TDC on compression as described in Section 3.

2 Remove the distributor as described in Chapter 5B.

3 Where a distributor base housing is fitted to the cylinder block, unscrew the single retaining bolt and lockwasher and remove the housing.

4 Look down into the distributor aperture and observe the position of the slot in the distributor driveshaft. With No 1 piston at TDC on compression, the slot should be positioned as shown according to engine type (carburettor engines or fuel injection engines) **(see illustrations)**. There is a degree of conflicting information from the manufacturer as to the correct position of this slot on later engines. As a general rule, when refitting the driveshaft, set the slot in the same position it was in prior to removal. If there is any doubt about the original position, set it as shown in the illustrations when refitting.

5 Screw into the end of the distributor driveshaft a 5/16 in UNF bolt. A tappet cover bolt (where fitted) is ideal for this purpose. The driveshaft can then be lifted out, the shaft being turned slightly in the process to free the

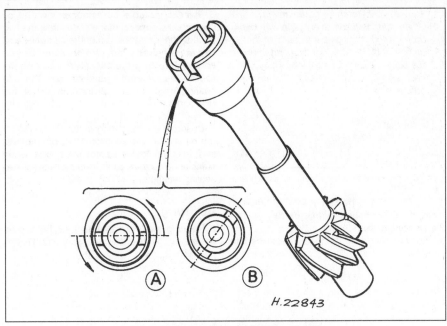

15.4b Distributor driveshaft fitting details – fuel injection engines

A Drive slot position prior to engagement with skew gear

B Correct drive slot position with shaft correctly installed

shaft skew gear from the camshaft skew gear **(see illustration)**.

Refitting

6 With the engine still positioned with No 1 piston at TDC, hold the driveshaft so that its slot is in the correct position for refitting, ie, so that its larger segment is uppermost (offset slot towards the bottom). Engage the driveshaft gear with the camshaft skew gear, and push the driveshaft fully into position. As the gear engages, the driveshaft will rotate anti-clockwise to the final, correct fitted position. If necessary, withdraw the driveshaft again and adjust its position as necessary until this is so.

7 Remove the bolt from the driveshaft.

8 Where applicable, refit the distributor base housing using a new O-ring and lock it in position with the single bolt and lockwasher.

9 The distributor can now be refitted as described in Chapter 5B.

15.5 Using a 5/16 in UNF bolt to remove the distributor driveshaft

in the dome of the hexagon nut, and bears against a machining in the block. When the oil pressure exceeds the specified pressure the cup is forced off its seat and the oil returns, via a drilling, directly to the sump.

4 Check the tension of the spring by measuring its free length. If it is shorter than the length shown in the Specifications it should be renewed. Check the condition of the cup checking carefully for wear ridges which would prevent the cup seating effectively. Renew the cup if its condition is suspect.

Refitting

5 Refitting is the reverse sequence to removal.

16 Oil pressure relief valve – removal, inspection and refitting

Removal

1 To prevent excessive oil pressure – for example when the engine is cold – an oil pressure relief valve is built into the right-hand side of the engine just below the oil delivery pipe union.

2 The relief valve is identified externally by a large domed hexagon nut. To remove the unit unscrew the nut and remove it, complete with the two fibre or copper sealing washers. The relief spring and the relief spring cup can then be easily extracted **(see illustration)**.

Inspection

3 In position, the metal cup fits over the opposite end of the relief valve spring resting

17 Oil filter housing and delivery pipe – removal and refitting

Removal

1 Drain the engine/transmission oil and remove the oil filter as described in Chapter 1.

2 On manual transmission models, Unscrew the banjo union bolt securing the delivery pipe to the cylinder block. Note that on later 1275 cc engines a tube nut and olive type fitting is used instead of the banjo union. At the other end of the pipe unscrew the nut securing the pipe to the oil filter housing **(see illustrations)**. Lift away the pipe and collect the two copper washers at the banjo union, or the rubber seals at the tube nut connections, according to type. Be prepared for oil spillage.

16.2 Removing the oil pressure relief valve

17.2a Oil feed pipe banjo union at the engine . . .

17.2b . . . and pipe nut attachment at the filter housing

3 On manual transmission models, unscrew the two nuts and slide the oil filter housing off the cylinder block studs. Recover the gasket.

4 On automatic transmission models, undo the two bolts and remove the filter housing from the top of the transmission casing flange. Recover the gasket.

5 Thoroughly clean the components and remove all traces of gasket from the mating surfaces.

6 If oil leakage from the pipe unions on later 1275 cc (12A) engines has been experienced, a modified pipe and tube nut assembly is available. Consult a Rover dealer for further information on this modification.

Refitting

7 Refitting is the reverse sequence to removal, bearing in mind the following points:
  a) Use a new filter housing gasket and new copper washers at the banjo union.
  b) When refitting the delivery pipe with banjo union fitting, engage the threads of the union nut at the filter housing first, then fit the banjo union with a copper washer on each side of the union head. Tighten the fittings securely.

18 Oil cooler – removal and refitting

Removal

1 Disconnect the battery negative terminal (refer to *Disconnecting the battery* in the Reference Chapter).

2 Remove the front grille as described in Chapter 11A.

3 Place a suitable container below the oil cooler. On Cooper S models, unscrew the two hose unions from the top of the oil cooler and move the hoses clear. On 1990-on 1275 cc engines, unscrew the banjo union bolt on the top of the oil cooler and recover the two sealing washers. On all models, cover the disconnected unions with tape to prevent entry of dust and dirt.

4 Unscrew the mounting bolts and withdraw the oil cooler. On 1990-on 1275 cc engines, unscrew the lower banjo union bolt when sufficient clearance exists and recover the two sealing washers.

Refitting

5 Refitting is a reversal of removal, but top-up the engine oil level as necessary (see *Weekly checks*).

Chapter 2 Part B:
Engine in-car repair procedures – October 1996 models onward

Contents

Compression test – description and interpretation 2
Crankshaft oil seals – renewal 10
Crankshaft pulley – removal and refitting 6
Cylinder head – removal and refitting 9
Engine oil and filter renewal . . . . .See Chapter 1
Engine oil level check . . . . .See *Weekly checks*
Engine/transmission mountings – renewal 12
Flywheel – removal and refitting 11
General information 1

Oil pressure relief valve – removal, inspection and refitting 13
Oil pressure switch – removal and refitting 14
Oil temperature sensor – removal and refitting 15
Rocker cover – removal and refitting 3
Rocker shaft assembly – removal, inspection and refitting 8
Timing chain, tensioner and sprockets – removal, inspection and
    refitting 7
Top Dead Centre (TDC) for number one piston – locating 4
Valve clearances – adjustment 5

Degrees of difficulty

Easy, suitable for novice with little experience	**Fairly easy,** suitable for beginner with some experience	**Fairly difficult,** suitable for competent DIY mechanic	**Difficult,** suitable for experienced DIY mechanic	**Very difficult,** suitable for expert DIY or professional

Specifications

Engine general

	Capacity	Bore	Stroke
Code:			
12A	1275 cc	70.61 mm	81.28 mm
Compression ratio	10.0:1		
Direction of crankshaft rotation	Clockwise (viewed from timing chain end of engine)		
Firing order	1-3-4-2 (No 1 cylinder at timing chain end of engine)		

Lubrication system

Oil pump type . . . . Eccentric rotor type directly driven off camshaft
Oil pressure at idling speed . . . . 0.5 bar
Oil pressure relief valve spring minimum length . . . . 72.5 mm

Valve clearances

Inlet and exhaust (engine cold) . . . . 0.27 to 0.33 mm

Torque wrench settings

	Nm	lbf ft
Auxiliary drivebelt tensioner bolts	22	16
Camshaft retaining plate bolts	11	8
Camshaft sprocket nut	90	66
Connecting rod big-end nuts	45	33
Crankshaft pulley bolt	150	111
Cylinder head nuts:		
Stage 1	34	25
Stage 2	68	50
Engine left-hand end plate bolts	11	8
Engine mountings:		
Left-hand engine mounting bracket to transmission	25	18
Left-hand engine mounting to mounting bracket	22	16
Left-hand engine mounting to subframe	22	16
Right-hand engine mounting to flywheel housing cover	18	13
Right-hand engine mounting to subframe	22	16
Engine lower tie-bar to subframe	40	30
Engine lower tie-bar to transmission bracket	40	30
Engine upper tie-bar to bulkhead	22	16
Engine upper tie-bar to cylinder head	22	16
Flywheel centre bolt*	150	111
Flywheel housing bolts	25	18
Flywheel housing cover bolts	10	7
Main bearing bolts	85	63
Oil pressure relief valve nut	60	44
Oil pressure switch	25	18
Oil pump bolts	11	8
Oil temperature sensor	60	44
Rocker cover bolts	5	4
Rocker shaft pedestal nuts	25	18
Timing chain tensioner bolts	22	16
Timing cover bolts	16	12
Transmission casing to engine	8	6
Water pump pulley bolts	10	7

Use a new bolt

---

1 General information

Using this Chapter

This Part of Chapter 2 is devoted to in-car engine repair procedures for October 1996 models onward. Similar information covering pre-October 1996 models will be found in Chapter 2A. All procedures concerning engine removal and refitting, and engine block/cylinder head overhaul for all engines can be found in Chapter 2C.

Refer to *Vehicle identification* in the Reference Section of this manual for details of engine code locations.

Most of the operations included in Chapter 2B are based on the assumption that the engine is still installed in the car. Therefore, if this information is being used during a complete engine overhaul, with the engine already removed, many of the steps included here will not apply.

Engine description

The Mini engine fitted to October 1996 models onward is a development of the earlier 1275 cc engine covered in Part A of this Chapter. The two power units are virtually identical apart from modifications to the cylinder block of the later unit. As a distributor is no longer fitted, the distributor driveshaft used on early engines has been deleted, and various internal changes to the lubrication system have also been made.

As with the earlier engine, the later unit is a four-cylinder, water-cooled, overhead valve type of 1275 cc displacement. The engine is bolted to the transmission assembly, which also forms the engine sump, and the complete power unit is supported, via rubber mountings, in the front subframe.

The cast iron cylinder head contains two valves per cylinder, mounted vertically and running in pressed-in valve guides. The valves are operated by rocker arms and pushrods via tubular cam followers from the camshaft, located in the front side of the cylinder block.

The inlet and exhaust manifolds are attached to the rear facing side of the cylinder head and are linked to the valves via five inlet and exhaust ports of siamese configuration.

The pistons are of anodised aluminium alloy with two compression rings and an oil control ring. The pistons are attached to the connecting rods by a gudgeon pin which is an interference fit in the connecting rod small-end bore. At the other end of the connecting rod, renewable big-end shell bearings are fitted.

The camshaft is supported in the cylinder block by three steel-backed metal bearings and is driven by a single row timing chain at the left-hand end of the engine via the crankshaft and camshaft sprockets. A spring-loaded tensioner is used to maintain the correct tension on the timing chain.

The statically and dynamically balanced forged steel crankshaft is supported by three renewable shell-type main bearings. Crankshaft endfloat is controlled by four semi-circular thrustwashers located in pairs on either side of the centre main bearing.

A forced feed system of lubrication is used, with oil circulated around the engine from the transmission casing/sump. The oil in the transmission casing/sump is also used to lubricate the transmission and differential.

The oil pump is mounted at the flywheel end of the cylinder block and is driven directly by the camshaft.

Oil is drawn from the sump through a gauze screen in the oil strainer and is sucked up the pick-up pipe and drawn into the oil pump. From the oil pump it is forced under pressure along a gallery in the cylinder block, and through drillings to the big-end, main and camshaft bearings. A small hole in each connecting rod allows a jet of oil to lubricate the cylinder wall with each revolution.

From the camshaft left-hand bearing, oil is fed through drilled passages in the cylinder block and head to the left-hand rocker pedestal where it enters the hollow rocker shaft. Holes drilled in the shaft allow for the lubrication of the rocker arms, and the valve stems and pushrod ends. This oil is at a reduced pressure to the oil delivered to the crankshaft bearings. Oil from the left-hand camshaft bearing also lubricates the timing chain. Oil returns to the sump by various passages; the tappets (cam followers) being lubricated by oil returning via the pushrod drillings in the block.

On all models a full-flow oil filter is fitted, and all oil passes through this filter before it reaches the main oil gallery.

The water pump and alternator are driven together by an auxiliary drivebelt from the crankshaft pulley.

Repair operations possible with the engine in the car

The following work can be carried out with the engine in the car:

a) Compression pressure – testing.
b) Crankshaft pulley – removal and refitting.
c) Valve clearances – adjustment.
d) Timing chain, tensioner and sprockets – removal and refitting.
e) Rocker shaft assembly – removal and refitting.
f) Cylinder head and valve gear – removal and refitting.
g) Cylinder head and pistons – decarbonising.
h) Crankshaft oil seals – renewal.
i) Flywheel – removal and refitting.
j) Engine mountings – renewal.
k) Oil pressure relief valve – removal, inspection and refitting.
l) Oil pressure switch and temperature sensor – removal and refitting.

2 Compression test – description and interpretation

1 When engine performance is down, or if misfiring occurs which cannot be attributed to the ignition or fuel systems, a compression test can provide diagnostic clues as to the engine's condition. If the test is performed regularly, it can give warning of trouble before any other symptoms become apparent.

2 The engine must be fully warmed-up to normal operating temperature, the battery must be fully charged, and the aid of an assistant will also be required.
3 Disable and depressurise the fuel system by removing the fuel pump fuse (fuse C7 in the passenger compartment fuseblock). Start the engine, and run it until it cuts out.
4 Disable the ignition system by disconnecting the wiring connector from the DIS module referring to Chapter 5C for further information.
5 Remove all four spark plugs and fit a compression tester to the No 1 cylinder spark plug hole – the type of tester which screws into the plug thread is to be preferred.
6 Have the assistant hold the throttle wide open, and crank the engine on the starter motor; after one or two revolutions, the compression pressure should build-up to a maximum figure, and then stabilise. Record the highest reading obtained.
7 Repeat the test on the remaining cylinders, recording the pressure in each.
8 All cylinders should produce very similar pressures; a difference of more than 2 bars between any two cylinders indicates a fault. Note that the compression should build-up quickly in a healthy engine; low compression on the first stroke, followed by gradually-increasing pressure on successive strokes, indicates worn piston rings. A low compression reading on the first stroke, which does not build-up during successive strokes, indicates leaking valves or a blown head gasket (a cracked head could also be the cause). Deposits on the undersides of the valve heads can also cause low compression.
9 If the pressure in any cylinder is low, carry out the following test to isolate the cause. Introduce a teaspoonful of clean oil into that cylinder through its spark plug hole, and repeat the test.
10 If the addition of oil temporarily improves the compression pressure, this indicates that bore or piston wear is responsible for the pressure loss. No improvement suggests that leaking or burnt valves, or a blown head gasket, may be to blame.
11 A low reading from two adjacent cylinders is almost certainly due to the head gasket having blown between them; the presence of

3.2 Release the accelerator cable adjusting nut from the mounting bracket and disconnect the cable end fitting from the throttle cam

coolant in the engine oil will confirm this.
12 If one cylinder is about 20 percent lower than the others and the engine has a slightly rough idle, a worn camshaft lobe could be the cause.
13 If the compression reading is unusually high, the combustion chambers are probably coated with carbon deposits. If this is the case, the cylinder head should be removed and decarbonised.
14 On completion of the test, refit the spark plugs, reconnect the DIS module and refit the fuel pump fuse.

3 Rocker cover – removal and refitting

Removal

1 Refer to Chapter 4C and remove the air cleaner assembly.
2 Release the accelerator cable adjusting nut from the mounting bracket, disconnect the inner cable end fitting from the throttle cam, and position the cable clear of the rocker cover (see illustration).
3 Undo the two rocker cover retaining bolts and lift out the bolts and washers (see illustration).
4 Collect the rocker cover retaining bolt dished washers from the top of the two rubber seals, then withdraw the seals from the rocker cover (see illustrations).

3.3 Unscrew the two rocker cover retaining bolts and lift out the bolts and washers

3.4a Collect the rocker cover retaining bolt dished washers . . .

3.4b . . . then withdraw the rubber seals from the rocker cover

5 Lift off the rocker cover and gasket, then remove the gasket from the cover **(see illustration)**.

6 Check the condition of the two retaining bolt rubber seals and, if necessary, obtain new seals for refitting, together with the new gasket.

Refitting

7 Prior to refitting, scrape away all traces of old gasket from the rocker cover, then thoroughly clean the cover and the cylinder head mating face.

8 Apply gasket sealant or a suitable adhesive to the gasket locating surface in the rocker cover to retain the gasket in place. Locate the new gasket in position in the cover, ensuring that it seats correctly in the flange around the edge of the cover.

9 Place the cover in position on the cylinder head and fit the two retaining bolt rubber seals.

10 Locate the dished washers over the rubber seals, then refit the retaining bolts and washers. Tighten the two bolts progressively to the specified torque.

11 Engage the accelerator cable end fitting with the throttle cam then refit the outer cable adjusting nut to the mounting bracket. Check the cable adjustment as described in Chapter 4C.

12 On completion, refit the air cleaner assembly as described in Chapter 4C.

---

4 Top Dead Centre (TDC) for number one piston – locating

1 Top dead centre (TDC) is the highest point in the cylinder that each piston reaches as the crankshaft turns. Each piston reaches its TDC position at the end of its compression stroke and then again at the end of its exhaust stroke. For the purpose of engine timing, TDC refers to the position of No 1 piston at the end of its compression stroke. On the engines covered by this manual, No 1 piston is at the timing chain end of the engine. It is necessary to set the engine in this position when carrying out certain operations in this Chapter. To do so, proceed as follows.

2 Remove the rocker cover as described in Section 3.

3 To allow the engine to be easily turned over, remove the spark plugs as described in Chapter 1.

4 Turn the engine over until No 1 piston is approaching TDC on the compression stroke. This can be checked by observing the valves of No 4 cylinder. The exhaust valve should be closing and the inlet valve just opening. The engine can be turned over quite easily by engaging top gear and moving the car forwards. This should only be done on level ground; and make sure that the car cannot run away.

5 Insert a screwdriver or similar tool into No 1

3.5 Lift off the rocker cover and gasket, then remove the gasket from the cover

cylinder spark plug hole so that it rests on the top of the piston. Continue to turn the engine very slowly until the screwdriver stops rising.

6 No 1 and 4 pistons should now be at TDC, with No 1 piston on the compression stroke. Verify this by observing the timing marks on the timing cover and crankshaft pulley. The marks consist of a TDC indicator line stamped on the timing cover and a notch on the outer rim of the crankshaft pulley **(see illustration)**. The marks are quite difficult to see and the use of a mirror is helpful. If necessary turn the engine further slightly until the timing marks are aligned. The engine is now set to TDC with No 1 piston on compression.

7 On completion, refit the rocker cover as described in Section 3, and refit the spark plugs as described in Chapter 1.

---

5 Valve clearances – adjustment

1 The valve clearance adjustments should be made with the engine cold. The importance of correct rocker arm/valve stem clearances cannot be overstressed as they vitally affect the performance of the engine. If the clearances are set too wide, the efficiency of the engine is reduced as the valves open later and close earlier than was intended. If, on the other hand the clearances are set too close, there is danger that the stems will expand upon heating and not allow the valves to close properly, which will cause burning of the valve head and seat, and possible warping.

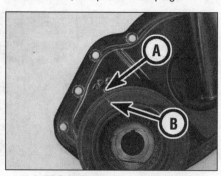

4.6 TDC indicator line on the timing cover (A) and crankshaft pulley notch (B)

2 To gain access to the rocker arms, remove the rocker cover as described in Section 3.

3 It is important that the clearance is set when the tappet of the valve being adjusted is on the heel of the cam (ie, opposite the peak). Turn the engine over until valve No 8 (nearest the flywheel end of the engine) is fully open. With the engine in this position, valve No 1 will be fully closed and ready to be checked. The engine can be turned over quite easily by engaging top gear and moving the car forwards. This should only be done on level ground; and make sure that the car cannot run away.

> **HAYNES HINT** *Turning the engine will be easier if the spark plugs are removed first – see Chapter 1.*

4 A feeler blade of the correct thickness should now be inserted between the valve stem and rocker arm. When the clearance is correct the feeler blade should be a smooth stiff sliding fit between the valve stem and rocker arm. The correct valve clearances are given in the Specifications at the start of this Chapter.

5 If the feeler blade is a tight or loose fit then the clearance must be adjusted. To do this, loosen the locknut of the adjustment stud and screw the adjuster stud in or out until the feeler blade can be felt to drag slightly when drawn from the gap **(see illustration)**.

6 Hold the adjuster firmly in this position and tighten the locknut. Recheck the gap on completion to ensure that it has not altered when locking the nut and stud.

7 Check each valve clearance in turn in the following sequence (which also avoids turning the engine more than necessary). The valves are numbered from the timing chain end of the engine.

Valve fully open	Check and adjust
Valve No 8	Valve No 1
Valve No 6	Valve No 3
Valve No 4	Valve No 5
Valve No 7	Valve No 2
Valve No 1	Valve No 8
Valve No 3	Valve No 6
Valve No 5	Valve No 4
Valve No 2	Valve No 7

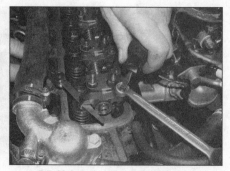

5.5 Valve clearance adjustment

6.3 Undo the two nuts (arrowed) and lift off the expansion tank

6.4a Disconnect the coolant temperature sensor wiring connector . . .

6.4b . . . and release the wiring harness cable clip from the expansion tank bracket

8 When all the valves have been checked and adjusted, refit the rocker cover as described in Section 3. Where removed, refit the spark plugs and HT leads (see Chapter 1).

6 Crankshaft pulley – removal and refitting

Removal

Note: *A new crankshaft pulley bolt locking washer will be required for refitting.*

1 Disconnect the battery negative terminal (refer to *Disconnecting the battery* in the Reference Chapter).
2 Refer to Chapter 1 and remove the auxiliary drivebelt.
3 Undo the two nuts securing the cooling system expansion tank to the mounting bracket

(see illustration). Lift the tank off the mounting bracket studs and position it to one side.
4 Disconnect the wiring connector from the coolant temperature sensor located in the thermostat housing. Release the sensor wiring harness cable clip from the expansion tank mounting bracket **(see illustrations).**
5 Working under the wheelarch, undo the two nuts securing the expansion tank mounting bracket to the body and remove the bracket **(see illustrations).**
6 Disconnect the horn wiring connector, then undo the two bolts securing the horn mounting bracket to the body **(see illustration).** Remove the horn and bracket from the engine compartment.
7 Undo the four water pump pulley retaining bolts and remove the pulley from the water pump spindle **(see illustration).**
8 Position a jack with interposed block of wood beneath the left-hand end of the

transmission. Raise the jack to just take the weight of the engine/transmission unit.
9 Undo the two through-bolts securing the left-hand engine/transmission mounting bracket to the transmission **(see illustration).** Raise the engine/transmission, by means of the jack, to allow access to the crankshaft pulley bolt.
10 Bend back the locking tab of the crankshaft pulley bolt locking washer, prising it back with a cold chisel or screwdriver. Using a suitable socket, unscrew and remove the bolt and locking washer **(see illustrations).** To prevent the crankshaft turning as the bolt is slackened, remove the starter motor (Chapter 5A) and lock the flywheel with a screwdriver or similar tool engaged with the ring gear teeth.
11 Placing two large screwdrivers behind the crankshaft pulley at 180° to each other, carefully lever the pulley off. It is preferable to

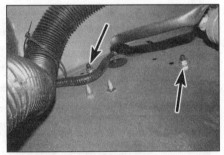

6.5a From under the wheelarch, undo the two expansion tank bracket retaining nuts (arrowed) . . .

6.5b . . . and remove the bracket from the inner wing panel

6.6 Undo the two bolts and remove the horn and mounting bracket

6.7 Undo the four bolts and remove the water pump pulley

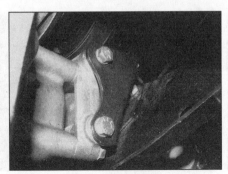

6.9 Left-hand engine/transmission mounting bracket through-bolts

6.10a Bend back the crankshaft pulley bolt locking washer tab . . .

6.10b . . . then unscrew and remove the bolt and locking washer

use a proper pulley extractor if this is available, but large screwdrivers or tyre levers are quite suitable, providing care is taken not to damage the pulley flange or timing cover.

Refitting

12 Thoroughly clean the crankshaft pulley then lubricate the oil seal contact surface with clean engine oil. Fit the pulley to the crankshaft, ensuring that the keyway engages with the Woodruff key.
13 Fit the new crankshaft pulley bolt locking washer and screw in the crankshaft pulley bolt. Tighten the bolt to the specified torque while using the same method to prevent crankshaft rotation as was used for removal.
14 Bend up the tab of the locking washer to secure the crankshaft pulley bolt.
15 Lower the jack until the holes in the left-hand engine/transmission mounting bracket and in the transmission casing are aligned.

Refit the two bolts and tighten them to the specified torque.
16 Refit the water pump pulley and tighten the four bolts to the specified torque.
17 Locate the horn and mounting bracket in position and secure with the retaining bolts.
18 Refit the expansion tank mounting bracket then locate the tank on the bracket and secure with the two nuts.
19 Reconnect the coolant temperature sensor wiring connector and harness cable clip.
20 Refer to Chapter 1 and refit the auxiliary drivebelt.
21 Refit the starter motor as described in Chapter 5A.

7 Timing chain, tensioner and sprockets – removal, inspection and refitting

Removal

1 Set the engine at TDC for No 1 piston as described in Section 4.
2 Remove the crankshaft pulley as described in Section 6, but check that the engine is still set at TDC for No 1 piston before the pulley is withdrawn from the crankshaft.
3 Undo the two bolts securing the auxiliary drivebelt tensioner to the alternator mounting bracket. Remove the bolts and tensioner and collect the spacer from the upper mounting bolt **(see illustration)**.
4 Disconnect the breather hose from the oil separator on the timing cover.

7.3 Undo the two bolts and remove the auxiliary drivebelt tensioner

5 Unscrew the eleven bolts securing the timing cover to the engine left-hand plate, noting that there are five large bolts and six small bolts.
6 Lift off the timing cover and gasket from the engine then, when sufficient clearance exists, release the cable clip securing the wiring harness to the side of the timing cover **(see illustration)**.
7 Withdraw the oil thrower from the end of the crankshaft **(see illustration)**.
8 Undo the two bolts and remove the timing chain tensioner **(see illustration)**.
9 Bend back the locking tab on the washer under the camshaft sprocket retaining nut and unscrew the nut, noting how the locking washer locating tag fits in the camshaft sprocket keyway **(see illustrations)**. Prevent the camshaft sprocket from turning as the nut is slackened using a suitable forked tool engaged with the holes in the sprocket.

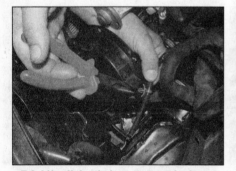

7.6 Lift off the timing cover and release the wiring harness cable clip

7.7 Withdraw the oil thrower from the end of the crankshaft

7.8 Undo the two bolts and remove the timing chain tensioner

7.9a Tap back the tab on the camshaft sprocket nut locking washer . . .

7.9b . . . then unscrew and remove the retaining nut . . .

7.9c . . . followed by the locking washer

7.11a Use a small chisel to extract the crankshaft sprocket Woodruff key . . .

7.11b . . . then collect the packing washers, where fitted

7.18 Using a straight-edge to check the camshaft and crankshaft sprocket alignment

10 To remove the camshaft and crankshaft sprockets complete with chain, ease each sprocket forward a little at a time, levering behind each one in turn with two large screwdrivers at 180° to each other. If the sprockets are locked solid, it will be necessary to use a suitable puller.

11 With both sprockets removed, extract the Woodruff key from the crankshaft by tapping it out with a small chisel. Note that there may be a number of very thin packing washers behind the crankshaft sprocket; if so carefully remove them **(see illustrations)**.

Inspection

12 Thoroughly clean all the components with paraffin or a suitable solvent and dry thoroughly. Pay particular attention to the timing cover and the mating face on the engine left-hand end plate, ensuring that all traces of old gasket are removed.

13 Examine the teeth on both the crankshaft and camshaft sprockets for wear. Each tooth forms an inverted V with the sprocket periphery and, if worn, the side of each tooth under tension will be slightly concave in shape when compared with the other side of the tooth. If any sign of wear is present, the sprockets must be renewed.

14 Examine the links of the chain for side slackness and renew the chain if any slackness is noticeable when compared with a new chain. It is a sensible precaution to renew the chain at about 60 000 miles, and at a lesser mileage if the engine is dismantled for a major overhaul. The rollers on a very badly worn chain may be slightly grooved.

15 Also check the condition of the timing chain tensioner arm contact face. If the tensioner arm rubber pad is severely grooved where it bears against the chain, it should also be renewed.

16 It is advisable to renew the timing cover oil seal at this stage, referring to the procedures contained in Section 10.

Refitting

17 If new sprockets are being fitted, the alignment between the two sprockets must be checked as follows.

18 Temporarily place the camshaft and crankshaft sprockets in position and place the straight-edge of a steel ruler from the side of the camshaft sprocket teeth to the crankshaft sprocket. Using feeler blades, measure the gap between the steel rule and the crankshaft sprocket **(see illustration)**. If a gap exists, a suitable number of packing washers (available from Rover dealers) must be placed on the crankshaft nose, behind the crankshaft sprocket, to bring it onto the same plane as the camshaft sprocket. Use the existing packing washers (if fitted) and supplement these with additional washers if necessary. Remove both sprockets once the alignment has been checked and, if necessary, corrected.

19 With the packing washers (where necessary) in position on the crankshaft, refit the Woodruff key to the crankshaft slot. Make sure that the upper surface of the key is parallel with the crankshaft and ensure that it is fully seated by gently tapping it into place. It is advisable at this stage to check that the crankshaft sprocket will slide onto the crankshaft without binding as it is very easy to have the key positioned slightly high at one end. If the sprocket binds, remove the Woodruff key and refit it again. If the edges of the key are burred they must be cleaned with a fine file.

20 Lay the two sprockets on a clean surface so that the timing marks are adjacent to each

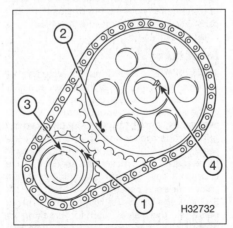

7.20 Timing mark locations relative to keyways

1 Crankshaft sprocket timing mark
2 Camshaft sprocket timing mark
3 Crankshaft sprocket keyway
4 Camshaft sprocket keyway

other. Slip the timing chain over them and pull the sprockets back into mesh with the chain so that the timing marks, although further apart are still adjacent to each other **(see illustration)**.

21 Check that the engine is still positioned at TDC for No 1 piston (Section 4). In this position the crankshaft Woodruff key should be at the 12 o'clock position and the camshaft Woodruff key should be at the 2 o'clock position.

22 Fit the timing chain and sprocket assembly onto the camshaft and crankshaft, keeping the timing marks adjacent. If the camshaft and crankshaft have been positioned accurately, it will be found that the keyways on the sprockets will match the position of the keys, although it may be necessary to rotate the camshaft a fraction to ensure accurate lining-up of the camshaft sprocket.

23 Fit the locking washer to the camshaft sprocket with its locating tab in the sprocket keyway.

24 Screw on the camshaft sprocket retaining nut and tighten the nut to the specified torque. Prevent the camshaft sprocket from rotating as the nut is tightened using the same method as was used for removal.

25 Bend up the locking tab of the locking washer to hold the camshaft retaining nut securely.

26 Refit the timing chain tensioner and screw in the two retaining bolts. Move the tensioner body inwards to apply tension to the chain and tighten the upper bolt sufficiently to hold the tensioner in this position. Now tighten both bolts to the specified torque.

27 Fit the oil thrower to the crankshaft with the F mark facing outwards (away from the chain) **(see illustration)**.

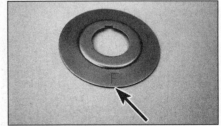

7.27 Fit the oil thrower with the F mark (arrowed) facing outward (away from the timing chain)

7.29 Insert two of the larger retaining bolts to locate the timing cover gasket in position

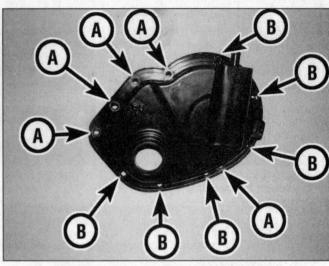

7.30 Timing cover retaining bolt identification

A Large bolts   B Small bolts

28 Lubricate the timing chain, sprockets and the inner lip of the timing cover oil seal with clean engine oil.

29 Position a new gasket on the timing cover and insert two of the larger retaining bolts to locate the gasket in position **(see illustration)**.

30 Hold the two bolts in place and fit the timing cover to the engine plate. Screw in the two bolts finger tight only to retain the cover and gasket. Refit the remaining bolts in their correct locations and also tighten them finger tight only at this stage **(see illustration)**.

31 Lubricate the oil seal contact surface on the crankshaft pulley, and temporarily locate the pulley on the crankshaft. With the pulley in place to centralise the timing cover, tighten the accessible bolts sufficiently to hold the timing cover in place.

32 Remove the crankshaft pulley and tighten all the timing cover retaining bolts to the specified torque.

33 Secure the wiring harness to the side of the timing cover using the cable clip.

34 Reconnect the breather hose to the oil separator on the timing cover.

35 Refit the auxiliary drivebelt tensioner to the alternator mounting bracket, ensuring that the spacer is correctly positioned on the upper bolt. Tighten the bolts to the specified torque.

36 Refit the crankshaft pulley as described in Section 6.

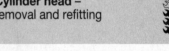

8 Rocker shaft assembly – removal, inspection and refitting

General information

1 The rocker shaft assembly is secured to the top of the cylinder head by the cylinder head inner studs and nuts. Although in theory it is possible to undo the head nuts and remove the rocker shaft assembly without removing the head, in practice, this is not recommended. Once the nuts have been removed, the head gasket will be disturbed, and the gasket will almost certainly leak or blow after refitting. For this reason, removal of the rocker shaft assembly cannot be done without removing the cylinder head and renewing the head gasket.

Removal

2 Remove the cylinder head as described in Section 9.

3 To dismantle the rocker shaft assembly, release the rocker shaft locating screw, remove the split pins, flat washers, and spring washers from each end of the shaft and slide from the shaft the pedestals, rocker arms, and rocker spacing springs. Keep all the components in order and make a note of each component's correct fitted position and orientation as it is removed, to ensure it is fitted correctly on reassembly.

Inspection

4 Check the rocker arms for wear of the rocker bushes, for wear at the rocker arm face which bears on the valve stem, and for wear of the adjusting ball-ended screws. Wear in the rocker arm bush can be checked by gripping the rocker arm tip and holding the rocker arm in place on the shaft, noting if there is any lateral rocker arm shake. If shake is present, and the arm is very loose on the shaft, renewal is necessary.

5 Check the tip of the rocker arm where it bears on the valve head for cracking or serious wear on the case hardening. If none is present re-use the rocker arm. Check the lower half of the ball on the end of the rocker arm adjusting screw. Wear on the ball and top of the pushrod is easily noted by the unworn 'pip' which fits in the small central oil hole on the ball. The larger this 'pip' the more wear has taken place to both the ball and the pushrod. Check the pushrods for straightness by rolling them on the bench. Renew any that are bent.

Refitting

6 To reassemble the rocker shaft fit the split pin, flat washer and spring washer at the right-hand end of the shaft and then slide on the rocker arms, rocker shaft pedestals, and spacing springs in the same order in which they were removed.

7 Screw in the rocker shaft locating screw and slip the locating plate into position. Finally, fit to the end of the shaft the spring washer, plain washer, and split pin, in that order.

8 Refit the cylinder head as described in Section 9.

9 Cylinder head – removal and refitting

Removal

1 Disconnect the battery negative terminal (refer to *Disconnecting the battery* in the Reference Chapter).

2 Remove the bonnet as described in Chapter 11B.

3 Remove the auxiliary drivebelt as described in Chapter 1.

4 Drain the cooling system as described in Chapter 1.

5 Refer to Chapter 4C and remove the air cleaner assembly.

6 Firmly apply the handbrake, then jack up the front of the car and support it securely on axle stands (see *Jacking and vehicle support*).

7 Working underneath the car, slacken and remove the nut and bolt securing the exhaust front pipe to its mounting bracket on the

transmission. Undo the three nuts securing the front pipe to the manifold, then disconnect it and recover the gasket.

8 Lower the car to the ground.

9 Disconnect the lambda sensor wiring connector located on the engine compartment bulkhead behind the throttle body **(see illustration)**. Release the wiring harness from any cable ties or clips.

10 Release the accelerator cable adjusting nut from the mounting bracket, release the inner cable from the throttle cam, and position the cable clear of the throttle body.

11 Depress the plastic collar on the quick-release fitting and disconnect the brake servo vacuum hose from the inlet manifold.

12 Disconnect the wiring connectors from the following components:

a) *Throttle potentiometer (on the side of the throttle body).*

b) *Idle air control valve (on the right-hand side of the inlet manifold).*

c) *Manifold absolute pressure sensor (on the left-hand side of the inlet manifold).*

d) *Inlet air temperature sensor (on the left-hand side of the inlet manifold).*

e) *Coolant temperature sensor (on the side of the thermostat housing).*

f) *Fuel injectors.*

13 Release the clip securing the engine wiring harness to the air cleaner mounting bracket at the front and move the harness to one side **(see illustration)**.

14 Release the clip securing the wiring harness at the rear of the air cleaner mounting bracket.

15 Bearing in mind the information contained in Chapter 4C concerning fuel system depressurisation, place absorbent rags around the fuel feed and return hose quick-release fittings. Remove the fuel tank filler cap to release any pressure in the tank. Depress the plastic collar on the quick-release fittings and disconnect the feed and return hoses from the pipes **(see illustration)**. Plug or cover each pipe and hose, to minimise the loss of fuel and prevent the entry of dirt into the system.

16 Disconnect the breather hose from each end of the breather hose on the cylinder head.

17 Release the retaining clip and disconnect the evaporative emission control purge hose from the inlet manifold.

18 Slacken the retaining clips and disconnect the radiator top hose, expansion tank hose and heater hose from the thermostat housing.

19 Undo the two bolts securing the radiator top hose support bracket and remove the bracket.

20 Make a note of the correct fitted positions of the HT leads, and disconnect them from the spark plugs.

21 Remove the alternator as described in Chapter 5A.

22 Remove the rocker cover as described in Section 3.

23 Slacken the four rocker pedestal nuts and the nine main cylinder head nuts, half a turn at

9.9 Disconnect the lambda sensor wiring connector located behind the throttle body

a time, in the reverse sequence to that shown **(see illustration 9.38)**. When the tension is released from all the nuts, they may then be removed, one at a time, from their studs.

24 Recover the pedestal plate then lift the rocker shaft assembly off the studs.

25 Lift out the pushrods, keeping them in order according to their respective valves.

 HAYNES HiNT *The easiest way to keep the pushrods in order is to push them through a sheet of thick paper or thin card, in the correct sequence, then number them 1 to 8.*

26 The cylinder head can now be removed by lifting upwards. If the head is jammed, try to rock it to break the seal. Under no circumstances try to prise it apart from the block with a screwdriver or cold chisel, as damage may be done to the faces of the head or block. If other methods fail to work, strike the head sharply with a soft-headed mallet, or with a metal hammer with an interposed piece of wood to cushion the blows. Do not hit the head directly with a metal hammer, as this may cause the casting to fracture. Several sharp taps with the mallet, at the same time pulling upwards, should free the head. Once free, lift the head up and off the studs, then recover the gasket.

27 If the cylinder head is to be dismantled for overhaul, refer to Part C of this Chapter. Refer to Section 8 if the rocker shaft assembly is to be dismantled.

9.13 Release the clip securing the engine wiring harness to the front of the air cleaner mounting bracket

Preparation for refitting

28 The mating faces of the cylinder head and cylinder block must be perfectly clean before refitting the head. Use a metal or hard plastic scraper to remove all traces of gasket and carbon. The same method can be used to clean the piston crowns. Take particular care during the cleaning operations, as the mating faces and piston crowns can be easily scored. Also, make sure that the carbon debris is not allowed to enter the oil and water passages – this is particularly important for the lubrication system, as carbon could block the oil supply to the engine's components. Using adhesive tape and paper, seal the water and oil and holes in the cylinder block.

 HAYNES HiNT *To prevent carbon debris entering the gap between the pistons and bores, smear a little grease in the gap. After cleaning each piston, use a small brush to remove all traces of grease and carbon from the gap, then wipe away the remainder with a clean rag.*

29 Check the mating surfaces of the cylinder block and the cylinder head for nicks, deep scratches and other damage. If slight, they may be removed carefully with a file, but if excessive, machining may be the only alternative to renewal.

30 If warpage of the cylinder head gasket surface is suspected, use a straight-edge to check it for distortion. Refer to Part C of this Chapter if necessary.

31 Check the condition of the cylinder head studs and nuts, and particularly their threads. Wash the nuts in a suitable solvent and wipe clean the studs. Check each for any sign of visible wear or damage, renewing any if necessary.

Refitting

32 Wipe clean the mating surfaces of the cylinder head and cylinder block, then place the new cylinder head gasket on the block. The gasket is marked FRONT and TOP and should be fitted in position according to these markings

9.15 Depress the plastic collar on the fuel hose quick-release fittings and disconnect the feed and return hoses

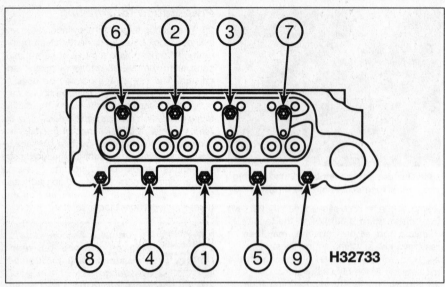

9.38 Cylinder head nut tightening sequence

33 With the gasket in position carefully lower the cylinder head onto the cylinder block.

34 Fit the cylinder head nuts and washers finger tight to the five cylinder head holding-down studs, which remain outside the rocker cover.

35 Lubricate the pushrods with clean engine oil and fit them in their original locations. Ensure that they locate properly in the stems of the tappets.

36 The rocker shaft assembly can now be lowered over its eight locating studs. Take care that the rocker arms are the right way round. Lubricate the ball-ends of the valve adjusting screws and position them in the pushrod cups. **Note:** *Failure to place the ball-ends in the cups can result in them seating on the edge of a pushrod or outside it when the head and rocker assembly is pulled down tight.*

37 Fit the pedestal plate then the four rocker pedestal nuts and washers, and the four cylinder head stud nuts and washers, which also serve to secure the rocker pedestals. Tighten all the nuts lightly at this time.

38 Working in the sequence shown, tighten the nine cylinder head nuts to the specified Stage 1 torque setting, and then to the Stage 2 setting **(see illustration)**. When the cylinder head nuts have been fully tightened, tighten the four smaller rocker pedestal nuts to the specified torque.

39 Adjust the valve clearances as described in Section 5.

40 The remainder of the refitting process is a direct reversal of the removal procedure, noting the following points:

a) *Ensure that all pipes/hoses are correctly reconnected, and (where necessary) are securely held in position by their retaining clips.*

b) *Tighten all nuts and bolts to the specified torque setting (where given).*

c) *Refit the rocker cover as described in Section 3.*

d) *Ensure that the mating faces of the exhaust manifold and front pipe are clean, and use a new gasket when connecting the front pipe flange.*

e) *Refit the alternator as described in Chapter 5A.*

f) *Adjust the accelerator cable and refit the air cleaner as described in Chapter 4C.*

g) *Refill the cooling system and refit the auxiliary drivebelt as described in Chapter 1.*

h) *Refit the bonnet as described in Chapter 11B.*

10 Crankshaft oil seals – renewal

Timing cover oil seal

1 Remove the timing cover as described in Section 7, paragraphs 1 to 6.

2 Thoroughly clean the timing cover with paraffin or a suitable solvent and dry thoroughly. Pay particular attention to the mating faces of the cover and the engine plate, ensuring that all traces of old gasket are removed.

3 Drive out the old seal and thoroughly clean the recess in the timing cover. Apply a smear of multipurpose grease to the outer edge of the new seal then, with the timing cover supported, tap the seal into place using a wooden block or the old seal to spread the load **(see illustrations)**. Ensure that the open side of the seal faces inward, towards the chain.

4 Refit the timing cover as described in Section 7, paragraphs 28 to 36.

Primary gear oil seal

Note 1: *The majority of clutch faults experienced on Mini power units are caused by oil contamination of the clutch friction linings due to the failure of the primary gear oil seal. It is therefore recommended that the seal is renewed whenever problems of this nature are encountered.*

Note 2: *Rover special tools 18G 1068B and 18G 1043 (or suitable alternatives) will be required for this operation. The accompanying photos in this Section depict the use of a typical alternative to the Rover special tools.*

5 Remove the flywheel and clutch assembly as described in Chapter 6.

6 The primary gear complete with oil seal can now be withdrawn from the crankshaft and flywheel housing as described below.

7 Remove the dust shield then lift off the C-shaped thrustwasher and backing ring that retain the primary gear in position **(see illustrations)**.

8 Now screw in the threaded centre bolt of special tool 18G 1068B until the base of the

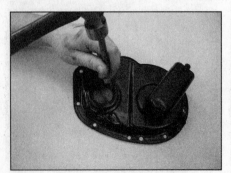

10.3a Drive out the timing cover oil seal using a hammer and punch . . .

10.3b . . . and tap the new seal into place using a wooden block or the old seal to spread the load

10.7a Remove the primary gear dust shield . . .

10.7b . . . then lift off the C-shaped washer . . .

10.7c . . . and backing ring

10.8 Engage the flange of the primary gear removal tool with the primary gear groove

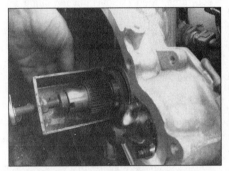

10.9 Tighten the tool centre bolt to draw off the primary gear and oil seal

10.10 Remove the tool and slide the primary gear and oil seal off the end of the crankshaft

10.12 Place a protective sleeve over the primary gear splines . . .

tool abuts the oil seal. Pull the primary gear outwards as far as it will go and slide the two collets of 18G 1068B between the groove at the rear of the primary gear splines and the base of the tool body. If an alternative tool is being used, engage the flange of the tool body with the primary gear groove **(see illustration)**.

9 Slowly unscrew the wing nut on tool 18G 1068B while holding the tool body. This will cause the primary gear to be withdrawn from the flywheel housing, bringing the oil seal with it. If an alternative tool is being used, position a suitable thrust pad on the end of the crankshaft and tighten the tool centre bolt against the thrust pad to draw off the primary gear and oil seal **(see illustration)**.

10 When the primary gear and oil seal are clear of the housing, lift them off the end of the crankshaft, remove the tool and slide the

oil seal off the primary gear **(see illustration)**.

11 To fit a new oil seal first slide the primary gear onto the crankshaft and secure with the C-shaped washer and backing ring.

12 To avoid damage to the oil seal as it is fitted, place the protective sleeve, special tool 18G 1043, over the primary gear, or if this tool is not available cover the primary gear splines and the stepped shoulder with masking tape **(see illustration)**.

13 Lubricate the lip of the oil seal, and very carefully slide it over the primary gear and into position against the flywheel housing **(see illustration)**. The open part of the seal must be facing towards the engine.

14 Screw on the threaded centre bolt of special tool 18G 1068B (or similar alternative) and, when the body of the tool contacts the seal, fully tighten the centre bolt, thus forcing the seal squarely into the housing **(see**

illustration). Remove the tool when the face of the seal is flush with the housing.

15 Refit the dust shield to the primary gear with the stepped face of the shield (marked FLYWHEEL SIDE) facing away from the engine **(see illustration)**.

16 The flywheel and clutch assembly can now be refitted as described in Chapter 6.

11 Flywheel – removal and refitting

The flywheel is removed complete with the clutch assembly, the components then being separated after removal. Full details of clutch and flywheel removal and refitting are contained in Chapter 6.

10.13 . . . then slide the new oil seal over the sleeve onto the primary gear

10.14 Use a suitable fitting tool to press the oil seal fully into the flywheel housing

10.15 Refit the primary gear dust shield with the stepped face marked FLYWHEEL SIDE (arrowed) facing away from the engine

12.3 Right-hand engine/transmission mounting retaining bolts (arrowed)

12 Engine/transmission mountings – renewal

General information

1 The engine/transmission is supported on two rubber mountings which are in turn bolted to the sides of the front subframe. One mounting is attached to a bracket on the transmission casing below the timing cover (left-hand mounting), and the other is attached to the base of the flywheel housing cover (right-hand mounting). Fore-and-aft movement of the power unit is controlled by an upper and lower tie-bar. One end of the upper tie-bar is attached to the engine, and the other to a bracket on the bulkhead. The lower tie-bar is bolted to the subframe at one end and to a bracket on the transmission at the other end. Rubber bushes are used at each end of the tie-bars to absorb vibration. A point worth noting is that the tie-bar rubber bushes are prone to wear and this is usually noticed as severe judder as the clutch is engaged, or excessive movement of the complete power unit when accelerating and decelerating.

Right-hand mounting

2 Remove the flywheel housing cover as described in Chapter 6.
3 With the cover removed, undo the bolts securing the engine mounting and lift off the mounting (see illustration).
4 Locate the new mounting in position on the cover and secure with the two bolts tightened to the specified torque.
5 Refit the flywheel housing cover as described in Chapter 6.

Left-hand mounting

6 Disconnect the battery negative terminal (refer to *Disconnecting the battery* in the Reference Chapter).

7 Firmly apply the handbrake, then jack up the front of the car and support it securely on axle stands (see *Jacking and vehicle support*).
8 Position a jack beneath the left-hand side of the transmission casing and just take the weight of the power unit. Use a block of wood interposed between the casing and the jack to spread the load.
9 Undo the bolt securing the radiator bottom hose support bracket to the engine mounting bracket (see illustration).
10 Undo the two bolts securing the engine mounting bracket to the transmission casing.
11 Undo and remove the two nuts, bolts and spring washers securing the mounting to the subframe, then remove the mounting and mounting bracket from under the car.
12 With the assembly on the bench, undo the two bolts and separate the mounting from the bracket.
13 Refitting is the reverse sequence to removal, ensuring that all nuts and bolts are tightened to the specified torque.

Upper tie-bar and bushes

14 Remove the air cleaner assembly as described in Chapter 4C.
15 Undo and remove the two bolts securing the tie-bar and mounting bracket to the right-hand side of the engine (see illustration opposite). Lift off the bracket then move the tie-bar sideways and recover the spacing washers.
16 Undo and remove the through-bolt and locknut securing the tie-bar to the bulkhead. Collect the engine earth strap then lift away the tie-bar.
17 With the tie-bar removed, slide out the rubber bushes and spacers and, if there is any sign of swelling or deterioration of the rubber whatsoever, renew the bushes.
18 Refitting is the reverse sequence to removal, ensuring that the engine earth strap and the spacing washers are correctly positioned. Tighten all nuts and bolts to the specified torque.

Lower tie-bar and bushes

19 Firmly apply the handbrake, then jack up the front of the car and support it securely on axle stands (see *Jacking and vehicle support*).
20 Undo the nut and bolt and collect the washers securing the lower tie-bar to the bracket on the flywheel housing (see illustration opposite). Similarly unbolt the other end of the tie-bar from the bracket on the subframe then remove the tie-bar from under the car.
21 With the tie-bar removed, slide out the rubber bushes and spacers and, if there is any sign of swelling or deterioration of the rubber whatsoever, renew the bushes.
22 Refitting is the reverse sequence to removal, ensuring that the mounting nuts and bolts are tightened to the specified torque.

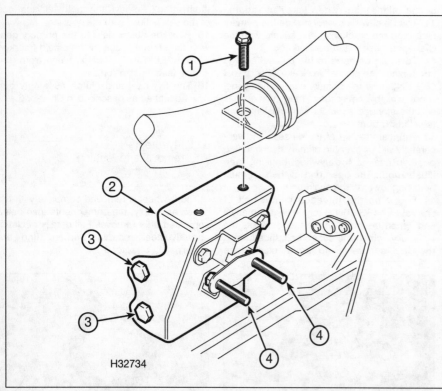

H32734

12.9 Left-hand engine/transmission mounting details

1 Bottom hose support bracket retaining bolt
2 Engine/transmission mounting bracket
3 Mounting bracket-to-transmission casing retaining bolts
4 Engine/transmission mounting-to-subframe retaining bolts

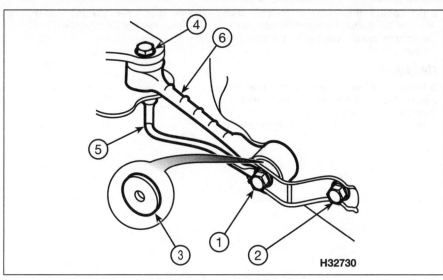

12.15 Upper tie-bar attachments

1 Tie-bar-to-engine retaining bolt
2 Tie-bar mounting bracket-to-engine retaining bolt
3 Spacing washer
4 Tie-bar-to-bulkhead retaining bolt
5 Earth strap
6 Tie-bar

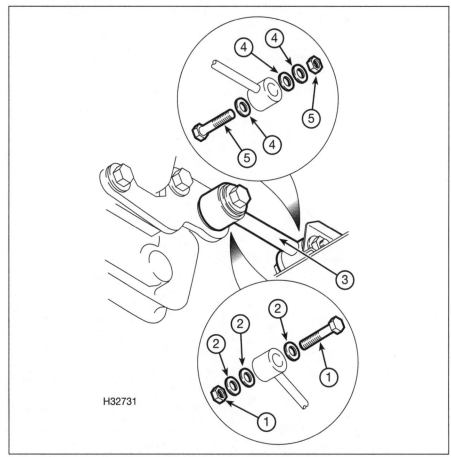

H32731

12.20 Lower tie-bar attachments

1 Tie-bar-to-flywheel housing bracket retaining nut and bolt
2 Packing washers
3 Lower tie-bar
4 Packing washers
5 Tie-bar-to-subframe retaining nut and bolt

13 Oil pressure relief valve – removal, inspection and refitting

Removal

1 To prevent excessive oil pressure – for example when the engine is cold – an oil pressure relief valve is built into the front facing side of the engine adjacent to the oil filter.
2 To gain access, remove the starter motor as described in Chapter 5A.
3 The relief valve is identified externally by a large domed hexagon nut. To remove the unit unscrew the nut and remove it, complete with the copper sealing washer. The relief spring and the relief spring cup can then be easily extracted.

Inspection

4 In position, the metal cup fits over the opposite end of the relief valve spring resting in the dome of the hexagon nut, and bears against a machining in the block. When the oil pressure exceeds the specified pressure the cup is forced off its seat and the oil returns, via a drilling, directly to the sump.
5 Check the tension of the spring by measuring its free length. If it is shorter than the length given in the Specifications, it should be renewed. Check the condition of the cup checking carefully for wear ridges which would prevent the cup seating effectively. Renew the cup if its condition is suspect.

Refitting

6 Refitting is the reverse sequence to removal. Use a new copper sealing washer and tighten the nut to the specified torque.

14 Oil pressure switch – removal and refitting

Removal

1 The oil pressure switch is located on the front facing side of the engine, adjacent to the engine oil dipstick. To gain access, remove the DIS module as described in Chapter 5C.
2 Disconnect the wiring connector then unscrew the switch from the cylinder block.

Refitting

3 Prior to refitting, thoroughly clean the threads on the switch body and its location in the cylinder block.
4 Apply Loctite 572 to the switch body threads and screw the switch into the cylinder block. Tighten the switch to the specified torque and reconnect the wiring connector.
5 Refit the DIS module as described in Chapter 5C.

15 Oil temperature sensor – removal and refitting

Removal

1 The oil temperature sensor is located on the front facing side of the engine, above the oil pressure relief valve.

2 Disconnect the wiring connector then unscrew the switch from the cylinder block. Collect the sealing washer as the switch is removed.

Refitting

3 Prior to refitting, thoroughly clean the mating faces of the switch body and its location in the cylinder block.

4 Screw the switch into the cylinder block, tighten it to the specified torque and reconnect the wiring connector.

Chapter 2 Part C:
Engine removal and overhaul procedures

Contents

Camshaft and tappets – removal, inspection and refitting 9
Crankshaft – refitting and running clearance check 17
Crankshaft – removal and inspection 12
Cylinder block/crankcase – cleaning and inspection 13
Cylinder head – dismantling, cleaning, inspection and reassembly . 8
Engine – initial start-up after overhaul and reassembly 19
Engine and automatic transmission – separation and reconnection . 6
Engine and manual transmission – separation and reconnection . . . 5
Engine overhaul – preliminary information 7
Engine overhaul – reassembly sequence 15
Engine/transmission (pre-October 1996 models) – removal and
  refitting 3

Engine/transmission (October 1996 models onward) – removal and
  refitting 4
Engine/transmission removal – methods and precautions 2
General information 1
Main and big-end bearings – inspection and selection 14
Oil pump – removal, inspection and refitting 10
Piston/connecting rod assemblies – refitting and big-end bearing
  clearance check 18
Piston/connecting rod assemblies – removal, inspection, separation
  and reconnection 11
Piston rings – refitting 16

Degrees of difficulty

Easy, suitable for novice with little experience	**Fairly easy,** suitable for beginner with some experience	**Fairly difficult,** suitable for competent DIY mechanic	**Difficult,** suitable for experienced DIY mechanic	**Very difficult,** suitable for expert DIY or professional

Specifications

Engine general
Engine codes:
85H	848 cc engines
99H	998 cc engines
10H	1098 cc engines
12H	1275 cc engines
12A	1275 cc engines

Valves
Valve head diameter:
Inlet:	
85H	27.76 to 27.89 mm
10H	29.23 to 29.36 mm
12H:	
1275 GT	33.20 to 33.32 mm
Cooper S Mk III	35.58 to 35.71 mm
12A	35.58 to 35.71 mm
Exhaust:	
85H, 99H and 10H	25.40 to 25.53 mm
12H:	
1275 GT	29.24 to 29.37 mm
Cooper S Mk III	30.83 to 30.96 mm
12A	29.25 to 29.38 mm
Valve stem diameter:	
Inlet	7.094 to 7.107 mm
Exhaust	7.082 to 7.094 mm
Valve stem-to-guide clearance:	
Inlet:	
85H, 99H and 10H	0.038 to 0.064 mm
12H and 12A	0.040 to 0.080 mm
Exhaust:	
85H, 99H and 10H	0.051 to 0.076 mm
12H and 12A	0.040 to 0.080 mm
Valve seat angle	45°

Valve springs

Valve spring free length:
85H and 99H	44.45 mm
10H	49.70 mm

12H:
1275 GT	49.70 mm
Cooper S Mk III outer spring	44.19 mm
Cooper S Mk III Inner spring	43.31 mm
12A	49.53 mm

Camshaft and camshaft bearings

Camshaft journal diameter:
Left-hand	42.304 to 42.316 mm
Centre	41.218 to 41.231 mm
Right-hand	34.857 to 34.887 mm

Bearing inside diameter (reamed after fitting):

85H:
Left-hand	42.342 to 42.355 mm
Centre	41.262 to 41.288 mm
Right-hand	34.908 to 34.938 mm

99H and 10H:
Left-hand	42.342 to 42.355 mm
Centre	41.225 to 41.267 mm
Right-hand	34.912 to 34.925 mm

12H and 12A:
Left-hand	42.342 to 42.355 mm
Centre	41.262 to 41.288 mm
Right-hand	34.908 to 34.938 mm

Bearing running clearance:

85H:
Left-hand	0.012 to 0.051 mm
Centre and right-hand	0.031 to 0.069 mm

All other engines:
Left-hand, centre and right-hand	0.025 to 0.051 mm
Camshaft endfloat	0.076 to 0.178 mm

Cylinder block

Bore diameter:
85H	62.94 mm
99H	64.59 mm
10H	64.59 mm
12H and 12A	70.61 mm

Maximum cylinder bore oversize (after reboring):
85H and 99H	+1.02 mm
All other engines	+0.51 mm
Maximum cylinder bore/liner taper*	0.10 mm
Maximum cylinder bore/liner ovality*	0.10 mm

*These are suggested figures, typical for this type of engine – no exact values are stated by Rover.

Pistons

Piston-to-bore clearance:

85H:
Top of skirt	0.066 to 0.81 mm
Bottom of skirt	0.015 to 0.030 mm

99H and 10H:
Top of skirt	0.060 to 0.085 mm
Bottom of skirt	0.010 to 0.026 mm

12H:

Top of skirt:
1275 GT	0.070 to 0.114 mm
Cooper S Mk III	0.063 to 0.072 mm

Bottom of skirt:
1275 GT	0.031 to 0.056 mm
Cooper S Mk III	0.048 to 0.063 mm

12A:
Top of skirt	0.074 to 0.114 mm
Bottom of skirt	0.023 to 0.064 mm

Piston oversizes available:
85H and 99H	+0.254 mm, +0.508 mm, +0.762 mm, +1.02 mm
All other engines	+0.254 mm, +0.508 mm

Piston rings

Piston ring end gap:

85H and 99H	0.178 to 0.305 mm
10H:	
Compression rings	0.178 to 0.305 mm
Oil control ring:	
Rails	0.305 to 0.711 mm
Side springs	2.54 to 3.81 mm
12H:	
Top compression ring:	
1275 GT	0.28 to 0.41 mm
Cooper S Mk III	0.20 to 0.33 mm
2nd and 3rd compression rings	0.20 to 0.33 mm
Oil control ring:	
1275 GT	0.254 to 1.02 mm
Cooper S Mk III	0.20 to 0.33 mm
12A:	
Top compression ring	0.25 to 0.45 mm
Second compression ring	0.20 to 0.33 mm
Oil control ring	0.38 to 1.04 mm
Ring-to-groove clearance (compression rings)	0.038 to 0.089 mm

Crankshaft

Main bearing journal diameter:

85H, 99H* and 10H	44.46 to 44.47 mm
12H:	
1275 GT	50.83 to 50.84 mm
Cooper S Mk III	50.81 to 50.82 mm
12A:	
No colour code	50.83 to 50.84 mm
Red colour code	50.81 to 50.82 mm
Green colour code	50.82 to 50.83 mm
Yellow colour code	50.83 to 50.84 mm
Minimum main bearing journal regrind diameter:	
85H, 99H* and 10H	43.45 mm
12H:	
1275 GT	49.78 mm
Cooper S Mk III	50.30 mm
12A	49.78 mm
Main bearing running clearance:	
85H, 99H* and 10H	0.025 to 0.068 mm
12H and 12A	0.017 to 0.058 mm
Big-end bearing journal diameter:	
85H, 99H* and 10H	41.28 to 41.29 mm
12H and 12A	44.44 to 44.46 mm
Minimum big-end journal regrind diameter:	
85H, 99H* and 10H	40.27 mm
12H and 12A	43.44 mm
Big-end bearing running clearance:	
85H, 99H* and 10H	0.025 to 0.063 mm
12H and 12A	0.038 to 0.081 mm
Crankshaft endfloat	0.051 to 0.076 mm

Refer to a Rover dealer for information on later models

Lubrication system

Oil pump shaft and rotor endfloat	0.127 mm
Oil pump rotor lobe clearance	0.152 mm
Oil pump rotor-to-body clearance	0.254 mm

Torque wrench settings

Refer to Chapter 2A or 2B as applicable

---

1 General information

Included in this Part of Chapter 2 are details of removing the engine/transmission from the car and general overhaul procedures for the cylinder head, cylinder block and all other engine internal components.

The information given ranges from advice concerning preparation for an overhaul and the purchase of replacement parts, to detailed step-by-step procedures covering removal, inspection, renovation and refitting of engine internal components.

After Section 7, all instructions are based on the assumption that the engine has been removed from the car. For information concerning engine in-car repair, as well as the removal and refitting of those external components necessary for full overhaul, refer to Part A or Part B of this Chapter and to Section 7. Ignore any preliminary dismantling operations described in Part A or B that are no longer relevant once the engine has been removed from the car.

2 Engine/transmission removal – methods and precautions

If you have decided that the engine must be removed for overhaul or major repair work, several preliminary steps should be taken.

Locating a suitable place to work is extremely important. Adequate work space, along with storage space for the car, will be needed. If a workshop or garage is not available, at the very least, a flat, level, clean work surface is required.

Cleaning the engine compartment and engine/transmission before beginning the removal procedure will help keep tools clean and organised.

An engine hoist will also be necessary. Make sure the equipment is rated in excess of the combined weight of the engine/transmission. Safety is of primary importance, considering the potential hazards involved in lifting the engine/transmission out of the car.

If this is the first time you have removed an engine, an assistant should ideally be available. Advice and aid from someone more experienced would also be helpful. There are many instances when one person cannot simultaneously perform all of the operations required when lifting the engine/transmission out of the vehicle.

Plan the operation ahead of time. Before starting work, arrange for the hire of or obtain all of the tools and equipment you will need. Some of the equipment necessary to perform engine/transmission removal and installation safely (in addition to an engine hoist) is as follows: a heavy duty trolley jack, complete sets of spanners and sockets as described at the rear of this manual, wooden blocks, and plenty of rags and cleaning solvent for mopping-up spilled oil, coolant and fuel. If the hoist must be hired, make sure that you arrange for it in advance, and perform all of the operations possible without it beforehand. This will save you money and time.

Plan for the car to be out of use for quite a while. An engineering works will be required to perform some of the work which the do-it-yourselfer cannot accomplish without special equipment. These places often have a busy schedule, so it would be a good idea to consult them before removing the engine, in order to accurately estimate the amount of time required to rebuild or repair components that may need work.

During the engine/transmission removal procedure, it is advisable to make notes of the locations of all brackets, cable ties, earthing points, etc, as well as how the wiring

harnesses, hoses and electrical connections are attached and routed around the engine and engine compartment. An effective way of doing this is to take a series of photographs of the various components before they are disconnected or removed. A simple inexpensive disposable camera is ideal for this and the resulting photographs will prove invaluable when refitting.

Always be extremely careful when removing and refitting the engine/transmission. Serious injury can result from careless actions. Plan ahead and take your time, and a job of this nature, although major, can be accomplished successfully.

The engine/transmission unit is removed upwards from the engine compartment on all models described in this manual.

3 Engine/transmission (pre-October 1996 models) – removal and refitting

Removal

1 Disconnect the battery negative terminal (refer to *Disconnecting the battery* in the Reference Chapter).

2 Drain the cooling system and the engine/transmission oil as described in Chapter 1.

3 Remove the bonnet and front grille as described in Chapter 11A.

4 On models equipped with an ignition shield mounted on the front of the engine, release the three retaining lugs and lift off the shield.

5 On carburettor engines, refer to Chapter 4A and remove the air cleaner assembly and carburettor(s). On fuel injection engines, slacken the accelerator cable locknuts, and free the outer cable from its mounting bracket. Release the inner cable from the throttle cam, and position the cable clear of the throttle body.

6 On fuel injection engines, remove the engine management ECU as described in Chapter 4B, Section 13.

7 Remove the starter motor and alternator as described in Chapter 5A.

8 Where applicable, undo and remove the screws securing the starter solenoid to the inner wing panel and position the solenoid clear of the engine.

9 On models equipped with a mechanical fuel pump, disconnect the fuel inlet hose and plug it with a suitable bolt or metal rod to prevent loss of fuel.

10 On fuel injection engines, undo the bolt and remove the retaining clip securing the injector housing fuel pipes to the bulkhead. Bearing in mind the information contained in Chapter 4B, concerning fuel system depressurisation, place absorbent rags around the fuel feed and return hose unions on the throttle body. Remove the fuel tank filler cap to release any pressure in the tank.

Using an open-ended spanner to retain each adapter, slacken the union nuts and disconnect the feed and return pipes from the throttle body assembly. Plug each pipe and adapter, to minimise the loss of fuel and prevent the entry of dirt into the system.

11 Where applicable, disconnect the cooling system hose from the expansion tank, which is located by the side of the radiator. Undo the retaining bolt and remove the expansion tank from the engine compartment.

12 On carburettor engines, slacken the retaining clips and remove the two heater hoses. Also slacken the two securing screws and withdraw the heater control cable from the valve on the cylinder head (where applicable). On fuel injection engines, Undo the heater control coolant valve mounting bolt, then slacken the retaining clips and disconnect the coolant valve hoses from the manifold and thermostat housing. Slacken the clip and disconnect the heater unit hose from its union with the bottom radiator hose (situated directly below the coolant valve).

13 If a fresh air heater/demister blower motor is mounted in the engine compartment, remove it.

14 Undo and remove the two nuts and bolts on the clamp, or the three flange nuts securing the exhaust front pipe to the manifold. Separate the front pipe from the manifold. **Note:** *On Cooper S models it will be necessary to remove the complete exhaust system as described in Chapter 4D.*

15 If the horn is mounted on the front body panel, disconnect the electrical leads, undo and remove the mounting bolts and withdraw the horn.

16 From beneath the right-hand front wing detach the heater fresh air ducting from the air inlet. Now withdraw the air inlet from the inner wing panel.

17 Disconnect the wiring from the following locations, after identifying the leads or wiring plugs for subsequent reconnection:

a) *Leads to the temperature gauge transmitter and oil pressure switch (where fitted).*

b) *LT leads at the ignition coil.*

c) *HT leads from the spark plugs and ignition coil, and the crankshaft sensor wiring connector on fuel injection engines.*

d) *On fuel injection engines, disconnect the wiring connectors from the injector housing, the throttle potentiometer and the stepper motor. Free the wiring from any relevant retaining clips, and position it clear of the throttle body assembly. Trace the wiring back from the exhaust system lambda sensor (which is screwed into the exhaust manifold), releasing it from any relevant cable-ties, and disconnect its wiring connector from the main harness.*

e) *Wiring connectors from the auxiliary cooling fan switch (where fitted), which is situated at the front bottom corner of the radiator.*

18 Spring back the distributor cap retaining clips, or undo the two screws and remove the cap and leads. Remove the rotor arm from the distributor shaft.

19 On manual transmission models, release the clutch slave cylinder return spring (where fitted) from the clutch operating lever. Undo and remove the two securing bolts and lift the slave cylinder off the flywheel housing or mounting bracket. Tie the cylinder out of the way from a convenient place on the engine bulkhead.

20 If an oil pressure gauge is fitted, slacken the clamp screw and pull the rubber hose off the feed pipe at the rear of the engine.

21 On fuel injection engines, release the retaining clip and disconnect the vacuum hose from the pipe situated just behind the thermostat housing. Disconnect the two vacuum hoses from the rear of the inlet manifold, noting their correct fitted positions; note that the hoses are colour-coded for identification purposes.

22 On later models, disconnect the oil separator breather hose from the right-hand end of the cylinder head. Undo the two bolts securing the separator to the flywheel housing, and remove the separator and hose assembly from the engine, along with its gasket.

23 Undo and remove the bolt securing the engine tie-bar to the side of the cylinder block. Slacken the tie-bar bulkhead mounting and move the bar back out of the way. Note that on later models the tie-bar retaining bolt also retains the engine earth strap.

24 Where fitted, remove the oil cooler as described in Part A of this Chapter.

25 On models fitted with a vacuum servo unit mounted in the engine compartment, refer to Chapter 9 and remove the servo and brake master cylinder. Unscrew the two union nuts securing the master cylinder brake pipes to the pressure-reducing valve, and remove both the pipes, noting their correct fitted positions. Plug the pressure-reducing valve ports, to minimise fluid loss and prevent the entry of dirt into the system.

26 Working under the front wheelarch undo and remove the screw securing the upper suspension arm rebound rubber to the subframe and withdraw the rubber. Place a solid wooden wedge of approximately the same thickness in its place. Repeat this procedure on the other side of the car.

27 Firmly apply the handbrake, then jack up the front of the car and support it securely on axle stands (see *Jacking and vehicle support*). Remove the front roadwheels.

28 On manual transmission models fitted with a direct engagement gear lever, undo and remove the retaining screws and lift off the interior rubber boot retaining plate. Now slide the rubber boot up the gear lever slightly. From under the car, undo and remove the two bolts securing the gear lever retaining plate to the rear of the differential housing. Withdraw the gear lever into the car and lift out the anti-rattle spring and plunger from the gear lever housing.

29 On manual transmission models fitted with the early type remote control extension housing, undo and remove the four shouldered bolts securing the housing to the mounting on the rear of the differential assembly. Pull the front of the extension housing downwards to disengage the linkage and then support the front of the housing on a block of wood.

30 On manual transmission models fitted with the later rod-change type remote control extension housing, drift out the roll pin securing the collar of the remote control extension rod to the selector shaft. Undo and remove the bolt securing the fork of the steady rod to the differential housing. Release the extension rod and the steady rod from the rear of the transmission.

31 On automatic transmission models, disconnect the gear selector cable from the transmission as described in Chapter 7B.

32 On early models undo and remove the bolt securing the engine earth strap to the flywheel/torque converter housing.

33 Undo and remove the nut securing the steering tie-rod balljoint to the steering arm on each side of the car. Release the balljoint tapers using a universal separator.

34 Undo and remove the nut securing the front suspension swivel hub balljoint to the upper suspension arm on each side of the car. Release the balljoint shanks from the upper suspension arms using a universal balljoint separator. Move the top of the two swivel hubs outwards and support them in this position. Take care not to strain the flexible brake hoses.

35 On early models equipped with rubber couplings at the inner end of each driveshaft, undo and remove the two U-bolt locknuts securing each coupling to the differential driving flanges. Withdraw the two U-bolts from each side and move the driveshafts away from the differential.

36 On later models equipped with offset sphere joints at the inner end of each driveshaft, release the joints from the differential using Rover special tool 18G 1240. If this tool cannot be obtained, it is possible to withdraw the joints using a tyre lever or similar tool pivoting against the end cover retaining bolt directly below the joint. Once the joints have been released, move the driveshafts away from the differential as far as possible.

37 On Cooper S and certain automatic transmission models, undo and remove the four nuts securing each universal joint flange to the differential driving flanges. Move the driveshafts away from the differential to separate the flanges.

38 On all models undo and remove the nut and bolt securing the exhaust pipe strap to the bracket on the side of the differential housing.

39 Undo and remove the nut and bolt securing the lower engine tie-bar to the bracket on the transmission casing. Slacken the nut and bolt securing the other end and move the tie-bar clear of the transmission.

3.44a Lift the engine/transmission out of the engine bay . . .

40 Position a crane or hoist over the engine and attach chains or ropes either to brackets bolted to the cylinder head or around each end of the transmission casing.

41 With the lifting gear in position, raise it slightly and just take the weight of the engine.

42 Undo and remove the two nuts and bolts securing the two engine mountings to the side of the front subframe.

43 Make a final check that all cables, pipes and hoses have been disconnected and that all removed parts are clear of the engine.

44 The engine/transmission can now be lifted out. Tilt it backwards as it is lifted out to allow the differential to clear the rear of the subframe. When the unit is halfway out or when sufficient clearance exists, unscrew the speedometer cable knurled retaining nut and lift the cable off the housing **(see illustrations)**. On fuel injection engines, disconnect the wiring connectors from the PTC heater and coolant temperature sensor situated on the underside of the inlet manifold. Release the wiring harness from any relevant retaining clips.

45 Now completely remove the power unit from the vehicle and position it on a bench or clean floor for separation.

Refitting

46 Refitting is the reverse sequence to removal, following where necessary the instructions given in the other Chapters of this manual. Note the following additional points:

a) *Tighten all nuts and bolts to the specified torque settings (where given).*

b) *On models fitted with offset sphere inner*

3.44b . . . until sufficient clearance exists to disconnect the speedometer cable

driveshaft joints, ensure that the joint circlips are properly located in their grooves, then apply a smear of graphite-based grease to the splines, and locate the joints in the transmission. Push them firmly into position, and check they are securely retained by the circlips.

c) Ensure that all wiring harnesses are properly routed, and are retained by any necessary cable ties or clips.

d) Reconnect and adjust the accelerator cable as described in Chapter 4A or 4B as applicable.

e) On automatic transmission models, adjust the selector cable as described in Chapter 7B.

f) On models fitted with a vacuum servo unit, refit the servo and brake master cylinder as described in Chapter 9.

g) Refill the cooling system as described in Chapter 1.

h) Refill the engine/transmission with the correct quantity and type of lubricant as described in Chapter 1.

4 Engine/transmission (October 1996 models onward) – removal and refitting

Removal

1 Disconnect the battery negative terminal (refer to *Disconnecting the battery* in the Reference Chapter).

2 Drain the cooling system and the engine/transmission oil as described in Chapter 1.

3 Remove the bonnet and front grille as described in Chapter 11B.

4 Remove the radiator as described in Chapter 3.

5 Remove the starter motor as described in Chapter 5A.

6 Remove the air cleaner assembly and the engine management ECU as described in Chapter 4C, Sections 2 and 12.

7 Remove the brake master cylinder and vacuum servo unit as described in Chapter 9.

8 Undo and remove the two bolts securing the engine earth strap, upper tie-bar and mounting bracket to the right-hand side of the engine. Lift off the bracket then move the tie-bar sideways and recover the spacing washers.

9 Undo and remove the through-bolt and locknut securing the tie-bar to the bulkhead. Collect the engine earth strap then lift away the tie-bar.

10 Disconnect the wiring connector from the coolant temperature sensor located in the thermostat housing. Release the sensor wiring harness cable clip from the expansion tank mounting bracket.

11 Slacken the retaining clips and disconnect the radiator top hose, expansion tank hose and heater hose from the thermostat housing.

12 Working under the wheelarch, undo the two nuts securing the expansion tank

mounting bracket to the body. Withdraw the tank and mounting bracket, disconnect the coolant hose from the base of the tank then remove the tank and mounting bracket from the engine compartment.

13 Disconnect the horn wiring connector, then undo the two bolts securing the horn mounting bracket to the body. Remove the horn and bracket from the engine compartment.

14 Remove the cover from the engine compartment fuseblock. Lift out the fusible link from the location in the fuseblock closest to the engine. Release the now exposed retaining tag and disconnect the wiring harness lead from the fuseblock.

15 Withdraw the fuseblock from the engine management ECU mounting bracket and position it to one side.

16 Release the clip securing the wiring harness to the ECU mounting bracket. Undo the mounting bracket retaining bolt and remove the bracket from the engine compartment.

17 Undo and remove the bolt, situated just to the right of the brake servo unit, securing the earth leads to the bulkhead.

18 Undo the bolts securing the wiring harness retaining clip and starter motor lead brackets to the flywheel housing.

19 Disconnect the wiring connector from the bonnet contact switch.

20 Working under the right-hand wheelarch, detach the heater air inlet hose from the air inlet duct. Remove the air inlet duct from the inner wing panel in the engine compartment.

21 Thoroughly clean the brake pipe unions and surrounding area on the brake pressure-reducing valve. Unscrew the union nuts and remove the brake pipes, noting their correct fitted positions. Plug the pressure-reducing valve ports and brake pipe unions, to minimise fluid loss and prevent the entry of dirt into the system.

22 Undo the two bolts securing the clutch slave cylinder to the mounting plate on the flywheel housing. Withdraw the slave cylinder from the pushrod and position it to one side.

23 Bearing in mind the information contained in Chapter 4C concerning fuel system depressurisation, place absorbent rags around the fuel feed and return hose quick-release fittings. Remove the fuel tank filler cap to release any pressure in the tank. Depress the plastic collar on the quick-release fittings and disconnect the feed and return hoses from the pipes. Plug or cover each pipe and hose, to minimise the loss of fuel and prevent the entry of dirt into the system.

24 Release the retaining clips and disconnect the two heater hoses at their bulkhead connections.

25 Release the accelerator cable adjusting nut from the mounting bracket, disconnect the inner cable end fitting from the throttle cam, and position the cable aside.

26 Release the retaining clip and disconnect the evaporative emission control purge hose from the inlet manifold.

27 Disconnect the wiring connector from the purge control valve situated behind the coolant expansion tank location.

28 Disconnect the engine wiring harness from the main harness at the multiplug connector on the bulkhead. Release the engine wiring harness multiplug from the bulkhead bracket.

29 Working under the front wheelarch, undo and remove the screw securing the upper suspension arm rebound rubber to the subframe and withdraw the rubber. Place a solid wooden wedge of approximately the same thickness in its place. Repeat this procedure on the other side of the car.

30 Firmly apply the handbrake, then jack up the front of the car and support it securely on axle stands (see *Jacking and vehicle support*). Remove the front roadwheels.

31 Remove the exhaust system front pipe as described in Chapter 4D.

32 From under the car, drift out the roll pin securing the collar of the gear change remote control extension rod to the selector shaft. Undo and remove the bolt securing the fork of the steady rod to the differential housing. Release the extension rod and the steady rod from the rear of the transmission.

33 Release the driveshaft inner CV joints from the differential using Rover special tool 18G 1240. If this tool cannot be obtained, it is possible to withdraw the joints using a tyre lever or similar tool pivoting against the end cover retaining bolt directly below the joint.

34 Undo and remove the nut securing the steering tie-rod balljoint to the steering arm on each side of the car. Release the balljoint tapers using a universal separator.

35 Undo and remove the nut securing the front suspension swivel hub balljoint to the upper suspension arm on each side of the car. Release the balljoint shanks from the upper suspension arms using a universal balljoint separator. Move the top of the two swivel hubs outwards and suitably support them in this position. Take care not to strain the flexible brake hoses.

36 Withdraw the driveshaft inner CV joints from the differential and suitably support them clear of the engine/transmission assembly.

37 Undo and remove the nut and bolt securing the lower engine tie-bar to the bracket on the transmission casing. Slacken the nut and bolt securing the other end and move the tie-bar clear of the transmission.

38 Position a crane or hoist over the engine and attach chains or ropes either to brackets bolted to the cylinder head or around each end of the transmission casing.

39 With the lifting gear in position, raise it slightly and just take the weight of the engine.

40 Undo and remove the two nuts and bolts securing the two engine mountings to the side of the front subframe.

41 Make a final check that all cables, pipes and hoses have been disconnected and that all removed parts are clear of the engine.

42 The engine/transmission can now be lifted

out. Tilt it backwards as it is lifted out to allow the differential to clear the rear of the subframe. When the unit is halfway out or when sufficient clearance exists, unscrew the speedometer cable knurled retaining nut and lift the cable off the housing.

Refitting

43 Refitting is the reverse sequence to removal, following where necessary the instructions given in the other Chapters of this manual. Note the following additional points:

a) *Tighten all nuts and bolts to the specified torque settings (where given).*

b) *Ensure that the driveshaft CV joint circlips are properly located in their grooves, then apply a smear of graphite-based grease to the splines, and locate the joints in the transmission. Push them firmly into position, and check they are securely retained by the circlips.*

c) *Ensure that all wiring harnesses are properly routed, and are retained by any necessary cable ties or clips.*

d) *Refit the brake vacuum servo unit and master cylinder as described in Chapter 9.*

e) *Reconnect and adjust the accelerator cable as described in Chapter 4C.*

f) *Refill the cooling system as described in Chapter 1.*

g) *Refill the engine/transmission with the correct quantity and type of lubricant as described in Chapter 1.*

---

5 Engine and manual transmission – separation and reconnection

Separation

Note: *A suitable puller will be required to release the flywheel from the crankshaft taper. Read through the entire procedure to familiarise yourself with the work involved, and obtain the relevant tools before proceeding.*

1 Remove the engine/transmission assembly from the car as described in Section 3 or 4 as applicable. Position the engine/transmission on the bench and proceed as follows.

2 If not already done, drain the engine/transmission oil as described in Chapter 1.

3 On later models, undo the three bolts securing the slave cylinder mounting plate to the flywheel housing, taking care to collect the spacer from the lower bolt. Remove the mounting plate from the housing.

4 Undo and remove the retaining bolts and lift off the flywheel housing cover and, if still in place, the starter motor **(see illustration)**.

5 On later models, undo the two bolts and remove the crankshaft position sensor from the flywheel housing.

6 On models without the later type Verto clutch assembly, withdraw the wire retaining clips and lift away the clutch thrust plate from the centre of the diaphragm spring housing **(see illustration)**. On models with the Verto

type clutch, withdraw the release bearing sleeve from the clutch hub.

7 Using a punch or small chisel, knock back the lockwasher tab(s) securing the large flywheel retaining bolt in the centre of the flywheel.

8 Rotate the flywheel until the timing marks on the flywheel periphery are at approximately the 3 o'clock position. This will prevent the primary gear retaining U-shaped washer from becoming dislodged as the flywheel is removed. On later models without timing marks, rotate the flywheel until the clutch hub slots are aligned horizontally.

9 With a large socket and extension handle, undo and remove the flywheel retaining bolt. Insert a screwdriver between the flywheel ring gear teeth and housing to prevent the flywheel from turning while the bolt is removed. Also have an assistant support the engine, as this bolt will be tight, requiring considerable leverage to remove it. When the bolt is removed, prise out the keyed drive washer from the end of the flywheel and crankshaft.

10 Where the bolt which retains the flywheel

5.4 Removing the flywheel housing cover

to the crankshaft has been secured with thread-locking compound or an encapsulated type of bolt is used, then prior to refitting, all threads in the crankshaft must be thoroughly cleaned. Preferably, this should be done by using a tap of the appropriate size. Discard the old retaining bolt, and use only a new encapsulated bolt incorporating a thread-locking compound patch on refitting.

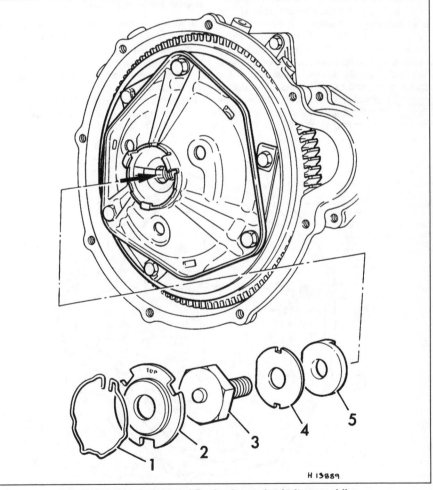

5.6 Clutch thrust plate and flywheel securing bolt assemblies – non-Verto type clutch shown

| 1 *Circlip* | 3 *Flywheel retaining* | 4 *Lockwasher* |
| 2 *Release bearing thrust plate* | *bolt* | 5 *Keyed drive washer* |

5.11 Using a commercially available puller to release the flywheel taper

11 The flywheel is a taper fit on the end of the crankshaft and a special puller will be needed to remove it. This puller is Rover special tool 18G 304 and adapter 18G 304M for models without the later type Verto clutch assembly, or 18G 1381 for models with a Verto type clutch (see Chapter 6 for identification of the two clutch types, if necessary). Note that there are a number of similar pullers readily obtainable from accessory shops or tool hire outlets if the manufacturer's tool is not available (see illustration).

12 Position the puller with the three studs or bolts inserted through the holes in the spring housing (non-Verto type) and screwed into the flywheel securely. Fit the thrust pad of the puller to the end of the crankshaft and then tighten the puller centre bolt. Prevent the flywheel from turning using a screwdriver inserted into the ring gear teeth.

13 Continue tightening the centre bolt of the puller until the flywheel breaks free from the taper. It is quite likely that the flywheel will be extremely tight requiring a great deal of effort to free it. If this is the case sharply strike the puller centre bolt with a medium hammer. This should 'shock' the flywheel off the taper. Take care when doing this as the flywheel may spring off and land on your feet.

14 Once the taper is released the complete clutch and flywheel assembly can be lifted off the end of the crankshaft.

15 With the flywheel and clutch removed, the flywheel housing can be separated from the engine/transmission casing as follows.

16 If a breather is fitted to the top of the housing undo and remove the retaining bolts and lift off the breather assembly.

17 Where fitted, remove the oil seal dust shield from the primary gear.

18 Observe the fasteners securing the flywheel housing to the cylinder block and transmission casing and proceed as follows according to type.

19 If a combination of nuts and bolts are used to secure the housing:

a) *Knock back the tabs on the lockwashers inside the housing. Note that new lockwashers will be required for refitting.*

b) *Undo and remove the nine nuts from the studs on the transmission casing (see illustration).*

c) *Undo and remove the six bolts from the cylinder block. Note the positions from which the shorter bolts are removed.*

20 If the housing is secured by bolts only (no nuts):

a) *Undo and remove the three upper outer bolts securing the housing to the cylinder block, noting that these bolts have a fine (UNF) thread.*

b) *Undo and remove the four lower outer bolts securing the housing to the transmission casing and collect the tie-bar bracket. Note that these bolts have a coarse (UNC) thread.*

c) *Undo and remove the eight inner bolts securing the housing to the cylinder block and transmission casing. Note that the three upper bolts securing the housing to the cylinder block have a fine (UNF) thread and the remaining five securing the housing to the transmission casing have a coarse (UNC) thread.*

21 The housing can now be carefully pulled off the locating dowels. As the housing is withdrawn a small quantity of oil will be released so have some old rags or a small container handy.

22 With the flywheel and flywheel housing removed, undo and remove the flange nuts, bolts and spring washers securing the engine to the transmission.

23 Where applicable, undo and remove the bolts securing the radiator lower mounting bracket to the engine mounting bracket.

24 Using a crane, or hoist and lifting slings, carefully lift the engine off the transmission casing. It may be necessary to tap the transmission casing downwards with a rubber or hide mallet to break the seal between the two mating faces. Once the engine is free, recover the engine/transmission joint gaskets, oil supply O-ring and left-hand main bearing cap oil seal.

25 With the engine removed, cover the top of the transmission to prevent dirt ingress.

Reconnection

Note 1: *Before reconnecting the engine and transmission, refer to Chapter 7A and adjust the endfloat of the transfer gears (primary gear and idler gear).*

Note 2: *New gaskets, oil seals, and other materials, together with certain special tools are required for this operation. Read through the entire procedure to familiarise yourself with the work involved, and obtain the necessary tools and materials before proceeding.*

26 Carefully scrape away any remaining traces of old gasket from the engine/transmission mating faces and flywheel housing joint.

27 Lightly smear the upper sides of the new engine/transmission joint gaskets with jointing compound and place them in position on the engine mating face.

28 Apply a bead of RTV sealant to all the mating surfaces of the new left-hand main bearing cap oil seal, then place seal in position between the left-hand main bearing cap and engine plate (see illustration).

29 Locate the new oil supply O-ring into its groove in the transmission casing face, and if

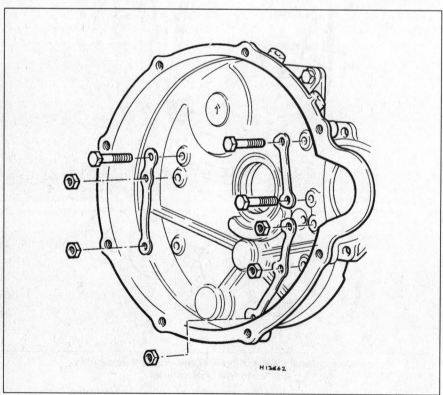

H12662

5.19 Flywheel housing attachments on early models

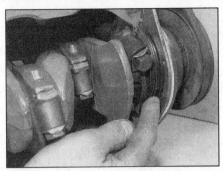

5.28 Fitting a new front main bearing cap oil seal . . .

5.29 . . . and a new O-ring to the transmission casing joint face

5.32 Position the primary gear thrustwasher on the crankshaft

necessary retain it in place with a trace of grease (see illustration).

30 Using suitable lifting gear and with the help of an assistant, carefully lower the engine onto the transmission casing. Have your assistant guide the engine, and lower it very slowly, as it is easy to dislodge the gaskets.

31 With the engine in position, refit and fully tighten the retaining nuts, bolts and spring washers and, where applicable, refit the radiator lower mounting bolts.

32 Refit the primary gear thrustwasher to the end of the crankshaft with its chamfered side toward the crankshaft flange (see illustration).

33 Slide on the primary gear (see illustration) and then turn the crankshaft until No 1 piston is at TDC on compression (refer to Part A or Part B of this Chapter, as applicable).

34 Refit the primary gear retaining ring and then secure the assembly in position with the C-shaped washer (see illustrations).

35 Refit the idler gear to its bearings in the transmission casing, turning it slightly to mesh with the other two gears as it is installed. Ensure that both the thrustwashers are in position, one each side of the idler gear: if the later type gear is being fitted, the longer boss goes toward the transmission casing.

36 The primary gear oil seal in the flywheel housing should be renewed before refitting the housing. Drive out the old seal and thoroughly clean the recess in the housing. Apply a smear of multipurpose grease to the outer edge of the new seal then, with the housing supported, tap the seal into place using a wooden block or the old seal to spread the load. Ensure that the open side of the seal faces inward, towards the engine.

37 Place a new flywheel housing gasket over the studs and/or dowels on the cylinder block and transmission casing.

38 To avoid damage to the oil seal as the housing is fitted, place the protective sleeve, special tool 18G 1043, over the primary gear, or if this tool is not available cover the primary gear splines and the stepped shoulder with masking tape

39 Lubricate the lip of the oil seal, then carefully refit the flywheel housing, taking care that the rollers on the first motion shaft bearing enter their outer race squarely. On no account force the housing. If it does not easily

push fully home, turn the bearing slightly and try again. Two or three attempts may be needed (see illustration).

40 Using a wire brush, clean the threads of the flywheel housing retaining bolts and apply Loctite 242 to the first three threads of each bolt.

41 Refer to the information contained in paragraphs 19 and 20 and refit the flywheel housing retaining nuts/bolts to their correct locations. Where nuts are used, new locktabs should also be fitted. Tighten the fixings to the specified torque and, where applicable, bend over the locktabs.

42 Carefully clean the mating tapers in the flywheel and on the end of the crankshaft, and make quite certain there are no traces of oil, grease, or dirt present.

43 Refit the flywheel on the end of the crankshaft and align the offset drive washer slot with the corresponding slot on the end of the crankshaft. Refit the drive washer which positively locates the flywheel.

44 Fit a new lockwasher under the head of the flywheel securing bolt. Remember to use only a new encapsulated bolt incorporating a thread-locking compound if that type of bolt was removed. Insert the bolt in the centre of the flywheel and tighten it to the specified torque.

45 On early models without the Verto type clutch, tap down the side of the lockwasher against the drive washer, and tap up the other side of the washer against the retaining bolt head. Refit the thrust plate and secure it in position with the circular retaining spring.

46 On models with a Verto type clutch, stake the lockwasher into the slots on the clutch hub, then refit the release bearing sleeve to the hub.

47 Refit the flywheel housing cover and fully tighten the retaining bolts.

48 On later models, refit the slave cylinder mounting plate to the flywheel housing and secure with the three bolts.

49 Where applicable, refit the crankshaft position sensor to the flywheel housing.

5.33 Slide on the primary gear . . .

5.34a . . . followed by the retaining ring . . .

5.34b . . . and the C-shaped washer

5.39 Refitting the flywheel housing

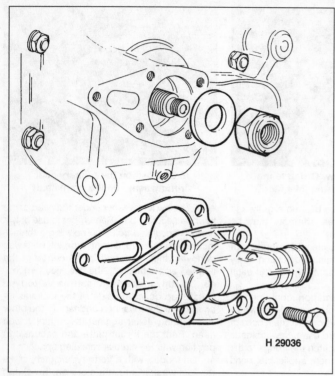

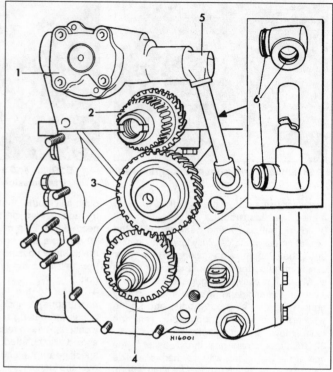

6.5 Low pressure valve assembly and input gear retaining nut – automatic transmission models

6.14 End view of the automatic transmission transfer gears with the converter housing removed

1	Main oil pump	4	Input gear
2	Converter output gear	5	Oil feed pipe
3	Idler gear	6	Sealing rings

6 Engine and automatic transmission – separation and reconnection

Separation

Note: *A suitable puller will be required to release the flywheel from the crankshaft taper. Read through the entire procedure to familiarise yourself with the work involved, and obtain the relevant tools before proceeding.*

1 Remove the engine/transmission assembly from the car as described in Section 3. Position the engine/transmission on the bench and proceed as follows.

2 If not already done, drain the engine/transmission oil as described in Chapter 1.

3 Undo and remove the retaining bolts and lift off the torque converter housing cover.

4 If still in place, remove the starter motor.

5 Undo and remove the five retaining bolts and lift off the low pressure valve assembly from its location beneath the torque converter **(see illustration)**.

6 Using a socket and bar, undo and remove the transmission input gear retaining nut. Use a large screwdriver inserted through the hole in the top of the converter housing and engaged with the ring gear teeth to prevent the torque converter from turning.

7 Knock back the locktabs, and undo and

remove three equally-spaced bolts from the centre of the converter. Leave the other three bolts in position.

8 Knock back the lockwasher securing the large converter centre retaining bolt. Using a large socket and bar, undo and remove the torque converter centre bolt. Use a screwdriver as previously described to prevent the converter from turning. Remove the lockwasher and the torque converter driving collar from the end of the crankshaft.

9 Rotate the crankshaft until the timing marks on the converter periphery are at approximately the 3 o'clock position.

10 The torque converter is a taper fit on the end of the crankshaft and it will be necessary to obtain Rover special tool 18G 1086 to remove it. The tool is bolted to the torque converter through the holes of the three previously-removed converter retaining bolts. With the adapter in position on the end of the crankshaft, tighten the tool centre bolt until the torque converter breaks free of the taper, and then lift it off the crankshaft.

11 Undo and remove the nuts, bolts and washers securing the converter housing to the engine and transmission casing.

12 Remove the selector bellcrank lever clevis pin and nut, and lift off the bellcrank lever. Remove the bellcrank lever pivot.

13 The converter housing can now be carefully withdrawn. As the housing is

withdrawn a small quantity of oil will be released so have some old rags or a small container handy.

14 With the torque converter and housing removed, carefully lever the main oil feed pipe from the transmission and oil pump **(see illustration)**.

15 Undo and remove the two retaining bolts and lift off the oil filter and housing assembly.

16 Unscrew the engine oil feed pipe union at the adapter on the transmission casing.

17 Undo and remove the flange nuts, bolts and spring washers securing the engine to the transmission.

18 Undo and remove the bolts securing the radiator lower mounting bracket to the engine mounting adapter.

19 Using a crane, or hoist and lifting slings, carefully lift the engine off the transmission casing. It may be necessary to tap the transmission casing downward with a rubber or hide mallet to break the seal between the two mating faces. Once the engine is free, recover the engine/transmission joint gaskets and left-hand main bearing cap oil seal.

20 With the engine removed cover the top of the transmission completely to prevent dirt ingress.

Reconnection

Note 1: *Before reconnecting the engine and transmission, the endfloat of the transfer gears* *(converter output gear and idler gear) must be adjusted. The procedure is the same as for manual transmission models and is described in Chapter 7A.*

Note 2: *New gaskets, oil seals, and other materials, together with certain special tools are required for this operation. Read through the entire procedure to familiarise yourself with the work involved, and obtain the necessary tools and materials before proceeding.*

21 Carefully scrape away any remaining traces of old gasket from the engine/transmission mating faces and flywheel housing joint.

22 Lightly smear the upper sides of the engine/transmission joint gaskets with jointing compound and place them in position on the engine mating face.

23 Apply a bead of RTV sealant to all the mating surfaces of the left-hand oil seal, then place seal in position between the left-hand main bearing cap and engine plate.

24 Using suitable lifting gear and with the help of an assistant, carefully lower the engine onto the transmission casing. Have your assistant guide the engine, and lower it very slowly, as it is easy to dislodge the gaskets.

25 With the engine in position, refit and fully tighten the retaining nuts, bolts and spring washers, and refit the radiator lower mounting bolts.

26 Refit the engine oil feed pipe to the union on the transmission casing.

27 Place a new gasket in position and refit the oil filter assembly.

28 Using new O-rings where necessary, carefully push the oil feed pipe into engagement with the oil pump and transmission casing orifice.

29 Place the converter output gear thrustwasher over the end of the crankshaft, with its chamfered face toward the crankshaft flange.

30 Now slide on the output gear. Turn the crankshaft until No 1 piston is at TDC (refer to Part A of this Chapter) then refit the output gear retaining ring and C-shaped washer.

31 With the thrustwashers located over each side of the idler gear, insert the gear into its needle roller bearing.

32 The converter housing oil seal should be renewed before refitting the housing. Note the fitted depth of the oil seal in the housing so that the new seal may be fitted in the same position. Using a hooked instrument, extract the oil seal and thoroughly clean the recess in the housing. Apply a smear of multipurpose grease to the outer edge of the new seal then, with the housing supported, tap the seal into place, with its open side toward the engine, using a wooden block or the old seal to spread the load. Ensure that the seal is fitted to the same depth as noted during removal otherwise it may cover an important oil drain hole in the housing.

33 Ensure that the mating faces of the engine/transmission and converter housing are clean, and then position a new gasket

over the studs on the transmission.

34 To avoid damage to the oil seal as the housing is fitted, place the protective sleeve, special tool 18G 1098, over the converter output gear, or if this tool is not available cover the output gear splines and the stepped shoulder with masking tape

35 Lubricate the lip of the oil seal and carefully refit the converter housing, pushing it squarely home over the transmission casting studs. Refit the retaining nuts and bolts, noting that the bolts with the coarse thread (UNC) are fitted to the transmission casing and the bolt with the copper washer is fitted to the hole adjacent to the selector rod. Tighten the nuts and bolts to the specified torque.

36 Refit the selector bellcrank lever pivot, lever, clevis pin and nut.

37 Before fitting the torque converter, it will be first necessary to refit the three central bolts removed to allow the special converter removal tool to be used during dismantling. Then remove each pair of bolts in turn from the converter centre and fit new locking plates. Tighten the six bolts to the specified torque wrench setting and bend over the lock tabs. *On no account remove all six bolts at any one time.* Then, with No 1 and 4 pistons still at the TDC position, slide the torque converter onto the end of the crankshaft, with the timing marks uppermost. Refit the driving collar, a new lockwasher and the retaining bolt. Tighten the retaining bolt to the torque given in the Specifications, and then knock back the lockwasher.

38 Refit the transmission input gear retaining nut and tighten the nut to the specified torque.

39 Position a new gasket on the transmission casing and refit the low pressure valve assembly.

40 Refit the converter housing cover and the starter motor.

7 Engine overhaul – preliminary information

It is much easier to dismantle and work on the engine if it is mounted on a portable engine stand. These stands can often be hired from a tool hire shop.

If a stand is not available, it is possible to dismantle the engine with it suitably supported on a sturdy, workbench or on the floor. Be careful not to tip or drop the engine when working without a stand.

If you intend to obtain a reconditioned engine, all ancillaries must be removed first, to be transferred to the replacement engine (just as they will if you are doing a complete engine overhaul yourself). These components include the following, according to engine type:

a) *Dynamo/alternator and mounting brackets.*

b) *Engine/transmission mountings and brackets (Part A or B of this Chapter).*

c) *Tappet block side covers – where fitted (Section 9).*

d) *The ignition system and HT components including all sensors, distributor cap and rotor arm (where fitted), HT leads and spark plugs (Chapter 1, 5B and 5C).*

e) *Distributor driveshaft – where fitted (Part A of this Chapter).*

f) *All electrical switches and sensors.*

g) *Emission control equipment – where applicable (Chapter 4D).*

h) *Thermostat and housing, water pump, heater control valve (Chapter 3).*

i) *Mechanical fuel pump – carburettor engines only (Chapter 4A).*

j) *Carburettor/fuel injection system components (Chapter 4A, 4B and 4C).*

k) *Inlet and exhaust manifolds (Chapter 4A, 4B, 4C and 4D).*

l) *Oil pump (Section 10).*

m) *Oil filter (Chapter 1).*

n) *Oil filter housing and delivery pipe – where applicable (Part A of this Chapter).*

Note: *When removing the external components from the engine, pay close attention to details that may be helpful or important during refitting. Note the fitted positions of gaskets, seals, washers, bolts and other small items.*

If you are obtaining a 'short' engine (cylinder block, crankshaft, pistons, camshaft and tappets, and connecting rods all assembled), then the cylinder head, timing chain (together with tensioner, sprockets and cover) will have to be removed also.

If a complete overhaul is planned, the engine can be dismantled in the order given below, referring to Part A and B of this Chapter unless otherwise stated.

a) *Inlet and exhaust manifolds (Chapter 4A, 4B, 4C and 4D).*

b) *Distributor driveshaft – where fitted.*

c) *Timing chain, sprockets and tensioner.*

d) *Cylinder head.*

e) *Camshaft and tappets (Section 9).*

f) *Oil pressure relief valve.*

g) *Oil filter housing and delivery pipe – where applicable.*

h) *Oil pump (Section 10).*

i) *Piston/connecting rod assemblies (Section 11).*

j) *Crankshaft (Section 12).*

8 Cylinder head – dismantling, cleaning, inspection and reassembly

Note: *New and reconditioned cylinder heads are available from the manufacturer, and from engine overhaul specialists. Be aware that some specialist tools are required for the dismantling and inspection procedures, and new components may not be readily available. It may therefore be more practical and economical for the home mechanic to purchase a reconditioned head, rather than dismantle, inspect and recondition the original head.*

8.4a Compress the valve springs with a spring compressor and lift off the split collets . . .

8.4b . . . then remove the compressor, valve cap and spring

Dismantling

1 Remove the cylinder head as described in Part A or Part B of this Chapter as applicable.

2 If not already done, remove the inlet and exhaust manifolds with reference to the relevant Part of Chapter 4.

3 With a pair of pliers, remove the spring clips (where fitted) holding the two halves of the split collets together.

4 Using a valve spring compressor, compress each valve spring in turn until the split collets can be removed. Release the compressor, and lift off the spring retainer, valve guide shield (early models) and the spring. Where fitted, slide the oil seal off the valve stem **(see illustrations)**. **Note:** *On 1275 cc engines the oil seal is positioned over the valve guide. On Cooper S models double valve springs are used.*

> **HAYNES HINT** *If, when the valve spring compressor is screwed down, the spring retainer refuses to free and expose the split collets, gently tap the top of the tool, directly over the retainer, with a light hammer. This will free the retainer.*

5 Withdraw the valve through the combustion chamber.

6 It is essential that each valve is stored together with its collets, retainer and spring(s). The valves should also be kept in their correct sequence, unless they are so badly worn that they are to be renewed. If they are going to be kept and used again, place each valve assembly in a labelled polythene bag or similar small container **(see illustration)**. Note that No 1 valve is nearest to the timing chain end of the engine.

Cleaning

7 Thoroughly clean all traces of old gasket material and sealing compound from the cylinder head mating surfaces. Use a suitable cleaning agent together with a putty knife or scraper, taking care not to scratch the head surface.

8 Remove the carbon from the combustion chambers and ports, then clean all traces of oil and other deposits from the cylinder head, paying particular attention to the valve guides and oilways.

9 Wash the head thoroughly with paraffin or a suitable solvent. Take plenty of time and do a thorough job. Be sure to clean all oil holes and galleries very thoroughly, dry the head completely and coat all machined surfaces with light oil.

10 Scrape off any heavy carbon deposits that may have formed on the valves, then use a power-operated wire brush to remove deposits from the valve heads and stems.

Inspection

Note: *Be sure to perform all the following inspection procedures before concluding that the services of an engineering works are required. Make a list of all items that require attention.*

Cylinder head

11 Inspect the head very carefully for cracks, evidence of coolant leakage, and other damage. If cracks are found, a new cylinder head should be obtained.

12 Use a straight-edge and feeler blade to check that the cylinder head gasket surface is not distorted. If it is, it may be possible to have it machined. Seek the advice of a Rover dealer or engine overhaul specialist if distortion is suspected.

13 Examine the valve seats in each of the combustion chambers. If they are severely pitted, cracked, or burned, they will need to be renewed or recut by an engine overhaul specialist. If they are only slightly pitted, this can be removed by grinding-in the valve heads and seats with fine valve-grinding compound, as described below.

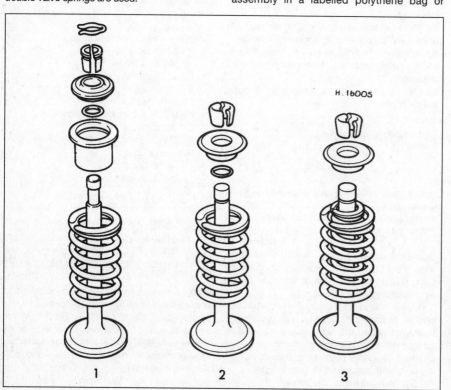

H. 16005

8.4c Valve assembly components

   1 Early type   *2 Later type*   *3 Cooper S type*

8.6 Keep all valve components together in a labelled plastic bag

14 Check the valve guides for wear by inserting the relevant valve, and checking for side-to-side motion of the valve. A very small amount of movement is acceptable. If the movement seems excessive, remove the valve. Measure the valve stem diameter (see below), and renew the valve if it is worn. If the valve stem is not worn, the wear must be in the valve guide, and the guide must be renewed. The renewal of valve guides is best carried out by a Rover dealer or engine overhaul specialist, who will have the necessary tools available.

15 If renewing the valve guides, the valve seats should be recut or reground only *after* the guides have been fitted.

Valves

16 Examine the head of each valve for pitting, burning, cracks, and general wear. Check the valve stem for scoring and wear ridges. Rotate the valve, and check for any obvious indication that it is bent. Look for pits or excessive wear on the tip of each valve stem. Renew any valve that shows any such signs of wear or damage.

17 If the valve appears satisfactory at this stage, measure the valve stem diameter at several points using a micrometer **(see illustration)**. Any significant difference in the readings obtained indicates wear of the valve stem. Should any of these conditions be apparent, the valve(s) must be renewed.

18 In order to reduce oil consumption, valve stem oil seals are fitted to the inlet valves of later 998 cc engines and to all the valves of 1275 cc (12A) engines. Fitting of the seals on 998 cc engines has required the incorporation of modified valves, with cotter grooves nearer the end of the stem. The valve spring seats have also been raised by 1.2 mm.

19 If renewing any valves, bear in mind that new-type valves and seals can be fitted to old type cylinder heads in complete sets only, with the addition of a shim 1.2 mm thick underneath each spring. These shims may also be found already fitted to engines which left the factory with the new-type valves and seals in unmodified heads. Consult a Rover dealer for further details of this modification.

20 If the valves are in satisfactory condition, they should be ground (lapped) into their respective seats, to ensure a smooth, gas-tight seal. If the seat is only lightly pitted, or if it has been recut, fine grinding compound *only* should be used to produce the required finish. Coarse valve-grinding compound should *not* be used, unless a seat is badly burned or deeply pitted. If this is the case, the cylinder head and valves should be inspected by an expert, to decide whether seat recutting, or even the renewal of the valve or seat insert (where possible) is required.

21 Valve grinding is carried out as follows. Place the cylinder head upside-down on a bench.

22 Smear a trace of (the appropriate grade

8.17 Measuring the valve stem diameter

8.25 Measuring valve spring free length

of) valve-grinding compound on the seat face, and press a suction grinding tool onto the valve head. With a semi-rotary action, grind the valve head to its seat, lifting the valve occasionally to redistribute the grinding compound. A light spring placed under the valve head will greatly ease this operation.

23 If coarse grinding compound is being used, work only until a dull, matt even surface is produced on both the valve seat and the valve, then wipe off the used compound, and repeat the process with fine compound. When a smooth unbroken ring of light grey matt finish is produced on both the valve and seat, the grinding operation is complete. *Do not* grind-in the valves any further than absolutely necessary, or the seat will be prematurely sunk into the cylinder head.

24 When all the valves have been ground-in, carefully wash off *all* traces of grinding compound using paraffin or a suitable solvent, before reassembling the cylinder head.

Valve components

25 Examine the valve springs for signs of damage and discoloration. Measure their free length and compare the dimension with the figures given in the Specifications **(see illustration)**.

26 Stand each spring on a flat surface, and check it for squareness. If any of the springs are damaged, distorted or shorter than the specified length, obtain a complete new set of springs. It is normal to renew the valve springs as a matter of course if a major overhaul is being carried out.

27 Renew the valve stem oil seals (where fitted) regardless of their apparent condition.

Reassembly

28 Lubricate the stems of the valves, and insert the valves into their original locations. If new valves are being fitted, insert them into the locations to which they have been ground.

29 As each valve is inserted, slip the oil seal into place just under the bottom of the collet groove. A much larger oil seal is used on the 1275 cc engines. This should be fitted over the top of the valve guide.

30 Refit the valve spring(s), valve guide shield (early models) and the spring retainer.

31 Compress the valve spring, and locate the split collets in the recess in the valve stem.

Release the compressor, then repeat the procedure on the remaining valves.

> **HAYNES HiNT** *Use a little dab of grease to hold the collets in position on the valve stem while the spring compressor is released.*

32 With all the valves installed, place the cylinder head face down on blocks on the bench and, using a hammer and interposed block of wood, tap the end of each valve stem to settle the components.

33 The cylinder head can then be refitted as described in Part A or B of this Chapter as applicable.

9 Camshaft and tappets –
removal, inspection and refitting

Note: *The camshaft can only be removed with the engine out of the car and on the bench. With the cylinder head, timing cover, gears and chain, fuel pump and distributor drivegear removed, proceed as follows.*

Removal

1 On 848, 998 and 1098 cc engines, undo and remove the bolt securing each tappet block side cover to the rear of the cylinder block and lift off the covers **(see illustration)**.

2 Lift out each tappet from its location in the cylinder block and ensure that they are kept in

9.1 Removing the tappet side covers

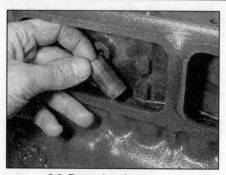

9.2 Removing the tappets

9.3 Undo the camshaft locating plate bolts and lift off the plate

the correct sequence in which they were removed **(see illustration)**. **Note:** *On 1275 cc engines, tappet block side covers are not fitted and the tappets can only be removed after removing the camshaft.*

3 Undo and remove the three bolts and spring washers securing the camshaft locating plate to the cylinder block plate. Lift off the plate **(see illustration)**.

4 On 848, 998 and 1098 cc engines, carefully withdraw the camshaft from the cylinder block, taking care not to damage the camshaft bearings with the cam lobes as it is withdrawn.

5 On 1275 cc engines position the engine on its side to prevent the tappets falling out, then slide out the camshaft. Recover the oil pump drive coupling from the end of the camshaft after removal. Now lift out each tappet, from inside the crankcase, keeping them in the correct sequence in which they were removed.

6 On all engines, if further dismantling is to be carried out, undo the bolts still remaining and lift off the engine plate. Recover the gasket and clean the mating surfaces of the plate and cylinder block.

Inspection

Camshaft and camshaft bearings

7 Carefully examine the camshaft bearings for wear. **Note:** *On 848 cc engines, only the left-hand camshaft bearing is renewable.* If the bearings are obviously worn or pitted or the metal underlay is showing through, then they must be renewed (where applicable). This

operation must be entrusted to a Rover dealer or engine reconditioning specialist as it demands the use of specialised equipment. The bearings are removed with a special drift, after which new bearings are pressed in, care being taken to ensure that the oil holes in the bearings line up with those in the block. With a special tool the bearings are then reamed in position.

8 The camshaft itself should show no signs of wear, but if very slight scoring on the cam lobes is noticed, the score marks can be removed by very gentle rubbing down with very fine emery cloth. The greatest care should be taken to keep the cam profiles smooth.

Tappets

9 Examine the bearing surface of the tappets which contact the camshaft lobes. Any indentation in this surface or any cracks indicate serious wear and the tappets should be renewed. Thoroughly clean them out, removing all traces of sludge. It is most unlikely that the sides of the tappets will prove worn, but, if they are a very loose fit in their bores and can readily be rocked, they should be renewed. It is very unusual to find any wear in the tappets, and any wear present is likely to occur only at very high mileage.

Refitting

10 On 1275 cc engines, generously lubricate the tappets internally and externally, and insert them in the bores from which they were removed.

11 Wipe the camshaft bearing journals clean and lubricate them generously with engine oil.

12 Insert the camshaft into the cylinder block, taking care not to damage the camshaft bearings with the sharp edges of the cam lobes.

13 Push the camshaft back as far as it will go and, if the oil pump is in position, ensure that the camshaft flange has mated with the pump drive.

14 Place a new gasket in position and refit the plate (if previously removed).

15 Now refit the camshaft locating plate and tighten the three retaining bolts. Temporarily refit the camshaft sprocket, then check the camshaft endfloat, referring to the figures given in the Specifications.

16 Refit the remaining plate bolts located inside the timing cover profile.

17 On 848, 998 and 1098 cc engines, refit the tappet block side covers using new gaskets and secure with the retaining bolts.

10 Oil pump –
removal, inspection and refitting

Removal

Note: *Prior to removing the pump, it will be necessary to remove the flywheel and flywheel housing, or torque converter and housing. The oil pump engages directly via a lip and slot or splined drive with the end of the camshaft.*

1 Bend back the locking tabs on the securing bolts which hold the pump to the block.

2 Unscrew and remove the bolts and lock tabs, then lift off the oil pump assembly.

Inspection

Note: *It is quite likely that after high mileage the rotor (or vanes), shaft, and internal body of the pump will be quite badly scored, requiring renewal of the pump. This is mainly due to the engine and transmission sharing the same lubricating oil, making thorough filtration of minute metallic particles impossible. It is therefore recommended that a very careful inspection of the pump be carried out and, if at all suspect, the pump renewed.*

3 Undo and remove the securing screw from the rear of the pump (early models) or the two screws on the front cover (later models) and lift off the cover, rotor and shaft.

4 Examine the rotor and shaft lobes (or vanes on certain early pumps) for scoring or wear ridges. Also check the inner circumference of the pump body. Renew the complete pump if wear is apparent.

5 If the pump is in a satisfactory condition, measure the endfloat and clearances between the shaft lobes and the side of the pump body **(see illustrations)**. If the clearances are outside the limits given in the Specifications the pump must be renewed.

6 Reassembly of the pump is the reverse sequence to dismantling. Fill the assembled pump with clean engine oil before refitting to the engine.

10.5a Measuring the oil pump rotor lobe clearance . . .

10.5b . . . and rotor-to-body clearance

Refitting

7 Ensure that the pump and cylinder block mating faces are clean then place a new gasket in position on the rear face of the block.

8 Check that the pump is filled with clean engine oil and then position it over the gasket, engaging the drive slot or coupling with the end of the camshaft.

9 Rotate the pump body until the offset holes in the pump, gasket and cylinder block are all in line, then refit the retaining bolts and new locktabs.

10 Tighten the bolts to the specified torque and bend over the locktabs.

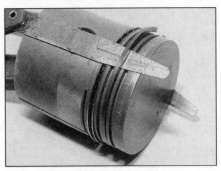

11.3 Removing a connecting rod big-end cap

---

11 Piston/connecting rod assemblies – removal, inspection, separation and reconnection

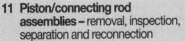

Removal

1 With the engine separated from the transmission and the cylinder head removed, the piston/connecting rod assemblies can be removed as follows.

2 Knock back the locking tabs on the big-end bearing cap retaining bolts, using a small chisel and remove the bolts and locking tabs. The 1275 cc engine does not have locking tabs and the big-end caps are retained by bolts and special multi-sided nuts.

3 Remove the big-end caps one at a time, taking care to keep them in the right order and the correct way round **(see illustration)**. Also ensure that the shell bearings are kept with their correct connecting rods and caps unless they are to be renewed. Normally, the numbers 1 to 4 are stamped on adjacent sides of the big-end caps and connecting rods, indicating which cap fits on which rod and which way round that cap fits. If no numbers or lines can be found then suitably mark the caps and rods using quick-drying paint or similar. This will ensure that there is no confusion later, as it is essential that the caps go back in the correct position on the connecting rods from which they were removed.

4 If the big-end caps are difficult to remove they may be gently tapped with a soft mallet.

5 To remove the shell bearings, press the bearing opposite the groove in both the connecting rod and the connecting rod caps, and the bearings will slide out easily.

6 Withdraw the pistons and connecting rods upwards and ensure that they are kept in the correct order for refitting in the same bore. Refit the connecting rod caps and bearings to the rods if the bearings do not require renewal, to minimise the risk of getting the caps and rods muddled.

Inspection

7 Before the inspection process can begin, the piston/connecting rod assemblies must be cleaned, and the original piston rings removed from the pistons.

8 Carefully expand the old rings over the top

of the pistons. The use of two or three old feeler blades will be helpful in preventing the rings dropping into empty grooves **(see illustration)**. Be careful not to scratch the piston with the ends of the ring. The rings are brittle, and will snap if they are spread too far. They are also very sharp – protect your hands and fingers. Always remove the rings from the top of the piston. Keep each set of rings with its piston if the old rings are to be re-used.

9 Scrape away all traces of carbon from the top of the piston. A hand-held wire brush (or a piece of fine emery cloth) can be used, once the majority of the deposits have been scraped away.

10 Remove the carbon from the ring grooves in the piston, using an old ring. Break the ring in half to do this (be careful not to cut your fingers – piston rings are sharp). Be careful to remove only the carbon deposits – do not remove any metal, and do not nick or scratch the sides of the ring grooves.

11 Once the deposits have been removed, clean the piston/connecting rod assembly with paraffin or a suitable solvent, and dry thoroughly. Make sure that the oil return holes in the ring grooves are clear.

12 If the pistons and cylinder bores are not damaged or worn excessively, the original pistons can be refitted. Normal piston wear shows up as even vertical wear on the piston thrust surfaces, and slight looseness of the top ring in its groove. New piston rings should always be used when the engine is reassembled.

13 Carefully inspect each piston for cracks around the skirt, around the gudgeon pin

11.16 Measuring the piston diameter

holes, and at the piston ring 'lands' (between the ring grooves).

14 Look for scoring and scuffing on the piston skirt, holes in the piston crown, and burned areas at the edge of the crown. If the skirt is scored or scuffed, the engine may have been suffering from overheating, and/or abnormal combustion which caused excessively high operating temperatures. The cooling and lubrication systems should be checked thoroughly. Scorch marks on the sides of the pistons show that blow-by has occurred. A hole in the piston crown, or burned areas at the edge of the piston crown, indicates that abnormal combustion (pre-ignition, knocking, or detonation) has been occurring. If any of the above problems exist, the causes must be investigated and corrected, or the damage will occur again. The causes may include incorrect ignition timing, or a carburettor or fuel injection system fault.

15 Corrosion of the piston, in the form of pitting, indicates that coolant has been leaking into the combustion chamber and/or the crankcase. Again, the cause must be corrected, or the problem may persist in the rebuilt engine.

16 Using a micrometer, measure the diameter of all four pistons at a point 10 mm from the bottom of the skirt, at right angles to the gudgeon pin axis **(see illustration)**. Record the measurements and use them to check the piston-to-bore clearance when the cylinder bores are measured later in this Chapter.

17 Hold a new piston ring in the appropriate groove and measure the ring-to-groove clearance using a feeler blade **(see illustration)**.

11.17 Measuring the piston ring-to-groove clearance

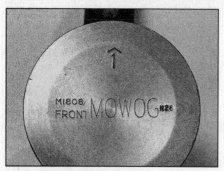

11.19 Identification markings on the piston crown

Note that the rings are of different types, so use the correct ring for the groove. Compare the measurements with those listed in the Specifications; if the clearances are outside the tolerance range, then the pistons must be renewed.

18 When new pistons are to be fitted, take great care to be sure to fit the exact size best-suited to the particular bore of your engine. Rover go one stage further than merely specifying one size piston for all standard bores. Because of very slight differences in cylinder machining during production, it is necessary to select just the right piston for the bore. A range of different sizes is available either from engine repair specialist or from a Rover dealer.

19 Examination of the cylinder block face will show, adjacent to each bore, a small diamond-shaped box with a number stamped in the metal. Careful examination of the piston crown will show a matching diamond and number **(see illustration)**. These are the standard piston sizes and will be the same for all bores. If the standard pistons are to be refitted or standard low compression pistons changed to standard high compression pistons, then it is essential that only pistons with the same number in the diamond are used. With oversize pistons fitted after a rebore, the amount of oversize is stamped in an ellipse on the piston crown.

20 Examine each connecting rod carefully for signs of damage, such as cracks around the big-end and small-end bearings. Check that the rod is not visibly bent or distorted. Damage is highly unlikely, unless the engine

11.22 Gudgeon pin clamped in place by a pinch-bolt (848 cc engines)

has been seized or badly overheated. Detailed checking of the connecting rod assembly can only be carried out by a Rover dealer or engine repair specialist with the necessary equipment.

Separation

21 Three different methods of gudgeon pin retention are employed, depending on the type and cubic capacity of the engine.

22 On the 848 cc engines the gudgeon pin is clamped firmly in place by a pinch-bolt located in the end of the connecting rod **(see illustration)**. To remove the piston from the connecting rod it is merely necessary to undo and remove the pinch-bolt and slide out the gudgeon pin. If it shows reluctance to move, do not force it as this may damage the piston. Immerse the piston in boiling water for a few minutes; the expansion of the aluminium should allow the pin to slide out easily.

23 On early 998 cc and all 1098 cc engines, fully-floating gudgeon pins are used, these being retained in position by a circlip at each end of the gudgeon pin bore in the piston. To remove the gudgeon pin and piston, withdraw the circlip from one end and push the pin out, immersing it in boiling water if it appears reluctant to move.

24 On later 998 cc and all 1275 cc engines the gudgeon pin is firmly held in the small-end of the connecting rod by an interference fit. Removal of the gudgeon pin calls for the use special tools and a good deal of experience to use them correctly. Therefore, piston and/or connecting rod renewal should be entrusted to a Rover dealer or engine repair specialist, who will have the necessary tooling to remove and install the gudgeon pins.

25 On early 998 cc and all 1098 cc engines, check the fit of the gudgeon pin in the connecting rod bush and in the piston. If there is perceptible play, a new bush or an oversize gudgeon pin must be fitted. Consult a Rover dealer or engine reconditioning specialist.

26 Examine all components and obtain any new parts required. If new pistons are purchased, they will be supplied complete with gudgeon pins and, where applicable, circlips. Circlips can also be purchased separately.

Reconnection

27 If the original pistons are being used, then they must be mated to the original connecting rod with the original gudgeon pin. If new pistons and gudgeon pins are being fitted, it does not matter which connecting rod they are used with.

28 The gudgeon pin may be a very tight fit in the piston when cold (particularly on pistons which have a small-end clamp bolt) but, because aluminium has a greater coefficient of expansion than steel, this fit will be much easier if the piston is heated in boiling water.

29 Lay the correct piston adjacent to its connecting rod and remember that the original rod and piston must go back into the

original bore. If new pistons are being used, it is only necessary to ensure that the right connecting rod is placed in each bore.

Gudgeon pins retained by clamp bolts

30 Locate the small-end of the connecting rod in the piston with the marking FRONT on the piston crown towards the front of the engine and the hole for the gudgeon pin bolt in the connecting rod towards the camshaft.

31 Note the indentation in the centre of the gudgeon pin, and insert the pin in the connecting rod, so that the indentation lines up with the clamp bolt hole in such a way that the bolt will pass through without touching the gudgeon pin.

32 For the gudgeon pin to fit correctly, it should slide in three quarters of its travel quite freely and for the remaining quarter have to be tapped in with a plastic or wooden-headed hammer. If the piston is heated in water then the pin will slide in the remaining quarter easily.

33 Fit a new spring washer under the head of the connecting rod bolt and secure it into position to the specified torque. Repeat this procedure for the remaining pistons and connecting rods.

Fully-floating gudgeon pins

34 Fit a gudgeon pin circlip in position at one end of the gudgeon pin hole in the piston.

35 Locate the connecting rod in the piston with the marking FRONT on the piston crown towards the front of the engine, and the connecting rod big-end caps towards the camshaft side of the engine.

36 Slide the gudgeon pin in through the hole in the piston and through the connecting rod small-end until it rests against the previously fitted circlip. Note that the pin should be a push fit.

37 Fit the second circlip in position. Repeat this procedure for the remaining pistons and connecting rods.

Interference fit gudgeon pins

38 As stated previously, removal and refitting of the gudgeon pin on these engines is a delicate operation requiring the use of special tools. This task must be entrusted to a Rover dealer or engine repair specialist.

12 Crankshaft – removal and inspection

Removal

1 With reference to Part A or Part B of this Chapter, and earlier Sections of this Part as applicable, carry out the following:
a) *Separate the engine from the transmission.*
b) *Remove the cylinder head.*
c) *Remove the piston/connecting rod assemblies.*
d) *Remove the timing cover, chain, tensioner and sprockets.*

e) *Remove the camshaft locating plate and engine plate.*

Note: *If no work is to be done on the pistons and connecting rods, then removal of the cylinder head and pistons will not be necessary. Instead, after disconnecting the connecting rods from the crankshaft, the pistons need only be pushed far enough up the bores so that they are positioned clear of the crankpins.*

2 Before removing the crankshaft it is advisable to check the endfloat using a dial gauge in contact with the end of the crankshaft. Push the crankshaft fully one way, and then zero the gauge. Push the crankshaft fully the other way, and check the endfloat. The result can be compared with the specified amount, and will give an indication as to whether new thrustwashers are required.

3 If a dial gauge is not available, feeler blades can be used. First push the crankshaft fully towards the flywheel end of the engine, then use feeler blades to measure the gap between the web of the crankpin and the thrustwasher **(see illustration)**.

4 If identification marks are not present on the main bearing caps, mark them suitably so that they may be refitted in their original positions and the correct way round.

5 Release the locktabs from the six bolts which hold the three main bearing caps in place. Note that locktabs are not used on 1275 cc engines.

6 Unscrew the bolts and remove them together with the locktabs.

7 Remove the main bearing caps and the bottom half of each bearing shell, taking care to keep the bearing shells in the right caps.

8 When removing the centre bearing cap, note the bottom semi-circular halves of the thrustwashers – one half lying on each side of the main bearing. Lay them with the centre bearing along the correct side **(see illustration)**.

9 Slightly rotate the crankshaft to free the upper halves of the bearing shells and thrust-washers, which should now be extracted and placed over the correct bearing cap.

10 Remove the crankshaft by lifting it away from the crankcase **(see illustration)**.

Inspection

11 Clean the crankshaft using paraffin or a suitable solvent, and dry it, preferably with compressed air if available. Be sure to clean the oil holes with a pipe cleaner or similar probe, to ensure that they are not obstructed.

 Warning: Wear eye protection when using compressed air.

12 Check the main and big-end bearing journals for uneven wear, scoring, pitting and cracking.

13 Big-end bearing wear is accompanied by distinct metallic knocking when the engine is running (particularly noticeable when the engine is pulling from low speed) and some loss of oil pressure.

12.3 Checking crankshaft endfloat using feeler blades

14 Main bearing wear is accompanied by severe engine vibration and rumble – getting progressively worse as engine speed increases – and again by loss of oil pressure.

15 Check the bearing journal for roughness by running a finger lightly over the bearing surface. Any roughness (which will be accompanied by obvious bearing wear) indicates that the crankshaft requires regrinding (where possible) or renewal.

16 If the crankshaft has been reground, check for burrs around the crankshaft oil holes (the holes are usually chamfered, so burrs should not be a problem unless regrinding has been carried out carelessly). Remove any burrs with a fine file or scraper, and thoroughly clean the oil holes as described previously.

17 Using a micrometer, measure the diameter of the main and big-end bearing journals, and compare the results with the Specifications **(see illustration)**. By measuring the diameter at a number of points around each journal's circumference, you will be able to determine whether or not the journal is out-of-round. Take the measurement at each end of the journal, near the webs, to determine if the journal is tapered. No actual figures are quoted by the manufacturer for crankshaft journal ovality or taper but a figure of 0.025 mm should be considered the maximum acceptable for an engine of this type. If in doubt, seek the advice of a Rover dealer or engine specialist.

18 Check the oil seal contact surfaces at each end of the crankshaft for wear and damage. If the seal has worn a deep groove in

12.8 Main bearing cap with thrustwashers in position

the surface of the crankshaft, consult an engine overhaul specialist; repair may be possible, but otherwise a new crankshaft will be required.

19 If the crankshaft journals have not been reground to their minimum regrind diameter, it may be possible to have the crankshaft reconditioned, and to fit oversize bearing shells (see Section 14). If the crankshaft has worn beyond the specified limits, it will have to be renewed. Consult your Rover dealer or engine specialist as to the best course of action.

13 Cylinder block/crankcase – cleaning and inspection

Cleaning

1 Remove all external components and electrical switches/sensors from the block.

2 Scrape all traces of gasket from the cylinder block/crankcase, taking care not to damage the gasket/sealing surfaces.

3 Remove all oil gallery plugs (where fitted). The plugs are usually very tight – they may have to be drilled out, and the holes retapped. Use new plugs when the engine is reassembled.

4 If the block is extremely dirty, it should be steam-cleaned.

5 After the block is returned, clean all oil holes and oil galleries one more time. Flush all internal passages with warm water until the water runs clear. Dry thoroughly, and apply a

12.10 Carefully lift out the crankshaft

12.17 Use a micrometer to measure the crankshaft bearing journal diameters

13.7 Using a tap to restore cylinder block threads

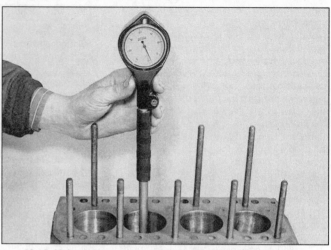

13.12 Using a bore gauge to check for cylinder bore wear

light film of oil to all mating surfaces, to prevent rusting, also oil the cylinder bores. If you have access to compressed air, use it to speed up the drying process, and to blow out all the oil holes and galleries.

 Warning: Wear eye protection when using compressed air.

6 If the cylinder block is not very dirty, you can do an adequate cleaning job with hot, soapy water and a stiff brush. Take plenty of time, and do a thorough job. Regardless of the cleaning method used, be sure to clean all oil holes and galleries very thoroughly, and to dry all components well. Protect the cylinder bores as described above, to prevent rusting.

7 All threaded holes must be clean, to ensure accurate torque readings during reassembly. To clean the threads, run the correct-size tap into each of the holes to remove rust, corrosion, thread sealant or sludge, and to

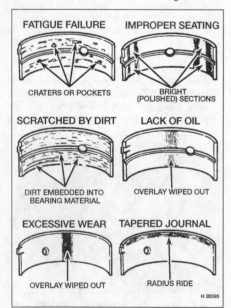

FATIGUE FAILURE
CRATERS OR POCKETS

IMPROPER SEATING
BRIGHT (POLISHED) SECTIONS

SCRATCHED BY DIRT
DIRT EMBEDDED INTO BEARING MATERIAL

LACK OF OIL
OVERLAY WIPED OUT

EXCESSIVE WEAR
OVERLAY WIPED OUT

TAPERED JOURNAL
RADIUS RIDE

H 28395

14.2 Typical bearing failures

restore damaged threads **(see illustration)**. If possible, use compressed air to clear the holes of debris produced by this operation.

8 Apply suitable sealant to the new oil gallery plugs, and insert them into the holes in the block. Tighten them securely.

9 If the engine is not going to be reassembled right away, cover it with a large plastic bag to keep it clean; protect all mating surfaces and the cylinder bores as described above, to prevent rusting.

Inspection

10 Visually check the castings for cracks and corrosion. Look for stripped threads in the threaded holes. If there has been any history of internal water leakage, it may be worthwhile having an engine overhaul specialist check the cylinder block/crankcase with special equipment. If defects are found, have them repaired if possible, or renew the assembly.

11 Check each cylinder bore for scuffing and scoring. Check for signs of a wear ridge at the top of the cylinder, indicating that the bore is excessively worn.

12 If the necessary measuring equipment is available, measure the bore diameter of each cylinder at the top (just under the wear ridge), centre, and bottom of the cylinder bore, parallel to the crankshaft axis **(see illustration)**.

13 Next, measure the bore diameter at the same three locations, at right-angles to the crankshaft axis. As no tolerance figures are actually stated by Rover, if there is any doubt about the condition of the cylinder bores, seek the advice of a Rover dealer or suitable engine reconditioning specialist.

14 Having measured the cylinder bores, subtract the piston diameters measured previously to obtain the piston-to-bore clearance for each cylinder. If the clearances are outside the tolerance range then, assuming that the cylinder bores are satisfactory, it will be necessary to fit new pistons of the correct size. If this is the case,

the bores should be honed, to allow the new rings to bed in correctly and provide the best possible seal. Honing is an operation that will be carried out for you by an engine reconditioning specialist.

15 If the cylinder bores are not in perfect condition, and providing they have not already been rebored to their maximum oversize limit, it should be possible to rectify any problems found by having the cylinder bores rebored and to fit matching oversize pistons.

16 After all machining operations are completed, the entire block/crankcase must be washed very thoroughly with warm soapy water to remove all traces of abrasive grit produced during the machining operations. When the cylinder block/crankcase is completely clean, rinse it thoroughly and dry it, then lightly oil all exposed machined surfaces, to prevent rusting.

14 Main and big-end bearings – inspection and selection

Inspection

1 Even though the main and big-end bearing shells should be renewed during the engine overhaul, the old shells should be retained for close examination, as they may reveal valuable information about the condition of the engine.

2 Bearing failure occurs because of lack of lubrication, the presence of dirt or other foreign particles, overloading the engine, and corrosion **(see illustration)**. Regardless of the cause of bearing failure, the cause must be corrected (where applicable) before the engine is reassembled, to prevent it from happening again.

3 When examining the bearing shells, remove them from the cylinder block/crankcase and main bearing caps, and from the connecting rods and the big-end bearing caps, then lay them out on a clean surface in the same general position as their location in the engine. This will enable you to match any bearing problems with the corresponding crankshaft journal.

4 Dirt or other foreign matter gets into the engine in a variety of ways. It may be left in the engine during assembly, or it may pass through filters or the crankcase ventilation system. It may get into the oil, and from there into the bearings. Metal chips from machining operations and normal engine wear are often present. Abrasives are sometimes left in engine components after reconditioning, especially when parts are not thoroughly cleaned using the proper cleaning methods. Whatever the source, these foreign objects often end up embedded in the soft bearing material, and are easily recognised. Large particles will not be embed in the material, and will score or gouge the shell and journal. The best prevention for this cause of bearing failure is to clean all parts thoroughly, and to keep everything spotlessly-clean during engine assembly. Frequent and regular engine oil and filter changes are also recommended.

5 Lack of lubrication (or lubrication breakdown) has a number of inter-related causes. Excessive heat (which thins the oil), overloading (which squeezes the oil from the bearing face) and oil leakage (from excessive bearing clearances, worn oil pump or high engine speeds) all contribute to lubrication breakdown. Blocked oil passages, which usually are the result of misaligned oil holes in a bearing shell, will also starve a bearing of oil, and destroy it. When lack of lubrication is the cause of bearing failure, the bearing material is wiped or extruded from the shell's steel backing. Temperatures may increase to the point where the steel backing turns blue from overheating.

6 Driving habits can have a definite effect on bearing life. Full-throttle, low-speed operation (labouring the engine) puts very high loads on bearings, which tends to squeeze out the oil film. These loads cause the shells to flex, which produces fine cracks in the bearing face (fatigue failure). Eventually, the bearing material will loosen in pieces, and tear away from the steel backing.

7 Short-distance driving leads to corrosion of bearings, because insufficient engine heat is produced to drive off condensed water and corrosive gases. These products collect in the engine oil, forming acid and sludge. As the oil is carried to the engine bearings, the acid attacks and corrodes the bearing material.

8 Incorrect shell refitting during engine assembly will lead to bearing failure as well. Tight-fitting shells leave insufficient bearing running clearance, and will result in oil starvation. Dirt or foreign particles trapped behind a bearing shell result in high spots on the bearing, which lead to failure.

9 Do not touch any shell's bearing surface with your fingers during reassembly; there is a risk of scratching the delicate surface, or of depositing particles of dirt on it.

Selection

10 Main and big-end bearing shells for the majority of the engines described in this Chapter are available in one standard size and, on earlier engines, in a range of undersizes to suit reground crankshafts.

11 Selective standard size main bearing shells are fitted to later 998 cc and 1275 cc engines. Red (R), Green (G) or Yellow (Y) codes are used to identify the bearing journal size, and the colours or RGY stamp will be found on the main bearing caps and the corresponding web of the crankshaft. The bearing shells are also identified in the same way. Undersize main and big-end bearing shells are no longer available from Rover dealers for these engines.

12 The relevant set of bearing shells required can be obtained by measuring the diameter of the crankshaft main bearing journals (see Section 12). This will show if the crankshaft is original or whether its journals have been reground, identifying if either standard or oversize bearing shells are required.

13 If access to the necessary measuring equipment cannot be gained, the size of the bearing shells can be identified by the markings stamped on the rear of each shell. Details of these markings should be supplied to your Rover dealer who will then be able to identify the size of shell fitted.

14 Whether the original shells or new shells are being fitted, it is recommended that the running clearance is checked as described in Section 17 prior to installation.

15 Engine overhaul – reassembly sequence

1 Before reassembly begins, ensure that all new parts have been obtained, and that all necessary tools are available. Read through the entire procedure to familiarise yourself with the work involved, and to ensure that all items necessary for reassembly of the engine are at hand.

2 In order to save time and avoid problems, engine reassembly can be carried out in the following order:

a) Crankshaft (Section 17).
b) Piston rings (Section 16)
c) Piston/connecting rod assemblies (Section 18).
d) Oil pump (Section 10).
e) Oil filter housing and delivery pipe – where applicable (Part A of this Chapter).
f) Oil pressure relief valve (Part A or B of this Chapter).
g) Camshaft and tappets (Section 9).
h) Cylinder head (Part A or B of this Chapter).
i) Timing chain, sprockets and tensioner (Part A or B of this Chapter).
j) Distributor driveshaft – where applicable (Part A of this Chapter).

k) Engine external components.

3 At this stage, all engine components should be absolutely clean and dry, with all faults repaired. The components should be laid out (or in individual containers) on a completely clean work surface.

16 Piston rings – refitting

1 Before fitting new piston rings, the ring end gaps must be checked as follows.

2 Lay out the piston/connecting rod assemblies and the new piston ring sets, so that the ring sets will be matched with the same piston and cylinder during the end gap measurement and subsequent engine reassembly.

3 Insert the top ring into the first cylinder, and push it down the bore using the top of the piston. This will ensure that the ring remains square with the cylinder walls. Position the ring near the bottom of the cylinder bore, at the lower limit of ring travel. On engines with tapered second and third compression rings, the top narrow side of the ring is marked with a T, or the word TOP **(see illustration)**.

4 Measure the end gap using feeler blades.

5 Repeat the procedure with the ring at the top of the cylinder bore, at the upper limit of its travel, and compare the measurements with the figures given in the Specifications.

6 If the gap is too small (unlikely if genuine Rover parts are used), it must be enlarged, or the ring ends may contact each other during engine operation, causing serious damage. Ideally, new piston rings providing the correct end gap should be fitted. As a last resort, the end gap can be increased by filing the ring ends very carefully with a fine file. Mount the file in a vice equipped with soft jaws, slip the ring over the file with the ends contacting the file face, and slowly move the ring to remove material from the ends. Take care, as piston rings are sharp, and are easily broken.

7 With new piston rings, it is unlikely that the end gap will be too large. If the gaps are too large, check that you have the correct rings for your engine and for the particular cylinder bore size.

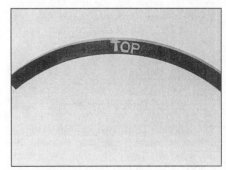

16.3 Piston ring identification markings

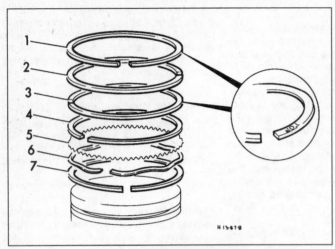

**16.10a Piston ring identification –
848 cc, 998 cc and 1098 cc engines**

1	Chrome plated	4	Top rail
	compression ring	5	Expander
2	Taper compression ring	6	Side spring
3	Taper compression ring	7	Bottom rail

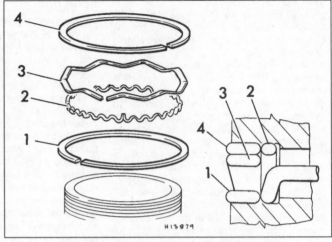

**16.10b Correct assembly of oil control ring
– 1275 cc engines**

1	Bottom rail	3	Oil control ring rail
2	Expander	4	Top rail

8 Repeat the checking procedure for each ring in the first cylinder, and then for the rings in the remaining cylinders. Remember to keep rings, pistons and cylinders matched up.

9 Once the ring end gaps have been checked and if necessary corrected, the rings can be fitted to the pistons.

10 Fit the piston rings using the same technique as for removal. Fit the bottom (oil control) ring first, and work up. When fitting a three piece oil control ring, first insert the expander and position its gap in line with the centre of the gudgeon pin. Fit the scraper rings with their gaps positioned either side of the expander gap. Where the oil control scraper is of one-piece type, position its gap 180° from the expander gap. Ensure that the second and third compression rings are fitted the correct way up, with their identification mark (either a T or the word TOP stamped on the ring surface) at the top **(see illustrations)**. Carefully examine all rings for this mark before fitting. Arrange the gaps of the compression rings equally around the piston. **Note:** *Always follow any instructions supplied with the new piston ring sets – different manufacturers may specify different procedures. Do not mix up the top and second compression rings, as they have different cross-sections.*

17 Crankshaft –
refitting and running clearance check

1 Crankshaft refitting is the first stage of engine reassembly following overhaul. It is assumed at this point that the cylinder block/crankcase and crankshaft have been cleaned, inspected and repaired or reconditioned as necessary.

2 Position the cylinder block on a clean level work surface, with the crankcase facing upwards. Unbolt the bearing caps and carefully release them from the crankcase; lay them out in order to ensure correct reassembly. If they're still in place, remove the old bearing shells from the caps and crankcase and wipe out the inner surfaces with a clean rag – they must be kept spotlessly clean.

3 Clean the backs of the bearing shells and insert them into position in the crankcase. If the original bearing shells are being used for the check, ensure that they are refitted in their original locations. Press the shells home so that the tangs engage in the recesses provided. When fitting the right-hand main bearing shell, it may be found that the cylinder block oilway is offset from the corresponding hole in the bearing shell. This condition is acceptable as long as a 2.3 mm diameter steel rod can be inserted into the exposed section of the hole.

4 Give the newly fitted bearing shells and the crankshaft journals a final clean with a rag.

17.7 Plastigauge in place on main bearing journal

Check that the oil holes in the crankshaft are free from dirt, as any left here will become embedded in the new bearings when the engine is started.

5 Carefully lay the crankshaft in the crankcase taking care not to dislodge the bearing shells.

Running clearance check

6 When the crankshaft and bearings are fitted, a clearance must exist between them to allow lubricant to circulate. This clearance is impossible to check using feeler blades, so Plastigauge is used. This consists of a fine thread of perfectly round plastic which is compressed between the bearing shell and the journal when the bearing caps are tightened up. When the cap and shell are removed, the width of the deformed plastic can be measured with a special card gauge supplied with the kit. The running clearance is determined from this gauge. The procedure for using Plastigauge is as follows.

7 Cut off three lengths of Plastigauge (they should be slightly shorter than the width of the main bearings) and place one length on each crankshaft journal axis **(see illustration)**.

8 Wipe the inner surface of the bearing caps and the backs of the lower bearing shells and fit the three bearing shells to their caps. Press the shells home so that the tangs engage in the recesses provided.

9 Ensure that all six tubular locating dowels are firmly in place, one on each side of the upper halves of the three main bearings, and then fit the main bearing caps in position ensuring that they locate properly on the dowels. Tighten their retaining bolts to the specified torque. Take care not to disturb the Plastigauge and **do not** rotate the crankshaft at any time during this operation.

10 Remove the main bearing caps again taking great care not to disturb the Plastigauge or rotate the crankshaft.

11 Compare the width of the crushed Plastigauge on each journal to the scale printed on the Plastigauge envelope to obtain the main bearing running clearance **(see illustration)**. Use the correct scale as both imperial and metric are printed. Compare the clearance measured with the running clearance dimension given in the Specifications.

12 If the clearance is significantly different from that expected, the bearing shells may be the wrong size (or excessively worn if the original shells are being re-used). Before deciding that the crankshaft is worn, make sure that no dirt or oil was trapped between the bearing shells and the caps or block when the clearance was measured. If the Plastigauge was wider at one end than at the other, the crankshaft journal may be tapered.

13 Before condemning the components concerned, seek the advice of your Rover dealer or suitable engine repair specialist. They will also be able to inform as to the best course of action and whether it is possible to have the crankshaft journals reground or whether renewal will be necessary.

14 Where necessary, obtain the correct size of bearing shell and repeat the running clearance checking procedure as described above.

15 On completion, carefully scrape away all traces of the Plastigauge material from the crankshaft and bearing shells using a fingernail or other object which is unlikely to score the bearing surfaces.

Final refitting

16 Lift the crankshaft out of the crankcase. Wipe the surfaces of the bearings in the crankcase and the bearing caps.

17 Wipe the recesses either side of the centre main bearings which locate the upper halves of the thrustwashers.

18 Generously lubricate the crankshaft journals and the upper and lower main bearing shells with clean engine oil and carefully place the crankshaft in position.

19 Introduce the upper halves of the thrustwashers (the halves without tabs) into their grooves on each side of the centre main bearing **(see illustration)**, rotating the crankshaft in the direction towards the main bearing tabs (so that the main bearing shells do not slide out). At the same time feed the thrustwashers into their locations with their oil grooves facing outwards away from the bearing.

20 Ensure that all six tubular locating dowels are still firmly in place, one on each side of the upper halves of the three main bearings, and then fit the main bearing caps in position ensuring that they locate properly on the dowels. The mating surfaces must be spotlessly clean or the caps will not seat properly.

21 When refitting the centre main bearing cap, ensure that the thrustwashers, generously lubricated, are fitted with their oil grooves facing outwards, and the locating tab of each washer is in the slot in the bearing cap.

22 Refit the one-piece locking tabs over the main bearing caps (where applicable) and refit the main bearing cap bolts, screwing them up finger-tight initially, then finally tightening to the torque setting given in the Specifications **(see illustration)**.

23 Test the crankshaft for freedom of rotation. Should it be very stiff to turn or possess high spots, recheck the running clearances as described above.

24 Carry out a check of the crankshaft endfloat as described in Section 12. If the thrust surfaces of the crankshaft have been checked and new thrustwashers have been fitted, then the endfloat should be within specification.

25 When all is satisfactory, secure the main bearing bolts by knocking up the locking tabs (where applicable) with a small chisel.

---

18 Piston/connecting rod assemblies – refitting and big-end bearing clearance check

Note: *At this point it is assumed that the crankshaft has been refitted to the engine as described in Section 17.*

Running clearance check

1 Clean the backs of the bearing shells, and the bearing locations in both the connecting rod and bearing cap.

2 Press the bearing shells into their locations, ensuring that the tab on each shell engages in the notch in the connecting rod and cap. If the original bearing shells are being used for the check, ensure that they are refitted in their original locations.

3 As with the main bearings (Section 17), a running clearance must exist between the big-end crankpin and its bearing shells to allow oil to circulate. There are two methods of checking the running clearance as described in the following paragraphs.

4 One method is to refit the big-end bearing

17.11 Measuring the width of the deformed Plastigauge using the card gauge supplied

cap to the connecting rod, with the bearing shells in place. With the cap retaining nuts or bolts correctly tightened, use an internal micrometer or vernier caliper to measure the internal diameter of each assembled pair of bearing shells. If the diameter of each corresponding crankshaft journal is measured and then subtracted from the bearing internal diameter, the result will be the big-end bearing running clearance.

5 The second, and more accurate method is to use Plastigauge (see Section 17).

6 Ensure that the bearing shells are correctly fitted. Place a strand of Plastigauge on each (cleaned) crankpin journal.

7 Temporarily refit the (clean) piston/connecting rod assemblies to the crankshaft, and refit the big-end bearing caps, using the marks made or noted on removal to ensure that they are fitted the correct way around.

8 Tighten the bearing cap nuts or bolts to the specified torque. Take care not to disturb the Plastigauge, nor rotate the connecting rod during the tightening sequence.

9 Dismantle the assemblies without rotating the connecting rods. Use the scale printed on the Plastigauge envelope to obtain the big-end bearing running clearance. Use the correct scale as both imperial and metric are printed.

10 If the clearance is significantly different from that given in the Specifications, the bearing shells may be the wrong size (or excessively worn, if the original shells are being re-used). Make sure that no dirt or oil was trapped between the bearing shells and

17.19 Refitting the crankshaft thrustwasher upper halves

17.22 Tighten the main bearing cap bolts to the specified torque

18.16 Refitting a piston with a piston ring clamp in position

the caps or block when the clearance was measured. If the Plastigauge was wider at one end than at the other, the crankshaft journal may be tapered.

11 Before condemning the components concerned, refer to your Rover dealer or engine reconditioning specialist for their advice on the best course of action to be taken.

12 On completion, carefully scrape away all traces of the Plastigauge material from the crankshaft and bearing shells. Use your fingernail, or some other object which is unlikely to score the bearing surfaces.

Final refitting

13 Ensure that the bearing shells are correctly fitted as described earlier. Wipe dry the shells and connecting rods with a clean cloth.

14 Lubricate the cylinder bores, the pistons, and piston rings, then lay out each piston/connecting rod assembly in its respective position.

15 Start with assembly No 1. Make sure that the piston rings are still spaced as described in Section 16, then clamp them in position with a piston ring compressor.

16 Insert the piston/connecting rod assembly into the top of cylinder No 1. Ensure that it is the correct piston/connecting rod assembly for that particular bore, that the connecting rod is the right way round, and that the front of the piston is towards the front of the engine. Using a block of wood or hammer handle against the piston crown, tap the assembly into the cylinder until the piston crown is flush with the top of the cylinder **(see illustration)**.

17 Ensure that the bearing shell is still correctly installed. Liberally lubricate the crankpin and both bearing shells. Taking care not to mark the cylinder bores, pull the piston/connecting rod assembly down the bore and onto the crankpin. As the big-end bosses on the connecting rods are offset, it will be obvious if they have been inserted the wrong way round because they will not fit over the crankpin. The centre two rods must be fitted with their offset bosses facing away from the centre main bearing, and the connecting rods at each extremity of the engine must be fitted with their offset bosses facing inwards **(see illustration)**. Fit the big-

end cap and retaining bolts with the one-piece locking tab under them (where applicable) and tighten the bolts to the specified torque. On 1275 cc engines the arrangement is slightly different, the caps being retained by nuts.

18 Once the bearing cap retaining nuts or bolts have been correctly tightened, rotate the crankshaft. Check that it turns freely; some stiffness is to be expected if new components have been fitted, but there should be no signs of binding or tight spots.

19 Refit the remaining three piston/connecting rod assemblies in the same way.

19 Engine –
initial start-up after overhaul and reassembly

1 Refit the remainder of the engine components in the order listed in Section 15 of this Chapter, referring to Part A or B where necessary. Reconnect the engine to the transmission (Section 5 or 6 as applicable), then refit the power unit to the car as described in Section 3 or 4 as applicable.

2 With the engine/transmission refitted, double-check the engine oil and coolant levels. Make a final check that everything has been reconnected, and that there are no tools or rags left in the engine compartment.

3 On fuel injection engines, disable the fuel system by removing the fuel pump fuse, located as follows (see Chapter 12 for additional information):

a) *Single-point fuel injection models with four-fuse fuseblock – remove line fuse 4 located in the line fuse cluster on the engine compartment bulkhead.*

b) *Single-point fuel injection models with twenty four-fuse fuseblock – remove fuse 11 located in the engine compartment fuseblock.*

c) *Multi-point fuel injection models – remove fuse C7 in the passenger compartment fuseblock.*

4 Remove the spark plugs. On engines with a distributor, disable the ignition system by disconnecting the ignition HT coil lead from the distributor cap, and earthing it on the cylinder block. Use a jumper lead or similar wire to make a good connection. On engines without a distributor, disable the ignition system by disconnecting the wiring connector from the DIS module referring to Chapter 5C for further information.

5 Turn the engine on the starter until the oil pressure warning light goes out. Refit the spark plugs, and reconnect the spark plug and distributor (HT) leads, referring to Chapter 1 for further information. Where applicable, refit the fuel pump fuse and reconnect the ignition coil wiring connector.

6 Start the engine, noting that this may take a little longer than usual, due to the fuel system components having been disturbed.

7 While the engine is idling, check for fuel, water and oil leaks. Don't be alarmed if there are some odd smells and smoke from parts getting hot and burning off oil deposits.

8 Assuming all is well, keep the engine idling until hot water is felt circulating through the top hose, then switch off the engine.

9 Check the ignition timing and the idle speed settings (as appropriate), then switch the engine off.

10 After a few minutes, recheck the oil and coolant levels as described in Chapter 1, and top-up as necessary.

11 If new pistons, rings or crankshaft bearings have been fitted, the engine must be treated as new, and run-in for the first 500 miles (800 km). *Do not* operate the engine at full-throttle, or allow it to labour at low engine speeds in any gear. It is recommended that the oil and filter be changed at the end of this period.

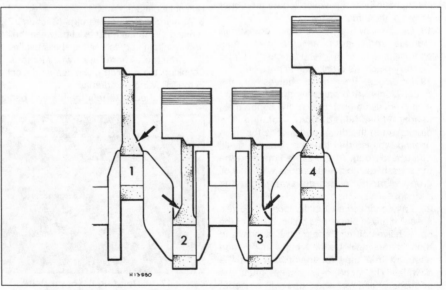

18.17 The correct positions of the offsets on the connecting rod big-ends

Chapter 3
Cooling, heating and ventilation systems

Contents

Antifreeze – general information	3
Auxiliary cooling fan (front-mounted radiator) – removal and refitting	11
Auxiliary cooling fan (side-mounted radiator) – information, removal and refitting	10
Auxiliary cooling fan thermostatic switch – removal, testing and refitting	12
Auxiliary drivebelt check and renewal	See Chapter 1
Coolant level check	See Weekly checks
Cooling system – draining	See Chapter 1
Cooling system – filling	See Chapter 1
Cooling system – flushing	See Chapter 1
Cooling system hoses – disconnection and renewal	2
Fresh air vent assembly – removal and refitting	17
General information and precautions	1
Heater assembly – dismantling and reassembly	16
Heater assembly – removal and refitting	15
Heater water valve – removal and refitting	14
Heater water valve control cable – removal and refitting	13
Radiator (front-mounted) – removal and refitting	5
Radiator (side-mounted) – removal and refitting	4
Thermostat (front-mounted radiator) – removal, testing and refitting	7
Thermostat (side-mounted radiator) – removal, testing and refitting	6
Water pump (front-mounted radiator) – removal and refitting	9
Water pump (side-mounted radiator) – removal and refitting	8

Degrees of difficulty

Easy, suitable for novice with little experience	**Fairly easy,** suitable for beginner with some experience	**Fairly difficult,** suitable for competent DIY mechanic	**Difficult,** suitable for experienced DIY mechanic	**Very difficult,** suitable for expert DIY or professional 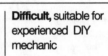

Specifications

General

System type	Pressurised, water pump assisted, thermo-syphon
Radiator/expansion tank pressure cap setting:	
Models with side-mounted radiator:	
Pre-1974 models	0.91 bar
1974 models onward	1.05 bar
Models with front-mounted radiator	0.5 bar

Thermostat

Type	Wax
Opening temperatures:	
Pre-1976 models:	
Standard	82°C
Hot climates	74°C
Cold climates	88°C
1976 models onward	88°C

Auxiliary cooling fan

Thermostatic switch settings:	
Models with side-mounted radiator:	
Switches on at	98°C
Switches off at	93°C
Models with front-mounted radiator:	
Switches on at	105°C
Switches off at	98°C

Torque wrench settings

	Nm	lbf ft
Auxiliary cooling fan thermostatic switch	10	7
Front-mounted radiator mounting bracket bolts	9	6
Thermostat housing	11	8
Water pump pulley	10	7
Water pump to cylinder block	22	16

1 General information and precautions

The cooling system is of the conventional pressurised, water pump-assisted thermo-syphon type comprising a radiator, water pump, thermostat and associated hoses.

On pre-October 1996 models, the radiator is located at the left-hand side of the engine compartment. Radiator cooling is provided by a fan mounted on the water pump and driven by a V-belt from the crankshaft pulley. As the radiator is mounted next to the wheelarch, the fan *pushes* cold air through the radiator matrix. An auxiliary electric cooling fan is fitted to later 1275 cc models, located beneath the left-hand front wheelarch. The fan provides an additional source of cooling for the radiator in conjunction with the belt-driven fan on the water pump.

On October 1996 models onward, the radiator is located at the front of the car directly behind the front grille panel. Radiator cooling is provided by the inrush of air when the car is in forward motion. The airflow is supplemented by an auxiliary electric cooling fan attached to the front of the radiator.

The cooling system functions by circulating cold coolant from the bottom of the radiator, up the lower radiator hose to the water pump where it is pumped around the water passages in the cylinder block.

The coolant then travels up into the cylinder head and circulates around the combustion chambers and valve seats. When the engine is at its correct operating temperature, the coolant travels out of the cylinder head, past the open thermostat, into the hose and into the top of the radiator. The coolant travels through the radiator where it is rapidly cooled by the passage of cold air through the radiator core. The coolant, now cool, reaches the bottom of the radiator where the cycle is repeated.

When the engine is cold, the thermostat (which is simply a temperature-sensitive valve), maintains the circulation of coolant in the engine by blocking the passage from the cylinder head to the radiator. Only when the opening temperature of the thermostat has been reached, does the thermostat allow the coolant to return to the radiator.

A basic heating and ventilation system is fitted which supplies warm or cold air to either the windscreen or car interior. A two-speed blower fan is fitted to supplement the airflow as required. Fresh air ventilation is provided by controllable air vents, located below the windscreen on each side of the car. These vents are independent of the main heater/blower unit and provide ambient air when the car is moving. The volume of air supplied is dependent on road speed.

Precautions

 Warning: Do not attempt to remove the radiator or expansion tank filler cap, or to disturb any part of the cooling system, while it or the engine is hot, as there is a very great risk of scalding. If the filler cap must be removed before the engine and radiator have fully cooled down (even though this is not recommended) the pressure in the cooling system must first be released. Cover the cap with a thick layer of cloth, to avoid scalding, and slowly unscrew the filler cap until a hissing sound can be heard. When the hissing has stopped, showing that pressure is released, slowly unscrew the filler cap further until it can be removed; if more hissing sounds are heard, wait until they have stopped before unscrewing the cap completely. At all times, keep well away from the filler opening.

 Warning: Do not allow antifreeze to come in contact with your skin, or with the painted surfaces of the vehicle. Rinse off spills immediately with plenty of water. Never leave antifreeze lying around in an open container, or in a puddle in the driveway or on the garage floor. Children and pets are attracted by its sweet smell, but antifreeze is fatal if ingested.

 Warning: On models with a front-mounted radiator, if the engine is hot, the electric cooling fan may start rotating even if the engine is not running. Be careful to keep your hands, hair, and any loose clothing well clear when working in the engine compartment.

2 Cooling system hoses – disconnection and renewal

Note: *Refer to the warnings given in Section 1 of this Chapter before proceeding. Hoses should only be disconnected once the engine has cooled sufficiently to avoid scalding.*

1 If the checks described in Chapter 1 reveal a faulty hose, it must be renewed as follows.

2 First drain the cooling system as described in Chapter 1. if the antifreeze is not due for renewal, the drained coolant may be re-used, if it is collected in a clean container.

3 To disconnect the main system hoses, use a pair of pliers to release the spring clamps (or a screwdriver to slacken screw-type clamps), then move them along the hose clear of the union. Carefully work the hose off its stubs. The hoses can be removed with relative ease when new – on an older vehicle, they may have stuck.

4 If a hose proves to be difficult to remove, try to release it by rotating it on its unions before attempting to work it off. Gently prise the end of the hose with a blunt instrument (such as a flat-bladed screwdriver), but do not apply too much force, and take care not to damage the pipe stubs or hoses. Note in particular that the radiator hose unions are fragile; do not use excessive force when attempting to remove the hoses.

 If all else fails, cut the hose with a sharp knife, then slit it so that it can be peeled off in two pieces. Although this may prove expensive if the hose is otherwise undamaged, it is preferable to buying a new radiator.

5 When refitting a hose, first slide the clamps onto the hose, then engage the hose with its unions. Work the hose into position, then check that the hose is settled correctly and is properly routed. Slide each clip along the hose until it is behind the union flared end, before tightening it securely.

 If the hose is stiff, use a little soapy water as a lubricant, or soften the hose by soaking it in hot water. Do not use oil or grease, which may attack the rubber.

6 On all engines except 1275 cc (12A) types, a bypass hose is fitted between the top of the water pump and the underside of the cylinder head. Renewal of the bypass hose is an awkward and tedious task which often presents problems. The easiest way to refit a bypass hose is to first place both clips in position on the hose. Fit the bottom of the hose to the water pump, bend the hose in half and then place the flat faces of a knife or feeler blade between the top of the hose and outlet in the cylinder head. Push the hose into an upright position and withdraw the blade. The hose should now be in position over the outlet. Several attempts may be necessary before the hose slides properly into position.

7 Refill the system with coolant as described in Chapter 1.

8 Check carefully for leaks as soon as possible after disturbing any part of the cooling system.

3 Antifreeze – general information

Note: *Refer to the warnings given in Section 1 of this Chapter before proceeding.*

1 The cooling system should be filled with a water/ethylene glycol-based antifreeze solution, of a strength which will prevent freezing down to at least –25°C, or lower if the local climate requires it. Antifreeze also provides protection against corrosion, and increases the coolant boiling point. As with all mixed metal engines, the corrosion protection properties of the antifreeze are critical. Only a top quality antifreeze should be used in the system and should never be mixed with different antifreeze types.

2 The cooling system should be maintained according to the schedule described in Chapter 1. If antifreeze is used that is not to

Rover's specification, old or contaminated coolant mixtures are likely to cause damage, and encourage the formation of corrosion and scale in the system.

3 Before adding antifreeze, check all hoses and hose connections, because antifreeze tends to leak through very small openings. Engines don't normally consume coolant, so if the level goes down, find the cause and correct it.

4 On models with a side-mounted radiator, a 30% to 50% mixture of antifreeze and clean soft water (by volume) should be used all year round to maintain maximum protection against freezing and corrosion. On models with a front-mounted radiator the manufacturer recommends that this ratio should be increased to a 50% to 60% mixture of antifreeze and clean soft water (by volume). Mix the required quantity in a clean container and then fill the system as described in Chapter 1 and *Weekly checks*. Save any surplus mixture for topping-up.

5 Towards the end of the 1999 model year, Rover introduced a new orange-coloured long-life antifreeze of a different formula to the blue-green type previously specified. As the new antifreeze must not be mixed with traditional ethylene glycol types, a label attached to the expansion tank filler neck indicates the type of antifreeze that should be used in the cooling system. Always consult this label, or seek the advice of a Rover dealer if in any doubt as to the type of antifreeze to obtain.

4 Radiator (side-mounted) – removal and refitting

Note: *Refer to the warnings given in Section 1 of this Chapter before proceeding.*

> **HAYNES HiNT**
>
> *If leakage is the reason for wanting to remove the radiator, bear in mind that minor leaks can often be cured using a radiator sealant with the radiator in situ.*

Removal

1 Drain the cooling system as described in Chapter 1.

2 Refer to Chapter 11A and remove the bonnet.

3 Slacken the two retaining clips and completely remove the radiator top hose.

4 If the bottom hose was not removed for draining, slacken the retaining clip, using a long thin screwdriver, and pull the hose off the radiator outlet.

5 Undo and remove the bolts and nuts securing the radiator upper support bracket to the fan cowling and thermostat housing. Lift away the bracket **(see illustration)**.

6 On later 1275 cc engines (except

carburettor engine Cooper models) disconnect the wiring connectors at the auxiliary cooling fan thermostatic switch in the bottom corner of the radiator.

7 At the base of the radiator undo and remove either the long through-bolt or the two short bolts (depending on model) that secure the lower support bracket to the engine

mounting **(see illustration)**. If necessary remove the front grille panel as described in Chapter 11A to provide greater access.

8 Undo and remove the bolts securing the fan cowlings to the radiator, move the cowlings as far as possible toward the engine and carefully lift out the radiator. If a two-piece cowling is fitted, lift off the top half.

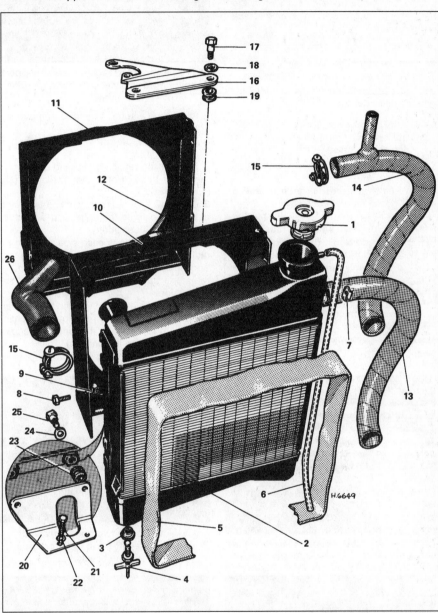

4.5 Exploded view of the side-mounted radiator and attachments

1 Filler cap	11 Cowl (upper – two piece type)	17 Bolt
2 Radiator	12 Cowl (lower – two-piece type)	18 Washer
3 Drain tap adapter		19 Rubber grommet
4 Drain tap or plug		20 Lower mounting
5 Rubber surround	13 Bottom hose (non-heater type)	21 Bolt
6 Overflow pipe		22 Washer
7 Retaining clip	14 Bottom hose (heater type)	23 Rubber grommet
8 Cowl fixing screw		24 Washer
9 Nut	15 Hose clip	25 Bolt
10 Cowl (one piece type)	16 Upper mounting	26 Top hose

Refitting

9 Refitting is the reverse sequence to removal.

 HINT *If the hose is stiff, use a little soapy water as a lubricant, or soften the hose by soaking it in hot water. Do not use oil or grease, which may attack the rubber.*

10 With the radiator in position, refill the cooling system as described in Chapter 1, and refit the bonnet and (if removed) the front grille panel as described in Chapter 11A.

5 Radiator (front-mounted) – removal and refitting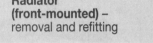

Note: *Refer to the warnings given in Section 1 of this Chapter before proceeding.*

 HINT *If leakage is the reason for wanting to remove the radiator, bear in mind that minor leaks can often be cured using a radiator sealant with the radiator in situ.*

Removal

1 Drain the cooling system as described in Chapter 1.

4.7 Side-mounted radiator lower support mounting bolt accessible through grille panel

2 Refer to Chapter 11B and remove the bonnet and front grille panel.
3 Remove the alternator as described in Chapter 5A.
4 Slacken the retaining clip and disconnect the top hose from the radiator **(see illustration)**.
5 Disconnect the auxiliary cooling fan wiring at the multiplug on the right-hand side of the radiator **(see illustration)**.
6 Undo the two bolts each side securing the radiator upper mounting brackets to the front body panel. Lift the two brackets off the radiator upper mounting studs **(see illustrations)**.
7 Lift the radiator, together with the auxiliary cooling fan, upwards off the lower mounting rubbers and remove it from the engine compartment **(see illustration)**.
8 If required the cooling fan can be removed

5.4 Slacken the clip and disconnect the top hose from the radiator – front-mounted radiator

from the radiator after undoing the four mounting bolts and the single bolt securing the wiring multiplug.

Refitting

9 Refitting is the reverse sequence to removal.

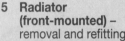 **HINT** *If the hose is stiff, use a little soapy water as a lubricant, or soften the hose by soaking it in hot water. Do not use oil or grease, which may attack the rubber.*

10 Refit the bonnet and front grille panel as described in Chapter 11B, and the alternator as described in Chapter 5A.
11 Refill the cooling system as described in Chapter 1.

5.5 Disconnect the cooling fan wiring at the multiplug – front-mounted radiator

5.6a Undo the two bolts (arrowed) securing the left-hand radiator upper mounting bracket . . .

5.6b . . . and lift the bracket off the mounting stud – front-mounted radiator

5.6c Similarly, undo the two bolts (arrowed) securing the right-hand radiator upper mounting bracket . . .

5.6d . . . and lift the bracket off the mounting stud – front-mounted radiator

5.7 Lift the radiator and fan upwards off the lower mounting rubbers – front-mounted radiator

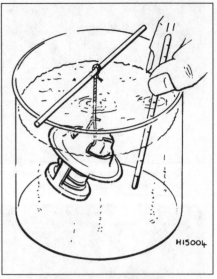

6.3b Thermostat housing and radiator upper mounting bracket (later models with side-mounted radiator)

6.8 Testing the thermostat

6.3a Exploded view of the thermostat housing components (early models with side-mounted radiator)

6 Thermostat (side-mounted radiator) – removal, testing and refitting

Note: *Refer to the warnings given in Section 1 of this Chapter before proceeding.*

Removal

1 Partially drain the cooling system (approximately 1 litre) as described in Chapter 1.

2 Undo the retaining bolts securing the upper radiator mounting bracket to the radiator cowl.

3 Undo the two nuts or bolts securing the upper radiator mounting bracket to the thermostat cover, or the single nut securing the bracket to the thermostat housing body **(see illustrations)**. Remove the bracket.

4 Slacken the radiator top hose retaining clip and disconnect the hose from the thermostat cover. Where applicable, disconnect the heater hose from the thermostat housing body and the wiring from the thermostatic switch or vacuum hoses from the thermostatic valve in the side of the housing body. Note the correct fitted positions of the vacuum hoses before disconnection.

5 Undo the remaining nut, or the three bolts (according to type) securing the thermostat cover, and lift off the cover and gasket. Where the cover is retained by nuts and studs, it is likely to be quite tight due to corrosion of the retaining studs. If so, apply liberal amounts of penetrating oil to the studs and allow time to

soak. Now very gently tap the cover from side-to-side, using a soft-faced mallet or block of wood. This should ease the corrosion and allow the cover to be lifted off.

6 With the cover removed, take out the thermostat.

7 On models with a separate thermostat housing body beneath the cover, lift off the housing body together with its lower gasket.

Testing

8 To test the thermostat for correct functioning, suspend it on a string in a saucepan of cold water together with a thermometer **(see illustration)**. Heat the water and note the temperature at which the thermostat begins to open. The correct opening temperatures are given in the Specifications at the beginning of this Chapter. Continue heating the water until the thermostat is fully open. Then let it cool down naturally.

9 If the thermostat does not fully open in boiling water, or does not close down as the water cools, then it must be discarded and a new one fitted. Should the thermostat be stuck open when cold, this will be apparent during removal.

Refitting

10 Refitting is the reverse sequence to removal bearing in mind the following points:

a) *Clean off all traces of old gasket from the component mating faces and renew any parts which show signs of corrosion.*

b) *Where the thermostat is located directly in*

the cylinder head, use a new gasket between the cylinder head and thermostat cover. On models with a separate thermostat housing body, use new gaskets on both sides of the housing body.

c) *Tighten the thermostat housing nuts/bolts to the specified torque.*

d) *Refill the cooling system as described in Chapter 1 on completion.*

7 Thermostat (front-mounted radiator) – removal, testing and refitting

Note: *Refer to the warnings given in Section 1 of this Chapter before proceeding.*

Removal

1 Partially drain the cooling system (approximately 1 litre) as described in Chapter 1.

2 Slacken the retaining clips and disconnect the expansion tank hose and radiator top hose from the thermostat cover **(see illustrations)**.

3 Disconnect the wiring connector from the coolant temperature sensor located in the thermostat housing body **(see illustration)**.

7.2a Slacken the retaining clips and disconnect the expansion tank hose . . .

7.2b . . . and radiator top hose from the thermostat cover – models with front-mounted radiator

7.3 Disconnect the wiring connector from the coolant temperature sensor . . .

7.4 . . . then disconnect the heater hose – models with front-mounted radiator

7.5a Undo the thermostat cover bolts and lift off the cover . . .

7.5b . . . followed by the gasket – models with front-mounted radiator

7.6a With the cover removed, take out the thermostat . . .

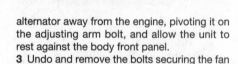

7.6b . . . then lift off the housing body . . .

4 Slacken the clip and disconnect the heater hose from the thermostat housing body **(see illustration)**.

5 Undo the three bolts securing the thermostat cover, lift off the cover and remove the gasket **(see illustrations)**.

6 With the cover removed, take out the thermostat then lift off the housing body and lower gasket **(see illustrations)**.

Testing

7 Refer to the information contained in Section 6.

Refitting

8 Refitting is the reverse sequence to removal bearing in mind the following points:

a) Clean off all traces of old gasket from the component mating faces and renew any parts which show signs of corrosion.

b) Use new gaskets on both sides of the

7.6c . . . and lower gasket – models with front-mounted radiator

thermostat housing body and tighten the cover retaining bolts to the specified torque.

c) Refill the cooling system as described in Chapter 1 on completion.

8 Water pump (side-mounted radiator) – removal and refitting

Note: *Water pump failure is indicated by water leaking from the gland or front of the pump, or by rough and noisy operation. This is usually accompanied by excessive play of the pump spindle which can be checked by moving the fan blades from side-to-side. Water pumps are relatively inexpensive items and the simplest course of action, should the above symptoms be evident, is to fit an exchange reconditioned unit. Refer to the warnings given in Section 1 of this Chapter before proceeding.*

Removal

Note: *If the car is fitted with exhaust emission control equipment, it will be necessary to remove the air pump and drivebelt, as described in Chapter 4D, Section 7, to provide access to the water pump.*

1 Remove the radiator as described in Section 4.

2 Remove the auxiliary drivebelt as described in Chapter 1, then undo and remove the two nuts, bolts and washers securing the dynamo or alternator to the mounting bracket and water pump flange. Move the dynamo or

alternator away from the engine, pivoting it on the adjusting arm bolt, and allow the unit to rest against the body front panel.

3 Undo and remove the bolts securing the fan and fan pulley to the water pump hub. Lift off the fan and pulley and, where fitted, recover the spacer. As a guide to reassembly, make a mark to indicate the outer face of the fan as it is quite easy to refit this component the wrong way round.

4 Slacken the hose clips and detach the radiator bottom hose from the water pump outlet and also from the heater take-off connection, where applicable. Now slacken the clip that secures the bypass hose to the outlet on the top of the pump.

5 Undo and remove the four bolts securing the water pump to the cylinder block. Lift off the pump, and at the same time detach the bypass hose. Recover the water pump gasket **(see illustration)**.

8.5 Removing the water pump (shown with engine removed)

Refitting

6 Before fitting the pump, clean off all traces of old gasket from the water pump and cylinder block mating faces, ensuring that the faces are smooth, clean and dry.

7 Refitting the water pump is the reverse sequence to removal, bearing in mind the following points:

a) *Always use a new gasket, which should be lightly smeared on both sides with jointing compound.*

b) *The bypass hose should be renewed as a matter of course, because these hoses sometimes prove unreliable and are extremely difficult to renew when the water pump is installed.*

c) *Tighten the retaining bolts to the specified torque.*

d) *Refit and adjust the auxiliary drivebelt as described in Chapter 1.*

e) *Refit the radiator as described in Section 4.*

9 Water pump (front-mounted radiator) – removal and refitting

Note: *Refer to the warnings given in Section 1 of this Chapter before proceeding.*

Removal

1 Remove the auxiliary drivebelt and drain the cooling system as described in Chapter 1.

2 Undo the four water pump pulley retaining bolts and remove the pulley from the water pump spindle.

3 Slacken the clip and detach the radiator bottom hose from the water pump outlet.

4 Undo and remove the four bolts securing the water pump to the cylinder block. Lift off the pump, and recover the gasket.

Refitting

5 Before fitting the pump, clean off all traces of old gasket from the water pump and cylinder block mating faces, ensuring that the faces are smooth, clean and dry.

6 Refitting the water pump is the reverse sequence to removal, bearing in mind the following points:

a) *Always use a new gasket, which should be lightly smeared on both sides with jointing compound.*

b) *Tighten the retaining bolts to the specified torque.*

c) *Refit and adjust the auxiliary drivebelt and refill the cooling system as described in Chapter 1.*

10 Auxiliary cooling fan (side-mounted radiator) – information, removal and refitting

General information

1 An auxiliary electric cooling fan is fitted to all later 1275 cc engine models. It is located

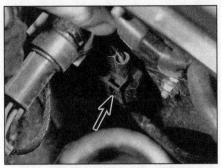

10.9 Auxiliary fan motor wiring connector (arrowed) – fuel injection models with side-mounted radiator

beneath the left-hand front wheelarch, and provides an additional source of cooling for the radiator in conjunction with the belt-driven fan on the water pump.

2 The auxiliary cooling fan is switched on and off by a thermostatic switch. On carburettor engine Cooper models, the switch is screwed into the thermostat housing body on the cylinder head, whereas on all other models it is situated in the front bottom corner of the radiator.

Removal

Carburettor engine Cooper models

3 Firmly apply the handbrake, then jack up the front of the car and support it securely on axle stands (see *Jacking and vehicle support*). Remove the left-hand front roadwheel.

4 Disconnect the air duct from the adapter beneath the front left-hand headlight.

5 Trace the fan motor wiring back to its connector, and disconnect it from the main wiring harness.

6 Slacken and remove the four cooling fan assembly shroud mounting nuts, and remove the assembly from underneath the wheelarch. Recover the mounting brackets, rubbers and spacers.

All other models

7 Remove the front grille panel as described in Chapter 11A.

8 Undo the three mounting bolts and remove the radiator upper mounting bracket. Loosen the lower radiator mounting bolt.

10.10 Removing the lower fan mounting nut (arrowed) – fuel injection models with side-mounted radiator

9 Disconnect the fan motor wiring connector, which is situated by the side of the radiator filler cap **(see illustration)**, and release the wiring grommet from the wing valance.

10 Slacken and remove the three (one lower and two upper) mounting nuts securing the fan shroud to the wing valance, then carefully withdraw the cooling fan assembly from underneath the wheelarch **(see illustration)**. Recover any relevant mounting rubbers and spacers.

Refitting

11 Refitting is the reverse sequence to removal, noting that the mounting rubbers should be renewed if they show any signs of wear or deterioration. Ensure that all disturbed nuts and bolts are securely tightened.

11 Auxiliary cooling fan (front-mounted radiator) – removal and refitting

Removal

Note: *Refer to the illustrations in Section 5 for details of the radiator attachments.*

1 Refer to Chapter 11B and remove the front grille panel.

2 Disconnect the cooling fan wiring at the multiplug on the right-hand side of the radiator.

3 Undo the two bolts each side securing the radiator upper mounting brackets to the front body panel. Lift the two brackets off the radiator upper mounting studs.

4 Undo the bolt securing the cooling fan wiring multiplug to the side of the radiator.

5 Carefully lift the radiator and fan assembly upwards off the lower mounting rubbers and move it towards the engine as far as possible.

6 Undo the four bolts securing the fan to the radiator and manoeuvre the fan from its location.

Refitting

7 Refitting is the reverse sequence to removal, ensuring that all attachments are tightened to the specified torque (where given).

12 Auxiliary cooling fan thermostatic switch – removal, testing and refitting

Note 1: *Refer to the warnings given in Section 1 of this Chapter before proceeding.*

Note 2: *The following procedures are only applicable to 1275 cc models with a side-mounted radiator. On models with a front-mounted radiator, the operation of the auxiliary cooling fan is controlled by the engine management ECU.*

Removal

1 When the engine and radiator are cold, either drain the cooling system as described in Chapter 1, or carefully unscrew the radiator filler cap to release any remaining pressure,

12.3 Auxiliary cooling fan switch location (arrowed) – fuel injection models with side-mounted radiator

and have ready a suitable plug that can be used temporarily to stop the escape of coolant while the switch is removed. If the latter method is used, take care not to damage the threads, and do not use anything which will leave foreign matter inside the cooling system.

2 On carburettor engine Cooper models, disconnect the wiring connectors, then unscrew the switch from the thermostat housing.

3 On all other models, if necessary, remove the front grille as described in Chapter 11A to improve access to the switch. Disconnect the two wiring connectors, then rotate the locking ring anti-clockwise to release it; withdraw the switch and rubber sealing ring from the bottom corner of the radiator **(see illustration)**. Examine the sealing ring for signs of damage or deterioration, and renew if necessary.

Testing

4 To carry out a thorough test of the switch, use two spare wires to connect it either to a multimeter (set to the resistance function) or to a battery-and-bulb test circuit. Suspend the switch in a pan of water which is being heated. Measure the temperature of the water with a thermometer. Do not let either the switch or the thermometer touch the pan itself.

5 The switch contacts should close to the 'on' position (ie, continuity should exist) when the water reaches the specified switch-on temperature given in the Specifications at the start of this Chapter. Stop heating the water, and allow it to cool down; the switch contacts should open at the specified switch-off temperature.

6 If the switch performance is significantly different from that specified, or if it does not work at all, it must be renewed.

Refitting

7 On carburettor engine Cooper models, ensure that the threads of the switch are clean, then apply a smear of suitable sealant to them. Refit the switch to the thermostat housing, tightening it to the specified torque, and reconnect the wiring connectors.

8 On all other models, fit the sealing ring to

the switch, then refit the switch to the radiator and secure it in position with the locking ring. Reconnect the wiring connectors, and refit the front grille (where removed).

9 On completion, either top-up or refill the cooling system as described in *Weekly checks* or Chapter 1.

13 Heater water valve control cable – removal and refitting

Removal

Pre-October 1996 models

1 Disconnect the battery negative terminal (refer to *Disconnecting the battery* in the Reference Chapter).

2 On pre-1989 models, slacken the inner cable trunnion screw and the outer cable clamp screw at the heater water valve on the cylinder head. Release the cable from the valve. On later models, release the outer cable retaining clip from the heater water valve on the engine compartment bulkhead. Disconnect the inner cable from the valve lever. Release the cable from its support clips.

3 From inside the car, undo and remove the screws, securing the centre console (where fitted). This will enable the console to be moved slightly to provide access to the control cable and heater.

4 Slacken the nut securing the rear of the heater unit to its mounting bracket.

5 Undo and remove the two screws securing the heater unit to the parcel shelf and lower the heater.

6 Detach the heater switch wire from the rear of the switch.

7 Undo and remove the two nuts securing the

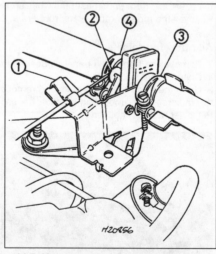

14.7 Heater water valve components – 1989 to October 1996 models

1 Outer cable retaining clip
2 Inner cable attachment
3 Coolant hose clip
4 Coolant hose clip

switch panel to the bracket under the parcel shelf.

8 Pull the switch panel backwards slightly, undo the control cable retaining nut, and pull the complete cable through into the car. Recover the nut and washer from the end of the cable as it is pulled through.

October 1996 models onward

9 Disconnect the battery negative terminal (refer to *Disconnecting the battery* in the Reference Chapter).

10 From inside the car, undo and remove the two screws securing the heater unit to the lower facia rail.

11 Reach up over the top of the heater water valve and undo the nut securing the valve mounting bracket to the facia rail, noting the earth lead which is also secured by the nut.

12 Release the outer cable retaining clip from the heater water valve mounting bracket. Disconnect the inner cable from the valve lever.

13 Undo and remove the two nuts securing the switch panel to the bracket under the lower facia rail.

14 Pull the switch panel backwards slightly, undo the control cable retaining nut, and withdraw the cable from the panel. Recover the nut and washer from the end of the cable as it is withdrawn.

Refitting

15 Refitting is the reverse sequence to removal, but check that the valve lever moves through its full range of travel. If necessary, adjust by repositioning the control outer cable in its clamp or retaining clip.

14 Heater water valve – removal and refitting

Note: *Refer to the warnings given in Section 1 of this Chapter before proceeding.*

Removal

Pre-1989 models

1 Drain the cooling system as described in Chapter 1.

2 Slacken the clip and disconnect the heater hose from the valve.

3 Slacken the inner cable trunnion screw and the outer cable clamp screw at the water valve, and release the control cable from the valve.

4 Undo the two nuts and remove the valve from the cylinder head studs.

5 Thoroughly clean the cylinder head and water valve mating faces and obtain a new gasket for refitting.

1989 to October 1996 models

6 Drain the cooling system as described in Chapter 1.

7 Slacken the clips and disconnect the heater hoses from both sides of the valve **(see illustration)**.

8 Release the outer cable retaining clip and disconnect the control cable from the valve lever.

9 Remove the valve assembly from the bulkhead.

October 1996 models onward

10 Drain the cooling system as described in Chapter 1.

11 Disconnect the demister duct from the side of the heater.

12 To prevent water damage to the carpets or upholstery, place polythene sheeting below the water valve and have a suitable container handy to collect the escaping coolant.

13 Release the clip securing the coolant feed hose to the heater. Position the container below the hose and disconnect the hose from the heater stub.

14 Operate the control cable to move the heater water valve lever to the open position and allow the coolant to drain into the container.

15 Reach up over the top of the water valve and undo the nut securing the valve mounting bracket to the facia rail, noting the earth lead which is also secured by the nut **(see illustration)**.

16 Lower the valve slightly and disconnect the heater hose from the top of the valve.

17 Release the control outer cable retaining clip from the water valve mounting bracket. Disconnect the inner cable from the valve lever and remove the valve assembly from the car.

Refitting

18 Refitting is the reverse sequence to removal, but check that the valve lever moves through its full range of travel. If necessary, adjust by repositioning the control outer cable in its clamp or retaining clip.

19 Refill the cooling system as described in Chapter 1.

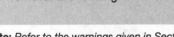

15 Heater assembly – removal and refitting

Note: *Refer to the warnings given in Section 1 of this Chapter before proceeding.*

Recirculating type (early models)

Removal

1 Disconnect the battery negative terminal (refer to *Disconnecting the battery* in the Reference Chapter).

2 Refer to Chapter 1 and drain the cooling system.

3 Make a note of their relative positions, then disconnect the heater motor wiring connectors.

4 Slacken the demister and water hose clips.

5 To prevent water damage to the carpets or upholstery, place polythene sheeting in the appropriate places on the floor and seating.

6 Undo and remove the screws that secure the heater unit to the parcel shelf and carefully lift away the heater unit.

14.15 Heater water valve location on October 1996 models onward

Refitting

7 Refitting is the reverse of removal, but the following additional points should be noted:

   a) *Open the heater tap on the rear of the engine and slowly refill the cooling system as described in Chapter 1.*

   b) *If the heater does not warm up, it is an indication that there is an air lock. To clear, disconnect the return hose from the lower radiator hose and plug the hole. Now extend the return hose to reach the radiator filler neck. Start the engine and observe the flow of water from the return hose. When the bubbles cease, switch off the engine and reconnect the hose.*

Fresh air type (later models)

Removal

8 Disconnect the battery negative terminal (refer to *Disconnecting the battery* in the Reference Chapter).

9 Refer to Chapter 1 and drain the cooling system.

10 On models with a centre console, remove the console and the facia glovebox securing screws. This will enable the console to be moved for greater access to the heater.

11 Carefully pull the demister and air inlet ducts out of the heater unit.

12 To prevent water damage to the carpets or upholstery, place polythene sheeting below the water valve and have a suitable container handy to collect the escaping coolant.

13 Release the clips, disconnect the heater water hoses and allow the coolant to drain into the container. Suitably plug the pipe stubs when the coolant has drained.

14 Undo and remove the two screws that secure the front of the heater to the parcel shelf or lower facia rail.

15 Slacken the nut that secures the rear of the heater to the body mounted bracket **(see illustration)**.

16 Make a note of the electrical connections to the blower motor and switch, then disconnect the wires. On later models, disconnect the wiring multiplug located above the heater.

17 Carefully lift the heater unit from the slotted rear brackets and lift the unit from the car.

Refitting

18 Refitting the heater assembly is the reverse sequence to removal. Refill the cooling system as described in Chapter 1 on completion.

16 Heater assembly – dismantling and reassembly

Recirculating type

1 Remove the heater assembly from the car as described in Section 15.

2 Detach the spring clips securing the demister flap to the cover plate and lift off the flap **(see illustration overleaf)**.

3 Undo and remove the screws securing the cover plate to the cowling and lift off the cover plate and motor assembly.

4 Prise the fan off the motor spindle, undo and remove the retaining nut and washer, then lift away the motor.

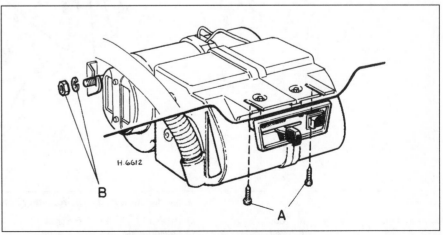

15.15 Fresh air heater attachment points

A Securing screws – heater to parcel shelf
B Nut and spring washer – heater to rear bracket

5 Undo and remove the screws securing the mounting bracket to the cowling, lift off the mounting bracket and withdraw the heater matrix.

6 Clean off all traces of rust and dirt from the matrix, and carefully inspect it for leaks or signs of excessive corrosion. The matrix should be renewed if it is badly corroded or leaking.

7 Reassembly is the reverse of the dismantling procedure.

Fresh air type

First version

8 Remove the heater assembly from the car as described in Section 15.

9 Undo and remove the two screws securing the control panel to the heater casing and lift off the panel **(see illustration opposite)**.

10 Carefully prise off the spring retaining clips and separate the two halves of the casing.

11 Withdraw the motor assembly and then lift out the heater matrix.

12 The two rotors may be removed from the blower motor by releasing the retaining clips and sliding off the rotors.

13 Clean off all traces of rust and dirt from the matrix, and carefully inspect it for leaks or signs of excessive corrosion. The matrix should be renewed if it is badly corroded leaking.

14 Reassembly is the reverse of the dismantling procedure.

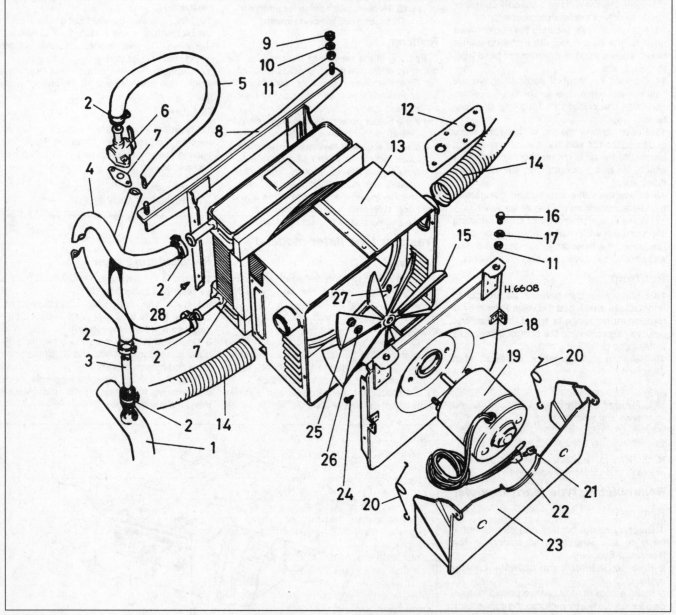

16.2 Exploded view of the recirculatory heater

1 Hose	6 Tap	11 Washer	16 Screw	20 Spring	25 Nut
2 Clip	7 Gasket	12 Sealing plate	17 Washer	21 Connector	26 Washer
3 Connection	8 Mounting bracket	13 Cowling	18 Motor	22 Sleeve	27 Fan retaining
4 Outlet hose	9 Nut	14 Demister hose	mounting	23 Flap	screw
5 Inlet hose	10 Washer	15 Fan	19 Motor	24 Screw	28 Screw

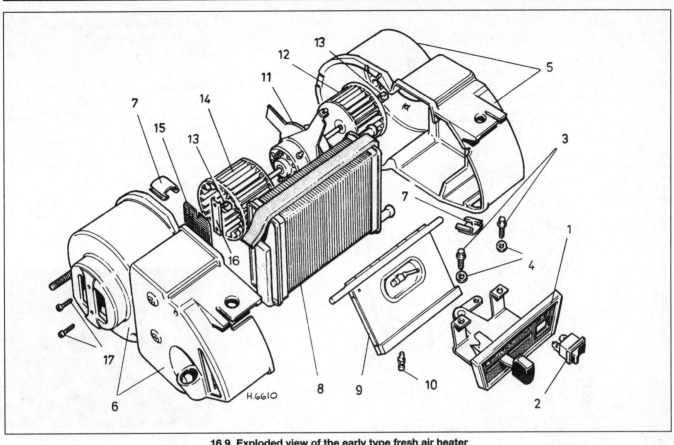

16.9 Exploded view of the early type fresh air heater

1 Control panel	4 Washer	8 Matrix	11 Fan motor	15 Flap valve
2 Fan switch	5 Heater casing	9 Air distribution	12 Air intake fan	16 Valve securing plate
3 Control panel securing	6 Heater casing	flap	13 Retaining clips	17 Valve securing
screws	7 Retaining clip	10 Trunnion screw	14 Recirculating fan	screws

Second version

15 Remove the heater assembly from the car as described in Section 15.

16 Detach the wire from the fan motor at the rear of the fan switch.

17 Undo and remove the three screws and lift off the heater control mounting plate.

18 Undo and remove the nine screws securing the right-hand end cover and lift off the cover.

19 Carefully slide out the heater matrix.

20 Undo and remove the screws securing the fan motor to the main casing, release the motor wires and grommet, and withdraw the motor assembly.

21 If necessary, remove the two fans from the motor spindle.

22 Clean off all traces of rust and dirt from the matrix, and carefully inspect it for leaks or signs of excessive corrosion. The matrix should be renewed if it is badly corroded or leaking. Note that on later models, the diameter and length of the heater inlet hose has been increased. If the heater matrix is to be renewed, it is important that the longer (1005.0 mm) hose is also fitted.

23 Reassembly is the reverse of the dismantling procedure.

Third version – 1985 models onward

24 Remove the heater assembly from the car as described in Section 15.

25 To remove the heater matrix, undo the two screws securing the matrix endplate, and withdraw the endplate, complete with matrix, from the heater casing.

26 Undo two screws each, and lift the pipe stubs off the matrix endplate **(see illustration)**.

27 Clean off the matrix, and carefully inspect it for leakage or corrosion. If it is leaking, renewal is recommended, as repairs are seldom successful unless done professionally.

28 Inspect the condition of the O-rings on the pipe stubs, and renew if necessary.

29 To remove the heater motor and fan, disconnect the motor switch wiring, undo the three screws, and withdraw the motor and fan from the casing **(see illustration overleaf)**.

30 Further dismantling of the motor and fan assembly is not possible, and if renewal is necessary, a complete assembly will be required.

31 Reassembly is the reversal of the dismantling procedure.

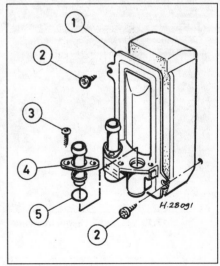

16.26 Later-type heater matrix

1 Matrix endplate
2 Endplate retaining screws
3 Pipe stub retaining screw
4 Pipe stub
5 O-ring

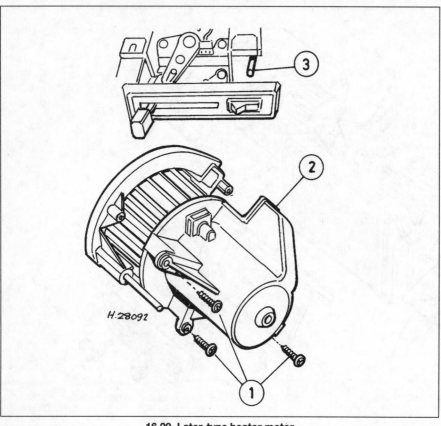

16.29 Later-type heater motor

1 Retaining screws	2 Heater motor	3 Switch wiring connector

17 Fresh air vent assembly – removal and refitting

Removal

1 Unscrew the fresh air vent retaining collar and, where fitted, lift away the binnacle **(see illustrations)**.
2 Turn the air vent anti-clockwise and remove it **(see illustration)**.

Refitting

3 Refitting is the reverse sequence to removal.

17.1a Unscrew the fresh air vent retaining collar . . .

17.1b . . . and lift away the binnacle (where fitted)

17.2 Turn the air vent anti-clockwise to remove

Chapter 4 Part A:
Fuel system – carburettor engines

Contents

Accelerator cable – removal and refitting 3
Accelerator pedal – removal and refitting 4
Air cleaner assembly – removal and refitting 2
Air cleaner element renewal .See Chapter 1
Anti-run-on valve (1990-on Cooper models) – removal and refitting . 17
Carburettor – general information 11
Carburettor – removal and refitting 12
Carburettor (SU HIF44 and HIF38) – fault diagnosis and overhaul . . 14
Carburettor (SU HIF44 and HIF38) – idle speed and mixture
    adjustment 16
Carburettor (SU HS2 and HS4) – fault diagnosis and overhaul 13
Carburettor (SU HS2 and HS4) – idle speed and mixture adjustment . 15

Choke cable – removal and refitting 5
Electric fuel pump – testing, removal and refitting 6
Fuel gauge sender unit – removal and refitting 8
Fuel system components, checks and lubrication . . . . .See Chapter 1
Fuel tank – removal and refitting 9
General information and precautions 1
Inlet manifold – removal and refitting 18
Mechanical fuel pump – testing, removal and refitting 7
Underbody and fuel/brake line check . . . . .See Chapter 1
Underbonnet check for fluid leaks and hose condition . .See Chapter 1
Unleaded petrol – general information and usage 10

Degrees of difficulty

Easy, suitable for novice with little experience	**Fairly easy,** suitable for beginner with some experience	**Fairly difficult,** suitable for competent DIY mechanic	**Difficult,** suitable for experienced DIY mechanic	**Very difficult,** suitable for expert DIY or professional

Specifications

General
System type . . . . Rear-mounted fuel tank, electric or mechanical fuel pump, single or twin SU variable choke (venturi) carburettor

Carburettor data

Mini 850 Saloon and variants, 848 cc (85H)

	1969-72	1972-74	1974-76	1976-on
Carburettor type	SU HS2	SU HS2	SU HS4	SU HS4
Piston spring	Red	Red	Red	Red
Jet size	2.3 mm	2.3 mm	2.3 mm	2.3 mm
Needle:				
Standard	EB	AAV	ABS	ADH
Rich	M	-	-	-
Weak	GG	-	-	-
Idle mixture CO%	-	3.5 to 4.5	3.5 to 4.5	3.0 to 4.5
Idle speed	500 rpm	800 rpm	800 rpm	750 rpm
Fast idle speed	900 rpm	1200 rpm	1200 rpm	1200 rpm

Mini Clubman and Mini 1000 Saloon and variants, 998 cc (99H)

Manual transmission up to 1974:	1969-72	1972-74
Carburettor type	SU HS2	SU HS2
Piston spring	Red	Red
Jet size	2.3 mm	2.3 mm
Needle:		
Standard	GX	AAV
Rich	M	-
Weak	GG	-
Idle mixture CO%	-	3.5 to 4.5
Idle speed	500 rpm	800 rpm
Fast idle speed	900 rpm	1200 rpm

Mini Clubman and Mini 1000 Saloon and variants, 998 cc (99H) (continued)

Automatic transmission up to 1974:
Carburettor type . . . . SU HS4
Piston spring . . . . Red
Jet size . . . . 2.3 mm
Needle:
  Standard . . . . AC
  Rich . . . . MI
  Weak . . . . HA
Idle speed . . . . 650 rpm
Fast idle speed . . . . 1050 rpm

Manual and automatic transmission 1974-89:

	1974-76	1976-78	1978-83	1983-89
Carburettor type	SU HS4	SU HS4	SU HS4	SU HS4
Piston spring	Red	Red	Red	Red
Jet size	2.3 mm	2.3 mm	2.3 mm	2.3 mm
Needle	ABX	ADE	ADE	AAC
Idle mixture CO%	3.5 to 4.5	3.0 to 4.5	3.0	2.5 ± 1.0
Idle speed	750 rpm	750 rpm	750 rpm	750 ± 50 rpm
Fast idle speed	1200 rpm	1250 rpm	1250 rpm	1100 ± 50 rpm

Manual and automatic transmission 1989-on:

	Low compression	High compression
Carburettor type	SU HS4	SU HS4
Piston spring	Red	Red
Jet size	2.3 mm	2.3 mm
Needle	ADE	AAC
Idle mixture CO%	2.5 ± 1.0	2.5 ± 1.0
Idle speed	750 ± 50 rpm	750 ± 50 rpm
Fast idle speed	1100 ± 50 rpm	1100 ± 50 rpm

Mini Clubman 1100, 1098 cc (10H)   1974-on
Carburettor type . . . . SU HS4
Piston spring . . . . Red
Jet size . . . . 2.3 mm
Needle . . . . ABP
Idle mixture CO% . . . . 3.0 to 4.5
Idle speed . . . . 750 rpm
Fast idle speed . . . . 1150 to 1300 rpm

Mini Cooper S Mk III, 1275 cc (12H)   1969-on
Carburettor type . . . . Twin SU HS2
Piston spring . . . . Red
Jet size . . . . 2.3 mm
Needle:
  Standard . . . . M
  Rich AH2
  Weak . . . . EB
Idle speed . . . . 600 rpm
Fast idle speed . . . . 1000 rpm

Mini 1275 GT, 1275 cc (12H)

	1969-72	1972-76	1976-77	1978-on
Carburettor type	SU HS4	SU HS4	SU HS4	SU HS4
Piston spring	Red	Red	Red	Red
Jet size	2.3 mm	2.3 mm	2.3 mm	2.3 mm
Needle:				
Standard	AC	AAV	ABB	AAT
Rich	BQ	-	-	-
Weak	HA	-	-	-
Idle mixture CO%	-	3.5 to 4.5	3.0 to 4.5	3.0 to 4.0
Idle speed	650 rpm	800 rpm	850 rpm	750 rpm
Fast idle speed	1050 rpm	1200 rpm	1300 rpm	1300 rpm

Mini Cooper, 1275 cc (12A)   1990-on
Carburettor type . . . . SU HIF44
Piston spring . . . . Red
Jet size . . . . 2.5 mm
Needle . . . . BFY
Idle mixture CO% . . . . 1.6 to 3.0 (measured at gas sampling pipe)
Idle speed . . . . 900 rpm
Fast idle speed . . . . 1200 ± 50 rpm

Mini Saloon and variants, 1275 cc (12A)	1992-on
Carburettor type	SU HIF38
Piston spring	Red
Jet size	2.3 mm
Needle	AEM
Idle mixture CO%	0.3 to 1.5 (measured at gas sampling pipe)
Idle speed	850 ± 50 rpm
Fast idle speed:	
Manual transmission	1300 rpm
Automatic transmission	1400 rpm

Recommended fuel

Minimum octane rating (see text Section 10):

All pre-1989 models*	Lead replacement petrol (LRP)
1989-on, 998 cc	95 RON unleaded or lead replacement petrol (LRP)
1990-on 1275 cc (12A) models	95 RON unleaded **only**

*Pre-1989 models with a 'Green pack' can be run on 95 RON unleaded petrol – see text for further information.
Note: Models with a catalytic converter **must** be run on unleaded petrol **only**.

Torque wrench setting	Nm	lbf ft
Manifold retaining nuts	20	15

1 General information and precautions

General information

The fuel system comprises a fuel tank, an electric or mechanical fuel pump and a variable choke (venturi) carburettor.

The fuel tank is located in the luggage compartment on Saloon models, and beneath the rear floor on the Estate, Van and Pick-up variants. On Cooper S versions twin fuel tanks are used, these being positioned on either side of the luggage compartment.

A number of the earlier vehicles covered by this manual are equipped with an SU electric fuel pump which is mounted on the left-hand member of the rear subframe. All later Mini models utilise a mechanical fuel pump bolted to the rear of the engine and operated by an eccentric on the camshaft.

A variable choke carburettor of SU manufacture is fitted to all models. Manual transmission versions manufactured up to 1974 utilise a single SU HS2 unit, the exception to this being the Cooper S model which incorporates a twin carburettor installation. Later vehicles are equipped with the larger SU HS4 carburettor, or its derivatives the HIF38 and HIF44. Further information on carburettor types will be found later in this Chapter.

Certain models are fitted with emission control equipment to reduce the level of harmful emissions in the exhaust gases. Information on the exhaust and emission control systems is contained in Part D of this Chapter.

Precautions

⚠️ **Warning: Petrol is extremely flammable – great care must be taken when working on any part of the fuel system. Do not smoke or allow** any naked flames or uncovered light bulbs near the work area. Note that gas-powered domestic appliances with pilot flames, such as heaters, boilers and tumble dryers, also present a fire hazard – bear this in mind if you are working in an area where such appliances are present. Always keep a suitable fire extinguisher close to the work area and familiarise yourself with its operation before starting work. Wear eye protection when working on fuel systems and wash off any fuel spilt on bare skin immediately with soap and water. Note that fuel vapour is just as dangerous as liquid fuel; a vessel that has just been emptied of liquid fuel will still contain vapour and can be potentially explosive. Petrol is a highly dangerous and volatile liquid, and the precautions necessary when handling it cannot be overstressed. Many of the operations described in this Chapter involve the disconnection of fuel lines, which may cause an amount of fuel spillage. Before commencing work, refer to the above Warning and the information in 'Safety first!' at the beginning of this manual.

⚠️ When working with fuel system components, pay particular attention to cleanliness – dirt entering the fuel system may cause blockages which will lead to poor running.

2 Air cleaner assembly – removal and refitting

Cooper S Mk III models

Removal

1 Undo and remove the two wing bolts and washers then disconnect the engine breather pipe and the throttle return spring. Lift off the air cleaner body and recover the two rubber sealing rings from the carburettor flanges.

Refitting

2 Refitting is the reverse sequence to removal but ensure that the rubber sealing rings are in position on the carburettor's flanges.

Cooper models

Removal

3 Unscrew the two nuts securing the air inlet duct to the rocker cover studs, then release the clip and disconnect the duct from the air cleaner (see illustration).

4 Unscrew and remove the nuts and washers, then lift the air cleaner from the carburettor and disconnect the hot air hose. Remove the sealing ring from the carburettor flange.

Refitting

5 Refitting is the reverse sequence to removal but ensure that the rubber sealing ring is in position on the carburettors flange.

2.3 Air cleaner and intake duct fitted to 1990-on Cooper models

1 Intake duct retaining nuts
2 Intake duct
3 Air cleaner mounting nuts

2.8a Remove the single wing nut on early models . . .

2.8b . . . or the two wing bolts on later models

2.9a If the air cleaner is retained by a single wing nut, lift off the top cover and withdraw the air cleaner body from the carburettor

2.9b Recover the sealing ring

Models with catalytic converter

Removal

6 Unscrew the two wing nuts, and lift the air cleaner assembly away from the carburettor. Recover the sealing ring from the carburettor flange.

Refitting

7 Refitting is the reverse sequence to removal but ensure that the rubber sealing ring is in position on the carburettors flange.

All other models

Removal

8 Undo and remove the single wing nut and washer on early models, or the twin wing bolts and washers on later models, securing the air cleaner to the carburettor **(see illustrations)**.
9 If the air cleaner is retained by a single wing nut lift off the air cleaner top cover. Detach the

rocker cover hose, then lift the air cleaner body off the carburettor, tip it up at the front and slide it sideways until it is clear of the long retaining stud and can be lifted away. Recover the sealing ring **(see illustrations)**.
10 If the air cleaner is retained by two wing bolts, detach the hot air duct (where fitted) and then lift the air cleaner body off the carburettor **(see illustrations)**.
11 With the air cleaner removed from the engine, recover the rubber sealing ring if it stayed behind on the carburettor flange.

Refitting

12 Refitting the air cleaner is the reverse sequence to removal. Ensure also that the rubber sealing ring is in position before refitting the air cleaner.
13 If the air cleaner body incorporates an adjustable air inlet spout, this should be positioned adjacent to the exhaust manifold in winter and away from it in summer.

2.10a If the air cleaner is retained by two wing bolts detach the hot air duct . . .

2.10b . . . and lift off the air cleaner body . . .

3 Accelerator cable – removal and refitting

Removal

1 Working in the engine compartment, disconnect the throttle return spring(s) and undo the nut and washer securing the cable to the bolt on the throttle lever **(see illustration)**. On later models the cable is attached to the throttle lever by means of a small clamp with a locking bolt through its centre. Hold the clamp and unscrew the bolt using either 4 BA or 7 BA spanners according to clamp type.
2 Pull the cable through the bolt or clamp and slide it out of the steady bracket on the rocker cover (if fitted).
3 From inside the car, depress the accelerator pedal and withdraw the ferrule on the cable from the slot in the top of the pedal arm.
4 The cable can now be withdrawn through the opening in the bulkhead and into the engine compartment.

Refitting

5 To refit the cable, feed it through the bulkhead and engage the ferrule into the slot on the pedal arm.
6 Now feed the other end of the cable through the brackets on the rocker cover and carburettor, and then insert the inner cable into the slotted bolt or clamp on the throttle lever.
7 Pull the cable through the bolt to take up any slack and then refit the washer and nut or the clamp locking bolt. Avoid straining or distorting the cable as the fixings are tightened.
8 Reconnect the return spring and check that

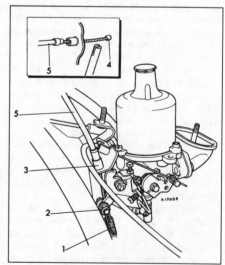

3.1 Accelerator cable attachments

1 *Throttle return spring*
2 *Cable-to-throttle lever securing bolt*
3 *Cable support bracket*
4 *Cable ferrule – pedal end*
5 *Outer cable*

a slight amount of free play exists between the pedal and cable.

9 Start the engine and check the operation of the cable.

4 Accelerator pedal – removal and refitting

Removal

1 Depress the accelerator pedal and detach the accelerator cable ferrule from the slot at the top of the pedal arm.

2 Undo and remove the two bolts securing the pedal assembly to the bulkhead and lift out the pedal.

Refitting

3 Refitting is the reverse sequence to removal.

5 Choke cable – removal and refitting

Removal

Note: On models fitted with a centre console it will be necessary to remove the centre console and console glovebox retaining screws. This will allow the console to be moved slightly to provide access for the following operations.

1 Disconnect the battery negative lead.

2 Refer to Section 2 and remove the air cleaner assembly.

3 Working in the engine compartment, disconnect the choke inner cable from the trunnion screw on the choke linkage and the outer cable from the support bracket (see illustration). Withdraw the complete cable from the carburettor.

4 From inside the car, undo and remove the two screws securing the heater assembly to the front of the parcel shelf. Now lower the heater slightly at the front.

5 Disconnect the heater switch wires from the switch.

6 Undo and remove the two nuts or screws which secure the auxiliary switch panel to the centre of the parcel shelf.

7 Draw the switch panel forward and unscrew the choke cable retaining nut, or extract the retaining clip (according to type) from the rear of the panel.

8 Pull the complete cable through the bulkhead grommet and switch panel, into the passenger compartment. Recover the retaining nut and lockwasher from the end of the cable.

Refitting

9 To refit the cable, slide it through the slot in the switch panel and then place the nut and washer over the cable.

10 Insert the cable through the bulkhead

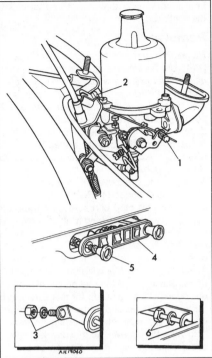

5.3 Choke cable attachments

1 Inner cable-to-linkage attachment
2 Outer cable support bracket
3 Switch panel retaining nuts
4 Switch panel
5 Choke cable
6 Cable retaining nut and washer

grommet and through to the engine compartment.

11 Screw on and fully tighten the choke cable retaining nut or refit the clip then refit the switch panel. Position the word LOCK on the cable knob at the top to ensure correct operation in use. Reconnect the heater switch leads and refit the heater securing screws.

12 Engage the other end of the cable into the support bracket and the inner cable into the trunnion on the choke linkage.

13 Ensure that the choke cable is pushed fully in, ie, in the 'off' position, then tighten the retaining screws on the support bracket and cable trunnion. Ensure that there is 1.5 mm of

6.8 Removing the fuel outlet pipe from the electric pump

free play on the cable before the cable starts to operate the choke linkage.

14 Refit the air cleaner, reconnect the battery and, where applicable, refit the centre console retaining screws.

6 Electric fuel pump – testing, removal and refitting

Note: Observe the precautions in Section 1 before working on any component in the fuel system.

Testing

1 To test the fuel pump, disconnect the fuel supply hose at the top of the carburettor float chamber and insert the end of the hose in a clean glass jar. With the ignition switched on there should be a steady flow of petrol from the end of the hose accompanied by a regular ticking noise from the pump.

⚠️ Warning: Carry out this operation in a well-ventilated area and take great care not to splash fuel onto hot engine components.

2 A rapid irregular ticking noise accompanied by a mixture of fuel and air bubbles flowing from the hose is indicative of an air leak on the suction side of the pump (ie, in the pipe between the pump and fuel tank). This will ultimately lead to fuel starvation and cutting out or misfiring if not corrected.

3 No fuel flow from the supply hose indicates a fault in the pump (perforated diaphragm, dirty contact points, etc), or a break in the electrical supply to the pump. If the electrical supply to the pump is sound but the pump is still not functioning, it should be taken to an auto-electrician for inspection and possible repair, or substituted with an exchange unit. Repair kits are unlikely to still be available from normal sources so an exchange unit may be the only alternative.

Removal

4 Disconnect the battery negative terminal (refer to Disconnecting the battery in the Reference Chapter).

5 Chock the front wheels then jack up the rear of the car and support it securely on axle stands (see Jacking and vehicle support).

6 Working under the car, disconnect the earth lead and the electrical supply wire from their terminals on the pump body.

7 Prepare to squeeze the rubber portion of the petrol pipe leading from the tank with a self-gripping wrench or similar tool, to ensure that the minimum amount of fuel is lost when the inlet pipe is removed from the pump. Plug the end of the pipe with a bolt or metal rod of suitable diameter immediately it is disconnected.

8 Remove the inlet and outlet fuel pipes by undoing the retaining clip screws and easing the pipes off the pump nozzles (see illustration). Remove the vent pipe connector, if fitted, at this stage.

9 Undo and remove the two nuts, bolts and spring washers securing the pump bracket to the subframe and lift off the pump assembly, complete with bracket and clamp.
10 To separate the pump from the bracket, slacken the clamp bolt and slide the pump out of the clamp.

Refitting

11 Refitting is the reverse sequence to removal, bearing in mind the following points:
   a) Arrows on the pump body indicate the correct locations of the inlet and outlet pipes. Ensure that these are fitted correctly and that the pump is installed with the outlet pipe at the top.
   b) Ensure that the electrical leads, particularly the earth, are clean and that a correct connection is made.

7	Mechanical fuel pump – testing, removal and refitting

Note: Observe the precautions in Section 1 before working on any component in the fuel system.

Testing

1 To test the fuel pump, disconnect the fuel supply hose at the top of the carburettor float chamber and insert the end of the hose in a clean glass jar. With an assistant cranking the engine on the starter, regular spurts of fuel should be ejected as the engine turns.

> ⚠ **Warning: Carry out this operation in a well-ventilated area and take great care not to splash fuel onto hot engine components.**

2 If the pump does not operate satisfactorily, it should be renewed. The AUF 700 series pump fitted to early models may be dismantled for inspection, but repair kits are unlikely to still be available from normal sources. The AUF 800 series pump fitted to later models is a sealed unit and cannot be dismantled.

Removal

Note: The fuel pump used on later models (1985-on) is different in appearance to those used previously, but is fully interchangeable. A modified kickdown rod will be required if a new type pump is fitted to older vehicles with automatic transmission. Details of the rod fitment should be obtained from your dealer.
3 Disconnect the battery negative terminal (refer to Disconnecting the battery in the Reference Chapter).
4 To provide greater access, remove the air cleaner, as described in Section 2.
5 Slacken the pipe clip screw on the outlet pipe connection and draw it off. Have a small container handy to collect what little fuel may drain from the pipe.
6 In all Saloon models, if the tank is more than half full, the fuel will drain from the tank under gravity when the fuel pump inlet pipe is disconnected, so provide for this situation by fitting a suitable clip or bung in the pipe if necessary. On all other models the tank is below the pump level, so this problem will not occur. Slacken the pipe clip screw on the inlet pipe connection and draw it off.
7 Slacken the two nuts which hold the pump to the crankcase on two studs through the lower body.
8 Ease the pump away from the crankcase slightly and release the insulating block and its two sealing gaskets. If they are stuck, carefully prise them off the crankcase using a knife or thin screwdriver. Now lift off the pump, insulating block and gaskets.

Refitting

9 Refitting the pump is the reverse sequence to removal bearing in mind the following points:
   a) Ensure that the mating faces of the pump and crankcase are thoroughly clean and dry.

   b) Ensure that the correct insulator block is used according to pump type. The insulator block fitted to the 700 series pump is different from the insulator block fitted to 800 series and AZX series pumps (see illustration). The 700 series pump requires an insulator block with a large inner aperture, whereas the 800 series and AZX pumps require an insulator block with a small aperture in order to retain the pump lever pivot. If the wrong insulator block is fitted, there is a possibility of the pivot and lever dropping into the sump/transmission.
   c) Use new sealing gaskets on either side of the insulating block but make sure that the original thickness is maintained otherwise the pump operation may be affected.

8	Fuel gauge sender unit – removal and refitting

Note: Observe the precautions in Section 1 before working on any component in the fuel system.

Removal

Saloon models

1 Disconnect the battery negative terminal (refer to Disconnecting the battery in the Reference Chapter). Disconnect the fuel gauge wires from their attachments to the sender unit mounted in the side of the tank (see illustration).
2 On early models, unscrew the screws which hold the gauge unit to the tank carefully, and lift the complete unit away, ensuring that the float lever is not bent or damaged in the process.
3 On later models, using crossed screwdrivers, remove the fuel gauge sender unit by turning the locking ring through 30° and lifting

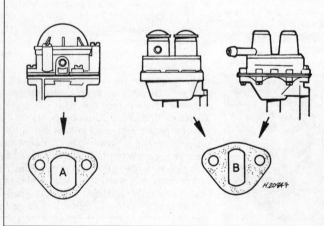

7.9 Mechanical fuel pump insulator block types

A 700 series type   *B 800 and AZX series type*

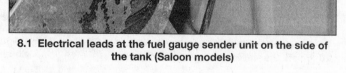

8.1 Electrical leads at the fuel gauge sender unit on the side of the tank (Saloon models)

away. Carefully lift the unit from the tank, ensuring that the float lever is not bent or damaged in the process.

Estate, Van and Pick-up models

4 Refer to Section 9 and remove the fuel tank from the car.
5 Removal and refitting of the sender unit now follows the procedure described for Saloon models.

Refitting

6 Refitting the unit is the reverse sequence to removal. To ensure a fuel-tight joint, scrape both the tank and sender unit mating flanges clean, and always use a new joint gasket and a suitable gasket sealer.

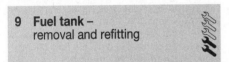

9 Fuel tank –
removal and refitting

Note: *Observe the precautions in Section 1 before working on any component in the fuel system.*

Saloon models except Cooper S

Removal

1 Before the tank can be removed, it must be drained of as much fuel as possible. To avoid the dangers and complications of fuel handling and storage, it is advisable to carry out this operation with the tank almost empty. Any fuel remaining can be drained as follows.
2 Disconnect the battery negative terminal (refer to *Disconnecting the battery* in the Reference Chapter).
3 Using a hand pump or syphon inserted through the filler neck, remove any remaining fuel from the bottom of the tank. **Note:** *A number of earlier models were fitted with a fuel tank incorporating a combined drain plug and tube. Access to this is from below the car, using a long box spanner.* In all cases carry out the draining or syphoning operation in a well-ventilated area, never in a garage or over an inspection pit.
4 Remove the spare wheel from its location in the luggage compartment.
5 Disconnect the wiring from the fuel gauge sender unit located on the side of the tank **(see illustration)**.
6 If the car is fitted with an electric fuel pump, slacken the clip and detach the fuel inlet hose from the pump inlet nozzle. Collect any remaining fuel in a suitable container.
7 When the tank is empty, slacken the clip and detach the fuel hose from the front of the tank.
8 Detach the fuel tank breather pipe and remove the filler cap.
9 Undo and remove the tank securing strap bolt and carefully manoeuvre the fuel tank from the luggage compartment.
10 If the tank is contaminated with sediment or water, remove the fuel gauge sender unit as described in Section 8 and swill the tank out

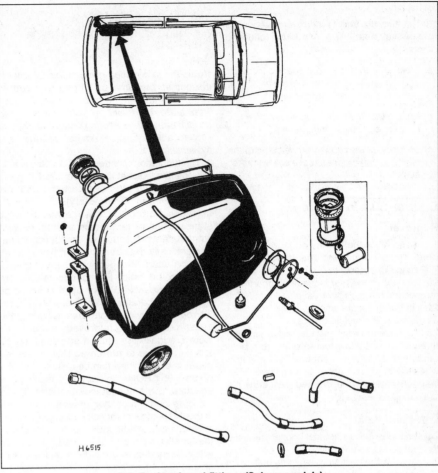

9.5 Fuel tank and fittings (Saloon models)

with clean fuel. If the tank is damaged or corroded it should be renewed. However, in certain cases it may be possible to have small leaks or minor damage repaired. Seek the advice of a Rover dealer or suitable specialist concerning tank repair.

Refitting

11 Refitting is the reverse sequence to removal.

Estate, Van and Pick-up models

12 Disconnect the battery negative terminal (refer to *Disconnecting the battery* in the Reference Chapter).
13 Chock the front wheels then jack up the rear of the car and support it securely on axle stands (see *Jacking and vehicle support*).
14 Remove the tank filler cap then, from underneath the car, undo and remove the drain plug, allowing the fuel to drain into a suitable container. Do this in a well-ventilated area, not in a garage or over an inspection pit. When drained, refit the drain plug and washer securely.
15 Disconnect the fuel outlet pipe and the fuel gauge wires from their connections on the sender unit on the side of the tank **(see illustration)**.

16 Undo and remove the six screws which hold the tank in place and remove the tank. It is helpful if a jack is positioned under the tank as the retaining screws are removed so that the tank does not drop out under its own weight. It may also be found easier to lower the tank slightly on the jack before disconnecting the sender unit leads, as with the tank half removed they are more accessible.
17 Refer to the information contained in paragraph 10.

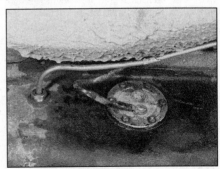

9.15 Fuel tank outlet pipe and fuel gauge sender unit (Estate, Van and Pick-up models)

Refitting

18 Refitting the tank is the reverse sequence to removal bearing in mind the following points:

a) *Make sure that the nylon spacers located at each retaining screw hole are in position before refitting the tank.*

b) *Ensure that the drain plug and washer are in place and securely tightened.*

c) *Ensure that the rubber ferrule beneath the filler cap makes an effective seal with the body.*

Cooper S twin fuel tanks

Removal

19 Disconnect the battery negative terminal (refer to *Disconnecting the battery* in the Reference Chapter).
20 Working in the rear luggage compartment remove the trimmed floor panel.
21 Lift out the spare wheel.
22 Remove the fuel filler caps.
23 Unscrew the left-hand fuel tank drain plug three turns and allow fuel to drain from both tanks into a suitable container. Do this in a well-ventilated area, not in a garage or over an inspection pit. When drained, resecure the drain plug.

Left-hand tank

24 Disconnect the electrical connectors from the fuel gauge sender unit.
25 Remove the tank strap securing bolt.
26 Detach the flexible pipe and the vent pipe from the fuel tank.
27 Carefully ease the fuel tank towards the centre of the luggage compartment and lift away.
28 Refer to the information contained in paragraph 10.

Right-hand tank

29 Completely remove the battery, referring to Chapter 5A if necessary.
30 Remove the tank strap securing bolt.
31 Detach the flexible hose from the left-hand tank.
32 Move the tank slightly from its mountings, taking extreme care not to damage the flexible fuel pipes.
33 The fuel tank will still contain a small amount of petrol which should be drained into a small container when the flexible fuel pipe is disconnected.
34 Disconnect the flexible fuel pipe.
35 Finally detach the vent pipe from the tank and lift the tank from the car.
36 Refer to the information contained in paragraph 10.

Refitting

37 Refitting either fuel tank is the reverse sequence to removal. Make sure that the seal around the drain plug housing is water-tight.

10 Unleaded petrol – general information and usage

Note: *The information given in this Chapter is correct at the time of writing. If updated information is thought to be required, check with a Rover dealer. If travelling abroad, consult one of the motoring organisations (or a similar authority) for advice on the fuel available.*

1 The fuel recommended by Rover is given in the Specifications at the start of this Chapter.
2 Models built up to October 1988 (as delivered from the factory) cannot use unleaded petrol; the valve seats fitted as standard will suffer serious premature wear without the protection of the petrol's lead content. Only 'lead-replacement petrol' (LRP) may be used, irrespective of the engine's compression ratio. Exceptions to this are those engines which have been modified as described in paragraph 5 below.
3 From October 1988 onwards (ie, during the 1989 model year), improved components were gradually introduced at the factory to enable engines to run on 95 RON unleaded petrol; these vehicles can be identified by the green '95 RON unleaded petrol' label attached to the bonnet lock platform. These vehicles can use either unleaded or LRP, without modification or risk of damage.
4 If you have a 1989 model and suspect that the label has become detached, check first with a Rover dealer whether the vehicle can or cannot use unleaded petrol; the VIN (Vehicle Identification Number) will be required for positive identification. Note, however, that as a general rule, 998 cc engines which can use unleaded petrol have the engine serial number prefix '99HE'.
5 As leaded petrol is no longer gererally available, a substitute known as 'lead-replacement petrol' (LRP) is now sold at the pumps. If your car cannot be run on unleaded petrol, there are few courses of action:

a) *Use lead-replacement petrol (LRP) instead of leaded 4-star. No ignition timing adjustment should be necessary.*

b) *Use a petrol additive. Some ignition timing adjustment may also be necessary.*

c) *Conversion kits are available (consisting basically of an exchange cylinder head known as 'Green Packs'), through Rover dealers. Any vehicle which has had such a conversion will have the letter U stamped between the engine prefix and the start of the serial number, and can use unleaded petrol.* **Note:** *Apart from any adjustment made during the fitting of a 'Green Pack' no alteration should be made to the ignition timing or carburation settings.*

6 If the ignition timing needs to be retarded to eliminate pinking, refer to the procedures contained in Chapter 5B.
7 Models equipped with a catalytic converter must be run on **unleaded petrol only.**

11 Carburettor – general information

SU HS2 and HS4

The variable choke (venturi) SU HS2 and HS4 carburettors are relatively simple instruments and are basically the same irrespective of type. They differ from most other carburettors in that, instead of having a number of various sized fixed jets for different conditions, only one variable jet is fitted to deal with all possible conditions.

The carburettor comprises four main assemblies; these are the carburettor body, the piston and dashpot assembly, the jet assembly and the float chamber. Fuel is carried from the float chamber to the base of the jet head by a nylon pipe, the float chamber being secured to the carburettor body by a horizontally positioned bolt and spacing washer.

The operation of the carburettor is as follows. Air passing rapidly through the carburettor creates a slight vacuum or depression over the jet, causing fuel to be drawn into the air stream, thus forming the fuel/air mixture. The amount of fuel drawn from the jet depends on the position of the tapered carburettor needle. This moves up or down the jet orifice according to engine load or throttle opening, thus effectively altering the size of the jet. This allows the right amount of fuel to be delivered for the prevailing road conditions.

The position of the tapered needle in the jet is determined by engine vacuum. The shank of the needle is held at its top end in a piston, which slides up and down the dashpot, in response to the degree of manifold vacuum. This is directly controlled by the throttle. The piston is necessary so that the depression over the jet needed to draw fuel into the air stream can be kept approximately constant. At slow engine speeds, the air entering the carburettor would not be travelling fast enough to create sufficient vacuum to draw fuel from the jet. By allowing the piston to partially restrict the opening through the carburettor, the incoming air is speeded up, causing an adequate depression over the jet.

With the throttle fully open, the full effect of inlet manifold vacuum is felt by the piston, which has an air bleed into the carburettor venturi on the outside of the throttle. This causes the piston to rise fully, bringing the needle with it. With the throttle partially closed, only slight inlet manifold vacuum is felt by the piston (although on the engine side of the throttle, the vacuum is now greater), and the piston only rises slightly.

To prevent piston flutter, and to give a richer mixture when the accelerator is suddenly depressed, an oil damper and light spring are located inside the dashpot.

For cold starting, when fuel enrichment is

necessary and very small amounts of air are drawn into the carburettor, actuation of the choke control causes the jet head to be lowered, thus effectively increasing the jet size.

The only portion of the piston assembly to come into contact with the piston chamber or dashpot is the central piston rod. All the other parts of the piston assembly, including the lower choke portion, have sufficient clearances to prevent any direct metal-to-metal contact, which is essential if the carburettor is to work properly.

The correct level of the petrol in the carburettor is determined by the level of the float in the float chamber. When the level is correct, the float rises and, by means of a lever resting on top of it, closes the needle valve in the cover of the float chamber. This closes off the supply of fuel from the pump. When the level in the float chamber drops, as fuel is used in the carburettor, the float sinks. As it does, the float needle comes away from its seat so allowing more fuel to enter the float chamber and restoring the correct level.

SU HIF44 and HIF38

The SU HIF44 and HIF38 carburettors are fitted to 1990-on Cooper models, and 1992-on 1275 cc models with open-loop catalytic converter respectively. These carburettors operate in a similar way to the SU HS2 and HS4 instruments described previously, but the float chamber has been incorporated into the main body of the carburettor, and a bi-metallic strip is fitted to the jet adjusting (mixture) screw mechanism; that is in order to compensate for the varying fuel densities which result from changes in fuel temperature.

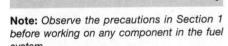

12 Carburettor – removal and refitting

Note: *Observe the precautions in Section 1 before working on any component in the fuel system.*

SU HS2 and HS4

Removal

1 Disconnect the battery negative terminal (refer to *Disconnecting the battery* in the Reference Chapter).
2 Remove the air cleaner assembly as described in Section 2.
3 Disconnect the distributor vacuum advance pipe from the carburettor (where fitted).
4 Slacken the retaining clip screw and withdraw the fuel inlet pipe from the top of the float chamber. Plug the disconnected pipe with a bolt or metal rod of suitable diameter.
5 Refer to Sections 3 and 5 and disconnect the accelerator and choke cables from the carburettor linkages.
6 Detach the throttle return spring from the

bracket on the exhaust manifold clamp. On Cooper S models detach the throttle and throttle linkage return springs from the heat shield. On automatic transmission models detach the governor control rod fork end from the throttle lever.
7 Detach the engine breather hose from the carburettor (where fitted).
8 Undo and remove the two nuts which secure the carburettor(s) to the inlet manifold studs and recover the spring washers.
9 Lift the carburettor carefully off the inlet manifold **(see illustration)**. If twin carburettors are being removed, lift off both carburettors together to avoid damaging the linkages that join the two carburettor spindles. These can be removed after the carburettors are lifted clear of the manifold studs.

Refitting

10 Refitting the carburettor(s) is the reverse sequence to removal, noting the following points:
   a) *Ensure that all mating surfaces are clean and dry, and use new gaskets.*
   b) *When refitting twin carburettors, ensure that the linkages joining the two spindles are in position, and that the operating forks are engaged in the slots on the carburettor spindles.*
   c) *Tighten the carburettor nuts evenly and progressively, to avoid possible distortion of the mounting flange.*
   d) *Refit the accelerator and choke cables with reference to Sections 3 and 5.*
   e) *Adjust the idle speed and mixture with reference to Section 15.*

SU HIF44 and HIF38

Removal

11 Disconnect the battery negative terminal (refer to *Disconnecting the battery* in the Reference Chapter).
12 Remove the air cleaner assembly as described in Section 2.
13 On Cooper models, remove the carburettor heat shield.
14 On models with an open-loop catalytic converter, release the retaining clip and disconnect the charcoal canister hose from the side of the carburettor.
15 On all models, disconnect the accelerator and choke cables from the carburettor linkages as described in Sections 3 and 5. Free the accelerator outer cable from its bracket, then release the retaining clip and detach the choke cable from the carburettor.
16 Disconnect the vacuum pipe from the top of carburettor mounting flange.
17 Release the retaining clip and disconnect the fuel supply hose from the carburettor. Plug the hose end to minimise fuel loss.
18 Release the retaining clip and disconnect the vent pipe from the float chamber.
19 Undo the mounting nuts and withdraw the carburettor from the inlet manifold, together with the throttle cable bracket, spacer and gaskets.

Refitting

20 Refitting is the reverse sequence to removal, noting the following points.
   a) *Ensure that all mating surfaces are clean and dry, and use new gaskets.*
   b) *Tighten the carburettor nuts evenly and progressively, to avoid possible distortion of the mounting flange.*
   c) *Refit the accelerator and choke cables with reference to Sections 3 and 5.*
   d) *Adjust the idle speed and mixture with reference to Section 16.*

13 Carburettor (SU HS2 and HS4) – fault diagnosis and overhaul

Fault diagnosis

1 If a carburettor fault is suspected, always check first that the ignition timing is correctly set, that the spark plugs are in good condition and correctly gapped, that the accelerator and choke cables are correctly adjusted, and that the air cleaner filter element is clean; refer to the relevant Sections of Chapter 1, Chapter 5B or this Chapter. If the engine is running very roughly, first check the valve clearances as described in Chapter 2A, then check the compression pressures as described in Chapter 2A.
2 If careful checking of all the above produces no improvement, the carburettor must be removed for cleaning and overhaul.
3 Prior to overhaul, check the availability of component parts before starting work; note that most sealing washers, screws and gaskets are available in kits, as are some of the major sub-assemblies.

Overhaul

Note: *Observe the precautions in Section 1 before working on any component in the fuel system.*
4 The SU carburettor is a straightforward unit to dismantle and service, but at the same time it is a delicate unit and clumsy handling can cause damage. In particular, it is easy to knock the finely tapering needle out of true, and the greatest care should be taken to keep all the parts associated with the dashpot in a

12.9 Removing the SU HS2 carburettor from the manifold

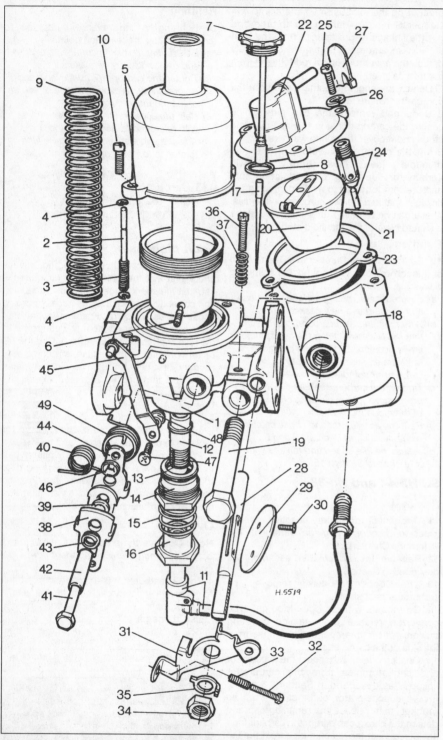

H.5519

the small sunken retaining screw in the side of the piston and lift out the needle. On later types equipped with a spring-loaded needle, recover the guide collar from the needle, and the spring from the piston, after removing the needle assembly.

9 Undo and remove the three retaining screws and lift off the float chamber cover and gasket. The float may be released from the cover by gently tapping out the float hinge pin. The fuel cut-off needle valve can now be withdrawn from its seat in the cover and the needle seat unscrewed if required.

10 Unscrew the union nut securing the nylon fuel pipe to the base of the float chamber and carefully withdraw the pipe. Note the position of the gland, ferrule and rubber sealing washer on the end of the pipe and make sure that the rubber washer has not been left behind in the float chamber as the pipe is withdrawn. If so, hook it out carefully with a small screwdriver.

11 If there is a tamperproof cap in position around the jet adjusting nut at the base of the carburettor, prise it apart with a screwdriver and discard it.

12 Release the jet link lever return spring from the cam lever on the linkage.

13 Undo and remove the small screw or release the clip that secures the jet link arm to the jet. Move the jet link arm to one side and

safe place and scrupulously clean. Prepare a clean and uncluttered working area before starting the dismantling, and have some small containers handy to store the small, easily-lost parts.

5 Begin by removing the carburettor(s) from the car as described in Section 12. Thoroughly clean the outside of the carburettor in paraffin or a suitable solvent and wipe dry.

6 Unscrew the piston damper assembly and

remove it from the top of the dashpot **(see illustrations)**.

7 Mark the base of the dashpot and carburettor body to ensure that on reassembly the dashpot is refitted in the same position. Now undo and remove the securing screws and lift off the dashpot.

8 Next lift off the piston spring and then carefully withdraw the piston and needle assembly from the carburettor body. Undo

13.6b Exploded view of the SU HS4 carburettor

1 Body	36 Washer
2 Piston lifting pin	37 Throttle return lever*
3 Spring	37a Throttle return lever
4 Sealing washer	38 Progressive throttle (snail cam)
5 Plain washer	
6 Circlip	39 Fast idle screw*
7 Dashpot	39a Fast idle screw and spring
8 Screw	
9 Piston	40 Lockwasher
10 Spring	41 Nut
11 Needle	42 Jet assembly – Capstat type
12 Needle tension spring	43 Sleeve nut
13 Needle guide collar	44 Washer
14 Locking screw	45 Gland
15 Piston damper	46 Ferrule
16 Identification tag	47 Jet bearing
17 Idle speed adjusting screw and O-ring*	48 Jet locating nut
	49 Jet adjustment nut and spring
18 Idle speed adjusting screw and spring	50 Rod link and pick-up lever
	51 Spring clip
19 Gaskets	52a Jet assembly
20 Insulator block	53a Pick-up lever non-Capstat type
21 Float chamber and spacer	
	53b Link
22 Gasket	53c Screw
23 Float	54 Pivot bolt
24 Hinge pin	55 Pivot bolt tube – inner
25 Needle and seat	
26 Float chamber cover	56 Pivot bolt tube – outer
	57 Distance washer
27 Baffle plate	58 Cam lever
28 Screw	59 Cam lever spring
29 Spring washer	60 Pick-up lever spring
30 Bolt	
31 Spring washer	61 Piston guide
32 Plain washer	62 Screw
33 Throttle spindle	
34 Throttle disc	
35 Screw	

Used with sealed adjustment carburettors

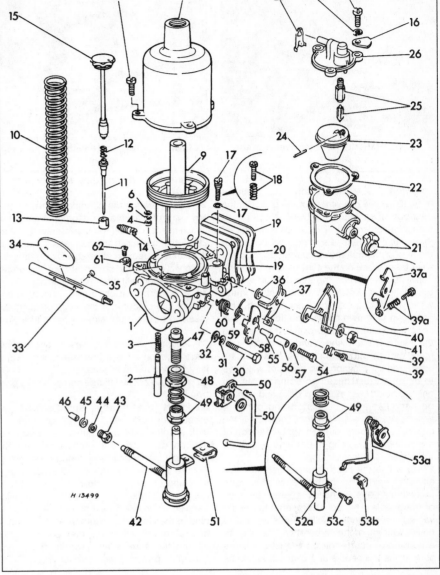

H 13499

withdraw the jet assembly, complete with fuel pipe from the jet housing.

14 It is not normally necessary to carry out any further dismantling of the SU carburettor. However, if the throttle spindle, jet housing, or float chamber are worn, damaged, or in any way suspect, the remainder of the carburettor may be dismantled as described below.

15 Bend back the small tab washer and then undo and remove the nut securing the throttle lever to the spindle. Lift off the lever.

16 Straighten the splayed ends of the two throttle disc retaining screws and then mark the position of the disc in relation to the spindle. Undo and remove the two screws, turn the disc to the fully open position and slide the disc out of the slot in the spindle. Note that new throttle disc retaining screws must be used when reassembling.

17 The spindle can now be removed from the carburettor body.

18 To remove the choke linkage undo the retaining pivot bolt and lift it off complete with linkage.

19 To dismantle the jet housing, first undo and remove the jet adjusting nut and lock spring. Next undo and remove the jet bearing locknut and withdraw the bearing.

20 The float chamber can be lifted off after unscrewing the retaining through-bolt. Recover the float chamber spacer, where fitted.

21 The carburettor is now completely dismantled with the exception of the piston lifting pin (omitted on later carburettors). The pin may be removed by prising off the small upper retaining circlip and lifting off the pin and spring.

22 Thoroughly clean all the carburettor components and dry thoroughly.

23 Carefully examine the throttle spindle and throttle disc for wear or distortion. If excessive wear is apparent on the spindle or spindle

bushes in the carburettor body, air will enter the carburettor, altering the mixture strength and causing uneven running. The throttle spindle is obtainable separately, but if the bushes are worn, a complete carburettor body will normally have to be obtained.

24 Closely inspect the carburettor needle. If this has not been running centrally in the jet orifice then the needle will have a tiny ridge worn on it. If a ridge can be seen then the needle must be renewed. SU carburettor needles are made to very fine tolerances and should a ridge be apparent no attempt should be made to rub the ridge down with emery paper.

25 If the needle is worn, it is likely that the jet will also be worn. If this is the case, also renew the jet. Also inspect the outside of the jet head where it bears against the jet bearing. Wear can take place here due to the action of the choke control moving the jet up and down in the jet bearing.

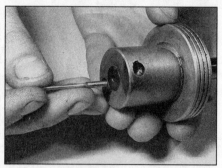

13.35a Refit the fixed jet needle to the piston . . .

13.35b . . . and secure with the retaining screw

26 The most critical components of the SU carburettor are the piston and dashpot assembly. Free movement of the piston in the dashpot is essential for the carburettor to function satisfactorily. The piston is machined to very fine tolerances so that it will not touch the side of the dashpot or carburettor body. If wear takes place on the centre guide tube or if deposits build up on the internal surfaces of the dashpot, the piston will come into contact with the side of the dashpot and will bind. This condition is known as piston sticking. If this condition cannot be improved after cleaning the inside of the dashpot and the piston with metal polish (harsh abrasives must not be used), then the piston and dashpot will have to be renewed. These two components are only obtainable as matched pairs and cannot be interchanged. The piston and dashpot assembly are in a satisfactory condition if the piston, having been pushed right to the top of the dashpot, will drop under its own weight without any trace of binding.

27 Examine the float chamber needle valve and seat next. After high mileage, it is quite likely that a ridge will have formed on the face of the needle. This could prevent the needle valve from shutting off the fuel supply and cause flooding of the carburettor. This is quite a common occurrence on SU carburettors and unless the needle and seat appear to be

in perfect condition, they should both be renewed.

28 Finally, check the condition of the float. If any signs of cracking or distortion are evident, which may allow fuel to enter, renew the float.

29 If the carburettor has been completely dismantled, begin reassembly by refitting the piston lifting pin and spring into the carburettor body and then refit the retaining circlip.

30 Place the float chamber in position and secure it in place, with the long retaining bolt inserted through the side of the carburettor body.

31 Refit the jet bearing, washer and locknut finger-tight only. Do not refit the lock spring or jet adjusting nut at this stage.

32 Refit the choke linkage and retaining pivot bolt.

33 Insert the throttle spindle into the carburettor body with the countersunk holes in the spindle facing outwards. Insert the throttle disc into the spindle, noting the assembly markings made during dismantling. Secure the disc to the spindle using new retaining screws, but do not tighten them. Snap the spindle open and shut to centralise the disc and make sure that the disc does not bind in the carburettor bore in any position. If necessary reposition the disc slightly. Now tighten the screws and spread their ends enough to prevent them from turning.

34 Slide the spacing washer and throttle lever onto the spindle, followed by the tab washer and retaining nut. Tighten the nut and bend over the tab washer.

35 On carburettors with a fixed jet needle, insert the needle into the piston, ensuring that the shoulder on the shank of the needle is flush with the underside of the piston. Refit and fully tighten the sunken retaining screw **(see illustrations)**.

36 On carburettors equipped with a spring-loaded needle, fit the spring and guide collar to the needle and insert this assembly into the piston. Position the guide collar so that it is flush with the underside of the piston and position the needle so that the small etch mark is between the two piston transfer holes. Secure the assembly with the sunken retaining screw **(see illustration)**.

37 If the jet housing has been removed, it will now be necessary to centralise the jet as follows.

38 With the jet bearing, washer and locknut in position as described in paragraph 31, refit the jet adjusting nut, without the lock spring, and screw it up as far as it will go. Now slide the jet assembly into the jet housing.

39 Carefully refit the piston and needle assembly to the carburettor body, followed by the spring and dashpot. Align the previously made marks on the dashpot and carburettor body and then refit the securing screws.

40 Slacken the jet bearing locknut and hold the piston down using a pencil inserted through the damper opening. Now tighten the jet bearing locknut.

41 Lift the piston and allow it to fall under its own weight. A definite metallic click should be heard, as the piston falls and contacts the bridge in the carburettor body.

42 Now fully lower the adjusting nut and note whether the piston still falls freely. If not, slacken the jet bearing locknut and repeat the centring procedure. It may be necessary to carry out the centring operation several times, until the piston will fall freely with the adjusting nut at the top and bottom of its travel.

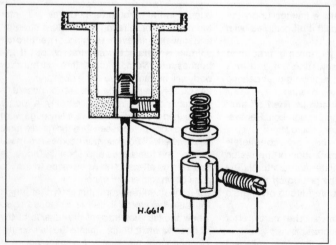

13.36 The spring-loaded needle assembly fitted to the later SU HS4 carburettors

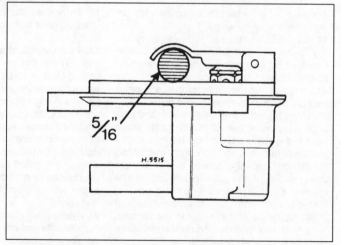

13.46 Method of setting the correct clearance of the float lever – early carburettors

43 With the jet correctly centralised, slide out the jet assembly and unscrew the adjusting nut. Now place the lock spring in position and refit the adjusting nut and jet assembly. Secure the jet link arm to the jet with the screw or retaining clip.

44 The flexible jet fuel supply tube can now be refitted to the base of the float chamber. Ensure that the small rubber sealing washer, nut and gland are in position on the tube and that there is at least 5.0 mm of pipe protruding through the washer. Push the tube into the float chamber and tighten the union nut.

45 Refit the fuel cut-off needle and seat to the float chamber cover. Place the float in position and tap in the float hinge pin until equal amounts of the pin are protruding either side of the mounting lugs.

46 On early carburettors equipped with a brass float, invert the float chamber cover so that the needle valve is closed. It should now just be possible to place a 5/16 inch (8.0 mm) diameter bar parallel to the float hinge pin and in the centre of the float chamber cover, without fouling the float. If the bar lifts the float or if the float stands clear of the bar, bend the float lever very slightly until the clearance is correct **(see illustration)**.

47 Later carburettors fitted with plastic floats incorporate either a plain steel needle or a spring-loaded needle enclosed in a plastic sheath. The adjustment procedure for the plain steel needle type is the same as described in paragraph 46. Float level adjustment for spring-loaded needles is as follows.

48 Invert the float chamber cover so that the needle valve is closed but the spring is not compressed. The gap between the float and the flange on the float chamber cover, at the centre of the cover, should be between 3.18 mm and 4.76 mm **(see illustration)**. If the gap is incorrect, bend the float lever slightly until the specified gap is obtained. In the case of floats having a moulded plastic hinge, increase or decrease the washer thickness under the needle seat to achieve the desired float level height.

49 Place a new gasket in position on the float chamber, refit the cover and secure it with the three retaining screws.

50 Fill the carburettor piston damper with the correct grade of oil, until the level is 13.0 mm above the top of the hollow piston rod. Now refit the damper plunger.

51 To obtain an initial jet setting and to allow the engine to be started, screw the jet adjusting nut up until the jet is flush with the bridge in the carburettor body. Now screw the nut down two complete turns on non-sealed carburettors and three complete turns on sealed units. **Note:** *The sealed type carburettors are identified by the throttle adjusting screw which is recessed within the carburettor body.*

52 The carburettor can now be refitted to the car as described in Section 12 and the idle speed and mixture adjustments carried out as described in Section 15.

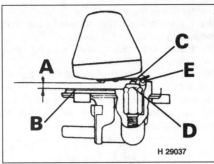

13.48 Method of setting the correct clearance of the float lever – later carburettors

A = 3.18 to 4.76 mm
B Machined lip
C Float lever adjustment point
D Float needle and seat assembly
E Lever hinge pin

14 Carburettor (SU HIF44 and HIF38) – fault diagnosis and overhaul

Fault diagnosis

1 Refer to Section 13.

Overhaul

2 Remove the carburettor from the car as described in Section 12, then clean the exterior surfaces thoroughly and wipe dry.

3 Mark the float chamber cover in relation to the carburettor body. Remove the screws, and withdraw the cover and sealing ring **(see illustration overleaf)**.

4 Unscrew and remove the mixture screw and spring, and withdraw the seal.

5 Unscrew the jet retaining screw, and remove the spring.

6 Withdraw the jet and bi-metal lever assembly. Disengage the lever from the jet.

7 Unscrew and remove the float pivot and seal.

8 Withdraw the float and the needle valve.

9 Unscrew and remove the needle valve seat.

10 Unscrew and remove the piston damper, and drain the oil.

11 Mark the dashpot in relation to the carburettor body. Remove the screws and withdraw the dashpot together with the piston.

12 Prise the clip from the top of the piston rod, then withdraw the piston and spring from the dashpot.

13 Unscrew the needle retaining grub screw. Remove the needle, guide and spring from the piston.

14 From underneath the main body, unscrew the jet bearing nut and withdraw the bearing.

15 Note how the spring is attached to the fast idle cam lever, then bend back the locktabs, unscrew the nut and remove the washer.

16 Hold the return spring against the main body, and use a screwdriver to prise the cam lever from the end of the cold start spindle. Remove the spring.

17 Remove the end cover and spindle seat.

18 Remove the two screws and withdraw the retaining plate, cold start body and gasket.

19 Remove the O-ring from the end of the cold start spindle, and withdraw the spindle from the main body. Remove the cold start seal.

20 Dismantling of the throttle spindle is not recommended, unless the components are damaged or excessively worn. If they are, first note how the return spring is attached to the throttle lever.

21 Mark the throttle valve in relation to the spindle and main body.

22 Remove the throttle valve screws while supporting the spindle with a block of wood if necessary.

23 Open the throttle and withdraw the valve disc.

24 Remove any burrs from the spindle screw holes with a fine file.

25 Bend back the locktabs and unscrew the spindle nut. Remove the lockwasher, plain washer, throttle lever, and return spring.

26 From the opposite end of the spindle, loosen the nut and bolt, and remove the throttle damper lever.

27 Check the threaded end of the spindle and main body in relation to each other, then withdraw the spindle. Remove the two seals.

28 Clean all the components dry thoroughly. Examine each item for damage and excessive wear. In particular, check the throttle spindle and bearings for wear. If excessive, renewal of the spindle may be sufficient, but if the bearings are worn, it may be necessary to renew the complete carburettor, as new bearings are not always available. Check the needle valve and seating for excessive ridging. Examine the main body for cracks, and for security of the brass fittings and piston key. Check the tapered needle, jet and jet bearing for wear. Shake the float, and listen for any trapped fuel which may have entered through a small crack or fracture. Renew the components as necessary, and obtain a complete set of gaskets and seals, and two new throttle valve screws if necessary.

29 Clean the inside of the dashpot and the periphery of the piston with methylated spirit. Do not use any form of abrasive. Lubricate the piston rod with engine oil, and insert it into the dashpot. Hold the two components horizontal, and spin the piston in several positions. The piston must spin freely, without touching the sides of the dashpot.

30 Commence reassembly by fitting the throttle spindle and two seals to the main body. The seals must be slightly recessed in their housings.

31 Locate the return spring and throttle lever on the end of the spindle, and fit the plain washer, lockwasher, and nut. Tighten the nut while holding the lever, and bend over the locktabs to lock.

32 Engage the return spring with the throttle lever and main body, and tension the spring.

33 Fit the throttle valve disc to the spindle in its original position, and insert the new screws, tightening them loosely (coat the threads with thread-locking fluid).

34 Open and close the throttle several times to settle the disc, then tighten the screws while supporting the spindle on a block of wood. Using a small chisel, spread the ends of the screws to lock them.

35 Locate the throttle damper lever loosely on the end of the spindle.

36 Locate the cold start seal in the main body with the cut-out uppermost.

37 Insert the cold start spindle (hole uppermost), and fit the O-ring.

38 Fit the cold start body with the cut-out uppermost, and the retaining plate with the slotted flange facing the throttle spindle. Use a new gasket, then insert and tighten the retaining screws.

39 Fit the spindle seat and end cover, followed by the spring, cam lever, lockwasher, and nut. Make sure that the spring is correctly engaged, then tighten the nut and bend over the locktabs to lock.

40 Insert the jet bearing and nut, and tighten the nut.

41 Connect the bi-metal lever with the fuel jet, making sure that the jet head moves freely in the cut-out.

42 Insert the mixture screw and seal into the main body. Fit the jet to the bearing, and at the same time engage the slot in the bi-metal lever with the small diameter of the mixture screw.

43 Insert the jet retaining screw with the spring, and tighten the screw.

44 Adjust the mixture screw so that the top of the jet is flush with the venturi bridge.

45 Insert and tighten the needle valve seat, and with the carburettor inverted, insert the needle valve.

46 Position the float, then insert the pivot and seal through the body and float, and tighten.

47 To check the float level adjustment, hold the carburettor inverted with the float keeping the needle valve shut. Using a straight edge and feeler blade, check that the centre portion of the float is 1.0 ± 0.5 mm below the surface of the float chamber face **(see illustration)**. If not, bend the tab which contacts the needle valve as necessary.

14.3 Exploded view of the SU HIF carburettor

1 Piston damper	21 Return spring
2 Dashpot	22 Dust cap
3 Piston spring and clip	23 Seal
	24 Retaining plate
4 Piston	25 Cold start body
5 Needle retaining screw	26 O-ring
	27 Cold start spindle
6 Spring	28 Cold start seal
7 Jet needle	29 Main body
8 Guide	30 Jet bearing
9 Lifting pin	31 Jet bearing nut
10 Lifting pin and circlip	32 Jet assembly
	33 Bi-metallic jet lever
11 Spindle seal	34 Jet (mixture) adjusting screw and seal
12 Throttle spindle	
13 Throttle valve and screw	
14 Return springs	35 Jet retaining screw and spring
15 Throttle lever and progressive throttle cam	
	36 Float
16 Fast idle adjustment screw	37 Float pivot and seal
17 Idle speed adjustment screw	38 Needle valve
	39 Needle valve seat
18 Spindle nuts and tab washers	40 Fuel strainer
	41 Float chamber cover
19 Return spring lever	42 Cover seal
20 Mixture control lever and fast idle cam	43 Screw and spring washer

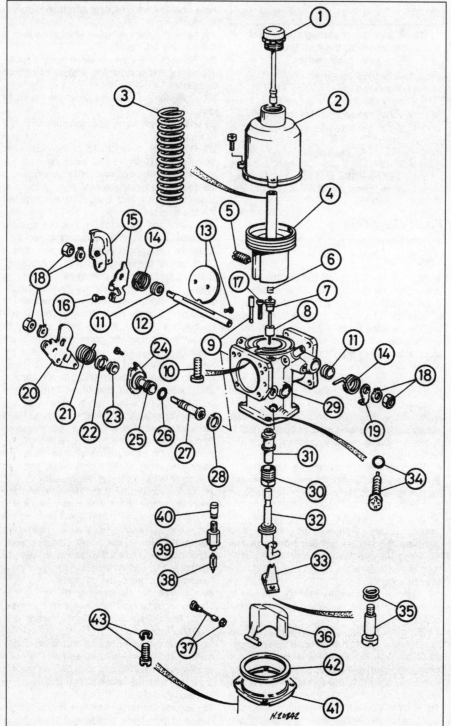

H.20842

48 Fit the float chamber cover in its original position, together with a new sealing ring. Tighten the screws in diagonal sequence.

49 Insert the spring, needle, and guide into the piston with the guide etch marks facing the dashpot transfer holes, and with the bottom face of the guide flush with the bottom face of the piston (**see illustration 13.36**).

50 Insert and tighten the guide retaining grub screw.

51 Lower the piston and needle assembly into the main body, at the same time engaging the slot with the piston key.

52 Locate the spring over the piston rod.

53 Hold the dashpot directly over the piston with its location mark aligned with the mark on the body, then lower it over the spring and piston rod. It is important not to tension the spring by twisting the dashpot.

54 Insert and tighten the dashpot retaining screws. Lift the piston with a finger, then release it and check that it returns to the venturi bridge without any assistance. If not, it may be necessary to loosen the retaining screws and slightly reposition the dashpot.

55 Hold the piston fully up, then fit the clip to the top of the piston rod.

56 Pour the specified type of oil into the top of the dashpot until the level is 13.0 mm above the top of the hollow piston rod. Refit and tighten the piston damper.

57 The carburettor can now be refitted to the car as described in Section 12 and the idle speed and mixture adjustments carried out as described in Section 16.

---

15 Carburettor
(SU HS2 and HS4) – idle speed and mixture adjustment

Preliminary information

1 Three adjustments are possible on the SU carburettor. These are the engine idling speed, fast idling speed and mixture strength. The mixture strength is particularly important as the initial setting, carried out with the engine idling, determines the mixture strength throughout the entire engine speed range. A good indication as to whether carburettor adjustment is necessary can be gained by checking the colour of the exhaust tailpipe and listening to the note of the exhaust at idling speed. If the tailpipe is black and the engine appears to be hunting, it is quite likely that the mixture is too rich. If the exhaust is light grey or white in appearance, accompanied by a rhythmic puffing sound, this would indicate a weak mixture. Ideally, the exhaust should be a medium grey colour and emit a steady even drone. The colour of the spark plugs will also give a good indication as to the mixture strength and general engine condition (see Chapter 1). These checks should only be carried out after a good run of about 5 to 10 miles. Idling in city traffic and stop/start motoring is bound to

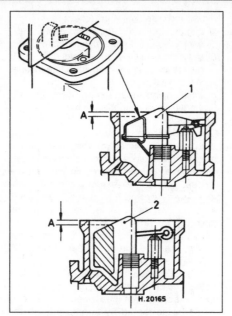

14.47 SU HIF carburettor float level adjustment A

    1 Type 1 float   A = 1.0 ± 0.5 mm
    2 Type 2 float

cause excessively dark exhaust pipe and spark plug deposits.

2 Before carrying out any adjustments to the carburettor, ensure that the ignition system is

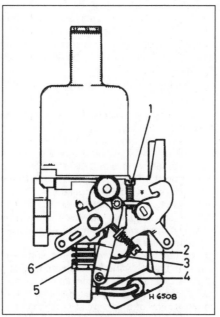

15.7a Carburettor adjustment points – SU HS2

    1 Throttle adjusting screw
    2 Fast idle adjusting screw
    3 Float chamber bolt
    4 Jet link securing screw
    5 Jet adjusting nut
    6 Jet locknut

in good condition, that the spark plugs, contact breaker points and ignition timing settings are correct, and that the engine is at normal operating temperature. Check also that the carburettor dashpot oil damper is topped-up to the correct level with the specified grade of oil.

3 Depending on year of manufacture either a sealed or non-sealed carburettor may be fitted. Early models are equipped with the non-sealed type, identified by the throttle and fast idle adjusting screws which are clearly visible and retained by a tension spring or locknut. On the sealed carburettors the throttle adjusting screw is located in a recessed hole in the carburettor body and may be covered by a small circular metal cap.

4 Carburettor adjustment is carried out as follows, according to type.

Single carburettor adjustment

Non-sealed type

5 Remove the air cleaner assembly as described in Section 2.

6 Connect a tachometer to the engine (if one is not already fitted to the car), following the manufacturer's instructions. If your ears can attune to slight changes in engine rpm or to alterations of the exhaust note, then it is possible to carry out the adjustments without the use of a tachometer.

7 Set the engine idling speed by turning the throttle adjusting screw until the specified idling speed is obtained (**see illustrations**). **Note:** *If the throttle adjusting screw is secured by a locknut, slacken the locknut before turning the adjusting screw and leave it slackened until all the carburettor adjustments have been completed.*

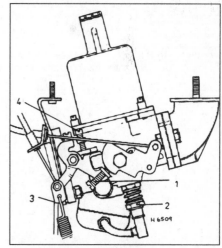

15.7b Carburettor adjustment points – SU HS4

    1 Fast idle adjusting screw
    2 Jet adjusting nut
    3 Governor control rod (automatic transmission)
    4 Throttle adjusting screw

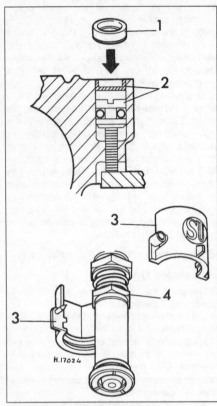

15.15 The tamperproof caps fitted to the later type sealed carburettors

1 *Throttle adjusting screw cap*
2 *Throttle adjusting screw showing cap in position*
3 *Jet adjusting nut seals*
4 *Jet adjusting nut*

8 To check the mixture strength, press the piston lifting pin (omitted on later models) on the side of the carburettor upwards, against light spring resistance, until it comes into contact with the piston. Now press it up a further 1.0 mm and listen to the engine speed.

15.27 Throttle and choke linkage (Cooper S models)

1 *Throttle spindle operating arms*
2 *Choke spindle operating arms*

This will indicate one of the following:
a) *If the speed of the engine increases appreciably, the mixture is too rich.*
b) *If the engine speed immediately decreases or the engine stalls, the mixture is too weak.*
c) *If the engine speed remains constant or increases very slightly, the mixture is correct.*

9 To enrich the mixture, rotate the jet adjusting nut located at the base of the carburettor in a clockwise direction as viewed from above, ie, downward. To weaken the mixture, rotate the jet adjusting nut anti-clockwise as viewed from above, ie, upward, while at the same time pushing the jet assembly upwards against the nut. When altering the mixture strength, only turn the nut one flat at a time and check the mixture with the lifting pin each time.

10 It is quite likely that there will be a slight increase or decrease in engine rpm, after the mixture adjustment has been made. This should be corrected by turning the throttle adjusting screw, until the specified idling speed is again obtained.

11 With the engine idling at the specified speed and the mixture correctly adjusted, check the fast idle adjustment as follows.

12 Rotate the choke linkage on the side of the carburettor, to the point where the linkage just starts to lower the jet. Hold the linkage in this position and rotate the fast idle adjustment screw until the specified engine fast idle speed is obtained.

13 When all adjustments are complete, disconnect the tachometer, refit the air cleaner and road test the car, carrying out any small adjustments that may be necessary on the road.

Sealed type without catalytic converter

14 Remove the air cleaner assembly as described in Section 2.

15 If the tamperproof seals are still in position over the throttle adjusting screw and mixture adjusting nut, remove and discard them **(see illustration)**. The seal over the throttle adjusting screw can be hooked out of the recess using a small screwdriver. The seal on the jet adjusting nut can be removed by prising it open with a screwdriver and then lifting away the two halves.

16 Connect a tachometer to the engine (if one is not already fitted to the car), following the manufacturer's instructions. If your ears can attune to slight changes in engine rpm or to alterations of the exhaust note, then it is possible to carry out the adjustments without the use of a tachometer.

17 Set the engine idling speed, by turning the throttle adjusting screw until the specified idling speed is obtained.

18 Turn the jet adjusting nut located at the base of the carburettor in a clockwise or anti-clockwise direction, one flat at a time, until the fastest possible engine speed consistent with

even running is obtained. Turning the nut clockwise as viewed from above, ie, downward, enriches the mixture. Turning the nut anti-clockwise as viewed from above, ie, upward, weakens the mixture.

19 It is quite likely that there will be a slight increase or decrease in engine rpm after the mixture adjustment has been made. This should be corrected by turning the throttle adjusting screw until the specified idling speed is again obtained.

20 The remainder of the adjustment procedure is the same as described previously for non-sealed carburettors in paragraphs 11 to 13.

Sealed type with catalytic converter

21 On 998 cc models equipped with an open-loop catalytic converter, the idle speed and mixture adjustments can be carried out as described previously in paragraphs 14 to 20, but using an exhaust gas analyser to check the CO content of the exhaust gas.

22 The gas analyser should be used in accordance with the maker's instructions and connected to the take-off point at the top of the exhaust system front pipe. To do this, it will first be necessary to jack up the front of the car and support it on axle stands.

23 Unscrew the threaded plug from the front pipe, and screw the gas sampling pipe adapter into the threaded hole; the adapter can be obtained from a Rover dealer. The gas analyser should then be connected to the end of the sampling pipe.

24 On completion, unscrew the sampling pipe, then refit the threaded plug and tighten it securely.

Twin carburettor adjustment

25 Before adjusting the mixture strength on models fitted with twin carburettors, it is necessary to ensure that the volume of air passing through each carburettor is the same. This is done as follows.

26 Remove the air cleaner assembly as described in Section 2.

27 Slacken the two clamp bolts on the throttle spindle operating arms and the two clamp bolts on the choke spindle operating arms **(see illustration)**.

28 Start the engine without depressing the accelerator and allow it to idle.

29 Using a proprietary balancing meter, in accordance with the manufacturer's instructions, balance the carburettors by altering the throttle adjusting screws until the airflow through both carburettors is the same.

30 Alternatively, use a length of small bore tubing, such as heater hose, approximately 500 mm long, to compare the intensity of the inlet hiss on both carburettors. Turn the throttle adjusting screws until the hiss sounds the same in both carburettors. It should be noted that this method is not really recommended, as it tends to be somewhat less accurate, and certainly more difficult, than using a balancing meter.

31 When the two carburettors are balanced, bring the engine idling speed back to the specified rpm by turning both throttle adjusting screws by equal amounts.

32 Now tighten the two clamp bolts, on the throttle spindle operating arms, making sure that a slight clearance exists between the peg and the lower edge of the fork. Ensure also that the arms are positioned in such a way that both carburettor throttles open at the same time when the accelerator pedal is depressed. If necessary, reposition one of the arms slightly to achieve this condition.

33 Now adjust the mixture strength for each carburettor using the procedure described in paragraphs 8 and 9.

34 If the idling speed requires adjustment after setting the mixture, turn both throttle adjusting screws by an equal amount in the desired direction.

35 The choke spindle operating arms can now be positioned and tightened using the method described previously for the throttle operating arms.

36 Finally, adjust the fast idle speed as follows.

37 Pull out the choke control knob or operate the linkage by hand, until the linkage just starts to lower the jets. Hold the linkage in this position and turn the fast idle adjusting screws, on both carburettors, until the specified fast idle speed is obtained and both carburettors are passing the same volume of air.

38 Adjustment of the carburettors is now complete. Refit the air cleaner and carry out a thorough road test.

---

16 Carburettor (SU HIF44 and HIF38) – idle speed and mixture adjustment

Note: *A tachometer and accurately calibrated exhaust gas analyser (CO meter) will be required for the following adjustments. If these instruments are not available, the car should be taken to a Rover dealer for the work to be carried out.*

Preliminary information

1 Refer to Section 15, paragraphs 1 and 2, then check the following items:
  a) *The crankcase ventilation hoses are secure and in good condition (Chapter 4D).*
  b) *The choke cable is correctly adjusted (Section 5).*
  c) *The accelerator cable is correctly adjusted (Section 3).*
  d) *The fast idle screw is correctly adjusted, so that there is clearance between the screw and the cam with the choke control off.*

2 Run the engine to normal operating temperature. Driving the car on the road for approximately 4 miles will achieve this.

3 The adjustments should be completed within two minutes of the engine reaching normal temperature, *before* the electric cooling fan operates. If the adjustments are not completed within the two minutes or if the cooling fan operates, wait for the fan to switch off, then increase the engine speed to 2000 rpm for approximately 30 seconds. The adjustments can then be resumed.

4 To adjust the mixture setting on Cooper models, it will be necessary to unscrew the plug from the gas sampling pipe which is situated on the right-hand end of the cylinder head, and connect an exhaust gas analyser to the end of the pipe **(see illustration)**. On all other models, the exhaust gas analyser should be connected to the take-off point on the exhaust system front pipe, using a gas sampling pipe adapter (which can be obtained from a Rover dealer). To fit the pipe, jack up the front of the car and support it on axle stands (see *Jacking and vehicle support*). Unscrew the threaded plug from the exhaust system front pipe, screw the gas sampling pipe into the threaded hole, and connect the exhaust gas analyser to the end of the sampling pipe.

Adjustment

Note: *If it has been noted that the engine idle speed has become erratic, and a high CO% reading is obtained during the following procedure, it is likely that the carburettor needle valve is faulty. Rover have produced a modified needle valve kit to overcome this problem. Refer to your Rover dealer for further information.*

5 Check that all electrical components are switched off.

6 Connect a tachometer to the engine in accordance with the maker's instructions.

7 Allow the engine to idle, and check that the idle speed is as given in the Specifications. If adjustment is necessary, turn the screw located on the dashpot base as necessary **(see illustration)**.

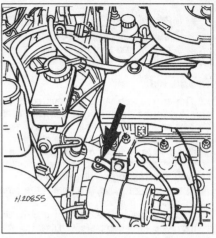

16.4 Gas sampling pipe location (arrowed) on 1990-on Cooper models

8 With the exhaust gas analyser connected as described in paragraph 4, and the engine idling, check that the mixture CO% is as given in the Specifications. If not, turn the adjustment screw located on the side of the carburettor body. Turn the screw by small increments, and allow the reading to stabilise between adjustments.

9 If necessary, re-adjust the idling speed as described in paragraph 7.

10 Check the fast idling speed by pulling out the choke until the arrow on the carburettor fast idle cam is aligned with the adjustment screw. If adjustment is necessary, turn the fast idle screw.

11 Stop the engine and disconnect the tachometer and exhaust gas analyser. On Cooper models, refit the plug to the sampling pipe. On all other models, remove the sampling pipe, refit and tighten the threaded plug, and lower the vehicle to the ground.

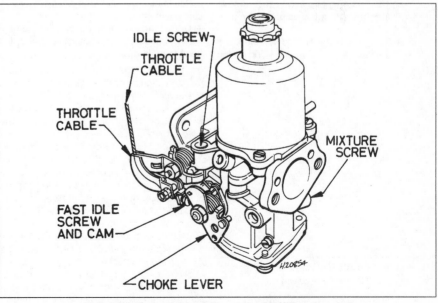

16.7 Adjusting point location on the SU HIF carburettor

17 Anti-run-on valve (1990-on Cooper models) – removal and refitting

Removal

1 The anti-run-on valve is mounted onto a bracket in the right-hand rear corner of the engine compartment. Its function is to prevent the engine running-on ('dieseling') after the ignition is switched off. If the valve is disconnected or damaged, it may prevent the engine from running or idling smoothly.
2 To remove the valve, disconnect the wiring connector and both hoses from it.
3 Unscrew the bracket retaining bolt, and remove the valve complete with its bracket.

Refitting

4 Refitting is a reverse of removal, ensuring that the wiring connector and hoses are securely connected.

18 Inlet manifold – removal and refitting

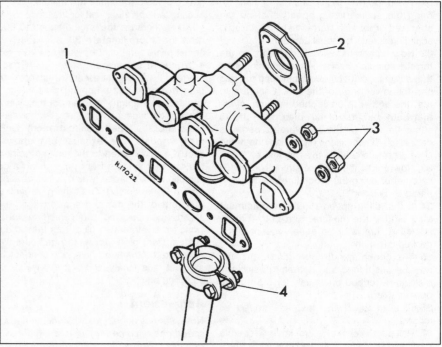

18.7 Inlet and exhaust manifold assembly

1 Manifold and gasket	3 Retaining nuts
2 Carburettor insulating block	4 Manifold-to-front pipe clamp

Removal

Note: *On vehicles fitted with emission control equipment it will be necessary to remove certain additional fittings, hoses and brackets to provide access to the inlet manifold. The items requiring removal will be obvious after a visual inspection, and full information regarding their removal will be found in Part D of this Chapter.*

1 Refer to Section 12 and remove the carburettor(s) from the inlet manifold.
2 On models fitted with a brake servo, slacken the retaining clip screw and remove the vacuum hose from the union on the inlet manifold.
3 If working on Cooper S models, undo and remove the nuts, large flat washers and spring washers securing the manifold to the cylinder head. Lift off the manifold. On all other models proceed as follows.
4 Firmly apply the handbrake, then jack up the front of the car and support it securely on axle stands (see *Jacking and vehicle support*).
5 From underneath the car, undo and remove the nut and bolt securing the exhaust front pipe support strap to the transmission bracket.
6 Undo and remove the two bolts and nuts securing the two halves of the exhaust manifold clamp to the front pipe. Lift away the clamp assembly.
7 Undo and remove the six nuts and flat washers securing the manifold to the cylinder head **(see illustration)**.

8 Lift off the hot air shroud, where fitted, and then slide the inlet and exhaust manifold assembly off the studs and withdraw it from the engine. Recover the manifold gasket.

Refitting

9 Refitting is the reverse sequence to removal bearing in mind the following points:

a) *Ensure that the mating surfaces of the manifold and cylinder head are clean, and use a new gasket.*
b) *Refit the exhaust manifold-to-front pipe clamp before tightening the front pipe support strap bolt.*

Chapter 4 Part B:
Fuel system – single-point fuel injection engines

Contents

Accelerator cable – removal, refitting and adjustment 4
Accelerator pedal – removal and refitting 5
Air cleaner air temperature control –information, testing and
   component renewal 3
Air cleaner assembly – removal and refitting 2
Air cleaner element renewal . . . . .See Chapter 1
Fuel filter renewal . . . . .See Chapter 1
Fuel gauge sender unit – removal and refitting 10
Fuel injection system – testing and adjustment 12
Fuel injection system components – removal and refitting 13
Fuel pump – removal and refitting 9

Fuel system – depressurisation 6
Fuel system – pressure check 7
Fuel tank – removal and refitting 8
General information and precautions 1
Inlet manifold – removal and refitting 15
Inlet manifold PTC heater – general information and component
   renewal 14
Underbody and fuel/brake line check . . . . .See Chapter 1
Underbonnet check for fluid leaks and hose condition . .See Chapter 1
Unleaded petrol – general information and usage 11

Degrees of difficulty

Easy, suitable for novice with little experience	Fairly easy, suitable for beginner with some experience	Fairly difficult, suitable for competent DIY mechanic 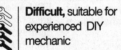	Difficult, suitable for experienced DIY mechanic	Very difficult, suitable for expert DIY or professional

Specifications

General

System type . . . .   Rover/Motorola Modular Engine Management System, using ECU-controlled single-point injection (MEMS-Spi) and speed/density method of airflow measurement

Fuel system data

Fuel pump type . . . .   Electric, immersed in fuel tank
Fuel pump regulated pressure . . . .   1.0 bar ± 4%
Injector and pressure regulator unit . . . .   JZX 3300
Throttle potentiometer voltage:
   Throttle closed . . . .   0 to 1 volt
   Throttle open . . . .   4 to 5 volts
Idle speed – nominal value, for reference only . . . .   850 ± 25 rpm
Idle mixture CO . . . .   0.5% maximum

Recommended fuel

Minimum octane rating . . . .   95 RON unleaded **only**

Torque wrench settings

	Nm	lbf ft
Brake servo vacuum hose union bolt	50	37
Fuel pump nuts	9	7
Fuel tank breather two-way valve nuts	9	7
Injector housing fuel pipe adapters	24	18
Injector housing fuel pipe union nuts	24	18
Injector housing screws	5	4
Inlet air temperature sensor	7	5
Manifold retaining nuts	22	16
Throttle body assembly nuts	10	7

1 General information and precautions

General information

The fuel system consists of a fuel tank, situated at the rear of the car, with an electric fuel pump immersed in it, a fuel filter, fuel feed and return lines, and the throttle body assembly (which incorporates the single fuel injector and the fuel pressure regulator), as well as the engine management electronic control unit (ECU) and the various sensors, electrical components and related wiring. The air cleaner contains a disposable paper filter element, and incorporates a flap valve air temperature control system, which allows cold air (from the outside of the car) and warm air (heated by the exhaust manifold) to enter the air cleaner in the correct proportions.

To reduce emissions and to improve driveability when the engine is cold, the inlet manifold is heated by the cooling system coolant and by an electric pre-heater system. Mixture enrichment for cold starting is a pre-programmed function of the system.

The ECU fully controls both the ignition and fuel injection systems, integrating the two in a complete engine management system; refer to Chapter 5B for information on the ignition side of the system.

The Rover/Motorola Modular Engine Management System uses ECU-controlled single-point injection (MEMS-Spi) and the speed/density method of airflow measurement. The whole system is best explained if considered as three sub-systems; the fuel delivery, air metering and electrical control systems.

The fuel delivery system incorporates the fuel tank with an electric fuel pump (immersed in a swirl pot to prevent aeration of the fuel) inside it. When the ignition is switched on, the pump is supplied with current via the fuel pump relay, under the control of the ECU; the pump feeds petrol via a non-return valve (to prevent fuel draining out of the system components and back to the tank when the pump is not working) to the fuel filter, and from the filter to the injector. Fuel pressure is controlled by the pressure regulator, which allows excess fuel to return to the tank swirl pot, where a venturi causes the returning fuel to draw cool fuel from the tank into the swirl pot. In the event of sudden deceleration (ie, an accident) an inertia switch cuts off the power to the pump, so that the risk of fire from fuel spraying out of broken fuel lines under pressure is minimised.

The air metering system includes the inlet air temperature control system and the air cleaner, but the main components are in the throttle body assembly. This incorporates the injector (which sprays fuel onto the back of the throttle disc), the throttle potentiometer (which is linked to the throttle disc spindle, and sends the ECU information on the rate of throttle opening by transmitting a varying voltage), and the stepper motor (which is controlled by the ECU, and operates the throttle disc spindle lever via a cam and pushrod to provide idle speed control).

The electrical control system consists of the ECU, with all the sensors that provide it with information, and the actuators by which it controls the whole system's operation. The ECU's manifold absolute pressure (MAP) sensor is connected, by hoses and a fuel (vapour) trap mounted on the bulkhead, to the inlet manifold; variations in manifold pressure are converted into graduated electrical signals, which are used by the ECU to determine the load on the engine. The inlet air temperature sensor is self-explanatory; the crankshaft position sensor provides the engine speed and crankshaft position; the coolant temperature sensor supplies the engine temperature, the accelerator pedal switch tells the ECU when the accelerator is closed; the throttle potentiometer is explained above, and the function of the lambda sensor is explained in Part D of this Chapter. The ECU also senses battery voltage, and can adjust the injector pulses width and use the stepper motor to increase the idle speed and, therefore, the alternator output if it is too low. Short-circuit protection and diagnostic capabilities are incorporated; the ECU can both receive and transmit information via the diagnostic connector, thus permitting engine diagnosis and tuning by Rover diagnostic equipment. If either the coolant temperature sensor, the inlet air temperature sensor or the manifold absolute pressure sensor circuits should fail, the ECU has a back-up facility which assumes a value corresponding to a coolant temperature of 60ºC, an inlet air temperature of 35ºC and an engine load based on the engine speed and throttle position; these are used to implement a back-up air/fuel mixture ratio.

All these signals are compared by the ECU, using digital techniques, with set values pre-programmed (mapped) into its memory. Based on this information, the ECU selects fuel and ignition settings appropriate to those values, and controls the ignition HT coil (varying the ignition timing as required), the fuel injector (varying its pulse width – the length of time the injector is held open – to provide a richer or weaker mixture, as appropriate), the stepper motor (controlling the idle and fast idle speeds), the fuel pump relay (controlling the fuel delivery), the manifold heater relay (controlling the inlet manifold pre-heater system) and the main relay, the purge control valve, and the lambda sensor and relay, accordingly. The mixture, idle speed and ignition timing are constantly varied by the ECU to provide the best settings for cranking, starting and engine warm-up (with either a hot or cold engine), idle, cruising, and acceleration. A rev-limiter circuit is built into the ECU, which switches off the injector earth (ie, the fuel supply) if the engine speed exceeds the recommended limit. The injector earth is also switched off on the overrun, to improve fuel economy and reduce exhaust emissions.

The ECU idle control is an adaptive system; it learns the engine load and wear characteristics over a period of time, and adjusts the idle speed to suit. If the ECU is renewed, or one from another car is fitted, it will take a short period of normal driving for the new ECU to learn the engine's characteristics and restore full idle control.

Precautions

Warning: Petrol is extremely flammable – great care must be taken when working on any part of the fuel system. Do not smoke or allow any naked flames or uncovered light bulbs near the work area. Note that gas-powered domestic appliances with pilot flames, such as heaters, boilers and tumble dryers, also present a fire hazard – bear this in mind if you are working in an area where such appliances are present. Always keep a suitable fire extinguisher close to the work area and familiarise yourself with its operation before starting work. Wear eye protection when working on fuel systems and wash off any fuel spilt on bare skin immediately with soap and water. Note that fuel vapour is just as dangerous as liquid fuel; a vessel that has just been emptied of liquid fuel will still contain vapour and can be potentially explosive. Petrol is a highly dangerous and volatile liquid, and the precautions necessary when handling it cannot be overstressed.

Many of the operations described in this Chapter involve the disconnection of fuel lines, which may cause an amount of fuel spillage. Before commencing work, refer to the above Warning and the information in 'Safety first!' at the beginning of this manual.

When working with fuel system components, pay particular attention to cleanliness – dirt entering the fuel system may cause blockages which will lead to poor running.

Note: *Residual pressure will remain in the fuel lines long after the vehicle was last used, when disconnecting any fuel line, it will be necessary to depressurise the fuel system as described in Section 6.*

2.1 Undo the three retaining screws . . .

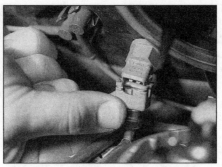

2.2a . . . then lift up the air cleaner assembly, and disconnect the intake air temperature sensor wiring connector . . .

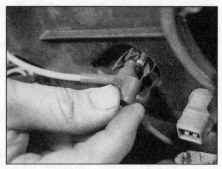

2.2b . . . and the thermac valve vacuum pipe

2 Air cleaner assembly – removal and refitting

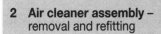

Removal

1 Slacken and remove the three screws securing the air cleaner assembly to the throttle body **(see illustration)**.
2 Lift up the assembly, then disconnect the wiring connector from the air temperature sensor, and the inlet manifold vacuum pipe from the thermac valve **(see illustrations)**.
3 Remove the air cleaner assembly, and recover its sealing ring from the throttle body flange.

Refitting

4 Refitting is the reverse sequence to removal, ensuring that the sealing ring is correctly located on the throttle body flange.

3 Air cleaner air temperature control – information, testing and component renewal

General information

1 The system is controlled by a thermac valve/switch mounted in the air cleaner assembly; when the engine is started from cold, the switch is closed, to allow inlet manifold depression to act on the air temperature control valve in the inlet duct. This raises a vacuum diaphragm in the valve assembly, and draws a flap valve across the cold air inlet, thus allowing only (warmed) air from the exhaust manifold to enter the air cleaner.
2 As the temperature of the exhaust-warmed air in the air cleaner rises, a bi-metallic strip in the thermac switch deforms, opening the switch to shut off the depression in the air temperature control valve assembly. The flap is lowered gradually across the hot air inlet until, when the engine is fully warmed-up to normal operating temperature, only cold air from the front of the inlet duct is entering the air cleaner.

Testing

3 To check the system, allow the engine to cool down completely, then unclip the inlet duct from the air cleaner body; the flap valve in the duct should be securely seated across the hot air inlet. Start the engine; the flap should immediately rise to close off the cold air inlet, and should then lower steadily as the engine warms-up, until it is eventually seated across the hot air inlet again.
4 To check the thermac switch, disconnect the vacuum pipe from the control valve when the engine is running, and place a finger over the pipe end. When the engine is cold, full inlet manifold vacuum should be present in the pipe, and when the engine is at normal operating temperature, there should be no vacuum in the pipe.
5 To check the air temperature control valve, unclip the inlet duct from the air cleaner body; the flap valve should be securely seated across the hot air inlet. Disconnect the vacuum pipe, and suck hard at the control valve stub; the flap should rise to shut off the cold air inlet.
6 If either component is faulty, it must be renewed as described below.

Component renewal

Thermac switch

7 Remove the air cleaner assembly as described in Section 2.
8 Release the lid retaining clips, then remove the lid and withdraw the air cleaner filter element.

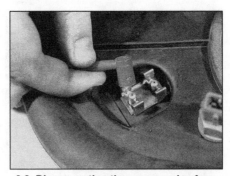

3.9 Disconnecting the vacuum pipe from the thermac valve

9 Disconnect the vacuum pipe **(see illustration)**, then bend up the tags on the switch clip. Remove the clip, then withdraw the switch and its seal.
10 Refitting is the reverse sequence to removal, ensuring that the switch mating surfaces are clean, and that the switch and seal are correctly located before fastening the clip.

Air temperature control valve

11 Disconnect the vacuum pipe from the valve, then unclip the inlet duct from the air cleaner and remove it from the engine compartment.
12 The air temperature control valve can be renewed only with the complete inlet duct assembly. If a new inlet duct assembly is being fitted, undo the three screws securing the hot air inlet adapter plate to the bottom of the duct, and transfer the adapter plate to the new duct **(see illustration)**.
13 Clip the duct into position in the air cleaner, and reconnect the vacuum pipe.

4 Accelerator cable – removal, refitting and adjustment

Removal

1 Remove the air cleaner assembly as described in Section 2.
2 Remove the engine management ECU as described Section 13.

3.12 Removing the air cleaner intake duct adapter

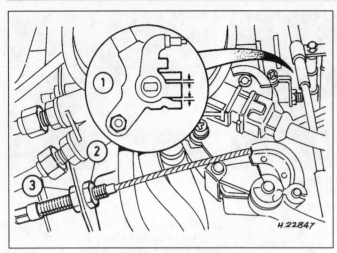

**4.8 Accelerator cable adjustment –
fuel-injected models**

1 Throttle lever-to-lost motion
   link clearance should be
   equal on each side

2 Adjuster locknut
3 Adjuster nut

4.9 To adjust the accelerator cable, index the stepper motor . . .

3 Slacken the accelerator cable locknuts, and free the outer cable from its mounting bracket. Release the inner cable from the throttle cam.
4 Work back along the outer cable, releasing it from any relevant retaining clamps and ties, and from the engine compartment bulkhead.
5 Working from inside the car release the heater duct from underneath the driver's side of the facia panel, to gain access to the upper end of the accelerator pedal.
6 Remove the accelerator cable retaining clip, then release the cable from the upper end of the accelerator pedal. Return to the engine compartment, and withdraw the cable from the bulkhead.

Refitting and adjustment

7 Refitting is the reverse sequence to removal, ensuring that the cable is correctly routed. Prior to tightening the cable locknuts, the cable should be adjusted as follows.
8 With the pedal fully released, position the locknuts so that there is equal clearance present on each side of the throttle lever at the lost motion link and no slack in the cable **(see illustration)**. Have an assistant fully depress the pedal, and check that the throttle cam opens fully, then check that it returns to the at-rest position when released.
9 To adjust the cable, switch on the ignition and position the stepper motor by moving the cam only to open, and fully close the throttle **(see illustration)**. Note that it is essential for accurate positioning of the stepper motor that the accelerator pedal switch contacts remain closed, so that the ECU recognises the throttle movement as a command, and indexes the stepper motor.
10 Slacken the adjuster locknut, then tighten the adjuster nut until the clearance is equal on each side of the throttle lever at the lost motion link, tighten the locknut without disturbing this setting **(see illustration)**.

Recheck the adjustment, and switch off the ignition.

5 Accelerator pedal – removal and refitting

Refer to Chapter 4A, Section 4.

6 Fuel system – depressurisation

Note: *Refer to the warning note in Section 1 before proceeding.*

⚠️ **Warning: The following procedure will merely relieve the pressure in the fuel system – remember that fuel will still be present in the system components, and take precautions accordingly before disconnecting any of them.**

1 The fuel system referred to in this Section is defined as the tank mounted fuel pump, the fuel filter, the fuel injector and the pressure regulator in the injector housing, and the metal

4.10 . . . then adjust the locknut and adjuster nut as described in text

pipes and flexible hoses of the fuel lines between these components. All these contain fuel which will be under pressure while the engine is running and/or while the ignition is switched on. The pressure will remain for some time after the ignition has been switched off, and must be relieved before any of these components are disturbed for servicing work.
2 Disconnect the battery negative terminal (refer to *Disconnecting the battery* in the Reference Chapter).
3 Place a suitable container beneath the relevant connection/union to be disconnected, and have a large rag ready to soak up any escaping fuel not being caught by the container.
4 Loosen the connection or union nut (as applicable) slowly to avoid a sudden release of pressure, and position the rag around the connection to catch any fuel spray which may be expelled. Once the pressure is released, disconnect the fuel line, and insert suitable plugs to minimise fuel loss and prevent the entry of dirt into the fuel system.

7 Fuel system – pressure check

Note: *The following procedure is based on the use of the Rover pressure gauge and adapter (service tool number 18G1500).*

1 Depressurise the fuel system as described in Section 6, then release the retaining clip and disconnect the flexible fuel feed hose at its union to the metal fuel pipe which is secured to the engine compartment bulkhead, just behind the throttle body assembly; the feed pipe is the lower of the two.
2 Connect the gauge into the fuel line between the hose and pipe, and check that it is securely retained.

3 Reconnect the battery and start the engine; the pressure should be steady at the specified regulated injection pressure. Stop the engine and watch the gauge; the pressure drop in the first minute should not exceed 0.7 bars.

4 If the regulated pressure recorded was too high, the pressure regulator must be renewed; this means renewing the complete injector housing assembly.

5 If the pressure first recorded was too low, or if it falls too quickly, check the system carefully for leaks. If no leaks are found, first renew the fuel filter (see Chapter 1), then check the pump by substituting a new one, and recheck the pressure. If the pressure does not improve, the fault is in the pressure regulator, and the complete injector housing assembly must be renewed; if this is the case, it is worth dismantling the regulator first to check that the fault is not due to its being jammed open with dirt, or similar.

8 Fuel tank –
removal and refitting

Note: *Observe the precautions in Section 1 before working on any component in the fuel system.*

Removal

1 Before the tank can be removed, it must be drained of as much fuel as possible. To avoid the dangers and complications of fuel handling and storage, it is advisable to carry out this operation with the tank almost empty. Any fuel remaining can be drained as follows.

2 Disconnect the battery negative terminal (refer to *Disconnecting the battery* in the Reference Chapter).

3 Using a hand pump or syphon inserted through the filler neck, remove any remaining fuel from the bottom of the tank. Do this in a well-ventilated area, not in a garage or over an inspection pit.

4 Remove the luggage compartment carpet and the spare wheel.

5 Release the two retaining studs, and remove the trim panel from the side of the fuel tank.

6 Disconnect the wiring connectors from the fuel gauge sender unit.

7 Release the retaining clip, and disconnect the vent pipe from the fuel tank.

8 Bearing in mind the information contained in Section 6 on depressurising the fuel system, release the retaining clips and disconnect the fuel feed and return hoses from the tank; the feed hose is marked with a yellow band, and the return hose is unmarked.

9 Undo the fuel tank strap retaining bolt, then remove the strengthening plate and move the strap to one side.

10 Release the fuel tank filler neck from its grommet, and remove the grommet from the car.

11 Peel back the rubber cover, then disconnect the wiring connector from the fuel pump, and remove the fuel tank from the vehicle.

Refitting

12 Refitting is the reverse sequence to removal, ensuring that all hoses are correctly reconnected and securely fastened so that there can be no risk of fuel leakage.

9 Fuel pump –
removal and refitting

Note: *Observe the precautions in Section 1 before working on any component in the fuel system.*

Removal

1 Remove the fuel tank as described in Section 8.

2 Release the retaining clip, and disconnect the two-way breather valve vent hose from the fuel tank. Unclip the valve and hose assembly from the tank seam, and remove it.

3 Slacken and remove the six fuel pump retaining nuts, then carefully withdraw the pump assembly from the tank, and remove the pump seal.

Refitting

4 Examine the pump seal for signs of damage or deterioration and, if necessary, renew it.

5 Ensure that the pump and tank mating surfaces are clean and dry, and fit the seal onto the fuel tank.

6 Carefully install the pump assembly, then refit the pump retaining nuts and tighten them to the specified torque.

7 Clip the two-way valve and hose assembly back onto the tank seam, then reconnect the vent hose to the tank, securing it in position with its retaining clip.

8 Refit the fuel tank as described in Section 8.

10 Fuel gauge sender unit –
removal and refitting

Refer to Chapter 4A, Section 8.

11 Unleaded petrol –
general information and usage

Note: *The information given in this Chapter is correct at the time of writing. If updated information is thought to be required, check with a Rover dealer. If travelling abroad, consult one of the motoring organisations (or a similar authority) for advice on the fuel available.*

All fuel injection models are designed to run on fuel with a minimum octane rating of 95 (RON). All models are equipped with catalytic converters, and therefore must be run on unleaded fuel **only**.

Super unleaded petrol (97/98 RON) can also be used in all models if wished, though there is no advantage in doing so.

12 Fuel injection system –
testing and adjustment

Testing

1 If a fault appears in the fuel injection system, first ensure that all the system wiring connectors are securely connected and free of corrosion. Ensure that the fault is not due to poor maintenance; ie, check that the air cleaner filter element is clean, the spark plugs are in good condition and correctly gapped, the valve clearances are correctly adjusted, the cylinder compression pressures are correct, and that the engine breather hoses are clear and undamaged, referring to Chapters 1 and 2A for further information.

2 If these checks fail to reveal the cause of the problem, the vehicle should be taken to a suitably-equipped Rover dealer for testing. A wiring block connector is incorporated in the engine management circuit, into which a special electronic diagnostic tester can be plugged. The tester will locate the fault quickly and simply, alleviating the need to test all the system components individually, which is a time-consuming operation that also carries a risk of damaging the ECU.

Adjustment

3 Experienced home mechanics with a considerable amount of skill and equipment (including a tachometer and an accurately calibrated exhaust gas analyser) may be able to check the exhaust CO level and the idle speed. However, if these are found to be in need of adjustment, the car *must* be taken to a suitably-equipped Rover dealer for further testing. **Note:** *There is no provision for the adjustment or alteration of these settings, except by reprogramming the ECU using Rover diagnostic equipment; if checking the idle speed, remember that it will vary constantly under ECU control.*

13 Fuel injection system components –
removal and refitting

Throttle body

Note: *Refer to the warning note in Section 1 before proceeding.*

Removal

1 Remove the air cleaner assembly, as described in Section 2.

13.2 Undo the retaining bolt (arrowed) and remove the fuel pipe retaining clip

13.3 Retain the adapters with an open-ended spanner whilst slackening the fuel pipe union nuts

13.6 Disconnect the breather and purge valve hoses from the front of the throttle body assembly

2 Slacken and remove the bolt and retaining clip securing the fuel pipes to the bulkhead (**see illustration**). Examine the injector housing fuel pipe feed and return unions for signs of leakage, then wipe them clean.

3 Bearing in mind the information contained in Section 6 on depressurising the fuel system, using an open-ended spanner to hold each adapter, unscrew the pipe union nuts, and release the fuel feed and return pipes from the adapters (**see illustration**). Plug each pipe and adapter, to minimise the loss of fuel and prevent the entry of dirt into the system.

4 Release the wire retaining clips, and disconnect the wiring connectors from the injector housing, the throttle potentiometer and the stepper motor.

5 Slacken the accelerator cable locknuts, and free the outer cable from its mounting bracket. Release the inner cable from the throttle cam.

6 Release the retaining clip(s), and disconnect the breather and purge valve hoses from the front of the throttle body (**see illustration**).

7 On models with automatic transmission, disconnect the governor control rod from the throttle linkage.

8 Slacken and remove the four nuts securing the throttle body to the inlet manifold, then remove the throttle body from the car. Remove the insulating spacer, and examine it for signs of wear or damage, renewing it if necessary.

9 If leakage was detected from the feed and return pipes or their union nuts, check the

sealing surfaces of the nuts and adapters, and renew the adapter or the pipe assembly as necessary. If leakage was detected from the adapters, unscrew each through one turn with a spanner, then through two turns by hand; if the adapter is still a tight fit in the housing, the threads are damaged, and the housing and adapters must be renewed as a set. If the threads are sound, fit new sealing washers to the adapters and refit them, tightening them to their specified torque wrench setting.

Refitting

10 Refitting is the reverse sequence to removal, noting the following points:
- a) Ensure that the mating surfaces of the throttle body and inlet manifold are clean, then fit the insulating spacer.
- b) Tighten the throttle body nuts and fuel pipe union nuts to their specified torque settings. Note that when tightening the injector housing fuel pipe union nuts, **do not** use an open-ended spanner to retain the adapters; this will ensure that the adapters are securely tightened in the injector housing.
- c) On completion, reconnect and adjust the accelerator cable as described in Section 4.

Injector housing

Note: Refer to the warning note in Section 1 before proceeding.

Removal

11 Carry out the operations described in paragraphs 1 to 3.

12 Release the wire retaining clip, and

disconnect the wiring connector from the injector housing (**see illustration**).

13 Remove the four screws securing the injector housing to the throttle body (**see illustration**), then lift off the injector housing and remove the gasket.

14 If leakage was detected from the fuel feed and/or return pipes, perform the checks described in paragraph 9.

Refitting

15 Refitting is the reverse sequence to removal, noting the following points:
- a) Ensure that the injector and throttle body mating surfaces are clean, and fit a new gasket.
- b) Apply thread-locking compound (Rover recommended Loctite Screwlock or Nutlock) to the threads of the injector housing screws, then tighten them to the specified torque.
- c) Tighten the fuel pipe union nuts to the specified torque setting, noting that when tightening the union nuts, **do not** use an open-ended spanner to retain the adapters; this will ensure that the adapters are securely tightened in the housing.

Fuel injector

Note: As a Rover replacement part, the injector is available only as part of the injector housing. Note, however, that it is a Bosch-manufactured component, and can be obtained separately through Bosch agents. Refer to the warning note in Section 1 before proceeding.

Removal

16 Disconnect the battery negative terminal (refer to Disconnecting the battery in the Reference Chapter).

17 Remove the air cleaner assembly as described in Section 2.

18 Slacken and remove the injector connector cap retaining screw, and lift off the connector cap (**see illustration**). As the screw is slackened, place a clean rag over the cap to catch any fuel spray which may be released. The injector can then be lifted out of the housing.

13.12 Disconnecting the injector housing wiring connector

13.13 Injector housing retaining screws (arrowed)

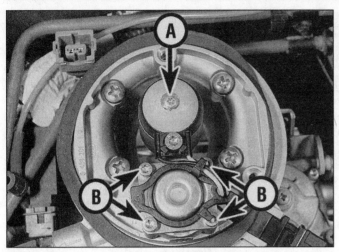

13.18 Injector cap retaining screw (A) and fuel pressure regulator retaining screws (B)

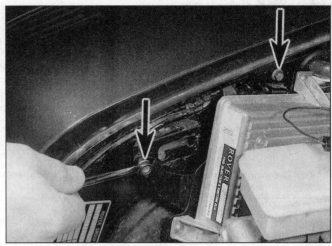

13.30 Undo the ECU mounting bracket-to-wing valance retaining bolts (arrowed) . . .

Refitting

19 Refitting is the reverse sequence to removal, ensuring that the connector cap makes good contact with the injector pins.

Fuel pressure regulator

20 The fuel pressure regulator is available only as part of the injector housing assembly. Refer to paragraphs 11 to 15 for details on removal and refitting.

Stepper motor

Removal

21 Remove the injector housing as described in paragraphs 11 to 14.
22 Release the retaining clip, and disconnect the stepper motor wiring connector.
23 Remove the four stepper motor retaining screws, and remove the stepper motor assembly from the throttle body. Do not attempt to dismantle the assembly.

Refitting

24 Refitting is the reverse sequence to removal, ensuring that the throttle body and motor mating surfaces are clean. On completion, adjust the accelerator cable as described in Section 4, to ensure that the stepper motor is correctly indexed.

Throttle potentiometer

Removal

25 Although not strictly necessary, access is greatly improved if the air cleaner assembly is first removed, as described in Section 2.
26 Disconnect the battery negative terminal (refer to *Disconnecting the battery* in the Reference Chapter).
27 Release the wire retaining clip, and disconnect the potentiometer wiring connector.
28 Remove the two screws, and remove the potentiometer from the throttle body, noting how its tongue engages with the throttle disc spindle lever. Withdraw the spacer if required.

Refitting

29 Refitting is the reverse sequence to removal, noting the following points:
a) *Carefully clean the mating surfaces of the throttle body, the spacer and the potentiometer, then refit the spacer.*
b) *Refit the potentiometer so that its tongue engages FORWARD of (ie, 'inside') the throttle disc spindle lever, then rotate the throttle cam to check the action of the lever and tongue.*
c) *Securely tighten the potentiometer screws, then recheck the potentiometer operation before reconnecting the wiring connector.*

Engine management ECU

Removal

30 Disconnect the battery negative terminal (refer to *Disconnecting the battery* in the Reference Chapter), then undo the two bolts securing the ECU mounting bracket to the right-hand wing valance **(see illustration)**.
31 Withdraw the ECU from the engine compartment, disconnecting its wiring connectors and the manifold absolute pressure sensor vacuum hose as they become accessible **(see illustration)**.

13.31 . . . then withdraw the ECU and disconnect the vacuum hose and wiring connectors

32 If necessary, undo the three screws and separate the ECU from its mounting bracket.

Refitting

33 Refitting is the reverse sequence to removal, ensuring that the wiring connectors and vacuum hose are securely reconnected. Due to the nature of the ECU, if a new or different ECU has been fitted, it may take a short while for full idle control to be restored.

Manifold absolute pressure (MAP) sensor

34 This is part of the ECU, and is removed and refitted as described in the previous sub-section.
35 The sensor's vacuum hose runs from the inlet manifold to the ECU via a fuel (vapour) trap mounted on the engine compartment bulkhead.
36 To remove the fuel trap, first remove the air cleaner assembly as described in Section 2. Release the fuel trap from its retaining clip, then disconnect the two vacuum hoses, noting their correct fitted positions, and remove it from the engine compartment **(see illustration)**.
37 On refitting, ensure that the vacuum hoses are reconnected to their original unions; the hoses are colour-coded to ensure correct reconnection.

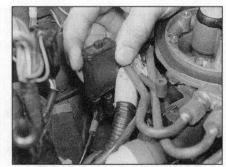

13.36 Removing the manifold absolute pressure (MAP) sensor fuel trap

13.40 Removing the intake air temperature sensor from the air cleaner housing

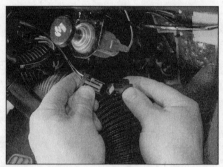

13.47 Disconnect the wiring connector . . .

13.48 . . . then undo the retaining bolt (arrowed) and remove the accelerator pedal switch assembly from the car

Inlet air temperature sensor

Removal

38 Disconnect the battery negative terminal (refer to *Disconnecting the battery* in the Reference Chapter).
39 Remove the air cleaner assembly as described in Section 2.
40 Unscrew the sensor, and remove it from the base of the air cleaner housing **(see illustration)**.

Refitting

41 Refitting is the reverse sequence to removal. Tighten the sensor to the specified torque wrench setting.

Coolant temperature sensor

Removal

42 The coolant temperature sensor is fitted to the underside of the inlet manifold, and access to the sensor is limited. Therefore, to remove the sensor, it will first be necessary to remove the inlet manifold as described in Section 15. The sensor can be unscrewed and removed from the manifold.

Refitting

43 Wipe clean the threads of the switch and inlet manifold. If a sealing washer is fitted, apply a smear of sealant to the switch threads.
44 Refit the switch to the manifold, and tighten it securely. Refit the manifold as described in Section 15.

Accelerator pedal switch

Removal

45 Working from inside the car, release the heater duct from underneath the driver's side of the facia panel, and position it clear of the accelerator pedal.
46 Using a suitable pair of pliers, unhook the accelerator pedal return spring from the pedal.
47 Release the switch wiring connector from its retaining clip, and disconnect it **(see illustration)**.
48 Slacken and remove the accelerator pedal switch mounting bracket retaining bolt, and remove the switch and bracket assembly from the car **(see illustration)**.
49 Prise off the C-clip, and remove the switch from the mounting bracket, noting the wave washer which is fitted between the switch and bracket.

Refitting

50 Refitting is the reverse sequence to removal.

Fuel cut-off inertia switch

51 The fuel cut-off inertia switch is mounted onto the left-hand side of the engine compartment bulkhead **(see illustration)**. If the switch has tripped, it can be reset by pressing in the button situated at the top of the switch.

Removal

52 Slacken and remove the two screws securing the cut-off switch to the bulkhead,

then disconnect the wiring connector and remove the switch.

Refitting

53 Reconnect the wiring connector, then refit the switch to the bulkhead and tighten its retaining screws securely. Reset the switch by depressing the button on the top of the switch.

Relay module

54 The relay module contains the four main relays which control the engine management system; the starter relay, the fuel pump relay, the main relay and the manifold PTC heater relay. If a fault develops in any one of the system relays, the complete relay module must be renewed; it is not possible to renew the relays individually.

Removal

55 Slide the relay off its mounting bracket in the right-hand rear corner of the engine compartment, then disconnect its wiring connectors and remove it from the car **(see illustration)**.

Refitting

56 Refitting is the reverse sequence to removal.

---

14 Inlet manifold PTC heater – general information and component renewal

General information

1 The system incorporates the manifold PTC (Positive Temperature Coefficient) heater, the relay and the coolant temperature sensor.
2 When the ignition is switched on and the engine is cold (coolant below 50°C), the relay-energising current is supplied by the engine management ECU, which then closes the relay contacts and allows current to flow from the battery to the heater. This ensures that the inlet manifold is warm enough, even before the effect of the coolant heating becomes apparent, to prevent fuel droplets condensing in the manifold, thus improving driveability and reducing exhaust emissions when the engine is cold.

13.51 Fuel cut-off inertia switch (arrowed) is mounted onto the left-hand side of the engine compartment bulkhead

13.55 Relay module is situated on the right-hand side of the engine compartment

3 As soon as the engine warms-up to temperatures above 50°C, the ECU switches off the supply current, and the relay cuts off the power supply to the manifold heater.

4 If the engine suddenly develops flat spots when cold, the system may be faulty.

Component renewal

PTC heater

5 The PTC heater is fitted to the underside of the inlet manifold, and access to the heater is limited. Therefore, to remove the heater, it will first be necessary to remove the inlet manifold as described in Section 15. With the manifold on the bench, using circlip pliers, remove the circlip and withdraw the heater. Inspect the rubber sealing ring for signs of damage or deterioration, and renew if necessary.

6 On refitting, ensure that the heater locating projection is correctly engaged in the manifold recess, then secure the switch in position with its circlip. Refit the manifold to the car as described in Section 15.

PTC heater relay

7 The manifold PTC heater relay is an integral part of the relay module, and can be removed and refitted as described in Section 13.

---

15 Inlet manifold – removal and refitting

Removal

1 Disconnect the battery negative terminal (refer to *Disconnecting the battery* in the Reference Chapter).

2 Remove the bonnet as described in Chapter 11A.

3 Remove the air cleaner assembly as described in Section 2.

4 Drain the cooling system as described in Chapter 1.

5 Carry out the operations described in paragraphs 2 to 7 of Section 13.

6 Undo the union bolt securing the brake servo vacuum hose to the manifold, and recover the hose union sealing washers **(see illustration)**.

7 Slacken the two hose clips, and disconnect the two coolant hoses from the left-hand side of the manifold.

8 Disconnect the two vacuum hoses from the rear of the inlet manifold, noting their correct fitted positions; the hoses are colour-coded for identification purposes.

9 Slacken and remove the four nuts securing the inlet manifold to the cylinder head, then remove the manifold from the engine, disconnecting the manifold PTC heater and coolant temperature sensor wiring connectors as they become accessible. Remove the two rings from the inlet manifold bore.

Refitting

10 Refitting is the reverse sequence to removal, noting the following points:

a) *Although not strictly necessary, it is also recommended that the exhaust manifold is removed, as described in Part D of this Chapter, so that the manifold gasket can be renewed before the inlet manifold is refitted.*

b) *If leakage was detected from the fuel feed and/or return pipes, perform the checks described in Section 13, paragraph 9.*

15.6 Inlet manifold brake servo unit vacuum hose union bolt (arrowed)

c) *Ensure that the manifold and gasket faces are clean, and that the two locating rings are in position in the manifold bores before refitting the manifold.*

d) *Tighten the manifold retaining nuts to the specified torque.*

e) *Ensure that all relevant hoses are reconnected to their original positions, and are securely held (where necessary) by the retaining clips.*

f) *Renew the vacuum servo unit vacuum hose banjo union sealing washers, and tighten the union bolt to the specified torque.*

g) *Prior to refitting the air cleaner assembly, adjust the accelerator cable as described in Section 4.*

h) *On completion, refill the cooling system as described in Chapter 1.*

Chapter 4 Part C:
Fuel system – multi-point fuel injection engines

Contents

Accelerator cable – removal, refitting and adjustment 3
Accelerator pedal – removal and refitting 4
Air cleaner assembly – removal and refitting 2
Air cleaner element renewal ....See Chapter 1
Fuel filter renewal ....See Chapter 1
Fuel gauge sender unit – removal and refitting 9
Fuel injection system – testing and adjustment 11
Fuel injection system components – removal and refitting 12
Fuel pump – removal and refitting 8

Fuel system – depressurisation 5
Fuel system – pressure check 6
Fuel tank – removal and refitting 7
General information and precautions 1
Inlet manifold – removal and refitting 13
Underbody and fuel/brake line check ....See Chapter 1
Underbonnet check for fluid leaks and hose condition ..See Chapter 1
Unleaded petrol – general information and usage 10

Degrees of difficulty

Easy, suitable for novice with little experience	**Fairly easy,** suitable for beginner with some experience	**Fairly difficult,** suitable for competent DIY mechanic 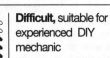	**Difficult,** suitable for experienced DIY mechanic 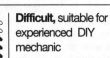	**Very difficult,** suitable for expert DIY or professional 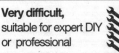

Specifications

General

System type	Rover/Motorola Modular Engine Management System, using ECU-controlled multi-point injection (MEMS-Mpi) and speed/density method of airflow measurement

Fuel system data

Fuel pump type	Electric, immersed in fuel tank
Fuel pump regulated pressure	1.0 to 1.3 bar ± 0.2 bar
Throttle potentiometer voltage:	
Throttle closed	0 to 1 volt
Throttle open 65°	3 to 4 volts
Throttle open 90°	4 to 5 volts
Idle speed – nominal value, for reference only	900 ± 50 rpm
Idle mixture CO%	0.4% maximum

Recommended fuel

Minimum octane rating	95 RON unleaded **only**

Torque wrench settings

	Nm	lbf ft
Air cleaner mounting bracket bolts	9	7
Camshaft position sensor	10	7
Coolant temperature sensor	15	11
Crankshaft position sensor	8	6
Fuel pump nuts	9	7
Idle air control valve	7	5
Inlet air temperature sensor	7	5
Manifold absolute pressure sensor	6	4
Manifold retaining nuts	22	16
Throttle body mounting bolts	8	6
Throttle potentiometer	2	1

1 General information and precautions

General information

The fuel system consists of a fuel tank, situated at the rear of the car, with an electric fuel pump immersed in it, a fuel filter, fuel feed and return lines, throttle body assembly, fuel pressure regulator, fuel rail with two injectors, as well as the engine management electronic control unit (ECU) and the various sensors, electrical components and related wiring.

The ECU fully controls both the ignition and fuel injection systems, integrating the two in a complete engine management system; refer to Chapter 5C for information on the ignition side of the system.

The Rover/Motorola Modular Engine Management System uses ECU-controlled multi-point injection (MEMS-Mpi) and the speed/density method of airflow measurement. The whole system is best explained if considered as three sub-systems; the fuel delivery, air metering and electrical control systems.

The fuel delivery system incorporates the fuel tank with an electric fuel pump (immersed in a swirl pot to prevent aeration of the fuel) inside it. When the ignition is switched on, the pump is supplied with current via the fuel pump relay, under the control of the ECU; the pump feeds petrol via a non-return valve (to prevent fuel draining out of the system components and back to the tank when the pump is not working) to the fuel filter, and from the filter to the fuel rail. Fuel pressure is controlled by the pressure regulator, which allows excess fuel to return to the tank swirl pot, where a venturi causes the returning fuel to draw cool fuel from the tank into the swirl pot. In the event of sudden deceleration (ie, an accident) an inertia switch cuts off the power to the pump, so that the risk of fire from fuel spraying out of broken fuel lines under pressure is minimised.

2.1 Undo and remove the three screws and remove the air cleaner from the throttle body

The air metering system includes the inlet air temperature sensor, the air cleaner and the throttle body assembly. The throttle body incorporates the throttle potentiometer (which is linked to the throttle disc spindle, and sends the ECU information on the rate of throttle opening by transmitting a varying voltage), and the idle air control valve (which is controlled by the ECU, and controls a by-pass air passage in the inlet manifold to provide idle speed control).

The electrical control system consists of the ECU, with all the sensors that provide it with information, and the actuators by which it controls the whole system's operation. The manifold absolute pressure (MAP) sensor is located in the inlet manifold and converts variations in manifold pressure into graduated electrical signals which are used by the ECU to determine the load on the engine. The inlet air temperature sensor is self-explanatory; the crankshaft position sensor provides the engine speed and crankshaft position; the coolant temperature sensor supplies the engine temperature; the camshaft position sensor provides information on inlet cam lobe position for each cylinder; the throttle potentiometer is explained above, and the function of the lambda sensor is explained in Part D of this Chapter. Short-circuit protection and diagnostic capabilities are incorporated; the ECU can both receive and transmit information via the diagnostic connector, thus permitting engine diagnosis and tuning by Rover diagnostic equipment. If certain sensor circuits should fail, the ECU has a back-up facility which assumes a basic sensor value and these are used to implement a back-up air/fuel mixture ratio.

All these signals are compared by the ECU, using digital techniques, with set values pre-programmed (mapped) into its memory. Based on this information, the ECU selects fuel and ignition settings appropriate to those values, and controls the ignition DIS module (varying the ignition timing as required), the fuel injectors (varying the pulse width – the length of time the injectors are held open – to provide a richer or weaker mixture, as appropriate), the idle air control valve (controlling the idle and fast idle speeds), the fuel pump relay (controlling the fuel delivery), the main relay, the purge control valve, and the lambda sensor and relay. The mixture, idle speed and ignition timing are constantly varied by the ECU to provide the best settings for cranking, starting and engine warm-up (with either a hot or cold engine), idle, cruising, and acceleration. A rev-limiter circuit is built into the ECU, which switches off the injector earth (ie, the fuel supply) if the engine speed exceeds the recommended limit. The injector earth is also switched off on the overrun, to improve fuel economy and reduce exhaust emissions.

The ECU idle control is an adaptive system; it learns the engine load and wear characteristics over a period of time, and adjusts the idle speed to suit. If the ECU is renewed, it will take a short period of normal driving for the new ECU to learn the engine's characteristics and restore full idle control.

Precautions

⚠️ *Warning: Petrol is extremely flammable – great care must be taken when working on any part of the fuel system. Do not smoke or allow any naked flames or uncovered light bulbs near the work area. Note that gas-powered domestic appliances with pilot flames, such as heaters, boilers and tumble dryers, also present a fire hazard – bear this in mind if you are working in an area where such appliances are present. Always keep a suitable fire extinguisher close to the work area and familiarise yourself with its operation before starting work. Wear eye protection when working on fuel systems and wash off any fuel spilt on bare skin immediately with soap and water. Note that fuel vapour is just as dangerous as liquid fuel; a vessel that has just been emptied of liquid fuel will still contain vapour and can be potentially explosive. Petrol is a highly dangerous and volatile liquid, and the precautions necessary when handling it cannot be overstressed.*

Many of the operations described in this Chapter involve the disconnection of fuel lines, which may cause an amount of fuel spillage. Before commencing work, refer to the above Warning and the information in 'Safety first!' at the beginning of this manual.

When working with fuel system components, pay particular attention to cleanliness – dirt entering the fuel system may cause blockages which will lead to poor running.

Note: *Residual pressure will remain in the fuel lines long after the vehicle was last used, when disconnecting any fuel line, it will be necessary to depressurise the fuel system as described in Section 5.*

2 Air cleaner assembly – removal and refitting

Removal

1 Undo and remove the three screws and washers securing the air cleaner assembly to the throttle body **(see illustration)**.

2 Lift the air cleaner assembly up and off the mounting bracket on the throttle body.

Refitting

3 Refitting is the reverse sequence to removal.

3.3a Release the accelerator cable adjusting nut from the mounting bracket . . .

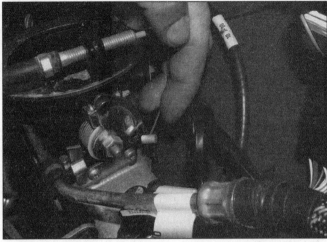

3.3b . . . then disconnect the inner cable end fitting from the throttle cam

3 Accelerator cable – removal, refitting and adjustment

Removal

1 Remove the air cleaner assembly as described in Section 2.
2 Remove the engine management ECU as described Section 12.
3 Release the accelerator cable adjusting nut from the mounting bracket, then disconnect the inner cable end fitting from the throttle cam **(see illustrations)**.
4 Work back along the outer cable, releasing it from any relevant retaining clamps and ties, and from the engine compartment bulkhead.
5 Working from inside the car release the heater duct from underneath the driver's side of the facia panel, to gain access to the upper end of the accelerator cable.
6 Remove the accelerator cable retaining clip, then release the cable from the upper end of the accelerator pedal. Return to the engine compartment, and withdraw the cable from the bulkhead.

Refitting and adjustment

7 Refitting is the reverse sequence to removal, ensuring that the cable is correctly routed. Prior to final refitting, the cable should be adjusted as follows.
8 Have an assistant fully depress the pedal, and check that the throttle cam opens fully, then check that it returns to the at-rest position when released. If this is not the case, alter the position of the adjusting nut on the threads of the accelerator outer cable.

4 Accelerator pedal – removal and refitting

Removal

1 Working from inside the car, release the heater duct from underneath the driver's side of the facia panel, to gain access to the upper end of the accelerator pedal.
2 Remove the accelerator inner cable retaining clip, then depress the pedal and detach the inner cable ferrule from the slot at the top of the pedal arm.
3 Disconnect the accelerator pedal return spring.
4 Undo and remove the two bolts securing the pedal assembly to the bulkhead and lift out the pedal.

Refitting

5 Refitting is the reverse sequence to removal, but adjust the accelerator cable as described in Section 3 on completion.

5 Fuel system – depressurisation

Note: *Refer to the warning note in Section 1 before proceeding.*

⚠️ *Warning: The following procedure will merely relieve the pressure in the fuel system – remember that fuel will still be present in the system components, and take precautions accordingly before disconnecting any of them.*

1 The fuel system referred to in this Section is defined as the tank-mounted fuel pump, the fuel filter, the fuel injectors and the pressure regulator in the fuel rail, and the metal pipes and flexible hoses of the fuel lines between these components. All these contain fuel which will be under pressure while the engine is running and/or while the ignition is switched on. The pressure will remain for some time after the ignition has been switched off, and must be relieved before any of these components are disturbed for servicing work.
2 Disconnect the battery negative terminal (refer to *Disconnecting the battery* in the Reference Chapter).
3 Remove the fuel tank filler cap to release any pressure in the tank.
4 Place a suitable container beneath the relevant connection/union to be disconnected, and have a large rag ready to soak up any escaping fuel not being caught by the container.
5 Release the connection union nut or quick-release fitting (as applicable) slowly, to avoid a sudden release of pressure, and position the rag around the connection to catch any fuel spray which may be expelled. Once the pressure is released, disconnect the fuel line, then suitably cover or seal the open union to minimise fuel loss and prevent the entry of dirt into the fuel system.

6 Fuel system – pressure check

Note: *The following procedure is based on the use of the Rover pressure gauge and adapter (service tool number 18G 1500).*

1 Disconnect the battery negative terminal (refer to *Disconnecting the battery* in the Reference Chapter).

2 Bearing in mind the information contained in Section 5, place absorbent rags around the fuel feed hose quick-release fitting in the engine compartment. Remove the fuel tank filler cap to release any pressure in the tank. Depress the plastic collar on the quick-release fitting and disconnect the feed hose from the pipes.

3 Connect the gauge into the fuel line between the hose and pipe, and check that it is securely retained.

4 Reconnect the battery and start the engine; the pressure should be steady at the specified regulated injection pressure. Stop the engine and watch the gauge; the pressure drop in the first minute should not exceed 0.7 bars.

5 If the regulated pressure recorded was too high, the pressure regulator must be renewed; this means renewing the fuel rail assembly.

6 If the pressure first recorded was too low, or if it falls too quickly, check the system carefully for leaks. If no leaks are found, first renew the fuel filter (see Chapter 1), then check the pump by substituting a new one, and recheck the pressure. If the pressure does not improve, the fault is in the pressure regulator.

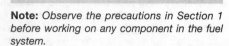

7 Fuel tank – removal and refitting

Note: *Observe the precautions in Section 1 before working on any component in the fuel system.*

Removal

1 Before the tank can be removed, it must be drained of as much fuel as possible. To avoid the dangers and complications of fuel handling and storage, it is advisable to carry out this operation with the tank almost empty. Any fuel remaining can be drained as follows.

2 Disconnect the battery negative terminal (refer to *Disconnecting the battery* in the Reference Chapter).

3 Using a hand pump or syphon inserted through the filler neck, remove any remaining fuel from the bottom of the tank. Do this in a well-ventilated area, not in a garage or over an inspection pit

4 Remove the luggage compartment carpet and the spare wheel.

5 Release the retaining studs, and remove the cover panel from the side of the fuel tank.

6 Disconnect the wiring connectors from the fuel gauge sender unit.

7 Release the retaining clip, and disconnect the vent pipe from the fuel tank.

8 Bearing in mind the information contained in Section 5, release the retaining clips and disconnect the fuel feed and return hoses from the tank; the feed hose is marked with a yellow band, and the return hose is unmarked.

9 Undo the fuel tank strap retaining bolt and move the strap to one side.

10 Release the fuel tank filler neck from its grommet, and remove the grommet from the car.

11 Disconnect the multiplug wiring connector from the fuel pump, and remove the fuel tank from the vehicle.

Refitting

12 Refitting is the reverse sequence to removal, ensuring that all hoses are correctly reconnected and securely fastened so that there can be no risk of fuel leakage.

8 Fuel pump – removal and refitting

Note: *Observe the precautions in Section 1 before working on any component in the fuel system.*

Removal

1 Remove the fuel tank as described in Section 7.

2 Release the retaining clip, and disconnect the two-way breather valve vent hose from the fuel tank. Unclip the valve and hose assembly from the tank seam, and remove it.

3 Slacken and remove the six fuel pump retaining nuts, then carefully withdraw the pump assembly from the tank, and remove the pump seal.

Refitting

4 Examine the pump seal for signs of damage or deterioration and, if necessary, renew it.

5 Ensure that the pump and tank mating surfaces are clean and dry, and fit the seal onto the fuel tank.

6 Carefully install the pump assembly, then refit the pump retaining nuts and tighten them to the specified torque.

7 Clip the two-way valve and hose assembly back onto the tank seam, then reconnect the vent hose to the tank, securing it in position with its retaining clip.

8 Refit the fuel tank as described in Section 7.

11.2 The diagnostic connector (arrowed) is located on the right-hand side of the heater unit

9 Fuel gauge sender unit – removal and refitting

Refer to Part A, Section 8.

10 Unleaded petrol – general information and usage

Note: *The information given in this Chapter is correct at the time of writing. If updated information is thought to be required, check with a Rover dealer. If travelling abroad, consult one of the motoring organisations (or a similar authority) for advice on the fuel available.*

All multi-point fuel injection models are designed to run on fuel with a minimum octane rating of 95 (RON). All models are equipped with catalytic converters, and therefore must be run on unleaded fuel **only**.

Super unleaded petrol (97/98 RON) can also be used in all models if wished, though there is no advantage in doing so.

11 Fuel injection system – testing and adjustment

Testing

1 If a fault appears in the fuel injection system, first ensure that all the system wiring connectors are securely connected and free of corrosion. Ensure that the fault is not due to poor maintenance; ie, check that the air cleaner filter element is clean, the spark plugs are in good condition and correctly gapped, the valve clearances are correctly adjusted, the cylinder compression pressures are correct, and that the engine breather hoses are clear and undamaged, referring to Chapters 1 and 2B for further information.

2 If these checks fail to reveal the cause of the problem, the vehicle should be taken to a suitably-equipped Rover dealer for testing. A diagnostic connector is incorporated in the engine management wiring circuit, into which a fault code reader, or Rover diagnostic tester can be plugged. The diagnostic connector is located in the passenger compartment, on a bracket on the right-hand side of the heater unit **(see illustration)**. A fault code reader or diagnostic tester will locate the fault quickly and simply, alleviating the need to test all the system components individually, which is a time-consuming operation that also carries a risk of damaging the ECU.

Adjustment

3 Experienced home mechanics with a considerable amount of skill and equipment (including a tachometer and an accurately calibrated exhaust gas analyser) may be able

12.4a Undo the bolts securing the air cleaner mounting bracket to the fuel rail . . .

12.4b . . . and inlet manifold (arrowed)

12.4c Release the wiring harness retaining clips and remove the mounting bracket

12.5a Disconnect the breather hose . . .

12.5b . . . and air bypass hose from the side of the throttle body

12.6 Disconnect the wiring multiplug from the throttle potentiometer

to check the exhaust CO level and the idle speed. However, if these are found to be in need of adjustment, the car *must* be taken to a suitably-equipped Rover dealer for further testing. **Note:** *There is no provision for the adjustment or alteration of these settings, except by reprogramming the ECU using Rover diagnostic equipment; if checking the idle speed, remember that it will vary constantly under ECU control.*

<table>
<tr><td>**12 Fuel injection system components –** removal and refitting</td><td>🔧</td></tr>
</table>

Throttle body

Note: *Refer to the warning note in Section 1 before proceeding.*

Removal

1 Disconnect the battery negative terminal (refer to *Disconnecting the battery* in the Reference Chapter).
2 Remove the air cleaner assembly, as described in Section 2.
3 Release the accelerator cable adjusting nut from the mounting bracket, release the inner cable from the throttle cam, and position the cable clear of the throttle body.
4 Undo the three bolts securing the air cleaner mounting bracket to the fuel rail and inlet manifold. Release the two clips securing the wiring harness to the mounting bracket then remove the bracket from the throttle body **(see illustrations)**.

5 Disconnect the breather hose and air bypass hose from the side of the throttle body **(see illustrations)**.
6 Disconnect the wiring multiplug from the throttle potentiometer **(see illustration)**.
7 Undo the three retaining bolts and lift the throttle body off the inlet manifold **(see illustration)**. Recover the O-ring seal, noting that a new seal will be required for refitting.

Refitting

8 Refitting is the reverse sequence to removal, noting the following points:
  a) *Thoroughly clean the mating surfaces of the throttle body and inlet manifold.*
  b) *Use a new throttle body O-ring lightly lubricated with silicone grease.*
  c) *Tighten the throttle body and air cleaner mounting bracket bolts to the specified torque.*

12.7 Undo the three retaining bolts and lift the throttle body off the inlet manifold

d) *On completion, reconnect and adjust the accelerator cable as described in Section 3.*

Fuel rail and injectors

Note: *Refer to the warning note in Section 1 before proceeding.*

Removal

9 Carry out the operations described in paragraphs 1 to 3.
10 Bearing in mind the information contained in Section 5, place absorbent rags around the fuel feed and return hose quick-release fittings. Remove the fuel tank filler cap to release any pressure in the tank. Depress the plastic collar on the quick-release fittings and disconnect the feed and return hoses from the pipes **(see illustration)**. Plug or cover each pipe and hose, to minimise the loss of fuel and prevent the entry of dirt into the system.

12.10 Depress the plastic collar on the quick-release fittings (arrowed) and disconnect the fuel feed and return hoses

12.12 Disconnect the fuel pressure regulator vacuum hose from the inlet manifold

12.13 Depress the plastic collar on the brake servo quick-release fitting and disconnect the vacuum hose

inlet air temperature sensor and the two fuel injectors (see illustrations). Move the wiring harness clear of the fuel rail.

15 Undo the three bolts securing the air cleaner mounting bracket to the fuel rail and inlet manifold. Release the two clips securing the wiring harness to the mounting bracket then remove the bracket from the throttle body.

16 Ease the two injectors from their locations in the inlet manifold and lift the fuel rail and injectors as an assembly off the engine (see illustration).

17 With the fuel rail on the bench, release the retaining clips and withdraw the injectors from the fuel rail (see illustrations). Remove the two sealing O-rings from each injector and obtain new O-rings for refitting.

Refitting

18 Refitting is the reverse sequence to removal, noting the following points:
   a) Fit new O-rings to the fuel injectors, lightly lubricated with silicone grease.
   b) Tighten the air cleaner mounting bracket bolts to the specified torque.
   c) On completion, reconnect and adjust the accelerator cable as described in Section 3.

Fuel pressure regulator

19 The fuel pressure regulator is available only as part of the fuel rail assembly. Refer to paragraphs 9 to 18 for details on fuel rail removal and refitting.

Idle air control valve

Removal

20 Remove the air cleaner as described in Section 2.

21 Disconnect the air bypass hose from the side of the throttle body.

22 Disconnect the wiring multiplug from the idle air control valve located on the right-hand side of the inlet manifold (see illustration).

23 Undo the two screws and remove the valve from the manifold. Remove the sealing O-ring from the valve and obtain a new O-ring for refitting.

Refitting

24 Refitting is the reverse sequence to removal, noting the following points:
   a) Fit a new O-ring to the valve, lightly lubricated with silicone grease.
   b) Tighten the retaining screws to the specified torque.

Throttle potentiometer

Removal

25 Remove the air cleaner as described in Section 2.

26 Disconnect the air bypass hose from the side of the throttle body.

27 Depress the plastic collar on the quick-release fitting and disconnect the brake servo vacuum hose from the inlet manifold.

28 Disconnect the wiring multiplug from the throttle potentiometer located on the right-hand side of the throttle body.

12.14a Disconnect the wiring multiplugs from the inlet air temperature sensor . . .

12.14b . . . and the two fuel injectors

11 Disconnect the breather hose from the throttle body and move it to one side.

12 Disconnect the fuel pressure regulator vacuum hose from the inlet manifold (see illustration).

13 Depress the plastic collar on the quick-release fitting and disconnect the brake servo vacuum hose from the inlet manifold (see illustration).

14 Disconnect the wiring multiplugs from the

12.16 Lift the fuel rail and injectors as an assembly off the engine

12.17a Release the retaining clips . . .

12.17b . . . and withdraw the injectors from the fuel rail

12.22 Disconnect the multiplug from the idle air control valve

12.32 Disconnect the inlet air temperature sensor wiring multiplug (arrowed)

12.36 Disconnect the MAP sensor wiring multiplug (arrowed)

12.40 Disconnect the coolant temperature sensor wiring multiplug (arrowed)

29 Undo the two screws and remove the specification plate from the throttle potentiometer. Note that new screws and wave washers will be required for refitting.

30 Carefully remove the throttle potentiometer from the throttle body, taking care not to twist or apply leverage to it as it is withdrawn.

Refitting

31 Refitting is the reverse sequence to removal, noting the following points:
 a) Carefully clean the mating surfaces of the throttle body and the potentiometer.
 b) Refit the potentiometer so that the machined flat on the throttle spindle is aligned with the mating portion of the potentiometer.
 c) Rotate the potentiometer in an anti-clockwise direction only to align the mounting holes.
 d) Secure the unit with new screws and wave washers tightened to the specified torque.
 e) Operate the throttle cam two or three times and check that full open and closed movement of the throttle disc is available.

Inlet air temperature sensor

Removal

32 Disconnect the wiring multiplug from the inlet air temperature sensor on the left-hand side of the inlet manifold (see illustration).

33 Unscrew the sensor and remove it from the manifold.

Refitting

34 Refitting is the reverse sequence to removal. Tighten the sensor to the specified torque.

Manifold absolute pressure (MAP) sensor

Removal

35 Remove the air cleaner as described in Section 2.

36 Disconnect the wiring multiplug from the MAP sensor located on the left-hand side of the inlet manifold (see illustration).

37 Undo the two screws and remove the sensor from the manifold. Remove the sealing O-ring from the sensor and obtain a new O-ring for refitting.

Refitting

38 Refitting is the reverse sequence to removal, noting the following points:
 a) Fit a new O-ring to the sensor, lightly lubricated with silicone grease.
 b) Tighten the retaining screws to the specified torque.

Coolant temperature sensor

Removal

39 When the engine and radiator are cold, either drain the cooling system as described in Chapter 1, or carefully unscrew the expansion tank filler cap to release any remaining pressure, and have ready a suitable plug that can be used temporarily to stop the escape of coolant while the sensor is removed. If the latter method is used, take care not to damage the threads, and do not use anything which will leave foreign matter inside the cooling system.

40 Disconnect the wiring multiplug, then unscrew the sensor from the thermostat housing (see illustration). Remove the sealing washer from the sensor and obtain a new washer for refitting.

Refitting

41 Ensure that the sensor threads and mating faces are clean, then refit the sensor to the thermostat housing using a new washer.

42 Tighten the sensor to the specified torque and reconnect the wiring multiplug.

43 On completion, either top-up or refill the cooling system as described in *Weekly checks* or Chapter 1.

12.48 Undo the bolt securing the ECU to the mounting bracket on the right-hand wing valance

Camshaft position sensor

Removal

44 Remove the air cleaner as described in Section 2.

45 Disconnect the wiring multiplug from the camshaft position sensor located on the rear facing side of the cylinder block.

46 Undo the retaining bolt and remove the sensor from the engine. Remove the sealing O-ring from the sensor and obtain a new O-ring for refitting.

Refitting

47 Refitting is the reverse sequence to removal, noting the following points:
 a) Fit a new O-ring to the sensor, lightly lubricated with silicone grease.
 b) Tighten the retaining bolt to the specified torque.

Engine management ECU

Note: *If a new ECU is to be fitted, this work should be entrusted to a Rover dealer. New units must be programmed with the vehicle anti-theft security code using Rover diagnostic equipment, before the engine can be started.*

Removal

48 Disconnect the battery negative terminal (refer to *Disconnecting the battery* in the Reference Chapter), then undo the bolt securing the ECU to the mounting bracket on the right-hand wing valance (see illustration).

49 Withdraw the ECU from the mounting bracket, disconnecting its two wiring connectors as they become accessible (see illustration).

12.49 Withdraw the ECU from the mounting bracket and disconnect the two wiring connectors

12.51 Fuel cut-off inertia switch location (arrowed) on the left-hand side of the engine compartment bulkhead

Refitting

50 Refitting is the reverse sequence to removal, ensuring that the wiring connectors are securely reconnected. Due to the nature of the ECU, if a new or different ECU has been fitted, it may take a short while for full idle control to be restored.

Fuel cut-off inertia switch

51 The fuel cut-off inertia switch is mounted onto the left-hand side of the engine compartment bulkhead **(see illustration)**. If the switch has tripped, it can be reset by pressing in the button situated at the top of the switch.

Removal

52 Slacken and remove the two screws securing the cut-off switch to the bulkhead, then disconnect the wiring connector and remove the switch.

Refitting

53 Reconnect the wiring connector, then refit the switch to the bulkhead and tighten its retaining screws securely. Reset the switch by depressing the button on the top of the switch.

Relay module

54 The relay module contains the four main relays which control the engine management system; the starter relay, the fuel pump relay, the main relay and the lambda sensor relay. If a fault develops in any one of the system relays, the complete relay module must be

13.11a Remove the inlet manifold from the cylinder head . . .

12.55 Slide the relay module off its mounting bracket and disconnect the wiring connectors

renewed; it is not possible to renew the relays individually.

Removal

55 Slide the relay module off its mounting bracket in the right-hand rear corner of the engine compartment, then disconnect its wiring connectors and remove it from the car **(see illustration)**.

Refitting

56 Refitting is the reverse sequence to removal.

13 Inlet manifold – removal and refitting

Removal

Note: *Refer to the illustrations in Section 12 for component locations and connector details.*

1 Disconnect the battery negative terminal (refer to *Disconnecting the battery* in the Reference Chapter).
2 For increased working clearance, remove the bonnet as described in Chapter 11B.
3 Remove the air cleaner assembly as described in Section 2.
4 Release the accelerator cable adjusting nut from the mounting bracket, release the inner cable from the throttle cam, and position the cable clear of the throttle body.
5 Depress the plastic collar on the quick-

13.11b . . . and remove the two locating rings from the cylinder head ports

release fitting and disconnect the brake servo vacuum hose from the inlet manifold.
6 Disconnect the wiring connectors from the following components:
  a) *Throttle potentiometer (on the side of the throttle body).*
  b) *Idle air control valve (on the right-hand side of the inlet manifold).*
  c) *Manifold absolute pressure sensor (on the left-hand side of the inlet manifold).*
  d) *Inlet air temperature sensor (on the left-hand side of the inlet manifold).*
  e) *Fuel injectors.*
7 Bearing in mind the information contained in Section 5, place absorbent rags around the fuel feed and return hose quick-release fittings. Remove the fuel tank filler cap to release any pressure in the tank. Depress the plastic collar on the quick-release fittings and disconnect the feed and return hoses from the pipes. Plug or cover each pipe and hose, to minimise the loss of fuel and prevent the entry of dirt into the system.
8 Undo the three bolts securing the air cleaner mounting bracket to the fuel rail and inlet manifold. Release the two clips securing the wiring harness to the mounting bracket then remove the bracket from the throttle body.
9 Release the retaining clip and disconnect the evaporative emission control purge hose from the inlet manifold.
10 Disconnect the breather hose located adjacent to the emission control purge hose on the inlet manifold.
11 Undo and remove the four nuts securing the inlet manifold to the cylinder head, then remove the manifold from the engine. Remove the two locating rings from the inlet manifold or cylinder head ports **(see illustrations)**.

Refitting

12 Refitting is the reverse sequence to removal, noting the following points:
  a) *Although not strictly necessary, it is also recommended that the exhaust manifold is removed, as described in Part D of this Chapter, so that the manifold gasket can be renewed before the inlet manifold is refitted.*
  b) *Ensure that the manifold and gasket faces are clean, and that the two locating rings are in position in the manifold bores before refitting the manifold.*
  c) *Tighten the manifold retaining nuts to the specified torque, working progressively, in a spiral sequence from the centre outward.*
  d) *Ensure that all relevant hoses are reconnected to their original positions, and are securely held (where necessary) by the retaining clips.*
  e) *Prior to refitting the air cleaner assembly, adjust the accelerator cable as described in Section 3.*

Chapter 4 Part D:
Exhaust and emission control systems

Contents

Air pump drivebelt check and renewal . . . . .See Chapter 1
Catalytic converter – general information and precautions 9
Crankcase emission control system – checking and component
   renewal 5
Emission control system check . . . . .See Chapter 1
Evaporative emission control system – checking and component
   renewal 6
Exhaust emission control (with catalytic converter) – checking and
   component renewal 8

Exhaust emission control (no catalytic converter) – checking and
   component renewal 7
Exhaust manifold – removal and refitting 4
Exhaust system check . . . . .See Chapter 1
Exhaust system (models with catalytic converter) – removal and
   refitting 3
Exhaust system (models without catalytic converter) – removal and
   refitting 2
General information 1
Underbonnet check for fluid leaks and hose condition . .See Chapter 1

Degrees of difficulty

Easy, suitable for novice with little experience	Fairly easy, suitable for beginner with some experience	Fairly difficult, suitable for competent DIY mechanic	Difficult, suitable for experienced DIY mechanic	Very difficult, suitable for expert DIY or professional

Specifications

Torque wrench settings	Nm	lbf ft
Front pipe-to-exhaust manifold flange nuts	22	16
Fuel tank breather two-way valve nuts	9	7
Lambda sensor	55	41
Manifold retaining nuts	22	16
Thermostatic vacuum valve – carburettor models	10	7

1 General information

Exhaust system

The exhaust system fitted to all Mini models covered by this manual, except Cooper S, consists of an exhaust manifold and a tubular steel exhaust system in either single or multiple sections. A single silencer is fitted to the rear section of early models; later versions incorporate an additional intermediate silencer and/or catalytic converter. The system fitted to Cooper S models comprises a three branch manifold, a front pipe and separate tailpipe incorporating a silencer. Certain versions have a second silencer located beneath the floor pan.

On all models the exhaust system is flexibly attached to the car by rubber mountings on the rear subframe and a bracket at the base of the transmission.

Crankcase emission control

To reduce the emissions of unburned hydrocarbons from the crankcase into the atmosphere, a positive crankcase ventilation system is used whereby the engine is sealed and the blow-by gases and oil vapour are drawn from inside the crankcase, through an oil separator, into the inlet tract to be burned by the engine during normal combustion.

Evaporative emission control

The evaporative emission control system is used to minimise the escape of unburned hydrocarbons into the atmosphere.

The fuel tank filler cap is sealed, and a

charcoal canister is mounted underneath the left-hand wheelarch to collect the petrol vapours generated in the tank, and on some models in the carburettor float chamber, when the car is parked. It stores them until they can be cleared from the canister into the inlet tract, to be burned by the engine during normal combustion.

On early carburettor models, the vapours were drawn into the inlet tract whenever the engine was running. On later catalytic converter-equipped carburettor models, a thermostatic vacuum valve screwed into the front of the thermostat housing controls the flow of vapour from the canister to the engine. To ensure that the engine runs correctly when it is cold, and to protect the catalytic converter from the effects of an over-rich mixture, the thermostatic vacuum valve does not open until the engine has warmed-up to approximately 70°C. The valve then allows inlet manifold vacuum to act upon the purge valve vacuum diaphragm fitted to the top of the charcoal canister, which in turn opens the canister and allows the stored vapour into the inlet tract.

On fuel injection models, the engine management ECU controls the flow of vapour from the canister to the engine, via an electrically-operated purge control valve.

The purge control valve is not opened by the ECU until the engine has warmed up to above 70°C, the engine speed exceeds 1500 rpm and manifold absolute pressure is below 30 kPa; the control valve solenoid is then modulated on and off to allow the stored vapour to pass into the inlet tract.

Exhaust emission control

Carburettor models without catalytic converter

The basis of this system, used on certain early models, is an air pump which supplies air under pressure to the cylinder head exhaust port of each cylinder, via an air injection manifold. A check valve is incorporated in the air delivery pipe to prevent a blow-back of exhaust gases from reaching the pump. Air from the pump is also supplied to the inlet manifold via a gulp valve to weaken the rich fuel/air mixture in the manifold during engine deceleration and overrun.

The air pump is of the rotary vane type and is mounted at the front of the cylinder head. Drive to the pump is by a V-belt from the water pump pulley. Air enters the pump through an extraction filter on early models, or through radial air inlets around the pulley on later versions. At high engine speeds, excess air is discharged to atmosphere through a relief valve.

A diverter valve is incorporated in the air delivery pipe between the air pump and check valve. The valve is operated by a cable on early models, or activated by a vacuum switch on later types, whenever the choke control is pulled out. During choke operation, air from the pump is cut off and diverted to atmosphere.

When the throttle is closed during deceleration or overrun, a rich fuel/air mixture is created in the inlet manifold. The gulp valve fitted between the air pump and manifold is activated by the depression also created in the manifold during these conditions, and opens to admit air from the air pump. The mixture is thus weakened preventing excessive exhaust emissions when the throttle is reopened. A restrictor is also fitted in the air feed to the gulp valve and prevents surging when the valve is in operation.

Carburettor models with catalytic converter

From approximately 1990 onwards certain models were fitted with an unregulated or 'open-loop' catalytic converter to minimise exhaust pollution. The converter consists of an element (or 'substrate') of ceramic honeycomb coated with a combination of precious metals (platinum and rhodium) in such a way as to produce a vast surface area over which the exhaust gasses must flow; the assembly being mounted in a stainless-steel box in the vehicle's exhaust system. The precious metals act as catalysts to speed up the reaction between the pollutants and the oxygen in the car's exhaust gases. HC and CO being oxidised to form H_2O and CO_2.

Fuel injection models

All fuel injection models are equipped with a catalytic converter in the exhaust system. The system, unlike that fitted to carburettor models, is a 'closed-loop' system. The lambda sensor in the exhaust manifold provides the engine management ECU with constant feedback on exhaust gas content, which enables the ECU to adjust the inlet fuel/air mixture to keep the converter operating at maximum efficiency.

The lambda sensor has a built-in heating element, controlled by the ECU through the lambda sensor relay to quickly bring the sensor's tip to an efficient operating temperature. The sensor's tip is sensitive to oxygen, and sends the ECU a varying voltage depending on the amount of oxygen in the exhaust gases; if the inlet air/fuel mixture is too rich, the exhaust gases are low in oxygen, so the sensor sends a low-voltage signal; the voltage rises as the mixture weakens and the amount of oxygen in the exhaust gases rises.

Peak conversion efficiency of all major pollutants occurs if the inlet air/fuel mixture is maintained at the chemically-correct ratio for the complete combustion of petrol – 14.7 parts (by weight) of air to 1 part of fuel (the 'stoichiometric' ratio). The sensor output voltage alters in a large step at this point, the ECU using the signal change as a reference point, correcting the inlet fuel/air mixture accordingly by altering the fuel injector pulse width.

2 Exhaust system (models without catalytic converter) – removal and refitting

All models except Cooper S

Removal

1 Working in the engine compartment, remove the air cleaner (see Part A of this Chapter) and detach the throttle return spring from the bracket on the exhaust manifold clamp.

2 Undo and remove the nuts and bolts and withdraw the manifold clamp **(see illustration)**.

3 Position the car over an inspection pit, or alternatively jack it up and support it on axle stands (see *Jacking and vehicle support*).

4 From underneath the car, undo and remove the nut and bolt securing the exhaust front pipe to the transmission or transmission bracket.

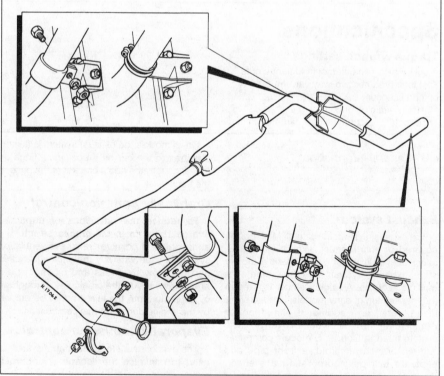

2.2 Typical exhaust system support brackets and mountings

3.2 Tailpipe-to-catalytic converter mounting flange and retaining nuts

3.3 Exhaust tailpipe and silencer mounting rubber attachment

5 Now undo and remove the nuts and spring washers securing the exhaust intermediate and rear mounting brackets to the rubber blocks on the rear subframe. Slide the brackets off the studs on the rubber blocks and lower the complete system to the ground.
6 Carefully inspect the rubber mounting blocks, the exhaust system brackets and clamps for signs of deterioration, corrosion or damage and renew as necessary.

Refitting

7 To refit the exhaust system, place it in position under the car and locate the brackets onto the rubber mounting blocks at the rear. Refit the nuts and spring washers but do not tighten at this stage.
8 Before positioning the bellmouth of the front pipe over the manifold flange, smear its mating surface with sealing paste. Doing this will reduce any risk of leakage. With the help of an assistant, locate the bellmouth squarely over the flange on the manifold. Hold the system in this position and refit the manifold clamp. Ensure that the pipe is square and that the clamp is seated properly over the pipe and manifold flanges otherwise leaks will occur at this joint.

> **HAYNES HiNT** *Position a jack under the exhaust front pipe and raise it just sufficiently to hold the bellmouth tightly against the manifold flange. This will ensure that the joint is properly seated as the clamp is fitted.*

9 Now fully tighten the manifold clamp securing bolts and refit the throttle return spring.
10 Check that the exhaust system is clear of the subframe and floor pan over its entire length and that it is not in tension. Now fully tighten the rear mountings.
11 Lower the car to the ground, refit the air cleaner, start the engine and check for leaks.

Cooper S models

Removal

12 Position the car over an inspection pit, or alternatively jack it up and support it on axle stands (see *Jacking and vehicle support*).
13 If the rear silencer and tailpipe only are to be removed, slacken the exhaust clamp securing the rear silencer to the front pipe and then remove the retaining clip securing the tailpipe to the rear mounting. Twist the rear silencer back-and-forth to separate the joint and then withdraw the tailpipe from under the car.

> **HAYNES HiNT** *Apply liberal amounts of releasing oil to the exhaust tailpipe-to-front pipe joint if it is reluctant to come free, and allow it time to soak in.*

14 To remove the complete system, slacken the front pipe to exhaust manifold clamp, and undo and remove the bolts securing the rear mountings to the subframe. Twist the complete system back-and-forth to free the joint and lower it to the ground.

Refitting

15 In all cases, refitting is the reverse of removal.

3 Exhaust system (models with catalytic converter) – removal and refitting

Tailpipe and silencer

Removal

1 Position the car over an inspection pit, or alternatively jack it up and support it on axle stands (see *Jacking and vehicle support*).
2 Slacken and remove the two nuts securing the tailpipe flange to the catalytic converter studs **(see illustration)**.

3 Either slacken and remove the nuts and bolts securing the tailpipe and silencer to its mounting brackets, or release it from its mounting rubbers (as applicable), then withdraw the assembly from underneath the car and recover the flange gasket **(see illustration)**.

Refitting

4 Refitting is the reverse sequence to removal, ensuring that the flange mating surfaces are clean and free of corrosion, and using a new gasket.

Catalytic converter

Removal

5 Remove the tailpipe and silencer assembly as described above.
6 Unscrew the two nuts securing the catalytic converter to the front pipe, then withdraw the catalytic converter from underneath the car and recover the flange gasket.

Refitting

7 Refitting is the reverse sequence to removal, ensuring that the flange mating surfaces are clean and free of corrosion and using new gaskets.

Front pipe

Removal

8 On carburettor models, remove the air cleaner assembly (see Part A of this Chapter).
9 Position the car over an inspection pit, or alternatively jack it up and support it on axle stands (see *Jacking and vehicle support*).
10 Slacken and remove the two nuts securing the catalytic converter to the front pipe. Unscrew the nut and bolt securing the front pipe to the bracket on the transmission **(see illustration)**.
11 On early Cooper models, undo the gas sampling pipe mounting bolts, then slacken its union nut and remove the pipe from the side of the exhaust front pipe.

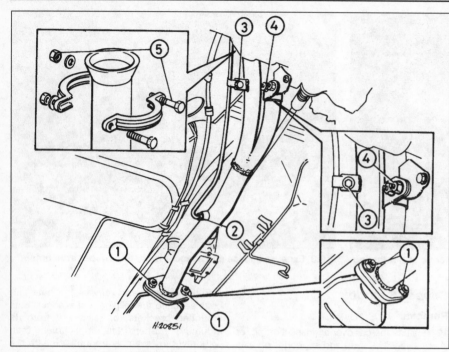

3.10 Exhaust front pipe fitted to models with catalytic converter

1 Catalytic converter flange nuts
2 Gas sampling pipe union nut
3 Gas sampling pipe mounting bolt
4 Front pipe mounting nut
5 Front pipe-to-manifold clamp and bolts

12 On all carburettor models, unbolt the exhaust front pipe-to-manifold clamp(s), then remove the front pipe from underneath the car, and recover the flange gasket from the catalytic converter.

13 On fuel injection models, undo the three nuts securing the front pipe to the exhaust manifold, then release the pipe from the manifold and catalytic converter studs. Remove the front pipe from underneath the car, and recover the flange gaskets.

Refitting

14 Refitting is the reverse sequence to removal, ensuring that the mating surfaces of the exhaust system are clean and free from corrosion. Fit a new gasket to the catalytic converter flange, and apply a smear of sealing paste to the front pipe-to-manifold joint, to alleviate any risk of leakage.

HAYNES HiNT *Position a jack under the exhaust front pipe and raise it just sufficiently to hold the bellmouth tightly against the manifold flange. This will ensure that the joint is properly seated as the clamp is fitted.*

Heat shields

15 Later catalytic converter-equipped models are fitted with two heat shields secured to the underside of the body, one above the catalytic converter and one above the tailpipe silencer.

Removal

16 Firmly apply the handbrake, then jack up the front of the car and support it securely on axle stands (see *Jacking and vehicle support*).

3.17 Undo the tailpipe heat shield retaining nuts . . .

3.18 . . . then slide the shield forward and manoeuvre it around and off the exhaust system

17 To remove the tailpipe heat shield, undo the four retaining nuts and lower the shield off the mounting studs **(see illustration)**.

18 Slide the shield forward then manoeuvre it around and off the exhaust system **(see illustration)**.

19 To remove the catalytic converter heat shield, first remove the tailpipe heat shield.

20 Undo the two remaining retaining nuts and lower the shield off the mounting studs. Slide the shield forward then manoeuvre it around and off the exhaust system.

Refitting

21 Refitting is the reverse sequence to removal, ensuring that the retaining nuts are securely tightened.

---

4 Exhaust manifold –
removal and refitting

Carburettor models

Except Cooper S

1 The exhaust manifold fitted to all carburettor models except Cooper S is removed as an assembly with the inlet manifold. Full details on this procedure will be found in Part A of this Chapter.

Cooper S

2 Remove the carburettors and inlet manifold as described in Part A of this Chapter.

3 Remove the complete exhaust system as described in Section 2 of this Part.

4 Undo and remove the nuts and flat washers securing the manifold to the cylinder head studs. Now ease the manifold off the studs and carefully manipulate it out of the engine compartment.

5 Before removing the LCB (long centre branch) exhaust manifold, refer to Chapter 8 and detach the right-hand driveshaft at the inboard end.

6 Refer to Chapter 10 and remove the right-hand front roadwheel, disconnect the steering tie-rod, the swivel hub at its upper and lower points, and partially withdraw the hub and driveshaft. Do not allow the assembly to hang from the brake hose.

7 Turn the differential driving flange so that it is upright. Release the exhaust manifold from the cylinder head, manoeuvre it to the right to clear the subframe and transmission casing before easing it upwards.

8 Refitting is the reverse sequence to removal, but use a new manifold gasket.

Fuel injection models

Single-point injection

9 Remove the inlet manifold as described in Part B of this Chapter.

10 Firmly apply the handbrake, then jack up the front of the car and support it securely on axle stands (see *Jacking and vehicle support*).

11 Working from underneath the vehicle,

4.20 Disconnect the lambda sensor wiring multiplug

4.21 Undo the bolt securing the breather pipe to the cylinder head

4.22 Release the breather pipe from the exhaust manifold studs

slacken and remove the single bolt securing the exhaust front pipe to its mounting bracket on the transmission. Undo the three nuts securing the front pipe to the exhaust manifold, and release the pipe from the manifold studs.

12 Track the wiring back from the exhaust manifold lambda sensor, releasing it from any relevant retaining clips, and disconnect it from the main wiring harness.

13 Slacken and remove the three heat shield retaining bolts, and remove the heat shield from the manifold.

14 Undo the two remaining exhaust manifold nuts, and slide the breather pipe off the manifold stud. Disengage the manifold from its mounting studs, and remove it from the engine compartment. Remove the manifold gasket, and discard it.

15 Examine all the exhaust manifold studs for signs of damage and corrosion; remove all traces of corrosion, and repair or renew any damaged studs.

16 Refitting is the reverse sequence to removal, noting the following points:

a) *Ensure that the exhaust manifold and cylinder head mating surfaces are clean and free from corrosion, and fit a new gasket onto the manifold studs.*

b) *Tighten the manifold nuts to the specified torque, not forgetting to first refit the breather pipe to the left-hand stud.*

c) *Fit a new gasket at the manifold to the front pipe flange joint, and securely tighten all other disturbed fasteners.*

Multi-point injection

17 Remove the inlet manifold as described in Part C of this Chapter.

18 Firmly apply the handbrake, then jack up the front of the car and support it securely on axle stands (see *Jacking and vehicle support*).

19 Working from underneath the vehicle, slacken and remove the single bolt securing the exhaust front pipe to its mounting bracket on the transmission. Undo the three nuts securing the front pipe to the exhaust manifold, and release the pipe from the manifold studs.

20 Disconnect the lambda sensor wiring multiplug located adjacent to the main wiring harness on the bulkhead **(see illustration)**.

21 Undo the bolt securing the breather pipe to the right-hand end of the cylinder head **(see illustration)**.

22 Undo the two remaining exhaust manifold nuts, and release the breather pipe from the manifold studs **(see illustration)**. Clearance between the breather pipe and manifold heat shield is limited and it may be necessary to unbolt the heat shield to increase the working clearance.

23 Disengage the manifold from its mounting studs, and remove it from the engine compartment. Remove the manifold gasket, and discard it **(see illustrations)**.

24 Examine all the exhaust manifold studs for signs of damage and corrosion; remove all traces of corrosion, and repair or renew any damaged studs.

25 Refitting is the reverse sequence to removal, noting the following points:

a) *Ensure that the exhaust manifold and cylinder head mating surfaces are clean and free from corrosion, and fit a new gasket onto the manifold studs.*

b) *One side of the gasket is marked 'manifold side' and should be fitted accordingly.*

c) *Tighten the manifold nuts to the specified torque, not forgetting to first refit the breather pipe to the manifold studs.*

d) *Fit a new gasket at the manifold to the front pipe flange joint, and securely tighten all other disturbed fasteners.*

4.23a Remove the manifold from the mounting studs . . .

4.23b . . . and collect the gasket

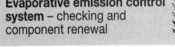

5 Crankcase emission control system – checking and component renewal

The crankcase emission control system consists simply of a number of ventilation hoses, an oil separator and a wire mesh filter in the engine oil filler cap.

The components of this system require no attention other than to check that the hoses are clear and undamaged and to renew the oil filler cap at regular intervals (see Chapter 1).

Component renewal is self-explanatory, but it may be necessary to detach surrounding components for improved access. Refer to the various Chapters of this manual as necessary if problems are encountered.

6 Evaporative emission control system – checking and component renewal

Checking

1 Poor idle, stalling and poor driveability can be caused by an inoperative canister purge valve, faulty thermostatic vacuum valve, a damaged canister, split or cracked hoses, or hoses connected to the wrong fittings. Check the fuel filler cap for a damaged or deformed gasket.

2 Fuel loss or fuel odour can be caused by liquid fuel leaking from fuel lines, a cracked or damaged canister, an inoperative canister

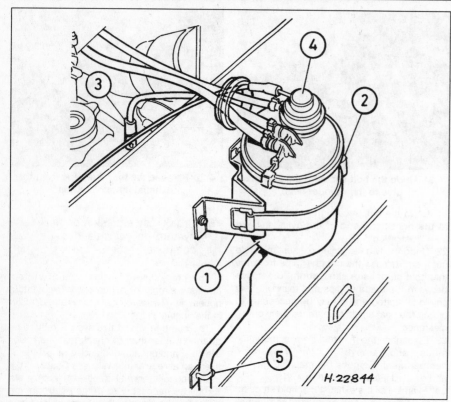

6.13 Charcoal canister fitted to carburettor models with catalytic converter

1 *Charcoal canister and mounting bracket*
2 *Rubber retaining strap*
3 *Fuel return pipe connection*
4 *Purge valve vacuum diaphragm*
5 *Vent hose*

purge valve, and disconnected, misrouted, kinked or damaged vapour or control hoses.

3 Inspect each hose attached to the canister for kinks, leaks and cracks along its entire length. If their condition is suspect, disconnect each hose in turn and blow through it to check for blockages. Repair or renew as necessary.

4 Inspect the canister. If it is cracked or damaged, renew it. Look for fuel leaking from the bottom of the canister. If fuel is leaking, renew the canister, and check the hoses and hose routing.

5 Checking of the thermostatic vacuum valve and purge control valve should be entrusted to a Rover dealer.

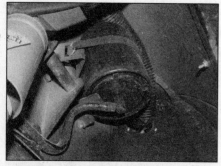

6.19 Charcoal canister attachments on fuel injection models

Charcoal canister renewal

Carburettor models

6 Disconnect the battery negative terminal (refer to *Disconnecting the battery* in the Reference Chapter).

7 Remove the air cleaner assembly as described in Part A of this Chapter.

8 Release the fasteners and detach the ignition cover from the front of the engine.

9 Release the retaining clips, and disconnect the charcoal canister hoses from the side of the carburettor and from the breather hose T-piece.

10 Disconnect the charcoal canister vacuum supply pipe from the thermostatic vacuum switch situated on the thermostat housing.

11 Release the clip and disconnect the canister hose from the fuel return pipe.

12 Firmly apply the handbrake, then jack up the front of the car and support it securely on axle stands (see *Jacking and vehicle support*).

13 Working from underneath the left-hand wing, release the rubber retaining strap, and free the canister from its mounting bracket **(see illustration)**. Disconnect the vacuum pipe from the purge valve diaphragm, then release the canister vent hose from the wing valance and withdraw the canister from underneath the wing.

14 Refitting is the reverse sequence to removal, noting that if a new canister is being installed, it will be necessary to remove the

vent hoses from the original canister and install them on the new one before fitting the canister to the car. Ensure that all hoses are correctly reconnected, and where necessary securely held by their retaining clips.

Fuel injection models

15 Disconnect the battery negative terminal (refer to *Disconnecting the battery* in the Reference Chapter).

16 Working in the engine compartment, release the retaining clip(s), and disconnect the canister hoses from the purge valve and fuel hose.

17 Firmly apply the handbrake, then jack up the front of the car and support it securely on axle stands (see *Jacking and vehicle support*).

18 From underneath the left-hand wheelarch, release the air inlet duct, and position it clear of the charcoal canister.

19 Release the canister vent hose from its retaining clips, then release the rubber retaining strap and remove the canister and hose assembly from underneath the wheelarch **(see illustration)**.

20 Refitting is the reverse sequence to removal, noting that if a new canister is being installed, it will be necessary to remove the vent hoses from the original canister and install them on the new one before fitting the canister to the car. Ensure that all hoses are correctly reconnected, and where necessary securely held by their retaining clips.

Vacuum valve renewal

Carburettor models

21 When the engine and radiator are cold, either drain the cooling system as described in Chapter 1, or unscrew the radiator filler cap to release any remaining pressure, and have ready a suitable plug that can be used temporarily to stop the escape of coolant while the switch is removed. If the latter method is used, take care not to damage the threads, and do not use anything which will leave foreign matter inside the cooling system.

22 Release the fasteners and remove the ignition cover from the front of the engine.

23 Disconnect the vacuum hoses from the thermostatic vacuum valve, which is screwed into the front of the thermostat housing **(see illustration)**.

24 Slacken the radiator top hose retaining clip, and slide the clip along the hose. Unscrew the valve from the front of the thermostat housing, and remove it along with its sealing washer. Where necessary, plug the housing aperture to minimise coolant loss.

25 On refitting, apply a smear of suitable sealant to the valve threads, then refit the valve and sealing washer to the thermostat housing, tightening it to the specified torque. Slide the radiator hose retaining clip back into position, and tighten it securely.

26 Reconnect the vacuum hoses to the valve, noting that the hose from the carburettor must be connected to the union of the valve marked CARB.

27 Refit the ignition cover, and refill or top-up the cooling system as described in Chapter 1 or *Weekly checks*.

Purge control valve renewal

Fuel injection models

28 Disconnect the battery negative terminal (refer to *Disconnecting the battery* in the Reference Chapter), then disconnect the wiring connector from the purge control valve **(see illustration)**.
29 Release the retaining clips, and disconnect the inlet and outlet hoses from the valve **(see illustration)**.
30 Prise out the C-clip which secures the inlet hose adapter to the mounting bracket **(see illustration)**, then withdraw the adapter, noting the O-ring which is fitted between the adapter and purge valve. Discard the O-ring; it must be renewed as a matter of course.
31 Slide the purge valve out of its mounting bracket, and remove the valve from the car.
32 Refitting is the reverse sequence to removal, using a new inlet hose adapter O-ring.

Fuel tank breather renewal

Fuel injection models

33 Remove the fuel tank as described in Part B or Part C of this Chapter, as applicable.
34 Release the retaining clip, and disconnect the two-way breather valve vent hose from the fuel tank. Unclip the valve and hose assembly from the tank seam, and remove it.
35 Release the retaining clips, disconnect the hose from the valve, then undo the two retaining nuts, and separate the valve from the mounting bracket.
36 Refitting is the reverse sequence to removal, tightening the valve retaining nuts to the specified torque, and ensuring that the hoses are securely reconnected.

7 Exhaust emission control (no catalytic converter) – checking and component renewal

Checking

1 Checking of the system as a whole entails a close visual inspection of all hoses, pipes and

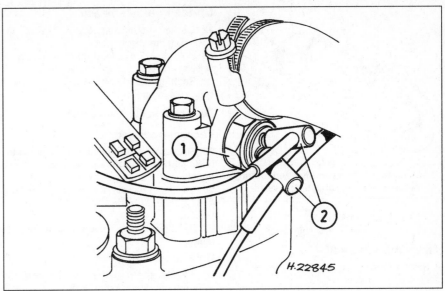

6.23 Thermostatic vacuum valve connections

1 Vacuum valve   *2 Vacuum hoses*

connections for condition and security. Ensure also that the air pump drivebelt is in satisfactory condition and correctly tensioned as described in Chapter 1.

Air pump and air manifold

2 Check the condition of the air pump bearings with the drivebelt removed by moving the pulley from side-to-side. Any appreciable movement indicates wear and will usually be accompanied by excessive noise from the unit when in operation. Apart from this, any known or suspected faults on either of these components should be attended to by a Rover dealer.

Check valve

3 Remove the valve as described later in this Section and test it by gently blowing into each end in turn. Air should pass through the valve from the air supply end only. If air will pass in both directions the valve is faulty and must be renewed. Do not use high pressure air or air from a tyre pump for this check or the valve will be damaged.

Vacuum-operated diverter valve

4 To test the operation of the valve, slacken

the hose clip and detach the diverter valve-to-check valve hose at the check valve end.
5 Start the engine and allow it to idle. Air pressure should be felt at the end of the disconnected hose.
6 Operate the choke control, and air pressure at the disconnected hose should be cut off completely. If air can still be felt at the end of the hose, the diverter valve is faulty and should be renewed.

Cable-operated diverter valve

7 The procedure for testing the cable-operated diverter valve is the same as for the vacuum type described previously. If the valve does not completely restrict the flow of air when the choke control is operated, make sure that the cable is correctly adjusted as described later in this Section and then carry out the test again. If the airflow is still not completely restricted, renew the valve.

Gulp valve

8 This component can only be tested satisfactorily using vacuum gauges. If the valve is suspect it is recommended that the testing is carried out by a Rover dealer.

6.28 Disconnecting the purge valve wiring connector

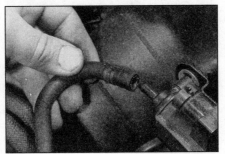

6.29 Release the retaining clip, and disconnect the outlet hose from the purge valve

6.30 Prise off the C-clip (arrowed), and remove the inlet hose adaptor from the purge valve

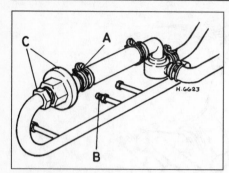

7.18 Air manifold assembly fitted to early models without catalytic converter

  A Check valve hose clip
  B Air manifold unions
  C Check valve and union nut

Air pump renewal

9 Remove the air pump drivebelt as described in Chapter 1.

10 Slacken the clips and detach the outlet hoses from the pump adapter.

11 Detach the HT lead and undo and remove No 1 cylinder spark plug.

12 Slacken the bolt securing the pump adjusting arm to the alternator pivot bolt.

13 Undo and remove the bolt securing the adjusting arm to the air pump.

14 Undo and remove the air pump pivot nut and bolt and lift off the pump.

15 Refitting is the reverse sequence to removal. Ensure that the drivebelt is correctly tensioned as described in Chapter 1.

Air manifold renewal

16 Release the three retaining lugs and remove the engine ignition shield, if fitted.

17 Detach the HT lead from No 1 cylinder spark plug.

18 Undo and remove the four air manifold unions from the cylinder head (see illustration).

19 Slacken the clip securing the check valve hose and lift away the air manifold complete with check valve.

20 Hold the air manifold union with a spanner and unscrew the check valve.

21 Refitting is the reverse sequence to removal.

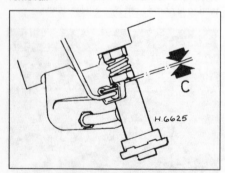

7.32 Correct position of jet assembly when testing diverter valve operation

C = 0.25 to 0.38 mm

Check valve renewal

22 Slacken the retaining clip and detach the hose from the check valve.

23 Hold the air manifold union to prevent it twisting and unscrew the check valve.

24 Refitting the check valve is the reverse sequence to removal.

Diverter valve renewal

Vacuum-operated valve

25 Slacken all the hose clips and detach the three air hoses and the small vacuum hose from the valve body.

26 Undo and remove the two retaining nuts and bolts and lift the valve off its mounting bracket.

27 Refitting is the reverse sequence to removal.

Cable-operated valve

28 Slacken the cable retaining screw and slide the cable and retainer out of the valve operating lever.

29 Slacken the hose clips and detach the three hoses from the valve body, then lift the valve off the engine.

30 Refitting the valve is the reverse sequence to removal. With the valve installed adjust the operating cable as follows.

31 Observe the movement of the jet housing beneath the carburettor while an assistant slowly operates the choke control.

32 When the jet housing has moved down away from the adjusting nut by 0.25 to 0.38 mm, lock the choke control to hold it in this position (see illustration).

33 The clearance between the diverter valve operating lever and the valve stem should now be 0.04 to 0.08 mm. Adjust the position of the cable retainer to obtain this dimension.

Gulp valve renewal

34 To remove the gulp valve slacken all the hose clips, and detach the air hoses and the vacuum hose from the valve body.

35 Undo and remove the two retaining nuts and bolts and lift the valve off its mounting bracket.

36 Refitting is the reverse sequence to removal.

---

8 Exhaust emission control (with catalytic converter) – checking and component renewal

Checking

1 Checking of the system as a whole entails a close visual inspection of all hoses, pipes and connections for condition and security. High exhaust gas CO content on carburettor models may be due to other fuel or ignition system faults such as dirty or choked air cleaner element, worn or incorrectly adjusted carburettor, worn or badly adjusted spark plugs or incorrect ignition timing. Apart from

these checks, and checks of the general engine condition, any known or suspected faults in the exhaust emission control system should be attended to by a Rover dealer.

Catalytic converter renewal

2 Removal and refitting procedures for the catalytic converter are contained in Section 3; general information and precautions are contained in Section 9.

Lambda sensor renewal

Fuel injection models

Note: *The lambda sensor is delicate, and will not work if it is dropped or knocked, if its power supply is disrupted, or if any cleaning materials are used on it.*

3 Remove the inlet manifold as described In Part B or Part C of this Chapter as applicable.

4 Trace the wiring back from the exhaust manifold lambda sensor, releasing it from any relevant retaining clips, and disconnect it from the main wiring harness (see illustration).

5 Unscrew the sensor from the manifold, and remove it with its sealing washer.

6 Prior to refitting, examine the sealing washer for signs of damage, and renew as necessary.

7 Ensure that the sensor and manifold threads are clean, then apply a smear of high-temperature anti-seize compound (Rover recommend 'Never-Seez') to the sensor's threads.

8 Fit the sealing washer to the sensor, then refit the sensor to the manifold, and tighten it to the specified torque.

9 Reconnect the sensor wiring connector, and secure the wiring in position with any relevant ties.

10 Refit the inlet manifold as described in Part B or Part C of this Chapter as applicable.

Lambda sensor relay renewal

Single-point fuel injection models

11 The lambda sensor relay is mounted onto the left-hand side of the engine compartment bulkhead, next to the fuel cut-off inertia switch. To remove the relay, undo its retaining screw and disconnect its wiring connector.

12 Refitting is the reverse sequence to removal.

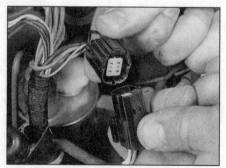

8.4 Disconnecting the exhaust system lambda sensor wiring connector

Multi-point fuel injection models

13 The lambda sensor relay is incorporated into the relay module located in the right-hand rear corner of the engine compartment. If a fault develops in the lambda sensor relay, the complete relay module must be renewed; it is not possible to renew the relays in the module individually.

14 Relay module removal and refitting details are contained in Part C, Section 12, of this Chapter.

9 Catalytic converter – general information and precautions

The catalytic converter is a reliable and simple device, which needs no maintenance in itself, but there are some facts of which an owner should be aware if the converter is to function properly for its full service life.

a) *DO NOT use leaded petrol in a vehicle equipped with a catalytic converter – the lead will coat the precious metals, reducing their converting efficiency, and will eventually destroy the converter.*

b) *Always keep the ignition and fuel systems well-maintained in accordance with the manufacturer's schedule (see Chapter 1).*

c) *If the engine develops a misfire, do not drive the vehicle at all (or at least as little as possible) until the fault is cured.*

d) *DO NOT push – or tow-start the vehicle – this will soak the catalytic converter in unburned fuel, causing it to overheat when the engine does start.*

e) *DO NOT switch off the ignition at high engine speeds, ie do not 'blip' the throttle immediately before switching off.*

f) *DO NOT use fuel or engine oil additives – these may contain substances harmful to the catalytic converter.*

g) *DO NOT continue to use the vehicle if the engine burns oil to the extent of leaving a visible trail of blue smoke.*

h) *Remember that the catalytic converter operates at very high temperatures. DO NOT, therefore, park the vehicle in dry undergrowth, over long grass or piles of dead leaves, after a long run.*

i) *Remember that the catalytic converter is FRAGILE. Do not strike it with tools during servicing work.*

j) *In some cases, a sulphurous smell (like that of rotten eggs) may be noticed from the exhaust. This is common to many catalytic converter-equipped vehicles. Once the vehicle has covered a few thousand miles, the problem should disappear – in the meantime, try changing the brand of petrol used.*

k) *The catalytic converter used on a well-maintained and well-driven vehicle should last for between 50 000 and 100 000 miles. If the converter is no longer effective, it must be renewed.*

Chapter 5 Part A:
Starting and charging systems

Contents

Alternator – removal and refitting 10
Alternator brushes – renewal 11
Alternator charging system – testing 9
Auxiliary drivebelt check and renewal ....See Chapter 1
Battery – removal and refitting 4
Battery – testing and charging 3
Battery check ....See Weekly Checks
Control box – adjustment 8
Control box cleaning and inspection ....See Chapter 1
Drive pinion assembly (inertia type starter) – removal and refitting . . 15
Dynamo – removal and refitting 6

Dynamo brushes – renewal 7
Dynamo charging system – testing 5
Dynamo check and lubrication ....See Chapter 1
Electrical fault finding – general information 2
Electrical system check ....See Weekly Checks
General information and precautions 1
Starter motor – removal and refitting 13
Starter motor – testing and overhaul 14
Starter solenoid – removal and refitting 16
Starting system – testing 12

Degrees of difficulty

Easy, suitable for novice with little experience		**Fairly easy,** suitable for beginner with some experience		**Fairly difficult,** suitable for competent DIY mechanic		**Difficult,** suitable for experienced DIY mechanic		**Very difficult,** suitable for expert DIY or professional	

Specifications

System type .... 12 volt, negative earth

Battery

Type .... Low maintenance or 'maintenance-free' sealed for life
Capacity .... 30 to 50 amp hour at 20 hour rate
Charge condition:
   Poor .... 12.5 volts
   Normal .... 12.6 volts
   Good .... 12.7 volts

Dynamo

Type .... Lucas C40/1
Maximum output .... 22 amps at 2250 rpm
Cut-in speed .... 1450 rpm at 13.5 volts
Minimum brush length .... 12.7 mm
Brush spring tension .... 510 g

Control box

Type .... Lucas RB106/2
Regulator:
   Open circuit setting at 3000 rpm (dynamo speed) at 20°C (68°F) ... 16.0 to 16.6 volts, decreasing by 0.1 volt for every increase of
      10°C (18°F) above 20°C (68°F)

Cut-out:
   Cut-in voltage .... 12.7 to 13.3 volts
   Drop-off voltage .... 8.5 to 11 volts
   Reverse current .... 5.0 amps (maximum)

Alternator

Type:
Pre-1982 models	Lucas 11AC or 16ACR
1982 to 1985 models	Lucas A115
1986 to October 1996 models	Lucas A127/45 or A127/55
October 1996 models onward	No information available

Maximum output:
11AC	43 amps
16ACR	34 amps
A115 and A127/45	45 amps
A127/55	55 amps

Minimum brush length:
11AC	3.9 mm
16ACR	7.5 mm
A115	10.0 mm
A127/45 and A127/55	5.0 mm

Starter motor

Type:
Pre-1986 models	Lucas M35G or M35J (inertia type)
1986 models onward	Lucas M79 (pre-engaged type)

Minimum brush length:
M35G and M35J	8.0 mm
M79	3.5 mm

Brush spring tension:
M35G	425 to 710 g
M35J	794 g
M79	N/A

1 General information and precautions

General information

The engine electrical system consists mainly of the charging and starting systems. Because of their engine-related functions, these components are covered separately from the body electrical devices such as the lights, instruments, etc (which are covered in Chapter 12). Information on the ignition system is covered in Part B and Part C of this Chapter.

The electrical system is of the 12 volt negative earth type.

The battery is of the low maintenance or 'maintenance-free' (sealed for life) type and is charged by the dynamo or alternator, which is driven by the auxiliary drivebelt.

The charging system on early models consists of a dynamo and control box incorporating a voltage regulator and cut-out. The voltage regulator controls the output from the dynamo depending on the state of the battery and the demands of the electrical equipment, and ensures that the battery is not over-charged. The cut-out is really an automatic switch and connects the dynamo to the battery when the dynamo is turning fast enough to produce a charge. Similarly it disconnects the battery from the dynamo when the engine is idling or stationary so that the battery does not discharge through the dynamo.

Later models are equipped with an alternator in place of the dynamo and control box. The Lucas 11AC alternator and separate 4TR control unit was used initially, but has been superseded by the 16ACR, A115 and A127 alternators with integral control units.

The alternators are all similar in construction, comprising basically an aluminium casing, housing a three-phase star connected stator. A rotor carrying the field windings rotates within the stator and is driven by the auxiliary drivebelt. The alternator output is controlled by a voltage regulator located in the separate control unit on the 11AC alternator and contained within the end housing on the other machines.

As its name implies, the alternator generates alternating current (ac) as opposed to direct current (dc) generated by the dynamo. The alternating current is rectified by diodes, located in the alternator end housing, into direct current, which is the current required for battery charging.

On early models an inertia type starter motor is fitted energised by a separate solenoid switch mounted on the front inner wing panel. When the ignition switch is turned, current flows from the battery to the starter motor solenoid, which causes it to become energised. Its internal plunger moves inwards and closes an internal switch, so allowing full starting current to flow from the battery to the starter motor. This causes a powerful magnetic field to be induced into the field coils which causes the armature to rotate.

Mounted on helical splines is the drive pinion which, because of the sudden rotation of the armature, is thrown forwards along the armature shaft and so into engagement with the ring gear. The engine crankshaft will then be rotated until the engine starts to operate on its own and, at this point, the drive pinion is thrown out of mesh with the ring gear.

A pre-engaged type starter motor is fitted to all models from 1986 onward. On starting, the integral solenoid moves the drive pinion into engagement with the flywheel ring gear before the starter motor is energised. Once the engine has started, a one-way clutch prevents the motor armature being driven by the engine until the pinion disengages from the flywheel.

Precautions

Further details of the various systems are given in the relevant Sections of this Chapter. While some repair procedures are given, the usual course of action is to renew the component concerned. The owner whose interest extends beyond mere component renewal should obtain a copy of the *Automobile Electrical & Electronic Systems Manual*, available from the publishers of this manual.

It is necessary to take extra care when working on the electrical system to avoid damage to semi-conductor devices (diodes and transistors), and to avoid the risk of personal injury. In addition to the precautions given in *Safety first!* at the beginning of this manual, observe the following when working on the system:

⚠️ *Always remove rings, watches, etc, before working on the electrical system. Even with the battery disconnected, capacitive discharge could occur if a component's live terminal is earthed through a metal object. This could cause a shock or nasty burn.*

Do not reverse the battery connections. Components such as the alternator, electronic control units, or any other components having semi-conductor circuitry could be irreparably damaged.

If the engine is being started using jump leads and a slave battery, connect the batteries positive-to-positive and negative-to-negative (see 'Jump starting'). This also applies when connecting a battery charger.

Never disconnect the battery terminals, the alternator, any electrical wiring or any test instruments when the engine is running.

Do not allow the engine to turn the alternator when the alternator is not connected.

Never 'test' for alternator output by 'flashing' the output lead to earth.

Never use an ohmmeter of the type incorporating a hand-cranked generator for circuit or continuity testing.

Always ensure that the battery negative terminal is disconnected when working on the electrical system.

Before using electric-arc welding equipment on the car, disconnect the battery, alternator and components such as the engine management electronic control unit to protect them from the risk of damage.

Several systems fitted to the vehicle require battery power to be available at all times, either to ensure their continued operation (such as the clock) or to maintain control unit memories or security codes which would be wiped if the battery were to be disconnected. To ensure that there are no unforeseen consequences of this action, Refer to 'Disconnecting the battery' in the Reference Section of this manual for further information.

2 Electrical fault finding – general information

Refer to the relevant Part of Chapter 12.

3 Battery – testing and charging

Testing

Standard & low maintenance battery

1 If the vehicle covers a small annual mileage, it is worthwhile checking the specific gravity of the electrolyte every three months to determine the state of charge of the battery. Use a hydrometer to make the check and compare the results with the following table. Note that the specific gravity readings assume an electrolyte temperature of 15°C (60°F); for

every 10°C (18°F) below 15°C (60°F) subtract 0.007. For every 10°C (18°F) above 15°C (60°F) add 0.007.

	Above 25°C (77°F)	Below 25°C (77°F)
Fully-charged	1.210 to 1.230	1.270 to 1.290
70% charged	1.170 to 1.190	1.230 to 1.250
Discharged	1.050 to 1.070	1.110 to 1.130

2 If the battery condition is suspect, first check the specific gravity of electrolyte in each cell. A variation of 0.040 or more between any cells indicates loss of electrolyte or deterioration of the internal plates.

3 If the specific gravity variation is 0.040 or more, the battery should be renewed. If the cell variation is satisfactory but the battery is discharged, it should be charged as described later in this Section.

Maintenance-free battery

4 In cases where a 'sealed for life' maintenance-free battery is fitted, topping-up and testing of the electrolyte in each cell is not possible. The condition of the battery can therefore only be tested using a battery condition indicator or a voltmeter.

5 If testing the battery using a voltmeter, connect the voltmeter across the battery and compare the result with those given in the Specifications under 'charge condition'. The test is only accurate if the battery has not been subjected to any kind of charge for the previous six hours. If this is not the case, switch on the headlights for 30 seconds, then wait four to five minutes before testing the battery after switching off the headlights. All other electrical circuits must be switched off, so check that the doors and tailgate are fully shut when making the test.

6 If the voltage reading is less than 12.2 volts, then the battery is discharged, whilst a reading of 12.2 to 12.4 volts indicates a partially-discharged condition.

7 If the battery is to be charged, remove it from the vehicle (see Section 4) and charge it as described later in this Section.

Charging

Standard & low maintenance battery

Note: *The following is intended as a guide only. Always refer to the manufacturer's recommendations (often printed on a label attached to the battery) before charging a battery.*

8 Charge the battery at a rate of 3.5 to 4.0 amps and continue to charge the battery at this rate until no further rise in specific gravity is noted over a four hour period.

9 Alternatively, a trickle charger charging at the rate of 1.5 amps can safely be used overnight.

10 Specially rapid 'boost' charges which are claimed to restore the power of the battery in 1 to 2 hours are not recommended, as they can cause serious damage to the battery plates through overheating.

11 While charging the battery, note that the temperature of the electrolyte should never exceed 37.8°C (100°F).

Maintenance-free battery

Note: *The following is intended as a guide only. Always refer to the manufacturer's recommendations (often printed on a label attached to the battery) before charging a battery.*

12 This battery type takes considerably longer to fully recharge than the standard type, the time taken being dependent on the extent of discharge, but it can take anything up to three days.

13 A constant voltage type charger is required, to be set, when connected, to 13.9 to 14.9 volts with a charger current below 25 amps. Using this method, the battery should be usable within three hours, giving a voltage reading of 12.5 volts, but this is for a partially discharged battery and, as mentioned, full charging can take considerably longer.

14 If the battery is to be charged from a fully discharged state (condition reading less than 12.2 volts), have it recharged by your Rover dealer or local automotive electrician, as the charge rate is higher and constant supervision during charging is necessary.

4 Battery – removal and refitting

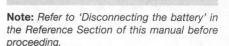

Note: *Refer to 'Disconnecting the battery' in the Reference Section of this manual before proceeding.*

Removal

1 The battery is located in a recess in the right-hand side of the luggage compartment floor on Saloon models, beneath the rear seat on Estate models, and behind the passenger seat on the Van and Pick-up.

2 Remove the cover (where fitted) then disconnect the negative and then the positive terminals from the battery after first removing the retaining screws or nuts and bolts from the terminal posts **(see illustration)**.

3 Remove the battery clamp and carefully lift the battery out of its compartment. Hold the battery upright to ensure that none of the electrolyte is spilled.

4.2 Disconnecting the battery negative terminal (Saloon model shown)

Refitting

4 Refitting is a direct reversal of this procedure. **Note:** *Refit the positive terminal before the negative terminal and smear the terminals with petroleum jelly. Never use an ordinary grease.*

5 Dynamo charging system – testing

Note: *Refer to the warnings given in 'Safety first!' and in Section 1 of this Chapter before starting work.*

1 If the ignition warning light fails to go out with the engine running, or if the battery does not appear to be receiving a charge, the dynamo may be at fault and should be tested while still in position on the engine as follows.

2 First check the auxiliary drivebelt condition and adjust the tension if necessary (see Chapter 1).

3 Check the leads from the dynamo to the control box (D and F), ensuring that they are firmly attached and that one has not come loose from its terminal.

4 To test the dynamo, first ensure that all electrical equipment is switched off and then pull the leads off the two dynamo terminals. Now join the two dynamo terminals together using a short length of non-insulated wire.

5 Attach to the centre of this short length of wire the positive clip of a 0 to 20 volt voltmeter. Connect the negative clip of the voltmeter to a good earth on the dynamo yoke.

6 Start the engine and allow it to run at a fast idle. A reading of approximately 15 volts should now be indicated on the voltmeter. If no reading is recorded, it is quite likely that the dynamo brushes or brush connections are at fault. If a very low reading is observed then the field windings or armature may be suspect.

7 Brush renewal is described in Section 7; any other repair should be entrusted to an auto-electrician who will be able to determine if repair is feasible, or whether an exchange reconditioned unit should be obtained.

8 If the voltmeter readings are satisfactory, switch off the engine and disconnect the

6.3 Disconnecting the coil leads

voltmeter. With the temporary link still in position, reconnect the two leads to the dynamo terminals and then disconnect the D and F terminals at the control box. Connect the positive clip of the voltmeter to the D lead and the negative clip to earth. Start the engine and allow it to run at a fast idle. The reading on the voltmeter should be identical to that recorded at the dynamo. If no voltage is recorded there is a break in the wire. If the voltage is less than previously recorded check the terminals for corrosion and the wire for chafing. Test the F lead in a similar fashion. If both readings are the same as recorded at the dynamo, then it will be necessary to test the control box as described in Section 8.

9 On completion of the tests remove the temporary link from the dynamo terminals and reconnect the leads to the dynamo and control box.

6 Dynamo – removal and refitting

Removal

1 Disconnect the battery negative terminal (refer to *Disconnecting the battery* in the Reference Chapter).

2 Slacken the two dynamo upper retaining bolts and the nut on the adjustment arm. Move the dynamo towards the engine and lift the auxiliary drivebelt off the pulley.

3 Disconnect the two leads from the dynamo terminals. If the ignition coil is mounted on the dynamo, slide back the rubber cover and disconnect the high tension lead from the centre of the coil, followed by the two low tension leads **(see illustration)**.

4 Undo and remove the lower bolt securing the adjustment arm to the dynamo and remove the two upper retaining bolts, nuts and washers. The dynamo can now be lifted off the engine.

Refitting

5 Refitting the dynamo is the reverse sequence to removal, ensuring that the auxiliary drivebelt is correctly tensioned as described in Chapter 1 before fully tightening the retaining bolts.

6 If a new or exchange dynamo is being fitted, ensure that the unit is correctly polarised as described below before installing.

7 In order for the dynamo to function it must be correctly polarised to suit the electrical installation to which it is being fitted. To polarise the dynamo to suit a negative earth system, connect a suitable length of wire from the battery earth terminal to the dynamo yoke or end bracket. Now connect another length of wire to the battery positive terminal and flick the other end of the wire several times on the dynamo F (small) terminal. This will induce a magnetism of the correct polarity into the dynamo field windings.

8 The correctly polarised dynamo can now be fitted to the car.

7 Dynamo brushes – renewal

1 Remove the dynamo from the car as described in Section 6.

2 If the ignition coil is mounted on the dynamo, undo and remove the clamp retaining bolts and lift off the coil.

3 Undo and remove the two long screws from the rear of the dynamo and lift off the commutator end bracket.

4 Now lift out the armature complete with drive end bracket and pulley from the dynamo yoke.

5 Undo and remove the brush lead retaining screws and lift the brushes out of their holders. If the brushes have worn to less than the minimum specified length, they must be renewed.

6 Check that the brushes slide freely and easily in their holders. If either of the brushes has a tendency to stick, clean the brushes with methylated spirit and a clean rag. If still stiff, lightly polish the sides of the brush with a very fine file until the brush moves quite freely and easily in its holder.

7 If the brushes are in a satisfactory condition and are to be re-used, ensure that they are refitted in the same holders from which they were removed. Check the tension of the brush springs using a small spring balance if possible. If the tension is insufficient, renew the springs.

8 Check the condition of the commutator. If the surface is dirty or blackened, clean it with methylated spirit and a clean rag. If the commutator is in good condition, the surface will be smooth and quite free from pits or burnt areas, and the insulated segments clearly defined. If the commutator is severely worn, seek the advice of an auto-electrician as to whether reconditioning is possible. Alternatively obtain a reconditioned dynamo.

9 If, after the commutator has been cleaned, pits and burnt spots are still present, then wrap a strip of glass paper round the commutator and rotate the armature.

10 Reassemble the dynamo using the reverse of the dismantling procedure. When refitting the commutator end bracket ease back the springs and lift the brushes half way out of their holders. Now rest the spring against the side of the brush to hold it in this position. This will prevent the brushes from fouling the commutator as the end bracket is fitted. With the end bracket in place, push the brushes down into contact with the commutator using a screwdriver inserted through the openings in the end bracket. As this is done the springs will jump into their correct position over the brushes.

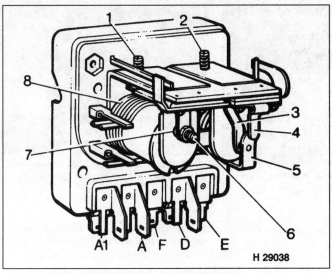

8.2 Control box components

1 Voltage adjusting screw
2 Cut-out adjusting
   screw
3 Fixed contact blade
4 Stop arm
5 Armature tongue and moving
   contact
6 Regulator fixed contact screw
7 Regulator moving contact
8 Regulator series windings

8.4 Mechanical setting of regulator

1 Core face and shim
2 = 0.533 mm
3 Armature
4 Fixed contact adjustment
   screw
5 Armature securing
   screws
6 Armature tension spring
7 Locknut
8 Voltage adjusting screw

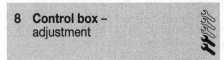

8 Control box –
adjustment

Note: *Refer to the warnings given in 'Safety first!' and in Section 1 of this Chapter before starting work.*

1 If the battery and dynamo are in sound condition but the operation of the charging circuit is still suspect, then the voltage regulator and cut-out in the control box should be checked, and if necessary adjusted as follows.

Voltage regulator adjustment

2 Check the regulator settings by removing the leads A and A1 from the control box and joining them together using a short length of wire **(see illustration)**. Connect the positive clip of a 0 to 20 volt voltmeter to the D terminal of the control box, and the negative clip to a good earth.
3 Start the engine and slowly increase its speed until the voltmeter needle flicks and then steadies. This should occur at about 2000 rpm.
4 If the voltage at which the needle steadies is outside the limits listed in the table, switch off the engine, remove the control box cover and turn the regulator adjusting screw a fraction of a turn at a time, clockwise to increase the setting and anti-clockwise to decrease it **(see illustration)**. Recheck the voltage reading after each adjustment.

Air temperature	Open circuit voltage
10°C (50°F)	16.1 to 16.7
20°C (68°F)	16.0 to 16.6
30°C (86°F)	15.9 to 16.5
40°C (104°F)	15.8 to 16.4

It is essential that the adjustments be completed within 30 seconds of starting the engine otherwise the heat from the shunt coil will affect the readings.

Cut-out adjustment

5 With the control box A and A1 leads joined together, and the voltmeter connected as described in paragraph 2, the cut-in voltage can be checked, and if necessary adjusted, as follows.
6 Switch on the headlights to provide an electrical load, start the engine and slowly increase its speed. The voltage reading will rise steadily, drop back and then rise again.

The point reached just before the drop back should be between 12.7 and 13.3 volts.
7 If the reading obtained is outside these limits, switch off the engine and turn the cut-out adjusting screw a fraction of a turn at a time clockwise to raise the voltage and anti-clockwise to lower it **(see illustration)**. Recheck the voltage reading after each adjustment. As with the voltage regulator, it is essential that the adjustments be completed within 30 seconds of starting the engine, otherwise the heat from the shunt coil will affect the readings.
8 After completing the adjustments remove the voltmeter, disconnect the control box leads and refit the cover.

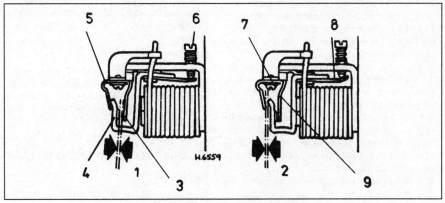

8.7 Mechanical setting of cut-out

1 = 0.25 to 0.51 mm
2 = 0.76 mm
3 Follow through = 0.25 to 0.51 mm
4 Armature tongue and moving
   contact
5 Stop arm
6 Output adjusting screw
7 Armature securing screw
8 Armature tension spring
9 Fixed contact blade

10.10a Undo the alternator upper mounting bolt . . .

10.10b . . . lower rear mounting bolt (arrowed) . . .

10.10c . . . and the longer lower front mounting stud (October 1996 models onward)

9 Alternator charging system – testing

Note: *Refer to the warnings given in 'Safety first!' and in Section 1 of this Chapter before starting work.*

1 If the ignition warning light fails to illuminate when the ignition is switched on, first check the alternator wiring connections for security. If satisfactory, check that the warning light bulb has not blown, and that the bulbholder is secure in its location in the instrument panel. If the light still fails to illuminate, check the continuity of the warning light feed wire from the alternator to the bulbholder. If all is satisfactory, the alternator is at fault and should be renewed or taken to an auto-electrician for testing and repair.

2 If the ignition warning light illuminates when the engine is running, stop the engine and check that the auxiliary drivebelt is correctly tensioned (see Chapter 1) and that the alternator connections are secure. If all is so far satisfactory, check the alternator brushes as described in Section 11. If the fault persists, the alternator should be renewed, or taken to an auto-electrician for testing and repair.

3 If the alternator output is suspect even though the warning light functions correctly, the regulated voltage may be checked as follows.

4 Connect a voltmeter across the battery terminals and start the engine.

5 Increase the engine speed until the voltmeter reading remains steady; the reading should be approximately 12 to 13 volts, and no more than 14 volts.

6 Switch on as many electrical accessories (eg, the headlights, heated rear window and heater blower) as possible, and check that the alternator maintains the regulated voltage at around 13 to 14 volts.

7 If the regulated voltage is not as stated, the fault may be due to worn brushes, weak brush springs, a faulty voltage regulator, a faulty diode, a severed phase winding, or worn or damaged slip rings. The brushes may be checked as described in Section 11, but if the fault persists, the alternator should be renewed or taken to an auto-electrician for testing and repair.

10 Alternator – removal and refitting

Pre-October 1996 models

Removal

Note: *If working on a pre-1990 car fitted with exhaust emission control equipment, it will be necessary to remove the air pump and drive-belt as described in Chapter 4D, Section 7, to provide access to the alternator.*

1 Disconnect the battery negative terminal (refer to *Disconnecting the battery* in the Reference Chapter).

2 On models fitted with an ignition shield over the front of the engine release the three retaining lugs and lift off the shield.

3 Release the spring clip and disconnect the wiring connector from the rear of the alternator.

4 Slacken the alternator adjusting arm nut and the bolt securing the adjusting arm to the alternator.

5 Slacken the two upper mounting nuts and bolts, move the alternator toward the engine and slip the drivebelt off the pulley.

6 Remove the two upper mounting nuts and bolts and the bolt securing the adjusting arm to the alternator. Lift the alternator off the engine.

Refitting

7 Refitting is the reverse sequence to removal. Ensure that the auxiliary drivebelt is correctly tensioned as described in Chapter 1 before finally tightening the mounting and adjustment arm bolts.

October 1996 models onward

Removal

8 Remove the auxiliary drivebelt as described in Chapter 1.

9 Undo the two nuts and disconnect the wiring connectors at the rear of the alternator.

10 Undo the alternator upper mounting bolt, lower rear mounting bolt and the longer lower front mounting stud **(see illustrations)**. Lift the alternator off the engine.

Refitting

11 Refitting is the reverse sequence to removal. Refit and tension the auxiliary drivebelt as described in Chapter 1 on completion.

11 Alternator brushes – renewal

Note: *If brush renewal is necessary on the alternator fitted to October 1996 models onward, seek the advice of an auto-electrician. Component parts for these later alternators are not available separately from Rover dealers.*

11AC alternator

1 Remove the alternator from the car as described in Section 10.

2 To remove the brushes, undo and remove the nut and spring washer, the large Lucar terminal and the plastic strip from the output terminal.

3 Undo and remove the two securing screws and withdraw the brush box. Note that there are two small washers between the brush box and end bracket.

4 Close up the retaining tongue at the root of each terminal blade and withdraw the brush, spring and terminal assemblies from the brush box.

5 With the brushes removed, measure their length, and renew them if worn to less than the minimum specified length.

6 Check that the brushes slide smoothly in their holders. Any sticking tendency may first be rectified by wiping with methylated spirit and a clean cloth, or if this fails, by carefully polishing with a very fine file where any binding marks may appear.

7 Refitting the brushes is the reverse sequence to removal. When refitting the terminal blades to the brush box bend the retaining tongue, at the root of each blade, out slightly to retain the blade in position.

16ACR alternator

8 Remove the alternator from the car as described in Section 10.

9 Undo and remove the two retaining screws and lift off the moulded end cover.

10 Detach the cable from the terminal blade on the outer of the three rectifier plates. Also detach the cable from the blade between the middle and inner of the three rectifier plates.

11 Undo and remove the four screws securing the brush assemblies to the brush holder.

12 Undo and remove the screw securing the surge protection diode cable to the brush holder.

13 Finally undo and remove the three bolts and lift off the brush holder and regulator assembly. Note that there is a small leaf spring fitted at the side of the inner brush.

14 Check the condition of the brushes as described in paragraphs 5 and 6.

15 Refitting the brushes is the reverse sequence to removal.

A115 alternator

16 Remove the alternator as described in Section 10.

17 Disconnect and remove the interference suppression capacitor from the end cover.

18 Undo the screws or nuts which secure the end cover, and remove the cover.

19 Unscrew the surge protection diode securing screw. Either move the diode carefully out of the way, or disconnect it from the rectifier board and remove it.

20 Make a careful note of the regulator lead colours and fitting arrangements, then disconnect the regulator leads from the rectifier board and remove it.

21 Remove the regulator screw and withdraw the regulator. Note that the regulator securing screw also holds one of the brush mounting plates in position.

22 Remove the two securing screws, and withdraw the brushbox. Extract the free brush, then undo the securing screw to release the other brush. Remove the sealing pad.

23 Renew the brushes if they are at, or approaching, the minimum specified length. Check the brush spring pressure with the brush ends flush with the end of the brushbox; renew the springs if they have become weak.

24 Refitting the brushes is the reverse sequence to removal.

A127 alternator

25 Remove the alternator as described in Section 10.

26 Undo the three small screws securing the regulator and brushbox assembly to the rear of the alternator.

27 Tip the assembly upwards at the edge, and withdraw it from its location. Disconnect the rectifier wiring connection, and remove the regulator and brushbox.

28 Measure the brush length, and renew the regulator and brushbox assembly if the brushes are worn below the figure given in the Specifications.

29 Refitting the brushes is the reverse sequence to removal.

12 Starting system – testing

Note: *Refer to the precautions given in 'Safety first!' and in Section 1 of this Chapter before starting work.*

1 If the starter motor fails to operate when the ignition key is turned to the appropriate position, the following possible causes may be to blame.
  a) The battery is faulty.
  b) The electrical connections between the switch, solenoid, battery and starter motor are somewhere failing to pass the necessary current from the battery through the starter to earth.
  c) The solenoid is faulty.
  d) The starter motor drive pinion may be jammed in the flywheel ring gear teeth (inertia type starters).
  e) The starter motor is mechanically or electrically defective.

2 To check the battery, switch on the headlights. If they dim after a few seconds, this indicates that the battery is discharged – recharge (see Section 3) or renew the battery. If the headlights glow brightly, operate the ignition switch and observe the lights. If they dim, then this indicates that current is reaching the starter motor, therefore the fault must lie in the starter motor. If an inertia type starter is fitted, check it is not jammed by placing the car in gear (manual transmission only) and rocking it to-and-fro. Alternatively, turn the armature with a small spanner on the square end protruding from the commutator end bracket. If the lights continue to glow brightly (and no clicking sound can be heard from the starter motor solenoid), this indicates that there is a fault in the circuit or solenoid – see following paragraphs. If the starter motor turns slowly when operated, but the battery is in good condition, then this indicates that either the starter motor is faulty, or there is considerable resistance somewhere in the circuit.

3 If a fault in the circuit is suspected, disconnect the battery leads (including the earth connection to the body), the starter/solenoid wiring and the engine/

transmission earth strap. Thoroughly clean the connections, and reconnect the leads and wiring, then use a voltmeter or test lamp to check that full battery voltage is available at the battery positive lead connection to the solenoid, and that the earth connection is sound.

> **HAYNES HINT** *Smear petroleum jelly around the battery terminals to prevent corrosion – corroded connections are amongst the most frequent causes of electrical system faults.*

4 If the battery and all connections are in good condition, check the circuit by disconnecting the wire from the solenoid blade terminal. Connect a voltmeter or test lamp between the wire end and a good earth (such as the battery negative terminal), and check that the wire is live when the ignition switch is turned to the 'start' position. If it is, then the circuit is sound – if not the circuit wiring can be checked as described in Chapter 12.

5 The solenoid contacts can be checked by connecting a voltmeter or test lamp between the battery positive feed connection on the starter side of the solenoid, and earth. When the ignition switch is turned to the 'start' position, there should be a reading or lighted bulb, as applicable. If there is no reading or lighted bulb, the solenoid is faulty and should be renewed.

6 If the circuit and solenoid are proved sound, the fault must lie in the starter motor. In this event, it may be possible to have the starter motor overhauled by a specialist, but check on the cost of spares before proceeding, as it may prove more economical to obtain a new or exchange motor.

13 Starter motor – removal and refitting

Pre-October 1996 models

Removal

1 Disconnect the battery negative terminal (refer to *Disconnecting the battery* in the Reference Chapter).

2 If an ignition shield is fitted to the front of the engine, release the three retaining lugs and lift off the shield.

3 For improved access if necessary, release the horn and horn bracket, and move them to one side.

4 On inertia type starters, undo and remove the nut and spring washer and then detach the starter motor cable from the terminal stud **(see illustration)**. On pre-engaged type starters, undo the nut, and disconnect the leads at the upper terminal on the solenoid.

13.4a Unscrew the nut securing the starter motor cable

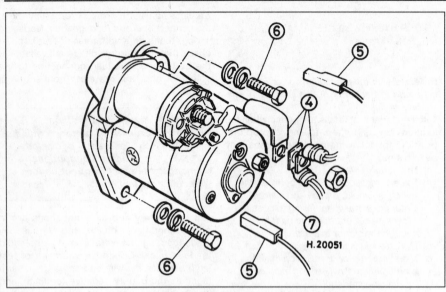

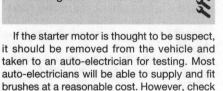

13.4b Pre-engaged starter motor attachments

4 *Solenoid upper terminal leads*
5 *Solenoid spade terminal leads*
6 *Retaining bolts*
7 *Starter motor*

Disconnect the leads at the two solenoid spade terminals, after identifying their positions **(see illustration)**.
5 If the ignition coil is mounted on a bracket secured to the cylinder head, undo and remove the nut securing the bracket to the head and place the coil to one side.
6 Undo and remove the two bolts securing the starter motor to the flywheel housing, then lift the motor upwards and out of the engine compartment.

Refitting

7 Refitting is the reverse sequence to removal.

October 1996 models onward

Removal

8 Disconnect the battery negative terminal (refer to *Disconnecting the battery* in the Reference Chapter).
9 Firmly apply the handbrake, then jack up the front of the car and support it securely on axle stands (see *Jacking and vehicle support*).
10 Remove the front grille panel as described in Chapter 11B.

11 Undo the two bolts each side securing the radiator upper mounting brackets to the front body panel. Lift the two brackets off the radiator upper mounting studs.
12 Lift the radiator off its lower mounting and move it sideways, away from the starter motor, as far as the hoses will allow.
13 Release the cable tie securing the wiring harness to the starter solenoid.
14 Undo the nut and disconnect the leads at the upper terminal on the solenoid. Disconnect the lead at the solenoid spade terminals.
15 Disconnect the wiring connector at the oil temperature gauge sender unit, located above the starter motor.
16 Undo and remove the two bolts securing the starter motor to the flywheel housing, then lift the motor out of the engine compartment through the front grille aperture **(see illustration)**. Note the location of the wiring harness support bracket which is also secured by the starter motor upper mounting bolt.

Refitting

17 Refitting is the reverse sequence to removal.

13.16 Removing the starter motor (October 1996 models onward)

16.2 Electrical connections at the remotely-mounted starter solenoid

14 Starter motor – testing and overhaul

If the starter motor is thought to be suspect, it should be removed from the vehicle and taken to an auto-electrician for testing. Most auto-electricians will be able to supply and fit brushes at a reasonable cost. However, check on the cost of repairs before proceeding as it may prove more economical to obtain a new or exchange motor.

Renewal of the solenoid and, on the inertia type starter motor the drive pinion assembly, is described in the following Sections.

15 Drive pinion assembly (inertia type starter) – removal and refitting

Removal

1 With the starter motor removed from the car (Section 13) use a starter motor pinion compressor tool (available from automobile accessory stores), to compress the mainspring until sufficient clearance exists to enable the circlip on the end of the shaft to be removed. Remove the pinion compressor and then slide off the locating washer and mainspring.
2 Slide the remaining parts off the armature shaft with a rotary action.
3 Examine the teeth of the drive pinion that engage with the flywheel ring gear. If they are badly worn on their leading edge, renew the pinion assembly. Bear in mind that if the drive pinion teeth are worn, the teeth on the flywheel ring gear are likely to be in a similar condition.
4 Inspect the remainder of the drive pinion components and renew the assembly if any are worn.

Refitting

5 Refitting the drive pinion is the reverse sequence to removal. **Note:** *It is most important that the drive pinion components are completely free from oil, grease and dirt before reassembly. Under no circumstances should any of the parts be lubricated, as this will attract dust from the clutch which could cause the drive pinion to stick.*

16 Starter solenoid – removal and refitting

Removal

Remotely-mounted solenoid

1 Disconnect the battery negative terminal (refer to *Disconnecting the battery* in the Reference Chapter).
2 Carefully ease back the rubber covers to gain access to the terminals **(see illustration)**.

3 Make a note of the Lucar terminal connectors and detach these terminals.

4 Undo and remove the heavy duty cable terminal connection nuts and spring washers. Detach the two terminal connectors.

5 Undo and remove the two securing screws and lift away the solenoid.

Integral solenoid

6 Remove the starter motor as described in Section 13.

7 Undo the nut and disconnect the lead at the lower terminal on the solenoid.

8 Undo the two bolts and remove the solenoid yoke **(see illustration)**.

9 Withdraw the plunger spring, unhook the plunger from the starter operating lever and remove the plunger.

Refitting

10 In all cases, refitting is the reverse sequence to removal.

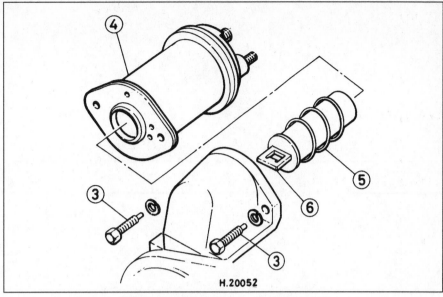

H.20052

16.8 Pre-engaged starter solenoid removal

3 *Retaining bolts*   4 *Solenoid yoke*   5 *Plunger spring*   6 *Plunger*

Chapter 5 Part B:
Distributor ignition system

Contents

Ballasted ignition system (carburettor models) – identification 2
Condenser – testing, removal and refitting 7
Contact breaker points – adjustment 5
Contact breaker points – renewal 6
Crankshaft position sensor (fuel injection models) – removal and
   refitting 11
Distributor – dismantling, inspection and reassembly 9
Distributor lubrication ....See Chapter 1
Distributor – removal and refitting 8
General information 1
Ignition coil – removal, testing and refitting 10
Ignition system check ....See Chapter 1
Ignition system (carburettor models) – testing 3
Ignition system (fuel injection models) – testing 4
Ignition timing – checking and adjustment 13
Reluctor ring (fuel injection models) – removal and refitting 12
Spark plug renewal ....See Chapter 1
Transmission-controlled ignition advance system – checking and
   component renewal 14

Degrees of difficulty

Easy, suitable for novice with little experience		**Fairly easy,** suitable for beginner with some experience		**Fairly difficult,** suitable for competent DIY mechanic		**Difficult,** suitable for experienced DIY mechanic		**Very difficult,** suitable for expert DIY or professional	

Specifications

Carburettor models

System type

All except 1990-on, 1275 cc models	Conventional contact breaker ignition
1990-on, 1275 cc models	Lucas electronic ignition

Distributor – contact breaker ignition

Type:
All models except Cooper S Mk III:	
Early type	Lucas 25D4
Later type	Lucas 45D4, 59D4 or Ducellier
Cooper S Mk III	Lucas 23D4
Direction of rotor arm rotation	Anti-clockwise
Contact breaker points gap	0.35 to 0.40 mm
Dwell angle:	
Lucas 23D4 and 25D4	60° ± 3°
Lucas 45D4:	
Non-sliding contacts	51° ± 5°
Sliding contacts	57° ± 5°
Lucas 59D4	54° ± 5°
Ducellier	57° ± 2° 30'
Firing order	1-3-4-2 (No 1 cylinder at timing chain end of engine)

Distributor – electronic ignition

Type	Lucas 65DM4 – Electronic
Ignition amplifier module	Lucas 9EM
Suppression capacitor	1 mf
Direction of rotor arm rotation	Anti-clockwise
Firing order	1-3-4-2 (No 1 cylinder at timing chain end of engine)

Ignition timing

Note: *If a Ducellier distributor is fitted, the timing setting is the same as the equivalent Lucas distributor.*

Vehicle type/distributor	Static	Stroboscopic (vacuum pipe disconnected)
Mini 850 Saloon and Estate, 848 cc, 1969-72:		
Lucas 25D4 41026 or 45D4 41411 distributor	TDC	3° BTDC at 600 rpm
Mini 850 Van and Pick-up, 848 cc, 1969-72:		
Lucas 25D4 41007 or 45D4 41410	7° BTDC	10° BTDC at 600 rpm
Mini 850 Saloon and variants, 848 cc:		
1972-74:		
Lucas 25D4 41026 or 45D4 41411 distributor	TDC	19° BTDC at 1000 rpm
Lucas 41569 or or 41570 distributor*	9° BTDC	14° BTDC at 1000 rpm
1974-76:		
Lucas 45D4 41570 distributor	6° BTDC	11° BTDC at 1000 rpm
1976-on:		
Lucas 45D4 41417 or 41767 distributor	–	7° BTDC at 1000 rpm
Mini 1000 Saloon and Estate, 998 cc, 1969-72:		
Lucas 25D4 40931, 41030 or 45D4 41412 distributor	5° BTDC	8° BTDC at 600 rpm
Mini 1000 Van and Pick-up, 998 cc, 1969-72:		
Lucas 25D4 41007 or 45D4 41410 distributor	7° BTDC	10° BTDC at 600 rpm
Mini 1000 Automatic, and Mini Clubman Automatic, 998 cc, 1969-74:		
Lucas 25D4 41134, 41242 or 45D4 41417 distributor	4° BTDC	6° BTDC at 600 rpm
Mini Clubman, 998 cc, 1969-72:		
Lucas 25D4 41030 or 45D4 41412 distributor	5° BTDC	8° BTDC at 600 rpm
Mini 1000 and Mini Clubman, Saloon and variants, 998 cc, 1972-74:		
Lucas 25D4 41254 or 45D4 41212 distributor	5° BTDC	11° BTDC at 1000 rpm
Lucas 41246 or 41418 distributor*	10° BTDC	13° BTDC at 1000 rpm
Mini 1000 and Mini Clubman, Saloon and variants, 998 cc, manual and automatic transmission:		
1974-76:		
Lucas 45D4 41418 distributor	4° BTDC	7° BTDC at 1000 rpm
1976-78:		
Lucas 45D4 41418 or 41793 distributor	–	7° BTDC at 1000 rpm
1978-on:		
Lucas 45D4 41406 or 41765 distributor	–	8° BTDC at 1000 rpm
Mini Saloon and variants, 998 cc, 1982-on:		
Lucas 59D4 41882 distributor:		
1983 to 1987	–	8° +0° –2° BTDC at 1500 rpm
1988 (category C)	–	10° +0° –2° BTDC at 1500 rpm
1989-on low-compression	–	8° +0° –2° BTDC at 1500 rpm
1989-on high-compression	–	10° +0° –2° BTDC at 1500 rpm
Mini Clubman 1100, 1098 cc:		
1974-76:		
Lucas 25D4 41246 or 45D4 41418 distributor	9° BTDC	12° BTDC at 1000 rpm
1976-on:		
Lucas 45D4 41418 or 41793 distributor	–	12° BTDC at 1000 rpm
Mini Cooper S Mk III, 1275 cc, 1969-72:		
Lucas 23D4 40819 or 41033 distributor	2° BTDC	4° BTDC at 600 rpm
Mini 1275 GT, 1275 cc:		
1969-72:		
Lucas 25D4 41257 or 45D4 41419 distributor	8° BTDC	10° BTDC at 600 rpm
1972-76:		
Lucas 25D4 41257, 41214 or 45D4 41419 distributor	8° BTDC	13° BTDC at 1000 rpm
1976-77:		
Lucas 45D4 41419 or 41768 distributor	–	13° BTDC at 1000 rpm
1978-on:		
Lucas 45D4 41419 or 41768 distributor	–	13° BTDC at 1000 rpm
Mini Saloon and variants, 1275 cc, 1990-on (electronic ignition)	–	5° +1° BTDC at 1500 rpm

* *Alternative distributor fitted to a limited number of 1974 models*

Timing mark locations	Marks on flywheel, pointer on housing (scale on timing cover, notch on pulley – later models)

Ignition coil

Type:
848 cc and 1098 cc engines	Lucas LA12

998 cc engines:
Pre-1982 models	Lucas LA12
1982 models	AC Delco 9977230 or Ducellier 520035A
1983 models on	GCL 144

1275 cc engines:

Pre-1990 models:
Except Cooper S Mk III and later 1275 GT	Lucas LA12
Cooper S Mk III	Lucas HA12
1275 GT, 1978 on	Lucas 15C6
1990 models on	GCL 143

Primary resistance at 20°C:
Lucas LA12 and 15C6	3.2 to 3.4 ohms
Lucas HA12	3.0 to 3.4 ohms
AC Delco 9977230 or Ducellier 520035A	1.2 to 1.5 ohms
GCL 144	1.3 to 1.5 ohms
GCL 143	0.70 to 0.86 ohms

Ballast resistance:
AC Delco 9977230 or Ducellier 520035A	1.3 to 1.5 ohms
GCL 144	1.5 ohms

Spark plugs .... See Chapter 1 Servicing specifications

Torque wrench settings	Nm	lbf ft
Distributor clamp	7	5

Fuel injection models

System type .... Rover/Motorola Modular Engine Management System (MEMS), fully electronic, controlled by ECU

Electronic control unit
Cooper models	MNE 10027
All other manual transmission models	MNE 10025
All other automatic transmission models	MNE 10026

Crankshaft position sensor
Type	ADU 7340

Distributor
Type	NJC 10034
Direction of rotor arm rotation	Anti-clockwise
Firing order	1-3-4-2 (No 1 cylinder at timing chain end of engine)

Timing mark locations .... Scale on timing cover, notch on pulley

Ignition timing
Nominal value	15° BTDC at idle*

This value will constantly vary under control of the ECU idle function (by as much as −11° to +10°) – see text for further information.

Ignition coil
Type	AUU 1326 or ADU 8779
Primary resistance at 20°C	0.71 to 0.81 ohms

Spark plugs .... See Chapter 1 Servicing specifications

Torque wrench settings	Nm	lbf ft
Crankshaft position sensor bolts	6	4
Distributor clamp	7	5

1 General information

Contact breaker ignition system

In order that the engine can run correctly, it is necessary for an electrical spark to ignite the fuel/air mixture in the combustion chamber at exactly the right moment in relation to engine speed and load. The ignition system is based on feeding low tension voltage from the battery to the coil, where it is converted to high tension voltage. The high tension voltage is powerful enough to jump the spark plug gap in the cylinders many times a second under high compression pressures, providing that the system is in good condition and that all adjustments are correct.

The ignition system is divided into two circuits: the low tension circuit and the high tension circuit.

The low tension (sometimes known as the primary) circuit consists of the battery, lead to the starter solenoid, lead to the ignition switch, lead from the ignition switch to the low tension or primary coil windings (coil terminal +), and the lead from the low tension coil windings (coil terminal −) to the contact breaker points and condenser in the distributor.

The high tension circuit consists of the high tension or secondary coil windings, the ignition king lead from the centre of the coil to the centre of the distributor cap, the rotor arm, the spark plug HT leads and the spark plugs.

The system functions in the following manner. Low tension voltage is changed in the coil into high tension voltage by the opening and closing of the contact breaker points in the low tension circuit. High tension voltage is then fed, via the carbon brush in the centre of the distributor cap, to the rotor arm of the distributor. The rotor arm revolves inside the distributor cap, and each time it comes in line with one of the four metal segments in the cap, which are connected to the spark plug leads, the opening and closing of the contact breaker points causes the high tension voltage to build up and jump the gap from the rotor arm to the appropriate metal segment. The voltage then passes, via the spark plug lead, to the spark plug, where it finally jumps the spark plug gap, before going to earth.

A ballasted ignition system is used on certain models to improve ignition performance, particularly when starting the engine. Ballast is provided by a low resistance lead incorporated in the supply from the ignition switch to the ignition coil + terminal. The starter solenoid circuit is wired so that upon operation of the starter, the ballast resistance is bypassed. This has the effect of slightly increasing coil primary voltage, which in turn temporarily increases HT output to improve starting.

The ignition is advanced and retarded automatically, to ensure that the spark occurs at just the right instant for the particular load at the prevailing engine speed. The ignition advance is controlled both mechanically and by a vacuum-operated system on all but Cooper S models. Automatic advance is mechanical only on Cooper S models. The mechanical governor mechanism comprises two lead weights, which move out from the distributor shaft, due to centrifugal force, as the engine speed rises. As they move outwards they rotate the cam relative to the distributor shaft, and so advance the spark. The weights are held in position by two light springs, and it is the tension of the springs which is largely responsible for correct spark advancement. The vacuum control consists of a diaphragm, one side of which is connected, via a small bore tube, to the carburettor, and the other side to the contact breaker plate. Depression in the inlet manifold and carburettor, which varies with engine speed and throttle opening, causes the diaphragm to move, so moving the contact breaker plate, and advancing or retarding the spark.

Certain models are also fitted with a transmission-controlled ignition advance system. The system consists of a vacuum line connected to the distributor-to-inlet manifold vacuum hose, which runs to an inhibitor switch located behind the gearchange remote control housing. A solenoid valve, operated by the inhibitor switch, is mounted in this vacuum line. When fourth gear is selected, the inhibitor switch energises the solenoid valve, and increased vacuum is applied to the advance

mechanism of the distributor. When anything other than fourth gear is selected, the system is de-energised; vacuum is vented to atmosphere, the vacuum line to the distributor is sealed, and the system reverts to normal operation.

Electronic ignition system

Carburettor models

The Lucas electronic ignition system used on later 1275 cc engines consists of a distributor, an amplifier module and a coil. Externally, the distributor resembles a conventional type, but internally, a reluctor and a pick-up unit take the place of the cam and contact breaker points.

Each time one of the reluctor arms passes through the magnetic field of the pick-up coil, an electrical signal is sent to the amplifier module, which then triggers the coil in the same way as the opening of the points in a conventional system. Both centrifugal and vacuum advances are used in the accustomed manner.

Because there are no contact breaker points to wear out, the electronic ignition system is extremely reliable. As long as the distributor is lubricated, the spark plugs inspected or renewed at the specified maintenance intervals, and the leads and connections kept clean and dry, it is very unlikely that trouble will be experienced.

Fuel injection models

The ignition system used on fuel injection models is fully-electronic in operation, incorporating the Electronic Control Unit (ECU) (situated on the right-hand side of the engine compartment), a distributor (driven off the camshaft via a skew gear), a crankshaft position sensor (mounted on the flywheel/torque converter housing, to register with the reluctor ring fixed to the rear of the flywheel/torque converter), as well as the spark plugs, HT leads, ignition coil, and associated wiring. The system is divided into two circuits; primary (low tension/LT) and secondary (high tension/HT). The primary circuit consists of the battery, ignition switch, ignition coil primary windings, ECU and wiring. The secondary circuit consists of the ignition coil secondary windings, the distributor cap and rotor arm, the spark plugs, and the HT leads connecting these.

The ECU controls both the ignition system and the fuel injection system, integrating the two in a complete engine management package; refer to Chapter 4B for information relating to the fuel injection side of the system.

As far as the ignition system is concerned, the ECU receives information in the form of electrical impulses or signals from the crankshaft position sensor, from the coolant temperature sensor (which supplies it with engine temperature), from the throttle pedal switch (which tells it when the throttle is closed) and from the manifold absolute

pressure sensor (which gives it the load on the engine). The crankshaft position sensor works in conjunction with the reluctor ring, which is bolted onto the back of the flywheel. The reluctor ring has thirty-four poles on it, spaced 10° apart, with two missing poles 180° apart; the missing poles identify the cylinder TDC positions. The sensor reads these poles, to provide an accurate assessment of the engine speed and crankshaft position to the ECU.

All the above signals are compared by the ECU, with set values preprogrammed (mapped) into its memory; based on this information, the ECU selects the ignition timing appropriate to those values, and controls the ignition coil accordingly.

Note that this means that the distributor is just that, a distributor of the HT pulse to the appropriate spark plug; it has no effect whatsoever on the ignition timing. Also, the system is so sensitive that, at idle speed, the ignition timing may be constantly changing; this should be remembered if trying to check the ignition timing.

2 Ballasted ignition system (carburettor models) – identification

1 As mentioned in Section 1, certain models may be fitted with a ballasted ignition system to improve ignition performance when starting.

2 To determine if a vehicle is equipped with a ballasted ignition system, check for the presence of a supplementary wiring harness, incorporating the white/pink ballast resistor lead, between the fuse block and the ignition coil LT terminal.

3 The ballast resistor lead replaces the original coil feed. The original lead is colour-coded white, and is retained in the harness to accommodate vehicles not fitted with a ballasted system. Do not connect this white lead to the ignition coil; it must remain taped to the harness.

4 Failure to observe this warning will result in coil overheating and premature contact breaker point failure. Similar damage will occur if a coil designed for use with a ballasted system is fitted to a non-ballasted system, this being due to the excessive primary current produced. Should it ever be necessary to renew the coil, ensure that the replacement is of the correct type.

3 Ignition system (carburettor models) – testing

Contact breaker ignition system

1 By far the majority of breakdown and running troubles are caused by faults in the ignition system, either in the low tension or high tension circuit. There are two main

symptoms indicating ignition faults. Either the engine will not start or fire, or the engine is difficult to start and misfires. If it is a regular misfire, ie, the engine is only running on two or three cylinders, the fault is likely to be in the secondary or high tension circuit. If the misfiring is intermittent, the fault could be in either the high or low tension circuits. If the engine stops suddenly or will not start at all, it is likely that the fault is in the low tension circuit. Loss of power and overheating, apart from carburettor settings, are normally due to faults in the distributor or incorrect ignition timing.

Engine fails to start

2 If the engine fails to start and the car was running normally when it was last used, first check there is fuel in the fuel tank. If the engine turns over normally on the starter motor and the battery is evidently well charged, then the fault may be in either the high or low tension circuits. First check the HT circuit. If the battery is known to be fully-charged, the ignition light comes on and the starter fails to turn the engine, check the tightness of the leads on the battery terminals and the security of the earth lead at its connection on the body (don't forget to check the engine to body earth strap as well). It is quite common for the leads to have worked loose, even if they look and feel secure. If one of the battery terminal posts gets very hot when trying to work the starter motor, this is a sure indication of a faulty connection to that terminal.

3 One of the most common reasons for bad starting is wet or damp spark plug HT leads and distributor. Remove the distributor cap. If condensation is visible internally, dry the cap with a rag and wipe over the HT leads. Refit the cap and spray the cap, leads and spark plugs with a water dispersant aerosol.

4 If the engine still fails to start, check that HT voltage is reaching the spark plugs by disconnecting each plug lead in turn at the spark plug end and holding the end of the cable about 5 mm away from the cylinder block. If the plug caps are not detachable, insert a nail or piece of stiff wire into the cap. Hold the lead with insulating material – eg a rubber glove, a dry cloth, or insulated pliers. With the ignition switched on, have an assistant crank the engine on the starter motor: a strong blue spark should be seen and heard to jump from the end of the lead to the block. If it does, this suggests that HT voltage is reaching the plugs, and that either the plugs themselves are defective, the ignition timing is grossly maladjusted, or the fault is not in the ignition system. If the spark is weak or absent, although the cranking speed is good, proceed with the checks below.

5 Remove the HT lead which enters the centre of the distributor cap. Hold the end near the block and repeat the check above. A good spark now, if there was none at the plug lead, indicates that HT voltage is not being transmitted to the plug leads. Check the rotor arm, distributor cap and HT leads thoroughly as described in Chapter 1. If there is no spark at the HT lead from the coil, check the connections at the coil end of the lead. If it is in order start checking the low tension circuit as follows.

6 Separate the contact breaker points with a piece of paper between their contact faces then switch on the ignition. Using a 12 volt voltmeter or a 12 volt bulb and two lengths of wire, test between the low tension wire to the coil (marked SW or +) and earth. No reading indicates a break in the supply from the ignition switch. Check the wiring and the connections at the switch and correct any problems found. A reading on the voltmeter or illumination of the test bulb indicates that voltage is reaching the coil and the problem is therefore a faulty coil, faulty condenser or a broken lead between the coil and distributor.

7 Remove the condenser from the baseplate on Lucas distributors or disconnect the condenser lead on the Ducellier version. With the contact breaker points open, test between the moving point and earth. If there is now a reading then the fault is in the condenser. Fit a new condenser and the engine should start.

8 With no reading from the moving point and earth, test between the coil negative terminal (marked CB or –) and earth. A reading here indicates a broken wire between the coil and distributor which must be repaired. No reading confirms that the coil has failed and must be renewed. If the coil is to be renewed, ensure that the correct type is obtained. The coils used on ballasted and non-ballasted systems are not interchangeable (see Section 2 for further details).

9 Where a ballasted ignition system is fitted, if the engine starts when the starter is operated, buts stops as soon as the ignition key is returned to the normal running position, the resistive wire may be open circuit. Connect a temporary lead between the coil positive (SW or +) terminal and the battery positive terminal. If the engine now runs correctly, renew the resistive wire. **Note:** *Bypassing the resistive wire in this way must only be done briefly for the purpose of this test. The wire must not be permanently bypassed, otherwise the coil will overheat and be irreparably damaged.*

Engine misfires

10 Uneven running and misfiring should first be checked by seeing that all leads, particularly HT, are dry and connected properly. Ensure that they are not shorting to earth through broken or cracked insulation. If they are, you should be able to see and hear it. If not, then check the plugs, contact breaker points and condenser just as you would in a case of total failure to start. A regular misfire can be isolated by removing each HT lead from its spark plug in turn (taking precautions against electric shock) while the engine is idling. Removing a good lead will accentuate the misfire, whilst removing the defective lead will make no difference.

11 Once the defective cylinder is located, switch off the engine, remove the lead from the spark plug again and hold the end about 5 mm away from the cylinder block. If the plug caps are not detachable, insert a nail or piece of stiff wire into the cap. Restart the engine. If the sparking is fairly strong and regular, the fault must lie in the spark plug. Remove and examine its condition as described in Chapter 1. If the spark plug is proved to be satisfactory, there may be an internal engine problem such as loss of compression on the defective cylinder. Carry out a compression test, as described in Chapter 2A to determine the condition of the engine internally.

12 If there is no spark at the end of the HT lead, or if it is weak and intermittent, check the entire length of the lead from the distributor cap to the spark plug. If the insulation is cracked or perished, renew the lead. Check the connections at the distributor cap at the same time.

13 If there is still no spark, carefully examine the condition of the distributor cap as described in Chapter 1, looking closely for signs of cracks or tracking between the internal segments.

14 Apart from the ignition timing being incorrect, other causes of misfiring have already been dealt with under the sub-Section dealing with the failure of the engine to start. To recap, these are:

a) *The coil may be faulty giving an intermittent misfire.*

b) *There may be a damaged wire or loose connection in the low tension circuit.*

c) *The condenser may be short-circuited.*

d) *There may be a mechanical fault in the distributor (incorrectly assembled contact breaker points or broken contact breaker spring).*

15 If the ignition timing is too far retarded it should be noted that the engine will tend to overheat and there will be a quite noticeable drop in power. If the engine is overheating and the power is down, and if the ignition timing is correct, then the carburettor should be checked as it is likely that this is where the fault lies.

Electronic ignition system

Note: *Refer to the warning given in Section 1 of Part A of this Chapter before starting work. Always switch off the ignition before disconnecting or connecting any component and when using a multi-meter to check resistances.*

General

16 Electronic ignition is normally very reliable; if it does fail, such failure tends to be complete. If a fault does occur, or if performance is suspect, the following test procedure should be used to isolate the problem area.

17 An electrical multimeter which can measure voltage and resistance (ohms) will be required for testing purposes.

⚠️ *Warning: Voltages produced by an electronic ignition system are considerably higher than those produced by conventional ignition systems. Extreme care must be taken when working on the system with the ignition switched on. Persons with surgically-implanted cardiac pacemaker devices should keep well clear of the ignition circuits, components and test equipment.*

Electronic ignition system test procedure

Test	Remedy
1 Is the battery voltage greater than 11.7 volts?	Yes: Proceed to Test 2 No: Recharge the battery
2 Is the voltage at the coil + terminal within 1 volt of battery voltage?	Yes: Proceed to Test 3 No: Faulty wiring or connector between ignition switch and coil, or faulty ignition switch
3 Is the resistance between the ignition coil + and – terminals between 0.4 and 0.9 ohms?	Yes: Proceed to Test 4 No: Renew the ignition coil
4 Is the resistance between the ignition coil + and HT terminals between 5.0 and 15.0 kohms?	Yes: Proceed to Test 5 No: Renew the ignition coil
5 Connect a low-wattage bulb across the ignition coil + and – terminals, and spin the engine on the starter. Does the bulb flash?	Yes: Proceed to Test 6 No: Proceed to Test 10
6 Is the resistance of any HT lead greater than 20 kohms?	Yes: Renew the HT lead No: Proceed to Test 7
7 Are there any signs of tracking on the ignition coil, distributor cap or rotor arm?	Yes: Renew the component as necessary No: Proceed to Test 8
8 Is the ignition timing correct?	Yes: Proceed to Test 9 No: Adjust ignition timing
9 Are the spark plugs in good condition?	Yes: Check carburettor settings and engine mechanical condition No: Renew the spark plugs
10 Are the ignition amplifier module connections sound?	Yes: Proceed to Test 11 No: See paragraphs 18 to 21 of this Section
11 With the module removed, is the resistance of the distributor pick-up coil between 950 and 1150 ohms?	Yes: See paragraphs 18 to 21 of this Section No: Renew the distributor pick-up coil

18 If, after carrying out the test procedures the ignition amplifier module is diagnosed as being faulty, make sure that the wiring is intact and secure.
19 As a double-check, remove the module, gasket and connector, and lightly squeeze together the terminals inside the connector. Clean the terminals in the module and distributor before refitting the module, and remember to apply heat-conducting silicone grease to the mounting face on the distributor.
20 Disconnect the wiring from the module, clean the terminals, and lightly squeeze together the terminals inside the connector before refitting it. Make sure that the connector is fully located over the base.
21 Check that the LT leads are correctly fitted to the ignition coil.

4 Ignition system (fuel injection models) – testing

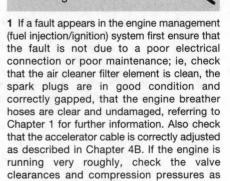

1 If a fault appears in the engine management (fuel injection/ignition) system first ensure that the fault is not due to a poor electrical connection or poor maintenance; ie, check that the air cleaner filter element is clean, the spark plugs are in good condition and correctly gapped, that the engine breather hoses are clear and undamaged, referring to Chapter 1 for further information. Also check that the accelerator cable is correctly adjusted as described in Chapter 4B. If the engine is running very roughly, check the valve clearances and compression pressures as described in Chapter 2A.
2 The only ignition system checks which can be carried out by the home mechanic are those described in Chapter 1, relating to the spark plugs, HT leads, rotor arm and distributor cap, and the ignition coil test described in Section 10 of this Chapter.
3 If these checks fail to reveal the cause of the problem the vehicle should be taken to a suitably-equipped Rover dealer for testing. A wiring block connector is incorporated in the engine management circuit into which a special electronic diagnostic tester can be plugged. The tester will locate the fault quickly and simply alleviating the need to test all the system components individually which is a time consuming operation that carries a high risk of damaging the ECU.

5 Contact breaker points – adjustment

1 If an ignition shield is fitted over the front of the engine, release the three plastic retaining lugs and lift away the shield. Detach the two spring clips or undo the two screws securing the distributor cap to the distributor body and lift off the cap **(see illustration)**.
2 On models that have a distributor shield attached to the inner front panel, remove the ignition coil HT lead from the centre of the distributor cap. Now detach the two

5.1 Removing the distributor cap

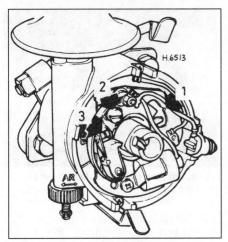

**5.6a Contact breaker points adjustment –
Lucas 25D4 distributor**

1 *Screwdriver slot for adjustment*
2 *Contact plate securing screw*
3 *Contact breaker points*

distributor cap securing spring clips or
screws. With careful manipulation it should be
possible to withdraw the distributor cap
upwards through the small space between the
rotor arm and the distributor shield. If difficulty
is experienced, undo and remove the
retaining screws and lift out the shield.
3 With the distributor cap removed, clean
and inspect it thoroughly as described in
Chapter 1.
4 Gently prise the contact breaker points
open to examine the condition of their faces. If
they are rough and pitted or dirty, they should
be renewed. Disregard any blue discoloration
which may be apparent on their faces. This is
due to the formation of tungsten oxide; it has
no detrimental effect on ignition performance
nor is it indicative of condenser failure.
5 Assuming that the points are in a
satisfactory condition, or that they have been
renewed, the gap between the two faces
should be measured using feeler blades. Note
however that on later models no contact
breaker points gap is quoted by the
manufacturers. On these models, the gap can
only be adjusted using the dwell angle
method described from paragraph 10 onward.
6 To adjust the gap using feeler blades, turn
the engine over until the heel of the contact
breaker arm is on the peak of one of the four
cam lobes. On manual transmission models,
the engine can be turned over quite easily by
engaging top gear and moving the car
backwards or forwards until the points are
fully open. This should only be done on level
ground; and make sure that the car cannot
run away. An alternative method, and the
method that should be used on automatic
transmission models, is to press the auxiliary
drivebelt midway between the water pump
pulley and dynamo or alternator pulley and
then turn the fan blades. With the points fully
open, a feeler blade equal to the contact

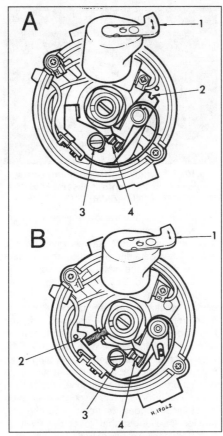

**5.6b Contact breaker points adjustment –
Lucas 45D4 and 59D4 distributor**

A *Non-sliding contact type*
B *Sliding contact type*
1 *Rotor arm*
2 *Screwdriver slot for adjustment*
3 *Contact plate securing screw*
4 *Contact breaker points*

breaker points gap, as stated in the
Specifications, should now just fit between
the contact faces **(see illustrations)**.

> **HAYNES HINT** *Turning the engine will be
> easier if the spark plugs are
> removed first – see Chapter 1.*

**5.6d Using feeler blades to check the
contact breaker points gap**

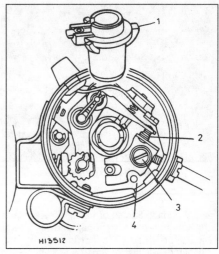

**5.6c Contact breaker points adjustment –
Ducellier distributor**

1 *Rotor arm*
2 *Contact breaker points*
3 *Contact plate securing screw*
4 *Screwdriver slot for adjustment*

7 If the gap is too large or too small, slacken
the contact breaker securing screw slightly
using a short screwdriver. Now insert the
screwdriver into the slot on the side or at the
rear of the contact breaker plate and move the
plate in the desired direction to increase or
decrease the gap **(see illustration)**.
8 Tighten the securing screw and recheck the
gap.
9 With the points correctly adjusted, refit the
distributor cap and ignition shield or
distributor shield if previously removed.
10 If a dwell meter is available, a far more
accurate method of setting the contact
breaker points gap is by measuring and
setting the distributor dwell angle.
11 The dwell angle is the number of degrees
of distributor cam rotation during which the
contact breaker points are closed, ie, the
period from when the points close after being
opened by one cam lobe until they are
opened again by the next cam lobe. The
advantages of setting the points by this
method are that any wear of the distributor
shaft or cam lobes is taken into account, and

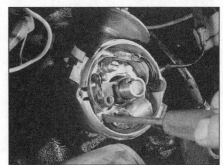

5.7 Adjusting the contact breaker points

6.8 Lift off the rotor arm . . .

6.10a . . . and with the retaining screw removed, lift the contact assembly off the baseplate

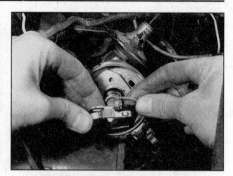

6.10b The LT terminal can then be detached from the tensioning arm

also the inaccuracies of using a feeler blade are eliminated. In general, a dwell meter should be used in accordance with the manufacturer's instructions. However, the use of one type of meter is outlined as follows.

12 To set the dwell angle, remove the distributor cap and rotor arm, and connect one lead of the dwell meter to the + terminal on the coil, and the other lead to the – coil terminal.

13 Whilst an assistant turns on the ignition and operates the starter, observe the reading on the dwell meter scale. With the engine turning over on the starter, the reading should be as stated in the Specifications. **Note:** *Fluctuation of the dwell meter needle indicates that the engine is not turning over fast enough to give a steady reading. If this is the case, remove the spark plugs and repeat the checks.*

14 If the dwell angle is too small, the contact breaker point gap is too wide, and if the dwell angle is excessive, the gap is too small.

15 Adjust the contact breaker points gap, while the engine is cranking using the method described in paragraph 7, until the correct dwell angle is obtained.

16 When the dwell angle is satisfactory, disconnect the meter and refit the rotor arm, distributor cap and ignition or distributor shield.

6 Contact breaker points – renewal

Note: *Carburettor models without electronic ignition may be fitted with either a Lucas 23D4, 25D4, 45D4, 59D4 or Ducellier distributor. Identify the unit being worked on by referring to the illustrations and then proceed as described below according to distributor type.*

Lucas 23D4 and 25D4

1 Remove the distributor cap as described in the previous Section then withdraw the rotor arm from the distributor spindle.

2 Undo and remove the small terminal nut, together with the washer under its head, if fitted. Lift off the flanged nylon insulator, the

condenser lead, and the low tension lead from the terminal post.

3 Using a short screwdriver, unscrew the single screw securing the adjustable contact breaker plate to the distributor baseplate. Lift off the screw and flat washer, taking care not to drop them inside the distributor. The contact breaker points can now be withdrawn.

4 To refit the points, first position the adjustable contact breaker plate and secure it with the retaining screw and washer. Fit the fibre washer to the terminal post (and pivot post where applicable), and then place the contact breaker arm over it. Insert the flanged nylon insulator with the condenser lead immediately under its head, and the low tension lead under that, over the terminal post. Place the washer over the terminal post and finally the retaining nut.

5 If a one-piece contact breaker point assembly is being refitted, position the contact assembly on the distributor baseplate and refit the retaining screw and washer.

6 Place the condenser lead and low tension lead under the head of the upper nylon insulator, and then fit the insulator to the terminal post. Finally refit the washer and retaining nut.

7 The contact breaker points gap should now be adjusted as described in the previous Section.

Lucas 45D4 and 59D4

8 Remove the distributor cap as described in the previous Section then withdraw the rotor arm from the distributor spindle **(see illustration)**.

9 Using a short screwdriver, unscrew the single screw securing the adjustable contact breaker plate to the distributor baseplate. Lift off the screw and washer, taking care not to drop them inside the distributor.

10 Lift the contact assembly off the baseplate and detach the tensioning arm from the insulator. Release the terminal containing the condenser and low tension leads from the end of the arm and then lift away the contact breaker points **(see illustrations)**.

11 To refit the points, first engage the terminal containing the condenser and low tension leads with the end of the tensioning arm. Make

sure that the black lead is uppermost.

12 Position the tensioning arm in the insulator, place the contact assembly on the baseplate and refit the retaining screw and washer.

13 The contact breaker points gap should now be adjusted as described in the previous Section.

Ducellier

14 Remove the distributor cap as described in the previous Section then withdraw the rotor arm from the distributor spindle.

15 Disconnect the contact breaker low tension lead at the connector.

16 Using a small screwdriver or pointed-nose pliers, carefully extract the circlip securing the moving contact arm to the pivot post. Remove the washer and lift off the moving contact arm and low tension lead assembly.

17 Unscrew the single screw securing the adjustable contact breaker plate to the baseplate. Lift off the screw and washer taking care not to drop them inside the distributor. Now lift away the breaker plate.

18 To refit the points first position the adjustable contact breaker plate on the baseplate and refit the retaining screw and washer.

19 Place the moving contact arm over the pivot post and engage the tensioning arm with the insulator. Refit the washer and circlip to the pivot post.

20 Enter the grommet of the low tension lead into the slot on the side of the distributor and reconnect the lead.

21 The contact breaker points gap should now be adjusted as described in the previous Section.

7 Condenser – testing, removal and refitting

Note: *Carburettor models without electronic ignition may be fitted with either a Lucas 23D4, 25D4, 45D4, 59D4 or Ducellier distributor. Identify the unit being worked on by referring to the illustrations accompanying Section 5, then proceed as described below according to distributor type.*

Testing

1 The purpose of the condenser (sometimes known as a capacitor) is to prevent excessive arcing of the contact breaker points, and to ensure that a rapid collapse of the magnetic field created in the coil, and necessary if a healthy spark is to be produced at the plugs, is allowed to occur.

2 The condenser is fitted in parallel with the contact breaker points. If it becomes faulty it will cause ignition failure, as the points will be prevented from cleanly interrupting the low tension circuit.

3 If the engine becomes very difficult to start, or begins to miss after several miles of running, and the contact breaker points show signs of excessive burning, then the condition of the condenser must be suspect. When examining the contact breaker points, disregard any blue discoloration which may be apparent on their faces. This is due to the formation of tungsten oxide, and has no detrimental effect on ignition performance; it is not indicative of condenser failure. A further test can be made by separating the points by hand, with the ignition switched on. If this is accompanied by an excessively strong flash, it indicates that the condenser has failed.

4 Without special test equipment, the only reliable way to diagnose condenser trouble is to renew the suspect unit and note if there is any improvement in performance.

5 Removal and refitting of the condenser varies according to distributor type as follows.

Removal

Lucas 23D4 and 25D4

6 Remove the distributor cap and rotor arm, referring to Section 5 if necessary.

7 Undo and remove the nut and washer (if fitted) from the contact breaker terminal post. Withdraw the flanged nylon insulator and release the condenser lead.

8 Undo and remove the small screw securing the condenser to the distributor baseplate and lift the condenser away.

Lucas 45D4 and 59D4

9 Remove the distributor cap and rotor arm, referring to Section 5 if necessary.

10 Release the contact breaker points tensioning arm from the insulator and detach the condenser and low tension lead terminal from the end of the arm.

11 Undo and remove the small screw securing the condenser to the distributor baseplate.

12 Disconnect the distributor low tension lead at the connector, push the lead and grommet into the inside of the distributor body and lift away the condenser complete with low tension lead assembly.

Ducellier

13 On the Ducellier distributor the condenser is mounted externally and removal consists of simply disconnecting the lead and undoing the retaining screw.

Refitting

14 In all cases, refitting is the reverse sequence to removal. On the Lucas 45D4 and 59D4 distributors, ensure that, when the terminal is connected to the tensioning arm, the black lead is uppermost.

8 Distributor –
removal and refitting

Removal

1 Release the three plastic retaining lugs and lift the ignition shield off the front of the engine. On models that have a distributor shield attached to the inner front panel, undo and remove the retaining screws and withdraw the shield.

2 Spring back the two distributor cap retaining clips or undo the screws then place the distributor cap to one side.

3 Gain access to the ignition timing marks by undoing the two bolts securing the inspection plate to the top of the flywheel housing and lifting off the plate. On models fitted with automatic transmission, withdraw the rubber grommet from the top of the converter housing. On later models there is a timing scale on the timing cover, together with a notch or pointer on the crankshaft pulley.

4 Turn the engine over until No 1 piston is approaching TDC on the compression stroke. This can be checked by removing No 1 spark plug and feeling the pressure being developed in the cylinder as the piston rises, or by removing the rocker cover and noting when the valves of No 4 cylinder are rocking, ie, the inlet valve just opening and the exhaust valve just closing. On manual transmission models, the engine can be turned over quite easily by engaging top gear and moving the car forwards. This should only be done on level ground; and make sure that the car cannot run away. An alternative method, and the method that should be used on automatic transmission models, is to press the auxiliary drivebelt midway between the water pump pulley and dynamo or alternator pulley and then turn the fan blades.

5 Continue turning the engine, in the correct direction of rotation, until No 1 piston is at TDC on the compression stroke. Verify this by checking that the timing marks are aligned. The timing marks on the flywheel (or torque converter), and the pointer on the housing, can be viewed through the inspection aperture using a small mirror **(see illustration)**. The 1/4 mark on the flywheel or torque converter indicates TDC and should be aligned with the pointer in the housing. On later models with a timing scale on the timing cover, the notch in the crankshaft pulley should be aligned with the 0 pointer on the timing cover scale.

6 The distributor rotor arm should now be pointing towards the No 1 spark plug HT lead

8.5 The timing marks on the flywheel can be viewed through the aperture in the housing using a mirror

segment in the distributor cap indicating that the crankshaft is correctly positioned with number 1 cylinder at TDC on its compression stroke. Temporarily place the cap in position to verify this if necessary. If the rotor arm is pointing at the No 4 HT lead segment in the cap, rotate the crankshaft one full turn (360º) until the TDC timing marks are realigned and the rotor arm is pointing at the No 1 segment.

7 On carburettor models, detach the distributor vacuum advance pipe from the vacuum unit (where applicable), then either disconnect the low tension (LT) lead at the connector or disconnect the ignition amplifier multiplug according to distributor type **(see illustration)**.

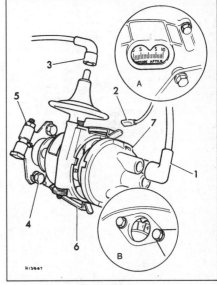

8.7 Distributor removal

1 HT lead
2 LT lead terminal connector
3 Vacuum pipe connection
4 Clamp securing bolts and spring washers
5 Clamp nut and bolt
6 Spring clip
7 Distributor cap
Inset: Timing marks:
   A   *Automatic transmission*
   B   *Manual transmission*

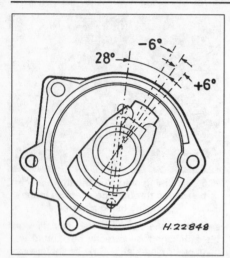

8.12 Correct distributor rotor arm offset and body position (No 1 cylinder at TDC on compression stroke) – fuel injection models

8 Using a dab of paint or a small file, make a mark between the distributor body and the clamping plate. This will ensure that the distributor is refitted in exactly the same position and that the timing is not lost.

9 If the distributor is retained by a clamping plate having a pinch-bolt and nut, slacken one of the bolts securing the clamping plate to the cylinder block and then slacken the pinch-bolt. If a C-shaped plate is used to retain the distributor, undo and remove the securing bolt and lift away the plate.

10 The distributor can now be withdrawn from the engine.

Refitting

11 Ensure that the crankshaft is still positioned so that number 1 cylinder is at TDC on its compression stroke, then refit the distributor to the engine, aligning the drive dog with the slot in the drive. When inserting the distributor into the engine aperture, press down lightly on the distributor body and at the same time rotate the distributor shaft slightly. When the lug on the distributor drive dog engages with the slot on the driveshaft, the distributor will move in toward the engine a further 6.3 mm.

12 If the original distributor is being refitted, align the marks made on removal between the distributor body and clamp plate. If a new distributor is being fitted to carburettor models, turn the distributor body until the rotor arm is pointing toward the No 1 HT lead segment in the distributor cap. If a new distributor is being fitted to fuel injection models, turn the distributor body until the rotor arm and body are aligned as shown **(see illustration)**.

13 With the distributor correctly positioned, tighten the pinch-bolt and clamp plate bolt or refit the C-shaped plate and tighten the bolt.

14 Refit the cap to the distributor, and secure with the clips or retaining screws.

15 If removed, refit the rocker cover and reconnect any disturbed spark plug HT leads.

16 On carburettor models, reconnect the distributor wiring and vacuum advance pipe.

17 Before refitting the remainder of the components on carburettor models, the ignition timing must be checked and adjusted as described in Section 13.

---

9 Distributor – dismantling, inspection and reassembly

Note: *The following procedures are applicable to the distributors fitted to carburettor models. The distributor fitted to fuel injection models consists simply of a shaft and housing and cannot be dismantled. Check the cost and availability of replacement parts before proceeding. If the distributor is excessively worn it may be beneficial (or necessary) to obtain a reconditioned unit.*

Dismantling

Lucas 23D4 and 25D4

1 Remove the distributor from the car as described in Section 8.

2 Withdraw the rotor arm from the distributor spindle and then remove the contact breaker points as described in Section 6.

3 Undo and remove the single retaining screw and lift off the condenser **(see illustration)**.

4 Unhook the vacuum unit operating spring from the post on the distributor baseplate (not 23D4).

5 Undo and remove the two small screws and spring washers which secure the baseplate to the distributor body. Note that one of these screws also retains the baseplate earth lead.

6 Now carefully lift out the baseplate.

7 Make a note of the position of the rotor arm drive slot, in the spindle, in relation to the offset driving dog at the opposite end of the distributor. It is essential that this is reassembled correctly, otherwise the ignition timing will be 180° out.

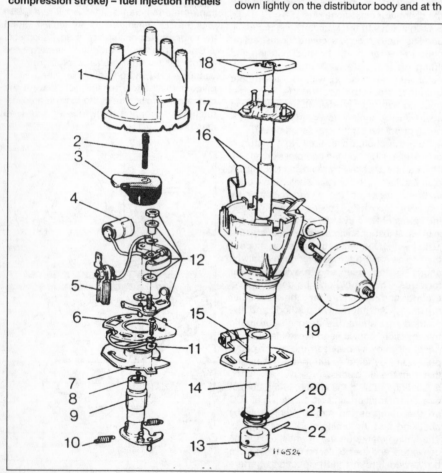

9.3 Exploded view of Lucas 25D4 distributor

1 Distributor cap	7 Fixed baseplate	13 Driving dog	18 Bob weights
2 Brush and spring	8 Cam screw	14 Bush	19 Vacuum unit
3 Rotor arm	9 Cam	15 Clamp plate	20 O-ring oil
4 Condenser	10 Advance spring	16 Cap retaining	seal
5 Terminal and	11 Earth lead	clips	21 Thrustwasher
lead	12 Contact breaker	17 Shaft and action	22 Taper pin
6 Moving baseplate	points	plate	

8 Undo and remove the cam spindle retaining screw which is located in the centre of the rotor arm drive.

9 Remove the two centrifugal advance weight tension springs and then lift off the cam spindle. It is quite likely that the cam spindle will prove difficult to remove and will not slide readily off the shaft. If this is the case, apply liberal amounts of penetrating oil to the top of the spindle and rotate it back-and-forth while at the same time pulling upward. This should free the spindle and allow it to be removed from the shaft.

10 With the cam spindle removed, the centrifugal advance weights can now be lifted out.

11 To remove the vacuum unit, prise off the small circlip located behind the knurled adjustment wheel. Now unscrew the adjustment wheel until the vacuum unit is released and then withdraw the vacuum unit from the distributor body. **Note:** *A vacuum unit is not fitted to the 23D4 type.*

12 As the unit is withdrawn, retrieve the adjustment wheel together with the tension spring and spring plate. The spring plate is responsible for the clicks when the adjustment wheel is turned. This spring plate together with the circlip are small and easily lost so put them in a safe place.

13 It is only necessary to remove the distributor driveshaft if it is thought to be excessively worn. With a thin punch, drive out the retaining pin from the driving dog on the bottom end of the distributor driveshaft. The shaft can then be removed.

Lucas 45D4 and 59D4

14 Remove the distributor from the car as described in Section 8.

15 Withdraw the rotor arm from the distributor spindle and then remove the contact breaker points as described in Section 6.

16 Push the low tension lead and grommet through into the inside of the distributor body **(see illustration)**. Undo and remove the single retaining screw and lift off the condenser and low tension lead assembly. Note that the condenser securing screw also retains the baseplate earth lead.

17 Undo and remove the two vacuum unit securing screws, tilt the vacuum unit to disengage the pullrod from the baseplate peg, and withdraw the unit.

18 Undo and remove the two screws securing the baseplate and the earth lead to the distributor body. Lift off the earth lead, lever the slotted segment of the baseplate out of its retaining groove and withdraw the baseplate.

19 The distributor driveshaft should only be removed if it is thought to be worn. After removal it cannot be further dismantled, and if necessary must be renewed as an assembly, complete with centrifugal advance weights and springs.

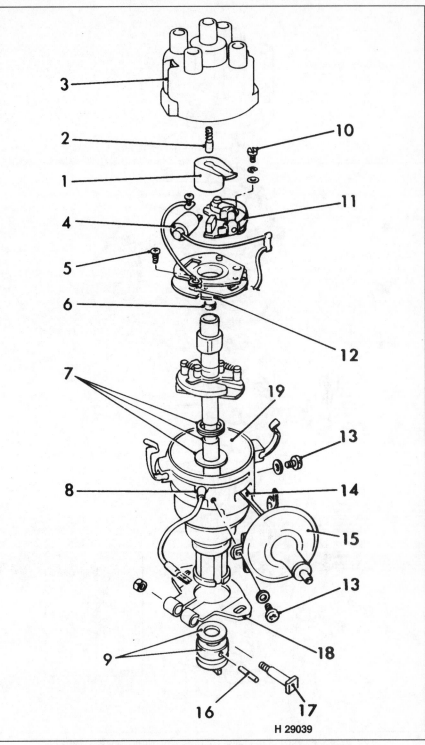

H 29039

9.16 Exploded view of Lucas 45D4 distributor (59D4 similar)

1 Rotor
2 Carbon brush and spring
3 Cap
4 Condenser (capacitor)
5 Baseplate securing screw
6 Felt pad
7 Shaft assembly with steel washer and spacer
8 Low tension lead and grommet
9 Drive dog and thrust washer
10 Contact set securing screw
11 Contact set
12 Baseplate
13 Vacuum unit retaining screws and washers
14 Vacuum unit link
15 Vacuum unit
16 Parallel pin
17 Pinch-bolt and nut
18 Lockplate
19 Distributor body

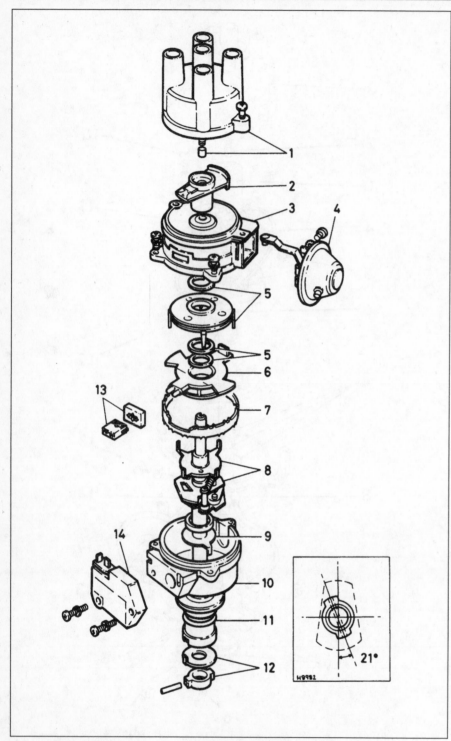

9.22 Exploded view of the Lucas 65DM4 electronic ignition distributor

1 Distributor cap, carbon brush and spring
2 Rotor arm
3 Upper housing
4 Vacuum unit
5 Stator pack, thrust washers and circlip

6 Pick-up winding
7 Clamp ring
8 Reluctor, centrifugal advance mechanism and shaft assembly
9 Thrustwasher
10 Lower housing

11 O-ring
12 Drive dog and thrustwasher
13 Connector and gasket
14 Amplifier module

Inset indicates correct rotor arm-to-drive dog offset (for carburettor models)

20 To remove the driveshaft, drift out the retaining pin from the driving dog using a thin punch. Remove the driving dog and thrustwasher and then lift out the driveshaft assembly.

Lucas 65DM4

21 Remove the distributor from the car as described in Section 8.
22 Pull off the rotor arm **(see illustration)**.
23 Remove the two screws and pull the amplifier module from the connector, then remove the gasket and pull off the connector.
24 Remove the screws, and separate the upper housing from the lower housing.
25 Remove the clamp ring and pick-up winding from the upper housing.
26 Remove the vacuum unit retaining screw, then extract the circlip and thrustwasher, withdraw the stator pack from the link arm, and remove the vacuum unit. Recover the remaining thrustwasher from the upper housing.
27 Further dismantling is not normally necessary. However, the shaft assembly may be removed from the lower housing by driving the roll pin from the drive dog, after marking the drive dog in relation to the shaft.
28 Clean and examine all the components, and renew them as required.

Ducellier

29 Remove the distributor from the car as described in Section 8.
30 Withdraw the rotor arm from the distributor spindle and then remove the contact breaker points as described in Section 6.
31 Undo and remove the two screws that secure the condenser, vacuum unit, and one of the distributor cap retaining clips to the distributor body **(see illustration opposite)**. Lift away the condenser and clip.
32 Using a small screwdriver, extract the circlip securing the serrated eccentric cam to the D-post. Mark the position of the eccentric cam in relation to the spring seat of the vacuum unit operating link.
33 Detach the vacuum unit operating link and the eccentric cam from the D-post and lift off the vacuum unit. Store the eccentric cam and the small circlip safely, as they are easily lost.
34 Undo and remove the screw securing the other distributor cap retaining clip and take off the clip.
35 The distributor baseplate can now be removed, taking care not to allow the nylon pressure pad and spring to fly off as the baseplate is withdrawn.
36 This is the limit of dismantling that can be carried out on these units. If the driveshaft, centrifugal advance weights or springs are thought to be worn, it will be necessary to obtain a complete new distributor assembly.

Inspection

37 Thoroughly clean all the mechanical parts in paraffin or a suitable solvent and wipe dry.

38 Examine the contact breaker points as described in Section 5 and renew them if necessary.

39 Check the distributor cap, HT leads and rotor arm as described in Chapter 1.

40 Check the vacuum unit for leaks of the internal diaphragm by sucking on the advance pipe union connection and observing the movement of the operating spring or arm. If, when suction is applied, a firm resistance builds-up and the spring or arm moves in toward the diaphragm then the unit is satisfactory. If no resistance to suction is felt, and the operating spring or arm does not move, then it is likely that the diaphragm is punctured and the vacuum unit should be renewed.

41 If working on a Lucas distributor, inspect the two halves of the baseplate. If the spring between the plates is damaged or if the two halves do not move freely, renew the baseplate.

42 On all distributors, check for excessive side movement of the distributor shaft in the bushes. Any excess side play here can greatly affect the accuracy of the ignition timing and the overall performance of the car. If wear is apparent it will be necessary to renew the complete distributor.

43 Examine the centrifugal advance weights and pivots for wear, and also check that the advance mechanism operates smoothly without binding. If these components are worn it will be necessary to renew the complete distributor in the case of the Ducellier unit, or the shaft assembly in the case of the Lucas 45D4. Advance weights and springs should be available separately for the Lucas 23D4 and 25D4 distributors.

Reassembly

Lucas 23D4 and 25D4

44 If the distributor shaft has been removed, lubricate the bearings in the distributor body with engine oil and refit the shaft. Position the thrustwasher and driving dog on the end of the shaft and tap in the retaining pin.

45 Slide the vacuum advance unit into its location on the side of the distributor body. Place the spring plate in position, slide the adjustment wheel tension spring over the threaded vacuum unit shaft, and then screw on the adjustment wheel.

46 Set the position of the vacuum unit by rotating the adjustment wheel until approximately half the marks on the vacuum unit vernier scale are visible. Now refit the small circlip to the end of the shaft.

47 Lay the centrifugal advance weights on the action plate of the distributor shaft. Lightly lubricate the shaft and the driving pins of the distributor spindle. Slide the spindle over the shaft and engage the driving pins with the advance weights. Check that when viewed from the base of the distributor, the large offset on the driving dog is to the left, with the rotor arm driving slot on the cam spindle

uppermost. If this is correct, refit the spindle retaining screw. If not, reposition the spindle by 180º.

48 Refit the two centrifugal advance weight tension springs to the posts on the action plate and spindle. Check the action of the weights by spinning the distributor shaft and ensure that they are not binding.

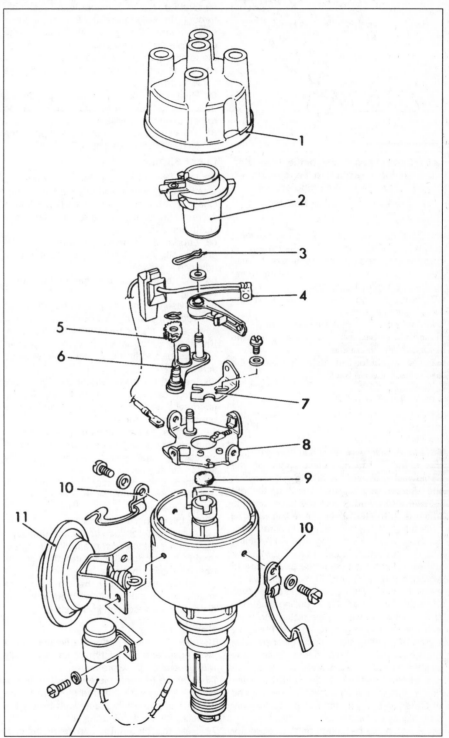

9.31 Exploded view of Ducellier distributor

1 Cap	5 Serrated cam	9 Felt pad
2 Rotor	6 Eccentric D-post	10 Cap retaining clips
3 Rocker arm clip	7 Fixed contact	11 Vacuum unit
4 Moving contact assembly	8 Baseplate	12 Condenser

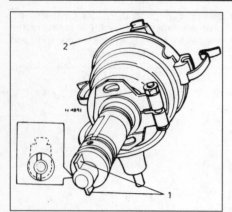

9.54 Correct positioning of the distributor driving dog in relation to the rotor arm – Lucas 45D4 distributor

1 Driving dog   2 Rotor arm
*   tongues*

49 Refit the baseplate and the two retaining screws, making sure that the earth lead is fitted under the head of the nearest screw. Reconnect the vacuum unit operating spring to the post on the baseplate.
50 Refit the condenser and secure with the single retaining screw.
51 Refit the contact breaker points as described in Section 6, and then place the rotor arm on the spindle.
52 The distributor can now be refitted to the car as described in Section 8.

Lucas 45D4 and 59D4

53 Begin reassembly by lubricating the distributor shaft assembly and sliding it into the distributor body.
54 Place the thrustwasher and driving dog on the shaft, with the raised pips of the thrustwasher toward the driving dog. Position the driving dog so that the tongues are parallel with the rotor arm electrode, and the offset is to the left of its centre line with the rotor arm pointing upward **(see illustration)**.
55 Secure the driving dog with the retaining pin. If a new shaft is being fitted, it must be drilled through the hole in the driving dog to accept the retaining pin. The drill size will be either 1/8 in or 3/16 in, depending on the type of driving dog fitted. When drilling, keep the shaft pressed down into the distributor body, and the driving dog tight against the body shank. After fitting the retaining pin, peen over the edges of the hole in the driving dog slightly to secure the pin. Make sure that there is a trace of endfloat of the shaft when the driving dog is fitted. If necessary, tap the end of the driving dog to flatten the thrustwasher pips slightly and increase the endfloat.
56 Position the baseplate on the distributor body so that the two downward pointing prongs straddle the screw hole below the distributor cap clip. Now press the baseplate into the body until it engages the undercut.
57 Refit the baseplate retaining screws and the earth lead.

58 Make sure that the baseplate prongs still straddle the screw hole and refit the vacuum unit. Engage the pullrod with the baseplate peg and secure the unit with the two screws.
59 Slide the low tension lead assembly through the hole in the distributor body and fully engage the grommet. Position the condenser on the baseplate and secure it with the retaining screw. Make sure that the other end of the earth lead is positioned under the screw head.
60 Refit the contact breaker points as described in Section 6, and then place the rotor arm on the spindle.
61 The distributor can now be refitted to the car as described in Section 8.

Lucas 65DM4

62 Refit the shaft assembly if removed, locate the drive dog, and drive in the roll pin. Check that the drive dog offset is positioned correctly in relation to the rotor arm (see illustration 9.22).
63 Lubricate the shaft bearing with a little engine oil. Also lubricate the centrifugal advance mechanism.
64 Locate the thrustwasher in the upper housing.
65 Grease the end of the link arm, then insert the vacuum unit in the upper housing, and engage the stator pack with the link arm. Retain the stator pack with the thrustwasher and circlip, and fit the vacuum unit retaining screw.
66 Insert the pick-up winding in the upper housing, centralise the terminals in the aperture, then fit the clamp ring with the cut-out over the aperture.
67 Fit the lower housing to the upper housing, and insert the screws finger-tight. Rotate the shaft several times, then fully tighten the screws.
68 Check that the reluctor arms do not touch the stator pack arms, as they can easily be bent inadvertently.
69 Fit the connector and gasket.
70 Apply heat-conducting silicone grease to the mounting face of the amplifier module, then fit the module and tighten the screws. Refit the rotor arm.
71 If necessary, renew the O-ring on the shank of the distributor, then refit the distributor, as described in Section 8.

Ducellier

72 Lubricate the centrifugal advance weight pivot posts and the distributor cam sparingly with general purpose grease.
73 Position the baseplate in the distributor body, making sure that the nylon pressure pad and spring are in place, with the pad in contact with the distributor shaft.
74 Refit the distributor cap retaining clip, located opposite to the vacuum unit, and secure with the retaining screw.
75 Position the operating link of the vacuum unit together with the eccentric cam, over the baseplate D-post. Turn the eccentric cam so that it is in the same position relative to the

spring seat of the operating link, as marked during dismantling. Now carefully refit the small retaining circlip.
76 Secure the vacuum unit, condenser, and the remaining distributor cap retaining clip to the distributor body, using the two screws.
77 Refit the contact breaker points as described in Section 6, and then place the rotor arm on the spindle.
78 The distributor can now be refitted to the car as described in Section 8.

---

10 Ignition coil –
    removal, testing and refitting

Removal

1 Release the fasteners, and remove the ignition shield from the front of the engine.
2 Where applicable, slide back the rubber cover fitted over the end of the coil to expose the wiring connectors. Disconnect the LT wiring from the coil terminals, noting their positions. Disconnect the HT lead from the centre of the coil.
3 If the coil is mounted on the dynamo, undo and remove the mounting bracket retaining bolts and lift off the coil. Slacken the clamp bolt and slide the coil out of its mounting bracket.
4 If the coil is mounted on the cylinder head, slacken and remove the nut securing the coil to the cylinder head stud, and remove the coil and bracket assembly from the engine. If necessary disconnect the suppressor, then slacken the clamp bolt and slide the coil out of its mounting bracket.

Testing

5 Testing the coil consists of using a multimeter set to its resistance function, to check the primary (LT + to – terminals) and secondary (LT + to HT lead terminal) windings for continuity. If the meter is used, the resistance of either winding can be checked and compared with the specified value; note that although no specified value is given by Rover for the secondary windings, as a guide, the reading should be in the region of 5 to 15 kohms. The resistance of the coil windings will vary slightly according to the coil temperature; those specified are accurate only when the coil is at 20ºC.
6 Using an ohmmeter or continuity tester, check that there is no continuity between the HT lead terminal and the coil body.
7 If the coil is faulty, it must be renewed. Ensure that the correct coil is obtained for the type of ignition system fitted.

Refitting

8 Refitting is the reverse sequence to removal, ensuring that the wiring connectors are securely reconnected.

11 Crankshaft position sensor (fuel injection models) – removal and refitting

Removal

Manual transmission models

1 Disconnect the battery negative terminal (refer to *Disconnecting the battery* in the Reference Chapter), then release the fasteners, and remove the ignition cover from the front of the engine.
2 Firmly apply the handbrake, then jack up the front of the car and support it securely on axle stands (see *Jacking and vehicle support*).
3 Remove the tie securing the crankshaft position sensor wiring to the starter motor solenoid, and undo the bolt securing the wiring connector to the mounting bracket **(see illustration)**.
4 Disconnect the sensor wiring connector, then undo the bolts securing the sensor to the flywheel housing, and remove the sensor from the car **(see illustration)**.

Automatic transmission models

5 Disconnect the battery negative terminal (refer to *Disconnecting the battery* in the Reference Chapter), then undo the two bolts securing the ECU mounting bracket to the right-hand wing valance, and position the ECU clear of the crankshaft position sensor.
6 Undo the bolt securing the wiring connector to the mounting bracket, then disconnect the sensor wiring connector.
7 Slacken and remove the two bolts securing the sensor to the torque converter housing, and remove the sensor from the car.

Refitting

8 On all models, refitting is the reverse sequence to removal, tightening the sensor mounting bolts to the specified torque.

12 Reluctor ring (fuel injection models) – removal and refitting

Manual transmission models

Removal

1 Remove the flywheel as described in Chapter 2A.
2 Slacken and remove the two retaining screws, and remove the reluctor ring from the rear of the flywheel.
3 Check the ring for obvious signs of wear or damage, and renew it if necessary.

Refitting

4 Refitting is the reverse sequence to removal, ensuring that the reluctor retaining screws are securely tightened.

Automatic transmission models

5 On automatic transmission models, the

11.3 Crankshaft position sensor wiring connector retaining bolt (arrowed) – manual transmission models

reluctor ring is an integral part of the torque converter assembly, and is not available separately. Refer to Chapter 2A for information on torque converter removal and refitting. If the reluctor ring is damaged, the completed torque converter assembly must be renewed.

13 Ignition timing – checking and adjustment

Carburettor models

1 In order that the engine can run efficiently, it is necessary for a spark to occur at the spark plug and ignite the fuel/air mixture at the instant just before the piston, on the compression stroke reached the top of its travel. The precise instant at which the spark occurs is determined by the ignition timing, and this is quoted in degrees before top dead centre (BTDC). On pre-1976 models the ignition timing may be checked with the engine stationary (this is the static ignition timing), or more accurately with the engine running, using a stroboscopic timing light. On post-1976 models a stroboscopic timing light must be used, as no static values are quoted by the manufacturer.

11.4 Crankshaft position sensor location (arrowed) on manual transmission models – viewed from underneath

2 If the distributor has been dismantled or renewed, or if its position on the engine has been altered, it will be necessary to reset the ignition timing using the following procedure.
3 First ensure that the contact breaker points are in good condition and that the gap is correctly set as described in Section 5.
4 To obtain the static timing setting, remove the distributor cap and place it to one side. Gain access to the ignition timing marks by undoing the two bolts securing the inspection plate to the top of the flywheel housing and lifting off the plate. On models fitted with automatic transmission, withdraw the rubber grommet from the top of the converter housing. On later models there is a timing scale on the timing cover, together with a notch or pointer on the crankshaft pulley.
5 The timing marks on the flywheel (or torque converter), and the pointer on the housing, can be viewed through the inspection aperture using a small mirror. The 1/4 mark on the flywheel or torque converter indicates TDC, and the 5, 10 and 15 marks indicate 5°, 10°, and 15° of advance before TDC respectively. On later models with a timing scale on the timing cover, each pointer on the scale represents 4° of ignition advance, with the larger pointer indicating TDC **(see illustrations)**.
6 Refer to the Specifications at the beginning of this Chapter for the correct ignition timing

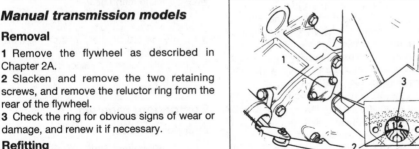

13.5a Ignition timing marks – manual transmission models

1 Inspection cover
2 Timing marks
3 Pointer

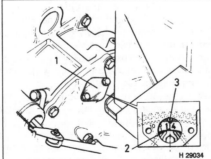

13.5b Location of timing marks on torque converter – automatic transmission models

A Detail showing alternative timing marks
B Insert screwdriver to turn converter

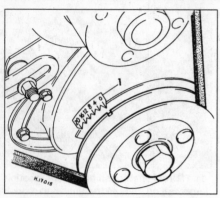

13.5c The timing scale located on the timing cover of later models

1 Timing scale

static setting. The distributor number will be found stamped on the side of the distributor body, usually just below the vacuum unit **(see illustration)**.

7 Having determined the correct setting, turn the engine over until No 1 piston is approaching TDC on the compression stroke. This can be checked by removing No 1 spark plug and feeling the pressure being developed in the cylinder as the piston rises, or by removing the rocker cover and noting when the valves of No 4 cylinder are rocking, ie, the inlet valve just opening and the exhaust valve just closing. If this check is not made, it is all too easy to set the timing 180° out, as both No 1 and No 4 pistons approach TDC at the same time, but only one is on the compression stroke. On manual transmission models, the engine can be turned over quite easily by engaging top gear and moving the car forwards. This should only be done on level ground; and make sure that the car cannot run away. An alternative method, and the method that should be used on automatic transmission models, is to press the auxiliary drivebelt midway between the water pump pulley and dynamo or alternator pulley and then turn the fan blades.

HAYNES HiNT *Turning the engine will be easier if the spark plugs are removed first – see Chapter 1.*

13.6 The distributor number is stamped on the body below the vacuum unit

8 Continue turning the engine, in the correct direction of rotation, until the appropriate timing mark on the flywheel or torque converter is in line with the pointer on the housing.

9 The distributor rotor arm should now be pointing towards the No 1 spark plug HT lead segment in the distributor cap. Temporarily place the cap in position to verify this if necessary.

10 With the engine set in the correct position and the rotor arm pointing towards the appropriate segment, turn the knurled vernier adjustment wheel, on the distributor (where applicable), until approximately half the marks on the vacuum unit timing scale are visible.

11 Next slacken the distributor clamp plate pinch-bolt and turn the distributor body clockwise until the points are *just* beginning to open. If they are already open, turn the distributor body anti-clockwise until they are fully closed, then turn it clockwise until they *just* begin to open. Now tighten the pinch-bolt. If the distributor incorporates a knurled vernier adjustment wheel on the vacuum unit a very fine degree of accuracy can be obtained. Turning the wheel in the direction A stamped on the vacuum unit advances the timing, and turning it towards R retards it. Eleven clicks of the wheel represents 1° of timing movement and each graduation of the vernier scale is equal to approximately 5° of timing movement.

12 Difficulty will probably be experienced in determining exactly when the contact breaker points open, so the following method can be used. Connect a 12 volt bulb in parallel with the contact breaker points (one lead to earth and the other to the distributor (–) low tension terminal on the coil). With the ignition switch on the bulb will light as the points open. The distributor body should be turned as in paragraph 11 until the point is reached where the bulb *just* lights up.

13 To adjust the ignition timing using a stroboscopic timing light, first connect the light in accordance with the manufacturer's instructions.

14 Remove the inspection cover from the flywheel or converter housing and shine the light beam into the aperture. Use a mirror to deflect the beam onto the flywheel or torque converter. On later models there is an additional and more easily visible timing scale on the timing cover, together with a notch or pointer on the crankshaft pulley

15 Start the engine and allow it to reach normal running temperature.

16 Refer to the Specifications for the appropriate ignition timing setting and the corresponding engine speed.

17 Disconnect the vacuum advance pipe from the distributor and adjust the engine speed to that specified (see Chapter 4A).

18 Turn the knurled adjustment wheel or slacken the distributor clamp or pinch-bolt and rotate the distributor body until the relevant timing marks and pointer appear stationary and directly in line with each other.

19 Tighten the clamp or pinch bolt, recheck that the timing is still correct, and then reconnect the vacuum pipe. After disconnecting the timing light, reset the engine idling speed to that specified (Chapter 4A).

20 Whichever method has been used to set the ignition timing, a thorough road test should be carried out to ensure that the engine performance is satisfactory under all engine load conditions. As a general guide, the timing is correct if very slight 'pinking' can be heard with the engine labouring (ie at the point where you would normally change to a lower gear). Any small corrections necessary can be made during the road test using the vernier adjustment wheel, or by turning the distributor body very slightly in the required direction.

Fuel injection models

21 While home mechanics with a timing light and a good-quality tachometer may be able to check the ignition timing, if it is found to be in need of adjustment, the car **must** be taken to a suitably-equipped Rover dealer; adjustments can be made only by reprogramming the fuel injection/ignition system ECU, using Rover diagnostic equipment connected to the system by the diagnostic connector. Note also that the timing and idle speed are under ECU control and may, therefore, vary significantly from the nominal values given; without full equipment, any check is therefore nothing more than a rough guide.

14 Transmission-controlled ignition advance – checking and component renewal

Note: *This procedure only applies to carburettor models.*

Checking

1 To check the operation of the system, chock the front wheels, apply the handbrake and start the engine.

2 Increase engine speed to approximately 2500 rpm.

3 Depress and hold the clutch pedal down while selecting fourth gear.

4 With fourth gear selected, engine speed should increase by 300 to 400 rpm.

5 Disengage fourth gear, release the clutch pedal, and stop the engine.

6 If the system does not respond as described, check the inhibitor switch adjustment as described below.

Component renewal

Inhibitor switch

7 Firmly apply the handbrake, then jack up the front of the car and support it securely on axle stands (see *Jacking and vehicle support*). Place the gear lever in neutral.

8 Disconnect the electrical leads from the inhibitor switch, located behind the gearchange remote control housing. Slacken the locknut securing the switch to its mounting bracket then unscrew the switch from the bracket.

9 Fit the switch to the mounting bracket and adjust as follows before tightening the locknut or reconnecting the leads.

10 Connect a self-powered test lamp to the terminals of the inhibitor switch, and screw the switch out of its mounting bracket until the lamp lights.

11 Now screw the switch in until the lamp goes out.

12 Screw the switch in a further one and one half to two flats, then tighten the locknut.

13 Check that the lamp lights only when the fourth gear is selected.

14 Remove the test lamp, reconnect the electrical leads, and carry out the test procedure previously described.

Solenoid valve

15 Pull the vacuum hoses from the solenoid valve.

16 Disconnect the electrical leads.

17 Remove the mounting screw, noting the earth lead, and remove the valve.

18 Refitting is the reverse sequence to removal, ensuring that the earth lead is fitted under the mounting bolt.

Chapter 5 Part C:
Distributorless ignition system

Contents

Crankshaft position sensor – removal and refitting 4
DIS module – testing, removal and refitting 3
General information 1
Ignition system check . . . . See Chapter 1
Ignition system – testing 2
Reluctor ring – removal and refitting 5
Ignition timing – checking and adjustment 6
Spark plug renewal . . . . .See Chapter 1

Degrees of difficulty

Easy, suitable for novice with little experience	Fairly easy, suitable for beginner with some experience	Fairly difficult, suitable for competent DIY mechanic	Difficult, suitable for experienced DIY mechanic 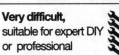	Very difficult, suitable for expert DIY or professional

Specifications

General
System type . . . .   Rover/Motorola Modular Engine Management System (MEMS), fully electronic, controlled by ECU
Firing order . . . .   1-3-4-2 (No 1 cylinder at timing chain end of engine)

Electronic control unit
Type MNE104290

Crankshaft position sensor
Type . . . .   ADU 7340

Ignition timing
Nominal value . . . .   12° BTDC at idle*
*This value will constantly vary under control of the ECU idle function (by as much as −11° to +10°) – see text for further information.

DIS module
Type NEC1000710
Primary resistance at 20°C . . . .   0.41 to 0.61 ohms
Secondary resistance at 20°C . . . .   6200 to 6700 ohms

Spark plugs . . . .   See Chapter 1

Torque wrench settings	Nm	lbf ft
Crankshaft position sensor bolts	6	4
DIS module mounting bolts	10	7

1 General information

General information

All Mini models from October 1996 onwards are equipped with a Distributorless Ignition System (DIS). The system is fully-electronic in operation, incorporating the Electronic Control Unit (ECU) (situated on the right-hand side of the engine compartment), a DIS module (attached to the front facing side of the cylinder block), engine sensors, spark plugs, HT leads and associated wiring. The system is divided into two circuits; primary (low tension/LT) and secondary (high tension/HT). The primary circuit consists of the battery, ignition switch, DIS module primary windings, ECU and wiring. The secondary circuit consists of the DIS module secondary windings, the spark plugs, and the HT leads connecting these.

The ECU controls both the ignition system and the fuel injection system, integrating the two in a complete engine management package; refer to Chapter 4C for information relating to the fuel injection side of the system.

As far as the ignition system is concerned, the ECU receives information in the form of electrical impulses or signals from the crankshaft position sensor (crankshaft position and speed), camshaft position sensor (camshaft position and cam lobe period), coolant temperature sensor (engine temperature), throttle position sensor (throttle position) and manifold absolute pressure sensor (engine load). The crankshaft position sensor works in conjunction with the reluctor ring, which is bolted onto the back of the flywheel. The reluctor ring has thirty-four poles on it, spaced 10° apart, with four missing poles at 30°, 60°, 210° and 250°; the missing poles identify the cylinder TDC positions. The sensor reads these poles, to provide an accurate assessment of the engine speed and crankshaft position to the ECU.

All the above signals are compared by the ECU, with set values pre-programmed (mapped) into its memory; based on this information, the ECU selects the ignition timing appropriate to those values, and controls the DIS module accordingly.

The DIS module consists of two ignition coils housed in a common casing. Each ignition coil supplies two spark plugs with HT voltage – thus, one spark is provided in a cylinder with its piston on the compression stroke, and one in a cylinder with its piston on the exhaust stroke. This results in a 'wasted spark' being supplied to one cylinder during each ignition cycle, but this has no detrimental effect. This system has the advantage that there are no moving parts – therefore there is no wear, and the system is largely maintenance-free.

2 Ignition system – testing

Warning: The HT voltage generated by an electronic ignition system is extremely high and, in certain circumstances, could prove fatal. Take care to avoid receiving electric shocks from the HT side of the ignition system. Do not handle HT leads, or touch the DIS module, when the engine is running. If tracing faults in the HT circuit, use well-insulated tools to manipulate live leads. Persons with surgically-implanted cardiac pacemaker devices should keep well clear of the ignition circuits, components and test equipment.

General

1 The components of the DIS ignition system are normally very reliable; most faults are far more likely to be due to loose or dirty connections, or to 'tracking' of HT voltage due to dirt, dampness or damaged insulation, than to the failure of any of the system components. **Always** check all wiring thoroughly before condemning an electrical component, and work methodically to eliminate all other possibilities before deciding that a particular component is faulty.

2 The practice of checking for a spark by holding the live end of an HT lead a short distance away from the engine is **not** recommended – not only is there a high risk of a powerful electric shock, but the DIS module or electronic control unit may be damaged.

3 Extreme care should be taken if attempts are to be made to test the system, as the electronic control unit is very sensitive, and if damaged, may prove very costly to renew.

4 Unless the correct special test equipment is available, entrust testing and fault diagnosis to a Rover dealer. It is far better to pay the labour charges involved in having the vehicle checked by someone suitably qualified, than to risk damage to the system or yourself. The engine management system has a self-diagnostic function, and any problems with the system are stored as fault codes, which can be read using suitable specialist diagnostic equipment.

Engine fails to start

5 If the engine either will not turn over at all, or only turns over very slowly, check the battery and starter motor. Connect a voltmeter across the battery terminals (meter positive probe to battery positive terminal). Disconnect the wiring multiplug from the DIS module, then note the voltage reading obtained while turning over the engine on the starter for a few seconds. If the reading obtained is less than approximately 8 volts, check the battery, starter motor and charging system (see Chapter 5A).

6 Testing of the ignition LT and HT circuits can only be carried out safely and effectively using special test equipment, and should be entrusted to a Rover dealer.

Engine misfires

7 Misfires are usually the result of partial or temporary failures in the system components, and the possible causes are too numerous to be eliminated without the use of special test equipment. The ignition system wiring and the spark plugs can be checked for signs of obvious faults as described in the following paragraphs, but if these checks do not reveal the source of the problem, take the vehicle to a Rover dealer, who will be able to test the full engine management system using the appropriate equipment.

8 An irregular misfire suggests a loose or dirty connection. With the ignition switched off, check the security and condition of the DIS module wiring, and the HT leads.

9 Regular misfiring is most likely to be due to a fault in the HT leads or spark plugs. Check that the HT leads are clean and dry. Check the leads themselves and the spark plugs (by substitution if necessary). Renew the spark plugs as a matter of course, if there is any doubt about their condition (refer to Chapter 1 for details of checking spark plugs).

3 DIS module – testing, removal and refitting

Testing

1 Testing of the DIS module can only be carried out safely, and without the risk of damage to the module, using the appropriate special test equipment. Testing should therefore be entrusted to a Rover dealer.

Removal

2 Disconnect the battery negative terminal (refer to *Disconnecting the battery* in the Reference Chapter).

3 Disconnect the HT leads from the spark plugs or from the DIS module, noting their locations to ensure correct refitting.

4 Unscrew the four bolts, and remove the module from its mounting plate **(see illustration)**.

3.4 Unscrew the four bolts, and remove the DIS module from its mounting plate

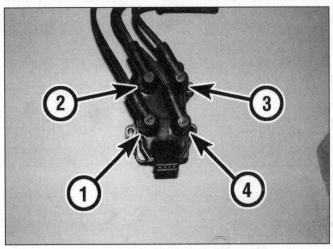

3.5 Disconnect the multiplug from the base of the DIS module

3.6 HT lead connections at the DIS module

5 Disconnect the multiplug from the base of the module **(see illustration)**.

Refitting

6 Refitting is a reversal of removal, ensuring that the HT leads are connected correctly **(see illustration)**.

4 Crankshaft position sensor – removal and refitting

Removal

1 Disconnect the battery negative terminal (refer to *Disconnecting the battery* in the Reference Chapter).
2 Firmly apply the handbrake, then jack up the front of the car and support it securely on axle stands (see *Jacking and vehicle support*).
3 Remove the cable tie securing the crankshaft position sensor wiring to the starter motor solenoid, and undo the bolt securing the wiring connector to the mounting

bracket **(see illustration)**.
4 Disconnect the sensor wiring connector, then undo the bolts securing the sensor to the flywheel housing, and remove the sensor from the car **(see illustration)**.

Refitting

5 Refitting is the reverse sequence to removal, tightening the sensor mounting bolts to the specified torque.

5 Reluctor ring – removal and refitting

Removal

1 Remove the flywheel as described in Chapter 2B.
2 Slacken and remove the two retaining screws, and remove the reluctor ring from the rear of the flywheel.
3 Check the ring for obvious signs of wear or damage, and renew it if necessary.

Refitting

4 Refitting is the reverse sequence to removal, ensuring that the reluctor retaining screws are securely tightened.

6 Ignition timing – checking and adjustment

While home mechanics with a timing light and a good-quality tachometer may be able to check the ignition timing, if it is found to be in need of adjustment, the car **must** be taken to a suitably-equipped Rover dealer; adjustments can be made only by reprogramming the fuel injection/ignition system ECU, using Rover diagnostic equipment connected to the system by the diagnostic connector. Note also that the timing and idle speed are under ECU control and may, therefore, vary significantly from the nominal values given; without full equipment, any check is therefore nothing more than a rough guide.

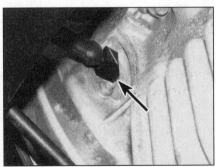

4.3 Crankshaft position sensor wiring connector retaining bolt (arrowed)

4.4 Crankshaft position sensor location (arrowed) – viewed from underneath

Chapter 6
Clutch

Contents

Clutch – inspection and renovation 13
Clutch and flywheel assembly (non-Verto type) – removal and refitting 11
Clutch and flywheel assembly (Verto type) – removal and refitting . . 12
Clutch fluid level check .... See *Weekly Checks*
Clutch hydraulic check .... See Chapter 1
Clutch hydraulic system – bleeding 3
Clutch master cylinder – dismantling, inspection and reassembly . . 7
Clutch master cylinder – removal and refitting 6
Clutch pedal – removal and refitting 8

Clutch release bearing – removal, inspection and refitting 14
Clutch return stop adjustment .... See Chapter 1
Clutch slave cylinder – dismantling, inspection and reassembly ... 5
Clutch slave cylinder – removal and refitting 4
Clutch throw-out stop – adjustment 2
Flywheel housing cover (carburettor engines) – removal and refitting 9
Flywheel housing cover (fuel injection engines) – removal and refitting 10
General information 1

Degrees of difficulty

| Easy, suitable for novice with little experience | | Fairly easy, suitable for beginner with some experience | | Fairly difficult, suitable for competent DIY mechanic | | Difficult, suitable for experienced DIY mechanic | | Very difficult, suitable for expert DIY or professional | |

Specifications

General

Type .... Diaphragm spring, single dry plate, hydraulically operated
Clutch disc diameter .... 180.9 mm
Clutch throw-out stop setting dimension (Verto clutch) .... 6.5 mm

Torque wrench settings	Nm	lbf ft
Diaphragm spring housing to pressure plate (non-Verto clutch)	22	16
Driving strap to flywheel (non-Verto clutch)	22	16
Engine lower tie-bar to subframe	40	30
Engine lower tie-bar to transmission bracket	40	30
Engine upper tie-bar to cylinder head	22	16
Flywheel centre bolt*	150	111
Flywheel housing cover bolts	10	7
Hydraulic pipe unions	14	10
Pressure plate-to-flywheel bolts (Verto clutch)	25	18
Right-hand engine mounting to subframe	22	16
Slave cylinder to mounting plate (Verto clutch)	37	27
Slave cylinder mounting plate to flywheel housing (Verto clutch)		
M8 bolts	37	27
M5 bolts	7	5

Use a new bolt

1 General information

Clutch type identification

All manual transmission models are equipped with a single dry plate diaphragm spring clutch. On early models, the design of the clutch is slightly unusual because there are major parts of the clutch assembly on both sides of the flywheel. Later models are fitted with a Verto clutch of a slightly more conventional design.

Externally, the two types can be quickly identified by observing the arrangement of the clutch slave cylinder and clutch release lever. Early (non-Verto type) models utilise a long release lever with the slave cylinder mounted directly on the flywheel housing. A return spring connects the release lever to the slave cylinder.

Later (Verto type) models have a short release lever and the slave cylinder is mounted on a bracket attached to the flywheel housing and cover. A return spring is not fitted.

Operation

Non-Verto clutch

The main parts of the clutch assembly on the outside of the flywheel are the spring housing, the thrust plate, the release bearing, the diaphragm spring and the three dividing straps. Located on the inside of the flywheel are the clutch disc and the pressure plate.

The spring housing is firmly bolted to the pressure plate by bolts and spring washers. The spring housing is held to the flywheel by dividing straps which are held a little away from the outer clutch by spacing washers.

The clutch disc is free to slide along the splines of the primary gear which is fitted to the end of the crankshaft. Friction lining material is riveted to the clutch disc, which has a segmented hub to help absorb transmission shocks and to ensure a smooth take-off.

The clutch is actuated hydraulically. The pendant clutch pedal is connected to the clutch master cylinder and hydraulic fluid reservoir by a short pushrod. The master cylinder and hydraulic reservoir are mounted on the engine side of the bulkhead in front of the driver. Depressing the clutch pedal moves the piston in the master cylinder forwards, so forcing hydraulic fluid through the clutch hydraulic pipe to the slave cylinder. The piston in the slave cylinder moves forward on the entry of the fluid and actuates the clutch release lever by means of a short pushrod. The opposite end of the release lever slots, by means of a balljoint, into a throw-out plunger. As the pivoted release lever moves backwards, it bears against the release bearing, pushing it forwards. This in turn bears against the clutch thrust plate, the spring housing, and the pressure plate which all move forward slightly, thus disengaging the pressure plate face from the clutch disc.

When the clutch pedal is released, the pressure plate springs force the pressure plate spring housing outwards, which, because it is attached to the pressure plate, brings the pressure plate into contact with the high friction linings on the clutch disc. At the same time the disc is forced firmly against the inner face of the flywheel and so the drive is taken up.

Verto clutch

The Verto clutch differs from all previous Mini clutches, in that the pressure plate and clutch disc are both on the 'outside' of the flywheel, ie, on the side furthest from the pistons.

The operation principle of the Verto clutch is the same as that of previous types. The clutch disc is sandwiched firmly between the flywheel and pressure plate friction surfaces when the clutch pedal is released; when the pedal is depressed, the release components cause the diaphragm spring to flex, and the grip of the pressure plate is relaxed.

The clutch is self-adjusting in use. Adjustment of the throw-out stop should only be necessary after dismantling has taken place.

2 Clutch throw-out stop – adjustment

Note: *At the base of the clutch release lever there is an adjustable collar and locknut threaded onto the end of the throw-out plunger. The position of this collar and locknut (known as the throw-out stop) determines the amount of travel of the release lever when the clutch pedal is depressed. Throw-out stop adjustment is normally only necessary after clutch overhaul and is carried out as described below.*

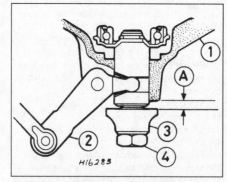

H16283

2.8 Clutch throw-out stop adjustment – Verto type clutch

1	Flywheel housing cover	3	Throw-out stop
2	Release lever	4	Locknut
		A	= 6.5 mm

Non-Verto clutch

1 Release the throw-out stop locknut and unscrew the locknut and throw-out stop to the end of their travel.

2 Engage the help of an assistant to depress the clutch pedal several times and then hold it down.

3 Screw in the throw-out stop and locknut until the stop contacts the boss on the flywheel housing cover.

4 Release the pedal, screw in the throw-out stop one further flat and then tighten the locknut.

Verto clutch

Pre-October 1996 models

5 On fuel injection engines, disconnect the battery negative terminal (refer to *Disconnecting the battery* in the Reference Chapter), then undo the two bolts securing the engine management ECU mounting bracket to the right-hand wing valance. Move the ECU and mounting bracket to one side.

6 Release the throw-out stop locknut and unscrew the locknut and throw-out stop to the end of their travel.

7 Pull the release lever out (away from the clutch cover) by hand until you can feel the release bearing make contact with the thrust sleeve.

8 Screw the throw-out stop in until the clearance between the end of the stop and the face of the cover is as given in the Specifications **(see illustration)**.

9 Tighten the locknut, taking care not to move the throw-out stop when doing so.

10 On fuel injection engines, refit the ECU and mounting bracket.

October 1996 models onward

11 Remove the engine management ECU as described in Chapter 4C, Section 12.

12 Withdraw the fusebox from the engine management ECU mounting bracket and position it to one side.

13 Release the clip securing the wiring harness to the ECU mounting bracket. Undo the mounting bracket retaining bolt and remove the bracket.

14 Adjust the throw-out stop clearance as described in paragraphs 6 to 9 above.

15 Refit the ECU mounting bracket and fusebox, then refit the ECU as described in Chapter 4C, Section 12.

3 Clutch hydraulic system – bleeding

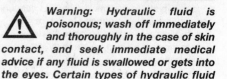

⚠️ *Warning: Hydraulic fluid is poisonous; wash off immediately and thoroughly in the case of skin contact, and seek immediate medical advice if any fluid is swallowed or gets into the eyes. Certain types of hydraulic fluid are inflammable, and may ignite when*

allowed into contact with hot components; when servicing any hydraulic system, it is safest to assume that the fluid IS inflammable, and to take precautions against the risk of fire as though it is petrol that is being handled. Hydraulic fluid is also an effective paint stripper, and will attack plastics; if any is spilt, it should be washed off immediately, using copious quantities of clean water. When topping-up or renewing the fluid, always use the recommended type, and ensure that it comes from a freshly-opened sealed container.

Note: If any of the clutch hydraulic system components have been disconnected on removal, or if the fluid level in the master cylinder reservoir has fallen appreciably, air will have been introduced into the system. For the clutch to function correctly all air must be removed from the system, and this process is known as bleeding.

1 To bleed the system first gather together a clean jar, a suitable length of rubber or clear plastic tubing, which is a tight fit over the bleed screw on the clutch slave cylinder, and a tin of the specified hydraulic fluid. The help of an assistant will also be required. If a one-man do-it-yourself bleeding kit for bleeding the brake hydraulic system is available, this can be used quite satisfactorily for the clutch also. Full information on the use of these kits may be found in Chapter 9.

2 On October 1996 models onward, remove the engine management ECU as described in Chapter 4C, Section 12.

3 Remove the filler cap from the master cylinder reservoir, and if necessary top-up the fluid. Keep the reservoir topped-up during subsequent operations.

4 Wipe clean the area around the bleed screw on the slave cylinder and remove the dust cap (if fitted).

5 Connect one end of the bleed tube to the bleed screw, and insert the other end of the tube in the jar containing sufficient clean hydraulic fluid to keep the end of the tube submerged.

6 Open the bleed screw half a turn and have your assistant depress the clutch pedal and then slowly release it. Continue this procedure until clean hydraulic fluid, free from air bubbles, emerges from the tube. Now tighten the bleed screw at the end of a downstroke.

7 Check the operation of the clutch pedal. After a few strokes it should feel normal. Any sponginess would indicate air still present in the system.

8 On completion remove the bleed tube and refit the dust cover. Top-up the master cylinder reservoir if necessary and refit the cap. Fluid expelled from the hydraulic system should now be discarded as it will be contaminated with moisture, air and dirt, making it unsuitable for further use.

4 Clutch slave cylinder – removal and refitting

Note: Refer to the warning at the beginning of Section 3 before proceeding.

Non-Verto clutch

Removal

1 Disconnect the clutch release lever return spring from the lever and from the tag on the slave cylinder bleed screw.

2 Clamp the flexible hydraulic hose with a suitable brake hose clamp or a self-gripping wrench with jaws protected. This will minimise hydraulic fluid loss when the hose is disconnected.

3 Wipe clean the area around the hose union on the slave cylinder and slacken the union half a turn.

4 Undo and remove the two bolts securing the slave cylinder to the top of the flywheel housing **(see illustration)**.

5 Move the slave cylinder to disengage the pushrod then, while supporting the hydraulic hose, turn the slave cylinder anti-clockwise to unscrew it from the hose. Take care not to lose the copper sealing washer when the hose is undone.

Refitting

6 Refitting the slave cylinder is the reverse sequence to removal. Take care not to kink the hose when refitting. With the cylinder installed, bleed the clutch hydraulic system as described in Section 3.

Verto clutch

Removal

7 Disconnect the battery negative terminal (refer to *Disconnecting the battery* in the Reference Chapter).

8 On fuel injection engines, remove the engine management ECU as described in Chapter 4B, Section 13, or 4C, Section 12, as applicable.

9 Disconnect the breather hose from the oil separator, then undo the two nuts securing the separator to the flywheel housing. Collect the two washers then remove the separator from the engine, along with its gasket.

10 Wipe clean the area around the bleed screw on the slave cylinder and remove the dust cap (if fitted).

11 Connect one end of a suitable bleed tube to the bleed screw, and insert the other end of the tube into a jar or similar receptacle.

12 Remove the filler cap from the clutch master cylinder, then open the bleed screw on the slave cylinder. Pump the clutch pedal until all the hydraulic fluid has drained from the master cylinder.

13 Close the bleed screw, remove the bleed tube and refit the master cylinder filler cap.

14 Wipe clean the hydraulic pipe unions at the clutch master cylinder and at the support

4.4 Undoing the clutch slave cylinder bolts – non-Verto type clutch

bracket on the bulkhead. Unscrew the union nuts and remove the hydraulic pipe. Suitably plug the open unions to prevent dirt ingress.

15 Unscrew the nut securing the slave cylinder hydraulic hose to the support bracket on the bulkhead. Collect the washer and slip the hose out of the bracket.

16 Undo the two bolts securing the clutch slave cylinder to the mounting plate on the flywheel housing **(see illustration)**. Withdraw the slave cylinder from the pushrod and remove it, complete with hydraulic hose from the engine.

17 To remove the hydraulic hose, clamp the slave cylinder in a soft-jawed vice and unscrew the hose or banjo union from the cylinder. Withdraw the hose and recover the sealing washer(s). Note that where a banjo union type fitting is used, there is a sealing washer on each side of the union.

Refitting

18 Refitting the slave cylinder is the reverse sequence to removal, bearing in mind the following points.

  a) Use new sealing washer when refitting the hose or banjo union to the slave cylinder.
  b) Tighten all nuts, bolts and hose/pipe unions to the specified torque (where given).
  c) On fuel injection engines, refit the engine management ECU as described in Chapter 4B, Section 13, or 4C, Section 12, as applicable.
  d) Bleed the clutch hydraulic system as described in Section 3 on completion.

4.16 Undo the bolts (arrowed) securing the slave cylinder to the mounting plate – Verto type clutch

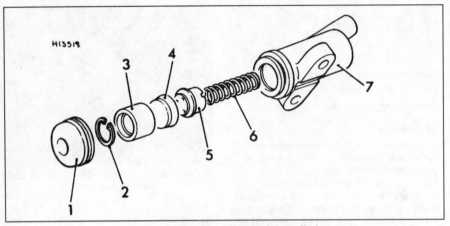

5.2 Exploded view of clutch slave cylinder

1 Dust cover	3 Piston	5 Cup filler	7 Cylinder
2 Circlip	4 Cup seal	6 Spring	body

5 Clutch slave cylinder – dismantling, inspection and reassembly

Note 1: *Refer to the warning at the beginning of Section 3 before proceeding.*
Note 2: *Check the availability of parts before dismantling the slave cylinder. On older models, slave cylinder repair kits may not be readily available and it may be necessary to obtain a complete new slave cylinder assembly.*

Dismantling

1 With the cylinder removed from the car, wipe off the exterior with a clean rag until it is free from dirt.
2 Lift off the dust cover, and then using circlip pliers, extract the circlip from the end of the cylinder bore **(see illustration)**.
3 Tap the cylinder on a block of wood until the piston emerges from the end of the cylinder. Now lift out the piston followed by the cup seal, cup filler and spring.
4 Thoroughly clean all the parts in clean hydraulic fluid and wipe dry with a lint-free rag.

Inspection

5 Carefully examine the piston and cylinder bore for signs of scoring, pitting or wear ridges, and if apparent renew the complete cylinder assembly. If these parts are in a satisfactory condition a new set of seals in the form of a slave cylinder repair kit should be obtained as a matter of course. Old seals should not be re-used as they will have deteriorated with age even though this may not be apparent during visual inspection.

Reassembly

6 Immerse all the internal components in clean hydraulic fluid and assemble them wet.
7 Reassemble the spring into the cylinder bore first, followed by the cup filler and then the cup seal, with its lip or larger diameter away from the piston.
8 Now slide the piston into position and secure the assembly with the circlip.
9 Slip the dust cover over the end of the cylinder bore and then refit the assembled unit to the car as described in Section 4.

6 Clutch master cylinder – removal and refitting

Note: *Refer to the warning at the beginning of Section 3 before proceeding.*

Removal

Carburettor engines

1 Disconnect the battery negative terminal (refer to *Disconnecting the battery* in the Reference Chapter).
2 Remove the air cleaner assembly as described in Chapter 4A.
3 Detach the flexible air inlet ducting from the side of the heater unit and withdraw it sufficiently to provide access to the clutch pedal.
4 Extract the split pin and withdraw the clevis pin securing the master cylinder pushrod to the clutch pedal.
5 Working in the engine compartment, wipe clean the area around the hydraulic pipe union on the top of the master cylinder. Unscrew the union nut and carefully lift out the pipe.
6 Undo and remove the two nuts securing the master cylinder mounting flange to the mounting bracket, and lift off the cylinder.

Fuel injection engines

7 Disconnect the battery negative terminal (refer to *Disconnecting the battery* in the Reference Chapter).
8 Remove the air cleaner assembly as described in Chapter 4B or 4C as applicable.
9 On single-point fuel injection models, undo the bolt securing the injector housing fuel

pipes to the bulkhead, and remove the retaining clip. Undo the two nuts, and release the fuel pipe bracket from the rear of the throttle body assembly.
10 On multi-point fuel injection models, remove the engine management ECU as described in Chapter 4C, Section 12.
11 On all models, slide the relay module out of its retaining bracket, and position it clear of the clutch master cylinder.
12 Wipe clean the area around the bleed screw on the slave cylinder and remove the dust cap (if fitted).
13 Connect one end of a suitable bleed tube to the bleed screw, and insert the other end of the tube into a jar or similar receptacle.
14 Remove the filler cap from the clutch master cylinder, then open the bleed screw on the slave cylinder. Pump the clutch pedal until all the hydraulic fluid has drained from the master cylinder.
15 Close the bleed screw, remove the bleed tube and refit the master cylinder filler cap.
16 Wipe clean the hydraulic pipe unions at the clutch master cylinder and at the support bracket on the bulkhead. Unscrew the union nuts and remove the hydraulic pipe. Suitably plug the open unions to prevent dirt ingress.
17 The master cylinder can then be removed as described previously in paragraphs 3 to 6.

Refitting

18 Refitting the master cylinder is the reverse sequence to removal, bearing in mind the following points.
a) *Tighten all nuts, bolts and hose/pipe unions to the specified torque (where given).*
b) *Refit the air cleaner and, where applicable, the ECU as described in the relevant Part of Chapter 4.*
c) *Bleed the clutch hydraulic system as described in Section 3 on completion.*

7 Clutch master cylinder – dismantling, inspection and reassembly

Note 1: *Refer to the warning at the beginning of Section 3 before proceeding.*
Note 2: *Check the availability of parts before dismantling the master cylinder. On older models, master cylinder repair kits may not be readily available and it may be necessary to obtain a complete new master cylinder assembly.*

Dismantling

1 Remove the master cylinder from the car as described in Section 6.
2 Remove the filler cap from the master cylinder, and drain and discard the hydraulic fluid from the reservoir.
3 With the cylinder on the bench, withdraw the rubber dust cover and slide it off over the end of the pushrod **(see illustration)**.
4 Using circlip pliers, extract and lift off the pushrod and dished washer.

5 Tap the master cylinder body on a block of wood until the piston emerges from the end of the cylinder bore.

6 Withdraw the piston from the cylinder followed by the piston washer, main cup seal, spring retainer and spring.

7 Lay the parts out in the order of removal and then very carefully remove the secondary cup seal by stretching it over the end of the piston.

8 Wash the components in clean hydraulic fluid and then dry with a lint-free cloth.

Inspection

9 Examine the cylinder bore and piston carefully for signs of scoring or wear ridges. If these are apparent renew the complete master cylinder. If the condition of the

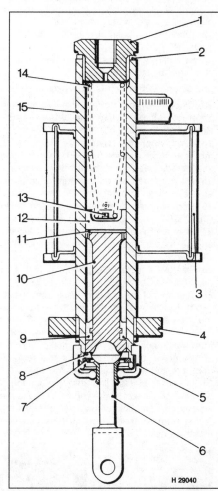

7.3 Sectional view of clutch master cylinder

1 End plug (early models only)	8 Stop washer
2 Washer (early models only)	9 Secondary cup seal
3 Reservoir	10 Piston
4 Mounting flange	11 Piston washer
5 Rubber dust cover	12 Main cup seal
6 Pushrod	13 Spring retainer
7 Circlip	14 Return spring
	15 Cylinder body

components appears satisfactory, a new set of rubber seals must be obtained. Never re-use old seals as they will have deteriorated with age, even though this may not be evident during visual inspection.

Reassembly

10 Begin reassembly by thoroughly lubricating the internal components and the cylinder bore in the clean hydraulic fluid.

11 Using fingers only, place the secondary cup seal in position on the piston with the lip of the cup facing the opposite (drilled) end of the piston.

12 Position the spring retainer over the smaller diameter of the spring and place this assembly into the cylinder bore, larger diameter first.

13 Now insert the main cup seal into the cylinder bore, lip end first then the washers.

14 Insert the piston assembly into the cylinder bore, followed by the pushrod, dished washer and circlip. Ensure that the circlip fully enters its groove.

15 Lubricate a new dust cover with rubber grease and stretch it over the pushrod and into position on the end of the cylinder.

16 The assembled master cylinder can now be refitted to the car as described in the previous Section.

8 Clutch pedal – removal and refitting

Removal

1 Detach the flexible air duct from the heater and from the air inlet under the right-hand front wheelarch. Move the duct away from the heater sufficiently to provide access to the clutch and brake pedals.

2 Slacken the nut securing the rear of the heater unit to the mounting bracket.

3 Undo and remove the two screws securing the front of the heater to the parcel shelf or lower facia rail and lower the unit to the floor.

4 Undo and remove the nut and washer securing the pedal cross-shaft to the pedal mounting bracket.

5 Extract the split pins and clevis pins securing the master cylinder pushrods to the clutch and brake pedals.

6 Slide the cross-shaft out of the mounting bracket, lift out the two pedals and detach the return spring.

7 Examine the pedal bushes and cross-shaft for wear and renew as necessary. The pedal bushes can be removed by drawing them out using a long bolt and nut, flat washers and a tube of suitable diameter. New bushes can be fitted in the same manner.

Refitting

8 Refitting the pedals is the reverse sequence to removal. Lightly lubricate the pedal shaft and bushes with general purpose grease prior to refitting.

9 Flywheel housing cover (carburettor engines) – removal and refitting

Removal

1 Disconnect the battery negative terminal (refer to *Disconnecting the battery* in the Reference Chapter).

2 Firmly apply the handbrake, then jack up the front of the car and support it securely on axle stands (see *Jacking and vehicle support*).

3 To provide greater access, remove the bonnet and front grille panel, referring to Chapter 11A if necessary.

4 If an ignition shield is fitted over the front of the engine, release the three fasteners and lift away the shield.

5 Detach the heater air duct from the air inlet under the right-hand front wing. Remove the air inlet from the inner wing panel.

6 Remove the starter motor as described in Chapter 5A.

7 Where applicable, undo and remove the screws securing the starter solenoid to the inner wing panel. Lift off the solenoid and position it out of the way.

8 If the ignition coil is mounted on the flywheel housing, or on a bracket secured to one of the cylinder head studs, remove the coil and mounting bracket and position it well clear.

9 On later Mini 850 and 1000 models, remove the horn and place it to one side.

10 On early models, disengage the return spring from the clutch release lever and slave cylinder, and lift away the spring.

11 On later models, undo the two bolts securing the clutch slave cylinder to the mounting plate on the flywheel housing. Withdraw the slave cylinder from the pushrod and position it to one side. Undo the three bolts securing the slave cylinder mounting plate to the flywheel housing and housing cover, taking care to collect the spacer from the lower bolt. Remove the mounting plate from the housing.

12 Undo and remove the two bolts securing the engine tie-bar and bracket to the side of the cylinder block. Note that on later models one of the bolts also retains the engine earth strap.

13 Undo the nut and bolt and collect the washers securing the engine lower tie-bar to the bracket on the flywheel housing. Push the tie-bar down slightly, clear of the flywheel housing cover.

14 Undo and remove the two nuts and two bolts securing the radiator upper support bracket to the radiator and thermostat housing. Withdraw the bracket. **Note:** *It is not necessary to remove the support bracket if a large clearance exists between the radiator and left-hand inner wing panel, as is the case on later Mini 850 and 1000 models.*

15 Place a jack beneath the flywheel housing end of the transmission casing and just take the weight of the power unit. Use a block of wood interposed between the transmission casing and the jack to spread the load.

16 From beneath the car undo and remove the two nuts and bolts securing the right-hand engine mounting to the subframe side-members. The best way to do this is to engage the help of an assistant to hold the bolts from above while you undo the nuts from below. The bolt heads are tucked away beneath the flywheel housing and can only be reached with a small open-ended spanner.

17 Having released the mounting, jack up the power unit sufficiently to enable the bolts securing the flywheel housing cover to be removed. Note that on early models one of the front bolts also retains the engine earth strap. On all models the rear bolts are fairly inaccessible, requiring a good deal of patience and a short spanner.

18 When all the bolts are undone, lift off the flywheel housing cover and, on early models, disengage the clutch release lever pushrod from the slave cylinder.

Refitting

19 Refitting is the reverse sequence to removal, bearing in mind the following points.
  a) Tighten all nuts and bolts to the specified torque (where given).
  b) Adjust the throw-out stop as described in Section 2 and, on early models, the return stop as described in Chapter 1 on completion.

10 Flywheel housing cover (fuel injection engines) – removal and refitting

Removal

Pre-October 1996 models

1 Disconnect the battery negative terminal (refer to Disconnecting the battery in the Reference Chapter).

2 Firmly apply the handbrake, then jack up the front of the car and support it securely on axle stands (see Jacking and vehicle support).

3 Remove the bonnet and front grille panel, referring to Chapter 11A if necessary.

4 Release the three fasteners and lift away the ignition shield from the front of the engine.

5 Remove the air cleaner assembly and the engine management ECU as described in Chapter 4B.

6 Remove the crankshaft position sensor as described in Chapter 5B.

7 Disconnect the horn wiring connectors, then undo the two mounting nuts and remove the horn.

8 If the ignition coil is mounted on the flywheel housing, or on a bracket secured to one of the cylinder head studs, remove the coil and mounting bracket and position it well clear.

9 Remove the starter motor as described in Chapter 5A.

10 Working under the right-hand wheelarch, detach the heater air inlet hose from the air inlet duct.

11 Remove the air inlet duct from the inner wing panel in the engine compartment.

12 Disconnect the oil separator breather hose from the right-hand end of the cylinder head, then undo the two bolts securing the separator to the flywheel housing. Remove the separator and hose assembly from the engine, along with its gasket.

13 Slacken and remove the bolt, situated just to the right of the brake servo unit, securing the earth leads to the bulkhead.

14 Undo the bolts securing the wiring harness retaining clip and starter motor lead brackets to the flywheel housing, then position the wiring harness to one side.

15 Undo the two bolts securing the clutch slave cylinder to the mounting plate on the flywheel housing. Withdraw the slave cylinder from the pushrod and position it to one side.

16 Undo the three bolts securing the slave cylinder mounting plate to the flywheel housing and cover, taking care to collect the spacer from the lower bolt. Remove the mounting plate from the housing.

17 Undo the three bolts securing the radiator upper support bracket to the radiator and cylinder head, then remove the bracket.

18 Undo the nut and bolt and collect the washers securing the engine lower tie-bar to the bracket on the flywheel housing. Push the tie-bar down slightly, clear of the flywheel housing cover.

19 Position a jack beneath the flywheel housing end of the transmission casing and just take the weight of the power unit. Use a block of wood interposed between the casing and the jack to spread the load.

20 From beneath the car undo and remove the two nuts and bolts securing the right-hand engine mounting to the subframe side-members. The best way to do this is to engage the help of an assistant to hold the bolts from above while the nuts are undone from below. The bolt heads are tucked away and can only be reached with a small open-ended spanner.

21 Having released the mounting, raise the power unit sufficiently to enable the bolts securing the flywheel housing cover to be removed. The rear bolts are fairly inaccessible, requiring a good deal of patience and a short spanner.

22 When all the bolts are undone, lift off the flywheel housing cover and remove it upwards through the gap between the engine and brake master cylinder.

October 1996 models onward

23 Disconnect the battery negative terminal (refer to Disconnecting the battery in the Reference Chapter).

24 Firmly apply the handbrake, then jack up the front of the car and support it securely on axle stands (see Jacking and vehicle support).

25 Remove the bonnet and front grille panel as described in Chapter 11B.

26 Remove the starter motor as described in Chapter 5A.

27 Remove the air cleaner assembly and the engine management ECU as described in Chapter 4C.

28 Remove the crankshaft position sensor as described in Chapter 5C.

29 Disconnect the breather hose from the oil separator, then undo the two nuts securing the separator to the flywheel housing. Collect the two washers then remove the separator from the engine, along with its gasket.

30 Remove the cover from the engine compartment fusebox **(see illustration)**.

31 Lift out the fusible link from the location in the fusebox closest to the engine. Release the now exposed retaining tag and disconnect the wiring harness lead from the fusebox **(see illustrations)**.

10.30 Remove the cover from the engine compartment fusebox

10.31a Lift out the fusible link from the location in the fusebox closest to the engine

10.31b Release the retaining tag and disconnect the wiring harness lead from the fusebox

10.33a Release the clip securing the wiring harness to the ECU mounting bracket

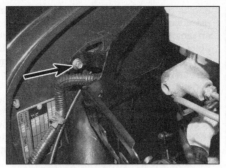

10.33b Undo the mounting bracket retaining bolt (arrowed) and remove the bracket

10.34 Undo the bolt (arrowed) securing the earth leads to the bulkhead

10.35 Undo the bolts (arrowed) securing the wiring harness clip and starter motor lead brackets to the flywheel housing

10.36 Remove the air inlet duct from the inner wing panel

10.38 Undo the slave cylinder mounting bolts and withdraw the cylinder from the pushrod

32 Withdraw the fusebox from the engine management ECU mounting bracket and position it to one side.

33 Release the clip securing the wiring harness to the ECU mounting bracket. Undo the mounting bracket retaining bolt and remove the bracket from the engine compartment **(see illustrations)**.

34 Slacken and remove the bolt, situated just to the right of the brake servo unit, securing the earth leads to the bulkhead **(see illustration)**.

35 Undo the bolts securing the wiring harness retaining clip and starter motor lead brackets to the flywheel housing, then position the wiring harness to one side **(see illustration)**.

36 Working under the right-hand wheelarch,

detach the heater air inlet hose from the air inlet duct. Remove the air inlet duct from the inner wing panel in the engine compartment **(see illustration)**.

37 Disconnect the wiring connector from the bonnet contact switch.

38 Undo the two bolts securing the clutch slave cylinder to the mounting plate on the flywheel housing. Withdraw the slave cylinder from the pushrod and position it to one side **(see illustration)**.

39 Undo the three bolts securing the slave cylinder mounting plate to the flywheel housing and cover, taking care to collect the spacer from the lower bolt **(see illustration)**. Remove the mounting plate from the housing.

40 Undo the nut and bolt and collect the washers securing the engine lower tie-bar to

the bracket on the flywheel housing **(see illustration)**. Push the tie-bar down slightly, clear of the flywheel housing cover.

41 Undo the two nuts and remove the washers securing the brake master cylinder to the servo **(see illustration)**. Ease the master cylinder off the two mounting studs taking care not to place undo strain on the hydraulic pipes.

42 Release the radiator top hose from the support clip above the DIS module.

43 Position a jack beneath the flywheel housing end of the transmission casing and just take the weight of the power unit. Use a block of wood interposed between the casing and the jack to spread the load.

44 From beneath the car undo and remove the two nuts and bolts securing the right-hand

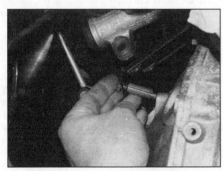

10.39 Undo the slave cylinder mounting plate bolts and collect the spacer from the lower bolt

10.40 Undo and remove the nut, bolt and washers from the lower tie-bar (arrowed)

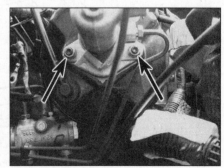

10.41 Undo and remove the two nuts and washers (arrowed) securing the brake master cylinder to the servo

10.46 Remove the flywheel housing cover through the gap between the engine and brake master cylinder

engine mounting to the subframe side-members. The best way to do this is to engage the help of an assistant to hold the bolts from above while the nuts are undone from below. The bolt heads are tucked away and can only be reached with a small open-ended spanner.

45 Having released the mounting, raise the power unit sufficiently to enable the nine bolts securing the flywheel housing cover to be removed. The rear bolts are fairly inaccessible, requiring a good deal of patience and a short spanner.

46 When all the bolts are undone, lift off the flywheel housing cover and remove it

upwards through the gap between the engine and brake master cylinder **(see illustration)**.

Refitting

47 Refitting is the reverse sequence to removal, bearing in mind the following points.
a) *Tighten all nuts and bolts to the specified torque (where given).*
b) *Adjust the throw-out stop as described in Section 2 on completion.*

11 Clutch and flywheel assembly (non-Verto type) – removal and refitting

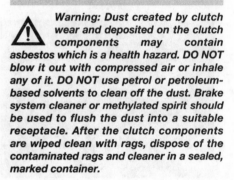

⚠ *Warning: Dust created by clutch wear and deposited on the clutch components may contain asbestos which is a health hazard. DO NOT blow it out with compressed air or inhale any of it. DO NOT use petrol or petroleum-based solvents to clean off the dust. Brake system cleaner or methylated spirit should be used to flush the dust into a suitable receptacle. After the clutch components are wiped clean with rags, dispose of the contaminated rags and cleaner in a sealed, marked container.*

Removal

Note: *A suitable puller will be required to release the flywheel from the crankshaft taper. Read through the entire procedure to familiarise yourself with the work involved, and obtain the relevant tools before proceeding.*

1 Remove the flywheel housing cover as described in Section 9.

2 Undo and remove the three bolts securing the diaphragm spring housing to the driving straps and lift off the housing **(see illustration)**.

3 Tap back the locking washer securing the large flywheel central retaining bolt.

4 Rotate the crankshaft until the driving slot in the flywheel, located just behind the retaining bolt head, is horizontal. If this is not done the crankshaft primary gear C-shaped thrustwasher may become dislodged, causing damage to the flywheel as it is removed.

5 Insert a large screwdriver through the starter motor aperture and engage the teeth of the ring gear to prevent the flywheel from turning.

6 Using a large socket and extension handle, undo and remove the flywheel retaining bolt and lift off the keyed drive washer.

7 Where the bolt which retains the flywheel to the crankshaft has been secured with thread-locking compound or an encapsulated type of bolt is used, then prior to refitting, all threads in the crankshaft must be thoroughly cleaned. Preferably, this should be done by using a tap of the appropriate size. Discard the old retaining bolt, and use only a new encapsulated bolt incorporating a thread-locking compound patch on refitting.

8 The flywheel is retained on the crankshaft by

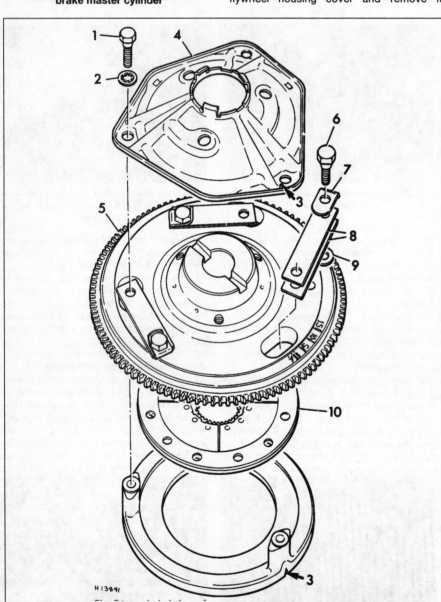

11.2 Exploded view of the non-Verto type clutch and flywheel assembly

1 Driving bolt	4 Diaphragm spring	7 Tab washer
2 Shakeproof	housing	8 Driving straps
washer	5 Flywheel	9 Distance washer
3 Alignment mark	6 Driving bolt	10 Clutch disc

11.13a Location of balance mark (A) on pressure plate . . .

11.13b . . . and diaphragm spring housing

11.15 Refitting the clutch disc

11.16 Refitting the flywheel

11.17 Refit the keyed drive washer, locking washer and retaining bolt

11.18 Refitting the diaphragm spring housing and retaining bolts

means of a taper, and a puller is necessary to separate it. The puller is Rover special tool No 18G 304 and adapter 18G 304M. There are, however, a number of similar pullers readily available from accessory shops or garages.

9 Position the puller with the three studs or bolts screwed into the flywheel securely. Fit the thrust pad of the puller to the end of the crankshaft and then tighten the puller centre bolt. Prevent the flywheel from turning using a screwdriver inserted into the ring gear teeth.

10 Continue tightening the centre bolt of the puller until the flywheel breaks free from the taper. It is quite likely that the flywheel will be extremely tight requiring a great deal of effort to free it. If this is the case sharply strike the puller centre bolt with a medium hammer. This should 'shock' the flywheel off the taper. When it does free it will release with a 'bang' giving the impression that something has broken. This, however, is quite normal and nothing to be alarmed about.

11 Once the taper is released, lift the flywheel off the end of the crankshaft, slide the clutch disc off the primary gear splines and lift out the pressure plate.

Refitting

12 Before refitting, check the primary gear endfloat as described in Chapter 7A, then lightly lubricate the primary gear splines with a lithium based grease.

13 Ensure that the flywheel and crankshaft tapers are clean and dry. Note also that the pressure plate and diaphragm spring housing are stamped with a balance mark (A) adjacent to one of the bolt holes. These marks must be

adjacent to each other when assembling, and aligned with the flywheel timing marks **(see illustrations)**.

14 Note the location of the balance mark A on the pressure plate and position the plate in the flywheel housing.

15 Slide the clutch disc over the primary gear splines with the hub facing inwards and then centralise the pressure plate over the disc **(see illustration)**.

16 Place the flywheel onto the crankshaft, ensuring that the lug of the pressure plate carrying the balance mark A enters the flywheel opening adjacent to the timing marks **(see illustration)**.

17 Refit the keyed drive washer, locking washer and retaining bolt. Remember to use only a new encapsulated bolt incorporating a thread-locking compound. Tighten the bolt to the specified torque and then bend over the locking washer **(see illustration)**.

12.2 Withdraw the release bearing sleeve from the clutch hub

18 Refit the diaphragm spring housing with the balance mark A adjacent to the flywheel timing marks. Ensure that the retaining bolts pass squarely through each set of driving straps and then progressively tighten the bolts to the specified torque **(see illustration)**.

19 The remainder of the reassembly procedure is a straightforward reverse of the removal sequence. Adjust the throw-out stop as described in Section 2, and the return stop as described in Chapter 1 on completion.

12 Clutch and flywheel assembly (Verto type) – removal and refitting

Removal

Note 1: *Refer to the warning at the beginning of Section 11 before proceeding.*

Note 2: *A suitable puller will be required to release the flywheel from the crankshaft taper. Read through the entire procedure to familiarise yourself with the work involved, and obtain the relevant tools before proceeding.*

1 Remove the flywheel housing cover as described in Section 9 or 10 as applicable.

2 Withdraw the release bearing sleeve from the clutch hub **(see illustration)**.

3 Rotate the crankshaft until the driving slot in the flywheel, located just behind the flywheel centre bolt head, is horizontal. If this is not done the crankshaft primary gear C-shaped thrustwasher may become dislodged, causing damage to the flywheel as it is removed.

12.4a Using a punch, relieve the lockwasher from the clutch hub slots . . .

12.4b . . . then undo the flywheel centre bolt using a large socket and extension handle

12.4c Remove the flywheel centre bolt . . .

12.4d . . . and the keyed drive washer from the crankshaft

12.8 Tighten the puller centre bolt until the flywheel breaks free from the crankshaft taper

12.9a Remove the flywheel/clutch unit from the engine

4 Relieve the lockwasher from the slots, then undo the flywheel centre bolt using a large socket and extension handle. Lock the flywheel by jamming a wide-bladed screwdriver between the starter ring gear and the flywheel housing. Remove the bolt and the keyed drive washer from the crankshaft **(see illustrations)**.

5 Where the bolt which retains the flywheel to the crankshaft has been secured with thread-locking compound or an encapsulated type of bolt is used, then prior to refitting, all threads in the crankshaft must be thoroughly cleaned. Preferably, this should be done by using a tap of the appropriate size. Discard the old retaining bolt, and use only a new encapsulated bolt incorporating a thread-locking compound patch on refitting.

6 The flywheel is retained on the crankshaft by means of a taper, and a puller is necessary

to separate it. The puller is Rover special tool No 18G 1381. There are, however, a number of similar pullers readily available from accessory shops or garages.

7 Position the puller with the three studs or bolts screwed into the flywheel securely. Fit the thrust pad of the puller to the end of the crankshaft and then tighten the puller centre bolt. Prevent the flywheel from turning using a screwdriver inserted into the ring gear teeth.

8 Continue tightening the centre bolt of the puller until the flywheel breaks free from the taper **(see illustration)**. It is quite likely that the flywheel will be extremely tight requiring a great deal of effort to free it. If this is the case sharply strike the puller centre bolt with a medium hammer. This should 'shock' the flywheel off the taper. When it does free it will release with a 'bang' giving the impression that something has broken. This, however, is

quite normal and nothing to be alarmed about.

9 Remove the flywheel/clutch unit. Unscrew the pressure plate bolts, half a turn at a time in a criss-cross sequence, and remove the pressure plate and clutch disc from the flywheel **(see illustrations)**.

Refitting

10 Before refitting check the primary gear endfloat, as described in Chapter 7A, then lightly lubricate the primary gear splines with a lithium based grease.

11 Fit the clutch disc to the flywheel, with the hub boss facing the flywheel. (The disc may be marked FLYWHEEL SIDE to confirm this orientation.)

12 Fit the pressure plate to the flywheel, and insert the retaining bolts. Only finger-tighten the bolts at this stage.

12.9b Unscrew and remove the pressure plate bolts . . .

12.9c . . . then remove the pressure plate . . .

12.9d . . . and clutch disc from the flywheel

13 If tool 18G 684 is available, use it to centralise the clutch disc relative to the flywheel and pressure plate. If the tool is not available, offer the flywheel/clutch assembly to the crankshaft. Providing the pressure plate bolts are not too tight, the clutch disc will be moved to the correct central position as it passes over the primary gear splines. Do not force the assembly onto the crankshaft if resistance is encountered, but remove it and check that the disc is just free to move, and approximately central.

14 When centralisation has been achieved, tighten the pressure plate retaining bolts in a criss-cross sequence to the specified torque **(see illustration)**.

15 If a centralisation tool was used, remove it and fit the flywheel/clutch assembly to the crankshaft.

16 Fit the keyed drive washer and the flywheel centre bolt. Remember to use only a new encapsulated bolt incorporating a thread-locking compound. Prevent the flywheel from rotating, and tighten the centre bolt to the specified torque. Stake the lockwasher into the slots of the clutch hub and refit the release bearing sleeve **(see illustration)**.

17 The remainder of the refitting process is a reversal of the removal procedure. Adjust the throw-out stop on completion as described in Section 2.

13 Clutch –
inspection and renovation

Note: *Refer to the warning at the beginning of Section 11 before proceeding.*

1 With the clutch removed as described in Section 11 or 12 as applicable, carefully inspect the clutch disc friction linings for wear and loose rivets, and the disc for rim distortion, cracks and worn splines. Renew the clutch disc if any of these conditions are apparent.

2 The disc should also be renewed if there is any sign of oil contamination of the friction linings. This is a common occurrence on Minis and can cause quite severe clutch judder or clutch slip. The cause of the contamination is oil leaking past the primary gear oil seal in the flywheel housing or up the centre of the gear between the bushes and the crankshaft. If this condition is evident it is recommended that the oil seal in the flywheel housing is renewed as described in Chapter 2A or 2B, as applicable. Also check that the endfloat of the primary gear is not excessive as this will encourage oil leakage through its centre. Full information regarding the primary gear running clearances will be found in Chapter 7A.

3 Inspect the machined faces of the flywheel and pressure plate for scores or deep grooving: if apparent they should be

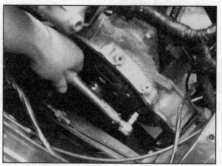

12.14 Tighten the pressure plate retaining bolts to the specified torque

machined until smooth. If the pressure plate is cracked or damaged it must be renewed. On the Verto type clutch the flywheel and pressure plate are not sold separately, but must be renewed as a matched assembly if wear or damage is evident. Deep grooving, cracks or crazing of the friction surfaces are grounds for renewal.

4 On the non-Verto type clutch, examine the diaphragm spring in the spring housing for cracks, and if evident renew the housing. Finally, examine the holes in the spring housing and driving straps for elongation or distortion, and the retaining bolts for ridges or shoulders. Renew any worn items as complete sets to preserve the balanced conditions.

5 On all clutch types, consideration should also be given to renewing the release bearing whilst it is easily accessible (see Section 14).

12.16 Tighten the flywheel centre bolt, then stake the lockwasher into the slots of the clutch hub

14 Clutch release bearing –
removal, inspection and refitting

Note: *Refer to the warning at the beginning of Section 11 before proceeding.*

Non-Verto clutch

Removal

1 Remove the flywheel housing cover as described in Section 9.

2 With the cover on the bench, undo and remove the throw-out stop and locknut from the release bearing throw-out plunger **(see illustration)**.

3 Extract the split pin, tap out the clevis pin and lift off the clutch release lever.

4 Now slide the release bearing and plunger out of the flywheel housing cover.

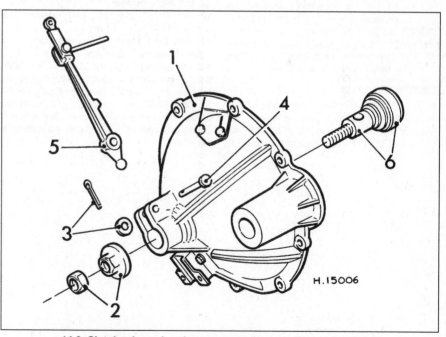

14.2 Clutch release bearing components – non-Verto type clutch

1 Flywheel housing cover	4 Clevis pin
2 Throw-out stop and locknut	5 Release lever
3 Washer and split pin	6 Release bearing and plunger assembly

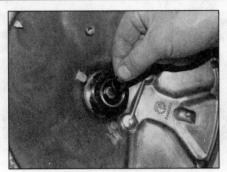 

14.16a Extract the retaining O-ring . . .

14.16b . . . and remove the release bearing assembly from the plunger – Verto type clutch

5 Support the underside of the release bearing and, on early models, tap out the plunger using a hammer and drift of suitable diameter. On later models, the bearing is removed after extracting the spring. Note that a new spring clip will be required for refitting.

Inspection

6 Examine the bearing for excess side-play or movement, and then spin the bearing and check for noisy operation or roughness. Renew the unit if any of these conditions are apparent.

7 Inspect the condition of the flywheel housing cover and in particular, the fit of the release bearing plunger in its location. Renew the cover if any signs of damage or distortion are evident. Note that from 1986, all replacement flywheel housing covers are supplied with the timing inspection hole blanked off by an aluminium membrane. If one of these later covers is to be fitted to an earlier engine which does not have timing marks on the timing chain cover and crankshaft pulley, then the aluminium membrane should be broken out to allow the timing marks on the flywheel to be seen.

Refitting

8 To refit the bearing on early models, place the plunger in position and then press the plunger into the bearing using a vice with protected jaws. Ensure that the bearing is pressed fully home until it is in contact with the shoulder of the plunger.

9 To address problems associated with clutch judder, later models are fitted with a self-aligning release bearing which is a loose fit on the plunger. This allows the bearing to move slightly when in operation and caters for any slight misalignment between the bearing and thrust plate. When refitting a bearing of this type always use a new retaining spring clip, and ensure that when installed, the clip has clamped the bearing firmly. Use a small diameter tube or socket to push the clip fully into position.

10 Smear the plunger with a graphite-based grease and insert it into the flywheel housing cover.

11 Smear the ball-end of the release lever with a graphite-based grease and position the lever on the cover, engaging the ball-end into the throw-out plunger.

12 Refit the clevis pin and washer then secure with a new split pin.

13 Refit the throw-out stop and locknut, but do not tighten at this stage.

14 The flywheel housing cover with release bearing installed can now be refitted using the reverse of the removal sequence contained in Section 9. When installation is complete adjust the throw-out stop as described in Section 2 and return stop as described in Chapter 1.

Verto clutch

Removal

15 Remove the flywheel housing cover as described in Section 9 or 10 as applicable.

16 Extract the O-ring and remove the release bearing assembly from the plunger **(see illustrations)**.

17 Separate the spring clip legs from the bearing retainer plate, then remove the bearing.

Inspection

18 Examine the bearing for excess side-play or movement, and then spin the bearing and check for noisy operation or roughness. Renew the unit if any of these conditions are apparent.

Refitting

19 Refitting is a reversal of removal, but note the following points:

a) The bearing seal faces away from the retainer plate.
b) Do not forget to fit the O-ring on the plunger.
c) Refit the flywheel housing cover as described in Section 9 or 10 as applicable.
d) Adjust the throw-out stop as described in Section 2 on completion of installation.

Chapter 7 Part A:
Manual transmission

Contents

Gearchange remote control housing – dismantling and reassembly 4
Gearchange remote control housing – removal and refitting 3
Gear lever – removal and refitting 2
General information 1
Oil seals – renewal 8

Transfer gear bearings – renewal 7
Transfer gears – general information 5
Transfer gears – removal and refitting 6
Transmission overhaul – general 10
Transmission – removal and refitting 9

Degrees of difficulty

Easy, suitable for novice with little experience	**Fairly easy,** suitable for beginner with some experience	**Fairly difficult,** suitable for competent DIY mechanic	**Difficult,** suitable for experienced DIY mechanic	**Very difficult,** suitable for expert DIY or professional

Specifications

General

Type .... Four forward and one reverse gear, synchromesh action on all forward gears

Transfer gear clearances

Primary gear endfloat .... 0.089 to 0.165 mm
Idler gear endfloat .... 0.101 to 0.177 mm

Torque wrench settings

	Nm	lbf ft
Differential end cover bolts	25	18
First motion shaft nut	207	153

---

1 General information

The manual transmission comprises four forward and one reverse gear with all forward gears being engaged through baulk ring synchromesh units. The transmission is housed within an aluminium casing bolted to the lower face of the engine, and shares the engine lubricating oil. The differential assembly is contained within a separate housing bolted to the rear of the main gearbox casing.

On early models, movement of the gear lever is transmitted to the selector forks by a selector lever, two relay shafts and a ball-and-socket joint. The gear lever is mounted either on the rear of the differential casing or externally in a remote control housing, which is in turn bolted to the rear of the differential. In this case an additional shaft transmits movement of the gear lever to the relay shafts.

A revised gear selector mechanism with a simpler and more positive rod-change remote control linkage is used on later transmissions. Movement of the gear lever is transmitted to the selector forks by an external selector rod, a selector shaft, and a bellcrank lever assembly. The gear lever is mounted in a remote control housing attached to the vehicle floor via rubber mountings.

2 Gear lever – removal and refitting

Removal

Direct engagement lever

1 Firmly apply the handbrake, then jack up the front of the car and support it securely on axle stands (see *Jacking and vehicle support*).
2 Lift up the front carpets and then undo and remove the screws securing the rubber boot retaining plate and rubber boot to the floor. Lift off the retaining plate and slide the boot up the gear lever slightly.
3 From underneath the car, undo and remove the two bolts and spring washers securing the gear lever retaining plate to the transmission casing **(see illustration)**.
4 Lift the gear lever out of its location and remove it from inside the car. As the gear lever is removed take out the small anti-rattle spring and plunger from the drilling in the side of the gear lever seat.

Early remote control lever

5 Working inside the car, lift up the carpets, undo and remove the screws securing the retaining plate and rubber boot to the floor.
6 Undo and remove the two screws and then

lift off the gear lever complete with retainer, distance piece, spring and flange.

Rod-change remote control lever

7 Lift up the carpets, and then undo and remove the screws securing the retaining plate and rubber boot to the floor.
8 Slide the rubber boot up the lever then press down and turn the bayonet cap fixing to release the lever from the remote control housing.
9 Lift out the gear lever, rubber boot and retainer.

Refitting

10 Refitting the lever is the reverse sequence to removal. Lubricate the gear lever ball with general purpose grease before refitting.

2.3 Removing the gear lever retaining plate

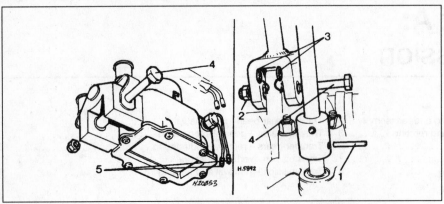

3.9 Removal of the rod-change type remote control assembly

1 Roll pin	3 Plain washers	5 Reversing light switch
2 Nut	4 Bolt	terminals

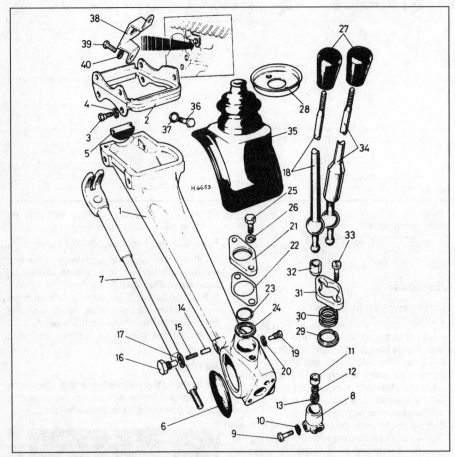

4.2 Exploded view of the early type remote control gearchange housing

1 Remote control housing	11 Thrust button	21 Retaining plate	32 Split bush
2 Front mounting	12 Inner spring	22 Gasket	33 Retaining screw
3 Shouldered bolt	13 Outer spring	23 Ring	34 Alternative gear lever
4 Washer	14 Anti-rattle plunger	24 Flange	35 Rubber boot
5 Grommet	15 Anti-rattle spring	25 Bolt	36 Bolt
6 Grommet	16 Nut	26 Washer	37 Washer
7 Primary shaft	17 Washer	27 Knob	38 Exhaust bracket
8 Shaft lever	18 Gear lever	28 Lever retainer	39 Bolt
9 Bolt	19 Locating pin	29 Nylon flange	40 Washer
10 Washer	20 Washer	30 Spring	
		31 Distance piece	

3 Gearchange remote control housing – removal and refitting

Removal

Early type

1 Firmly apply the handbrake, then jack up the front of the car and support it securely on axle stands (see *Jacking and vehicle support*).
2 Remove the gear lever (see Section 2).
3 From the rear of the housing, undo and remove the nut and washer securing the rubber mounting to the support bracket.
4 From the front of the housing, undo and remove the four shouldered bolts securing the front mounting to the housing.
5 Pull the housing down at the front to disengage the linkage, and then move it forward and out of the rear support bracket.

Rod-change type

6 Firmly apply the handbrake, then jack up the front of the car and support it securely on axle stands (see *Jacking and vehicle support*).
7 Remove the gear lever (see Section 2).
8 Working beneath the car, disconnect the reversing light switch wiring.
9 Unscrew the nut securing the rear of the steady rod to the remote control housing and remove the washer. There is no need to remove the steady rod from the differential housing on the transmission except for examination of the rod. Furthermore, with the remote control housing fitted it may be difficult to remove the front rod bolt as it may foul the exhaust downpipe **(see illustration)**.
10 Using a parallel pin punch drift out the roll pin securing the collar to the gearchange extension rod or gearbox shaft. Note that although there is radial play between the collar and shaft/rod, the roll pin should be a tight fit in both components.
11 Unscrew and remove the nut and through-bolt securing the remote control housing to the mounting bracket, then withdraw the housing from the steady rod and remove from under the car.

Refitting

12 Refitting the remote control housing is the reverse sequence to removal. When engaging the front of the housing with the mounting on the early type assembly, it may be necessary to move the gear lever slightly to align the linkage and enable the front of the housing to be pushed fully home.

4 Gearchange remote control housing – dismantling and reassembly

Early type

Dismantling

1 Remove the remote control housing from the car as described in Section 3.

2 Undo and remove the anti-rattle spring, plunger retaining nut and washer and take out the spring and plunger **(see illustration opposite)**.

3 Prise off the large grommet from the side of the housing and then, using a socket, undo and remove the primary shaft pinch-bolt.

4 Slide the primary shaft forward to disengage the shaft lever and then lift out the shaft and lever.

5 Examine the primary shaft and the nylon bush in the shaft lever for wear and renew as necessary. The bush in the lever may be prised out with a screwdriver, and a new bush simply pushed into place. Check that the anti-rattle spring is not weak or broken as this will cause a sizzling noise to be emitted from the gear lever during hard acceleration. Also inspect the front and rear mountings for deterioration of the rubber, and renew if suspect.

Reassembly

6 Lubricate all the components with general purpose grease and reassemble using the reverse of the dismantling procedure. Ensure that the machined groove in the end of the primary shaft is in line with the pinch-bolt hole in the shaft lever when reassembling these components.

Rod-change type

Dismantling

7 Remove the remote control housing from the car as described in Section 3.

8 Undo and remove the six screws and lift off the bottom cover plate **(see illustration)**.

9 Undo and remove the locknut, washer and steady rod from the housing.

10 Using a parallel pin punch, drift out the roll pin securing the gearchange extension rod to the rod eye and then withdraw the extension rod.

11 Drift out the second roll pin that secures the rod eye to the support rod and then withdraw the rod eye and support rod.

12 Examine the dismantled components for wear or corrosion and renew as necessary. Pay particular attention to the nylon bush in the rod eye and renew this item if it shows any signs of wear or deformation. Also check the rubber mountings, and renew these if there are signs of cracking or deterioration of the rubber.

Reassembly

13 Reassembly is the reverse sequence to removal. Lubricate all the parts with general purpose grease before reassembly.

Drive is transmitted from the clutch to the transmission by means of three transfer gears. On the end of the crankshaft is the

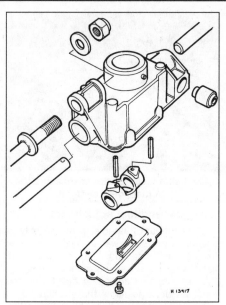

4.8 Component parts of the rod-change type remote control housing

primary gear. When the clutch pedal is depressed the primary gear remains stationary while the crankshaft revolves inside it. On releasing the clutch pedal the drive is taken up and the primary gear revolves with the crankshaft at crankshaft speed.

Drive is taken from the primary gear, through an intermediate (idler) gear, to the first motion shaft drivegear, which is a splined fit on the nose of the first motion shaft.

6 Transfer gears –
removal and refitting

Note: *To provide access to the idler gear and first motion shaft gear it will be necessary to remove the engine/transmission from the car as described in Chapter 2C. The flywheel and flywheel housing must also be removed; full information on this procedure will also be found in Chapter 6. Access to the primary gear can, however, be gained with the engine/transmission still in the car. Refer to the crankshaft oil seal renewal procedures contained in Chapter 2A and 2B for further information.*

Removal

1 With the flywheel housing removed, the transfer gears are now exposed. The primary gear can be removed first by lifting off the U-shaped ring and retaining washer and sliding the gear off the end of the shaft **(see illustration)**. Now slide off the thrustwasher.

2 Lift the idler gear out of its needle roller bearing in the transmission casing. Make sure that the thrustwashers (one on each side) are kept in their correct relative positions.

3 To remove the first motion shaft gear, first extract the circlip and withdraw the roller bearing, using a puller or two screwdrivers, from the first motion shaft **(see illustration)**. Now bend back the lockwasher and undo and remove the nut. To prevent the first motion shaft from turning as the nut is undone, put

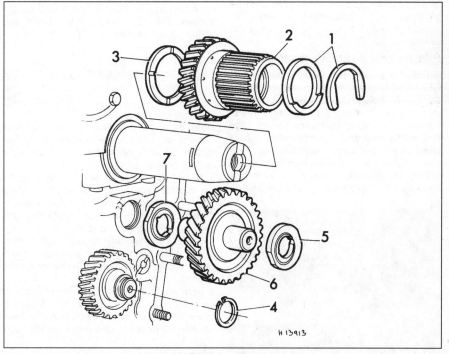

6.1 Transfer geartrain

1	*Retaining washer and U-ring*	4	*Circlip*	6	*Idler gear*
2	*Primary gear*	5	*Thrustwasher*	7	*Thrustwasher*
3	*Thrustwasher*		

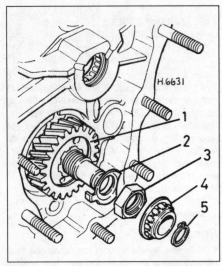

6.3 First motion shaft gear and bearing assembly

1 First motion shaft gear	3 Retaining nut
2 Lockwasher	4 Roller bearing
	5 Circlip

the transmission in gear and then lock the drive flanges using blocks of wood between the flanges and transmission casing. On later models Rover tool 18G 1088 may be needed.
4 Lift off the lockwasher and slide the gear off the first motion shaft.

Refitting

5 Refitting the transfer gears is the reverse sequence to removal. However, the endfloat of the primary gear and idler gear must be checked, and if necessary adjusted, as described below before finally refitting the flywheel housing.

Primary gear endfloat adjustment

6 Refit the primary gear thrustwasher with its chamfered bore against the crankshaft flange. Slide on the gear and secure with the retaining washer and U-shaped ring. Using feeler blades measure the clearance between the end of the gear and the thrustwasher (see illustration). The correct endfloat is given in the Specifications. If the measured endfloat is outside the specified limits, selective thrust-washers are available from your Rover dealer.

6.8 Checking the endfloat of the idler gear

6.6 Using feeler blades to measure the primary gear endfloat

Idler gear endfloat adjustment

7 The endfloat of the idler gear can only be accurately measured with the engine removed from the transmission. If a new idler gear, thrustwashers, transmission casing or flywheel housing are being fitted then this must be done to allow the endfloat to be accurately measured. If, however, the original components are being refitted, it can be assumed that the endfloat will be as before and therefore satisfactory.
8 To check the endfloat, refit the flywheel housing after making sure the mating faces are clean. Tighten the retaining nuts to the specified torque and then, using feeler blades, measure the clearance between the thrustwasher and the side of the casing (see illustration). The endfloat should be as specified. Selective thrustwashers are available from your Rover dealer to correct any deficiency. The flywheel housing can now be removed, the engine positioned on the transmission and the transfer gears and housing finally refitted.

7 Transfer gear bearings – renewal

Note: *If the idler gear bearings in the flywheel housing or transmission casing, or the first motion shaft support bearing outer race require renewal, proceed as follows.*
1 Remove the engine/transmission from the car and then remove the flywheel and flywheel housing as described in Chapters 2C and 6.
2 Heat the flywheel housing in boiling water. *On no account apply a direct flame to the housing.* If a receptacle large enough to hold the flywheel housing is not available, slowly pour boiling water over the area round the bearing.
3 Remove the retaining ring (where fitted) and carefully prise the bearing out of the casing, taking great care not to damage the bearing housing. If possible use Rover service tool 18G 581.
4 When fitting a new bearing carefully drift it into position (having previously heated the housing as described above) until it is just clear of the retaining ring recess (where fitted).

On no account press the bearing right into the recess in the housing, as this would mask the bearing oil supply hole which is at the rear of the recess.
5 To renew the idler gear needle roller bearing in the transmission casing, separate the engine from the transmission, remove the circlip and drift the bearing out of the casing. Alternatively, if Rover service tool 18G 581 is obtainable, the engine need not be separated from the transmission.
6 To refit the bearing, carefully drive it into position using a suitable drift and refit the circlips.
7 If the outer race of the first motion shaft roller bearing requires renewal, use the procedure described in paragraphs 2 and 3, or preferably obtain Rover service tool 18G 617A.

8 Oil seals – renewal

Driveshaft flange oil seals

1 Drain the engine/transmission oil as described in Chapter 1.
2 Firmly apply the handbrake, then jack up the front of the car and support it securely on axle stands (see *Jacking and vehicle support*). Remove the relevant front roadwheel.

Inner rubber coupling or Hardy-Spicer joint

3 Undo and remove the retaining nut and spring washer securing the swivel hub balljoint to the upper suspension arm.
4 Using a universal balljoint separator, release the taper of the balljoint shank from the upper suspension arm.
5 From underneath the car, undo and remove the rubber drive coupling retaining U-bolts and locknuts then lift off the coupling. On Cooper S models, undo and remove the universal joint flange retaining nuts and separate the flanges.
6 Move the driveshaft as far as possible away from the differential to provide sufficient clearance to enable the driveshaft flanges to be removed.
7 Extract the split pin, where fitted, and then undo and remove the driveshaft flange castellated retaining nut or bolt. Prevent the flange from turning by placing a block of wood between the flange and transmission casing, or where applicable, use a screwdriver across the retaining studs and against the casing.
8 Now slide the driveshaft flange off the splined gearshaft.

Inner offset sphere type joint

9 From underneath the car, ease the offset sphere joint out of the differential using Rover special tool 18G 1240. If this tool cannot be borrowed, it is possible to make do with a tyre lever or similar strip of thick metal. Engage the end of the lever between the differential end

8.9 Using a cranked bar to release the offset sphere joint from the differential

8.12a Recover the preload shim fitted behind the left-hand end cover

8.12b Recover the detent sleeve . . .

cover and the body of the joint. Pivot the lever against the bolt head directly beneath the end cover. Strike the other end of the lever with a few sharp hammer blows until the joint is released and moves out slightly **(see illustration)**.

10 Undo and remove the retaining nuts securing both the upper and lower swivel hub balljoints to the suspension arms. Separate the balljoint tapers using a universal balljoint separator.

11 Support the swivel hub to avoid stretching the flexible brake hose and withdraw the driveshaft, complete with inner offset sphere joint, out of the differential sufficiently to allow removal of the end cover. Temporarily locate the upper balljoint into the suspension arm and refit the nut loosely to support the swivel hub.

All models

12 Undo and remove the five bolts and spring washers securing the relevant end cover to the side of the differential housing. Lift off the end cover together with its gasket and, if working on the left-hand side, recover the preload shim fitted behind the end cover **(see illustration)**. **Note:** *If working on the right-hand side end cover of the later rod-change type transmission take care not to lose the selector shaft detent sleeve, spring and ball which will be released as the cover is withdrawn **(see illustrations)**.*

13 Using a screwdriver or suitable lever, prise the oil seal from the end cover **(see illustration)**. Carefully press in a new seal or tap it in using a flat block of wood to distribute the load. Ensure that the seal enters the end cover squarely and that the open side of the seal faces inwards.

14 Clean off all traces of old gasket from the mating faces of the end cover and differential housing, and ensure that the faces are clean and dry.

15 Refitting is the reverse sequence to removal, bearing in mind the following points:

a) *Use a new end cover gasket lightly smeared on both sides with jointing compound.*

b) *Tighten all nuts and bolts to the specified torque, referring to Chapter 8 for torque wrench settings applicable to the driveshaft and suspension components.*

8.12c . . . spring and ball fitted behind the right-hand end cover on later models

c) *When refitting an offset sphere driveshaft joint ensure that the joint is fully engaged on the differential gearshaft. If necessary wrap a long worm-drive hose clip around the joint and tap the head of the clip with a mallet until the joint is fully home.*

d) *Refill the engine/transmission with oil as described in Chapter 1 on completion.*

Selector shaft oil seal

General information

16 Oil leakage from the gear selector shaft oil seal is a common occurrence on the rod-change type transmissions and may re-occur quite quickly even after renewing the oil seal.

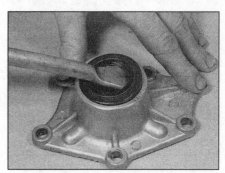

8.13 Levering out the end cover oil seal

If the problem persists it may be cured by fitting a nylon bush and O-ring seal, obtainable from your dealer, behind the main oil seal **(see illustration)**. The bush will align the shaft centrally in the seal, making the seal more effective.

17 Later transmissions are fitted with a larger type of nylon bush during production, and should not need modifying. Note however that this later bush is not suitable for use on any transmission to which it has not been fitted as standard.

18 After fitting a nylon bush to the selector shaft, check selection of all gears; any stiffness evident will indicate that the transmission is not suitable for modification, and the bush should be removed.

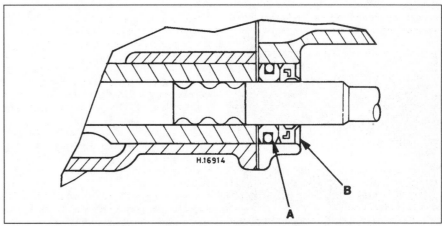

8.16 Selector shaft nylon bush and O-ring (A) fitted behind main oil seal (B)

Renewal

19 Drain the engine/transmission oil as described in Chapter 1.

20 Firmly apply the handbrake, then jack up the front of the car and support it securely on axle stands (see *Jacking and vehicle support*).

21 Using a parallel pin punch, drift out the roll pin securing the gearchange extension shaft collar to the selector shaft.

22 Undo and remove the nut and bolt securing the gearchange steady rod to the differential housing. Move the steady rod rearwards slightly and withdraw the extension rod collar off the selector shaft.

23 Withdraw the rubber gaiter (if fitted) and then hook out the oil seal with a small screwdriver **(see illustration)**.

24 Before refitting a new seal wrap adhesive tape around the selector shaft to avoid damaging the seal lips as it is installed. If possible, obtain the protector sleeve, Rover special tool No 18G 1238 and place this over the selector shaft.

25 Lubricate the new seal in clean engine oil and slide it over the shaft with the open side of the seal toward the differential.

26 Tap the seal fully into position using a tube of suitable diameter **(see illustration)**.

27 Remove the adhesive tape or protector sleeve and then refit the gearchange extension shaft and the steady rod **(see illustration)**.

28 Lower the car to the ground and refill the engine/transmission with oil as described in Chapter 1.

9 Transmission – removal and refitting

The engine and transmission are removed from the car as a complete assembly and the two units are then separated after removal. Details of removal, separation, reconnection and refitting are given in Chapter 2C.

10 Transmission overhaul – general

Overhauling a manual transmission is a difficult and involved job for the DIY home mechanic. In addition to dismantling and reassembling many small parts, clearances must be precisely measured and, if necessary, changed by selecting shims and spacers. Internal transmission components are also often difficult to obtain, and in many instances, are extremely expensive. Because of this, if the transmission develops a fault or becomes noisy, the best course of action is to have the unit overhauled by a specialist repairer, or to obtain an exchange reconditioned unit.

Nevertheless, it is not impossible for the more experienced mechanic to overhaul the transmission, provided the special tools are available, and that the job is done in a deliberate step-by-step manner so that nothing is overlooked.

The tools necessary for an overhaul may include internal and external circlip pliers, bearing pullers, a slide hammer, a set of pin punches, a dial test indicator, and possibly a hydraulic press. In addition, a large, sturdy workbench and a vice will be required.

During dismantling of the transmission, make careful notes of how each component is fitted, to make reassembly easier and accurate.

Before dismantling the transmission, it will help if you have some idea which area is malfunctioning. Certain problems can be closely related to specific areas in the gearbox, which can make component examination and replacement easier.

8.23 Hook out the selector shaft oil seal with a small screwdriver

8.26 Tap the new seal into position using a tube of suitable diameter

8.27 Refit the gearchange extension shaft and secure with the roll pin

Chapter 7 Part B:
Automatic transmission

Contents

Automatic transmission – removal and refitting 10
Automatic transmission overhaul – general information 11
Driveshaft flange oil seal – renewal 9
Gear selector cable – checking and adjustment 4
Gear selector lever housing and cable – dismantling and
  reassembly 7
Gear selector lever housing and cable – removal and refitting 6
General information 1
Governor control rod – adjustment 5
Reversing light switch – adjustment 3
Starter inhibitor switch – adjustment 2
Transfer gears – removal and refitting 8

Degrees of difficulty

Easy, suitable for novice with little experience	**Fairly easy,** suitable for beginner with some experience	**Fairly difficult,** suitable for competent DIY mechanic	**Difficult,** suitable for experienced DIY mechanic	**Very difficult,** suitable for expert DIY or professional

Specifications

General

Type	Automatic, four forward speeds and reverse
Make	Automotive Products (AP)

Torque wrench settings

	Nm	lbf ft
5/16 in UNF bolts	26	19
3/8 in UNF bolts	41	30
Converter housing bolts	25	18
Engine to transmission casing	16	12
Reversing light switch locknut	5	4
Selector cable clamp screw	4	3
Starter inhibitor switch locknut	5	4

1 General information

The automatic transmission fitted as an optional extra to Mini models incorporates a three-element fluid torque converter, with a maximum conversion of 2.1, coupled to a bevel geartrain assembly.

The final drive is transmitted from a drivegear to a conventional type differential unit, which in turn transmits engine torque through two flange type coupling driveshafts to the roadwheels.

The complete geartrain assembly, including the reduction gears and differential units, runs parallel to, and below, the crankshaft and is housed in the transmission casing, which also serves as the engine sump.

The system is controlled by a selector lever within a gated quadrant marked with seven positions and mounted centrally on the floor of the car. The park, reverse, neutral, and drive positions are for normal automatic driving, with the first, second and third positions used for manual operation or over-ride as required. This allows the system to be used as a fully automatic four-speed transmission from rest to maximum speed, with the gears changing automatically according to throttle position and load. If a lower gear is required to obtain greater acceleration, an instant full throttle position (ie, kickdown on the accelerator) immediately produces the change.

Complete manual control of all four forward gears by use of the selector lever provides rapid changes. However, it is very important that downward changes are effected at the correct road speeds otherwise serious damage may result to the automatic transmission. The second, third and top gears provide engine braking whether driving in automatic or manual conditions. In first gear a freewheel condition exists when decelerating. Manual selection to third or second gear gives engine braking and also allows the driver to stay in a particular low gear to suit road conditions or when descending steep hills.

Due to the complexity of the automatic transmission, any repair or overhaul work must be left to a Rover dealer with the necessary special equipment for fault diagnosis and repair. The contents of the following Sections are therefore confined to supplying general information, and any service information and instructions that can be used by the owner.

2 Starter inhibitor switch – adjustment

Early models

1 The starter inhibitor switch is located on the rear of the gear selector lever housing (see illustration). Early switches have two terminals which are connected through the ignition/starter circuit. On later versions two additional terminals are used to actuate the reversing lights. The purpose of the switch is

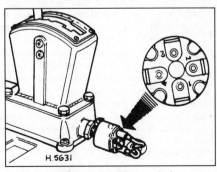

2.1 Starter inhibitor switch

to ensure that the engine will only start when the gear selector lever is in the N position.

2 The switch terminals marked 2 and 4 are used in the ignition/starter circuit and both the electrical leads are interchangeable to the 2 and 4 positions of the switch.

3 When the reversing light is fitted, terminals 1 and 3 are used for this light.

4 Before making any adjustments to the switch, ensure that the gear selector cable adjustment is correct as described in Section 4.

5 To adjust the switch, move the selector lever to the N position.

6 Disconnect the electrical connections from the rear of the switch.

7 Slacken the locknut and screw out the switch as far as possible.

8 Connect a test light and battery across the switch terminals numbered 2 and 4.

9 Screw the switch into the housing until the lamp *just* lights and then screw it in a further one half turn. Hold the switch in this position and tighten the locknut.

10 Remove the test equipment and reconnect the electrical leads to the appropriate terminals.

11 Check that the starter motor will operate with the selector lever in the N position. When reversing lights are fitted check that they only come on when R is selected.

Later models

12 On later models, the starter inhibitor switch is screwed into the base of the transmission, instead of into the rear of the gear selector housing as on earlier models. The switch is adjusted as follows.

13 Check and, if necessary, adjust the gear selector cable as described later in Section 4.

14 Chock the rear wheels then jack up the front of the car and support it on axle stands (see *Jacking and vehicle support*).

15 Position the selector lever in the D position.

16 Undo the two retaining bolts, and remove the inhibitor switch cover from the transmission. Disconnect the inhibitor switch wiring connector.

17 Slacken the inhibitor switch locknut, and connect a multimeter, set to the resistance function, across the switch terminals. Unscrew the switch until continuity exists between the switch terminals. From this point, screw the switch slowly into the transmission until the point is reached where continuity no longer exists between the terminals. From here, screw the switch in a further half turn. Hold the switch stationary, then tighten the locknut to the specified torque setting. Check that continuity only exists between the switch terminals when the selector lever is in the P or N positions, then disconnect the multimeter.

18 Connect the wiring connector, then refit the switch cover, tightening its retaining bolts securely.

19 Lower the vehicle to the ground, and check that the engine will only start when the selector lever is in the P or N position.

Note: *On early models the reversing light switch is incorporated in the starter inhibitor switch and is adjusted as described in Section 2. On later models, the reversing light switch is fitted to the rear of the selector lever housing (in the same position as the starter inhibitor switch on earlier models). On these models, the switch is adjusted as follows.*

1 Firmly apply the handbrake, then jack up the front of the car and support it securely on axle stands (see *Jacking and vehicle support*).

2 Position the selector lever in the R position.

3 Disconnect the wiring connectors from reversing light switch, and slacken the switch locknut.

4 Connect a multimeter, set to the resistance function, across the switch terminals, then unscrew the switch until an open-circuit is present between the switch terminals. From this point, screw the switch slowly into the transmission until the point is reached where there is continuity between the terminals. From here, screw the switch in a further half turn. Hold the switch stationary, then tighten the locknut to the specified torque setting. Check that continuity only exists between the switch terminals when the selector lever is in the R position, then disconnect the multimeter.

5 Reconnect the wiring connectors, then lower the vehicle to the ground and check the operation of the reversing lights.

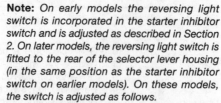

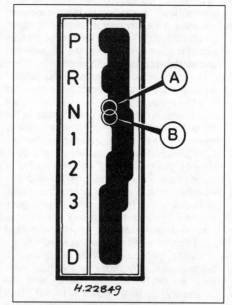

H.22849

4.4 Selector mechanism adjustment checking details

A Reverse gear disengagement point
B First gear disengagement point

Checking

1 First check the cable setting as follows before carrying out any adjustment.

2 Apply the handbrake firmly, select N and start the engine.

3 With the footbrake firmly applied, move the selector lever to the R position and check that reverse gear is engaged.

4 Move the lever slowly towards N and check that reverse is disengaged just before or exactly as the lever locates the N position **(see illustration)**.

5 Repeat the above procedure with the first gear 1 position.

6 If the checks show the cable to be in need of adjustment, proceed as follows.

Adjustment

Early models

7 Firmly apply the handbrake, then jack up the front of the car and support it securely on axle stands (see *Jacking and vehicle support*).

8 From underneath the car undo and remove the two bolts securing the bellcrank cover plate to the right-hand end of the transmission casing **(see illustration opposite)**.

9 Undo and remove the nut and bolt securing the cable fork to the bellcrank lever.

10 Move the bellcrank lever to pull the transverse rod fully out and then move it back two detents.

11 From inside the car move the selector lever to the N position.

12 Slacken the two selector cable adjusting nuts and position the cable so that the pivot bolt can be easily inserted through the cable fork and bellcrank lever.

13 Hold the cable in this position, tighten the adjusting nuts and check that the position of the cable has not altered.

14 Refit the pivot bolt and nut followed by the bellcrank cover plate.

15 Lower the car to the ground and recheck the cable setting as described in paragraphs 2 to 5 inclusive.

Later models

16 Firmly apply the handbrake, then jack up the front of the car and support it securely on axle stands (see *Jacking and vehicle support*). Ensure that the selector lever is in the P position.

17 Undo the two retaining bolts, and remove the selector cable cover from the underside of the transmission **(see illustration opposite)**.

18 Slacken the clamp screw securing the selector cable to the transmission bellcrank, then rotate the bellcrank fully anti-clockwise to position the transmission valve rod in its fully-out (park) position.

19 From inside the car, unscrew the selector lever knob, then carefully unclip the lever

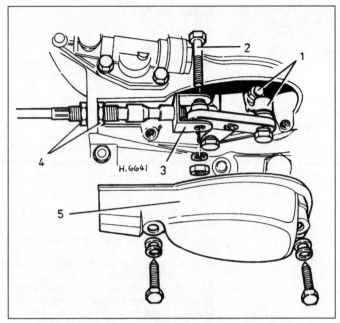

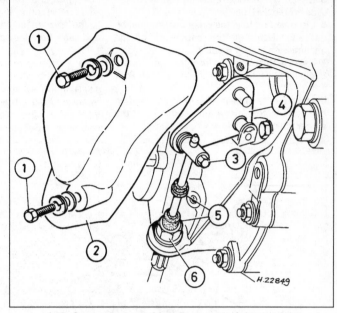

4.8 Gear selector cable adjustment – early models

1 Transverse rod-to-bellcrank lever adapter
2 Cable fork-to-bellcrank lever retaining bolt
3 Cable fork
4 Cable adjusting nuts
5 Bellcrank cover plate

4.17 Gear selector cable adjustment – later models

1 Selector cable cover retaining bolts
2 Selector cable cover
3 Clamp screw
4 Transmission bellcrank
5 Rubber sleeves
6 Outer cable retaining nut

indicator panel (taking care not to lose its four retaining clips) and lift it off the lever.
20 Insert a feeler blade of 0.76 to 0.89 mm thickness between the selector lever and the end of the slot in the selector gate. Have an assistant keep the selector lever tight against the feeler blade then, from underneath the car, tighten the selector cable clamp screw.
21 Refit the selector cable cover to the transmission, and securely tighten its retaining bolts.
22 From inside the vehicle, ensure that the four retaining clips are correctly fitted to the

indicator panel, then slide the panel over the selector lever, and clip it into position. Refit the selector lever knob.
23 Lower the vehicle to the ground, and carry out the checks as described above to ensure that the cable is correctly adjusted.

5 Governor control rod – adjustment

1 Start the engine and run it until it reaches

normal operating temperature.
2 Refer to Chapter 4A and ensure that the carburettor settings are correct.
3 Disconnect the governor control rod at the throttle linkage **(see illustration)**.
4 Insert a 6.4 mm diameter rod through the hole in the governor control rod bellcrank lever and into the hole in the transmission casing.
5 Slacken the locknut and adjust the length of the rod to suit the carburettor linkage in the tickover position.
6 Reconnect the governor control rod to the throttle linkage. Tighten the balljoint locknut and remove the checking rod from the bellcrank lever.

6 Gear selector lever housing and cable – removal and refitting

Early models

Removal

1 Firmly apply the handbrake, then jack up the front of the car and support it securely on axle stands (see *Jacking and vehicle support*).
2 From underneath the car, undo and remove the two bolts securing the bellcrank cover plate to the right-hand end of the transmission casing.
3 Undo and remove the nut washer and pivot bolt securing the selector cable fork to the bellcrank lever.
4 Slacken the fork retaining nut and unscrew the fork from the cable.

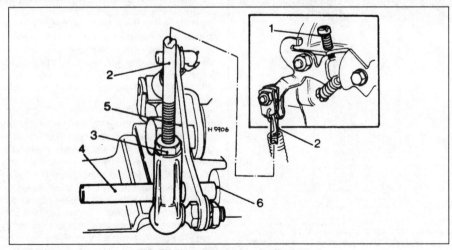

5.3 Governor control rod adjustment

1 Throttle adjusting screw
2 Governor control rod
3 Locknut
4 6.4 mm diameter rod
5 Intermediate bellcrank lever
6 Transmission case

5 Unscrew the fork retaining nut and then slide off the two rubber ferrules.

6 Undo and remove the outer cable adjusting nut and then pull the cable out of the transmission casing bracket.

7 Release the cable clip from the floor panel.

8 Working inside the car lift up the front floor covering.

9 Make a note of their relative positions, then disconnect the electrical leads from the starter inhibitor switch.

10 Undo and remove the four nuts and washers securing the selector lever housing to the floor panel, and withdraw the housing and cable from the car **(see illustration)**.

Refitting

11 Refitting is the reverse sequence to removal. Adjust the cable as described in Section 4 and the inhibitor switch as described in Section 2 after refitting.

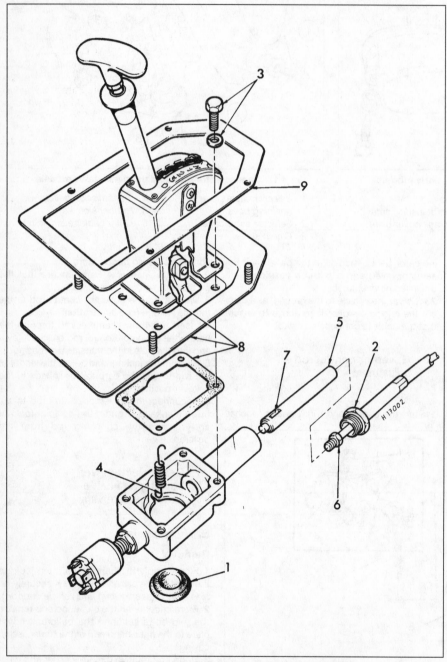

6.10 Exploded view of the gear selector lever housing

1 Grommet	*4 Reverse return spring*	*7 Operating plunger slot*
2 Outer cable locknut	*5 Operating plunger*	*8 Quadrant, plate and gasket*
3 Quadrant securing bolts	*6 Inner cable locknut*	*9 Upper gasket*

Later models

Removal

12 Firmly apply the handbrake, then jack up the front of the car and support it securely on axle stands (see *Jacking and vehicle support*). Position the selector lever at the P position.

13 Undo the two retaining bolts, and remove the selector cable cover from the underside of the transmission.

14 Slacken the clamp screw securing the cable to the transmission bellcrank, then disconnect the inner cable, and slide the rubber sleeves off the end of the inner cable. Unscrew the outer cable retaining nut, then disconnect the cable from the transmission and remove the flat washer.

15 Work back along the length of the cable, and release it from any relevant retaining clamps or ties.

16 Disconnect the wiring connectors from the reversing light switch.

17 From inside the car, unscrew the selector lever knob, then carefully unclip the lever indicator panel (taking care not to lose its four retaining clips) and lift it off the lever.

18 Slacken and remove the four bolts securing the cable housing to the selector lever housing.

19 From underneath the vehicle, detach the selector cable housing from the lever housing, and recover the gasket.

20 Unscrew the selector cable, and withdraw it from the housing. Slacken the inner cable locknut, and unscrew the cable from the plunger.

21 Make a note of their relative positions, then disconnect the electrical leads from the reversing light switch.

22 Undo and remove the four nuts and washers securing the selector lever housing to the floor panel, and withdraw the housing and gasket from the car.

Refitting

23 Using a new gasket if necessary, refit the lever housing and secure with the four nuts.

24 Ensure that the cable housing and plunger are clean, and apply a smear of multi-purpose grease to their contact surfaces.

25 Screw the plunger fully onto the selector inner cable, and securely tighten its locknut.

26 Slide the plunger into position, and screw the outer cable into the cable housing, tightening it securely.

27 Rotate the inner cable so that the chamfered end of the plunger hole is uppermost, so that it will engage easily with the selector lever. Fit the gasket to the cable housing, then refit the selector cable housing to the base of the selector lever. Have an assistant refit the housing retaining bolts and tighten them securely. Move the selector lever, and check the cable plunger is correctly engaged before proceeding further.

28 Refit the rubber sleeves and flat washer to the transmission end of the cable, then locate the cable with the transmission and securely tighten the outer cable retaining nut.

29 Engage the inner cable with the bellcrank clamp, and adjust the selector cable as described in Section 4.

7 Gear selector lever housing and cable – dismantling and reassembly

Dismantling

1 Remove the assembly (see Section 6).
2 Prise out the rubber grommet at the base of the selector mechanism and then mount the assembly in a vice.
3 Slacken the nut securing the outer cable to the housing.
4 If not already done during the removal procedure, undo and remove the four bolts securing the quadrant to the housing, release the reverse return spring and lift off the quadrant and lever.
5 Unscrew the outer cable and withdraw it from the housing.
6 Insert a screwdriver into the slot of the operating plunger to prevent it turning, and slacken the nut securing the cable to the plunger.
7 Finally, unscrew the plunger from the cable.
8 Inspect all the parts for wear and renew as necessary.

Reassembly

9 Reassembly is the reverse of the dismantling procedure. Lubricate all moving parts with general purpose grease before reassembling.

8 Transfer gears – removal and refitting

The procedure for removing and refitting the transfer gears on vehicles equipped with automatic transmission is the same as described in Part A, Section 6, for manual transmission models with the exception of the input (first motion shaft) gear which should not be disturbed.

To provide access to the transfer gears it will be necessary to remove the engine/transmission from the car and then remove the torque converter and converter housing as described in the appropriate part of Chapter 2.

9 Driveshaft flange oil seal – renewal

Refer to Part A, Section 8.

10 Automatic transmission – removal and refitting

The engine and transmission are removed from the car as a complete assembly and the two units are then separated after removal. Details of removal, separation, reconnection and refitting are given in Chapter 2C.

11 Automatic transmission overhaul – general information

In the event of a fault occurring with the transmission, it is first necessary to determine whether it is of an electrical, mechanical or hydraulic nature, and to do this, special test equipment is required. It is therefore essential to have the work carried out by a Rover dealer if a transmission fault is suspected.

Do not remove the transmission from the car for possible repair before professional fault diagnosis has been carried out, since most tests require the transmission to be in the vehicle.

Chapter 8
Driveshafts

Contents

Constant velocity joint – removal, inspection and refitting 5
Constant velocity joint rubber gaiter – renewal 4
Driveshaft – removal and refitting 2
Driveshaft gaiter check . . . . .See Chapter 1
Driveshaft overhaul – general information 3
General information 1
Hardy-Spicer universal joint – overhaul 7
Inner offset sphere joint – dismantling, inspection and reassembly . 9
Inner offset sphere joint – removal and refitting 8
Inner rubber drive coupling – removal and refitting 6

Degrees of difficulty

Easy, suitable for novice with little experience	**Fairly easy,** suitable for beginner with some experience	**Fairly difficult,** suitable for competent DIY mechanic	**Difficult,** suitable for experienced DIY mechanic	**Very difficult,** suitable for expert DIY or professional 

Specifications

Type . . . . Solid shaft reverse spline, with constant velocity outer joint and rubber coupling, Hardy-Spicer, or offset sphere type inner joint – depending on model and year of production

Torque wrench settings	Nm	lbf ft
Driveshaft retaining nut:		
Disc brake models:		
With multiple split pin holes in driveshaft	207	153
With single split pin hole in driveshaft	255 to 270	188 to 199
Drum brake models	83	61
Rubber coupling U-bolts	14	10
Swivel hub balljoint to suspension arm	54	40
Tie-rod balljoint nut	30	22

1 General information

Drive is transmitted from the differential to the front wheels by means of two equal length driveshafts. A constant velocity joint is fitted to the outer end of each shaft to cater for steering and suspension movement. The constant velocity (CV) joint comprises a driving member (splined to the driveshaft), six caged steel balls, and a driven member (splined to the wheel hub flange). The driven member pivots freely on the steel balls to any angle, thus allowing the drive to be smoothly transmitted to the front wheels throughout the full range of steering and suspension travel.

To allow for vertical movement of the driveshaft with the suspension, models equipped with manual transmission incorporate either a flexible rubber drive coupling or an offset sphere type CV joint at the inner end of each driveshaft. A Hardy-Spicer universal joint is used at each driveshaft inner end on Cooper S Mk III

models and certain vehicles equipped with automatic transmission. On models fitted with offset sphere type inner joints, lateral movement of the driveshaft is catered for by the sliding components within the joint. On all other models each driveshaft incorporates a sliding spline at the inner end.

The CV joint, offset sphere joint and the driveshaft sliding spline are housed within flexible rubber gaiters to prevent water and dirt entry and to retain the lubricating grease.

2 Driveshaft – removal and refitting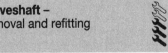

Removal

1 Working under the wheelarch, undo and remove the single retaining screw and lift out the upper suspension arm rebound rubber. Position a solid packing piece of approximately the same thickness in its place **(see illustration)**.

2 Firmly apply the handbrake, then jack up

the front of the car and support it securely on axle stands (see *Jacking and vehicle support*). Remove the front roadwheel.

2.1 Fitting a solid packing wedge in place of the suspension rebound rubber

1 *Screw*   3 *Solid packing*
2 *Rebound rubber*   *piece*

2.3a Removing the driveshaft retaining nut . . .

2.3b . . . and thrustwasher

3 Extract the split pin from the driveshaft retaining nut and, with an assistant firmly depressing the brake pedal, undo and remove the driveshaft nut using a socket and extension bar. Remove the washer or split-collar, as applicable, located behind the driveshaft nut **(see illustrations)**. Note that on disc brake models, the driveshaft retaining nut is extremely tight and it may be beneficial to adopt the following procedure to prevent the hub rotating when undoing the nut.

H30004

Using a fabricated tool to hold the front hub stationary whilst the driveshaft retaining nut is slackened.

An alternative method of releasing the balljoint tapered shank is to refit the locknut to the balljoint and screw it on two or three turns. Using a medium hammer, sharply strike the end of the steering arm until the shock separates the taper. Now remove the locknut and lift the joint off the arm.

4 Fabricate a tool from two lengths of steel strip (one long, one short) and a nut and bolt; the nut and bolt form the pivot of a forked tool. Attach the tool to the hub using two wheel nuts, and hold the tool to prevent the hub from rotating **(see Tool Tip)**. Slacken the hub nut using a socket and a long extension bar, then remove the nut and split-collar.
5 The procedure now varies slightly according to the type of inner joint fitted to the driveshaft.

Inner rubber coupling or Hardy-Spicer joint

6 From underneath the car, suitably mark the driveshaft flanges to ensure correct reassembly. Undo and remove the four outer locknuts from the U-bolts securing the driveshaft flange to the rubber coupling. On models fitted with Hardy-Spicer universal joints, undo and remove the four locknuts securing the two flanges together.
7 Undo and remove the steering tie-rod ball-joint retaining locknut then release the balljoint tapered shank from the steering arm using a universal balljoint separator **(see Tool Tip)**.

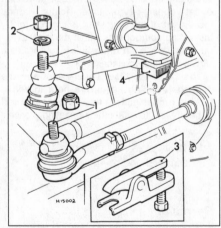

H15002

2.8 Releasing the tie-rod and swivel hub balljoints

1 Tie-rod balljoint and nut
2 Swivel hub upper balljoint and nut
3 Universal balljoint separator
4 Solid packing piece

8 Undo and remove the nuts and spring washers securing the upper and lower suspension arms to the swivel hub balljoints **(see illustration)**.
9 Using the method described in paragraph 7, separate the upper and lower suspension arms from the tapered shanks of the balljoints.
10 Support the swivel hub to avoid stretching the flexible brake hose. Tap the end of the driveshaft with a soft-faced mallet to free the shaft from the hub.
11 Slide the driveshaft fully out of the hub and then withdraw it from the car outwards through the aperture in the subframe. With the driveshaft removed refit the swivel hub balljoint to the upper suspension arm and screw on the retaining nut two or three turns.

Inner offset sphere type joint

12 Release the driveshaft from the swivel hub, and the swivel hub from the suspension and steering arms, using the procedure described in paragraphs 7 to 10 inclusive.
13 Withdraw the swivel hub off the end of the driveshaft **(see illustration)** and then tie the hub assembly out of the way from a convenient place under the wheelarch. Avoid placing excessive strain on the flexible brake hose.
14 The inner end of the driveshaft must now be removed from the offset sphere joint. If Rover special tool No 18G 1243 can be obtained this will greatly simplify the task of removing the driveshaft from the joint **(see illustration)**. If this tool is not available the following procedure should be used.
15 Insert a flat metal bar or similar tool through the aperture in the subframe so that it rests on the driveshaft and is in contact with the flange of the joint. Take care not to pinch the rubber gaiter with the bar as it is easily punctured.
16 Pull the driveshaft outwards approx-imately 25 mm and firmly hold it in this position. The help of an assistant may be useful here.
17 Strike the end of the bar with a few sharp hammer blows. This will force the flange of the joint inwards and release it from the end of the driveshaft. The driveshaft can now be withdrawn from the car **(see illustration)**.

2.13 Withdraw the swivel hub from the end of the driveshaft

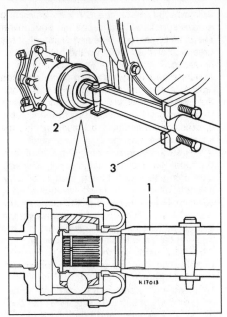

2.14 Removal of driveshaft inner end from offset sphere joint

1 Special tool 18G 1243
2 Tool in contact with joint flange
3 Tool plate engaged with driveshaft groove

Refitting

Models with front drum brakes

18 Refitting the driveshaft is the reverse sequence to removal, bearing in mind the following points:

a) Ensure that the hub bearing water shield is in place on the driveshaft CV joint and positioned approximately 6 mm from the shoulder of the joint **(see illustration)**.

b) When refitting the driveshaft to the offset sphere type inner joint, ensure that the circlip is in position on the shaft **(see illustration)** and lubricate the splines with a graphite-based grease. Push the driveshaft smartly into the joint to lock the shaft in position.

c) Tighten all nuts and bolts to the specified torque.

d) Tighten the driveshaft retaining nut to the specified torque, then tighten the nut

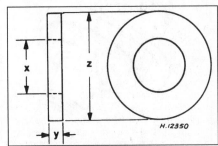

2.17 Withdrawing the driveshaft assembly

further to align the split pin holes in the driveshaft and nut. Secure the nut with a new split pin.

Models with front disc brakes

19 Refitting the driveshaft is the reverse sequence to removal, bearing in mind points a, b and c detailed in paragraph 18. Additionally, the following procedure must be observed on models with disc brakes, otherwise it is possible that the split-collar fitted beneath the driveshaft retaining nut will become clamped on the shaft before the shaft is fully home in the hub bearings.

20 Insert the driveshaft through the swivel hub, but do not fit the split collar. Obtain a plain washer of the dimensions shown **(see illustration)**. If necessary, make the washer from mild steel.

21 Fit the plain washer over the driveshaft end. Fit the driveshaft retaining nut and, using the same procedure as for removal to prevent the hub rotating, tighten the nut to the specified torque to seat the shaft in the hub bearings. Note that there are two different torque settings for the driveshaft nut; one for driveshafts with multiple split pin holes, and a higher setting for driveshafts with a single split pin hole. Now remove the nut and washer and smear engine oil over the driveshaft threads.

22 Examine the split-collar, and renew it if damaged or worn. Fit the collar and driveshaft retaining nut, and once again tighten it to the specified torque. Tighten the nut further to align the split pin holes in the driveshaft and nut, then secure the nut with a new split pin.

3 Driveshaft overhaul – general information

1 The driveshaft assembly consists of the outer constant velocity joint, the inner sliding spline and rubber coupling on early models, the inner offset sphere joint on later models, and the Hardy-Spicer universal joint on Cooper S Mk III and automatic transmission models. All of these components are subject to wear after high mileage, and the following tests can be used to isolate a suspect unit prior to overhaul.

Constant velocity joint

2 This is a well publicised weak spot on Minis. Wear is easily recognised as a metallic clicking from the front of the car as it is driven slowly in a circle with the steering on full lock. The noise is caused by excessive clearance between the balls in the joint and the recesses in which they operate. If the noise is only slight it may be nothing more serious than a lack of grease in the joint due to a split or damaged rubber gaiter. The best course of action if a clicking noise is apparent is to remove the joint as described in Section 5 and carry out a visual inspection. If wear is excessive the joint must be renewed.

Inner sliding splines

3 To check for wear on these components it will be necessary to position the car over a ramp or pit, or to jack it up and support it on axle stands (see Jacking and vehicle support). Grasp the driveshaft with one hand and the inner flange with the other and attempt to turn them in opposite directions. If this is possible to any appreciable degree then wear has taken place and both the driveshaft and flange should be renewed. Also check the condition of the rubber gaiter; if damaged or split it too should be renewed.

Inner rubber coupling

4 Wear in the rubber coupling can often be experienced on the road as a thumping, consistent with road speed and felt through the steering and body, usually on the overrun.

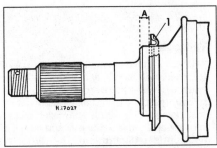

2.18a Correct positioning of water shield on CV joint

1 Water shield   A = 6 mm

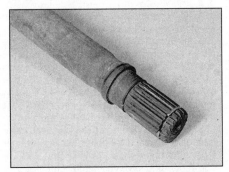

2.18b Ensure that the circlip is in position before refitting the driveshaft

2.20 Details of special washer required for fitting the driveshaft on disc brake models

X = 25 mm   Y = 6.5 mm   Z = 50 mm

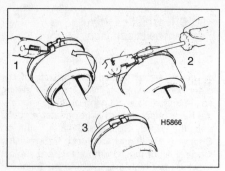

4.9 When clips are used to secure the rubber gaiter, pull clips tight and secure in order shown

Arrow indicates forward rotation of shaft

A closer inspection can be carried out from beneath the vehicle with it over a ramp or pit, or jacked up and supported on axle stands (see *Jacking and vehicle support*). Check for swelling or deterioration of the rubber or for oil contamination. Place a flat bar or stout screwdriver between the flanges and apply gentle leverage. Appreciable movement indicates wear in the joint. In more advanced stages of wear the rubber may have worn to such an extent that the inner metal spider will be visible. If the rubber has swollen due to oil contamination, the joint will rub on the rear face of the transmission casing, with the obvious disastrous results if this is allowed to continue.

Offset sphere joint

5 These joints are quite reliable and seldom give trouble. However, a vibration felt through the car, particularly during acceleration, may indicate wear in the joint. If the vibration is only slight it may be due to a lack of grease caused by a damaged rubber gaiter. If the joint is suspect it should be removed from the car and carefully inspected as described in Sections 8 and 9. It is possible to renew the rubber gaiter separately, but if the internal components of the joint are worn it will be necessary to renew the complete unit.

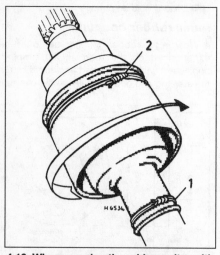

4.10 When securing the rubber gaiter with soft iron wire, ensure that the wire ends (1 and 2) are bent away from forward direction of rotation – arrowed

Hardy-Spicer universal joint

6 Wear in the needle roller bearings of these joints is characterised by vibration in the transmission, clonks on taking up the drive, and in extreme cases of lack of lubrication, metallic squeaking, and ultimately grating and shrieking as the needle bearings break up. With the car over a ramp or pit, or jacked up and supported on axle stands (see *Jacking and vehicle support*), attempt to turn the shaft with one hand while holding the inner drive flange with the other. If any movement exists, this indicates that considerable wear has taken place. Also try lifting the joint, noting any appreciable movement. If the joint is worn it may be overhauled using a repair kit consisting of a new spider, bearings, seals and circlips. This is described in detail in Section 7.

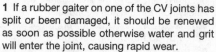

4 Constant velocity joint rubber gaiter – renewal

1 If a rubber gaiter on one of the CV joints has split or been damaged, it should be renewed as soon as possible otherwise water and grit will enter the joint, causing rapid wear.
2 To renew the rubber gaiter, begin by removing the driveshaft from the car as described in Section 2.
3 On models equipped with a rubber drive coupling or universal joint at the inner end of the driveshaft, remove the retaining clips or wire from the small inner rubber gaiter and then slide the flange and gaiter off the end of the driveshaft.
4 Now remove the retaining clips or wire from the constant velocity joint rubber gaiter. Slide the gaiter along the shaft and off the splined end.
5 Thoroughly clean all traces of rubber, old grease and dirt from the shaft and CV joint. **Note:** *If the car has been operated for a considerable length of time with a defective rubber gaiter, or if the grease appears contaminated with grit, it is essential that the CV joint is thoroughly washed out with paraffin or a suitable solvent.*
6 New CV joint rubber gaiters are available in the form of a repair kit from your local dealer. The kit comprises the CV joint gaiter, the gaiter retaining clips and a tube of special grease. It is most important that only this type of grease is used. When purchasing a replacement gaiter kit, if possible take along the old item for comparison, and check that the mouldings around the inner circumference of both old and new items are identical. Later type gaiters have a V-section rib around their inner circumference which fits into a corresponding groove in the joint housing body. *Under no circumstances fit a new type of gaiter to an old type joint.*

7 Thoroughly pack the CV joint using the grease supplied in the repair kit. Manipulate the joint from side-to-side and ensure that the grease is worked well into the balls and ball recesses.
8 Now slide the new CV joint gaiter over the splined end of the driveshaft and position it onto the joint. Ensure that the moulded lips or V-section rib of the gaiter fit into the shallow depressions machined in the outer circumference of the joint and on the driveshaft.
9 Place the larger retaining clip supplied in the repair kit over the CV joint with the end containing the tabs facing away from the forward direction of shaft rotation. Using pliers, pull the other end of the clip over the end containing the tabs and press down the first set of tabs using a screwdriver. Pull the free end tight and fold it over the compressed tabs. Now bend over the second set of tabs, trapping the free end of the clip underneath **(see illustration)**.
10 Alternatively secure the gaiter using two or three turns of soft iron wire. Twist the ends of the wire together and bend them over to face away from the forward direction of rotation of the shaft. Ensure that the wires are correctly located on the area of the gaiter directly over the shallow depressions in the joint **(see illustration)**.
11 Secure the smaller diameter of the CV joint gaiter to the driveshaft using the same method as described in paragraphs 9 and 10 above.
12 The remaining operations only apply to models fitted with a rubber drive coupling or universal joint at the inner end of the driveshaft.
13 Slide the smaller rubber gaiter over the splines until the moulded lip fits in the shallow depression on the shaft.
14 Liberally smear the splines on the driveshaft and the flange with the remains of the grease supplied in the repair kit.
15 Slide the flange onto the end of the shaft and pull the larger lip of the rubber gaiter over the end of the flange, engaging the lip into the shallow depression on the flange.
16 Secure the rubber gaiter using soft iron wire as described in paragraph 10.
17 The driveshaft can now be refitted to the car as described in Section 2.

5 Constant velocity joint – removal, inspection and refitting

Removal

1 Remove the driveshaft from the car as described in Section 2, and the rubber gaiters from the driveshaft as described in Section 4.
2 Firmly grasp the driveshaft or support it in a vice. Using a hide or plastic mallet, sharply strike the outer edge of the joint and drive it off the shaft **(see illustration)**. The CV joint is retained on the driveshaft by an internal circular section circlip, and striking the joint in the manner described forces the circlip to contract into a groove, so allowing the joint to slide off.

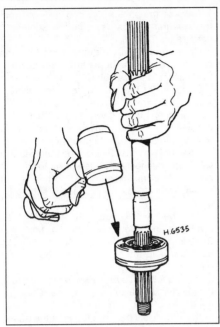

5.2 Using a soft-faced mallet to remove the CV joint

Inspection

3 With the CV joint removed from the drive-shaft, thoroughly wash out the joint using paraffin or a suitable solvent and dry it, preferably using compressed air. Carry out a careful visual inspection of the CV joint, paying particular attention to the following areas.

4 Move the inner splined driving member from side-to-side to expose each ball in turn at the top of its track. Examine the balls for cracks, flat spots or signs of surface pitting.

5 Inspect the ball tracks on the inner and outer members. If the tracks have widened, the balls will no longer be a tight fit. At the same time check the ball cage windows for wear or for cracking between the balls. Wear in the balls, ball tracks and ball cage windows will lead to the characteristic clicking noise on full lock described in Section 3.

6 It is no longer possible to obtain a CV joint overhaul kit consisting of a new ball cage and associated components. Therefore, if wear is apparent in the above mentioned areas, it will be necessary to renew the CV joint.

7 If a new joint has been obtained, or if the original joint was found to be in a satisfactory condition and is being refitted, a repair kit comprising a new CV joint rubber gaiter, gaiter retaining clips and a tube of special grease should be obtained from your local dealer. Only use this type of grease in the CV joint.

Refitting

8 The help of an assistant will be necessary whilst refitting the CV joint to the driveshaft. Ensure that the circlip is correctly located in its groove in the driveshaft. Position the CV joint over the splines on the end of the shaft until it abuts the circlip.

9 Using two small screwdrivers placed either side of the circlip, compress the circlip and at the same time have your assistant firmly strike the end of the CV joint with a hide or plastic mallet.

10 The joint should slide over the compressed circlip and into position on the shaft. It will probably require several attempts before you achieve success. If the joint does not spring into place the moment it is struck, remove it, reposition the circlip and try again. Do not force the joint otherwise the circlip will be damaged.

11 With the CV joint in place and in contact with the spring collar on the shaft, the joint should now be lubricated and the rubber gaiters refitted as described in Section 4, paragraphs 7 to 16 inclusive. The assembled driveshaft can then be refitted to the car as described in Section 2.

6 Inner rubber drive coupling – removal and refitting

Removal

1 Working under the wheelarch, undo and remove the single retaining screw and lift out the upper suspension arm rebound rubber. Place a solid packing piece of approximately the same thickness in its place.

2 Firmly apply the handbrake, then jack up the front of the car and support it securely on axle stands (see *Jacking and vehicle support*). Remove the front roadwheel.

3 Undo and remove the nut and spring washer securing the upper suspension arm to the swivel hub balljoint.

4 If a universal balljoint separator is available, use the separator to release the tapered shank of the balljoint from the upper suspension arm. Alternatively, use the procedure described in Section 2, paragraph , to free the taper.

5 With the upper balljoint disconnected, pull the upper part of the hub assembly away from the car and allow it to hang in this position. Avoid placing undue strain on the flexible brake hose.

6.6 Remove the rubber coupling U-bolt locknuts

6 From underneath the car, undo and remove the eight locknuts securing the retaining U-bolts to the coupling flanges **(see illustration)**.

7 Withdraw the U-bolts from the flanges, using a screwdriver to lever them out, and then lift off the rubber coupling.

Refitting

8 Refitting is the reverse sequence to removal. Ensure that the U-bolt locknuts and swivel hub balljoint retaining nut are tightened to the specified torque.

7 Hardy-Spicer universal joint – overhaul

1 Remove the driveshaft from the car as described in Section 2.

2 Remove the retaining wire securing the sliding spline protective rubber gaiter to the yoke flange and slide the yoke off the end of the driveshaft.

3 Thoroughly clean the exterior of the universal joint and yoke using paraffin or a suitable solvent and dry with a lint-free cloth.

4 Using circlip pliers, remove the four circlips securing the universal joint bearing cups to the yokes. If the circlips are tight, tap the bearing cups downward to relieve the tension on the circlip using a hammer and brass drift.

5 Support the underside of the yoke on the top of a vice **(see illustration)**. Tap the outer

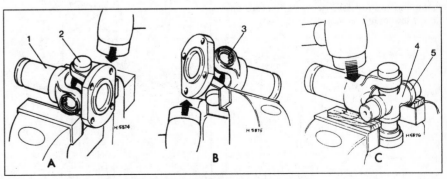

7.5 Universal joint removal procedure

1 Yoke	3 Circlip in	4 Journal spider
2 Needle bearing race	position	5 Rubber seal

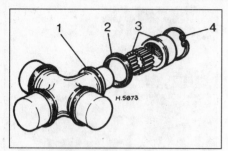

7.11 Universal joint components

1 Journal spider
2 Rubber seal
3 Needle rollers and bearing cup
4 Circlip

circumference of the other yoke with a soft-faced mallet until the bearing cup emerges from the top of the yoke.

6 Turn the assembly over and grip the exposed bearing cup between protected vice jaws. Now tap the yoke upwards until the bearing cup is released.

7 Repeat paragraphs 5 and 6 on the opposite bearing cup and then lift the yoke off the spider.

8 Position the two exposed bearing trunnions on the spider over the top of the protected vice jaws. Tap the yoke downwards until the bearing cup emerges from the top of the yoke.

9 Turn the yoke over and grip the exposed bearing cup between the protected vice jaws. Tap the yoke upwards until the bearing cup is released.

10 Repeat paragraphs 8 and 9 on the opposite bearing cup and then lift the spider out of the yoke.

11 Inspect the needle roller bearings, spider and bearing cups for lack of lubrication, surface pitting or load markings. If wear is apparent a new universal joint must be fitted **(see illustration)**.

12 Before refitting the universal joint, ensure that each bearing cup contains a complete set of rollers and that the rubber seals are in position on the bearing cups. Smear the inside of each cup with general purpose grease to retain the needle roller bearings in position.

13 Check that the bearing cup apertures in the yokes are clean and dry, paying particular attention to the circlip grooves. Remove any burrs that may exist using a small file.

14 Insert one of the bearing cups into the yoke aperture and then place the spider in position pushing it up into the cup to hold the needle bearings in place.

15 Using a hammer and soft drift, tap the bearing cup fully into the yoke and then refit the circlip.

16 Place the bearing cup in the opposite side of the yoke in position and move the spider up slightly until it just engages the needles.

17 Now tap the bearing cup fully into the yoke and refit the circlip.

18 Repeat paragraphs 14 to 17 inclusive for the remaining two bearing cups.

19 If the assembled joint appears to bind, tap the top of the bearing cups lightly using the soft drift to relieve the pressure of the bearing cups on the spider.

20 Smear the splines on the driveshaft and yoke with grease, and then refit the yoke to the driveshaft.

21 Engage the lip of the rubber gaiter over the yoke and secure with two or three turns of soft iron wire. Twist the ends of the wire together and then bend them down to face away from the forward direction of rotation of the driveshaft.

22 Refit the driveshaft to the car as described in Section 2.

8 Inner offset sphere joint – removal and refitting

Removal

1 Working under the wheelarch, undo and remove the single retaining screw and lift out the upper suspension arm rebound rubber. Position a solid packing piece of approximately the same thickness in its place.

2 Firmly apply the handbrake, then jack up the front of the car and support it securely on axle stands (see *Jacking and vehicle support*). Remove the front roadwheel.

3 Drain the engine/transmission oil as described in Chapter 1.

4 Release the steering tie-rod balljoint from the steering arm as described in Section 2, paragraphs 7 and 8.

5 Undo and remove the nut and spring washer securing the upper suspension arm to the swivel hub balljoint. Using the same method as for the steering tie-rod balljoint, separate the upper suspension arm from the tapered shank of the swivel hub balljoint.

6 The inner end of the driveshaft must now be removed from the offset sphere joint. If Rover special tool No 18G 1243 can be obtained this will greatly simplify the task of removing the driveshaft from the joint. If this tool is not available the following procedure should be used.

7 Tip the swivel hub outwards slightly, pivoting it on the lower balljoint. Take care not to stretch the flexible brake hose. Have an assistant hold the hub and driveshaft in this position.

8 Insert a flat metal bar or similar tool through the aperture in the subframe so that it rests on the driveshaft and is in contact with the flange of the joint. Take care not to pinch the rubber gaiter with the bar, as it is easily damaged.

9 Strike the end of the bar with a few sharp hammer blows. This will force the flange of the joint inwards and release it from the end of the driveshaft.

10 Fully withdraw the driveshaft from the joint flange and temporarily position the end of the shaft over the differential housing out of the way.

11 Using Rover special tool 18G 1240, release the offset sphere joint from the differential **(see illustrations)**. Alternatively, use a suitable cranked bar with a flattened end such as a tyre lever. Insert the flattened end of the bar between the joint inner face and the differential end cover **(see illustration)**. Pivot the bar against the end cover lower retaining bolt head. If the bar is not sufficiently cranked to reach the bolt head, use suitable spacers. Do not lever against the end cover. Strike the bottom of the bar with a few sharp hammer blows towards the centre of the car. This will release the joint from the retaining circlip on the differential shaft. Once the joint has moved outward slightly it can be removed the rest of the way by hand.

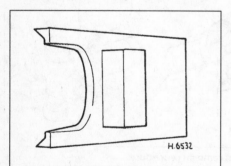

8.11a Special tool 18G 1240 for removing the offset sphere joint

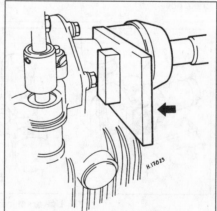

8.11b Using the special tool to release the joint from the differential

8.11c Using a cranked bar to release the offset sphere joint from the differential

12 With the offset sphere joint removed, recover the oil flinger, noting the direction of fitting.

Refitting

13 Refitting the joint is the reverse sequence to removal, bearing in mind the following points:

a) *Ensure that the oil flinger is in position before refitting the joint to the differential (see illustration).*

b) *Position a large worm-drive hose clip (or two joined together) around the joint and strike the head of the clip to force the joint fully into the differential.*

c) *When refitting the driveshaft ensure that the circlip is in position on the shaft and lubricate the splines with a graphite-based grease. Push the driveshaft smartly into the joint to lock the shaft in position.*

d) *Tighten all nuts and bolts to the specified torque.*

e) *Refill the engine/transmission with oil as described in Chapter 1.*

9	Inner offset sphere joint – dismantling, inspection and reassembly

Dismantling

1 With the joint removed from the car as described in Section 8, remove and discard the two retaining rings and the rubber gaiter.

2 Withdraw the joint inner member and ball cage assembly from the outer members **(see illustration)**.

3 Using a screwdriver inserted between each ball in turn and the joint inner member, release the balls from the ball cage.

4 Turn the ball cage until the grooves on the inside of the cage are aligned with the lands on the inner member and then lift off the ball cage.

Inspection

5 Wash off all the parts in paraffin or a suitable solvent and dry with a lint-free cloth.

8.13 Ensure that the oil flinger is in position before refitting

6 Carefully inspect the balls and the inner and outer members for signs of pitting, scoring, wear ridges or breakdown of the surface hardening. Examine the ball cage for elongation of the ball locations. If any of the components are worn, it will be necessary to renew the complete joint, as the internal parts are not available separately. If the joint is in a satisfactory condition, obtain a new rubber gaiter, gaiter retaining clips and a tube of the special lubricant from your Rover dealer.

Reassembly

7 Begin reassembly by refitting the ball cage to the inner member, noting that the long tapered end of the ball cage faces the driveshaft end of the inner member.

8 Press each of the balls in turn into the locations in the ball cage.

9 Slide the assembled inner member into the joint outer member.

10 Position a new retaining ring onto the inner neck of the rubber gaiter with the chamfered end of the ring toward the inside of the gaiter.

11 Fold back the gaiter and, using a tube of suitable diameter, push the gaiter onto the inner member.

12 Pack the assembled joint with the contents of the tube of special lubricant, working it well into the ball tracks and cage.

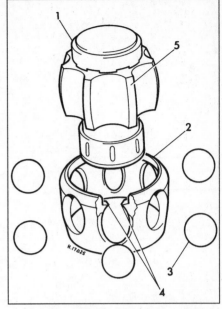

9.2 Dismantling the offset sphere joint

1. *Inner member*
2. *Ball cage*
3. *Balls*
4. *Ball cage internal grooves*
5. *Inner member lands*

13 Position the larger diameter of the rubber gaiter over the joint outer member. Place the retaining clip over the gaiter with the end containing the tabs facing away from the forward direction of joint rotation. Using pliers, pull the other end of the clip over the end containing the tabs and press down the first set of tabs using a screwdriver. Pull the free end tight and fold it over the compressed tabs. Now bend over the second set of tabs, trapping the free end of the clip underneath.

14 The offset sphere joint can now be refitted to the car as described in Section 8.

Chapter 9
Braking system

Contents

Brake disc – inspection, removal and refitting 9
Brake drum – removal, inspection and refitting 4
Brake fluid level check .... See *Weekly checks*
Brake fluid renewal .... See Chapter 1
Brake pad wear check .... See Chapter 1
Brake pedal – removal and refitting 23
Brake shoe wear check .... See Chapter 1
Disc brake caliper – removal, overhaul and refitting 8
Disc brake pads – renewal 7
Drum brake adjustment .... See Chapter 1
Drum brake shoes – renewal 5
Drum brake wheel cylinder – removal, overhaul and refitting 6
General information 1
Handbrake adjustment .... See Chapter 1
Handbrake cable – removal and refitting 10
Handbrake lever – removal and refitting 11
Hydraulic pipes and hoses – renewal 3

Hydraulic system – bleeding 2
Master cylinder (single circuit system) – removal, overhaul and
  refitting 12
Pressure differential warning actuator (dual circuit system) – removal,
  overhaul and refitting 20
Pressure reducing valve (dual circuit system) – removal and refitting 19
Pressure regulating valve (single circuit system) – removal, overhaul
  and refitting 18
Tandem master cylinder (dual circuit system) – identification and
  modifications 13
Tandem master cylinder (type 1) – removal, overhaul and refitting .. 14
Tandem master cylinder (type 2) – removal, overhaul and refitting .. 15
Tandem master cylinder (type 3) – removal, overhaul and refitting .. 16
Tandem master cylinder (type 4) – removal, overhaul and refitting .. 17
Underbody and fuel/brake line check .... See Chapter 1
Vacuum servo unit – removal and refitting 21
Vacuum servo unit air filter (1989 models onward) – renewal 22

Degrees of difficulty

Easy, suitable for novice with little experience	**Fairly easy,** suitable for beginner with some experience	**Fairly difficult,** suitable for competent DIY mechanic	**Difficult,** suitable for experienced DIY mechanic	**Very difficult,** suitable for expert DIY or professional

Specifications

System type

Footbrake	Lockheed single or dual circuit hydraulic, servo assisted on later models
Handbrake	Mechanical by cables to rear brakes

Front drum brakes

Type	Twin leading shoe
Drum diameter	178.0 mm
Minimum brake shoe lining thickness	3.0 mm

Front disc brakes

Type	Disc with twin piston caliper
Disc diameter:	
Cooper S models	190.5 mm
All other models	213.4 mm
Maximum disc run-out	0.15 mm
Minimum brake pad thickness	3.0 mm

Rear brakes

Type	Single leading shoe drum
Drum diameter	178.0 mm
Minimum brake shoe lining thickness	3.0 mm

Torque wrench settings

	Nm	lbf ft
Brake caliper retaining bolts	52	38
Brake disc to hub flange	57	42
Driveshaft retaining nut (disc brake models):		
With multiple split pin holes in driveshaft	207	153
With single split pin hole in driveshaft	255 to 270	188 to 199
Master cylinder body outlet plugs	39	29
Master cylinder pressure differential piston end plug	45	33
Master cylinder to servo unit	25	18
Pressure differential warning actuator end plug	35	26
Pressure differential warning actuator failure switch	19	14
Vacuum servo unit to mounting bracket	25	18
Vacuum servo mounting bracket-to-bulkhead	25	18

1 General information

Drum brakes are fitted to the front and rear wheels on all early models except Cooper S and 1275 GT versions. These, and all later models, have disc brakes at the front. The braking system is operated hydraulically by a master cylinder, which is actuated by the brake pedal. Later disc brake models are servo assisted by a vacuum servo unit mounted in the engine compartment.

The hydraulic system on early models is of the single circuit type, whereby both the front and rear brakes are operated by the same hydraulic system from the master cylinder. On later models a dual circuit system is used, whereby the brakes at each pair of wheels are operated by a separate hydraulic system from a tandem master cylinder. In the event of hydraulic failure in one circuit, full braking force will still be available at two wheels. On early dual circuit systems a diagonal split is used, each circuit supplying one front and one diagonally opposite rear brake. Later versions employ a front-to-rear split whereby both front and both rear brakes are operated by a separate hydraulic circuit.

A pressure differential warning actuator is fitted to certain models to inform the driver of a hydraulic circuit failure via an illuminated warning light, and also to restrict the flow of hydraulic fluid into the failed circuit. This unit is either mounted separately on the engine compartment bulkhead, or incorporated in the master cylinder. On single circuit and certain dual circuit systems, a pressure reducing valve is incorporated in the rear brake circuit. This valve reduces hydraulic fluid pressure to the rear brakes and prevents rear wheel lock-up due to forward weight transfer under heavy braking. On models not equipped with a pressure reducing valve, the same effect is achieved by reducing the rear wheel cylinder piston diameters.

A low brake fluid warning light is also fitted to later models operated by a float-type switch in the master cylinder reservoir filler cap.

On models fitted with front drum brakes, the brake shoes are operated by two single piston wheel cylinders at each front wheel. Models with front disc brakes utilise a twin piston fixed type caliper at each front wheel. At the rear on all models, one twin piston wheel cylinder operates each wheel's leading and trailing brake shoes.

The handbrake provides an independent mechanical means of rear brake shoe application.

Adjustment of the drum brakes is provided by two adjusters on each front brake and a single adjuster on each rear brake. Periodic adjustment is necessary to compensate for wear on the brake shoe friction linings. The front disc brakes do not require adjustment, as the pistons in the caliper automatically compensate for brake pad wear.

Note: *When servicing any part of the system, work carefully and methodically; also observe scrupulous cleanliness when overhauling any part of the hydraulic system. Always renew components (in axle sets, where applicable) if in doubt about their condition, and use only genuine Rover replacement parts, or at least those of known good quality. Note the warnings given in 'Safety first!' and at relevant points in this Chapter concerning the dangers of asbestos dust and hydraulic fluid.*

2 Hydraulic system – bleeding

Warning: Hydraulic fluid is poisonous; wash off immediately and thoroughly in the case of skin contact, and seek immediate medical advice if any fluid is swallowed or gets into the eyes. Certain types of hydraulic fluid are inflammable, and may ignite when allowed into contact with hot components; when servicing any hydraulic system, it is safest to assume that the fluid IS inflammable, and to take precautions against the risk of fire as though it is petrol that is being handled. Hydraulic fluid is also an effective paint stripper, and will attack plastics; if any is spilt, it should be washed off immediately, using copious quantities of clean water. Finally, it is hygroscopic (it absorbs moisture from the air). The more moisture is absorbed by the fluid, the lower its boiling point becomes, leading to a dangerous loss of braking under hard use. Old fluid may be contaminated and unfit for further use. When topping-up or renewing the fluid, always use the recommended type, and ensure that it comes from a freshly-opened sealed container.

General

1 The correct functioning of the brake hydraulic system is only possible after removing all air from the components and circuit; this is achieved by bleeding the system.

2 During the bleeding procedure, add only clean, fresh hydraulic fluid of the specified type; never re-use fluid that has already been bled from the system. Ensure that sufficient fluid is available before starting work.

3 If there is any possibility of incorrect fluid being used in the system, the brake lines and components must be completely flushed with uncontaminated fluid and new seals fitted to the components.

4 If brake fluid has been lost from the master cylinder due to a leak in the system, ensure that the cause is traced and rectified before proceeding further.

5 Park the car on level ground, switch off the ignition and select first gear (manual transmission) or Park (automatic transmission) then chock the wheels and release the handbrake.

6 Check that all pipes and hoses are secure, unions tight, and bleed screws closed. Remove the dust caps and clean any dirt from around the bleed screws.

7 Unscrew the master cylinder reservoir cap, and top-up the reservoir. Refit the cap loosely, and remember to keep the reservoir topped-up throughout the procedure, otherwise there is a risk of further air entering the system.

8 There is a number of one-man, do-it-yourself, brake bleeding kits currently available from motor accessory shops. It is recommended that one of these kits is used wherever possible, as they greatly simplify the bleeding operation, and also reduce the risk of expelled air and fluid being drawn back into the system. If such a kit is not available, collect a clean glass jar of reasonable size and a suitable length of plastic or rubber tubing, which is a tight fit over the bleed screw.

9 If a kit is to be used, prepare the car as described previously, and follow the kit manufacturer's instructions, as the procedure may vary slightly according to the type being used; generally, they are as outlined in the text below.

10 The procedure for bleeding varies according to whether the car is equipped with a single or dual circuit braking system, and also with dual circuit systems, the type of master cylinder that is fitted. Identify the type of system being worked on by referring to the illustrations, and to Section 13, then proceed according to type.

Single circuit system

11 To bleed the system, clean the area around the bleed screw of the wheel to be bled. If the hydraulic system has only been partially disconnected, and suitable precautions were taken to prevent further loss of fluid, it should only be necessary to bleed that part of the system. However, if the entire system is to be bled, proceed in the sequence ABCD for right-hand drive cars, and BADC for left-hand drive vehicles (see illustration).

12 Remove the master cylinder reservoir filler cap and top-up the reservoir. Periodically check the fluid level during the bleeding operation and top-up as necessary.

13 If a one-man brake bleeding kit is being used, connect the outlet tube to the bleed screw (see illustration) and then open the screw approximately one turn. Position the unit so that it can be viewed from the car then depress the brake pedal to the floor and rapidly release it. The one-way valve in the kit will prevent expelled air from returning to the system at the end of each stroke. Repeat this operation until clean hydraulic fluid, free from air bubbles, can be seen coming through the tube. Then tighten the bleed screw and remove the outlet tube.

14 If a one-man brake bleeding kit is not available, connect one end of the plastic tubing to the bleed screw and immerse the other end in the jar containing sufficient clean hydraulic fluid to keep the end of the tube submerged.

15 Open the bleed screw approximately one turn and have your assistant depress the brake pedal to the floor, and then rapidly release it. Tighten the bleed screw at the end of each downstroke to prevent expelled air from being drawn back into the system.

16 Repeat this operation until clean hydraulic fluid, free from air bubbles, can be seen coming through the tube. Then tighten the bleed screw on a downstroke and remove the plastic tube.

17 If the entire system is being bled the procedures described previously should now be repeated at each wheel in the correct sequence.

18 When completed, check the fluid level in the master cylinder, top-up if necessary, and refit the cap. Check the feel of the brake pedal, which should be firm and free from any sponginess; this would indicate air still present in the system.

19 Discard any used hydraulic fluid, as the minute air bubbles and contamination which will be present in the fluid make it unsuitable for further use in the hydraulic system.

Dual circuit system

Early type

20 The following procedure is applicable to the type 1 tandem master cylinder (see Section 13) fitted to diagonally-split hydraulic systems.

21 To bleed the system, clean the area around the bleed screws of the wheels to be bled. If only half of the hydraulic system has been disconnected, it should only be necessary to bleed that half, provided no air has entered the other half. However, if the entire system is to be bled, proceed in the sequence ABCD for right-hand drive cars and BADC for left-hand drive vehicles (see illustration).

22 The procedure is now the same as described in paragraphs 12 to 19 for the single circuit system, except that the brake pedal should be depressed rapidly, held down for three seconds and then released slowly. A delay of fifteen seconds should then be allowed before repeating.

23 When bleeding is complete, check the operation of the pressure differential warning actuator as described in Section 20.

Later type

24 The following procedure is applicable to the type 2, 3 and 4 tandem master cylinders (see Section 13) fitted to diagonally-split and front-to-rear split hydraulic systems.

25 Before commencing the bleeding operation, unscrew the brake failure warning switch (where fitted) from the side of the master cylinder body. (No fluid loss will occur unless there is internal pressure differential piston seal failure.) **Note:** *If the system is being bled following renewal of the master cylinder, check whether a plastic spacer is fitted between the pressure switch and master cylinder body. If a spacer is present, leave it in position during the bleeding operation and then discard it.*

26 To bleed the system, clean the area

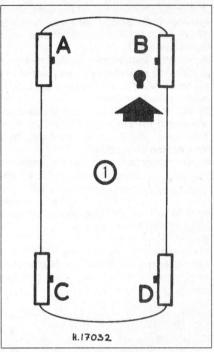

2.11 Bleeding sequence for single circuit braking systems

around the bleed screws of the wheels to be bled. If only half of the hydraulic system has been disconnected, it should only be necessary to bleed that half, provided no air has entered the other half. However, if the entire system is to be bled, it must be done in the following sequence.

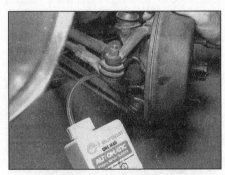

2.13 One-man brake bleeding kit connected to the front bleed screw

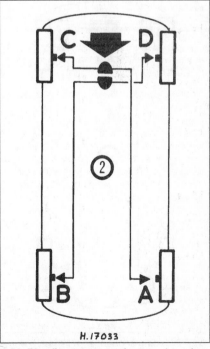

2.21 Bleeding sequence for type 1 tandem master cylinder – see text

27 For diagonally split systems, proceed in the order ABCD for right-hand drive cars, and CDAB for left-hand drive vehicles **(see illustration)**.

28 For front-to-rear split systems with type 2 and 3 tandem master cylinders, proceed in the order ABCD, irrespective of driving position **(see illustration)**.

29 For all type 4 tandem master cylinders, proceed in the order ABCD for right-hand drive cars, and BADC for left-hand drive vehicles **(see illustration)**.

30 The procedure is now the same as described in paragraphs 12 to 19 for the single circuit system, except that the brake pedal should be depressed rapidly, held down for three seconds, and then released slowly. A delay of fifteen seconds should then be allowed before repeating.

31 Where applicable, refit the brake failure warning switch and tighten it to the specified torque after completing the bleeding operation.

3 Hydraulic pipes and hoses – renewal

Note: *Before starting work, refer to the warning at the beginning of Section 2 concerning the dangers of hydraulic fluid.*

1 If any pipe or hose is to be renewed, minimise hydraulic fluid loss by removing the master cylinder reservoir cap, placing a piece of plastic film over the reservoir and sealing it with an elastic band. Alternatively, flexible hoses can be sealed, if required, using a proprietary brake hose clamp; metal brake pipe unions can be plugged (if care is taken not to allow dirt into the system) or capped immediately they are disconnected. Place a wad of rag under any union that is to be disconnected, to catch any spilt fluid.

2 If a flexible hose is to be disconnected, unscrew the brake pipe union nut before undoing the nut which secures the hose to its mounting. At the front, the other end of the hose will be screwed into its tapped hole in the wheel cylinder or brake caliper.

3 To unscrew the union nuts, it is preferable to obtain a brake pipe spanner of the correct size; these are available from most large motor accessory shops. Failing this, a close-fitting open-ended spanner will be required, though if the nuts are tight or corroded, their flats may be rounded-off if the spanner slips. In such a case, a self-locking wrench is often the only way to unscrew a stubborn union, but it follows that the pipe and the damaged nuts must be renewed on reassembly. Always clean a union and surrounding area before disconnecting it. If disconnecting a component with more than one union, make a careful note of the connections before disturbing any of them.

4 If a brake pipe is to be renewed, it can be obtained, cut to length and with the union nuts and end flares in place, from Rover dealers. All that is then necessary is to bend it to shape, following the line of the original, before fitting it to the car. Alternatively, most motor accessory shops can make up brake pipes from kits, but this requires very careful measurement of the original, to ensure that the replacement is of the correct length. The safest answer is usually to take the original to the shop as a pattern.

5 Before refitting, blow through the new pipe or hose with dry compressed air. Do not overtighten the union nuts. It is not necessary to exercise brute force to obtain a sound joint.

6 If flexible rubber hoses are renewed, ensure that the pipes and hoses are correctly routed, with no kinks or twists, and that they are secured in the clips or brackets provided.

7 After fitting, bleed the hydraulic system as described in Section 2, wash off any spilt fluid, and check carefully for fluid leaks.

4 Brake drum – removal, inspection and refitting

Note: *Before starting work, refer to the warning at the beginning of Section 5 concerning the dangers of asbestos dust.*

Removal

1 Chock the wheels then jack up the front or rear of the car as applicable and support it on axle stands (see *Jacking and vehicle support*). Remove the relevant roadwheels. Release the handbrake if necessary.

2 Slacken off the brake shoe adjuster(s) from behind the backplate **(see illustrations)**.

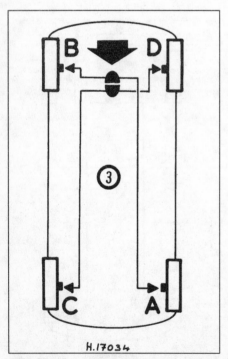

2.27 **Bleeding sequence for type 2, 3 and 4 tandem master cylinders with diagonal split dual circuit braking systems – see text**

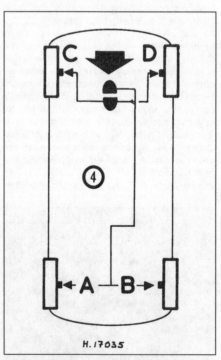

2.28 **Bleeding sequence for type 2 and 3 tandem master cylinders with front-to-rear split dual circuit braking systems – see text**

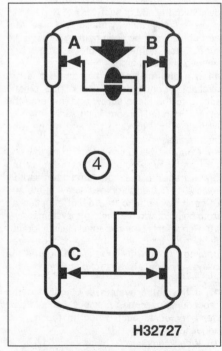

2.29 **Bleeding sequence for type 4 tandem master cylinders with front-to-rear split dual circuit braking systems – see text**

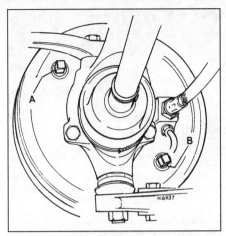

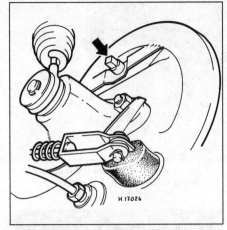

4.2a Location of the two front brake adjusters – A and B

4.2b Location of the rear brake adjuster – arrowed

4.3 On later models, if working on the rear brakes, lift off the wheel spacer, if fitted

based solvents to clean brake parts; use brake cleaner or methylated spirit only.

1 Remove the brake drum as described in Section 4.

2 Brush the dust and dirt from the shoes, backplate and drum.

3 Before removing the brake shoes, make a note of the positions of the shoes and the return springs and then remove the brake shoes as follows.

Front brakes

4 First release the small hook springs (where fitted) securing the brake shoes to the wheel cylinder pistons. Now lift the end of each shoe off the pivot side of each wheel cylinder, and then the other end off the wheel cylinder pistons. Detach the return springs and withdraw the shoes (see illustrations).

5 If necessary, position a rubber band over the wheel cylinders to prevent the pistons coming out. Should there be evidence of brake fluid leakage from the wheel cylinder, renew it or overhaul it, as described in Section 6.

6 Refitting the front brake shoes is the reverse sequence to removal, bearing in mind the following points:

a) Before refitting the shoes, smear a trace of high-melting-point brake grease to the pivot areas of the wheel cylinder, brake adjuster and backplate.

b) Do not allow any grease or hydraulic fluid to come into contact with the brake shoe linings.

c) Ensure that the shoes are refitted correctly and the return springs are in their correct holes.

4.4a Remove the brake drum retaining screws . . .

4.4b . . . and withdraw the drum

3 On later models, if working on the rear brakes, lift off the wheel spacer, if fitted (see illustration).

4 Undo the two brake drum retaining screws, then remove the brake drum from the wheel hub (see illustrations). If the drum is tight, gently tap its circumference with a soft-faced mallet.

Inspection

4 Brush the dust and dirt from the brake drum and carefully inspect the drum interior.

5 If the drum is grooved, owing to failure to renew worn brake shoes or after a very high mileage has been covered, then it may be possible to regrind it, provided the grooving is not excessive.

6 Even if only one drum is in need of grinding both drums must be reground to the same size in order to maintain even braking characteristics.

7 Judder or a springy pedal felt when the brakes are applied can be caused by a distorted (out-of-round) drum. Here again it may be possible to regrind the drums, otherwise a new drum will be required.

Refitting

8 Refitting is the reverse sequence to removal. Adjust the brakes as described in Chapter 1 before lowering the car to the ground.

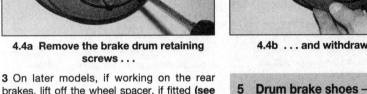

5 Drum brake shoes – renewal

⚠️ **Warning: Brake shoes must be renewed on both front or both rear wheels at the same time – never renew the shoes on only one wheel, as uneven braking may result. Also, the dust created by wear of the shoes may contain asbestos, which is a health hazard. Never blow it out with compressed air, and don't inhale any of it. An approved filtering mask should be worn when working on the brakes. DO NOT use petrol or petroleum-**

5.4a Remove the front brake shoes from the wheel cylinder pivot end first . . .

5.4b . . . and then from the piston end

5.7a Withdraw the rear brake shoes from the brake adjuster pivots, detach the return spring . . .

5.7b . . . then lift off the front and rear shoe from the wheel cylinder and handbrake lever

5.9a Smear a trace of high-temperature brake grease to the contact areas of the wheel cylinder . . .

5.9b . . . brake adjuster . . .

5.9c . . . and backplate

d) *Repeat all the above operations on the opposite front brake.*

e) *With the brake shoes assembled and drums refitted, adjust the brakes as described in Chapter 1.*

Rear brakes

7 Lift the top of both shoes off the brake adjuster pivots and detach the top brake shoe return spring. Now lift the bottom of the front shoe off the wheel cylinder piston and disengage the handbrake operating lever **(see illustrations)**. Repeat this for the rear shoe and lift away both shoes and lower return spring.

8 If necessary, position a rubber band over the wheel cylinders to prevent the pistons coming out. Should there be evidence of brake fluid leakage from the wheel cylinder, renew it or overhaul it, as described in Section 6.

9 Refitting the rear brake shoes is the reverse sequence to removal, bearing in mind the following points:

a) *Before refitting the shoes, smear a trace of high-temperature brake grease to the contact areas of the wheel cylinder, brake adjuster and backplate (see illustrations).*

b) *Do not allow any grease or hydraulic fluid to come into contact with the brake shoe linings.*

c) *Ensure that the shoes are refitted correctly and the return springs are in their correct holes. Ensure that the lower rear return spring does not rub on the wheel hub when refitted.*

d) *Repeat all the above operations on the opposite rear brake.*

e) *With the brake shoes assembled and drums refitted, adjust the brakes as described in Chapter 1.*

6 Drum brake wheel cylinder – removal, overhaul and refitting

Note: *Before starting work, refer to the*

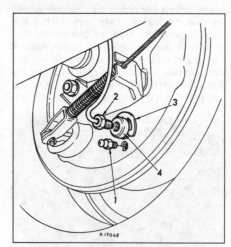

6.12 Rear wheel cylinder removal

1 Bleed screw
2 Hydraulic pipe union
3 Retaining circlip
4 Wheel cylinder

warning at the beginning of Section 2 concerning the dangers of hydraulic fluid, and to the warning at the beginning of Section 5 concerning the dangers of asbestos dust.

Removal

Front wheel cylinder

1 Remove the brake shoes from the relevant wheel as described in Section 5.

2 Thoroughly clean the rear of the backplate in the area around the wheel cylinder.

3 Clamp the flexible brake hose leading to the wheel cylinder with a proprietary brake hose clamp, or a self-gripping wrench with their jaws suitably protected. This will minimise hydraulic fluid loss when the hose or pipe is disconnected.

4 Disconnect the interconnecting brake pipe from the rear of the two wheel cylinders.

5 Undo and remove the two bolts securing each cylinder to the backplate.

6 If removing the cylinder containing the bleed screw, undo and remove the screw and lift off the cylinder.

7 If removing the cylinder containing the flexible brake hose, slacken the hose union at the wheel cylinder half a turn. Withdraw the wheel cylinder from the backplate and when it is clear, turn the cylinder anti-clockwise to unscrew it from the hose, taking care not to lose the copper sealing washer.

8 If the hose has not been clamped, suitably plug its end to prevent fluid loss and dirt ingress.

Rear wheel cylinder

9 Remove the brake shoes from the relevant wheel as described in Section 5.

10 Thoroughly clean the rear of the backplate in the area around the wheel cylinder.

11 Clamp the flexible hose located at the front of the rear suspension arm with a proprietary brake hose clamp, or a self-gripping wrench with its jaws suitably protected. This will minimise hydraulic fluid loss when the hydraulic pipe is disconnected.

12 Undo and remove the brake bleed screw and the hydraulic pipe union from the rear of the wheel cylinder **(see illustration)**. Suitably protect the end of the brake pipe against dirt ingress.

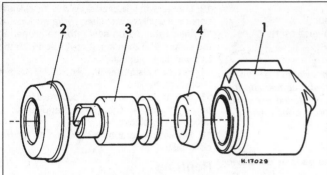

6.15a **Exploded view of a front wheel cylinder**

1 *Cylinder body*   3 *Piston*
2 *Dust cover*   4 *Rubber seal*

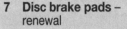
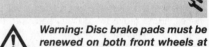

6.15b **Exploded view of a rear wheel cylinder**

1 *Cylinder body*   3 *Piston assemblies*
2 *Dust covers*   4 *Rubber seals*

13 Using a screwdriver, prise off the retaining circlip from the rear of the cylinder and then withdraw the wheel cylinder from the backplate.

Overhaul

Note: *Check the availability of parts before dismantling the wheel cylinder. On older models, wheel cylinder repair kits may not be readily available and it may be necessary to obtain a complete wheel cylinder assembly.*

14 Thoroughly clean off the exterior of the cylinder, then prepare a clean working area on the bench.

15 Lift off the rubber dust cover(s) from the end of the wheel cylinder and withdraw the piston(s) and rubber seal(s), noting their precise location in relation to each other **(see illustrations)**.

16 Thoroughly wash the components in clean hydraulic fluid or methylated spirit and dry with a lint-free cloth.

17 Carefully inspect the surface of the piston(s) and the internal bore of the cylinder body for scoring, pitting or other signs of wear. If any of these conditions are apparent the cylinder must be renewed.

18 If the wheel cylinder is in a satisfactory condition, a new set of rubber seals should be obtained. Never re-use old seals as their condition is bound to be suspect.

19 To reassemble the wheel cylinder, immerse the piston and the new internal rubber seals in clean hydraulic fluid.

20 Carefully fit the seal(s) to the piston(s) with their lip or larger diameter facing away from the main part of the piston(s).

21 Slide the piston into the cylinder bore and then refit the dust cover(s) after first lubricating with the rubber grease supplied in the kit.

Refitting

22 Refitting the front and rear wheel cylinders is the reverse sequence to removal, bearing in mind the following points:

a) *Where a wheel cylinder has been unscrewed from a flexible hose, use a new copper washer and ensure that the hose is not kinked when the cylinder is refitted.*

b) *Ensure that the retaining spring circlip is correctly located in the groove in the rear wheel cylinder body.*

c) *After fitting the wheel cylinder and refitting the brake shoes and drum, bleed the hydraulic system as described in Section 2. Providing the hoses were clamped as instructed, it should only be necessary to bleed the relevant wheel and not the entire system.*

7 Disc brake pads – renewal

> *Warning: Disc brake pads must be renewed on both front wheels at the same time – never renew the pads on only one wheel as uneven braking may result. Dust created by wear of the pads may contain asbestos, which is a health hazard. Never blow it out with compressed air and do not inhale any of it. DO NOT use petroleum-based solvents to clean brake parts. Use brake cleaner or methylated spirit only. DO NOT allow any brake fluid, oil or grease to contact the brake pads or disc. Also refer to the warning at the start of Section 2 concerning the dangers of hydraulic fluid.*

1 Firmly apply the handbrake, then jack up the front of the car and support it securely on axle stands (see *Jacking and vehicle support*). Remove the front roadwheels.

2 Straighten the ends of the two brake pad retaining split pins then extract the split pins from the brake caliper **(see illustration)**.

3 Lift away the pad retaining spring plate then, using a pair of pliers, carefully withdraw the two brake pads and (where fitted) their anti-rattle shims from the front of the caliper **(see illustrations)**.

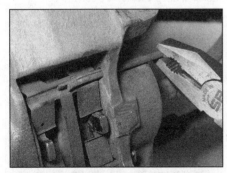

7.2 **Extract the brake pad split pins from the caliper**

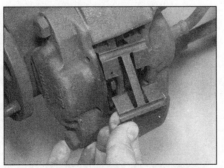

7.3a **Lift away the pad retaining spring plate . . .**

7.3b **. . . then withdraw the two brake pads**

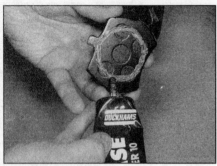

7.8 Smear high-temperature brake grease to the pad backing plates

4 Carefully inspect the pads and renew them if the friction material has worn down to less than the minimum specified thickness.

5 Thoroughly clean all traces of dirt and dust from the recesses in the caliper in which the brake pads lie, and the exposed face of each piston.

6 If new brake pads are being fitted it will be necessary to move the pistons back into the caliper to accommodate the new, thicker pads. This will cause a quantity of hydraulic fluid to be returned to the master cylinder reservoir, causing the fluid level to rise and possibly overflow. To protect the surrounding paintwork, remove the reservoir filler cap and place a large rag beneath the reservoir to absorb any fluid that may overflow. Alternatively, syphon off a quantity of fluid from the reservoir first.

 HAYNES HiNT *An ideal way to remove fluid from the master cylinder reservoir is to use a clean syringe or an old poultry baster.*

7 Using a flat bar or large screwdriver, lever the piston in each half of the caliper back into its cylinder as far as it will go.

8 Smear a small amount of high-temperature brake grease onto the edges and rear of the pad backing plates which contact the calipers and pistons **(see illustration)**. Do not allow any grease onto the friction material of the brake pads.

9 Check that the cutaway face of each piston is facing upwards and then place the anti-rattle shims in position.

10 Slide in the brake pads, refit the pad retaining spring plate, then secure the assembly using new split pins. Spread the ends of the split pins to retain them in position **(see illustration)**.

11 Depress the brake pedal several times (it will probably go right to the floor on the first stroke), to centralise the pads, and then check that the disc turns reasonably freely with the pedal released.

12 Repeat the above operations on the other front brake.

13 Refit the roadwheels and lower the car to the ground.

8 Disc brake caliper – removal, overhaul and refitting

Note: *Before starting work, refer to the warning at the beginning of Section 2 concerning the dangers of hydraulic fluid, and to the warning at the beginning of Section 7 concerning the dangers of asbestos dust.*

Removal

1 Remove the disc brake pads as described in Section 7.

2 If the caliper is being removed for overhaul, slowly and carefully depress the brake pedal to bring the caliper pistons nearly into contact with the brake disc. This will assist subsequent removal of the pistons.

3 Using a proprietary brake hose clamp, or a self-gripping wrench with its jaws suitably protected, clamp the flexible brake hose leading to the caliper. This will eliminate any hydraulic fluid loss when the hose is disconnected.

4 Slacken the flexible hose union on the side of the caliper half a turn.

5 Undo and remove the two bolts securing the caliper to the swivel hub, and then withdraw the caliper forward and off the hub.

6 With the caliper clear of the hub and brake disc, support the flexible hose and turn the caliper anti-clockwise to unscrew it. With the hose disconnected, recover the copper sealing washer and plug its end to prevent dirt ingress.

Overhaul

7 Carefully withdraw the two pistons one at a time from the caliper body. Do not attempt to separate the caliper halves.

8 Taking great care not to scratch the cylinder walls of the caliper, hook out the dust seal and piston seal from each caliper cylinder.

9 Thoroughly clean the caliper and pistons in clean hydraulic fluid or methylated spirit and dry with a lint-free cloth.

10 Inspect the pistons and caliper bores in the caliper for wear, score marks or surface pitting, and if evident renew the complete caliper assembly.

11 If the caliper and pistons are in a satisfactory condition, a new set of seals should be obtained. *Never re-use old seals.*

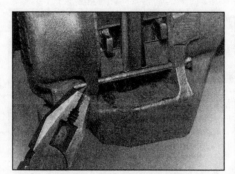

7.10 Spread the ends of the split pins to retain them in position

12 Lubricate the pistons, seals and the cylinder bores in the caliper with clean hydraulic fluid.

13 Insert the piston seal into the groove in the caliper and then insert the piston with the cutaway facing upwards.

14 Push the piston into its cylinder until 8.0 mm remains protruding.

15 Now carefully insert the dust seal into the outer groove in the caliper and push it squarely into place.

16 Repeat paragraphs 13, 14 and 15 for the other piston.

Refitting

17 Refitting the brake caliper is the reverse sequence to removal, bearing in mind the following points:

a) Use a new copper washer on the flexible brake hose and ensure that with the caliper in position, the hose is not kinked or twisted.

b) Tighten the caliper retaining bolts to the specified torque.

c) Refit the brake pads as described in Section 7 then bleed the hydraulic system as described in Section 2. If the flexible hose was clamped as described, it should not be necessary to bleed the entire system.

9 Brake disc – inspection, removal and refitting

Note: *Before starting work, refer to the warning at the beginning of Section 7 concerning the dangers of asbestos dust.*

Inspection

Note: *If a disc requires renewal, BOTH discs should be renewed at the same time to ensure even and consistent braking. New brake pads should also be fitted.*

1 Remove the disc brake pads as described in Section 7.

2 Inspect the disc friction surfaces for cracks or deep scoring (light grooving is normal and may be ignored). A cracked disc must be renewed; a scored disc can often be reclaimed by machining provided that the thickness is not significantly reduced. Consult your Rover dealer as to the best course of action if deep scoring is evident.

3 Check the disc run-out using a dial test indicator with its probe positioned near the outer edge of the disc. If the run-out exceeds the figures given in the *Specifications*, machining may be possible, otherwise disc renewal will be necessary.

HAYNES HiNT *If a dial test indicator is not available, check the run-out by positioning a fixed pointer near the outer edge, in contact with the disc face. Rotate the disc and measure the maximum displacement of the pointer with feeler blades.*

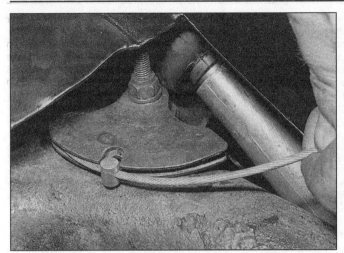

10.7 Removing the handbrake cable from the moving sector

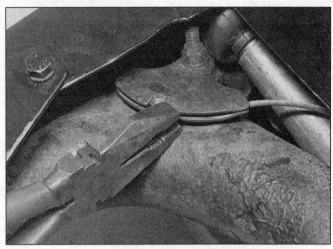

10.10 Pinching the ends of the moving sector to retain the handbrake cable

4 Excessive disc thickness variation can also cause judder. Check this using a micrometer. No actual thickness variation figures are provided by the manufacturer, but as a general guide, 0.010 mm should be considered a maximum.

Removal

5 If not already done, chock the rear wheels then jack up the front of the car and support it on axle stands (see *Jacking and vehicle support*). Remove the front roadwheel.
6 Extract the split pin from the driveshaft retaining nut. If the brake pads have not been removed, have an assistant firmly depress the brake pedal, while you undo and remove the driveshaft nut using a socket and extension bar. Remove the split-collar located behind the driveshaft nut. If the brake pads have already been removed for disc inspection, temporarily refit them to allow the driveshaft nut to be undone or, alternatively, fabricate a home-made tool to prevent the hub flange rotating when undoing the nut (see Chapter 8, Section 2). Note that the driveshaft retaining nut is extremely tight and it may be beneficial to use the home-made tool even if the pads are still fitted.
7 Undo and remove the brake caliper retaining bolts. Lift off the caliper complete with brake pads (where applicable), with the brake hose still attached, and tie it out of the way from a convenient place under the wheelarch. Take care not to stretch the flexible hose.
8 Withdraw the front hub flange and brake disc from the swivel hub and driveshaft.
9 To separate the disc from the hub flange, first mark the two components to ensure that they are refitted in the same position.
10 Undo and remove the bolts securing the hub flange to the disc and lift away the disc.

Refitting

11 Ensure that the mating surfaces between disc and hub flange are thoroughly clean then place the disc in position and refit the retaining bolts. If the original disc is being refitted, ensure that the marks made on removal are aligned.
12 Locate the hub flange and disc assembly over the driveshaft and in position on the swivel hub. Smear engine oil over the driveshaft threads and fit the split-collar and driveshaft retaining nut. Tighten the nut finger tight only at this stage.
13 Refit the brake caliper and secure with the two bolts tightened to the specified torque.
14 If removed, refit the brake pads as described in Section 7.
15 Using the same procedure as for removal to prevent the hub rotating, tighten the nut to the specified torque. Note that there are two different torque settings for the driveshaft nut; one for driveshafts with multiple split pin holes, and a higher setting for driveshafts with a single split pin hole. Tighten the nut further to align the split pin holes in the driveshaft and nut, then secure the nut with a new split pin.
16 Refit the roadwheel and lower the car to the ground.

---

10 Handbrake cable –
  removal and refitting

Early models

1 Chock the front wheels then jack up the rear of the car and support it securely on axle stands (see *Jacking and vehicle support*). Remove the rear roadwheel and ensure that the handbrake is off.
2 From inside the car, undo and remove the cable adjusting nut at the handbrake lever, then pull the cable out of the lever trunnion. Slide the two washers and tension spring off the threaded end of the cable.
3 Lift up the carpets to expose the cable guide plates located at the point where the cable passes through the floor.

4 Engage the help of an assistant to hold the two nuts from underneath the car while the two cable guide retaining screws are removed from above. Lift off the guide and sealing pad.
5 From beneath the car, pull the end of the cable through the opening in the floor and out of the passenger compartment.
6 Bend back the tags slightly on the guide channel located on the forward crossmember of the rear subframe. Lift the cable out of the guide channel.
7 Similarly bend up the pinched ends of the moving sector located at the front of the rear suspension arm. Lift the cable and the locating peg out of the sector **(see illustration)**, and then pull the disconnected end of the cable through the opening in the side of the subframe.
8 At the other end of the cable, extract the split pin and withdraw the clevis pin securing the cable end to the handbrake operating arm.
9 Release the cable from the abutment bracket at the rear of the brake backplate and lift the cable off the car.
10 Refitting the cable is the reverse sequence to removal, bearing in mind the following points:
  a) With the cable in position, pinch the ends of the moving sector and subframe guide channel slightly to retain the cable **(see illustration)**.
  b) Ensure that the guide channel in the subframe is well-lubricated.
  c) Adjust the handbrake as described in Chapter 1 on completion.

Later models – front cable

Up to October 1996

11 Chock the front wheels then jack up the rear of the car and support it securely on axle stands (see *Jacking and vehicle support*). Ensure that the handbrake is off.
12 Tilt the front seats forward and lift up the carpet around the handbrake lever.

13 Slacken the locknut, and then unscrew the cable adjusting nut until the cable can be withdrawn from the lever assembly **(see illustration)**.

14 Undo and remove the screws securing the cable guide plate to the floor. Have an assistant hold the two nuts from under the car as the screws are undone.

15 Lift off the guide plate and pass the cable through the hole in the floor.

16 Pull the cable rearwards and remove it from the compensator on the rear cable.

17 Refitting is the reverse sequence to removal. Adjust the handbrake as described in Chapter 1 on completion.

October 1996 models onward

18 Remove the front seat on the driver's side as described in Chapter 11B.

19 Remove the front seat belt stalk and front seat belt lower mounting on the driver's side as described in Chapter 11B.

20 Release the carpet from the door seal and from the retaining clips, then fold back the carpet for access to the handbrake lever.

21 Slacken the locknut, and then unscrew the cable adjusting nut until the cable can be withdrawn from the lever assembly.

22 Chock the front wheels then jack up the rear of the car and support it securely on axle stands (see *Jacking and vehicle support*). Ensure that the handbrake is off.

23 Remove the exhaust system tailpipe heat shield as described in Chapter 4D.

24 Undo and remove the screws securing the cable guide plate to the floor. Have an assistant hold the two nuts from under the car as the screws are undone.

25 Lift off the guide plate and pass the cable through the hole in the floor.

26 Extract the retaining clip securing the front cable to the compensator on the rear cable. Pull the cable rearwards and remove it from the compensator.

27 Refitting is the reverse sequence to removal, referring to Chapter 11B for details of refitting the seat belts and front seat. Adjust the handbrake as described in Chapter 1 on completion.

Later models – rear cable

28 Remove the front cable as described previously.

29 Extract the split pins and withdraw the clevis pins securing the cable ends to the handbrake operating arms at the rear of each brake backplate. Release the cable and tension springs from the abutment brackets on the backplate.

30 Bend back the tags slightly on the guide channels located on the forward crossmember of the rear subframe.

31 Similarly bend up the pinched ends of the moving sectors located at the front of each rear suspension arm. Lift the cable and locating pegs out of the sectors, pull the disconnected ends of the cable through the openings in the side of the subframe, and lift away the cable complete with compensator.

32 Refitting the rear cable is the reverse sequence to removal bearing in mind the following points.

a) *With the cable in position pinch the ends of the moving sectors and subframe guide channels slightly to retain the cable.*

b) *Ensure that the guide channels in the subframe are well-lubricated.*

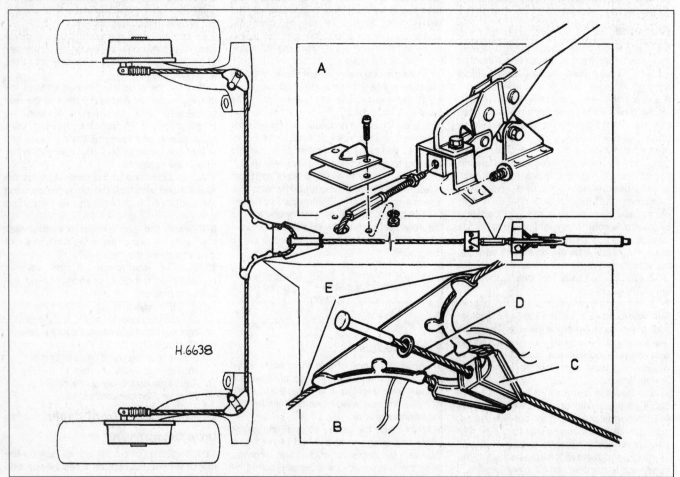

H.6638

10.13 Handbrake cables and lever assembly fitted to later models

A Front cable adjustment detail	C Compensator	E Rear cable
B Rear cable and compensator detail	D Front cable	

11 Handbrake lever – removal and refitting

Removal

1 On early models lift up the front seats, unscrew the two handbrake cable adjusting nuts and pull the cables out of the trunnion on the lever. On later models slacken the locknut, unscrew the cable adjusting nut and withdraw the cable.

2 Undo and remove the two nuts, bolts and spring washers securing the handbrake lever to the bracket on the floor (see illustration). Lift off the lever and withdraw it from the car.

3 The handbrake lever cannot be dismantled, and if worn or faulty must be renewed as a complete assembly.

Refitting

4 Refitting is the reverse sequence to removal. Adjust the handbrake as described in Chapter 1 on completion.

12 Master cylinder (single circuit system) – removal, overhaul and refitting

Note: *Before starting work, refer to the warning at the beginning of Section 2 concerning the dangers of hydraulic fluid.*

Removal

1 From inside the car release the heater air inlet ducting from the side of the heater unit and wheelarch. Remove the ducting from under the parcel shelf.

2 Extract the split pin and withdraw the clevis pin securing the master cylinder pushrod to the brake pedal (see illustration).

3 Working in the engine compartment, unscrew the brake pipe union from the top of the master cylinder and carefully pull the pipe clear.

4 Undo and remove the two nuts and spring washers securing the master cylinder to the bulkhead and lift off the cylinder.

Overhaul

Note: *Check the availability of parts before dismantling the master cylinder. On older models, master cylinder repair kits may not be readily available and it may be necessary to obtain a complete master cylinder assembly.*

5 Remove the filler cap from the master cylinder then drain and discard the hydraulic fluid from the reservoir.

6 With the cylinder on the bench, withdraw the rubber dust cover and slide it off over the end of the pushrod (see illustration).

7 Using circlip pliers, extract the circlip and lift off the pushrod and dished washer.

8 Tap the master cylinder body on a block of wood until the piston emerges from the end of the cylinder bore.

11.2 Handbrake lever retaining nuts and bolts

9 Withdraw the piston from the cylinder, followed by the piston washer, main cup seal, spring retainer, spring and non-return valve.

10 Lay the parts out in the order of removal, and then very carefully remove the secondary cup seal from the piston by stretching it over the end of the piston.

11 Wash the components in clean hydraulic fluid or methylated spirit and dry with a lint-free rag.

12 Examine the cylinder bore and piston carefully for signs of scoring, or wear ridges. If

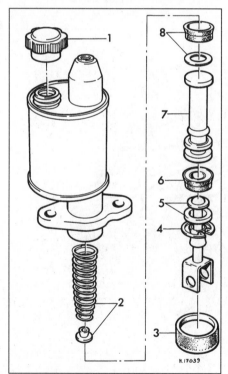

12.6 Exploded view of the single circuit master cylinder

1 *Filler cap*
2 *Spring and spring retainer*
3 *Dust cover*
4 *Circlip*
5 *Pushrod and stop washer*
6 *Secondary cup seal*
7 *Piston*
8 *Piston washer and main cup seal*

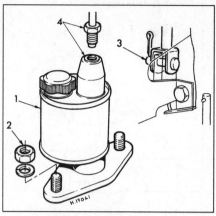

12.2 Removal of the single circuit master cylinder

1 *Master cylinder*
2 *Retaining nuts*
3 *Pushrod-to-brake pedal attachment*
4 *Hydraulic pipe union*

these are apparent, renew the complete master cylinder. If the condition of the components appears satisfactory, a new set of rubber seals must be obtained. Never re-use old seals as they will have deteriorated with age even though this may not be evident during visual inspection.

13 Begin reassembly by thoroughly lubricating the internal components and the cylinder bore in clean hydraulic fluid.

14 Using fingers only, place the secondary cup seal in position on the piston with the lip of the cup facing the opposite (drilled) end of the piston.

15 Position the non-return valve over the larger diameter of the spring and the spring retainer over the smaller diameter, and place this assembly into the cylinder bore, larger diameter first.

16 Now insert the main cup seal into the cylinder bore, lip end first followed by the washer.

17 Insert the piston assembly into the cylinder bore followed by the pushrod, dished washer and circlip. Ensure that the circlip fully enters its groove.

18 Lubricate a new dust cover with rubber grease and stretch it over the pushrod and into position on the end of the cylinder.

Refitting

19 Refitting is the reverse sequence to removal. Bleed the complete hydraulic system as described in Section 2 on completion.

13 Tandem master cylinder (dual circuit system) – identification and modifications

Identification

1 Four different versions of tandem brake master cylinder have been fitted to Mini models covered by this manual. The removal, refitting and overhaul procedures for the four

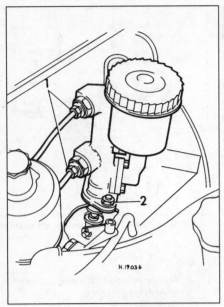

13.2a Identification and removal of the type 1 tandem master cylinder

1 *Hydraulic pipe unions*
2 *Retaining nuts*

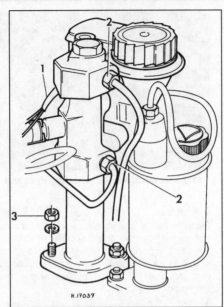

13.2b Identification and removal of the type 2 tandem master cylinder

1 *Electrical wiring to failure switch*
2 *Hydraulic pipe unions*
3 *Retaining nuts*

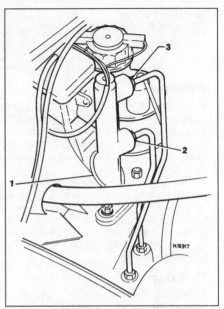

13.2c Identification and removal of the type 3 tandem master cylinder

1 *Yellow band*
2 *Larger pipe union*
3 *Smaller pipe union*

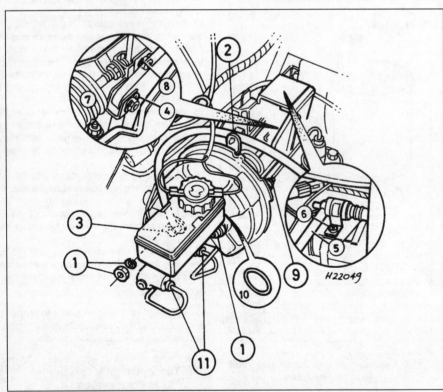

13.2d Identification and removal of the type 4 tandem master cylinder

1 *Master cylinder mounting nuts*
2 *Vacuum hose retaining clip*
3 *One-way vacuum valve*
4 *Brake pedal clevis pin*
5 *Anti-run-on valve hoses (where fitted)*
6 *Anti-run-on valve (where fitted)*
7 *Servo mounting bracket nuts*
8 *Servo pushrod clevis pin*
9 *Servo-to-mounting bracket nuts*
10 *O-ring*
11 *Brake pipe union nuts*

versions are distinctly different and it is important to correctly identify the unit being worked on before proceeding.

2 For identification purposes only, the master cylinders will be referred to in this Chapter as types 1, 2, 3 or 4. Identification is as follows:

• *Type 1: Vertically-mounted and incorporating a circular plastic transparent fluid reservoir with large flat filler cap **(see illustration)**. Separate pressure differential warning actuator located on engine compartment bulkhead.*

• *Type 2: Vertically-mounted and incorporating a rectangular plastic transparent fluid reservoir with small flat filler cap possibly with brake fluid level warning indicator. Upper and lower hydraulic pipe union nuts of the same size. Pressure differential warning actuator integral with master cylinder, operating a brake failure warning switch fitted to the side of the cylinder body **(see illustration)**.*

• *Type 3: Vertically-mounted and incorporating a rectangular plastic transparent fluid reservoir with brake fluid level warning indicator in the filler cap. Upper hydraulic pipe union nut larger than the lower nut. A yellow plastic identification band should also appear around the cylinder body **(see illustration)**. Fitted to models manufactured from November 1985 to 1989 and as a retro-fit replacement for type 2 units.*

• *Type 4: Horizontally-mounted on the front of the vacuum servo unit. Fitted to models manufactured from 1989 onwards **(see illustration)**.*

Modifications

3 In November 1985, the type 3 tandem master cylinder with a revised front/rear split was introduced to replace the type 2. This new cylinder has a stepped bore, and the primary and secondary circuits have been reversed.

4 Should a type 2 master cylinder require renewal, a type 3 unit will be supplied by Rover dealers.

5 To fit the type 3 cylinder to pre-November 1985 vehicles, two modified brake pipes will be required and, on vehicles without a brake fluid level warning indicator, a conversion wiring loom will also be required. These modified components should be available from Rover dealers.

6 To fit a type 3 master cylinder in place of a type 2 master cylinder, proceed as follows.

7 Remove the master cylinder, as described in Section 15. **Note:** *On vehicles equipped with a fluid level indicator, disconnect the wiring connectors from the switch on the reservoir filler cap.*

8 Remove the existing hydraulic pipes from the pressure-reducing valve (which run to the brake master cylinder).

9 Fit the new pipes to the pressure reducing valve.

10 Fit the new brake master cylinder, which is a reversal of removal, then connect the new pipes to it.

11 To fit the wiring conversion loom, first cut the connector from the end of the two black and white wires removed from the brake warning switch on the old cylinder **(see illustration)**.

12 Join the two wires together, fit a Lucar connector, and connect it to one terminal of the fluid level warning switch on the new master cylinder.

13 Using black cable, make up an earth lead with a Lucar connector at one end and an eyelet at the other.

14 The earth lead should be 533.0 mm long, and is connected to the other connector on the fluid level warning switch, and routed along the wiring loom in the engine bay to the existing earth screw.

15 Fill and bleed the hydraulic system, as described in Section 2, and check the operation of both the brake warning light and the low fluid level warning light.

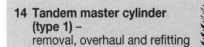

14 Tandem master cylinder (type 1) – removal, overhaul and refitting

Note: *Before starting work, refer to the warning at the beginning of Section 2 concerning the dangers of hydraulic fluid.*

Removal

1 Place a cloth around the master cylinder to catch any spilled fluid then unscrew the hydraulic pipe unions from the master cylinder

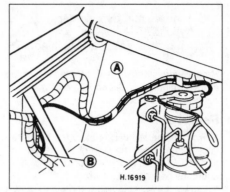

13.11 Braking system conversion wiring loom details

A Loom   *B Earth screw*

and carefully pull the pipes clear. Plug or tape over the disconnected unions to prevent dirt entry.

2 Undo and remove the two nuts and spring washers securing the master cylinder to the bulkhead. Lift off the master cylinder, leaving the pushrod attached to the brake pedal.

Overhaul

Note: *Check the availability of parts before dismantling the master cylinder. On older models, master cylinder repair kits may not be readily available and it may be necessary to obtain a complete master cylinder assembly.*

3 Remove the filler cap from the master cylinder, then drain and discard the hydraulic fluid from the reservoir.

4 Mount the master cylinder In a vice with protected jaws, so that the mouth of the cylinder bore is uppermost.

5 Slide off the rubber boot, compress the return spring and, using a small screwdriver, remove the Spirolex ring from its groove in the primary piston **(see illustration)**. Take care not to distort the coils of the ring or score the bore of the cylinder.

6 Using a pair of circlip pliers, remove the piston retaining circlip.

7 Carefully move the piston up-and-down in the bore so as to free the nylon guide bearing and cap seal. Lift away the guide bearing seal.

8 Lift away the plain washer.

9 Using a pair of circlip pliers, remove the inner circlip.

10 The primary and secondary piston assembly, complete with the stop washer, may now be withdrawn from the cylinder bore.

11 Lift away the stop washer.

12 Compress the spring that separates the two pistons then, using a small diameter parallel pin punch, drive out the roll pin that retains the piston link.

13 Inspect and note the location of the rubber cups (look for the moulded indentations) then remove the cups and washers from the pistons.

14 Undo and remove the four bolts that secure the plastic reservoir to the body and lift away the reservoir.

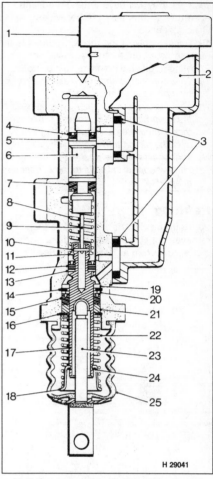

14.5 Cross-sectional view of the type 1 tandem master cylinder

1 Filler cap	*14 Circlip*
2 Plastic reservoir	*15 Cup*
3 Reservoir seals	*16 Circlip*
4 Main cap	*17 Piston*
5 Piston washer	*18 Spring*
6 Piston	*retainer*
7 Main cup	*19 Stop washer*
8 Spring	*20 Washer*
9 Piston link	*21 Bearing*
10 Pin	*22 Spring*
11 Pin retainer	*23 Pushrod*
12 Main cup	*24 Spirolex ring*
13 Piston washer	*25 Rubber boot*

15 Recover the two reservoir sealing rings.

16 Unscrew and remove the hydraulic pipe connection adapters, discard the copper gaskets and recover the spring and trap valves.

17 Wash all parts in clean hydraulic fluid or methylated spirit and dry with a lint-free cloth.

18 Examine the bore of the cylinder carefully for any signs of scores or ridges. If this is found to be smooth all over, new seals can be fitted. If, however, there is any doubt of the condition of the bore, then a new cylinder must be obtained and fitted. *Never re-use old* seals as they will have deteriorated with age even though this may not be evident during visual inspection.

19 Reassembly of the master cylinder is the reverse sequence to removal, but the following additional points should be noted:

a) *All components should be assembled wet by dipping in clean brake fluid.*

b) *Locate the piston washer over the head of the secondary piston, convex surface first, then carefully ease the secondary cup over the piston and seat it with its flat surface against the washer.*

c) *Fit new copper gaskets to the connection adapters.*

Refitting

20 Refitting is the reverse sequence to removal. On completion, bleed the complete hydraulic system as described in Section 2.

15 Tandem master cylinder (type 2) –
removal, overhaul and refitting

Note: *Before starting work, refer to the warning at the beginning of Section 2 concerning the dangers of hydraulic fluid.*

Removal

1 From inside the car, release the heater air inlet ducting from the side of the heater unit and wheelarch. Remove the ducting from under the parcel shelf.

2 Extract the split pin and withdraw the clevis pin securing the master cylinder pushrod to the brake pedal.

3 Working in the engine compartment, disconnect the wiring connector from the brake warning switch on the master cylinder body.

4 Place a cloth around the master cylinder to catch any spilled fluid then unscrew the hydraulic pipe unions from the side of the master cylinder body and carefully pull the pipes clear. Plug or tape over the disconnected unions to prevent dirt entry.

5 Unscrew the two nuts securing the master cylinder to the bulkhead and lift the unit off.

Overhaul

Note: *Check the availability of parts before dismantling the master cylinder. On older models, master cylinder repair kits may not be readily available and it may be necessary to obtain a complete type 3 master cylinder assembly.*

6 Remove the filler cap from the master cylinder, and drain and discard the hydraulic fluid from the reservoir.

7 Mount the cylinder in a vice with protected jaws, so that the reservoir is uppermost.

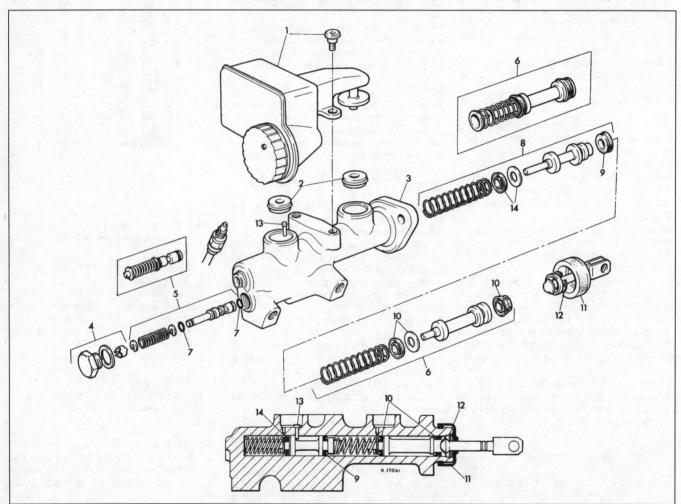

15.8 Exploded view of the type 2 tandem master cylinder

1 *Reservoir and retaining screw*
2 *Reservoir sealing washers*
3 *Master cylinder body*
4 *End plug assembly*
5 *Pressure differential piston (insert shows alternative assembly)*

6 *Primary piston and spring (inset shows alternative assembly)*
7 *Piston rubber seals*
8 *Secondary piston and spring*
9 *Secondary piston seals*

10 *Primary piston seals*
11 *Dust cover*
12 *Circlip*
13 *Stop pin*
14 *Secondary piston seals*

8 Unscrew the two reservoir retaining screws and lift the reservoir off the master cylinder body **(see illustration opposite)**. Carefully withdraw the two reservoir sealing washers from the outlets.

9 Push in the pushrod as far as possible, and using pliers, extract the secondary piston stop pin from its recess.

10 Release the pushrod rubber boot from the end of the cylinder, push the pushrod in and extract the retaining circlip. Now lift away the pushrod assembly.

11 Remove the master cylinder from the vice, tap it on a block of wood and withdraw the primary and secondary piston assemblies from the cylinder bore.

12 Unscrew the brake failure switch from the cylinder body.

13 Unscrew the end plug and washer, then remove the distance piece and pressure differential piston assembly.

14 Note the position and direction of fitting of the rubber seals on the piston assemblies, and then carefully remove them.

15 Wash all the parts in clean hydraulic fluid or methylated spirit and dry with a lint-free cloth.

16 Examine the bore of the master cylinder carefully for any signs of scores or ridges. If this is found to be smooth all over, new seals can be fitted. If, however, there is any doubt about the condition of the bore, then a new cylinder must be obtained and fitted. *Never re-use old seals*, as they will have deteriorated with age even though this may not be evident during visual inspection.

17 Reassembly of the master cylinder is the reverse sequence to removal, but the following additional points should be noted:

a) *Thoroughly lubricate all components in clean hydraulic fluid and assemble them wet.*

b) *Refit the seals onto the pistons using fingers only, and ensure that they are fitted the correct way round.*

c) *When refitting the secondary piston assembly, push the piston down the bore using a soft metal rod and insert the stop pin. The primary piston and remaining components can then be fitted.*

Refitting

18 Refitting is the reverse sequence to removal. On completion, bleed the complete hydraulic system as described in Section 2.

16 Tandem master cylinder (type 3) – removal, overhaul and refitting

Removal, refitting and overhaul of the type 3 master cylinder is essentially the same as for the type 2 unit and reference should be made to the procedures contained in Section 15. Bear in mind also the differences between the two types outlined in Section 13.

17 Tandem master cylinder (type 4) – removal, overhaul and refitting

Note: *Before starting work, refer to the warning at the beginning of Section 2 concerning the dangers of hydraulic fluid.*

Removal

1 If necessary, for improved access to the front and rear bleed screws, firmly apply the handbrake, then jack up the front of the car and support it securely on axle stands (see *Jacking and vehicle support*).

2 Connect a bleed tube to both the front caliper and rear wheel cylinder bleed screws on the right-hand side, and place the ends of the tubes in suitable containers.

3 Open both bleed screws and depress the brake pedal until the master cylinder is completely empty, then tighten the screws.

4 Disconnect the low fluid level warning light wiring from the fluid reservoir filler cap.

5 Place a cloth around the master cylinder to catch any spilled fluid then unscrew the hydraulic pipe unions from the master cylinder and carefully pull the pipes clear. Plug or tape over the disconnected unions to prevent dirt entry.

6 Unscrew the mounting nuts securing the master cylinder to the vacuum servo unit, then withdraw it from the engine compartment, taking care not to spill any brake fluid on the bodywork.

7 Remove the O-ring from the recess in the master cylinder.

Overhaul

Note: *Check the availability of parts before dismantling the master cylinder. On older models, master cylinder repair kits may not be readily available and it may be necessary to obtain a complete master cylinder assembly.*

8 Remove the filler cap from the master cylinder, and drain and discard the hydraulic fluid from the reservoir.

9 Mount the cylinder in a vice with protected jaws, so that the reservoir is uppermost.

10 Tap out the retaining roll pin and lift the reservoir off the master cylinder body **(see illustration)**. Carefully withdraw the two reservoir sealing washers from the outlets followed by the metal seating washers.

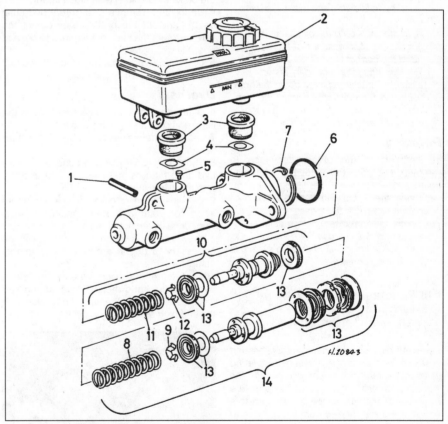

17.10 Exploded view of the type 4 tandem master cylinder

1 Roll pin	6 O-ring	11 Secondary spring
2 Brake fluid reservoir	7 Circlip	12 Spring retainer
3 Sealing washers	8 Primary spring	13 Seal and
4 Metal seating washers	9 Spring retainer	washer
5 Secondary piston stop pin	10 Secondary piston components	14 Primary piston components

11 Push in the primary piston and, using pliers, extract the secondary piston stop pin from its recess.

12 Extract the retaining circlip from the end of the master cylinder bore.

13 Remove the master cylinder from the vice, tap it on a block of wood and withdraw the primary and secondary piston assemblies from the cylinder bore.

14 Note the position and direction of fitting of the rubber seals on the piston assemblies, then carefully remove them.

15 Wash all the parts in clean hydraulic fluid or methylated spirit and dry with a lint-free cloth.

16 Examine the bore of the master cylinder carefully for any signs of scores or ridges. If this is found to be smooth all over, new seals can be fitted. If, however, there is any doubt about the condition of the bore, then a new cylinder must be obtained and fitted. *Never re-use old seals*, as they will have deteriorated with age even though this may not be evident during visual inspection.

17 Reassembly of the master cylinder is the reverse sequence to removal, but the following additional points should be noted:

a) *Thoroughly lubricate all components in clean hydraulic fluid and assemble them wet.*

b) *Refit the seals onto the pistons using fingers only, and ensure that they are fitted the correct way round.*

c) *When refitting the secondary piston assembly, push the piston down the bore using a soft metal rod and insert the stop pin. The primary piston and remaining components can then be fitted.*

Refitting

18 Refitting is the revere sequence to removal, but note the following additional points:

a) *Smear the O-ring with clean brake fluid before fitting it in the recess.*

b) *On completion, bleed the hydraulic system as described in Section 2.*

c) *Check that the low fluid warning system is functioning correctly.*

18 Pressure regulating valve (single circuit system) – removal, overhaul and refitting

Note: *All models with single circuit braking systems incorporate a pressure regulating valve in the rear brake hydraulic circuit. The valve regulates the hydraulic pressure available at the rear wheels, and therefore prevents the rear brakes from locking due to forward weight transfer under heavy braking. Before starting work, refer to the warning at the beginning of Section 2 concerning the dangers of hydraulic fluid.*

Removal

1 Chock the front wheels then jack up the rear of the car and support it securely on axle

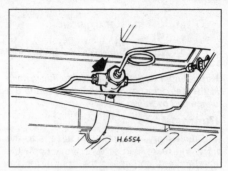

18.3 Location of pressure regulating valve on rear subframe

stands (see *Jacking and vehicle support*). Remove the rear roadwheels.

2 Remove the brake master cylinder filler cap, top-up the reservoir, place a thin piece of polythene over the filler neck and refit the cap. This will reduce hydraulic fluid loss when the rear brake pipes are removed from the regulating valve.

3 Thoroughly clean the exterior of the valve, located on the rear subframe, ensuring that all dirt and grit is removed from the area around the brake pipe unions **(see illustration)**.

4 Undo and remove the three hydraulic unions and lift the brake pipes out of the valve. Protect the ends of the pipes to prevent possible dirt ingress.

5 Undo and remove the retaining nut and bolt and lift the valve off its mounting.

Overhaul

6 Clamp the valve in a vice and remove the large end plug and sealing washer.

7 Lift out the valve assembly and return spring.

8 Thoroughly clean the components in clean hydraulic fluid or methylated spirit and dry with a lint-free cloth.

9 Examine the valve, cylinder bore and rubber seals for wear and renew as necessary. Rubber seals are not supplied separately, and if they appear swollen or worn it will be necessary to obtain a new valve assembly complete with seals.

10 Lubricate the components in clean hydraulic fluid and then refit the spring and valve assembly into the valve body. Now refit the end plug and sealing washer.

19.6 Pressure reducing valve hydraulic pipe unions

Refitting

11 Refitting the valve is the reverse sequence to removal. Bleed the hydraulic system as described in Section 2 on completion. If hydraulic fluid loss has been kept to a minimum it should only be necessary to bleed the rear brakes.

19 Pressure reducing valve (dual circuit system) – removal and refitting

Note: *On certain models fitted with dual circuit braking systems a pressure reducing valve is used to limit the braking force at the rear wheels. The operation of the valve is similar to the pressure regulating valve used on single circuit systems. Before starting work, refer to the warning at the beginning of Section 2 concerning the dangers of hydraulic fluid.*

Removal

Pre-October 1996 models

1 On fuel injection engines, disconnect the battery negative terminal (refer to *Disconnecting the battery* in the Reference Chapter), then undo the two bolts securing the engine management ECU mounting bracket to the right-hand wing valance. Move the ECU and mounting bracket to one side.

October 1996 models onward

2 Disconnect the battery negative terminal (refer to *Disconnecting the battery* in the Reference Chapter), then remove the engine management ECU as described in Chapter 4C, Section 12.

3 Withdraw the fusebox from the engine management ECU mounting bracket and position it to one side.

4 Release the clip securing the wiring harness to the ECU mounting bracket. Undo the mounting bracket retaining bolt and remove the bracket.

All models

5 Remove the brake master cylinder filler cap, top-up the reservoir, and place a thin piece of polythene over the filler neck. Secure the polythene with an elastic band or by refitting the cap. This will reduce hydraulic fluid loss when the brake pipes are disconnected from the valve.

6 Unscrew the four pipe unions from the reducing valve and carefully lift out the pipes. Protect the disconnected unions to prevent possible dirt ingress **(see illustration)**.

7 Undo and remove the retaining bolt and lift off the valve.

8 The pressure reducing valve is a sealed unit and cannot be dismantled. If the valve is faulty it must be renewed as a complete assembly.

Refitting

9 Refitting is the reverse sequence to removal. Bleed the hydraulic system as described in Section 2 on completion.

20 Pressure differential warning actuator (dual circuit system) – removal, overhaul and refitting

Note: *On early type dual circuit braking systems, a separate pressure differential warning actuator, located on the engine compartment bulkhead, informs the driver of failure of one of the braking hydraulic circuits. On later systems so equipped, the warning actuator is incorporated in the master cylinder. Before starting work, refer to the warning at the beginning of Section 2 concerning the dangers of hydraulic fluid.*

Removal

1 Unscrew the brake master cylinder filler cap, place a piece of polythene over the filler neck and refit the cap. This will reduce hydraulic fluid loss when the brake pipes are disconnected.
2 Detach the electrical connector from the switch on the side of the warning actuator body.
3 Unscrew the hydraulic pipe unions and carefully remove the pipes. Protect the disconnected unions from possible dirt ingress.
4 Undo and remove the retaining bolt and lift off the unit.

Overhaul

Note: *Check the availability of parts before dismantling the actuator. On older models, repair kits may not be readily available and it may be necessary to obtain a complete actuator assembly.*

5 Clean off the exterior of the unit and make sure it is free from dirt and grit.
6 Undo and remove the end plug and discard the copper washer **(see illustration)**.
7 Unscrew the warning light switch.
8 Tap the warning actuator body on a block of wood to release the shuttle valve piston assembly and withdraw it from the bore.
9 Remove the two rubber seals from the piston.
10 Wash the components in clean hydraulic fluid or methylated spirit and dry with a lint-free cloth.
11 Carefully inspect the piston and the casing bore for scoring and damage. If the bore and piston are not in perfect condition, renew the complete pressure differential warning actuator. If the components are in a satisfactory condition obtain new seals and a new copper sealing washer. *Do not re-use the old seals.*
12 Reassembly of the unit is the reverse of the dismantling sequence. Lubricate all the parts with clean hydraulic fluid and assemble them wet. Observe the specified torque wrench settings when refitting the end plug and warning failure switch.

Refitting

13 Refitting is the reverse sequence to

removal. Bleed the hydraulic system as described in Section 2 after refitting.
14 After bleeding the braking system, switch on the ignition and observe the brake failure warning light. If the light is illuminated, press the brake pedal hard: the light should go out and stay out when the pedal is released. If the light fails to go out, the pressure in the braking system is unbalanced or there is a fault in the warning actuator or its switch. Bleed the braking system again, and if this fails to cure the trouble, investigate the warning actuator and the switch.
15 If the brake failure warning light is not illuminated when the brake pedal is depressed, but does come on when the test-push on the switch is operated, then the system is functioning satisfactorily.

21 Vacuum servo unit – removal and refitting

Pre-1989 models

Removal

1 Unscrew the brake master cylinder filler cap, place a piece of polythene over the filler neck and refit the cap. This will minimise hydraulic fluid loss when the servo is removed.
2 From under the right-hand front wing detach the inlet ducting from the inlet unit and then withdraw the inlet unit from inside the engine compartment.
3 Disconnect the vacuum pipe from the one-way valve on the servo unit.

4 Remove the securing bracket from the end of the servo unit.
5 Unscrew the hydraulic pipe unions and carefully withdraw them from the servo. Protect the disconnected unions against possible dirt ingress.
6 Undo and remove the nuts securing the servo to its mounting bracket and lift away the unit.

Refitting

7 Refitting is the reverse sequence to removal. Bleed the hydraulic system as described in Section 2 on completion.

1989 models onward

Removal

8 On fuel injection engines, slide the engine management relay module out of its retaining bracket, and position it to one side.
9 Disconnect the low brake fluid level warning light wiring from the master cylinder fluid reservoir filler cap.
10 Unscrew the master cylinder mounting nuts from the servo unit.
11 Position a container beneath the master cylinder, then loosen (but do not remove) the hydraulic pipe union nuts, to prevent damage to the pipes when the master cylinder is moved from the servo unit. Move the master cylinder clear of the servo unit, then retighten the union nuts.
12 Disconnect the vacuum hose from the servo unit and release it from the clip.
13 Extract the split pin, and withdraw the clevis pin securing the pushrod to the brake pedal.

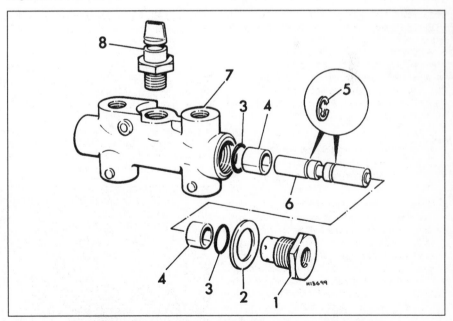

20.6 Exploded view of the pressure differential warning actuator

1 End adapter	4 Sleeve	7 Body
2 Copper washer	5 Circlip	8 Switch
3 O-ring	6 Piston	

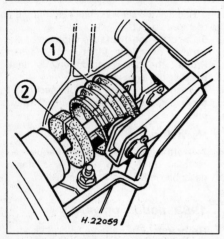

22.1 Vacuum servo unit air filter

1 Rubber boot   *2 Air filter*

14 Where fitted, disconnect the anti-run-on valve hoses, and plug them.

15 Unscrew the bolt securing the anti-run-on valve to the servo mounting bracket.

16 Unscrew the mounting nuts and bolts, and withdraw the servo unit and bracket assembly from the engine compartment.

17 Separate the servo unit from the bracket by disconnecting the clevis and unscrewing the nuts. Prise the O-ring from the recess in the master cylinder.

18 Refitting is the reverse sequence to removal. Smear the O-ring with clean brake hydraulic fluid and bleed the hydraulic system as described in Section 2 on completion.

22 Vacuum servo unit air filter (1989 models onward) – renewal

1 Working in the engine compartment, prise back the rubber boot from the rear of the servo, and slide it along the pushrod **(see illustration)**.

2 Prise the air filter from inside the servo body.

3 Cut the new air filter in one place with a sharp knife, then locate it over the pushrod and push it into the servo body.

4 Refit the rubber boot.

23 Brake pedal – removal and refitting

The brake pedal is removed together with the clutch pedal, and full information on the removal and refitting procedure will be found in Chapter 6.

Chapter 10
Suspension and steering

Contents

Front hub bearings – renewal 4
Front lower suspension arm – removal and refitting 6
Front shock absorber (models with rubber cone suspension) – removal
  and refitting 11
Front subframe mountings – renewal 12
Front suspension Hydrolastic displacer unit – removal and refitting . 10
Front suspension rubber cone spring – removal and refitting 9
Front suspension tie-bar – removal and refitting 7
Front swivel hub – removal and refitting 3
Front swivel hub balljoints – removal and refitting 5
Front upper suspension arm – removal and refitting 8
General information 1
Hydrolastic suspension system – principles of operation 2
Rack-and-pinion steering gear – lubrication 29
Rack-and-pinion steering gear – removal and refitting 27
Rack-and-pinion steering gear overhaul – general information 28
Rear helper spring (models with Hydrolastic suspension) – removal
  and refitting 17
Rear hub bearings – renewal 13

Rear Hydrolastic displacer unit – removal and refitting 15
Rear radius arm – removal and refitting 18
Rear rubber cone spring – removal and refitting 14
Rear shock absorber (models with rubber cone suspension) – removal
  and refitting 16
Rear subframe – removal and refitting 20
Rear subframe mountings – renewal 19
Steering and suspension check ....See Chapter 1
Steering and suspension lubrication ....See Chapter 1
Steering column – dismantling and reassembly 24
Steering column (October 1996 models onward) – removal and
  refitting 23
Steering column (pre-October 1996 models) – removal and refitting 22
Steering rack rubber gaiter – removal and refitting 26
Steering tie-rod outer balljoint – removal and refitting 25
Steering wheel – removal and refitting 21
Tyre condition and pressure checks ....See *Weekly Checks*
Wheel alignment and steering angles – general information 30

Degrees of difficulty

Easy, suitable for novice with little experience	**Fairly easy,** suitable for beginner with some experience	**Fairly difficult,** suitable for competent DIY mechanic	**Difficult,** suitable for experienced DIY mechanic	**Very difficult,** suitable for expert DIY or professional

Specifications

Front suspension

Type:
Rubber cone suspension .... Independent by rubber cone springs and unequal length upper and
  lower suspension arms
Hydrolastic suspension .... Independent by interconnected Hydrolastic displacers and unequal
  length upper and lower suspension arms

Rear suspension

Type:
Rubber cone suspension .... Independent by rubber cone springs and trailing radius arms
Hydrolastic suspension .... Independent by interconnected Hydrolastic displacers, trailing radius
  arms and coil hold-down springs

Steering

Type .... Rack-and-pinion
Turns lock-to-lock 2.7
Lubricant capacity (see text):
Early models .... 0.2 litre
Later models .... 0.1 litre
Lubricant type (see text):
Early models .... Gear oil, viscosity SAE 90EP
Later models .... Sterak semi fluid grease, specification 31.815.252 in accordance with
  specification 31.820.194

Wheel alignment and steering angles

Front wheel*:
Toe setting	1.58 mm toe-out
Castor angle	3° ± 1° positive
Camber angle	2° ± 1° positive
Swivel hub inclination	9° 30'
Trim height (models with Hydrolastic suspension)	343.0 mm ± 9.5 mm

Rear wheel*:
Toe setting	3.17 mm toe-in
Camber angle	0.5° to 2.5° positive

Note: *Information applicable to pre-October 1996 models only. At time of writing, information on later models was unavailable.*

Tyres

Tyre size	5.20 x 10, 145 SR x 10, 145/70 SR x 12, 165/70 HR x 10, 165/60 R x 12, 175/50 VR x 13, according to model
Tyre pressures	See *Weekly Checks*

Torque wrench settings

	Nm	lbf ft
Front suspension		
Driveshaft retaining nut:		
Disc brake models:		
With multiple split pin holes in driveshaft	207	153
With single split pin hole in driveshaft	255 to 270	188 to 199
Drum brake models	83	61
Lower suspension arm pivot bolt nut	45	33
Swivel hub balljoint domed nut	102	75
Swivel hub balljoint to suspension arm	54	40
Tie-bar to subframe	30	22
Tie-bar to suspension arm	26	19
Upper suspension arm pivot shaft nut	72	53
Rear suspension		
Radius arm pivot shaft nut	72	53
Rear hub retaining nut	81	60
Steering		
Steering column lower clamp pinch-bolt	16	12
Steering column upper clamp:		
Pre-October 1996 models	19	14
October 1996 models onward	25	18
Steering rack tie-rod ball housing collar	52	38
Steering rack U-bolts	15	11
Steering wheel nut	47	35
Tie-rod balljoint nut	30	22
Roadwheels		
Roadwheel nuts	60	44

1 General information

The front and rear suspension assemblies and associated components are mounted on subframes which are bolted to the underside of the bodyshell. The subframes are of welded all-steel construction, the front subframe also providing mounting points for the engine/transmission assembly.

The front suspension on all Mini models is of the independent type, each side consisting of an upper and lower suspension arm. The lower arm is supported in rubber bushes at its inner end, while the inner end of the upper arm pivots on two caged needle roller bearings.

The outer ends of the two suspension arms are bolted to the tapered shanks of the swivel hub balljoints. Fore-and-aft movement of each front suspension assembly is controlled by a tie-bar bolted at one end to the lower suspension arm and mounted at the other end, via rubber bushes, to the subframe. The swivel hubs contain tapered roller or ball bearings which support the outer ends of the driveshafts, and also provide mounting points for the drum brake backplate or disc brake calipers. Suspension and steering movement of the swivel hubs is catered for by adjustable balljoints.

The rear suspension on all models is also independent by means of two trailing radius arms. The forward end of each radius arm contains a needle roller bearing and bronze bush, which allows the arm to pivot on a shaft bolted to the subframe. The brake backplate is bolted to the rear end of each radius arm, as is the stub axle which carries the rear wheel hub and bearings.

While all Mini models share the same suspension component layout, two different types of springing and damping have been employed. All models are now equipped with dry suspension, whereby a rubber cone spring and telescopic shock absorber are fitted to the suspension assembly at each wheel. Early Clubman and 1275GT models were equipped with Hydrolastic suspension, whereby a displacer unit which combines the actions of both spring and shock absorber is fitted to each suspension assembly, in place of the rubber cone. The displacer units are interconnected front-to-rear on each side of the vehicle and are filled with a water-based, non-corrosive fluid under pressure. The principles of operation of the Hydrolastic suspension system are described in detail in Section 2.

The steering gear is of the conventional rack-and-pinion type with tie-rods connected to the swivel hub steering arms by tie-rod outer balljoints. Further balljoints on the inner ends of the tie-rods are screwed into the rack. The upper splined end of the helically-toothed pinion protrudes from the rack housing and engages with the splined end of the steering column. The pinion spline is grooved and the steering column is held to the pinion by a clamp bolt which partially rests in the pinion groove.

2 Hydrolastic suspension system – principles of operation

Component layout

The Hydrolastic suspension system consists of a Hydrolastic unit (known as a displacer) fitted to the suspension assembly at each wheel, and two metal pipes which interconnect the displacer units on each side of the vehicle, front to rear. The system is filled with a water-based, non-corrosive antifreeze fluid under pressure.

Each displacer consists of a rubber spring fitted to the upper part of the unit. This rubber spring is the actual springing and damping medium, and is shaped in such a way as to give a progressive rate characteristic similar to the rubber cone spring fitted to non-Hydrolastic Minis. At the lower end of the displacer unit a tapered piston, attached to a diaphragm, operates within a tapered cylinder. The diaphragm seals off the lower part of the displacer and the piston is coupled to the suspension assembly. Internally the displacer unit is divided into an upper and lower chamber by a separator plate, which also contains the damper valves and a bleed hole.

Operation

Movement of the vehicle suspension actuates the displacer piston, causing fluid to be displaced through the separator plate and into the upper chamber either via the bleed hole, if suspension movement is small, or through the damper valve if the movement is more vigorous. This causes the upper chamber to deflect upwards against the resistance of the rubber spring, thus damping the suspension movement. In addition to this, fluid in the upper chamber will be displaced via the transfer pipe to the displacer unit connected to the other suspension assembly, on the same side of the car. This will cause the piston in this displacer to move downwards and act on the suspension,

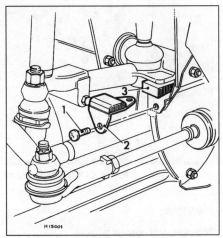

3.1 Fitting a solid packing wedge in place of the suspension rebound rubber

1 Screw
2 Rebound rubber
3 Solid packing piece

ensuring that the vehicle remains in a level attitude. In the event of both suspension assemblies on the same side of the car deflecting together (ie, body roll when cornering), no fluid movement between the two displacers will occur and the entire fluid pressure will be applied simultaneously to both displacer pistons giving a very high resistance to the rolling movement.

As the relative front end weight of the Mini is high, the normal ride attitude of the car would be tail high, as the partially deflected front suspension would transfer fluid to the rear suspension, causing it to rise. To overcome this, non-adjustable coil hold-down springs are fitted between the chassis and each rear suspension arm. Thus, fluid is transferred from rear to front and a near level attitude is maintained.

Servicing

The Hydrolastic system is completely sealed, and therefore virtually maintenance-free. It is advisable, however, at periodic intervals, to inspect the external condition of the displacer units, hoses and pipe unions. Any seepage of fluid from the union between displacer hose and transfer pipe, or from any other part of the system, will cause the vehicle

3.5 Remove the steering tie-rod balljoint with a universal separator

suspension to sag on the affected side.

It will be necessary when working on certain suspension components to remove or disconnect the displacer units or transfer pipes. Before doing this, the system must be depressurised by a Rover dealer who will have the equipment required to remove the fluid and evacuate the system. The vehicle can be driven for short distances at slow speeds (ie, below 30 mph/48 kph) in a depressurised condition, providing it is driven carefully. On completion of the work the system must be repressurised, again by a dealer.

The pressure in the system determines the trim height of the vehicle and this should also be checked periodically to ensure that it has not altered appreciably. The trim height is measured from the centre of the front wheel hub to the top of the wheelarch. It is important to ensure that the correct height is maintained otherwise the steering geometry may be affected, resulting in uneven tyre wear and insensitive handling.

3 Front swivel hub – removal and refitting

Removal

1 Working under the wheelarch, undo and remove the single retaining screw and lift out the upper suspension arm rebound rubber. Position a solid packing piece of approximately the same thickness in its place **(see illustration)**.

2 Firmly apply the handbrake, then jack up the front of the car and support it securely on axle stands (see *Jacking and vehicle support*). Remove the relevant front roadwheel.

3 Extract the split pin from the driveshaft retaining nut and, with an assistant firmly depressing the brake pedal, undo and remove the driveshaft nut using a socket and extension bar. Remove the washer or split-collar, as applicable, located behind the driveshaft nut. Note that on disc brake models, the driveshaft retaining nut is extremely tight and it may be beneficial to fabricate a home-made tool to prevent the hub rotating when undoing the nut (see Chapter 8).

4 On disc brake models, undo and remove the brake caliper retaining bolts. Lift off the caliper complete with brake pads, and tie it out of the way from a convenient place under the wheelarch. On models fitted with drum brakes, clamp the flexible brake hose with a proprietary brake hose clamp or a self-gripping wrench with its jaws suitably protected. Now slacken the brake hose union at the wheel cylinder by half a turn.

5 Undo and remove the steering tie-rod balljoint retaining locknut and then release the balljoint tapered shank from the steering arm using a universal balljoint separator **(see illustration and Tool Tip)**.

An alternative method of releasing the balljoint tapered shank is to refit the locknut to the balljoint and screw it on two or three turns. Using a medium hammer, sharply strike the end of the steering arm until the shock separates the taper. Now remove the locknut and lift the joint off the arm.

6 Undo and remove the nuts and spring washers securing the swivel hub balljoints to the upper and lower suspension arms **(see illustration)**.

7 Using the method described in paragraph 5, separate the upper and lower suspension arms from the tapered shanks of the balljoints.

8 Carefully lift the swivel hub assembly off the two suspension arms. At the same time, tap the centre of the driveshaft, using a soft-faced mallet, until the driveshaft can be withdrawn from the rear of the swivel hub assembly.

9 On disc brake models, withdraw the swivel hub assembly and then lift off the driving flange and disc. On models with drum brakes, support the flexible brake hose to avoid stretching it and then rotate the complete swivel hub assembly anti-clockwise to unscrew it from the hose **(see illustration)**. The hub can now be lifted away and the end of the brake hose protected to prevent dirt ingress. Collect the copper sealing washer from the end of the hose as the hose is removed. Note that a new washer will be required for refitting.

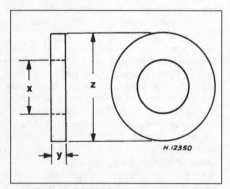

3.12 Details of special washer required for fitting the driveshaft on disc brake models

X = 25 mm   Y = 6.5 mm   Z = 50 mm

3.6 Remove the lower swivel hub balljoint retaining nut

Refitting

Models with drum brakes

10 Refitting is the reverse sequence to removal, bearing in mind the following points:

a) *Ensure that the hub bearing water shield is in place on the driveshaft CV joint and positioned approximately 6 mm from the shoulder of the joint.*

b) *Use a new copper washer on the flexible brake hose and ensure that the hose is not twisted when refitting the swivel hub. Bleed the hydraulic system at the appropriate wheel on completion (see Chapter 9).*

c) *Tighten all nuts and bolts to the specified torque.*

d) *Tighten the driveshaft retaining nut to the specified torque, then tighten the nut further to align the split pin holes in the driveshaft and nut. Secure the nut with a new split pin.*

Models with disc brakes

11 Refitting is the reverse sequence to removal, bearing in mind points a and c detailed in paragraph 10. Additionally, the following procedure must be observed, otherwise it is possible that the split-collar fitted beneath the driveshaft retaining nut will become clamped to the shaft before the shaft is fully home in the hub bearings.

12 Insert the driveshaft through the swivel hub, but do not fit the split collar. Obtain a plain washer of the dimensions shown **(see illustration)**. If necessary, make the washer from mild steel.

13 Fit the plain washer over the driveshaft end. Fit the driveshaft retaining nut and, using the same procedure as for removal to prevent the hub rotating, tighten the nut to the specified torque to seat the shaft in the hub bearings. Note that there are two different torque settings for the driveshaft nut; one for driveshafts with multiple split pin holes, and a higher setting for driveshafts with a single split pin hole. Now remove the nut and washer and smear engine oil over the driveshaft threads.

14 Examine the split-collar, and renew it if damaged or worn. Fit the collar and driveshaft retaining nut, and once again tighten it to the specified torque. Tighten the nut further to align the split pin holes in the driveshaft and nut, then secure the nut with a new split pin.

3.9 Withdraw the swivel hub from the end of the driveshaft

4 Front hub bearings – renewal

Drum brake models

1 Remove the swivel hub assembly as described in Section 3.

2 With the assembly on the bench, slacken the brake adjusters, remove the two brake drum retaining screws and lift off the drum. If it is tight, tap it gently using a soft-faced mallet.

3 Arrange two wooden blocks approximately 250 mm high on the bench, far enough apart for the drive flange to lie freely between them, with the brake shoes resting on the top of the blocks. Using a tube or drift of suitable diameter, tap the drive flange out of the hub. It is likely that the inner race of the outer bearing together with the oil seal and the outer bearing distance piece will come away with the flange **(see illustration opposite)**. If this happens, carefully remove these items from the flange with the aid of a puller.

4 Undo and remove the four bolts securing the brake backplate to the swivel hub and lift off the backplate with brake shoes still in position.

5 Clean away any surplus grease from the centre of the hub between the bearings, and then prise out the two oil seals using a screwdriver. Note that there is a spacer fitted between the rear oil seal and the bearing outer race.

6 Using a tube or drift of suitable diameter tap out the bearing inner races away from the centre of the hub. Take care not to lose the balls which will be dislodged as the inner races are released, and recover the spacer (if fitted) between the two bearings.

7 Firmly support the swivel hub in a vice and drift out the two bearing outer races from each side of the hub.

8 Clean the bearings and swivel hub thoroughly using paraffin or a suitable solvent and dry with a lint-free rag. Remove any burrs or score marks from the hub bore with a fine file or scraper.

9 Examine carefully the bearing inner and outer races, the balls and ball cage for pitting, scoring or cracks, and if at all suspect renew the bearings. It will also be necessary to renew the oil seals as they will have been damaged during removal.

10 If the old bearings are in a satisfactory condition and are to be re-used, reassemble the balls to the ball cage, place it in the outer race and then press the inner race into position.

11 Before refitting the bearings to the hub, pack them thoroughly with a high melting-point grease. Do not fill the space between the bearings in the swivel hub with grease.

12 Place one of the bearings in position on the hub with the word THRUST or the markings stamped on the outer race facing toward the centre of the hub. **Note:** *Certain*

later models are fitted with bearings having lengthened inner races which butt against each other. On these assemblies the bearing spacer is omitted and the bearings are fitted with the identification markings facing away from the centre of the hub. Using a tube of suitable diameter or a drift, press the outer race into the hub between the vice jaws or very carefully tap it into position. Ensure that the outer race does not tip slightly and bind as it is being fitted. If this happens, the outer race will crack so take great care to keep it square. Ensure that the bearing seats firmly against the shoulder in the centre of the hub when fitted.

13 Now place the bearing spacer in position and repeat the previous paragraph for the

second bearing. **Note:** *Some makes of bearing have lengthened inner races which butt against each other. In this case the bearing spacer is no longer needed.*

14 Tap a new oil seal into place over the outer bearing using a block of wood to keep it square. Note that both oil seals are fitted with their sealing lips inwards and that the inner seal has a second lip on its inner circumference.

15 Refit the split spacer against the inner bearing and tap in the inner oil seal using a tube of suitable diameter.

16 Refit the brake backplate to the swivel hub and secure with the four retaining bolts, tightened securely.

17 Place the distance piece over the driving

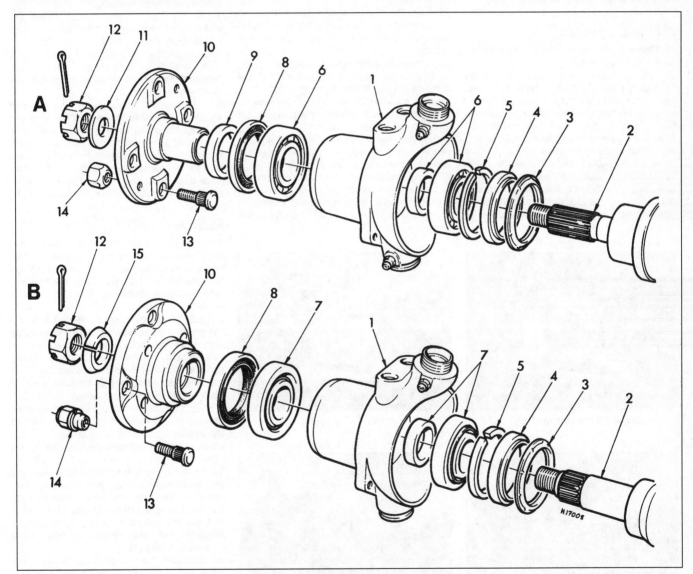

4.3 Exploded view of the front hub components

A Drum brake models	2 Driveshaft	6 Ball bearing and spacer set	8 Outer oil seal	12 Castellated hub nut
	3 Water shield		9 Distance ring	13 Wheel stud
B Disc brake models	4 Inner oil seal	7 Taper roller bearing and spacer set	10 Driving flange	14 Wheel nut
1 Swivel hub	5 Oil seal spacer		11 Thrustwasher	15 Thrust washer

flange with the chamfer towards the flange. With the inner race of the inner bearing suitably supported, tap the driving flange into the bearings. Ensure that the flange enters the distance piece between the two bearings squarely, otherwise the bearing inner race will be dislodged with possible damage to the oil seal.

18 The brake drum and its retaining screws can now be refitted and the complete swivel hub assembly refitted to the car as described in the Section 3. When refitting the hub assembly, ensure that the water shield on the driveshaft is packed with grease around its sealing face and positioned approximately 6.00 mm from the end of the shaft. Adjust the brakes as described in Chapter 1 before lowering the car to the ground.

Disc brake models

19 Remove the swivel hub assembly as described in Section 3.

20 With the assembly on the bench, lift off the tapered collar (fitted to certain models) from the front of the outer bearing and then prise out the two oil seals using a screwdriver. Now lift out the inner bearing spacer, the two taper roller bearings and the distance piece.

21 Using a suitable drift, tap out the two bearing outer races from each side of the hub.

22 Thoroughly clean the bearings and swivel hub using paraffin or a suitable solvent and dry with a lint-free rag. Remove any burrs or score marks from the hub bore with a fine file or scraper.

23 Carefully examine the bearing outer races, the rollers and roller cages for pitting, scoring, or cracks, and if at all suspect renew the bearings. It will also be necessary to renew the oil seals as they will have been damaged during removal.

24 Begin reassembly by refitting the bearing outer races to the hub, with their smaller diameter toward the hub centre. Press the outer races into the hub using a tube of suitable diameter and a vice, or very carefully tap them into place using a brass drift. Ensure that the race does not tip slightly and bind as it is being installed. If this happens, the outer race will crack so take great care to keep it square. The outer race must seat firmly against the shoulder in the centre of the hub when fitted.

25 Pack the two roller bearings with a high melting-point grease and position them in their outer races with the distance piece in between.

26 Install the two new oil seals with their sealing lips inwards and use a tube of suitable diameter to tap them fully home. Note that there is a spacer fitted behind the inner oil seal and that the inner seal also has a second lip on its inner circumference.

27 Position the tapered collar over the outer bearing (where fitted), and refit the swivel hub assembly to the car as described in Section 3. When refitting the swivel hub, ensure that the water shield on the driveshaft is packed with grease around its sealing face and positioned approximately 6.00 mm from the end of the shaft.

5 Front swivel hub balljoints – removal and refitting

Removal

1 Remove the swivel hub assembly as described in Section 3 and mount it firmly in a vice, with the balljoint requiring attention uppermost.

2 Remove the rubber dust cover, tap back the lockwasher, and using a large socket or box spanner, undo and remove the domed retaining nut.

3 Lift off the ball-pin, ball-pin seat, and if working on the lower balljoint assembly, the ball-pin seat tension spring.

4 Lift off the shims located over the lockwasher, then remove the grease nipple and lift away the lockwasher.

5 Clean all the components thoroughly and then carefully inspect the ball-pin, ball-pin seat and domed nut for pitting, score marks or corrosion.

6 If the components are worn, a balljoint repair kit, consisting of new ball-pin, ball-pin seat, spring, shims, lockwasher and retaining nut should be obtained from your dealer. If the old parts are in a satisfactory condition they may be re-used and any slackness that may have been previously felt in the joint can be taken up by adjustment of the shim sizes.

Refitting

7 Before final reassembly of the balljoint, it is necessary to determine the correct number and size of shims required to provide a snug fit of the ball-pin with the domed retaining nut fully tightened. This is done in the following way.

8 Place the lockwasher in position and refit the grease nipple. Now place all the available shims over the lockwasher and then refit the ball-pin seat, the ball-pin and domed retaining nut. Assemble all the parts without grease at this stage, and if working on the lower balljoint *do not* fit the ball-pin seat tension spring.

9 Fully tighten the retaining nut and then check the movement of the ball-pin. With all the available shims fitted, it should be quite slack with considerable up-and-down movement.

10 Using a trial-and-error process, remove the retaining nut, take out a shim and then refit the nut and recheck the movement of the ball-pin. Continue doing this until it is possible to move the ball-pin in all directions, without binding, but with slight resistance to movement being felt.

11 Dismantle the joint again, lubricate all the parts with general purpose grease and finally reassemble the joint. If working on the lower assembly, the ball-pin seat tension spring should now be fitted (see illustrations).

12 Tighten the retaining nut fully, check that the ball-pin still moves freely with only slight

5.11a Fit the lockwasher . . .

5.11b . . . spring . . .

5.11c . . . ball-pin seat . . .

5.11d . . . and shims

5.12a Refit the ball-pin and nut . . .

5.12b . . . screw in the grease nipple . . .

5.12c . . . and fully tighten the nut

resistance, and if satisfactory bend up the lockwasher to secure the retaining nut (**see illustrations**).

13 Refit the rubber dust cover to the balljoint (**see illustration**) and then refit the swivel hub as described in Section 3.

6 Front lower suspension arm – removal and refitting

Removal

1 Working under the wheelarch, undo and remove the single retaining screw and lift out the upper suspension arm rebound rubber. Position a solid packing piece of approximately the same thickness in its place (**see illustration 3.1**).

2 Firmly apply the handbrake, then jack up the front of the car and support it securely on axle stands (see *Jacking and vehicle support*). Remove the relevant front roadwheel.

3 Undo and remove the nut and washer securing the swivel hub balljoint to the lower suspension arm. Release the taper of the balljoint shank using a universal balljoint separator, or the alternative method described in Section 3, paragraph 5.

4 Move the lower suspension arm downwards to disengage the balljoint shank.

5 Undo and remove the nut and bolt securing the tie-bar to the suspension arm and then move the tie-bar sideways out of the way.

6 Undo and remove the nut and washer from the rear of the pivot bolt securing the lower suspension arm to the subframe (**see illustration**).

7 Lever the pivot bolt forward and off the subframe, then lift out the lower suspension arm.

8 Lift the rubber bushes off the suspension arm and inspect them carefully for swelling, cracks or deterioration of the rubber. Also inspect the pivot bolt for wear or damage. Renew any worn components.

Refitting

9 Refitting is the reverse sequence to removal, bearing in mind the following points:

5.12d Bend up the lockwasher . . .

5.13 . . . and fit the dust cover

a) Ensure that the flat of the pivot bolt head locates under the tab on the subframe.
b) Tighten all nuts and bolts to the specified torque.
c) Do not fully tighten the pivot bolt retaining nut until the car has been lowered to the ground.

7 Front suspension tie-bar – removal and refitting

Removal

1 Firmly apply the handbrake, then jack up the front of the car and support it securely on axle stands (see *Jacking and vehicle support*). Remove the relevant front roadwheel.

2 Undo and remove the locknut securing the front end of the tie-bar to the subframe (**see**

6.6 Lower suspension arm inner mounting

illustration). Now lift off the thrustwasher and the rubber thrust bush.

3 Undo and remove the bolt, nut and spring washer securing the other end of the tie-bar to the lower suspension arm. Disengage the tie-bar from the suspension arm and subframe, then lift it off the car. Slide the remaining rubber thrust bush off the tie-bar end.

4 Carefully inspect the tie-bar thrust bushes for swelling, compression damage or deterioration of the rubber and check the tie-bar for straightness and elongation of the mounting bolt holes. Also check the securing bolt for wear of its shank. If any of the components are defective a new tie-bar kit should be obtained from your local dealer.

Refitting

5 Refitting is the reverse sequence to removal.

7.2 Tie-bar front mounting

8.6 Subframe tower mounting bolt fitted to later models

8 Front upper suspension arm – removal and refitting

Note: *Before carrying out this operation on cars fitted with Hydrolastic suspension, it will be necessary to have the Hydrolastic system depressurised by a Rover dealer. If working on cars equipped with rubber cone suspension, Rover special tool 18G 574B will be required to compress the rubber cone.*

Removal

1 Firmly apply the handbrake, then jack up the front of the car and support it securely on axle stands (see *Jacking and vehicle support*). Remove the relevant front roadwheel.
2 Undo and remove the nut and washer securing the swivel hub balljoint to the upper suspension arm. Release the taper of the balljoint shank using a universal balljoint separator, or the alternative method described in Section 3, paragraph 5.

Models with Hydrolastic suspension

3 Undo and remove the single retaining screw and lift out the upper suspension arm rebound rubber.
4 Lift up the rubber dust cover around the knuckle joint located on the top of the upper suspension arm. Withdraw the ball-end of the

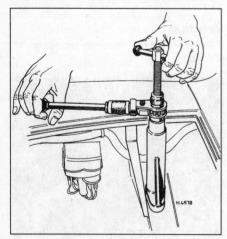

8.7 Use of special tool to compress rubber cone spring

knuckle joint from its seat in the upper arm and then prise the shank of the knuckle joint out of the displacer unit using a screwdriver. The shank of the knuckle joint is a simple push fit in the displacer unit; however, corrosion may make it initially tight to remove. Recover the spacer (where fitted) from the shank.

Models with rubber cone suspension

5 Undo and remove the nut and flat washer securing the shock absorber to the upper suspension arm. Now move the shock absorber sideways until it is clear of the mounting stud.
6 Working in the engine compartment, undo and remove the two bolts (or nuts) securing the subframe tower to the bulkhead crossmember. Lift off the locking plate and then refit the bolts (or nuts). On later models undo and remove the large hexagon-headed plug that is used instead of the two bolts or nuts **(see illustration)**.
7 It is now necessary to compress the rubber cone spring using service tool 18G 574B as follows. Position the body of the tool over the two subframe tower retaining bolts (or nuts) and turn the tool centre screw, nine complete turns, to engage the threads in the rubber cone. Now turn the ratchet handle of the tool until it contacts the tool body. Hold the centre screw and turn the ratchet handle clockwise until all tension is removed from the strut which interconnects the rubber cone and the upper suspension arm **(see illustration)**.
8 Undo and remove the single retaining screw and lift out the upper suspension arm rebound rubber.
9 Lift up the rubber dust cover around the knuckle joint located at the base of the spring strut.
10 Withdraw the ball-end of the knuckle joint from its seat in the upper arm and then lift out the spring strut assembly from the rubber cone. If it is tight, prise it out using a screwdriver **(see illustration)**.

All models

11 Undo and remove the nut and spring washer from each end of the upper arm pivot shaft.
12 Undo and remove the two nuts, bolts and spring washers securing the pivot shaft thrust collar retaining plate, thrust collar and seal and then withdraw the pivot shaft forward and out of the upper suspension arm.
13 Now take out the rear thrust collar and seal and then manipulate the upper arm out of the subframe.
14 With the upper arm removed, inspect the pivot shaft and the needle roller bearings for wear, and if necessary renew them. The needle roller bearings can be removed from the upper arm by tapping them out of each side using a long thin drift inserted through the other side. Press in new bearings using a vice, or drift them in using a tube of suitable diameter or a shouldered mandrel. Ensure that the marked ends of the bearings face outwards.
15 Also carefully inspect the ball-end of the

knuckle joint and its plastic cup seat in the upper arm. If the ball-end is corroded, worn or pitted or if the plastic cup seat is cracked or worn, renew the joint. The plastic cup seat can be removed by prising out with a screwdriver. The new knuckle joint will be supplied fully assembled and the plastic cup seat can be fitted to the arm with the joint in this condition. The rubber dust cover and ball-end will then have to be removed to allow refitment of the upper arm.

Refitting

16 Refitting is the reverse sequence to removal bearing in mind the following points:
a) *Lubricate all parts with general purpose grease during reassembly.*
b) *If the original knuckle joint is being refitted, pack the cup seat with Dextragrease Super GP (or a suitable alternative) available from Rover dealers.*
c) *Ensure that the dust cover is correctly located over the knuckle joint cup, when refitting, otherwise dirt and road grit will enter the joint.*
d) *Ensure that all nuts and bolts are tightened to the specified torque.*
e) *On models with Hydrolastic suspension, do not drive the car (except to your nearest Rover dealer) until the system has been repressurised.*

9 Front suspension rubber cone spring – removal and refitting

Removal

1 Remove the front upper suspension arm as described in Section 8.

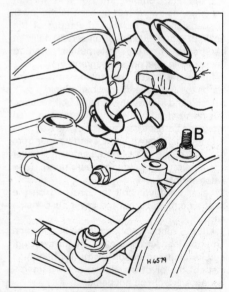

8.10 Suspension strut removal – rubber cone spring suspension

A Upper suspension arm
B Upper swivel hub balljoint

11.2a Shock absorber upper . . .

11.2b . . . and lower mounting

11.6 Remove the plastic collar from the shock absorber piston

11.7a Using a small screwdriver inserted through the top of the dust cover . . .

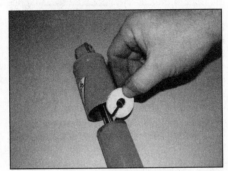

11.7b . . . release the rebound rubber and remove it from the piston

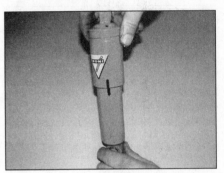

11.10 Make an alignment mark on the shock absorber body and dust cover

2 The service tool (18G 574B) used to compress the rubber cone must now be released by turning the ratchet anti-clockwise until all tension in the rubber cone is released.
3 Unscrew the service tool and withdraw the rubber cone from its location in the subframe.

Refitting

4 Refitting is the reverse sequence to removal.

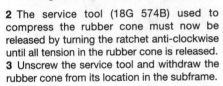

10 Front suspension Hydrolastic displacer unit – removal and refitting

Removal

1 Remove the front upper suspension arm as described in Section 8.
2 Using two large spanners, undo and remove the displacer hose from the transfer pipe union on the engine compartment bulkhead.
3 Push the displacer unit upward, undo and remove the two screws securing the displacer retaining bracket to the subframe tower.
4 Rotate the displacer anti-clockwise and withdraw it from its location on the subframe.

Refitting

5 Refitting is the reverse sequence to removal. When installing the displacer, rotate it clockwise to engage the registers on the locating plate.

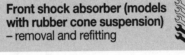

11 Front shock absorber (models with rubber cone suspension) – removal and refitting

Removal

1 Firmly apply the handbrake, then jack up the front of the car and support it securely on axle stands (see *Jacking and vehicle support*). Remove the relevant front roadwheel.
2 Undo and remove the shock absorber upper and lower retaining nut and washers and lift off the shock absorber (**see illustrations**).
3 Examine the shock absorber for leaks or damage of the outer casing. Hold the shock absorber upright and fully compress and extend it six times. Now slowly extend and compress it again. If 'dead' areas are apparent, if there is free travel when changing direction, or if the unit is damaged or leaking, it must be renewed.

Adjustment

October 1996 models onward

Note: *The following adjustment must be carried out on both shock absorbers otherwise the handling qualities of the vehicle may be impaired.*

4 On later models, the shock absorbers may be adjusted to compensate for reduced damping characteristics due to vehicle mileage.
5 With the shock absorber removed, clamp the lower eye in a vice and fully extend the piston rod.

6 Remove the plastic collar from the shock absorber piston (**see illustration**).
7 Remove the rebound rubber from the dust cover, using a small screwdriver inserted through the hole in dust cover to release it from its location (**see illustrations**).
8 Compress the shock absorber, while at the same time turning the dust cover anti-clockwise until the adjusting pins engage with the shock absorber body.
9 Keeping the shock absorber compressed, turn the dust cover anti-clockwise until it stops.
10 Using a felt-tipped pen, mark the relationship of the dust cover to the shock absorber body (**see illustration**).
11 Adjust the shock absorber by turning the dust cover one half a turn clockwise for every 48 000 miles completed (**see illustration**).
12 On completion, refit the rebound rubber and plastic collar.

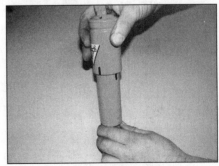

11.11 Adjust the shock absorber by turning the dust cover

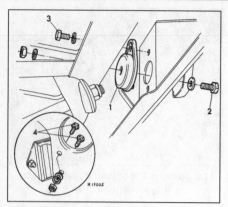

12.3 Front subframe mountings

1 *Front mounting*
2 *Mounting-to-subframe retaining bolt*
3 *Mounting-to-body retaining bolt*
4 *Rear mounting-to-subframe retaining bolts*

Refitting

13 Refitting is the reverse sequence to removal. Hold the shock absorber in an upright position and fully compress and extend it six times to expel any air before fitting.

12 Front subframe mountings – renewal

Note: *The following information is applicable to later models equipped with bonded rubber mountings between the front subframe and vehicle underbody. The mountings can be renewed with the subframe in position as follows.*

Front mountings

1 Firmly apply the handbrake, then jack up the front of the car and support it securely on axle stands (see *Jacking and vehicle support*).
2 Support the subframe with a jack on the side to be released.
3 Undo and remove the nut and bolt securing the mounting to the subframe and the nut and bolt securing the mounting to the body **(see illustration)**.
4 Undo and remove the two nuts and bolts securing the subframe to the rear mounting.
5 Lower the jack slightly, lever the subframe rearwards, and extract the front mounting.

Collect any shims that may be fitted between the mounting and the subframe.
6 Refitting is the reverse sequence to removal. With the mounting attached to the body, it is important to measure the gap between the rear of the mounting and the subframe, and then to select an appropriate number of shims of the same thickness for fitting in the gap. The shims are slotted and square in shape, and are 1.32 mm thick. They are located over the mounting bolt shanks.

Rear mounting

7 Chock the front wheels then jack up the rear of the car and support it securely on axle stands (see *Jacking and vehicle support*).
8 Support the subframe with a jack on the side to be released.
9 Undo and remove the two nuts and bolts securing the subframe to the mounting.
10 Lift up the carpets inside the car and have an assistant hold the two bolts securing the mounting to the body. Undo and remove the nuts from below and lift off the mounting.
11 Refitting is the reverse sequence to removal.

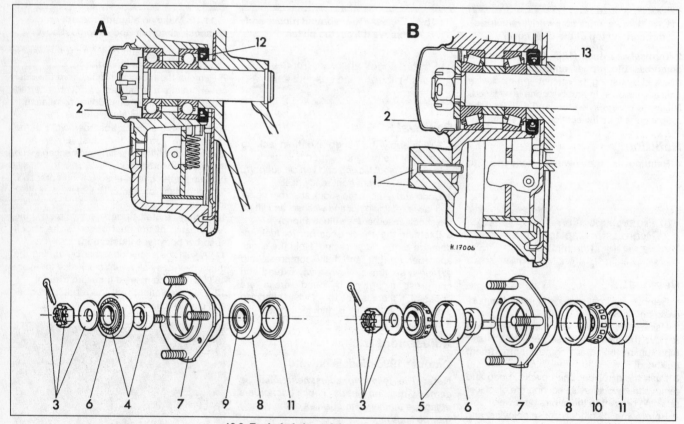

13.3 Exploded view of the rear hub components

A *Ball bearing type*
B *Taper roller bearing type*
1 *Brake drum and retaining screw*
2 *Hub cap*
3 *Hub retaining nut assembly*
4 *Outer ball bearing inner race and spacer*

5 *Outer taper roller bearing inner race and spacer*
6 *Outer bearing outer race*
7 *Rear hub*
8 *Inner bearing outer race*
9 *Inner ball bearing inner race*

10 *Inner taper roller bearing inner race*
11 *Oil seal*
12 *Oil seal installed with lips facing inwards*
13 *Oil seal installed with lips facing outwards*

13 Rear hub bearings – renewal

1 Chock the front wheels then jack up the rear of the car and support it securely on axle stands (see *Jacking and vehicle support*). Remove the relevant rear roadwheel, then release the handbrake.

2 Slacken off the brake adjuster, unscrew the two brake drum retaining screws and lift off the drum. If it is tight, tap it gently using a soft-faced mallet.

3 By judicious tapping and levering, extract the hub cap and withdraw the retaining split pin from the hub securing nut **(see illustration opposite)**.

4 Using a large socket, undo and remove the hub securing nut and thrustwasher. Note that the **left-hand hub nut** has a **left-hand thread** and the right-hand hub nut has a right-hand thread.

5 Withdraw the hub from the stub axle using a hub puller. Alternatively, lever it off using two stout screwdrivers or flat bars.

6 With the hub assembly removed from the car, prise out the rear oil seal, then tap out the two bearing inner races using a brass drift. Take care not to lose the balls which will be released as the inner races are removed. On certain models, taper roller bearings are fitted and the inner races are simply lifted out.

7 Withdraw the distance piece (if fitted) located between the two bearings and then drive out the two outer races away from the hub centre.

8 Thoroughly clean all the parts in paraffin or a suitable solvent and dry with a lint-free cloth.

9 Carefully examine the bearing inner and outer races, and the ball cage and balls for scoring, pitting or wear ridges; renew as necessary. The hub oil seal must be renewed as it will have been damaged during removal. If the bearings are in a satisfactory condition, reassemble the balls and ball cage to the outer race and then press the inner race back into position.

10 Before refitting the bearings remove any burrs that may be present in the bore of the hub. Use a fine file or scraper.

11 Pack the bearings using a general purpose lithium based grease and fit the inboard bearing to the hub with the narrow edge of the bearing outer race facing away from the hub centre. Press or tap the bearing into position, using the outer race only, with a tube of suitable diameter until the bearing abuts the shoulder in the hub. Take great care to keep the bearing square as it is installed, otherwise it will jam in the hub bore, and could cause the outer race to crack.

12 Fit a new oil seal to the rear of the hub with its lip facing towards the ball bearing. On models fitted with taper roller bearings, the oil seal lip faces away from the bearing.

13 Place the distance piece in position and fit the outboard bearing into the hub, again ensuring that the narrow edge of the bearing outer race faces away from the hub centre. **Note:** *Some makes of plain ball bearings have lengthened inner races which butt against each other. In this case the bearing distance piece is no longer needed.*

14 With the bearings installed, refit the hub to the stub axle and gently tap it home using a soft-faced mallet. Ensure that the stub axle squarely enters the distance piece between the two bearings.

15 Place the thrustwasher over the stub axle, chamfered side toward the bearing, then refit the securing nut and tighten it to the specified torque. Align the next split pin hole and fit a new split pin.

16 Refit the hub cap, brake drum and road-wheel, readjust the brakes (see Chapter 1) then lower the car to the ground.

14 Rear rubber cone spring – removal and refitting

Removal

1 Chock the front wheels then jack up the rear of the car and support it securely on axle stands (see *Jacking and vehicle support*). Remove the relevant rear roadwheel.

2 Support the radius arm using a jack or block of wood, then undo and remove the shock absorber retaining locknut and washers from the arm. Slide the end of the shock absorber off the radius arm stud then remove the jack and lower the arm as far as it will go.

3 Using a screwdriver or thin flat bar, prise the rear end of the spring strut out of the rubber cone **(see illustration)**. Now disengage the ball-end of the knuckle joint at the front of the spring strut from its seat and lift the strut off the car.

4 The rubber cone spring can now be levered off its location in the subframe and withdrawn from the car **(see illustration)**.

Refitting

5 Before refitting the rubber cone spring, drift the ball-end of the knuckle joint out of its location in the spring strut; examine it and its seat in the radius arm for scoring, corrosion and damage. Renew the complete knuckle joint if worn. If the joint is in a satisfactory condition, pack the cup seat with Dextragrease GP (or a suitable alternative) available from Rover dealers, then refit the ball-end of the knuckle joint to the cup seat. Ensure that the rubber dust cover is correctly located, otherwise water and grit will enter the joint.

6 The remainder of refitting is the reverse sequence to removal. When refitting the shock absorber, be sure that the spring strut and knuckle joint are properly engaged as the radius arm is raised.

14.3 Remove the rear rubber cone spring strut . . .

15 Rear Hydrolastic displacer unit – removal and refitting

Note: *To enable the displacer unit to be removed it will first be necessary to have the Hydrolastic system depressurised by a Rover dealer.*

Removal

1 Chock the front wheels then jack up the rear of the car and support it securely on axle stands (see *Jacking and vehicle support*). Remove the relevant rear roadwheel.

2 Place a block of wood or a jack beneath the rear radius arm, then undo and remove the nut, spring and flat washers securing the helper spring to the radius arm.

3 Lower the radius arm as far as it will go.

4 Undo and remove the single retaining screw and lift the bump rubber off the subframe.

5 Disconnect the flexible Hydrolastic hose from its union at the rear of the subframe.

6 Pull the displacer strut rearwards to disengage the knuckle joint ball from its seat, then withdraw the strut from the displacer unit.

7 Rotate the displacer anti-clockwise and lift it from its location on the subframe.

Refitting

8 Before refitting the displacer unit, examine the knuckle joint ball-end (assuming that it was released from its seat as the strut was removed) and seat for scoring, pitting or

14.4 . . . and rubber cone spring

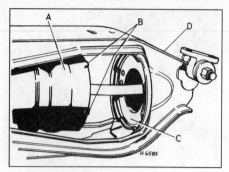

15.9 Rear Hydrolastic displacer unit
separated from locating plate

A *Displacer unit*   C *Locating plate*
B *Locating lugs*   D *Subframe*

corrosion. Renew the complete knuckle joint if
worn. If the joint is in a satisfactory condition,
pack the cup seat with Dextragrease GP (or a
suitable alternative) available from Rover
dealers, then refit the ball-end of the knuckle
joint to the cup seat. Ensure that the rubber
dust cover is correctly located, otherwise
water and grit will enter the joint.

9 The remainder of refitting is the reverse
sequence to removal, bearing in mind the
following points:

a) *When installing the displacer, turn it
   clockwise to lock it into the registers on the
   subframe locating plate (see illustration).*
b) *As the radius arm is lifted to refit the helper
   spring, ensure that the strut correctly
   locates in the knuckle joint and displacer.*
c) *When refitting is complete, have the
   Hydrolastic system repressurised at your
   nearest Rover dealer.*

16 Rear shock absorber (models with rubber cone suspension) – removal and refitting

Removal

1 Chock the front wheels then jack up the
rear of the car and support it securely on axle
stands (see *Jacking and vehicle support*).
Remove the relevant rear roadwheel.
2 If removing the left-hand shock absorber on
Saloon models, or either of the rear shock
absorbers on Cooper S models equipped with
twin fuel tanks, it will first be necessary to
remove the fuel tank(s) as described in the
relevant Part of Chapter 4.
3 Support the radius arm using a jack or
block of wood, then undo and remove the
shock absorber retaining locknut and washers
from the radius arm (see illustration).
4 Working inside the car or luggage
compartment, lift off the protective rubber
cap, then undo and remove the two locknuts
from the upper end of the shock absorber
(see illustration).
5 Lift off the thrustwasher and rubber bush,
and then withdraw the shock absorber from
under the car.

16.3 Remove the shock absorber lower . . .

6 Examine the shock absorber for leaks or
damage to the outer casing. Hold the shock
absorber upright, and fully compress and
extend it six times. Now slowly compress and
extend it once more. If 'dead' areas are
apparent, if there is free travel when changing
direction, or if the unit is damaged or leaking,
it must be renewed.
7 On later models the shock absorbers can
be adjusted to compensate for vehicle
mileage. Refer to Section 11 for details.

Refitting

8 Refitting is the reverse sequence to
removal. Hold the shock absorber in an
upright position and fully compress and
extend it six times to expel any air before
installing.

17 Rear helper spring (models with Hydrolastic suspension) – removal and refitting

The procedure is the same as described in
Section 16 for removal and refitting of the
shock absorber.

18 Rear radius arm – removal and refitting

Note: *Before carrying out this operation on
cars fitted with Hydrolastic suspension, it will
be necessary to have the Hydrolastic system
depressurised by a Rover dealer.*

18.7 The small distance piece is fitted to
the handbrake moving sector

Removal

1 Remove the rear shock absorber as
described in Section 16 if working on vehicles
fitted with rubber cone suspension, or the rear
helper spring (Section 17) if Hydrolastic
suspension is fitted.
2 Lower the radius arm as far as it will go.
When working on vehicles fitted with rubber
cone suspension, extract the spring strut from
the cone spring. Then pull the strut rearwards,
to disengage the ball-end of the knuckle joint
from its cup seat in the radius arm. If
Hydrolastic suspension is fitted, pull the
displacer strut rearwards to disengage the strut
from the knuckle joint (or the ball-end of the
knuckle joint from its seat) and then move the
strut forwards and out of the displacer unit.
3 Undo and remove the retaining screws and
lift off the finisher panel from the end of the
body side sills (where fitted).
4 On models fitted with Hydrolastic suspension, undo and remove the retaining screw
and lift off the bump rubber from the subframe.
5 Clamp the flexible brake hose, located over
the top of the radius arm, with a brake hose
clamp or self-gripping wrench with jaws
suitably protected. Now undo the union nut
securing the metal pipe to the hose and undo
and remove the nut securing the hose to its
bracket. Plug the ends of the hose and pipe
after removal to prevent dirt ingress.
6 Extract the split pin and withdraw the clevis
pin securing the end of the handbrake cable
to the brake operating lever. Detach the cable
and tension spring from the bracket at the
rear of the brake backplate.
7 The handbrake cable moving sector is
secured to the front of the radius arm either by
a through-bolt and lower locknut, or by an
upper retaining spire clip, thrustwasher and
spring washer. In the case of the through-bolt,
undo and remove the lower locknut and then
remove the sector from the bolt. Take care not
to lose the small distance tube from the centre
of the sector (see illustration). If the sector is
retained by a spire clip, prise the clip off the
upper end of the pivot pin, lift off the washers
and then withdraw the sector and pivot from
the radius arm.
8 From underneath the car undo and remove
the radius arm pivot shaft inner retaining nut
and spring washer. Undo and remove the
pivot shaft outer retaining nut and washer.

16.4 . . . and upper mounting

9 Undo and remove the four bolts securing the radius arm outer bracket to the subframe. Note that two of these bolts can only be removed using a socket and extension or box spanner inserted between the radius arm and subframe or bracket **(see illustration)**. Lift away the bracket.

10 Carefully lift the radius arm off the subframe, taking care not to lose the thrustwashers and rubber seal fitted at each end of the radius arm pivot shaft.

11 If there is any doubt about the condition of the radius arm pivot bearings, they should be inspected as follows.

12 Lift off the rubber seal and thrustwasher from each end of the pivot shaft and then slide the pivot shaft out of the bearings **(see illustrations)**.

13 Wipe away all traces of grease from the pivot shaft and the bearings, and carefully inspect these components. Signs of wear will be most obvious on the pivot shaft in the form of scoring, pitting, wear, ridges or deterioration of the surface hardening. If any of these conditions are apparent, the shaft and bearings require renewal.

14 The removal and refitting of both the bearings, and the line-reaming of the bronze bearing to suit the outside diameter of the pivot shaft, entails the use of several special tools. As there is no other way of satisfactorily carrying out this work, it is strongly recommended that the arm is taken to a Rover dealer for the complete bearing removal, refitting and reaming to be carried out.

Refitting

15 Refitting is the reverse sequence to removal bearing in mind the following points:
- a) When refitting the ball-end of the knuckle joint to the seat in the radius arm, pack the cup seat with Dextragrease GP (or a suitable alternative) available from Rover dealers.
- b) Bleed the hydraulic system at the disconnected side as described in Chapter 9.
- c) When refitting is complete, have the Hydrolastic system repressurised at your nearest Rover dealer.

18.9 Rear radius arm outer bracket retaining bolts (subframe shown removed)

19 Rear subframe mountings – renewal

Note: *The subframe front and rear mountings and rubber bushes can be renewed with the subframe still in position in the car as described below.*

Front mounting

1 Remove the relevant radius arm assembly from the car as described in Section 18.

2 Undo and remove the nut and washer securing the support bolt to the subframe.

3 Undo and remove the two bolts and spring washers securing the mounting to the body.

4 Lever the subframe down slightly and lift off the mounting assembly.

5 The support bolt and rubber bushes can now be removed from the mounting.

6 Refitting is the reverse sequence to removal, noting that the step in the mounting and the short bolt must be at the top (where applicable).

Rear mounting

7 Chock the front wheels then jack up the rear of the car and support it securely on axle stands (see *Jacking and vehicle support*). Remove the relevant rear roadwheel.

8 Undo and remove the nut and washer securing the mounting to the subframe.

9 On Estate, Van and Pick-up models, undo and remove the two bolts securing the mounting to the body. On Saloon models

have an assistant hold the bolts from inside the luggage compartment while the retaining nuts are removed from below.

10 Lever the subframe down slightly and slide the mounting assembly sideways and off the subframe.

11 The rubber bushes can now be removed from the mounting.

12 In all cases, refitting is the reverse sequence to removal, noting that the step in the mounting and the short bolt must be at the front.

20 Rear subframe – removal and refitting

Note: *Corrosion of the rear subframe is a common occurrence on Minis, particularly older models, and is one of the main causes of MOT test failure on these cars. Where corrosion has reached an advanced stage, renewal of the subframe is the only satisfactory cure. Despite its reputation for being an extremely difficult task, removal of the rear subframe is in fact a fairly straightforward operation. Before carrying out this work on cars fitted with Hydrolastic suspension, it will be necessary to have the system depressurised by a Rover dealer.*

Removal

1 Firmly apply the handbrake, then jack up the front of the car and support it securely on axle stands (see *Jacking and vehicle support*).

2 Where the battery positive lead is routed through the subframe, disconnect the negative, then the positive lead from the battery terminals and pull the positive lead clear of the frame, noting its routing for reference when refitting.

3 On early models undo and remove the two adjusting nuts securing the ends of the two handbrake cables to the trunnion on the handbrake lever **(see illustration overleaf)**. Pull the cables out of the trunnion and then slide off the washers and tension spring. **Note:** *On later models a single front cable is used and the tension springs are omitted.*

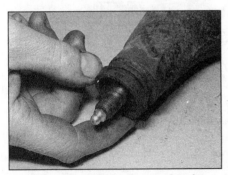

18.12a Lift off the radius arm bearing rubber seal . . .

18.12b . . . and thrustwasher . . .

18.12c . . . then slide out the pivot shaft

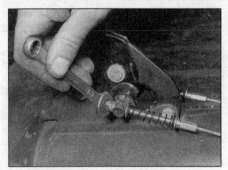

20.3 Remove the handbrake cable adjusting nuts on early models

20.5a Hold the cable guide retaining nuts from below . . .

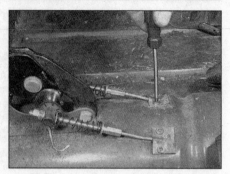

20.5b . . . and unscrew from above

4 Lift up the carpets to expose the cable guide plates located at the point where the cable passes through the floor.

5 Engage the help of an assistant to hold the nuts from underneath the car while the cable guide retaining screws are removed from above **(see illustrations)**. Lift off the guides and sealing pads, and from underneath the car, pull the ends of the cable through the opening in the floor and out of the passenger compartment.

6 Remove the brake master cylinder reservoir filler cap and place a piece of polythene over the filler neck, then refit the cap. This will help prevent fluid loss when the rear pipes are

disconnected. From underneath the rear of the car, undo and remove the brake hydraulic pipe union from the centre of the pressure regulating valve on early models. On models equipped with a dual circuit braking system, unscrew the pipe unions at the pipe connectors on each side of the subframe front crossmember. On later dual circuit systems unscrew the pipe union from the three-way connector on the rear subframe.

7 On fuel injection models, undo the two nuts and release the fuel filter mounting bracket from the subframe.

8 Refer to Chapter 4D, if necessary, and

remove the complete exhaust system from the car.

9 If an electric fuel pump is fitted, disconnect the electrical leads, slacken the clips and detach the fuel inlet and outlet hoses from the pump. **Note:** *During this operation, clamp the hoses using a self-gripping wrench with suitably protected jaws to prevent loss of fuel. Plug both hoses with a bolt or suitable metal rod upon removal.*

⚠️ **Warning: Refer to the precautions contained in Chapter 4A, Section 1, before carrying out any work on the fuel system.**

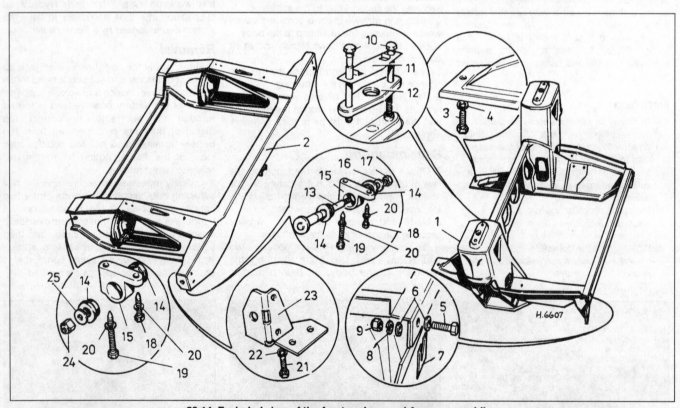

20.14 Exploded view of the front and rear subframe assemblies

1 Front subframe	6 Washer	11 Washer	16 Washer	21 Screw
2 Rear subframe	7 Packing piece	12 Pressure pad	17 Nut	22 Washer
3 Screw	8 Washer	13 Support pin	18 Screw	23 Bracket
4 Washer	9 Nut	14 Bush	19 Screw	24 Nut
5 Bolt	10 Screw	15 Mounting	20 Washer	25 Washer

10 On models fitted with Hydrolastic suspension, undo and remove the transfer pipe unions from the pressure valves at the rear of the subframe.

11 Place a block of wood under the rear wheels or jack up the radius arms slightly. From inside the car or luggage compartment, undo and remove the shock absorber upper mounting on models with rubber cone suspension, or the helper spring upper mounting on models with Hydrolastic suspension. On Saloon models, it will be necessary to detach the fuel tank retaining strap and move the tank slightly to provide access to the left-hand mounting.

12 Undo and remove the retaining screws and lift off the finisher panels from each end of the body side sills (where fitted).

13 Place a jack under each side of the subframe, or a trolley jack in the centre, with a substantial plank of wood running transversely across the subframe, and just take the weight of the frame on the jacks.

14 Undo and remove the two bolts securing each of the four subframe mountings to the body (see illustration opposite). If the bolts are tight, use liberal amounts of penetrating oil on them and allow time for the oil to soak in.

15 With the mounting bolts removed, engage the help of an assistant to steady the subframe and then slowly lower the jacks until the subframe can be withdrawn from the rear of the car.

Refitting

16 Refitting is the reverse sequence to removal, bearing in mind the following points:

a) Line up the subframe mountings and fit the bolts finger tight first, before progressively tightening.

b) Bleed the complete hydraulic system on completion as described in Chapter 9.

c) On models fitted with Hydrolastic suspension, have the system repressurised at your nearest Rover dealer.

21 Steering wheel – removal and refitting

Models without an airbag

Removal

1 Depending on model, either undo and remove the retaining screws and lift off the trim, or carefully prise up the steering wheel central motif (see illustration).

2 Set the front roadwheels in the straight-ahead position.

3 Using a suitable socket, slacken the nut which retains the wheel on the steering column by two turns, then lift the wheel off the splines on the column. If the wheel is tight, tap it up near the centre, using the palm of your hand, or twist it from side-to-side, whilst pulling upwards to release it from the shaft

21.1 Where fitted, prise up the central motif for access to the steering wheel nut

splines. Once free, remove the retaining nut and lockwasher (if fitted) and lift off the wheel. Note that if the nut is of the self locking type, a new nut will be required for refitting.

Refitting

4 Make sure that the roadwheels are in the straight-ahead position and that the small triangle on the direction indicator switch bush is pointing toward the horn push (later models only).

5 Refit the steering wheel to the column with the wheel spokes centralised.

6 Refit the lockwasher and new retaining nut (where applicable), then tighten the nut to the specified torque.

7 Refit the trim or central motif.

Models with an airbag

> **Warning: Make sure that the safety recommendations given in Chapter 12B are followed, to prevent personal injury.**

Removal

8 Remove the airbag as described in Chapter 12B.

9 Disconnect the horn wiring multiplug from the rotary coupling (see illustration).

10 Set the front roadwheels in the straight-ahead position.

11 Using a suitable socket, slacken the nut which retains the wheel on the steering column by two turns, then lift the wheel off the splines on the column. If the wheel is tight, tap it up near the centre, using the palm of your hand, or twist it from side-to-side, whilst pulling upwards to release it from the shaft

21.11a With the steering wheel released from the splines, remove the retaining nut . . .

21.9 Disconnect the horn wiring multiplug from the rotary coupling

splines. Once free, remove the retaining nut and lift off the wheel (see illustrations). Note that a new nut will be required for refitting.

12 With the steering wheel removed, attach tape to the edge of the rotary coupling to retain it in the centred position.

Refitting

13 Ensure that the roadwheels are in the straight-ahead position, then remove the tape used to retain the rotary coupling in the centred position. If the coupling has moved appreciably from the centred position, follow the instructions contained on the label on the front face of the coupling to centralise it.

14 Set the direction indicator cancelling cam in the vertical position, engage the rotary coupling and fit the wheel to the steering column shaft. Ensure that the steering wheel spokes are horizontal.

15 Secure the steering wheel with a new retaining nut tightened to the specified torque.

16 Connect the horn wiring multiplug to the rotary coupling, then refit the airbag as described in Chapter 12B.

22 Steering column (pre-October 1996 models) – removal and refitting

Removal

1 Disconnect the battery negative terminal (refer to *Disconnecting the battery* in the Reference Chapter).

21.11b . . . then lift the steering wheel off the column shaft

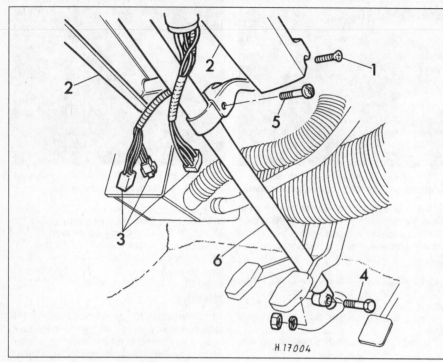

22.3 Steering column removal – pre-October 1996 models

1 Column shroud retaining screw
2 Column shroud halves
3 Multiplug connectors
4 Pinch-bolt
5 Upper column support clamp bolt
6 Steering column

2 Undo and remove the screws securing the two halves of the steering column shroud to the column and lift off the shroud.

3 Disconnect the electrical wiring multiplug connectors located under the parcel shelf (see illustration).

4 At the base of the column, undo and remove the pinch-bolt securing the inner column clamp to the pinion shaft.

5 Undo and remove the upper column support clamp bolt at the parcel shelf. On later models where a shear bolt is used, cut a slot in the bolt and use a screwdriver to unscrew it, or drill a small hole and remove it with a stud extractor.

6 Position the roadwheels in the straight-ahead position, pull the column upwards and remove it from the car.

Refitting

7 Make sure that the roadwheels are still in the straight-ahead position.

8 Lift up the front carpets and slacken the steering rack U-bolt locknuts sufficiently to allow sideways movement of the rack housing.

9 Slacken the upper column support clamp mounting bracket bolts, to allow movement of the bracket.

10 Lift out the rubber grommet in the

passenger side floor, then remove the plastic plug from the rack housing. Insert a 6.0 mm diameter centralising pin (a bolt or drill bit are ideal) into the hole (see illustration). Move the rack sideways slightly until the pin fully engages with the hole in the rack, thus centralising the assembly. Engage the steering inner column clamp with the pinion shaft ensuring that the steering wheel spokes are horizontal/centre spoke vertical.

11 Refit the column clamp bolt and then remove the centralising pin. Refit the plastic plug and grommet.

12 Refit the upper column support clamp bolt, using a new shear bolt on later models. Ensure that there is no twist or strain on the column as the bolt is inserted. Reposition the clamp and bracket if necessary.

13 The remainder of the refitting procedure now varies according to model as described below.

Single stalk multifunction switch

14 Tighten the steering column clamp and bracket retaining bolts and the steering rack U-bolt locknuts to the specified torque.

15 Reconnect the electrical multiplugs under the parcel shelf.

16 Adjust the direction indicator switch cancelling stud so that it just trips the switch levers as the wheel is turned.

17 With the roadwheels in the straight-ahead position and the steering column installed, the direction indicator stalk should be at 20° to the horizontal, with the cancelling levers of the switch (see illustration). If this is not the case, slacken the steering column support bracket clamp and rotate the column as necessary.

18 Refit the steering column shrouds and the carpets, then reconnect the battery.

Twin stalk multifunction switch

19 Position the outer column to give 2.0 mm clearance between the steering wheel hub and the boss of the multifunction switch, then tighten the shear bolt until the head breaks off.

20 Reconnect the electrical multiplugs under the parcel shelf.

21 Refit the steering column shrouds and the carpets, then reconnect the battery.

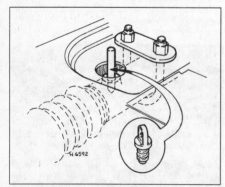

22.10 Use of a dowel to centralise the steering rack

Inset shows plastic plug

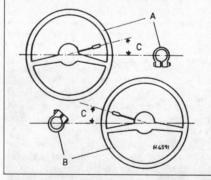

22.17 Correct position of clamp bolt and direction indicator lever when refitting the early type steering column

A RHD models
B LHD models
C = 20°

23 Steering column (October 1996 models onward) – removal and refitting

Removal

1 Remove the steering wheel as described in Section 21.

2 Remove the airbag rotary coupling as described in Chapter 12B, Section 22.

3 Withdraw the direction indicator cancelling cam from the steering column shaft.

4 Disconnect the wiring multiplugs from the rear of the steering column multifunction switch assembly.

5 Undo the two screws securing the multifunction switch assembly to the steering column and lift off the switch assembly.

6 Disconnect the ignition switch wiring multiplug located under the facia.

7 At the base of the column, undo and remove the pinch-bolt securing the inner column clamp to the pinion shaft.

8 Undo and remove the upper column support clamp bolt under the facia, then pull the column upwards and remove it from the car.

Refitting

9 Make sure that the roadwheels are still in the straight-ahead position.

10 Lift out the rubber grommet in the passenger side floor, then remove the plastic plug from the rack housing. Insert a 6.0 mm diameter centralising pin (a bolt or drill bit are ideal) into the hole **(see illustration 22.10)**. Have an assistant move the roadwheels slightly until the pin fully engages with the hole in the rack, thus centralising the assembly.

11 Engage the steering inner column clamp with the pinion shaft then refit the column clamp bolt and tighten it to the specified torque.

12 Refit the upper column support clamp bolt and tighten it to the specified torque.

13 Reconnect the ignition switch wiring multiplug.

14 Refit the steering column multifunction switch assembly, secure with the two screws and reconnect the multiplugs.

15 Refit the direction indicator cancelling cam, setting it in the vertical position.

16 Refit the airbag rotary coupling as described in Chapter 12B, and the steering wheel as described in Section 21.

17 Remove the steering rack centralising pin and refit the plastic plug and grommet.

24 Steering column – dismantling and reassembly

Dismantling

1 With the steering column removed from the car as described in Section 22 or 23 as applicable, remove the steering wheel as described in Section 21 if not already done.

2 If still in place, undo and remove the retaining screws and withdraw the multifunction switch from the column.

3 On early models, undo and remove the direction indicator cancelling stud and locknut from the inner column.

4 The inner column can now be withdrawn from the lower end of the outer column tube. Before doing this insert the ignition key into the switch and turn it to the I position. This will release the steering lock and allow the inner column to be removed.

5 Prise the top bush out of the column if necessary using a screwdriver. The lower felt bush is removed by simply sliding it out of the outer column.

6 To remove the steering lock/ignition switch, drill out the shear bolt heads, or alternatively drill a hole in the shear bolts and unscrew them using a stud extractor **(see illustration)**. The clamp plate and lock switch assembly can then be removed.

7 With the steering column assembly dismantled, check the inner and outer column for straightness by rolling them on a flat surface. Renew the parts if distortion is obvious.

Reassembly

8 Begin reassembly by lubricating the upper polythene bush with graphite grease. Insert the bush into the top of the outer column, chamfered end first. Tap the bush fully into position, ensuring that the shouldered slot engages with the detent in the outer column.

9 Insert the inner column into the lower end of the outer column and slide it in approximately half way.

10 Soak the lower felt bush in engine oil and then wrap it around the inner column until its ends are butted together. Now carefully slide the inner column fully home.

11 On pre-October 1996 models, refit the multifunction switch assembly, and on early models the direction indicator cancelling stud and locknut.

12 Refit the steering lock ignition switch using new shear bolts. Do not shear the heads off the bolts until the steering column has been refitted and the operation of the steering lock tested.

13 On pre-October 1996 models, refit the steering column to the car as described in Section 22 then, when the column is correctly positioned in relation to the steering gear, refit the steering wheel (Section 21).

14 On October 1996 models onward, refit the steering column to the car as described in Section 23.

25 Steering tie-rod outer balljoint – removal and refitting

Removal

1 Firmly apply the handbrake, then jack up the front of the car and support it securely on axle stands (see *Jacking and vehicle support*). Remove the relevant front roadwheel.

2 Slacken the locknut securing the balljoint to the steering tie-rod by a quarter of a turn.

3 Undo and remove the balljoint shank locknut and separate the taper of the shank using a universal balljoint separator or the alternative method described in Section 3, paragraph 5.

4 Hold the steering tie-rod with a self-gripping wrench and unscrew the balljoint from the tie-rod, counting the number of turns necessary to remove it.

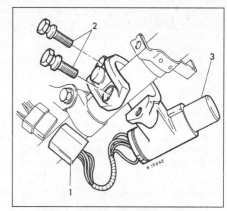

24.6 Steering lock/ignition switch assembly

A Multiplug connector
2 Shear bolts
3 Steering lock/ignition switch

Refitting

5 Screw the new balljoint onto the tie-rod by the same number of turns as counted during removal.

6 Clean the taper surfaces then fit the balljoint shank to the steering arm. Refit and tighten the shank locknut to the specified torque.

 If difficulty is experienced in tightening the balljoint shank locknut due to the tapered shank turning in the steering arm, apply pressure with a jack or long lever to the underside of the balljoint to lock the taper in its conical seat.

7 Tighten the locknut securing the balljoint to the steering tie-rod

8 Refit the roadwheel and lower the car to the ground.

9 On completion, have the front wheel toe setting checked (see Section 30).

26 Steering rack rubber gaiter – removal and refitting

Note: *Should the rubber gaiters at each end of the steering rack become damaged, split or show any other signs of deterioration, they must be renewed immediately, otherwise the lubricant will be lost from the rack unit, and water and road grit will enter the assembly, causing rapid internal wear.*

Removal

1 Remove the steering tie-rod outer balljoint as described in Section 25.

2 Mark the position of the locknut on the tie-rod so that it can be refitted in the same place, then unscrew it from the tie-rod.

3 Place a suitable container beneath the rubber gaiter to catch any oil that may spill from the rack (early models only).

4 Undo and remove the two retaining clips or cut off the wire clips, then slide the gaiter off the rack housing and tie-rod.

Refitting

5 Refitting is the reverse sequence to removal. With the gaiter in position refill the rack with the appropriate lubricant, as described in Section 29, before refitting the retaining clips or wire.

27 Rack-and-pinion steering gear – removal and refitting

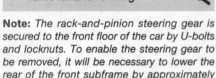

Note: *The rack-and-pinion steering gear is secured to the front floor of the car by U-bolts and locknuts. To enable the steering gear to be removed, it will be necessary to lower the rear of the front subframe by approximately 76.0 mm to provide the necessary working clearances.*

Removal

1 Remove the air cleaner assembly as described in the relevant Part of Chapter 4.

2 Remove the steering column as described in Section 22 or 23 as applicable.

3 Firmly apply the handbrake, then jack up the front of the car and support it securely on axle stands (see *Jacking and vehicle support*). Remove the front roadwheels.

4 On Cooper S models, and all October 1996 models onward, remove the complete exhaust system as described in Chapter 4D. On all other models, undo and remove the nuts and bolts securing the exhaust pipe-to-manifold clamp and lift off the clamp. Undo and remove the nut and bolt securing the exhaust pipe support to the bracket on the side of the transmission.

5 Undo and remove the bolt securing the engine tie-rod to the side of the cylinder block.

6 Detach the clutch operating lever return spring (where fitted), then undo and remove the two bolts securing the clutch slave cylinder to the flywheel housing or mounting plate. Tie the slave cylinder out of the way from a convenient place on the bulkhead.

7 Undo and remove the two bolts (or nuts) each side securing the subframe towers to the bulkhead crossmember. On later models undo and remove the large hexagon-headed plug used in place of the bolts or nuts.

8 Lift up the carpets and then undo and remove the four steering rack U-bolt locknuts.

9 On manual transmission models fitted with a remote control gearchange, undo and remove the bolts securing the rear of the remote control housing to the floor. On automatic transmission models it should be

possible to lower the subframe sufficiently for removal of the steering gear without disconnecting the gear selector cable. However, if during subsequent operations the cable appears to be under tension, disconnect it from the transmission as described in Chapter 7B.

10 On models with rubber cone suspension, disconnect the front shock absorbers from the upper suspension arms.

11 Undo and remove the locknuts securing the steering tie-rod outer balljoint shanks to the steering arms on the swivel hubs. Release the tapers using a universal balljoint separator or the alternative method described in Section 3, paragraph 5.

12 Support the subframe securely on jacks and then undo and remove the nuts and bolts securing the subframe to the rear mountings or to the floor.

13 Slacken the bolt securing the front of the subframe or subframe mountings to the body.

14 Carefully lower the jacks, allowing the subframe to drop by approximately 76.0 mm at the rear.

15 Lift off the rack-and-pinion retaining U-bolts and clamp pads and then manoeuvre the rack assembly out from between the subframe and body on the driver's side.

Refitting

16 Refitting is the reverse sequence to removal bearing in mind the following points:

a) *Do not tighten the U-bolt locknuts until the steering column is fitted and secure.*

b) *Refit the steering column as described in Section 22 or 23, as applicable.*

28 Rack-and-pinion steering gear overhaul – general information

Examine the steering gear assembly for signs of wear or damage, and check that the rack moves freely throughout the full length of its travel, with no signs of roughness or excessive free play between the steering gear pinion and rack. If wear or damage is evident, the best course of action is to obtain an exchange reconditioned unit. Although it is possible to overhaul the steering gear assembly fitted to early models, it is an involved procedure and this task should be entrusted to a Rover dealer. Note also, that certain parts may no longer be available. The steering gear fitted to later models (approximately 1992 onward) is a sealed unit and cannot be overhauled. The only components which can be renewed easily by the home mechanic are the steering rack gaiters and the tie-rod outer balljoints. These procedures are covered in Sections 26 and 25 respectively.

29 Rack-and-pinion steering gear – lubrication

1 The steering gear is filled with lubricant during manufacture and then sealed. Additional lubricant will only be required in service if a leak develops, either from the rubber gaiters or from any of the joints, or if the steering gear has been dismantled.

2 The steering gear fitted to early models, identified by black rubber gaiters, is filled with oil. The steering gear fitted to later models, identified by transparent rubber gaiters, is filled with semi-fluid grease. The grade and quantity of lubricant for both types is given in the Specifications.

3 Should it be necessary to refill the rack, proceed as follows.

4 Firmly apply the handbrake, then jack up the driver's side of the car and support it securely on axle stands (see *Jacking and vehicle support*). Remove the front roadwheel.

5 Centralise the steering gear so that the wheels are in the straight-ahead position.

6 Slacken the retaining clips or remove the wire securing the rubber gaiter to the rack housing and tie-rod. Slide the rubber gaiter down the tie-rod sufficiently to provide access.

7 Using an oil can or grease gun filled with the specified grade and quantity of lubricant, fill the rack housing.

8 Refit the rubber gaiter and secure it with the retaining clips or soft iron wire.

9 Turn the steering from lock-to-lock to distribute the lubricant, refit the roadwheel and lower the car to the ground.

30 Wheel alignment and steering angles – general information

General

1 A car's steering and suspension geometry is defined in four basic settings – all angles are expressed in degrees (toe settings are also expressed as a measurement); the relevant settings are camber, castor, swivel hub inclination, and toe-setting. Front wheel toe-setting is readily adjustable but all other settings are established during manufacture and will not normally require attention. It is possible to alter the front castor angle by fitting a longer or shorter tie-bar to the relevant side, and to alter the rear wheel toe setting by fitting spacers between the rear radius arm outer brackets and the subframe. Should there be any reason to suspect that the front castor angle is incorrect (insensitive steering, pulling to one side, etc) or the rear wheel toe setting is incorrect (excessive rear tyre wear) then the settings should be checked and if necessary altered by a Rover dealer.

Front wheel toe setting

2 Due to the special measuring equipment necessary to accurately check the wheel alignment, and the skill required to use it properly, checking and adjustment is best left to a Rover dealer or similar expert. Note that most tyre-fitting shops now possess sophisticated checking equipment. The following is provided as a guide, should the owner decide to carry out a DIY check.

3 The front wheel toe setting is checked by measuring the distance between the front and rear inside edges of the roadwheel rims. Proprietary toe measurement gauges are available from motor accessory shops. Adjustment is made by screwing the tie-rod outer balljoints in or out of their tie-rods, to alter the effective length of the tie-rod assemblies.

4 For **accurate** checking, the vehicle **must** be at kerb weight, ie, unladen and with a full tank of fuel, and on models with Hydrolastic suspension, the trim height must be correct (see Section 2).

5 Before starting work, check the tyre pressures and tread wear, the condition of the hub bearings, the steering wheel free play, and the condition of the front suspension components (see Chapter 1). Correct any faults found.

6 Park the vehicle on level ground, check that the front roadwheels are in the straight-ahead position, then rock the rear and front ends to settle the suspension. Release the handbrake, and roll the vehicle backwards 1 metre, then forwards again, to relieve any stresses in the steering and suspension components.

7 Measure the distance between the front edges of the wheel rims and the rear edges of the rims. Subtract the rear measurement from the front measurement, and check that the result is as given in the Specifications.

8 If adjustment is necessary, apply the handbrake, then jack up the front of the vehicle and support it securely on axle stands (see *Jacking and vehicle support*). Turn the steering wheel onto full-left lock, and record the number of exposed threads on the right-hand tie-rod. Now turn the steering onto full-right lock, and record the number of threads on the left-hand side. If there are the same number of threads visible on both sides, then subsequent adjustment should be made equally on both sides. If there are more threads visible on one side than the other, it will be necessary to compensate for this during adjustment. **Note:** *It is most important that after adjustment, the same number of threads are visible on each tie-rod.*

9 First clean the tie-rod threads; if they are corroded, apply penetrating fluid before starting adjustment. Release the rubber gaiters outboard clips (where necessary), and slide back the gaiters; apply a smear of grease to the gaiter seat on the tie-rod, so that the gaiters will not be twisted or strained as their respective tie-rods are rotated.

10 Use a straight-edge and a scriber or similar to mark the relationship of each tie-rod to its outer balljoint then, holding each tie-rod in turn, unscrew its outer balljoint locknut fully.

11 Alter the length of the tie-rods, bearing in mind the note made in paragraph 8. Screw them into or out of their outer balljoints, rotating the tie-rod using a suitable pair of grips or self-locking wrench. Shortening the tie-rods (screwing them into their outer balljoints) will reduce toe-in/increase toe-out.

12 When the setting is correct, hold the tie-rods and securely tighten the outer balljoint locknuts. Count the exposed threads to check the length of both tie-rods. If they are not the same, then the adjustment has not been made equally, and problems will be encountered with tyre scrubbing in turns; also, the steering wheel spokes will no longer be horizontal when the wheels are in the straight-ahead position.

13 If the tie-rod lengths are the same, lower the vehicle to the ground and re-check the toe setting; re-adjust if necessary. When the setting is correct, securely tighten the outer balljoint locknuts. Ensure that the rubber gaiters are seated correctly, and are not twisted or strained, and secure them in position with new retaining clips or wire (where necessary).

Chapter 11 Part A:
Bodywork and fittings – pre-October 1996 models

Contents

Bodywork seam trim strips – general information 30
Bodywork, paint and exterior trim check . . . . See Chapter 1
Bonnet – removal and refitting 13
Bonnet lock – removal and refitting 15
Bonnet lock release cable – removal and refitting 14
Boot lid – removal and refitting 16
Boot lid lock – removal and refitting 17
Centre console – removal and refitting 28
Door hinge – removal and refitting 8
Door, boot and bonnet check and lubrication . . . . See Chapter 1
Doors – removal and refitting 7
Facia top rail cover – removal and refitting 27
Front and rear bumpers – removal and refitting 31
Front door exterior handle (Saloon and Estate models) – removal and
 refitting 11
Front door glass – removal and refitting 9
Front door interior trim panel (Saloon and Estate models) – removal
 and refitting 6
Front door lock assembly – removal and refitting 10
Front door striker plate – removal and refitting 12
Front grille panel – removal and refitting 29
General information 1
Maintenance – bodywork and underframe 2
Maintenance – upholstery and carpets 3
Major structural damage or corrosion – general information 5
Minor body damage – repair 4
Rear door lock (Estate and Van models) – removal and refitting . . . 19
Rear door window (Estate and Van models) – removal and refitting . 23
Rear doors (Estate and Van models) – removal and refitting 18
Rear quarterlight glass (Saloon models) – removal and refitting 24
Rear side screen window (Estate models) – removal and refitting . . 25
Rear window (Saloon and Pick-up models) – removal and refitting . 22
Sunroof components – general information 32
Tailgate (Pick-up models) – removal and refitting 20
Windscreen – removal and refitting 21
Wooden facia – removal and refitting 26

Degrees of difficulty

Easy, suitable for novice with little experience	**Fairly easy,** suitable for beginner with some experience	**Fairly difficult,** suitable for competent DIY mechanic	**Difficult,** suitable for experienced DIY mechanic	**Very difficult,** suitable for expert DIY or professional

1 General information

Although the Mini has been produced in many forms since its introduction, the principle of construction has remained the same. The body and floor pan are of a monocoque all-steel, welded construction creating a very strong and torsionally rigid shell. The front and rear suspension assemblies are mounted on subframes, bolted to the underside of the bodyshell. The front subframe also provides mounting points for the engine/transmission.

Although the Mini bodyshell is extremely strong, it is likely to have suffered to some degree, particularly on older models, from the effects of rust and corrosion. Common problem areas are the front wings, body side sills and the rear subframe. Particular attention should be paid to the rear subframe and areas around its mountings, as well as the side sills, as these are load bearing areas; corrosion here, if left unchecked, could seriously affect the roadworthiness of the vehicle. The subframes are covered in detail in Chapter 10 and full information regarding the treatment of rust and corrosion and body repairs will be found in subsequent Sections of this Chapter.

2 Maintenance – bodywork and underframe

The general condition of a vehicle's bodywork is the one thing that significantly affects its value. Maintenance is easy but needs to be regular. Neglect, particularly after minor damage, can lead quickly to further deterioration and costly repair bills. It is important also to keep watch on those parts of the vehicle not immediately visible, for instance the underside, inside all the wheelarches and the lower part of the engine compartment.

The basic maintenance routine for the bodywork is washing preferably with a lot of water, from a hose. This will remove all the loose solids which may have stuck to the vehicle. It is important to flush these off in such a way as to prevent grit from scratching the finish. The wheelarches and underframe need washing in the same way to remove any accumulated mud which will retain moisture and tend to encourage rust. Oddly enough, the best time to clean the underframe and wheelarches is in wet weather when the mud is thoroughly wet and soft. In very wet weather the underframe is usually cleaned of large accumulations automatically and this is a good time for inspection.

Periodically, except on vehicles with a wax-based underbody protective coating, it is a good idea to have the whole of the underframe of the vehicle steam cleaned, engine compartment included, so that a thorough inspection can be carried out to see what minor repairs and renovations are necessary. Steam cleaning is available at many garages and is necessary for removal of the accumulation of oily grime which sometimes is allowed to become thick in certain areas. If steam cleaning facilities are not available, there are one or two excellent grease solvents available which can be brush applied; the dirt can then be simply hosed off. Note that these methods should not be used on vehicles with wax-based underbody protective coating or the coating will be removed. Such vehicles should be inspected annually, preferably just prior to winter, when the underbody should be washed down and any damage to the wax coating repaired using underseal. Ideally, a completely fresh coat should be applied. It would also be worth considering the use of such wax-based protection for injection into door panels, sills, box sections, etc, as an additional safeguard against rust damage where such protection is not provided by the vehicle manufacturer.

After washing paintwork, wipe off with a chamois leather to give an unspotted clear finish. A coat of clear protective wax polish will give added protection against chemical pollutants in the air. If the paintwork sheen has dulled or oxidised, use a cleaner/polisher combination to restore the brilliance of the shine. This requires a little effort, but such dulling is usually caused because regular washing has been neglected. Care needs to be taken with metallic paintwork as special non-abrasive cleaner/polisher is required to avoid damage to the finish.

Always check that the door and ventilator opening drain holes and pipes are completely clear so that water can be drained out. Bright work should be treated in the same way as paint work. Windscreens and windows can be kept clear of the smeary film which often appears by the use of a proprietary glass cleaner. Never use any form of wax or other body or chromium polish on glass.

3 Maintenance – upholstery and carpets

Mats and carpets should be brushed or vacuum cleaned regularly to keep them free of grit. If they are badly stained remove them from the vehicle for scrubbing or sponging and make quite sure they are dry before refitting. Seats and interior trim panels can be kept clean by wiping with a damp cloth and a proprietary upholstery cleaner. If they do become stained (which can be more apparent on light coloured upholstery) use a little liquid detergent and a soft nail brush to scour the grime out of the grain of the material. Do not forget to keep the headlining clean in the same way as the upholstery. When using liquid cleaners inside the vehicle do not over-wet the surfaces being cleaned. Excessive damp could get into the seams and padded interior causing stains, offensive odours or even rot. If the inside of the vehicle gets wet accidentally it is worthwhile taking some trouble to dry it out properly, particularly where carpets are involved. *Do not leave oil or electric heaters inside the vehicle for this purpose.*

4 Minor body damage – repair

Repair of minor scratches in bodywork

If the scratch is very superficial, and does not penetrate to the metal of the bodywork, repair is very simple. Lightly rub the area of the scratch with a paintwork renovator, or a very fine cutting paste, to remove loose paint from the scratch, and to clear the surrounding bodywork of wax polish. Rinse the area with clean water.

Apply touch-up paint to the scratch using a fine paint brush; continue to apply fine layers of paint until the surface of the paint in the scratch is level with the surrounding paintwork. Allow the new paint at least two weeks to harden: then blend it into the surrounding paintwork by rubbing the scratch area with a paintwork renovator or a very fine cutting paste. Finally, apply wax polish.

Where the scratch has penetrated right through to the metal of the bodywork, causing the metal to rust, a different repair technique is required. Remove any loose rust from the bottom of the scratch with a penknife, then apply rust-inhibiting paint, to prevent the formation of rust in the future. Using a rubber or nylon applicator fill the scratch with bodystopper paste. If required, this paste can be mixed with cellulose thinners, to provide a very thin paste which is ideal for filling narrow scratches. Before the stopper-paste in the scratch hardens, wrap a piece of smooth cotton rag around the top of a finger. Dip the finger in cellulose thinners, and then quickly sweep it across the surface of the stopper-paste in the scratch; this will ensure that the surface of the stopper-paste is slightly hollowed. The scratch can now be painted over as described earlier in this Section.

Repair of dents in bodywork

When deep denting of the vehicle's bodywork has taken place, the first task is to pull the dent out, until the affected bodywork almost attains its original shape. There is little point in trying to restore the original shape completely, as the metal in the damaged area will have stretched on impact and cannot be reshaped fully to its original contour. It is better to bring the level of the dent up to a point which is about 3 mm below the level of the surrounding bodywork. In cases where the dent is very shallow anyway, it is not worth trying to pull it out at all. If the underside of the dent is accessible, it can be hammered out gently from behind, using a mallet with a wooden or plastic head. Whilst doing this, hold a suitable block of wood firmly against the outside of the panel to absorb the impact from the hammer blows and thus prevent a large area of the bodywork from being 'belled-out'.

Should the dent be in a section of the bodywork which has a double skin or some other factor making it inaccessible from behind, a different technique is called for. Drill several small holes through the metal inside the area – particularly in the deeper section. Then screw long self-tapping screws into the holes just sufficiently for them to gain a good purchase in the metal. Now the dent can be pulled out by pulling on the protruding heads of the screws with a pair of pliers.

The next stage of the repair is the removal of the paint from the damaged area, and from an inch or so of the surrounding 'sound' bodywork. This is accomplished most easily by using a wire brush or abrasive pad on a power drill, although it can be done just as effectively by hand using sheets of abrasive paper. To complete the preparation for filling, score the surface of the bare metal with a screwdriver or the tang of a file, or alternatively, drill small holes in the affected area. This will provide a really good 'key' for the filler paste.

To complete the repair see the Section on filling and re-spraying.

Repair of rust holes or gashes in bodywork

Remove all paint from the affected area and from an inch or so of the surrounding 'sound' bodywork, using an abrasive pad or a wire brush on a power drill. If these are not available a few sheets of abrasive paper will do the job just as effectively. With the paint removed you will be able to gauge the severity of the corrosion and therefore decide whether to renew the whole panel (if this is possible) or to repair the affected area. New body panels are not as expensive as most people think and it is often quicker and more satisfactory to fit a new panel than to attempt to repair large areas of corrosion.

Remove all fittings from the affected area except those which will act as a guide to the original shape of the damaged bodywork (eg headlight shells etc). Then, using tin snips or a hacksaw blade, remove all loose metal and any other metal badly affected by corrosion. Hammer the edges of the hole inwards in order to create a slight depression for the filler paste.

Wire brush the affected area to remove the powdery rust from the surface of the remaining metal. Paint the affected area with rust inhibiting paint; if the back of the rusted area is accessible treat this also.

Before filling can take place it will be necessary to block the hole in some way. This can be achieved by the use of aluminium or plastic mesh, or aluminium tape.

Aluminium or plastic mesh or glass fibre matting is probably the best material to use for a large hole. Cut a piece to the approximate size and shape of the hole to be filled, then position it in the hole so that its edges are below the level of the surrounding bodywork. It can be retained in position by several blobs of filler paste around its periphery.

Aluminium tape should be used for small or very narrow holes. Pull a piece off the roll and trim it to the approximate size and shape required, then pull off the backing paper (if used) and stick the tape over the hole; it can be overlapped if the thickness of one piece is insufficient. Burnish down the edges of the tape with the handle of a screwdriver or similar, to ensure that the tape is securely attached to the metal underneath.

Bodywork repairs – filling and re-spraying

Before using this Section, see the Sections on dent, deep scratch, rust holes and gash repairs.

Many types of bodyfiller are available, but generally speaking those proprietary kits which contain a tin of filler paste and a tube of resin hardener are best for this type of repair; some can be used directly from the tube. A wide, flexible plastic or nylon applicator will be found invaluable for imparting a smooth and well contoured finish to the surface of the filler.

Mix up a little filler on a clean piece of card or board – measure the hardener carefully (follow the maker's instructions on the pack) otherwise the filler will set too rapidly or too slowly. Using the applicator, apply the filler paste to the prepared area; draw the applicator across the surface of the filler to achieve the correct contour and to level the filler surface. As soon as a contour that approximates to the correct one is achieved, stop working the paste – if you carry on too long the paste will become sticky and begin to 'pick up' on the applicator. Continue to add thin layers of filler paste at twenty-minute intervals until the level of the filler is just proud of the surrounding bodywork.

Once the filler has hardened, excess can be removed using a metal plane or file. From then on, progressively finer grades of abrasive paper should be used, starting with a 40 grade production paper and finishing with 400 grade wet-and-dry paper. Always wrap the abrasive paper around a flat rubber, cork, or wooden block – otherwise the surface of the filler will not be completely flat. During the smoothing of the filler surface the wet-and-dry paper should be periodically rinsed in water. This will ensure that a very smooth finish is imparted to the filler at the final stage.

At this stage the 'dent' should be surrounded by a ring of bare metal, which in turn should be encircled by the finely 'feathered' edge of the good paintwork. Rinse the repair area with clean water, until all of the dust produced by the rubbing-down operation has gone.

Spray the whole repair area with a light coat of primer – this will show up any imperfections in the surface of the filler. Repair these imperfections with fresh filler paste or bodystopper, and once more smooth the surface with abrasive paper. If bodystopper is used, it can be mixed with cellulose thinners to form a really thin paste which is ideal for filling small holes. Repeat this spray and repair procedure until you are satisfied that the surface of the filler, and the feathered edge of the paintwork are perfect. Clean the repair area with clean water and allow to dry fully.

The repair area is now ready for final spraying. Paint spraying must be carried out in a warm, dry, windless and dust free atmosphere. This condition can be created artificially if you have access to a large indoor working area, but if you are forced to work in the open, you will have to pick your day very carefully. If you are working indoors, dousing the floor in the work area with water will help to settle the dust which would otherwise be in the atmosphere. If the repair area is confined to one body panel, mask off the surrounding panels; this will help to minimise the effects of a slight mis-match in paint colours. Bodywork fittings (eg chrome strips, door handles etc) will also need to be masked off. Use genuine masking tape and several thicknesses of newspaper for the masking operations.

Before commencing to spray, agitate the aerosol can thoroughly, then spray a test area (an old tin, or similar) until the technique is mastered. Cover the repair area with a thick coat of primer; the thickness should be built up using several thin layers of paint rather than one thick one. Using 400 grade wet-and-dry paper, rub down the surface of the primer until it is really smooth. While doing this, the work area should be thoroughly doused with water, and the wet-and-dry paper periodically rinsed in water. Allow to dry before spraying on more paint.

Spray on the top coat, again building up the thickness by using several thin layers of paint. Start spraying in the centre of the repair area and then, with a single side-to-side motion, work outwards until the whole repair area and about 50 mm of the surrounding original paintwork is covered. Remove all masking material 10 to 15 minutes after spraying on the final coat of paint.

Allow the new paint at least two weeks to harden, then, using a paintwork renovator or a very fine cutting paste, blend the edges of the paint into the existing paintwork. Finally, apply wax polish.

Plastic components

With the use of more and more plastic body components by the vehicle manufacturers (eg bumpers, spoilers, and in some cases major body panels), rectification of more serious damage to such items has become a matter of either entrusting repair work to a specialist in this field, or renewing complete components. Repair of such damage by the DIY owner is not really feasible owing to the cost of the equipment and materials required for effecting such repairs. The basic technique involves making a groove along the line of the crack in the plastic using a rotary burr in a power drill. The damaged part is then welded back together by using a hot air gun to heat up and fuse a plastic filler rod into the groove. Any excess plastic is then removed and the area rubbed down to a smooth finish. It is important that a filler rod of the correct plastic is used, as body components can be made of a variety of different types (eg polycarbonate, ABS, polypropylene).

Damage of a less serious nature (abrasions, minor cracks etc) can be repaired by the DIY owner using a two-part epoxy filler repair material. Once mixed in equal proportions, this is used in similar fashion to the bodywork filler used on metal panels. The filler is usually cured in twenty to thirty minutes, ready for sanding and painting.

If the owner is renewing a complete component himself, or if he has repaired it with epoxy filler, he will be left with the problem of finding a suitable paint for finishing which is compatible with the type of plastic used. At one time the use of a universal paint was not possible owing to the complex range of plastics encountered in body component applications. Standard paints, generally speaking, will not bond to plastic or rubber satisfactorily. However, it is now possible to obtain a plastic body parts finishing kit which consists of a pre-primer treatment, a primer and coloured top coat. Full instructions are normally supplied with a kit, but basically the method of use is to first apply the pre-primer to the component concerned and allow it to dry for up to 30 minutes. Then the primer is applied and left to dry for about an hour before finally applying the special coloured top coat. The result is a correctly coloured component where the paint will flex with the plastic or rubber, a property that standard paint does not normally possess.

5 Major structural damage or corrosion – general information

1 Because the body is built on the monocoque principle and is integral with the underframe, major damage must be repaired by specialists with the necessary welding and hydraulic straightening equipment.
2 Although subframes are used front and rear, they act in the main as supports and locations for the power units and suspension systems.
3 If the damage is severe, it is vital that on completion of the repair the body and subframes are in correct alignment. Less severe damage may also have twisted or distorted the body or subframes, although this may not be visible immediately. It is therefore always best on completion of repair to check for twist and squareness to make sure all is well.
4 To check for twist, position the car on a clean level floor, place a jack under each jacking point, raise the car and take off the wheels. Raise or lower the jacks until the sills are parallel with the ground. Depending where the damage occurred, using an accurate

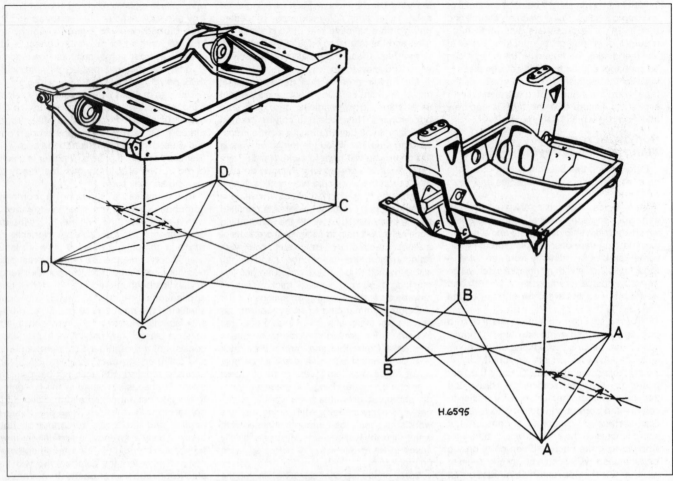

H.6595

5.5 Body and subframe horizontal alignment check

AA Width between centres of the front subframe front mounting bolts = 660.4 mm
BB Width between centres of the front subframe rear mounting bolts = 412.65 mm
CC Width between centres of the rear subframe front mounting block lower bolts = 1282.7 mm
DD Width between centres of the rear subframe rear mounting block bolts = 977.9 mm

scale, take measurements at the suspension mounting points and if comparable readings are not obtained it is an indication that the body is twisted.

5 After checking for twist, check for squareness by taking a series of measurements on the floor **(see illustration)**. Drop a plumb line and bob weight from various mounting points on the underside of the body and mark these points on the floor with chalk. Draw a straight line between each point and measure and mark the middle of each line. A line drawn on the floor starting at the front and finishing at the rear should be quite straight and pass through the centres of the other lines. Diagonal measurements can also be made as a check for squareness.

6 On older Minis, rust or corrosion of the vehicle underframe is a common occurrence and, if the corrosion has reached an advanced state, may be grounds for failure of the annual MOT test.

7 Where serious rust or corrosion has affected a load bearing area, it will be necessary to

have this repaired immediately either by fitting a new body section or, in less serious cases, by plating over the affected area. The load-bearing areas of the Mini consist of the subframe, the side sills (inner and outer) and any area of the vehicle structure within 300 mm of a suspension, steering, subframe, or seat belt anchorage point.

6.1 Remove the interior pull handle retaining screws and handle

8 Repairs of this nature are best left to a body repair specialist, as any new section or plating that may be necessary must be welded in place to restore the original structural rigidity of the bodyshell. The repair of corrosion to structural areas using fibreglass, body filler, or the retention of new sections with pop rivets, or screws, is not acceptable to legal requirements.

6 Front door interior trim panel (Saloon and Estate models) – removal and refitting

Removal

1 Undo and remove the two screws and lift off the interior pull handle **(see illustration)**.
2 Undo and remove the retaining screws and lift away the door lock remote control handle followed by the window regulator handle and surround **(see illustrations)**. On later models,

6.2a Remove the door lock remote control handle . . .

6.2b . . . and the window regulator handle

6.3 Ease off the interior lock control surround . . .

the screw securing the window regulator handle is covered with a trim cap, which must be carefully prised out for access to the screw.

3 Carefully ease off the interior lock control surround **(see illustration)**.

4 On later models undo and remove the retaining screws and lift away the storage bin.

5 If the top edge of the trim panel incorporates a trim capping, undo the two screws, then carefully ease the capping away from the door using a wide-bladed screwdriver or flat strip of metal. This will release the three retaining studs behind the capping, allowing the capping to be lifted away. If any of the studs break during removal, extract the broken stud and glue a new one in its place.

6 Using a wide-bladed screwdriver or flat strip of metal inserted between the trim panel and the door, carefully detach the trim panel clips from the door panel **(see illustration)**.

7 When all the clips are released, the panel can be withdrawn.

8 If it is wished to gain access to the internal door components, carefully peel off the waterproof covering.

Refitting

9 Refitting is the reverse sequence to removal, but ensure that the waterproof covering is in position before refitting the panel. If the panel incorporates a trim capping, refit by placing the capping in position and pushing the studs fully home. Secure with the three retaining screws.

7 Doors –
removal and refitting

All models except Van & Pick-up

Removal

1 Refer to Chapter 3 and remove the fresh air vent assembly (if fitted) adjacent to the door pillar.

2 Gently ease the door sealing rubber from the door pillar around the area where it retains the facia inner trim.

3 Undo and remove the retaining screws (if fitted), and then carefully fold back the facia inner trim to give access to the door check strap aperture.

4 Extract the split pin and clevis pin from the door check strap.

5 Support the weight of the door on blocks, or engage the help of an assistant. Undo and remove the four nuts and two washer plates, accessible from inside the front wheelarch.

6 Carefully lift the door assembly, complete with hinges, off the body, noting the position of any alignment shims that may be fitted to the hinges.

Refitting

7 Refitting the door is the reverse sequence to removal.

Van & Pick-up models

Removal

8 Upon inspection it will be seen that each door is held in place by two hinges and a check strap.

9 To remove a door, first unscrew and remove the two set screws and washers that secure the door check strap coupling bracket which is located on the inside of the door pillars. To gain access it will be necessary to ease back the side trim first.

10 Open the door carefully and pull out the interior lining of the door.

11 Undo and remove the cross-head screw and nut from the door side of each of the two hinges.

6.6 . . . then detach the panel clips and withdraw the trim panel

12 The door can now be lifted away from the body, leaving the hinges still attached to the body.

Refitting

13 Refitting the door is the reverse sequence to removal.

8 Door hinge –
removal and refitting

All models except Van & Pick-up

Removal

1 Remove the door as described in Section 7.

2 The hinges can now be removed from the door by simply undoing the retaining screws and lifting off.

Refitting

3 Refitting is the reverse sequence to removal.

Van & Pick-up models

Removal

4 Refer to Section 7 and remove the door.

5 Two nuts/bolts hold each hinge to the inside of the front wing. The heads of the nuts/bolts are very difficult to get at because they are surrounded at the top and bottom by the sides of the support brackets. This is particularly applicable to the top hinge, inside bolt.

6 Using a socket and universal coupling, undo and remove the nuts and bolts and lift away the hinge.

7 If the head on one of the bolts has become so burred that the spanner will no longer fit and provide a positive grip, very carefully examine a new hinge and decide on the exact position of the old bolt by comparison.

8 The old bolt can then be carefully drilled out from the outside of the hinge.

Refitting

9 Refitting the door hinge is the reverse sequence to removal.

9 Front door glass – removal and refitting

All models except Van & Pick-up

Removal

1 Refer to Section 6, and remove the door interior trim panel.

2 Carefully ease off the waist rail finisher strips from the top of the door edge, taking care not to damage them as they are lifted away from the clips.

3 Wind the window approximately half-way down so that the two arms of the regulator mechanism are as near vertical as they can be. With a piece of wood, wedge the window glass at the sill in this position.

4 Remove the regulator mechanism securing screws **(see illustration)**.

5 Pull the regulator away from the door panel enough to move it forwards so that the rear arm comes out of the window channel. Then move the mechanism back to release the arm from the front channel and lift it away.

6 Support the glass with one hand, remove the wedge and tilt the forward edge down into the door so that the top rear corner of the glass comes inside the top of the window frame. The glass can then be lifted out.

Refitting

7 Refitting is the reverse sequence to removal, bearing in mind the following points:

a) *Make sure that the window is located snugly in the frame glazing channels before wedging it in the half-way position.*

b) *Check that the waist rail finisher clips are evenly spaced before fitting the finishers back on. With the inner finisher, butt the forward end against the glazing channel rubber seal before fitting the rest.*

c) *Before securing the regulator mechanism to the door panel, apply a suitable sealer to the edge of the plate. This compensates for any irregularities in the panel which could cause rattles. Ensure that the lip on the front edge of the plate is engaged inside the panel.*

Van & Pick-up models

Removal

8 Undo and remove the retaining screw, boss and washer securing the catches to the glass. Lift off the catches and sealing rubbers.

9 Slide the front glass rearwards and then undo and remove the screw securing the lower channel to the door. If the screw is very tight or badly corroded, apply liberal amounts of penetrating oil to the screw and allow it to soak in. Give the screw a sharp tap with a hammer and drift to break the corrosion. It should now be possible to unscrew it.

10 Move both glasses forward and repeat the above procedure, if necessary, on the other lower channel retaining screw.

11 Ease the glasses, lower channel, and glass catch strip towards the centre of the car at the bottom, then lift the assembly off the door. The two sliding glasses can then be removed from the lower channel.

Refitting

12 Refitting is the reverse sequence to removal.

10 Front door lock assembly – removal and refitting

All models except Van & Pick-up

Removal

1 Refer to Section 6 and remove the door interior trim panel.

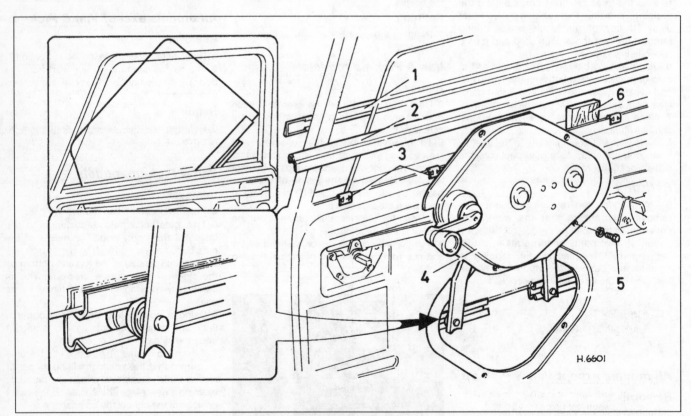

9.4 Removal of front door glass

Inset shows regulator arm and position of door glass ready for removal

| 1 | Waist rail finisher (outer) | 3 | Securing clips for finishers | 5 | Regulator securing screws |
| 2 | Waist rail finisher (inner) | 4 | Window regulator | 6 | Wedge (to hold glass) |

10.2 Remove the door inner remote control handle retaining screws . . .

10.3 . . . the interior lock control retaining screws . . .

10.4 . . . and the door lock retaining screws

2 Undo and remove the screws securing the door inner remote control handle to the door panel **(see illustration)**.

3 Undo and remove the screws securing the interior lock control to the door panel **(see illustration)**.

4 Undo and remove the screws securing the door lock to the side of the door **(see illustration)**.

5 Slide the door lock out of its location in the door and carefully release the two small circlips securing the remote control handle and interior lock operating rods to the door lock assembly.

6 Lift away the door lock, then withdraw the remote control and interior lock control from the door panel.

Refitting

7 Refitting is the reverse sequence to removal, bearing in mind the following points:

a) *Ensure that the small link rod on the lock assembly is engaged with the operating link of the exterior door handle.*

b) *If problems are experienced with the operation of the lock, it is likely that the inner remote control handle assembly is incorrectly positioned. If the door fails to lock, loosen the three retaining screws, and move the remote control handle assembly forwards to correct the*

operation. If the door fails to unlock, move the assembly rearwards.

Van & Pick-up models

Removal

8 Undo and remove the three screws that secure the lock body to the inner door panel **(see illustration)**.

9 Undo and remove the screw located at the end of the locking handle spindle.

10 Slacken the inner handle clamp screw (where fitted) and slide out the outer handle and escutcheon. Now lift off the lock body.

Refitting

11 Refitting is the reverse sequence to removal.

---

11 Front door exterior handle (Saloon and Estate models) – removal and refitting

Removal

1 Refer to Section 6 and remove the door interior trim panel.

2 Undo and remove the screws securing the interior lock control to the inner door panel.

3 Undo and remove the screws securing the door lock assembly to the side of the door, and move the lock up at the bottom and away from the door.

4 Undo and remove the screws securing the exterior handle to the door and lift the handle off **(see illustration)**.

5 With the handle removed, the lock barrel and push button can be withdrawn as follows.

6 Prise off the retaining clip securing the lock barrel to the handle.

7 Insert the key into the lock and withdraw the lock barrel.

8 Undo and remove the screw securing the retaining plate to the exterior handle.

9 Lift off the retaining plate, operating link, washer, and spring. Now withdraw the push button.

Refitting

10 Refitting is the reverse sequence to removal. On the earlier type door handle the push button plunger incorporates an adjustable nylon cap over the plunger. The adjustment of this cap is set during manufacture, but if necessary it can be screwed in or out slightly to give 1.0 to 1.5 mm of free play before contacting the door lock release lever **(see illustration)**.

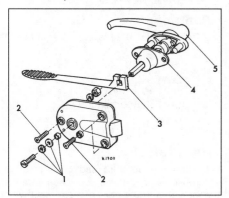

10.8 Exploded view of the door lock and handle assembly fitted to Van and Pick-up models

1 *Lock handle spindle fixings*
2 *Lock body retaining screws*
3 *Interior handle*
4 *Seal*
5 *Exterior handle*

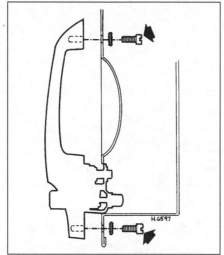

11.4 Exterior door handle securing screws (arrowed) – Saloon and Estate models

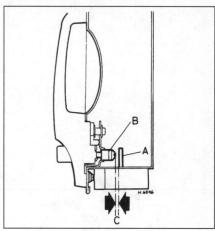

11.10 Door handle push button plunger adjustment

A *Lock release lever*
B *Plunger cap*
C = *1.0 to 1.5 mm*

12 Front door striker plate – removal and refitting

All models except Van & Pick-up

Removal

1 Remove the striker plate cover from the body pillar.
2 Undo and remove the striker plate retaining screws, lift out the striker lock and remove the striker plate.

Refitting

3 Refitting is the reverse sequence to removal. Adjust the striker plate so that as the door is closed, the striker lock passes through the door lock without fouling. It should also be possible to push the door in slightly against compression of the sealing rubber when the door is closed.

Van & Pick-up models

Removal

4 To remove the striker on these models, simply undo and remove the retaining screws and lift off.

Refitting

5 When refitting the striker plate, adjust it so that the door sealing rubber is just compressed and the door is flush with the adjoining bodywork when closed.

13 Bonnet – removal and refitting

Removal

1 Open the bonnet and support on its stay.
2 With a pencil, mark the outline of the hinge on the bonnet to assist correct refitting.
3 An assistant should now take the weight of the bonnet. Undo and remove the bonnet-to-hinge retaining nuts, spring and plain washers at both hinges **(see illustration)**. Carefully lift away the bonnet over the front of the car.

Refitting

4 Refitting is the reverse sequence to removal. Alignment in the body may be made by leaving the securing nuts slightly loose and repositioning by trial-and-error.

14 Bonnet lock release cable – removal and refitting

Removal

1 From inside the car, slacken the retaining nut, and release the cable and handle assembly from the bracket under the facia.
2 In the engine compartment, remove the ignition splash shield, then undo the two bolts securing the bonnet lock to the front panel.
3 Disconnect the return spring and the release cable from the bonnet lock, and remove the lock.
4 Undo the bolt and move the relay located at the rear of the right-hand inner wing, for access to the cable-to-bulkhead grommet.
5 Release the cable from the cable clip, push the cable grommet through the bulkhead, and withdraw the cable from inside the car.

Refitting

6 Refitting is the reverse sequence to removal, but adjust the bonnet lock alignment before finally tightening the two lock retaining bolts.

15 Bonnet lock – removal and refitting

Removal

1 Open the bonnet and support it on its stay.
2 On models having an ignition splash shield attached to the body front panel, undo and remove the retaining screws and withdraw the shield.
3 Detach the slider catch return spring.
4 Undo and remove the two screws securing the lock assembly to the front panel and lift off the lock and guide plate.

Refitting

5 Refitting is the reverse sequence to removal.

16 Boot lid – removal and refitting

Removal

1 Open the boot lid and disconnect the number plate light electrical leads from their connectors in the boot compartment wiring harness.
2 Support the boot lid and undo and remove the screws securing the two stays to the sides of the boot lid.
3 Undo and remove the nuts, spring and plain washers securing the hinges to the boot lid and lift off the boot lid **(see illustration)**.

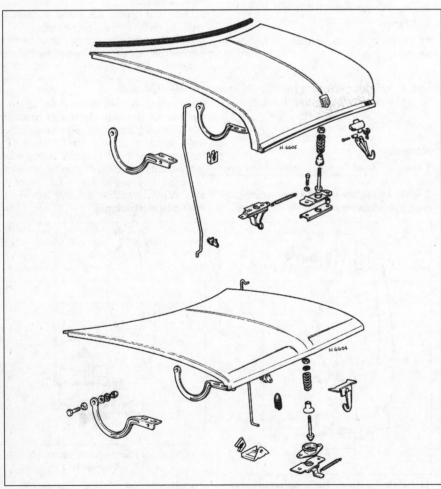

13.3 Bonnet hinge and lock assemblies

Refitting

4 Refitting is the reverse sequence to removal.

17 Boot lid lock –
removal and refitting

Removal

1 Open the boot lid, undo and remove the retaining screws, and lift off the lock assembly.
2 To remove the lock handle, undo and remove the two nuts and washers and lift off the handle and joint washer.
3 If it is wished to remove the lock barrel from the handle, extract the spring clip and slide off the flat and wavy washers from the end of the handle.
4 Take out the small lock barrel retaining pin and then slide out the barrel. Recover the locking pin from the end of the handle.

Refitting

5 Reassembly and refitting of the lock is the reverse sequence to removal. When reassembling the lock barrel, position the small retaining pin in the slot of the locking pin before refitting.

18 Rear doors
(Estate and Van models) – removal and refitting

Removal

1 Open both doors and disconnect the door support stays by undoing the nut, washer and bolt at the end of each stay.
2 Preferably have an assistant hold the door,

or place a support under it, and then bend down the tab washer on each door hinge.
3 Undo and remove the nut, tab washer, hinge centre bolt, and the spherical bush from each of the door hinges in turn.

Refitting

4 Refitting is the reverse sequence to removal.

19 Rear door lock
(Estate and Van models) – removal and refitting

Removal

1 Undo and remove the screws securing the lock to the door.
2 Disengage the lock assembly from the handle, lift it up to release the lower stay from its guide, lower it to release the upper stay, and then withdraw the complete assembly.
3 Slacken the nuts securing the stays to the lock and then unscrew the stays.
4 To remove the door handle, release the door seal retaining clips from the hole in the door panel.
5 Undo and remove the nuts and washers securing the door handle to the door. Lift off the handle and recover the joint washer.
6 To remove the lock barrel, first remove the retaining circlip and slide off the cover, spring washer and brass washers.
7 Withdraw the handle yoke, extract the lock barrel retaining pin, and remove the lock barrel and locking pin.

Refitting

8 Reassembly and refitting is the reverse sequence to removal. When refitting the stays note that the cranked stay is refitted to the top with the crank to the right.

20 Tailgate
(Pick-up models) – removal and refitting

Removal

1 Undo and remove the number plate light cover retaining screw and lift off the cover and lens.
2 Detach the electrical leads from the number plate light bulbholders and withdraw the leads from the tailgate.
3 Support the tailgate in the open position, then undo and remove the tailgate stays securing screws.
4 Undo and remove the screws securing the tailgate hinges to the tailgate and carefully lift away the tailgate.

Refitting

5 Refitting is the reverse sequence to removal.

21 Windscreen –
removal and refitting

Removal

1 Remove the wiper arms from their spindles by using a screwdriver to ease them up, then lift off.
2 If a self-adhesive interior mirror is fitted to the windscreen, remove it by gently warming the mirror base and the area of screen around it. Use a hair dryer or rag soaked in warm water as a heat source.
3 Using a small screwdriver, carefully ease up one end of the finishing strip from its groove in the windscreen sealing rubber and then pull the entire length of the strip out of the rubber.
4 If an undamaged windscreen is being removed, from inside the car firmly push the screen outwards, starting at one of the top corners. Carefully remove the complete windscreen from the sealing rubber and lift if off the car. Withdraw the sealing rubber from the windscreen aperture in the body.
5 If a shattered windscreen is being removed, lay some old blankets or sheets over the bonnet and in the car interior, making sure that the demister vents are well covered. Break the remaining glass onto the blankets or sheets, and then withdraw the sealing rubber from the windscreen aperture. Discard the shattered glass and clean up any fragments using a vacuum cleaner.

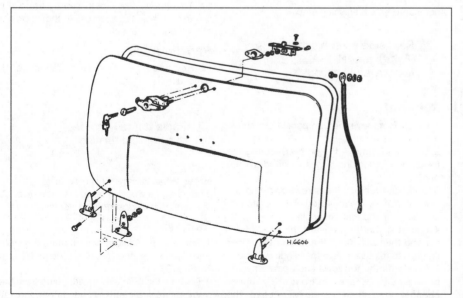

16.3 Boot lid hinge and lock assemblies

HAYNES HINT *When cleaning up after a shattered windscreen, operate the heater in all positions with the fan motor running to dislodge any trapped glass, but watch out for flying fragments which may be blown out of the ducting.*

Refitting

6 To fit the windscreen, first inspect the sealing rubber for hardness or deterioration and renew if necessary. It is advisable to renew the sealing rubber as a matter of course when fitting a new windscreen.

7 Position the sealing rubber over the windscreen, and then insert a length of string around the circumference of the rubber, ensuring that it seats into the body flange groove of the rubber. Position the string so that the two ends protrude by at least 300 mm at the bottom centre of the screen.

8 Mix a concentrated soap and water solution and apply it liberally to the flange of the windscreen aperture.

9 Place the windscreen and rubber seal in position on the car, and engage the help of an assistant to apply firm pressure to the outside of the screen. From inside the car use the string to pull the rubber lip over the body flange, working slowly around the screen until the string has been fully withdrawn.

10 Starting at the top centre of the rubber seal, use a wide-bladed screwdriver to spread the lips of the seal, while at the same time pressing the finishing strip into place. Work around the entire circumference of the windscreen in this way.

11 With the screen in position and the finishing strip fitted, the wiper arms can now be refitted to their spindles, and the mirror (where fitted) resecured using a suitable adhesive.

22 Rear window (Saloon and Pick-up models) – removal and refitting

The removal and refitting procedure for the rear window or its sealing rubber is the same as described in Section 21 for the windscreen.

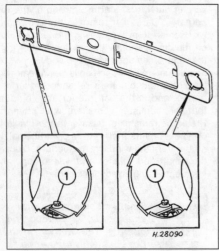

26.6 Wooden facia attachment points

1 Mounting bracket locations accessible through fresh air vent apertures

On later models, it will also be necessary to disconnect the electrical supply and earth leads to the heated rear window element before removal.

23 Rear door window (Estate and Van models) – removal and refitting

The removal and refitting procedure for the rear door window or its sealing rubber is the same as described in Section 21 for the windscreen. Note, however, that the sealing rubber does not incorporate a finishing strip.

24 Rear quarterlight glass (Saloon models) – removal and refitting

Hinged type

Removal

1 Open the window and then undo and remove the screws securing the catch to the body.

2 With the window supported, undo and remove the screws securing the hinge(s) to the body pillar.

3 Lift away the window, and if required undo and remove the retaining screw and window glass surround.

Refitting

4 Refitting is the reverse sequence to removal.

Fixed type

5 Removal and refitting of the fixed type window follows the same procedure as described for the windscreen in Section 21. Note, however, that the sealing rubber does not incorporate a finishing strip.

25 Rear side screen window (Estate models) – removal and refitting

Removal

1 Carefully remove the trim panel from above the windows.

2 Undo and remove the screw securing the fixed window locking peg and withdraw the peg.

3 Undo and remove the screws securing the front, upper, and rear glazing channels and lift out the front and rear channels.

4 Slide the windows toward the front of the car and then pull down the rear of the upper channel to release it from the window frame.

5 Now slide the windows and upper channel rearwards to release the front of the upper channel, and then carefully remove the channel and windows.

Refitting

6 Refitting is the reverse sequence to removal.

26 Wooden facia – removal and refitting

Removal

1 Disconnect the battery negative terminal (refer to *Disconnecting the battery* in the Reference Chapter).

2 Open the doors, and carefully release the door seal weatherstrip from the area near the ends of the facia.

3 Remove the complete steering column assembly as described in Chapter 10.

4 Remove the fresh air vent assemblies from both sides of the facia as described in Chapter 3.

5 Remove the radio as described in Chapter 12A.

6 Working through the fresh air vent apertures, slacken the two bolts, one each side, securing the facia mounting brackets **(see illustration)**.

7 Release the facia and withdraw it forward from its location.

8 Disconnect the wiring to the glovebox light, clock and instruments, then remove the facia from the car.

9 The glovebox can be removed, if desired, by undoing the screws securing the lid hinges and the glovebox liner, and lifting these components away **(see illustration opposite)**.

10 The instrument panel can be removed by undoing the 12 screws securing the panel to the rear of the facia and lifting away, complete with instruments. Removal of the instruments from the panel is as described in Chapter 12A.

11 To remove the clock, simply undo the clamping bracket nut, and slide the clock out of the front of the facia.

Refitting

12 Refitting is the reverse sequence to removal.

27 Facia top rail cover – removal and refitting

Note: *When removing the facia top rail on models with a wooden facia, the facia must be removed first as described in Section 26.*

Removal

1 Remove the fresh air vent assemblies from both sides of the facia as described in Chapter 3.

2 Release the door seal weatherstrip from the body pillar sufficiently to clear the top rail cover.

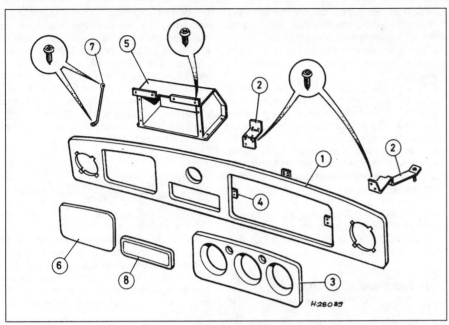

26.9 Wooden facia components

1 Facia panel	4 Instrument panel retaining plates	7 Glove box lid strap
2 Facia mounting brackets	5 Glove box liner	8 Radio blanking plate (where fitted)
3 Instrument panel	6 Glove box lid	

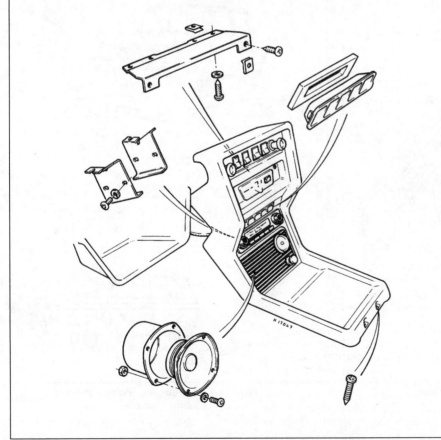

28.2 Centre console components and attachments

3 Withdraw the left-hand facia inner trim panel.

4 Undo and remove the four nuts securing the top rail cover, lift the front of the cover upwards to release the four studs, and then withdraw the cover from the car.

Refitting

5 Refitting is the reverse sequence to removal.

28 Centre console – removal and refitting

Removal

1 Disconnect the battery negative terminal (refer to *Disconnecting the battery* in the Reference Chapter).

2 Undo and remove the centre console retaining screws **(see illustration)**.

3 Carefully ease off the radio knobs and finishers, and then undo and remove the radio securing wing nuts.

4 Engage fourth gear, while at the same time moving the console rearwards. Undo and remove the radio retaining screws and ease the radio clear of the console.

5 Disconnect the wiring from the clock and cigarette lighter, and detach the speaker plug from the radio.

6 Release the gear lever grommet then remove the centre console from the car.

7 With the console removed, release the clamp and lift out the cloth. Unscrew the cigarette lighter body and withdraw it. Unclip and remove the speaker grille, then lift out the speaker after undoing the retaining screws.

Refitting

8 Refitting the components to the console and the console to the car is the reverse sequence to removal.

29 Front grille panel – removal and refitting

Except Clubman & 1275 GT

Removal

1 Undo and remove the self-tapping screws securing the edge trim to each side of the grille panel and lift off the trim **(see illustration overleaf)**.

2 Undo and remove the remaining screws securing the centre panel of the grille and withdraw the panel.

Refitting

3 Refitting is the reverse sequence to removal.

Clubman and 1275 GT

Removal

4 Undo and remove the self-tapping screws securing the grille panel and the headlight extension panels.

5 Lift off the extension panels, disengage the lugs on the lower edge of the grille from the grommets in the lower body panel, and lift off the grille.

Refitting

6 Refitting is the reverse sequence to removal.

30 Bodywork seam trim strips – general information

1 The welded seams on the exterior of the Mini bodywork are covered by protective metal and push-fit trim strips which are either chromium plated or sprayed to match the exterior colour scheme. Additionally, a chrome, black, or body-coloured trim strip is used to cover the side sill seams and, on models without flared wheelarch extensions, the wheelarch edges. On most models, this is a one-piece plastic moulding running the full length of the car.

2 The side seam trim strips are removed by carefully prising up with a screwdriver and lifting off.

3 To refit the strips, ensure that the small retaining clips are in sound condition and simply push the trim into place, giving it a firm push with the palm of your hand to ensure that it is fully home.

4 The wheelarch and side sill plastic moulding is removed after first drilling out the pop rivet that retains each end of the trim to the wheelarch.

5 Before fitting a new trim, heat it slightly in a warm oven until it is pliable and then carefully position it over the wheelarch edges and side sill seams. Secure each end with a pop rivet or self-tapping screw.

31 Front and rear bumpers – removal and refitting

The layout of the bumpers and their method of attachment varies considerably according to model type and year of manufacture. The location and type of retaining nuts, bolts or screws will be obvious after a visual inspection, and no problems should be encountered (see illustration). On models with a full width wrap-around bumper, it is helpful to engage the aid of an assistant to support the bumper, thus ensuring that the paintwork is not scratched as it is removed.

32 Sunroof components – general information

The sunroof is a complex piece of equipment, consisting of a large number of components. Adjustment and/or repair of the sunroof is outside the scope of this manual, and it is recommended that work of this nature should be entrusted to your Rover dealer.

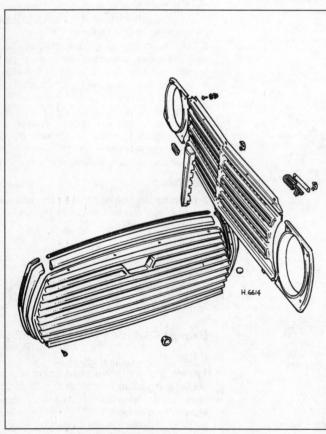

29.1 **Front grille panels and attachments**

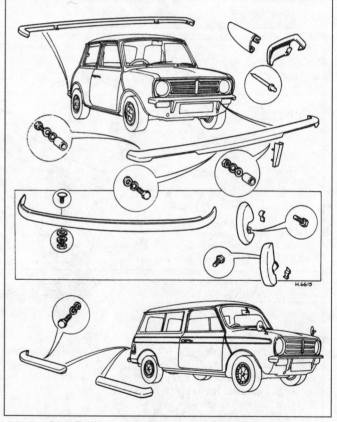

31.1 **Front and rear bumpers and attachments – Clubman models**

Chapter 11 Part B:
Bodywork and fittings system – October 1996 models onward

Contents

Bodywork, paint and exterior trim check .... See Chapter 1
Bonnet – removal and refitting 12
Bonnet lock – removal and refitting 14
Bonnet lock release cable – removal and refitting 13
Boot lid – removal and refitting 15
Boot lid lock – removal and refitting 16
Door, boot and bonnet check and lubrication .... See Chapter 1
Doors – removal and refitting 7
Facia – removal and refitting 19
Facia top rail – removal and refitting 20
Front and rear bumpers – removal and refitting 23
Front door exterior handle – removal and refitting 10
Front door glass – removal and refitting 8
Front door interior trim panel – removal and refitting ... 6
Front door lock assembly – removal and refitting 9

Front door striker plate – removal and refitting 11
Front grille panel – removal and refitting 21
General information 1
Interior trim – removal and refitting 27
Maintenance – bodywork and underframe 2
Maintenance – upholstery and carpets 3
Major structural damage or corrosion – general information 5
Minor body damage – repair 4
Rear quarterlight glass – removal and refitting 18
Seat belt components – removal and refitting 26
Seats – removal and refitting 25
Sunroof components – general information 24
Wheelarch extensions – removal and refitting 22
Windscreen – removal and refitting 17

Degrees of difficulty

Easy, suitable for novice with little experience	**Fairly easy,** suitable for beginner with some experience	**Fairly difficult,** suitable for competent DIY mechanic	**Difficult,** suitable for experienced DIY mechanic	**Very difficult,** suitable for expert DIY or professional

Specifications

Torque wrench settings	Nm	lbf ft
Front seat belt mountings:		
Inertia reel	30	22
Lower anchorage bolt	30	22
Seat belt pre-tensioner-to-companion box:		
Nut	6	4
Bolt	2	1
Seat belt stalk	32	24
Upper anchorage bolt	32	24
Rear seat belt mountings (all)	30	22

1 General information

Although the Mini has been produced in many forms since its introduction, the principle of construction remains the same even on later models. The body and floor pan are of a monocoque all-steel, welded construction creating a very strong and torsionally rigid shell. The front and rear suspension assemblies are mounted on subframes, bolted to the underside of the bodyshell. The front subframe also provides mounting points for the engine/transmission.

2 Maintenance – bodywork and underframe

Refer to Chapter 11A, Section 2.

3 Maintenance – upholstery and carpets

Refer to Chapter 11A, Section 3.

4 Minor body damage – repair

Refer to Chapter 11A, Section 4.

5 Major structural damage or corrosion – general information

Refer to Chapter 11A, Section 5.

6.2a Undo the screws and remove the door handle . . .

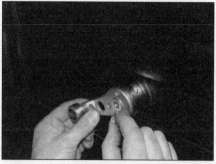

6.2b . . . followed by the window regulator handle . . .

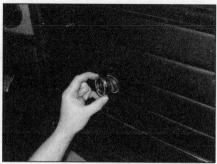

6.2c . . . and surround

6 Front door interior trim panel – removal and refitting

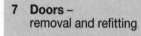

Removal

1 If the top edge of the trim panel incorporates a wooden trim finisher, undo the three screws and remove the finisher from the door.

2 Undo and remove the retaining screws and lift away the door handle followed by the window regulator handle and surround (**see illustrations**). Depending on model, it may be necessary to prise out the trim cap for access to the window regulator handle retaining screw.

3 Undo and remove the two screws and lift off the interior pull handle (**see illustration**).

4 Undo and remove the retaining screws and lift away the storage bin (**see illustrations**).

5 Carefully ease off the interior lock control surround (**see illustration**).

6 Using a wide-bladed screwdriver or flat strip of metal inserted between the trim panel and the door, carefully detach the trim panel clips from the door panel (**see illustration**).

7 When all the clips are released, the panel can be withdrawn.

8 If it is wished to gain access to the internal door components, carefully peel off the waterproof covering.

Refitting

9 Refitting is the reverse sequence to removal, but ensure that the waterproof covering is in position before refitting the panel.

7 Doors – removal and refitting

Removal

1 Extract the split pin and clevis pin from the door check strap.

2 Support the weight of the door on blocks, or engage the help of an assistant. Undo and remove the four nuts and two washer plates, accessible from inside the front wheelarch.

3 Carefully lift the door assembly, complete with hinges, off the body, noting the position of any alignment shims that may be fitted to the hinges.

4 If required, the hinges can now be removed from the door by undoing the retaining screws and lifting off.

Refitting

5 Refitting the door is the reverse sequence to removal.

8 Front door glass – removal and refitting

1 Refer to the procedures contained in Chapter 11A, Section 9, but remove and refit the door interior trim panel as described in Section 6 of this Chapter.

6.3 Undo the two screws and remove the interior pull handle

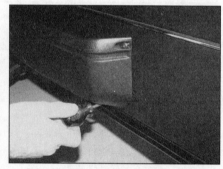

6.4a Undo and remove the retaining screws . . .

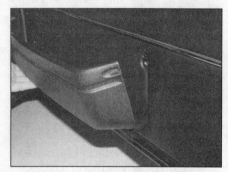

6.4b . . . and lift away the storage bin

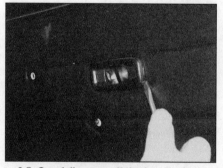

6.5 Carefully ease off the interior lock control surround

6.6 Detach the trim panel clips and remove the door panel

19.2a Unscrew the passenger's side facia fresh air vent retaining collar . . .

19.2b . . . turn the air vent anti-clockwise to remove . . .

19.2c . . . then withdraw the air vent hose

9 Front door lock assembly – removal and refitting

1 Refer to the procedures contained in Chapter 11A, Section 10, but remove and refit the door interior trim panel as described in Section 6 of this Chapter.

10 Front door exterior handle – removal and refitting

1 Refer to the procedures contained in Chapter 11A, Section 11, but remove and refit the door interior trim panel as described in Section 6 of this Chapter.

11 Front door striker plate – removal and refitting

Refer to Chapter 11A, Section 12.

12 Bonnet – removal and refitting

Refer to Chapter 11A, Section 13.

13 Bonnet lock release cable – removal and refitting

Removal

1 From inside the car, undo the retaining nut, and release the cable and handle assembly from the bracket under the facia.
2 In the engine compartment, disconnect the return spring from the bonnet lock, then undo the two bolts securing the bonnet lock to the front body panel.
3 Lift off the bonnet lock and disconnect the cable from the lock lever.
4 Release the cable retaining clip located behind the engine management ECU.

5 Pull the cable through the bulkhead grommet and remove it from inside the car.

Refitting

6 Refitting is the reverse sequence to removal, but adjust the bonnet lock alignment before finally tightening the two lock retaining bolts.

14 Bonnet lock – removal and refitting

Removal

1 In the engine compartment, disconnect the return spring from the bonnet lock, then undo the two bolts securing the bonnet lock to the front body panel.
2 Lift off the bonnet lock and disconnect the release cable from the lock lever. Remove the lock assembly.

Refitting

3 Refitting is the reverse sequence to removal, but adjust the bonnet lock alignment before finally tightening the two lock retaining bolts.

15 Boot lid – removal and refitting

Refer to Chapter 11A, Section 16.

16 Boot lid lock – removal and refitting

Refer to Chapter 11A, Section 17.

17 Windscreen – removal and refitting

Refer to Chapter 11A, Section 21.

18 Rear quarterlight glass – removal and refitting

Refer to Chapter 11A, Section 24.

19 Facia – removal and refitting

Removal

1 Disconnect the battery negative terminal (refer to *Disconnecting the battery* in the Reference Chapter).
2 Unscrew the passenger's side facia fresh air vent retaining collar, then turn the air vent anti-clockwise and remove it. Withdraw the air vent hose **(see illustrations)**. Remove the vent on the driver's side in the same way.
3 Remove the radio/cassette player as described in Chapter 12B.
4 Working through the radio/cassette player and fresh air vent apertures, undo the three nuts securing the facia retaining brackets to the body **(see illustration)**.
5 Release the retaining brackets and carefully pull the facia free for access **(see illustration)**.
6 Reach behind the facia and disconnect the speedometer cable by depressing the locking tab on the cable end fitting **(see illustration)**.

19.4 Undo the facia centre retaining bracket securing nut, working through the radio/cassette aperture

19.5 Release the retaining brackets and carefully pull the facia free

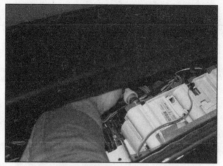

19.6 Reach behind the facia and disconnect the speedometer cable end fitting

19.7 Disconnect the wiring connectors

7 Disconnect the wiring connectors at the headlight levelling switch, anti-theft alarm warning light, tachometer and instrument panel **(see illustration)**.
8 Ease the facia from its location, checking that all wiring has been disconnected and moved clear, then remove the facia from inside the car **(see illustration)**.

Refitting

9 Refitting is the reverse sequence to removal.

20 Facia top rail – removal and refitting

Removal

1 Remove the facia as described in Section 19.
2 Remove the windscreen as described in Section 17.
3 Undo the three nuts securing the facia top rail to the body.
4 Withdraw the facia top rail from its location and disconnect the two demister ducts. Remove the rail from the car.

Refitting

5 Refitting is the reverse sequence to removal.

19.8 With all wiring disconnected, remove the facia from inside the car

21 Front grille panel – removal and refitting

Removal

1 Where fitted, slacken the mounting bolts and move the auxiliary driving lights forward as far as they will go.
2 Undo the eight screws, along the top and around the side, securing the front grille panel to the body and withdraw the grille panel **(see illustration)**.

Refitting

3 Refitting is the reverse sequence to removal. Set the auxiliary lights in the horizontal position and tighten the mounting bolts. The auxiliary light beam alignment should be checked by a suitably-equipped service station at the earliest opportunity.

22 Wheelarch extensions – removal and refitting

Front
Removal

1 Remove the front bumper as described in Section 23.
2 Firmly apply the handbrake, then jack up the front of the car and support it securely on axle stands (see *Jacking and vehicle support*).
3 Using a 5.0 mm drill bit, drill out the pop rivet securing the lower rear end of the wheelarch extension to the body.
4 From under the wheelarch, undo the five securing nuts and remove the extension from the front wing.

Refitting

5 Clean the mating faces of the wheelarch extension and the front wing and ensure that the rubber seal is correctly fitted to the extension.
6 Locate the extension in position and secure with the five retaining nuts.
7 Pop rivet the lower rear end of the extension to the body.

8 Refit the front bumper as described in Section 23 and lower the vehicle to the ground.

Rear
Removal and refitting

9 The procedure for removal and refitting of the rear wheelarch extensions is the same as described previously for the front extensions bearing in mind the following points.
  a) If working on the left-hand side, it will be necessary to remove the fuel tank for access to the wheelarch extension mounting nuts. Details of fuel tank removal and refitting are contained in Chapter 4C.
  b) If working on the right-hand side, move the washer reservoir to one side for access to the mounting nuts.

23 Front and rear bumpers – removal and refitting

Removal

1 The front and rear bumpers are secured to the body by three nuts, one each side and one in the centre. After unscrewing the nuts and removing the washers, the bumpers are simply lifted from their locations.

Refitting

2 Refitting is the reverse sequence to removal.

21.2 Removing the front grille panel

24 Sunroof components – general information

The sunroof is a complex piece of equipment, consisting of a large number of components. Adjustment and/or repair of the sunroof is outside the scope of this manual, and it is recommended that work of this nature should be entrusted to your Rover dealer.

25 Seats – removal and refitting

Front seats

Removal

1 Move the seat fully rearwards.
2 Undo the two nuts and bolts securing the seat to the mounting brackets at the front.
3 Release the rear seat access lever to release the seat from the floor then remove the seat from the car.

Refitting

4 Refitting is the reverse sequence to removal. Tighten the seat mounting bolt nuts so that the seat can still be tipped forward without binding.

Rear seat cushion

Removal

5 Lift the rear seat cushion from its location.
6 Undo the two screws securing the cushion retaining straps to the body and remove the cushion (see illustration).

Refitting

7 Refitting is the reverse sequence to removal.

Rear seat back

Removal

8 Remove the rear seat cushion as described previously.
9 From inside the luggage compartment undo the screw each side securing the seat back to the parcel shelf (see illustration).

25.6 Undo the two screws securing the rear seat cushion retaining straps to the body

10 Move the seat belt harness to one side, release the seat back from its location and remove it from the car.

Refitting

11 Refitting is the reverse sequence to removal.

26 Seat belt components – removal and refitting

Note: *Record the positions of the washers and spacers on the seat belt anchors, and ensure they are refitted in their original positions.*

Front seat belt

⚠️ *Warning: The front seats are equipped with pyrotechnic seat belt pre-tensioners and must be treated with the same precautions as for the airbag assembly. Refer to Chapter 12B for the precautions which should be observed when dealing with an airbag system. Do not tamper with the seat belt pre-tensioner unit in any way, and do not attempt to test the unit. Note that the unit is triggered if the mechanism is supplied with an electrical current (including via an ohmmeter), or if the assembly is subjected to a temperature of greater than 100°C.*

Removal

1 Remove the rear quarter companion box as described in Section 27.

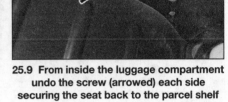

25.9 From inside the luggage compartment undo the screw (arrowed) each side securing the seat back to the parcel shelf

2 Undo the nut and bolt securing the seat belt pre-tensioner to the side of the companion box.
3 Prise off the trim cap from the seat belt upper anchorage bolt then undo the bolt and remove the washers (see illustration).
4 Undo the lower anchorage bolt and the inertia reel mounting bolt (after removing the trim cap) and remove the seat belt and pre-tensioner assembly from the car (see illustrations).
5 Undo the bolt and remove the washers securing the seat belt stalk to the body and remove the stalk.

Refitting

6 Refitting is the reverse sequence to removal. Ensure that all washers and/or spacers are positioned as noted before removal, and tighten all mounting bolts to the specified torque.

Rear seat belt

Removal

7 Remove the rear quarter companion box as described in Section 27.
8 Remove the rear seat cushion as described in Section 25.
9 Prise off the trim cap from the seat belt upper anchorage bolt then undo the bolt and remove the washers.
10 Undo the lower anchorage bolt and remove the washers.
11 Undo the inertia reel mounting bolt and remove the rear seat belt assembly from the car.

26.3 Prise off the trim cap from the front seat belt upper anchorage bolt then undo the bolt and remove the washers

26.4a Undo the front seat belt lower anchorage bolt (arrowed) . . .

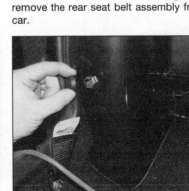

26.4b . . . and the inertia reel mounting bolt after removing the trim cap

27.2a Undo the front . . .

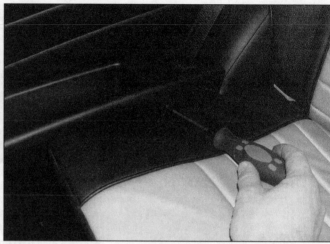

27.2b . . . and rear screws securing the top of the companion box to the body

12 Undo the bolt and remove the washers securing the seat belt buckles to the body.

Refitting

13 Refitting is the reverse sequence to removal. Ensure that all washers and/or spacers are positioned as noted before removal, and tighten all mounting bolts to the specified torque.

27 Interior trim – removal and refitting

Removal

Rear quarter companion box

1 Release the two seat belt guides from the top of the companion box.
2 Undo the two screws securing the top of the companion box to the body **(see illustrations)**.
3 Lift the companion box from its location and release the seat belts through the slots in the box **(see illustration)**.
4 Remove the companion box from the car.

Rear quarter wooden finisher

5 Undo the two screws securing the finisher to the body and remove the finisher.

Rear quarter trim pad

6 Remove the rear quarter companion box and rear quarter wooden finisher as described previously.
7 Release the retaining clips and remove the trim pad from the body.

Refitting

8 Refitting is the reverse sequence to removal.

27.3 Withdraw the companion box and release the seat belts through the slots in the box

Chapter 12 Part A:
Body electrical system – pre-October 1996 models

Contents

Anti-theft alarm system components – removal and refitting 19
Bulbs (exterior lights) – renewal 5
Bulbs (interior lights) – renewal 6
Dim-dip lighting system components – removal and refitting 8
Electrical fault finding – general information 2
Fuses and relays – general information 3
General information and precautions 1
Headlight beam alignment – checking and adjusting 7
Horn – removal, refitting and adjustment 9
Instrument panel – dismantling and reassembly 16
Instrument panel – removal and refitting 15

Radio – removal and refitting 18
Speedometer cable – removal and refitting 17
Switches – removal and refitting 4
Windscreen washer fluid level check . . . . .See *Weekly Checks*
Windscreen washer pump – removal and refitting 14
Windscreen wiper arms – removal and refitting 10
Windscreen wiper motor – dismantling and reassembly 12
Windscreen wiper motor – removal and refitting 11
Windscreen wiper wheelbox – removal and refitting 13
Wiper blade check . . . . .See *Weekly Checks*

Degrees of difficulty

Easy, suitable for novice with little experience	Fairly easy, suitable for beginner with some experience	Fairly difficult, suitable for competent DIY mechanic	Difficult, suitable for experienced DIY mechanic	Very difficult, suitable for expert DIY or professional

Specifications

General
System type . . . .   12 volt negative earth

Main fuses (two-fuse fuseblock)

Fuse connecting	Rating (amp)	Circuits protected
1 and 2	35	Interior light, horn and auxiliary units which operate with the ignition switched on or off
3 and 4	35	Direction indicators, windscreen wiper motor, heater blower, stop-lights and auxiliary units which operate only when the ignition is switched on

Note: *The fitting of additional accessories which are required to operate independently of the ignition circuit should be connected to the '2' terminal; accessories which are required to operate only when the ignition is switched on should be connected to the '4' terminal.*

Line fuses (two-fuse fuseblock)

Rating (amp)	Circuits protected
8	Side and tail lights
35	Hazard flasher

Main fuses (four-fuse fuseblock – early models)

Fuse connecting	Rating (amp)	Circuits protected
1 and 2	35	Stop-lights, reversing lights, direction indicators, heated rear window. These systems will only operate with the ignition switch at position II
3 and 4	25	Horn, headlight flasher, brake failure circuit. These systems operate independently of the ignition switch
5 and 6	25	Heater blower motor, windscreen wipers/washers, radio. These systems will operate with the ignition switch at position I or II
7 and 8	15	Side and tail lights, instrument panel lights

Note: *The fitting of additional accessories which are required to operate independently of the ignition circuit should be connected to the '4' terminal.*

Line fuses (four-fuse fuseblock – early models)

Rating (amp)	Circuits protected
15	Hazard flashers, interior light
–	Radio (rating to be as specified by the manufacturer)

Main fuses (four-fuse fuseblock – later models)

Fuse connecting	Rating (amp)	Circuits protected
1 and 2	35	Stop-lights, reversing lights, direction indicator relay, heated rear window, headlight dim-dip relay. These systems will only operate with the ignition switch at position II
3 and 4	25	Horn, headlight flasher, brake failure circuit, radio memory. These systems operate independently of the ignition switch
5 and 6	25	Heater blower motor, windscreen wipers/washers, instruments. These systems will operate with the ignition switch at position I or II
7 and 8	15	Left-hand side and tail lights, instrument panel lights, headlight dim-dip relay

Note: *The fitting of additional accessories which are required to operate independently of the ignition circuit should be connected to the '4' terminal*

Line fuses (four-fuse fuseblock – later models)

Rating (amp)	Circuits protected
15	Right-hand side and tail lights
10	Direction indicators/hazard flashers, interior light
15	Dim-dip lighting
10	Rear foglight

Fuses (twenty four-fuse fuseblock)

Fuse connecting	Rating (amp)	Circuits protected
1	15	Heated rear window
2	15	Reversing lights, stop-lights, headlight dim/dip*, direction indicator relay
3	15	Auxiliary cooling fan
4	15	Headlight dim/dip*
5	15	Heater blower motor, sunroof motor*
6	15	Wipers/washers
7	20	Headlight flasher, horn, anti-theft alarm*
8	10	Tachometer*, engine management ECU*, fuel pump relay*, anti-theft alarm*
9	10	Radio/cassette, cooling fan relay, automatic gear selector light*
10	10	Radio memory*, interior light, direction indicators, hazard flasher, anti-theft alarm LED*, brake test circuit*
11	10	Fuel pump*
12	10	Starter signal
13	10	Left-hand, side and tail lights
14	10	Right-hand, side and tail lights, instrument illumination
15	10	Left-hand headlight main beam
16	10	Right-hand headlight main beam, main beam warning light
17	10	Left-hand headlight dip beam
18	10	Right-hand headlight dip beam
19	20	Not used
20	15	Not used
21	10	Not used
22	20	Not used
23	Not used	
24	10	Rear foglight

* depending on model

Bulbs

	Wattage	Type
Auxiliary driving lights	55	453
Direction indicator side repeaters	5	501
Direction indicators	21	382
Footwell light	5	239
Glovebox light	10	245
Headlights:		
Europe (except France – dip vertical)	45/40	410
France – dip vertical	45/40	411
LHD (except Europe – dip right)	50/40	415
Sealed beam without sidelight, dip left (not UK)	60/54	101
Sealed beam with sidelights, dip left (UK only)	60/45	104
Illuminated switches	0.75	284
Interior light:		
Early models	6	254
Later models	10	245

Bulbs (continued)

	Wattage	Type
Number plate light:		
Estate, Van and Pick-up	5	989
Saloon	6	254
Panel and warning lights	2.2	987
Rear foglight	21	382
Reversing lights	21	382
Sidelights:		
Bayonet type	5	989
Capless type	5	501
Sidelights and front direction indicators	21/5	380
Stop/tail lights	21/5	380

Windscreen wiper motor

Brush spring pressure	140 to 200 g
Minimum brush length	4.8 mm
Armature endfloat	0.05 to 0.02 mm
Maximum pull to move rack in guide tubes	2.7 kg

1 General information and precautions

⚠️ **Warning: Before carrying out any work on the electrical system, read through the precautions given in 'Safety first!' at the beginning of this manual, and in Chapter 5A.**

1 The electrical system is of the 12 volt negative earth type. Power for the lights and all electrical accessories is supplied by a lead-acid type battery, which is charged by the dynamo or alternator.

2 This Chapter covers repair and service procedures for the various electrical components not associated with the engine. Information on the battery, dynamo, alternator and starter motor can be found in Chapter 5A.

3 It should be noted that, prior to working on any component in the electrical system, the battery negative terminal should first be disconnected, to prevent the possibility of electrical short-circuits and/or fires.

Caution: Before proceeding, refer to 'Disconnecting the battery' in the Reference Chapter for further information.

2 Electrical fault finding – general information

Note: Refer to the precautions given in 'Safety first!' and in Section 1 of this Chapter before starting work. The following tests relate to testing of the main electrical circuits, and should not be used to test delicate electronic circuits, particularly where an electronic control unit is used.

General

1 A typical electrical circuit consists of an electrical component, any switches, relays, motors, fuses, fusible links or circuit breakers related to that component, and the wiring and connectors which link the component to both the battery and the chassis. To help to pinpoint a problem in an electrical circuit, wiring diagrams are included at the end of this Chapter.

2 Before attempting to diagnose an electrical fault, first study the appropriate wiring diagram, to obtain a complete understanding of the components included in the particular circuit concerned. The possible sources of a fault can be narrowed down by noting if other components related to the circuit are operating properly. If several components or circuits fail at one time, the problem is likely to be related to a shared fuse or earth connection.

3 Electrical problems usually stem from simple causes, such as loose or corroded connections, a faulty earth connection, a blown fuse, a melted fusible link, or a faulty relay. Visually inspect the condition of all fuses, wires and connections in a problem circuit before testing the components. Use the wiring diagrams to determine which terminal connections will need to be checked in order to pinpoint the trouble-spot.

4 The basic tools required for electrical fault-finding include a circuit tester or voltmeter (a 12 volt bulb with a set of test leads can also be used for certain tests); an ohmmeter (to measure resistance and check for continuity); a battery and set of test leads; and a jumper wire, preferably with a circuit breaker or fuse incorporated, which can be used to bypass suspect wires or electrical components. Before attempting to locate a problem with test instruments, use the wiring diagram to determine where to make the connections.

5 To find the source of an intermittent wiring fault (usually due to a poor or dirty connection, or damaged wiring insulation), a 'wiggle' test can be performed on the wiring. This involves wiggling the wiring by hand to see if the fault occurs as the wiring is moved. It should be possible to narrow down the source of the fault to a particular section of wiring. This method of testing can be used in conjunction with any of the tests described in the following sub-Sections.

6 Apart from problems due to poor connections, two basic types of fault can occur in an electrical circuit – open-circuit or short-circuit.

7 Open-circuit faults are caused by a break somewhere in the circuit, which prevents current from flowing. An open-circuit fault will prevent a component from working.

8 Short-circuit faults are caused by a 'short' somewhere in the circuit, which allows the current flowing in the circuit to 'escape' along an alternative route, usually to earth. Short-circuit faults are normally caused by a breakdown in wiring insulation, which allows a feed wire to touch either another wire, or an earthed component such as the bodyshell. A short-circuit fault will normally cause the relevant circuit fuse to blow.

Finding an open-circuit

9 To check for an open-circuit, connect one lead of a circuit tester or the negative lead of a voltmeter either to the battery negative terminal or to a known good earth.

10 Connect the other lead to a connector in the circuit being tested, preferably nearest to the battery or fuse. At this point, battery voltage should be present, unless the lead from the battery or the fuse itself is faulty (bearing in mind that some circuits are live only when the ignition switch is moved to a particular position).

11 Switch on the circuit, then connect the tester lead to the connector nearest the circuit switch on the component side.

12 If voltage is present (indicated either by the tester bulb lighting or a voltmeter reading, as applicable), this means that the section of the circuit between the relevant connector and the switch is problem-free.

13 Continue to check the remainder of the circuit in the same fashion.

14 When a point is reached at which no voltage is present, the problem must lie between that point and the previous test point with voltage. Most problems can be traced to a broken, corroded or loose connection.

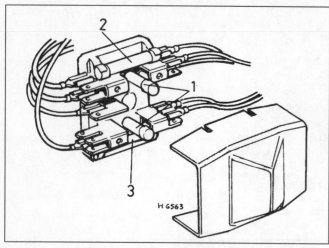

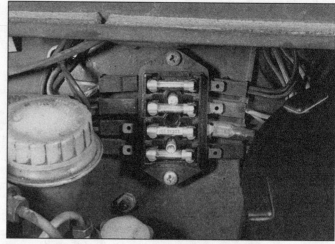

3.1a Two-fuse type fuseblock details

3.1b Four-fuse type fuseblock location

1 Spare fuses   *2 35 amp fuse*   *3 35 amp fuse*

Finding a short-circuit

15 To check for a short-circuit, first disconnect the load(s) from the circuit (loads are the components which draw current from a circuit, such as bulbs, motors, heating elements, etc).

16 Remove the relevant fuse from the circuit, and connect a circuit tester or voltmeter to the fuse connections.

17 Switch on the circuit, bearing in mind that some circuits are live only when the ignition switch is moved to a particular position.

18 If voltage is present (indicated either by the tester bulb lighting or a voltmeter reading, as applicable), this means that there is a short-circuit.

19 If no voltage is present during this test, but the fuse still blows with the load(s) reconnected, this indicates an internal fault in the load(s).

Finding an earth fault

20 The battery negative terminal is connected to 'earth' – the metal of the engine/transmission and the vehicle body – and many systems are wired so that they only receive a positive feed, the current returning via the metal of the car body. This means that the component mounting and the body form part of that circuit. Loose or corroded mountings can therefore cause a range of electrical faults, ranging from total failure of a circuit, to a puzzling partial failure. In particular, lights may shine dimly (especially when another circuit sharing the same earth point is in operation), motors (eg, wiper motors) may run slowly, and the operation of one circuit may have an apparently-unrelated effect on another. Note that on many vehicles, earth straps are used between certain components, such as the engine/transmission and the body, usually where there is no metal-to-metal contact between components, due to flexible rubber mountings, etc.

21 To check whether a component is

properly earthed, disconnect the battery and connect one lead of an ohmmeter to a known good earth point. Connect the other lead to the wire or earth connection being tested. The resistance reading should be zero; if not, check the connection as follows.

22 If an earth connection is thought to be faulty, dismantle the connection, and clean both the bodyshell and the wire terminal (or the component earth connection mating surface) back to bare metal. Be careful to remove all traces of dirt and corrosion, then use a knife to trim away any paint, so that a clean metal-to-metal joint is made. On reassembly, tighten the joint fasteners securely; if a wire terminal is being refitted, use serrated washers between the terminal and the bodyshell, to ensure a clean and secure connection. When the connection is remade, prevent the onset of corrosion in the future by applying a coat of petroleum jelly or silicone-based grease, or by spraying on (at regular intervals) a proprietary ignition sealer, or a water-dispersant lubricant.

3 Fuses and relays – general information

Main fuses

1 The main fuses are located in a block which is mounted on the right-hand wing valance on early models, and on the right-hand side of the engine compartment bulkhead on later models **(see illustrations)**. The fuseblock is covered by a plastic push-on cover. Upon inspection it will be seen that there are two main fuses on early models and either four or twenty four main fuses on later versions. In both cases, spare fuses are contained within the fuseblock or cover. The fuse positions and circuits protected are listed in the Specifications.

2 To remove a fuse, simply withdraw it from the contacts in the fuseblock; the wire within the fuse should be visible; if the fuse is blown, the wire will be broken or melted. Before refitting a new fuse ensure that the contacts

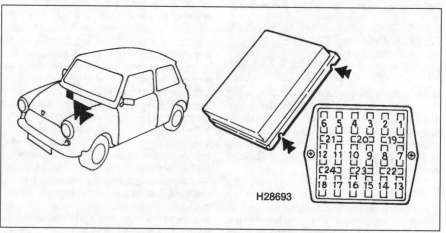

3.1c Twenty-four fuse type fuseblock location

Arrows indicate fuseblock cover locating notches

are clean and free from corrosion. If necessary the contacts may be cleaned with a fine grade emery paper.

3 Always renew a fuse with one of an identical rating; never use a fuse with a different rating from the original or substitute anything else. Never renew a fuse more than once without tracing the source of the trouble.

4 Persistent blowing of a particular fuse indicates a fault in the circuit(s) protected. Where more than one circuit is involved, switch on one item at a time until the fuse blows, so showing in which circuit the fault lies.

5 Besides a fault in the electrical component concerned, a blown fuse can also be caused by a short-circuit in the wiring to the component. Look for trapped or frayed wires allowing a live wire to touch vehicle metal, and for loose or damaged connectors.

6 After renewing a fuse, refit the fuseblock cover, ensuring that it is pushed fully into place. The cover for the twenty four fuseblock has two notches on one side to ensure that it is fitted correctly.

Line fuses

7 A line fuse is fitted to protect an individual unit or circuit. Line fuses are located in clusters on the engine compartment bulkhead, behind the facia or instrument panel, and under the bonnet lock platform. The number of fuses, and the circuits protected, depends on model and equipment fitted. To change a line fuse, hold one end of the container, press and twist off the other end.

Relays

8 A relay is an electrically-operated switch, which is used for the following reasons:

a) *A relay can switch a heavy current remotely from the circuit in which the current is flowing, allowing the use of lighter gauge wiring and switch contacts.*

b) *A relay can receive more than one control input, unlike a mechanical switch.*

4.5 Remove the securing screws and lift off the steering column shroud

c) *A relay can have a timer function – for example an intermittent wiper delay.*

9 On later Mini models, relays are used to operate a number of circuits, mainly in the engine management and emission control systems. The engine management system relays are contained in a sealed module mounted on the engine compartment bulkhead – these cannot be individually renewed and in the event of a fault in this area, the complete module must be renewed. A relay for the lambda (oxygen) sensor is mounted separately, also on the bulkhead. Further information on the engine management system relays will be found in Chapter 4B.

10 Relays for circuits such as the direction indicator/hazard flasher system, and auxiliary cooling fan are also used according to model, year, and equipment fitted.

11 If a circuit which includes a relay develops a fault, remember that the relay itself could be faulty. Testing is by substitution of a known good relay. Do not assume that relays which look similar are necessarily identical for purposes of substitution.

12 Make sure that the ignition is switched off, then pull the relay from its socket. Push the new

relay firmly in to refit. **Note:** *The engine management system relays can only be renewed as a complete module (see Chapter 4B, Section 13).*

4 Switches – removal and refitting

Note: *Disconnect the battery negative terminal (refer to 'Disconnecting the battery' in the Reference Chapter) before removing any switch, and reconnect the terminal after refitting the switch.*

Steering column switches

Single stalk multifunction switch

1 Undo and remove the screws securing the two halves of the steering column shroud to the column and lift off the two halves.

2 Undo and remove the two screws securing the switch retaining strap and lift the switch off the column.

3 Disconnect the wiring harness connector under the parcel shelf and lift away the switch.

4 Refitting is the reverse sequence to removal.

Twin stalk multifunction switch

5 Undo and remove the retaining screws and lift off the two halves of the steering column shroud **(see illustration)**.

6 Refer to Chapter 10 and remove the steering wheel.

7 Disconnect the two switch multiplug connectors under the parcel shelf **(see illustration)**.

8 Undo and remove the retaining screw and lift out the direction indicator cancelling block.

9 Slacken the switch clamp screw and slide the switch off the end of the steering column.

10 If it is wished to renew either of the switches they may be renewed as a complete assembly or individually. If they are to be renewed individually, it will be necessary to drill out the two rivets securing the windscreen washer/wiper switch to the mounting plate and unwrap the insulating tape securing the harnesses together.

11 Refitting is the reverse sequence to removal. Ensure that the striker dog on the nylon switch centre is in line with and adjacent to the direction indicator switch stalk.

Facia switches

12 Undo and remove the lower heater retaining nut and the two screws securing the heater to the parcel shelf. Lower the heater to the floor. **Note:** *On models fitted with a centre console, it will be necessary to remove the console and facia glovebox retaining screws to allow the console to be moved, if necessary, for access.*

13 On models fitted with toggle switches, unscrew the locking ring securing the switch to the panel and withdraw the switch. Make a note of the electrical connections at the rear of the switch and disconnect them.

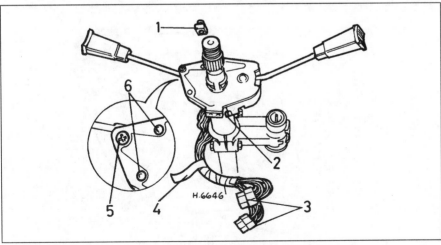

H.6646

4.7 Steering column multifunction switch

1	*Cancelling ring drive block*	*3*	*Multiplug connectors*	*5*	*Screw*
2	*Clamp screw*	*4*	*Insulating tape*	*6*	*Rivet*

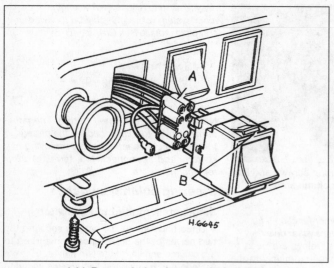

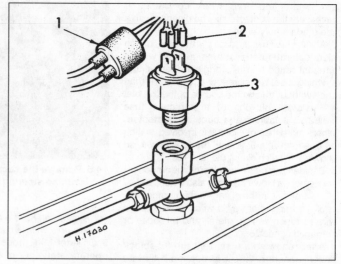

4.14 Removal of rocker type facia switch

A Multiplug connector   B Switch retaining tabs

4.19 Hydraulic stop-light switch removal

1 Rubber cover (where fitted)   2 Electrical leads
     3 Stop-light switch

14 On models fitted with rocker switches simply push the switch out of the panel and detach the multiplug **(see illustration)**.
15 In both cases refitting is the reverse sequence to removal.

Door pillar switch

16 The interior light door pillar switches are retained by either being a push-fit in the pillars, or by a single securing screw. Prise out the push-fit type or remove the screw, disconnect the electrical lead and lift away the switch.

Tape the wiring to the door pillar, to prevent it falling back into the pillar. Alternatively, tie a piece of string to the wiring to retrieve it.

17 The switch is refitted in the reverse way.

Stop-light switch

Note: *The stop-lights are operated either hydraulically by a pressure-sensitive switch incorporated in the braking system or electrically by an on/off switch mounted above the brake pedal.*

Hydraulically-operated type

18 Remove the brake master cylinder filler cap and place a piece of polythene over the filler neck. Now refit the cap. This will prevent loss of hydraulic fluid when the stop-light switch is removed.
19 Lift up the rubber cover, if fitted, and disconnect the two wires from the stop-light switch located on the right-hand side of the front subframe beneath the flywheel housing **(see illustration)**.
20 Using a large socket and extension bar, remove the switch from the pipe connector.
21 Refitting the switch is the reverse sequence to removal. If precautions were

taken to prevent fluid loss, it should not be necessary to bleed the hydraulic system. However, if the brake pedal now feels spongy, bleed the system as described in Chapter 9.

Electrically-operated type

22 Disconnect the two wires at the switch, accessible from below the parcel shelf.
23 Undo and remove the locknut and then withdraw the switch from its mounting bracket.
24 Refitting is the reverse sequence to removal. Adjust the position of the switch and locknuts so that the stop-lights operate after 6.3 mm of brake pedal travel.

Ignition switch

25 Undo and remove the securing screws and lift off the two halves of the steering column shroud.

26 Disconnect the ignition switch multiplug connector **(see illustration)**.
27 Inspect the top of the ignition switch housing, and if a small screw is present, unscrew it. The ignition switch can now be withdrawn from the steering lock housing.
28 If a small retaining screw is not visible, then the ignition switch is of the sealed type and can only be removed with the steering lock housing as a complete assembly. This procedure is described fully in Chapter 10, Section 24; there is no need to remove the steering column.
29 Refitting the ignition switch is the reverse sequence to removal.

Reversing light switch

Manual transmission models

Note: *The following procedures apply to later*

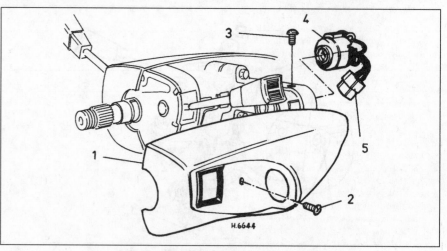

4.26 The later type ignition/starter switch

1 Steering column shroud   3 Ignition switch securing screw   4 Ignition switch
2 Shroud retaining screw   5 Multiplug connector

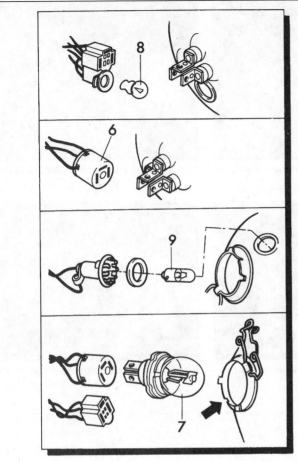

5.1 Headlight bulb assemblies

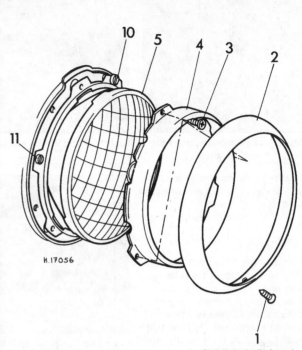

H.17056

1 *Outer rim retaining screw*	8 *Sidelight bulb (used with*
2 *Outer rim*	*sealed beam light unit)*
3 *Inner rim retaining screw*	9 *Sidelight bulb (used with*
4 *Inner rim*	*bulb type light unit)*
5 *Light unit*	10 *Vertical adjustment screw*
6 *Three-pin connector*	11 *Horizontal adjustment*
7 *Headlight bulb*	*screw*

Mini Saloon models having reversing lights incorporated in the rear light clusters. The switch is located in the gearchange remote control housing and is actuated by the gearchange lever when reverse is selected.

30 Firmly apply the handbrake, then jack up the front of the car and support it securely on axle stands (see *Jacking and vehicle support*).

31 Working underneath the car, disconnect the two switch wires, slacken the locknut and unscrew the switch from the remote control housing.

32 Refitting is the reverse sequence to removal.

33 Adjustment is carried out as follows. With the wires disconnected, screw the switch into the housing until slight resistance is felt.

34 Connect the wires, select reverse gear and switch on the ignition. Continue screwing the switch in until the reversing lights just come on and then screw the switch in a further quarter of a turn.

35 Tighten the locknut and check that the reversing lights are illuminated with the gear lever in reverse and extinguished in all other gear positions. Lower the car to the ground on completion.

Automatic transmission models

36 Refer to Chapter 7B.

Starter inhibitor switch

37 Refer to Chapter 7B.

5 Bulbs (exterior lights) – renewal

Note: *With all light bulbs, remember that if they have just been in use, they may be very hot. Switch off the power before renewing a bulb. With quartz halogen bulbs (headlights and similar applications), use a tissue or clean cloth when handling the bulb; do not touch the bulb glass with the fingers. Even small quantities of grease from the fingers will cause blackening and premature failure. If a bulb is accidentally touched, clean it with methylated spirit and a clean rag.*

Headlight

1 Either sealed beam or renewable bulb light units are fitted to all Minis, depending on model type and year of manufacture **(see illustration)**.

2 To remove the headlight unit on Clubman and 1275 GT models, undo and remove the four screws and lift off the grille panel

extension around the light unit. On all other models undo and remove the outer rim securing screw and ease the bottom of the outer rim forwards, lift it up and off the retaining lugs at the top of the light unit **(see illustrations)**.

3 Proceed as follows according to light unit type.

Sealed beam type

4 Undo and remove the three small inner rim securing screws and withdraw the inner rim **(see illustrations)**. Lift out the light unit.

5.2a On Clubman models remove the grille panel extension for access to the headlight

5.2b On non-Clubman models, undo the outer rim securing screw . . .

5.2c . . . and lift the rim off the upper lugs

5.4a Unscrew the inner rim securing screws . . .

5 Withdraw the three pin connector from the rear of the reflector and lift away the complete unit **(see illustration)**.

6 Refitting is the reverse sequence to removal.

Renewable bulb type

7 Undo and remove the three small inner rim securing screws and withdraw the inner rim. Lift out the light unit.

8 Withdraw the three pin connector from the rear of the reflector and disengage the spring clip from the reflector lugs. Lift away the bulb. Note the locating pip on the reflector and mating indentation in the bulb rim.

9 Refitting is the reverse sequence to removal. Ensure that the indentation in the bulb rim locates over the locating pip on the reflector.

Alternative renewable bulb type

10 On certain models an alternative bulb type headlight assembly of slightly different design to the standard unit may be fitted **(see illustration)**.

11 To renew a bulb on these units, first remove the outer rim as described in paragraph 2.

12 Carefully pull the three adjusting screws one at a time out of their locations and lift out the reflector.

13 Withdraw the three-pin connector from the rear of the reflector and disengage the spring clip from the reflector lugs. Lift away the bulb. Note the position of the projection on the bulb rim in relation to the bulb locator and ensure that the new bulb is fitted correctly.

14 Refitting is the reverse sequence to removal. Ensure that the projection on the bulb rim is correctly engaged with the bulb locator.

Auxiliary driving light

Cooper models

15 Undo and remove the screw and release the clamp securing the reflector to the light unit.

16 Withdraw the reflector and disconnect the bulb wiring connector.

17 Disengage the spring clip from the reflector lugs and lift away the bulb.

18 Refitting is the reverse sequence to removal.

5.4b . . . and lift off the inner rim

5.5 Detach the electrical connector and lift away the light unit

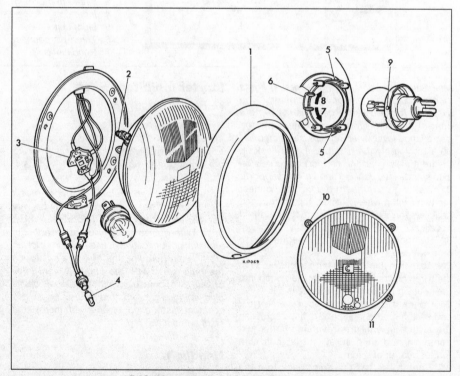

5.10 Alternative type headlight assembly

1 Outer rim	6 Bulb locator	9 Projection on bulb
2 Adjusting screws	7 Position of bulb locator for	10 Horizontal adjustment
3 Three-pin connector	right-hand drive vehicles	screw
4 Sidelight bulb	8 Position of bulb locator for	11 Vertical adjustment
5 Spring clip	left-hand drive vehicles	screw

5.24 Undo the two screws and lift off the lens

5.27a Fold back the rubber flange and remove the rim . . .

5.27b . . . and lens

Front sidelight

Except Clubman & 1275 GT

19 Undo and remove the headlight outer rim securing screw and ease the bottom of the outer rim forwards, lift it up and off the retaining lugs at the top of the light unit.

20 Undo and remove the three small headlight inner rim securing screws and withdraw the inner rim. Lift out the light unit.

21 Where a sealed beam headlight unit is fitted, disconnect the headlight bulb wiring connector and remove the sidelight bulb from the wiring connector block; it will be either a push-fit or bayonet type fitting.

22 Where a renewable bulb type light unit is fitted, withdraw the sidelight bulbholder from the rear of the reflector. Remove the bayonet fitting type bulb from the holder.

23 Refit the bulb and headlight unit using the reverse sequence to removal.

Clubman & 1275 GT

24 Undo and remove the two screws that secure the lens to the light body. Carefully lift away the lens (see illustration).

25 Push in the bayonet fitting bulb slightly and turn it anti-clockwise to remove.

26 Refitting is the reverse sequence to removal. Take care not to overtighten the two lens retaining screws as the lenses can be easily cracked.

Front direction indicator

Except Clubman & 1275 GT

27 To renew a bulb, very carefully fold back the rubber flange with the aid of a screwdriver and remove the plated rim and lens (see illustrations). On later models the lens is secured by two screws.

28 Push the bulb in slightly and turn it anti-clockwise to remove it (see illustration).

29 Refitting is the reverse of the removal procedure, but ensure that the plated rim is secured all round by the rubber flange, if applicable.

Clubman & 1275 GT

30 The procedure is the same as described previously for the front sidelight bulb.

Direction indicator side repeater

31 Access to the rear of the light and the bulbholder is gained through the front wheelarch (see illustration).

32 Push the bulbholder in and rotate it, this will release it from the rear of the light unit and allow the holder and electrical lead to be drawn down out of the wheelarch.

33 The push-fit bulb can now be removed from the holder.

34 Refitting is the reverse of removal.

5.28 Push and turn the bulb anti-clockwise to remove

Stop/tail & rear direction indicator

35 Undo the three screws to release the light lenses (see illustrations).

36 The direction indicator bulb is fitted in the top compartment and the stop/tail bulb in the lower compartment (or centre compartment on later models).

37 Both bulbs have bayonet fixings; to remove push in slightly, and rotate anti-clockwise.

38 Refitting is the reverse sequence to removal. Take care not to overtighten the lens securing screws as the lenses can easily be cracked.

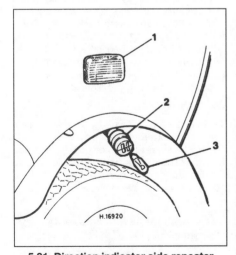

5.31 Direction indicator side repeater details

| 1 | Light unit | 3 | Bulb |
| 2 | Bulbholder | | |

5.35a Rear light cluster lens removed for bulb renewal – Saloon models

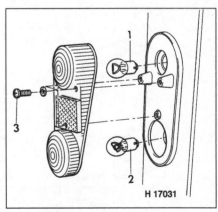

5.35b Rear light bulb renewal – Estate, Van and Pick-up models

| 1 | Direction indicator bulb | 2 | Stop/tail bulb |
| | | 3 | Securing screws |

5.44 Removal of the number plate lens and bulbholder on Saloon models

5.47 On Estate, Van and Pick-up models lift off the cover and lens . . .

5.48 . . . and remove the bulbs by turning them anti-clockwise

Reversing light

39 On later models the rear light clusters are increased in size to accommodate a reversing light bulb.

40 The reversing light bulb is fitted to the lower of the three compartments in the rear light clusters and its renewal is the same as for the stop/tail and direction indicator bulbs described previously.

Rear foglight

41 Access to the bulb is gained by removing the two lens cover screws and pulling off the lens.

42 The bayonet-fit bulb can now be removed from the holder by pushing in slightly, and rotating anti-clockwise.

43 Refitting is the reverse sequence to removal.

Number plate light

Saloon models

44 Undo and remove the lens securing screws and carefully ease the lens and bulbholder out of the light unit. In some cases it will be found that the lens and bulbholder cannot be withdrawn due to the wires fouling the light unit. If this happens, open the boot lid, remove the three retaining screws and lift

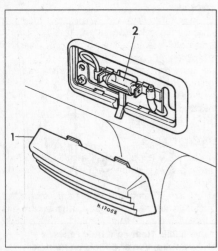

6.1 Interior light bulb renewal

1 Lens   *2 Bulb*

off the light unit. The lens and bulbholder can now be removed **(see illustration)**.

45 The festoon type bulb is removed by simply withdrawing it from the bulbholder contacts.

46 Refitting is the reverse sequence to removal.

Estate, Van and Pick-up models

47 Undo and remove the retaining screw and lift off the cover and lens **(see illustration)**.

48 Remove the bulbs by turning anti-clockwise and lifting out **(see illustration)**.

49 Refitting is the reverse sequence to removal.

6 Bulbs (interior lights) – renewal

Note: *With all light bulbs, remember that if they have just been in use, they may be very hot. Switch off the power before renewing a bulb.*

Interior courtesy light

Early type

1 Carefully squeeze the two sides of the courtesy light plastic lens together until the retaining lugs of the lens are clear of the sockets in the light base **(see illustration)**.

2 Draw the lens from the light base.

3 The festoon bulb may now be detached from the contact blades.

4 Refitting the bulb and lens is the reverse sequence to removal.

Later type

5 Release the light unit by carefully prising out the end furthest from the switch.

6 The bayonet-fit bulb can now be removed from the bulbholder by pushing in slightly, and rotating anti-clockwise.

7 Refitting is the reverse sequence to removal.

Footwell light

8 Release the light unit from its mounting below the facia.

9 The festoon bulb may now be detached from the contact blades.

10 Refitting is the reverse sequence to removal.

Switch illumination

11 To renew a bulb in the illuminated switches fitted to later models, insert a small screwdriver under the notch on both sides of the switch rocker. Depress the notch slightly and lever off the rocker. The bulb may be unscrewed for renewal using the outer plastic casing of a wiring connector which is a snug fit over the bulb lens.

12 Refit the bulb and push the switch rocker back into place.

Instrument and warning lights

Central instrument panel

13 Access to the instrument panel warning lights and panel illumination lights is gained from the engine compartment by withdrawing the push type bulbholders from the speedometer and instruments.

14 On later models it may be helpful to remove the air cleaner assembly as described in the relevant Part of Chapter 4 to provide greater access.

Offset instrument panel

15 On models having an instrument panel in front of the driver, access to the bulbs is through an access panel beneath the parcel shelf and from the side of the panel after the facia trim has been eased back. Alternatively, for greater access, the instrument panel may be removed as described in Section 15.

16 The bulbholders are a push-fit in the rear of the instrument panel and the capless bulbs are also a push-fit in the holders.

Glovebox light

17 Release the light unit by carefully prising out the end furthest from the switch.

18 The bayonet-fit bulb can now be removed from the bulbholder by pushing in slightly, and rotating anti-clockwise.

19 Refitting is the reverse sequence to removal.

7 Headlight beam alignment – checking and adjusting

1 The headlights may be adjusted for both vertical and horizontal beam positions by means of the two adjusting screws. On the

7.1 Headlight vertical position (A) and horizontal position (B) adjusting screws

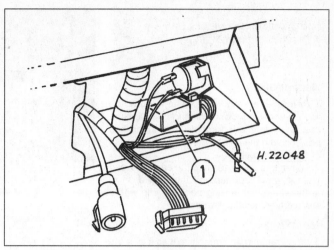

8.2 Location of dim-dip lighting unit (1) behind the instrument panel

standard fitting sealed beam and bulb type headlight units, the upper spring-loaded screw adjusts the vertical position and the side spring-loaded screw adjusts the horizontal position **(see illustration)**. On the alternative type headlight units, the two diametrically opposite screws are used for adjustment. The upper screw adjusts the horizontal setting and the lower screw adjusts the vertical setting (see illustration 5.10).

2 The lights should be set so that on full or high beam, the beams are set slightly below parallel with a level road surface. Do not forget that the beam position is affected by how the car is normally loaded for night

driving, and set the beams with the car loaded to this position.

3 Although this adjustment can be approximately set at home, it is recommended that beam alignment is be carried out by a Rover dealer or other specialist heaving the necessary optical alignment equipment.

8 Dim-dip lighting system components – removal and refitting

Dim-dip unit

Removal

1 Remove the instrument panel as described in Section 15.

2 Disconnect the dim-dip unit from the wiring loom connector **(see illustration)**.

Refitting

3 Refitting is the reverse sequence to removal.

Dim-dip resistor

Removal

4 Disconnect the battery negative terminal (refer to *Disconnecting the battery* in the Reference Chapter).

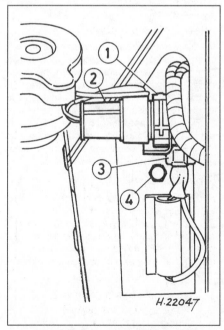

8.5 Location of dim-dip resistor

1 Wiring loom connector
2 Resistor plug
3 Wiring loom clip
4 Mounting plate bolt

9.1 Horn location showing electrical leads and mounting nuts

5 Open the bonnet, and unclip the wiring loom connector on the right-hand side of the engine compartment **(see illustration)**.

6 Pull the resistor plug from the connector, and release the wiring loom.

7 Unscrew the mounting bolt, and withdraw the resistor and mounting plate.

Refitting

8 Refitting is the reverse sequence to removal.

9 Horn – removal, refitting and adjustment

Removal and refitting

1 The horn is located in the engine compartment and is attached to a bracket, which is in turn secured to the front body panel by two small nuts and bolts **(see illustration)**.

2 To remove the unit, disconnect the horn wiring then undo the retaining bracket nuts and bolts. Remove the horn, complete with bracket, then remove the bracket. The horn is not repairable and should not be dismantled.

3 Refitting is the reverse sequence to removal.

Adjustment

4 On early type horns an adjustment is provided to compensate for wear of the moving parts.

5 Adjustment is by means of a screw on the broad rim of the horn nearly opposite the two terminals. Do not confuse this with the large screw in the centre.

6 Turn the adjustment screw anti-clockwise until the horn just fails to sound. Then turn the screw a quarter of a turn clockwise, which is the optimum setting.

10 Windscreen wiper arms – removal and refitting

Removal

1 Before removing a wiper arm, turn the windscreen wiper switch on and off, to ensure that the arms are in their normal parked position with the blades parallel to the bottom of the windscreen.

2 To remove the arm, pivot the arm back and pull the wiper arm head off the splined drive, at the same time easing back the clip with a screwdriver **(see illustration)**.

Refitting

3 When refitting an arm, place it so it is in the correct relative parked position and then press the arm head onto the splined drive until the retaining clip clicks into place.

11 Windscreen wiper motor – removal and refitting

Removal

1 Remove the wiper arms from the spindles as described in Section 10.

2 Disconnect the battery negative terminal (refer to *Disconnecting the battery* in the Reference Chapter).

3 Withdraw the electrical cable terminal

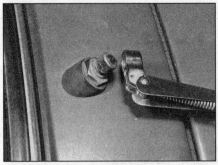

10.2 The wiper arm is a push-fit on the wiper spindle splines

connector from the motor, and if a separate earth wire is fitted, detach this from the wing valance.

4 Undo the nut securing the cable rack guide tube to the wiper motor gearbox **(see illustration)**.

5 Undo and remove the two motor strap retaining screws and lift off the strap.

6 Carefully withdraw the motor assembly pulling the cable rack from the guide tubes.

Refitting

7 To refit the motor, lightly lubricate the cable rack with a general purpose grease.

8 Enter the cable rack into the guide tubes and carefully push it through, ensuring that it engages the wheelbox gear teeth.

9 Refit the motor retaining strap and the guide tube retaining nut.

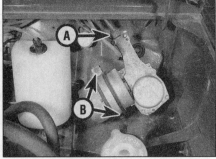

11.4 Cable rack guide tube retaining nut (A) and motor strap retaining screws (B)

10 Reconnect the electrical leads and the battery terminal.

11 Switch on the wipers, check the function of the motor and then turn it off. With the motor now in the 'park' position, refit the wiper arms.

12 Windscreen wiper motor – dismantling and reassembly

Dismantling

1 Due to the limited availability of spare parts, the only repair which can be effectively undertaken on the motor is the renewal of the brushes and the limit switch. Anything more serious than this will mean exchanging the complete motor or having a repair undertaken by an automobile electrician.

12.2 Exploded view of the windscreen wiper motor and gearbox

1	Cover screw	10	Armature thrust screw
2	Gearbox cover	11	Dished washer
3	Circlip	12	Limit switch assembly
4	Plain washers	13	Brush gear
5	Connecting rod	14	Bush gear screw
6	Shaft and gear	15	Armature
7	Cross-head and rack	16	Yoke assembly
8	Gearbox	17	Yoke bolts
9	Limit switch screw		

2 With the motor removed from the car as described in Section 11, undo and remove the four gearbox cover retaining screws and lift away the cover **(see illustration opposite)**. Release the circlip and flat washer securing the connecting rod to the crankpin on the shaft and gear. Lift away the connecting rod followed by the second flat washer.

3 Raise the circlip and flat washer securing the shaft and gear to the gearbox body.

4 De-burr the gearshaft and lift away the gear, making a careful note of the location of the dished washer.

5 Scribe a mark on the yoke assembly and gearbox to ensure correct reassembly, and unscrew the two yoke bolts from the motor yoke assembly. Part the yoke assembly, including armature, from the gearbox body. As the yoke assembly has residual magnetism ensure that the yoke is kept well away from metallic dust.

6 Unscrew the two screws securing the brushgear and the terminal and switch assembly, and remove both the assemblies.

7 Inspect the brushes for excessive wear. If the main brushes are worn to less than the minimum specified length, or the narrow section of the third brush is worn to the full width of the brush, fit a new brushgear assembly. Ensure that the three brushes move freely in their boxes.

8 If either the brushes or the limit switch are to be renewed on early motor assemblies, it will be necessary to unsolder the wires at the switch and then resolder the new wires. On later types the wires are retained by Lucar connectors which are simply detached. In all cases make a note of the wire positions before disconnecting.

Reassembly

9 Reassembly of the windscreen wiper motor is the reverse sequence to dismantling.

13 Windscreen wiper wheelbox – removal and refitting

Removal

1 Remove the windscreen wiper motor as described in Section 11.

2 Carefully lift back the engine compartment bulkhead insulation to provide access to the wheelboxes.

3 Undo and remove the retaining nut and spacer from each wheelbox **(see illustration)**.

4 Slacken the nuts that clamp the guide tubes between the wheelbox plates and then lift out the guide tubes.

5 The wheelboxes can now be lifted out.

6 With the wheelboxes removed, withdraw the wheelbox plates and lift out the spindle and gear. Examine the gear teeth for wear and renew as necessary.

Refitting

7 Refitting is the reverse sequence to removal; bearing in mind the following points.

 a) *Lightly lubricate the spindles and gear teeth with a general purpose grease.*

 b) *Do not tighten the nuts that clamp the guide tubes between the wheelbox plates until the motor and cable rack have been refitted.*

 c) *Ensure that the bend radius on the guide tube nearest to the motor is not less than 230.0 mm.*

14 Windscreen washer pump – removal and refitting

Manual pump

1 Disconnect the battery negative terminal (refer to *Disconnecting the battery* in the Reference Chapter).

2 Undo and remove the retaining nut at the rear of the heater and the two screws securing the front of the heater to the parcel shelf. Lower the heater to the floor.

3 Unscrew the locking ring securing the washer pump to the centre of the switch panel and pull the pump out from the rear of the panel.

4 Detach the two water hoses from the rear of the pump and lift it away.

5 Refitting is the reverse sequence to removal.

Electric pump

Early models

6 Disconnect the battery negative terminal (refer to *Disconnecting the battery* in the Reference Chapter).

7 Refer to Chapter 4A or 4B as applicable and remove the air cleaner.

8 Disconnect the two electrical wires and the two water hoses from the pump.

9 Undo and remove the two securing screws and lift off the pump.

10 Refitting is the reverse sequence to removal. Make sure that the water hoses are connected to the correct outlets. Arrows on the pump body indicate the direction of water flow.

Later models

11 On later models the washer pump and reservoir are located in the luggage compartment. The pump is clipped into the side of the reservoir **(see illustration)**.

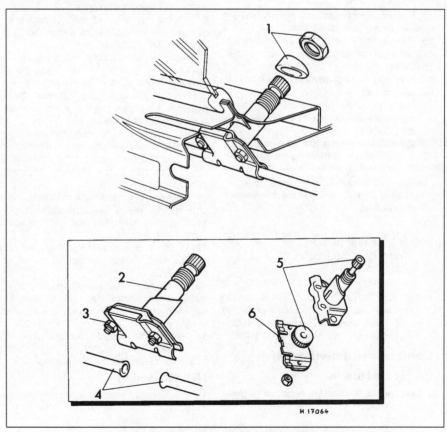

H.17064

13.3 Windscreen wiper wheelbox assembly

1 *Retaining nut and spacer*	3 *Wheelbox plate retaining screw*	5 *Spindle and gear*
2 *Wheelbox body*	4 *Wiper rack guide tubes*	6 *Lower plate*

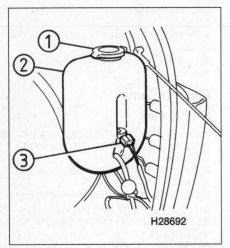

14.11 Washer pump and reservoir location in the luggage compartment on later models

1 Filler cap	3 Pump and wiring
2 Reservoir	multiplug

12 To renew either item, first disconnect the battery negative terminal (refer to *Disconnecting the battery* in the Reference Chapter).

13 Carefully prise the wiring connector from the pump.

14 Pull the reservoir upwards from its retaining bracket. Drain the fluid into a container.

15 Release the washer tube from the pump. The reservoir can now be removed completely.

16 Detach the pump from the reservoir.

17 Refitting is the reverse sequence to removal, noting the following:

a) *Use a new pump seal. Fit the seal in the reservoir and lubricate it before refitting the pump.*

b) *If the washer tube is difficult to replace onto the pump, soften it by immersing it in hot water for a few minutes.*

c) *Top-up the reservoir with reference to 'Weekly Checks' and test the operation of the washers.*

15 Instrument panel – removal and refitting

Note: *On models with a wooden facia, refer to the removal and refitting procedures for the facia as described in Chapter 11A, which include details of instrument panel removal.*

Central instrument panel

Except Mini 850

1 Disconnect the battery negative terminal (refer to *Disconnecting the battery* in the Reference Chapter).

2 Carefully ease out the trim panels at the rear of the facia on either side of the instrument panel.

3 Fold back the parcel shelf cover around the front of the instrument panel.

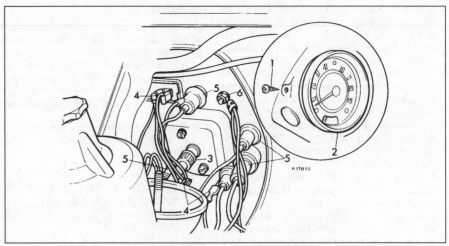

15.18 Instrument panel removal – 850 models

1 Retaining screw	3 Speedometer cable	5 Bulbholders
2 Instrument panel	4 Wiring connectors	6 Earth lead

4 Slacken the nut securing the heater unit to the rear mounting bracket. Undo and remove the two screws securing the front of the heater to the parcel shelf and lower the unit to the floor.

5 Undo and remove the screws securing the instrument panel to the facia.

6 Working in the engine compartment, remove the air cleaner as described in the relevant Part of Chapter 4.

7 Unscrew the knurled nut securing the speedometer cable to the rear of the speedometer and withdraw the cable.

8 Remove the clip that secures the oil pressure gauge pipe to the engine compartment bulkhead.

9 From inside the car draw the instrument panel away from the facia and disconnect the wires and bulbholders from the instruments. Label each wire as it is removed to prevent confusion when refitting.

10 Unscrew the union nut and release the oil pipe from the rear of the oil pressure gauge.

11 Unscrew the knurled retaining nuts and lift out the instruments.

12 Undo and remove the two securing screws and lift out the speedometer and sealing ring.

13 If required, the fuel gauge and voltage stabiliser may be removed from the rear of the speedometer after removing the retaining screws and nuts.

14 Reassembly and refitting of the instruments and panel is the reverse sequence to dismantling and removal.

Mini 850 models

15 Disconnect the battery negative terminal (refer to *Disconnecting the battery* in the Reference Chapter).

16 Working in the engine compartment, remove the air cleaner as described in the relevant Part of Chapter 4.

17 Withdraw the sound insulation from speedometer aperture.

18 Unscrew the knurled retaining nut and detach the speedometer cable from the speedometer **(see illustration)**.

19 Disconnect the wires from the fuel gauge and voltage stabiliser. Label each wire as it is removed to prevent confusion when refitting.

20 Note the locations of the bulbholders and remove them from the rear of the speedometer.

21 Disconnect the earth wire.

22 From inside the car undo and remove the two screws securing the speedometer to the cowling and then lift out the speedometer.

23 Refitting is the reverse sequence to removal.

Offset instrument panel

24 Disconnect the battery negative terminal (refer to *Disconnecting the battery* in the Reference Chapter).

25 Hold both sides of the instrument nacelle and carefully pull it off the instrument cluster **(see illustration)**. On some models the nacelle is secured by screws.

26 Remove the upper plastic trim strip to gain access to the panel upper retaining screws.

27 Undo and remove the side and upper retaining screws securing the instrument panel to the mounting brackets **(see illustrations)**.

15.25 Remove the instrument cluster nacelle

15.27a Undo the side . . .

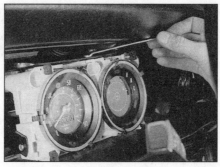

15.27b . . . and upper retaining screws

15.28a Detach the speedometer cable . . .

28 Draw the panel outward and detach the speedometer cable, the wiring multiplug connector and (where fitted) the two electrical leads at the rear of the tachometer **(see illustrations)**.

29 Carefully lift away the instrument panel, taking care not to damage the printed circuit.

30 Refitting is the reverse sequence to removal.

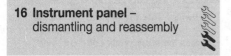

16 Instrument panel –
dismantling and reassembly

Note: *On models fitted with a centrally*

mounted panel the instruments and components are withdrawn as part of the instrument panel removal sequence (see Section 15). The following procedure is therefore applicable to models having an offset instrument panel mounted in front of the driver.

Dismantling

1 Remove the instrument panel as described in Section 15.

Fuel and temperature gauge

2 Ease off the spring clips securing the instrument lens glass and carefully remove the glass, sealing rings and printed face plate **(see illustration)**.

15.28b . . . and the multiplug connector, then lift away the instrument panel

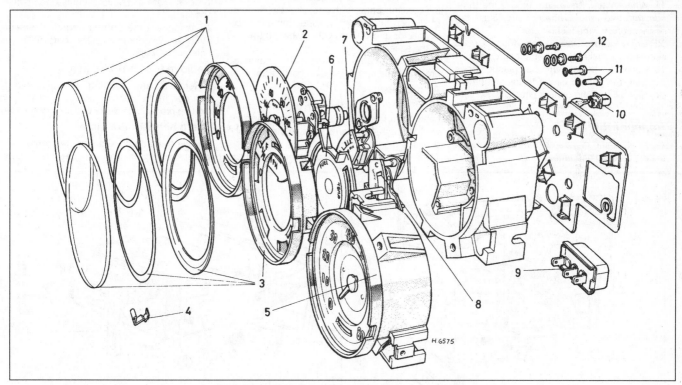

16.2 Exploded view of the offset instrument cluster

1 *Speedometer lens and faceplate assembly*	6 *Fuel/temperature gauge facing*
2 *Speedometer unit*	7 *Fuel gauge*
3 *Fuel/temperature gauge lens and faceplate assembly*	8 *Temperature gauge*
4 *Lens securing clips*	9 *Voltage stabiliser*
5 *Tachometer assembly (where fitted)*	10 *Panel lamp bulb and holder*
	11 *Fuel/temperature gauge securing screws*
	12 *Speedometer securing screws*

3 Undo and remove the three small screws and lift out the instrument facing.

4 At the rear of the instrument panel, undo and remove the two screws securing the gauge to the panel body and remove the gauge.

Speedometer

5 Ease off the spring clips securing the speedometer lens glass and carefully remove the glass, sealing rings and printed face plate.

6 At the rear of the instrument panel undo and remove the two screws securing the speedometer to the panel body and remove the speedometer.

Tachometer

7 Detach the voltage stabiliser lead and bulbholder from the rear of the tachometer.

8 Carefully prise up the pegs securing the printed circuit to the tachometer body and lift the unit away.

Printed circuit & voltage stabiliser

9 Pull the voltage stabiliser carefully out of its location in the printed circuit at the rear of the instrument panel **(see illustration)**.

10 Withdraw the panel and warning light bulbholders.

11 Where fitted, undo and remove the three screws and the voltage stabiliser tag connections for the tachometer.

12 Undo and remove the four screws securing the fuel and temperature gauges.

13 Carefully prise out the plastic pegs securing the printed circuit to the instrument panel and lift off the printed circuit.

Reassembly

14 In all cases reassembly is the reverse of the dismantling sequence.

17 Speedometer cable – removal and refitting

Removal

Central instrument panel

1 Disconnect the battery negative terminal (refer to *Disconnecting the battery* in the Reference Chapter).

2 Working in the engine compartment, detach the speedometer cable from the rear of the speedometer by unscrewing the knurled retaining nut and pulling the cable into the engine compartment.

3 Release the cable from the cable clip on the bulkhead

Offset instrument panel

4 Disconnect the battery negative terminal (refer to *Disconnecting the battery* in the Reference Chapter).

5 Hold both sides of the instrument nacelle and carefully pull it off the instrument panel. On some models the nacelle is secured by screws.

6 Remove the upper trim strip to gain access to the upper instrument panel retaining screws.

7 Undo and remove the side and upper retaining screws securing the instrument panel to the mounting brackets.

8 Draw the panel outward slightly, depress the lug on the side of the speedometer cable connector and withdraw the cable off the end of the speedometer.

9 Pull the cable through the bulkhead grommet and into the engine compartment.

All models

10 Working under the car disconnect the cable from the transmission. To gain access, work through the aperture above the left-hand driveshaft.

11 Should the cable securing nut be tight to turn by hand, remove the bolt that secures the speedometer drive and withdraw the cable complete with the drive assembly. The cable may then be detached from the drive assembly.

Refitting

12 Refitting the speedometer cable is the reverse sequence to removal but the following additional points should be noted:

a) *If the speedometer drive was removed, always fit a new joint washer.*

b) *To lubricate the inner cable, withdraw the inner cable and lightly grease it except for 200 mm at the speedometer end. Refit the inner cable and wipe away any surplus grease.*

18 Radio – removal and refitting

Note: *If the radio incorporates an anti-theft system, once the battery has been disconnected, the radio unit cannot be re-activated until the appropriate security code has been entered. Do not remove the unit unless the appropriate code is known.*

Removal

1 De-activate the radio security code (where applicable).

2 Disconnect the battery negative terminal (refer to *Disconnecting the battery* in the Reference Chapter).

Radio in the centre console

3 Removal and refitting of the radio is included in the centre console removal and refitting procedures described in Chapter 11A.

Radio beneath the facia

4 Prise the side covers from the radio, then loosen the two small screws **(see illustration)**.

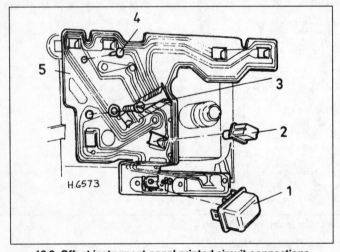

16.9 Offset instrument panel printed circuit connections

1	*Voltage stabiliser*	3	*Fuel and temperature gauge securing screws*
2	*Panel light*	4	*Printed circuit securing stud*
		5	*Printed circuit*

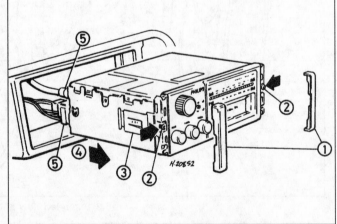

18.4 Radio fixings on 1989-on models

1	*Side covers*	4	*Direction of removal*
2	*Retaining screws*	5	*Multiplug and aerial lead*
3	*Holding clips*		

5 Press the two screws in to release the radio securing clips.

6 Push the radio out from behind the facia, and disconnect the wiring connectors and aerial lead.

7 Refitting is a reversal of removal, but make sure that the radio is fully engaged with the clips.

Radio in the facia

8 Two special DIN standard removal tools, available from in-car entertainment specialists, are required for removal.

9 Where fitted, prise the side covers from the radio.

10 Insert the removal tools into the holes on each side of the radio front plate, and push them in until they snap into place.

11 Push the tools apart to depress the internal retaining clips, then pull the tools outwards to withdraw the radio.

12 Disconnect the wiring connectors and the aerial lead from the rear of the radio. Release the removal tools.

13 To refit, reconnect the wiring and aerial lead, push the radio into its aperture until the retaining clips engage and, where applicable, refit the side covers.

Refitting

14 Refitting is the reverse sequence to removal. Where applicable, re-activate the security code on completion.

19 Anti-theft alarm system components – removal and refitting

Removal

Electronic control unit (ECU)

1 On models fitted with a wooden facia, remove the facia as described in Chapter 11A.

2 On models without a wooden facia, remove the left-hand fresh air vent assembly as described in Chapter 3, then release the left-hand door seal weatherstrip to gain access to the bulkhead trim. Remove the two edge clips, and peel back the bulkhead trim for access to the ECU.

3 On all models, undo the two ECU retaining screws and disconnect the wiring multiplugs.

4 Cut the cable-ties to release the receiver lead, and remove the ECU.

Bonnet switch

5 Open the bonnet, and undo the screw securing the switch to the front panel.

6 Lift off the switch and disconnect the wiring.

Boot switch

7 Open the boot, and disconnect the wiring from the switch.

8 Undo the switch retaining screw, and remove the switch from its bracket.

Refitting

9 Refitting is the reverse sequence to removal. Secure the receiver lead with new cable-ties when refitting the ECU.

Key to wiring diagrams 1 to 9 inclusive

Some of the components listed in this key may not be fitted to individual models

1	Dynamo or alternator	30	RH rear flasher light	95	Tachometer
2	Control box	31	LH rear flasher light	110	RH repeater flasher
3	Battery (12 volt)	32	Heater or fresh-air blower switch	111	LH repeater flasher
4	Starter solenoid	33	Heater or fresh-air blower	115	Rear window demister switch
5	Starter motor	34	Fuel gauge	116	Rear window demister unit
6	Lighting switch	35	Fuel gauge tank unit	139	Alternative connections for two-speed wiper motor and switch
7	Headlight dip switch	36	Windscreen wiper switch		
8	RH headlight	37	Windscreen wiper motor	150	Rear window demist warning light
9	LH headlight	38	Ignition/starter stitch	152	Hazard warning light
10	Main beam warning light	39	Ignition coil	153	Hazard warning switch
11	RH sidelight/parking light	40	Distributor	154	Hazard warning flasher unit
12	LH sidelight/parking light	41	Fuel pump	158	Printed circuit instrument panel
14	Panel lights	42	Oil pressure switch	159	Brake pressure warning light and light test switch
15	Number plate light(s)	43	Oil pressure gauge or warning light		
16	RH stop and tail light	44	Ignition warning light	160	Brake pressure failure switch
17	LH stop and tail light	45	Speedometer (headlight flasher switch on Canadian Mini 1000)	164	Ballast resistor
18	Stop light switch			168	Ignition key audible warning buzzer
19	Fuse block	46	Water temperature gauge	170	RH front side marker light
20	Interior light	47	Water temperature transmitter	171	LH front side marker light
21	RH door switch(es)	49	Reversing light switch	172	RH rear side marker light
22	LH door switch(es)	50	Reversing light	173	LH rear side marker light
23	Horn(s)	64	Bi-metallic instrument voltage stabiliser	198	Driver's seat belt switch
24	Horn push	67	Line fuse (35 amp)	199	Passenger's seat belt switch
25	Flasher unit	75	Automatic transmission inhibitor switch (when fitted)	200	Passenger's seat switch
26	Direction indicator headlight flasher and dip switch			201	Seat belt warning gearbox switch
		77	Windscreen washer motor	202	Seat belt warning light
27	Direction indicator warning light(s)	78	Windscreen washer switch	203	Seat belt warning code
28	RH front flasher light	83	Induction heater and thermostat		
29	LH front flasher light	84	Suction chamber heater		

Cable colour code

B	Black	N	Brown	U	Blue
G	Green	O	Orange	W	White
K	Pink	P	Purple	Y	Yellow
LG	Light Green	R	Red		

When a cable has two colour code letters the first denotes the main colour and the second denotes the tracer colour

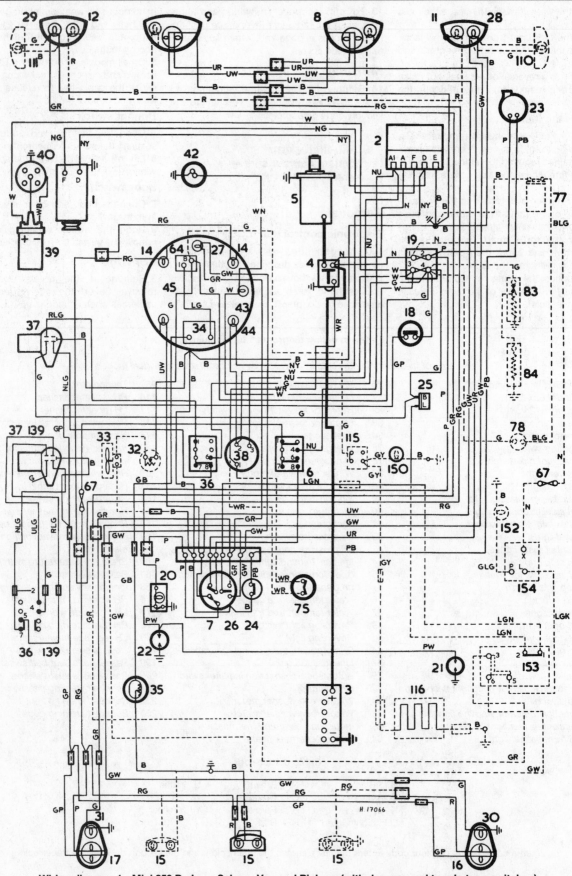

Wiring diagram 1 - Mini 850 De Luxe Saloon, Van and Pick-up (with dynamo and toggle type switches)

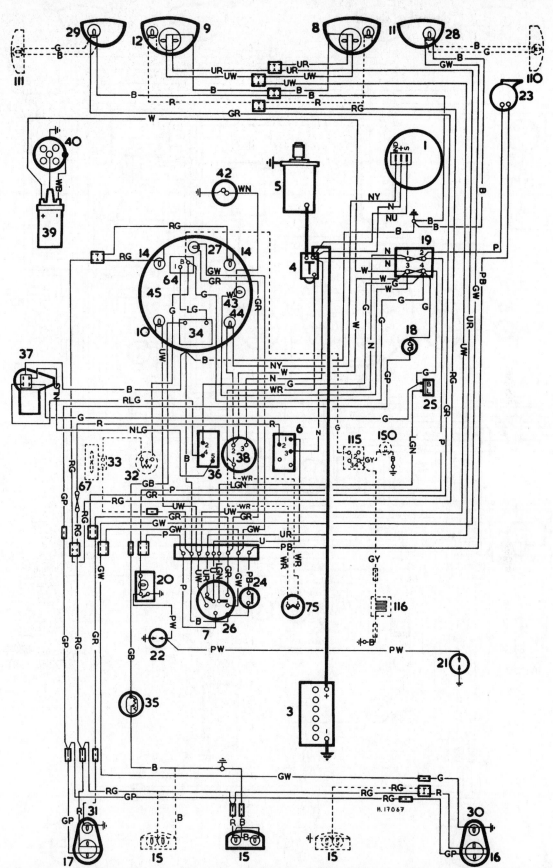

Wiring diagram 2 - Mini 850 De Luxe Saloon, Van and Pick-up (with alternator and rocker type switches) - pre 1976

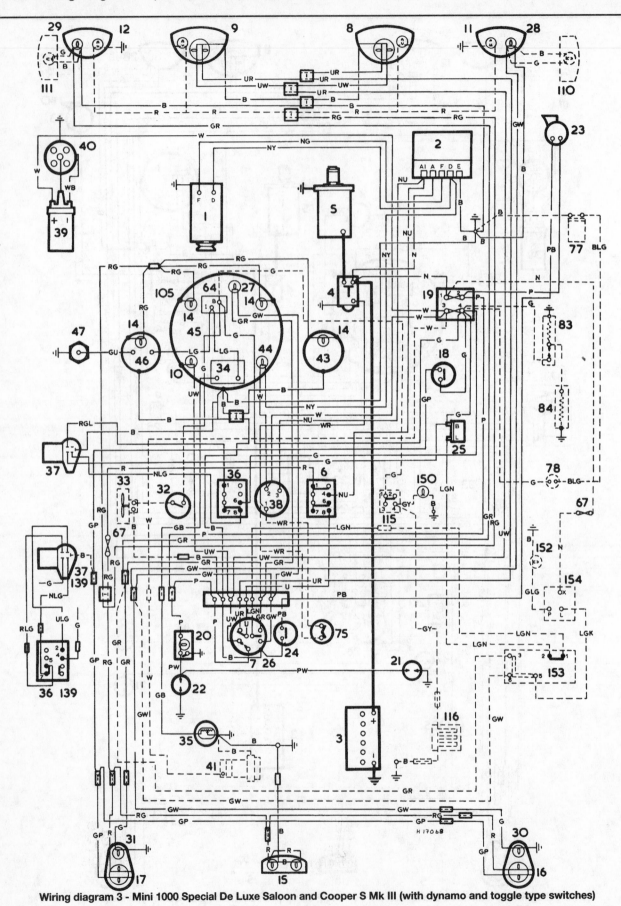

Wiring diagram 3 - Mini 1000 Special De Luxe Saloon and Cooper S Mk III (with dynamo and toggle type switches)

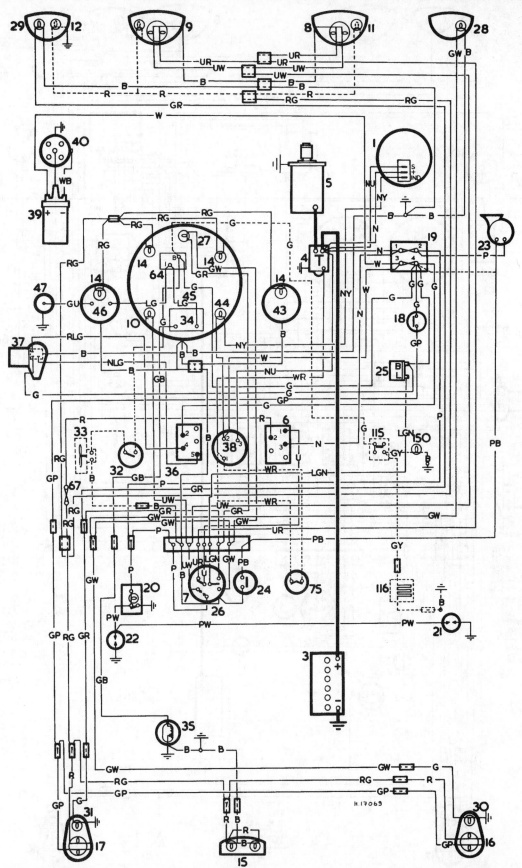

Wiring diagram 4 - Mini 1000 Special De Luxe Saloon (with alternator and rocker type switches) - pre 1976

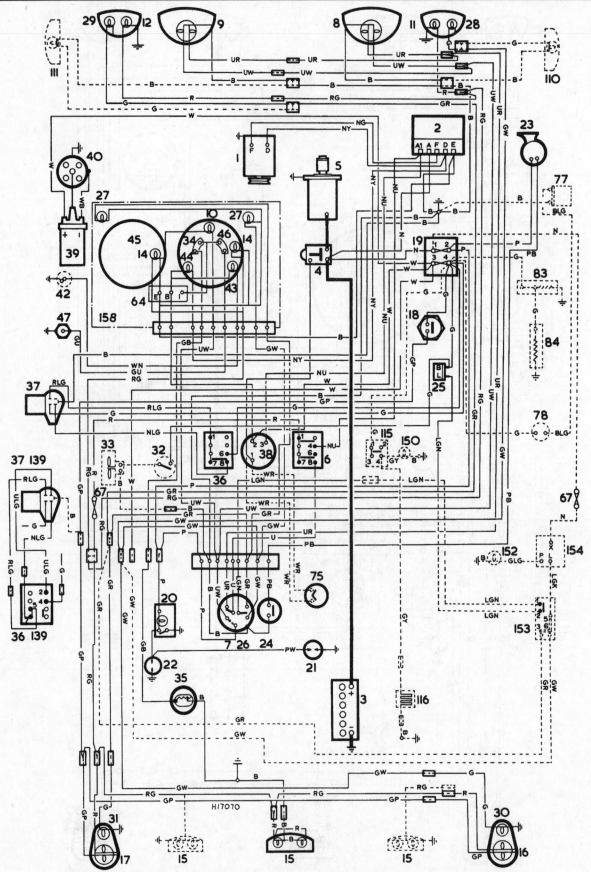

Wiring diagram 5 - Mini Clubman Saloon and Estate (with dynamo and toggle type switches)

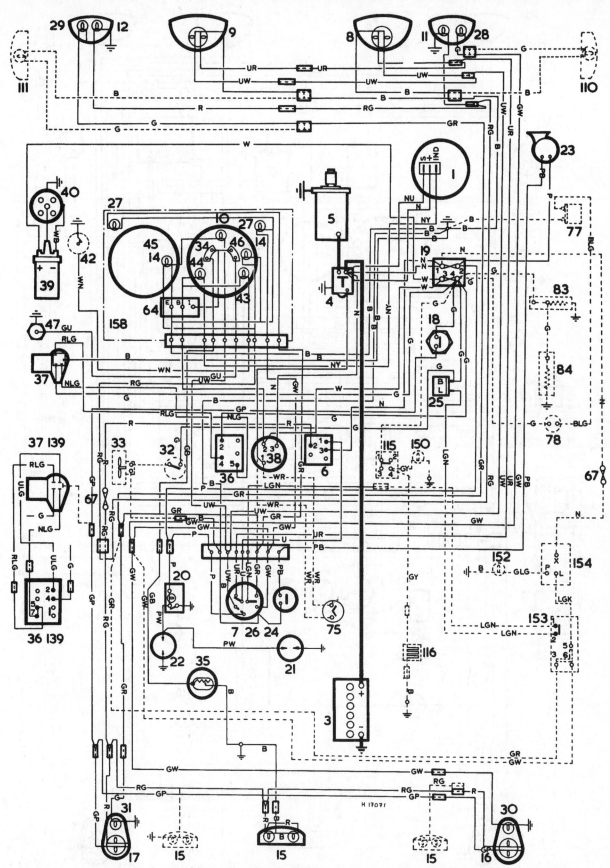

Wiring diagram 6 - Mini Clubman Saloon and Estate (with alternator and rocker type switches) - pre 1976

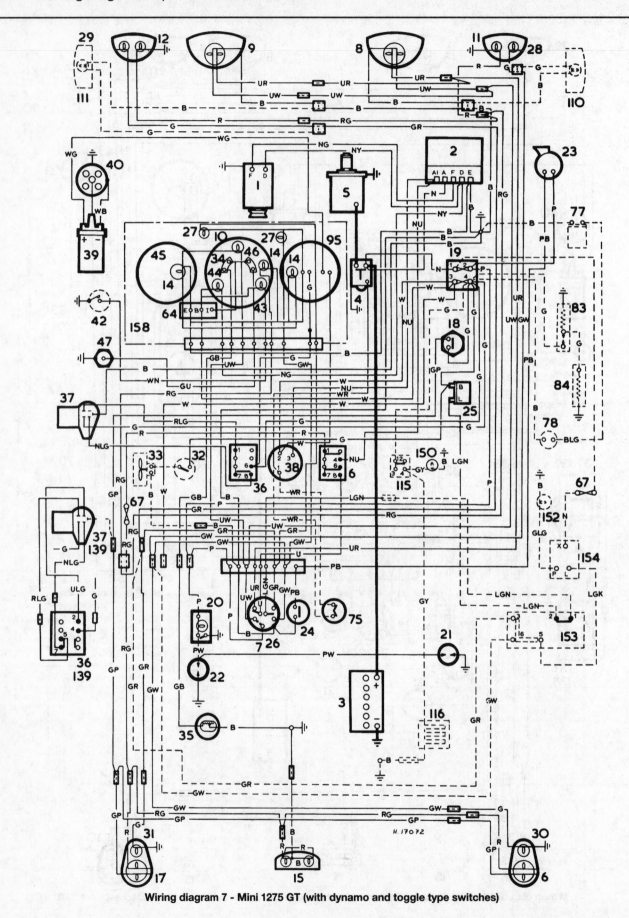

Wiring diagram 7 - Mini 1275 GT (with dynamo and toggle type switches)

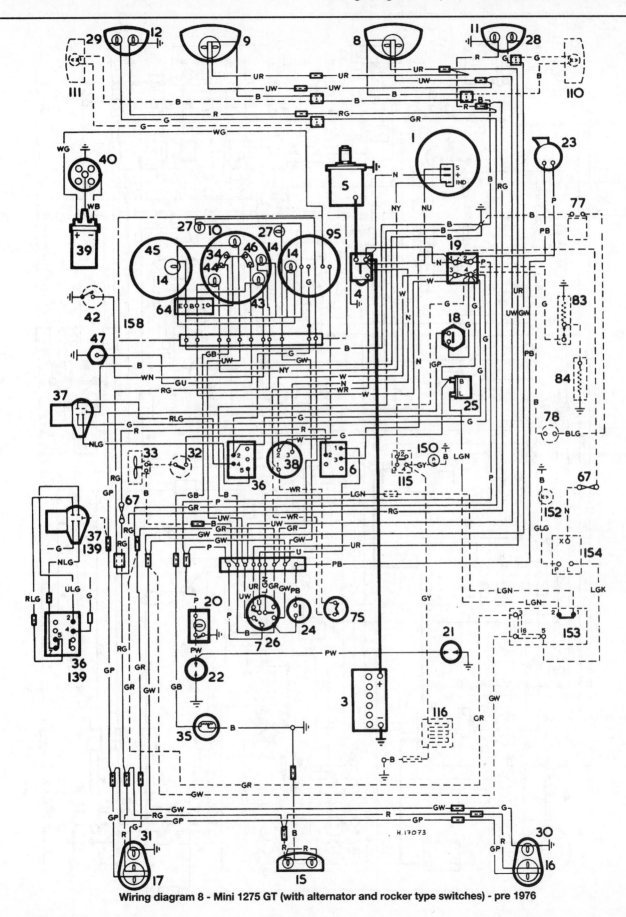

Wiring diagram 8 - Mini 1275 GT (with alternator and rocker type switches) - pre 1976

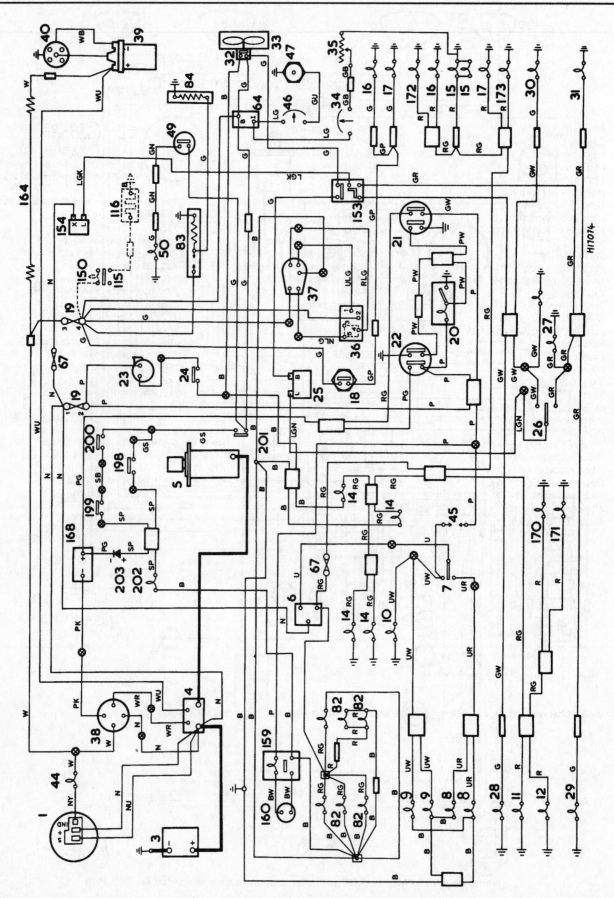

Wiring diagram 9 - Mini 1000 Saloon (Canada) - pre 1977

Key to wiring diagrams 10 to 15 inclusive

Some of the components listed in this key may not be fitted to individual models

1	Alternator	34	Fuel level indicator	152	Hazard warning light
3	Battery	35	Fuel level indicator tank unit	153	Hazard warning switch
4	Starter solenoid	37	Windscreen wiper motor	154	Hazard warning flasher unit
5	Starter motor	38	Ignition switch	158	Printed circuit instrument panel
6	Lighting switch	39	Ignition coil	159	Brake failure test switch and warning
7	Headlight dip switch	40	Distributor		light
8	Headlight dip beam	42	Oil pressure switch	160	Brake pressure differential switch
9	Headlight main beam	43	Oil pressure warning light	164	Resistive cable
10	Main beam warning light	44	No charge warning light	165	Handbrake switch
11	Sidelight - RH	45	Headlight flasher switch	166	Handbrake warning light
12	Sidelight - LH	46	Water temperature indicator	168	Ignition key warning buzzer
14	Panel illumination lights	47	Water temperature transmitter	169	Buzzer door switch
15	Number plate illumination lights	49	Reversing light switch	170	RH front side marker light
16	Stop lights	50	Reversing light	171	LH front side marker light
17	Tail light - RH	56	Clock (if fitted)	172	RH rear side marker light
18	Stop light switch (hydraulic)	57	Cigar lighter (if fitted)	173	LH rear side marker light
18	Stop light switch (mechanical)	60	Radio	198	Driver's seat belt switch
19	Fuse box	64	Voltage stabiliser	199	Passenger's seat belt switch
20	Interior light	67	Line fuse	200	Passenger seat switch
21	Interior light switch (door)	75	Automatic transmission inhibitor switch	201	Seat belt warning gearbox switch
22	Tail light - LH	77	Windscreen washer motor	202	Seat belt warning light
23	Horn	82	Switch illumination light	203	Blocking diode - seat belt warning
24	Horn-push	83	Induction heater and thermostat	208	Cigar lighter illumination
25	Indicator flasher unit	84	Suction chamber heater	210	Panel illumination rheostat
26	Indicator switch	95	Tachometer	211	Heater control illumination
27	Indicator warning light	110	Indicator repeater lights	286	Rear fog guard switch
28	Front indicator light - RH	115	Heated rear screen switch	287	Rear fog guard warning light
29	Front indicator light - LH	116	Heated rear screen	288	Rear fog guard light
30	Rear indicator light - RH	118	Combined windscreen washer and	291	Brake warning relay
31	Rear indicator light - LH		wiper switch	314	Clock illumination
32	Heater switch	132	Brake warning light		
33	Heater motor	150	Heated rear screen warning light		

Cable colour code

B	Black	N	Brown	U	Blue
G	Green	O	Orange	W	White
K	Pink	P	Purple	Y	Yellow
LG	Light Green	R	Red		

When a cable has two colour code letters the first denotes the main colour and the second denotes the tracer colour.

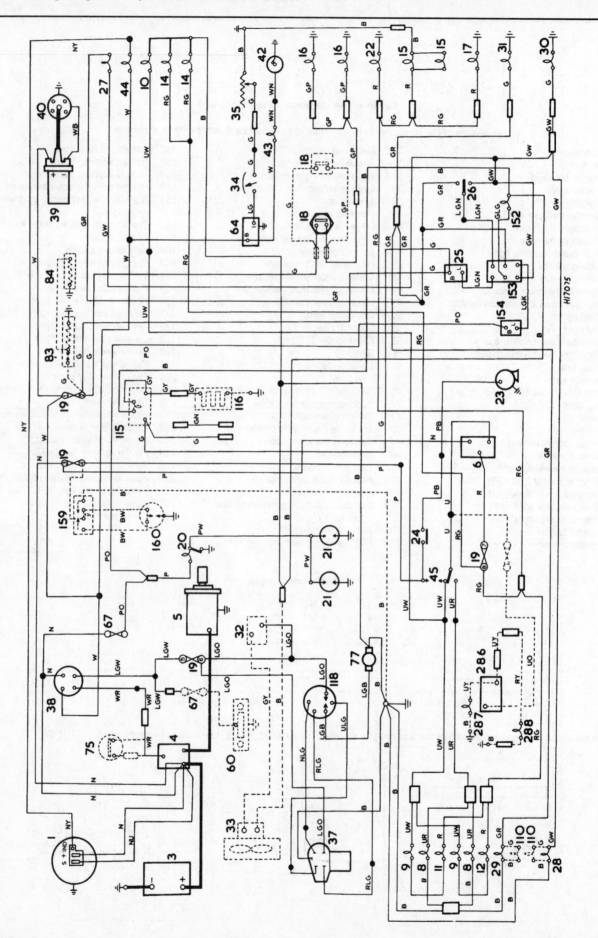

Wiring diagram 10 – Mini 850 Saloon, Van and Pick-up – 1976 onwards

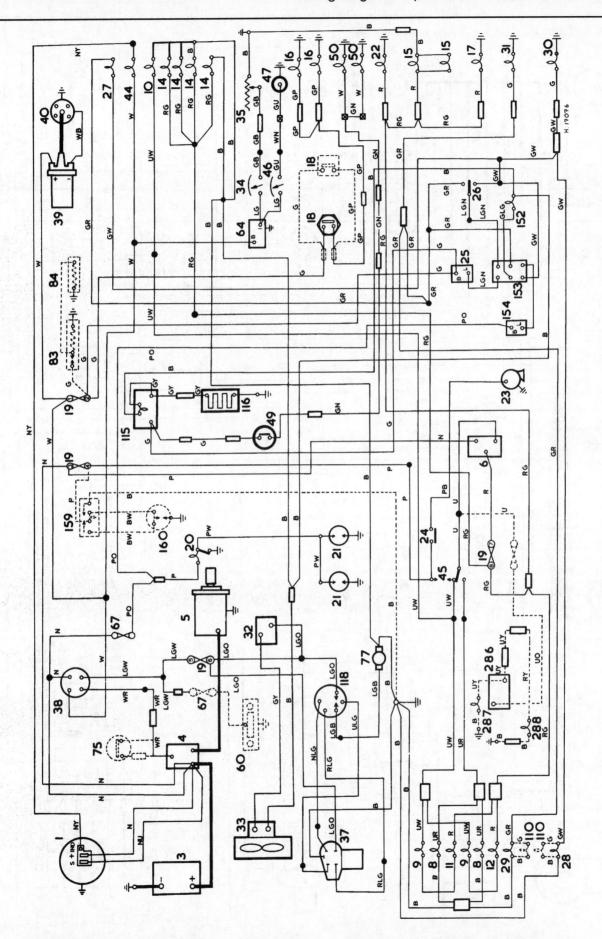

Wiring diagram 11 - Mini 1000 Saloon (triple instrument facia) - 1976 onwards (UK, Europe, Sweden); and Mini Special (triple instrument facia) - 1976 to 77

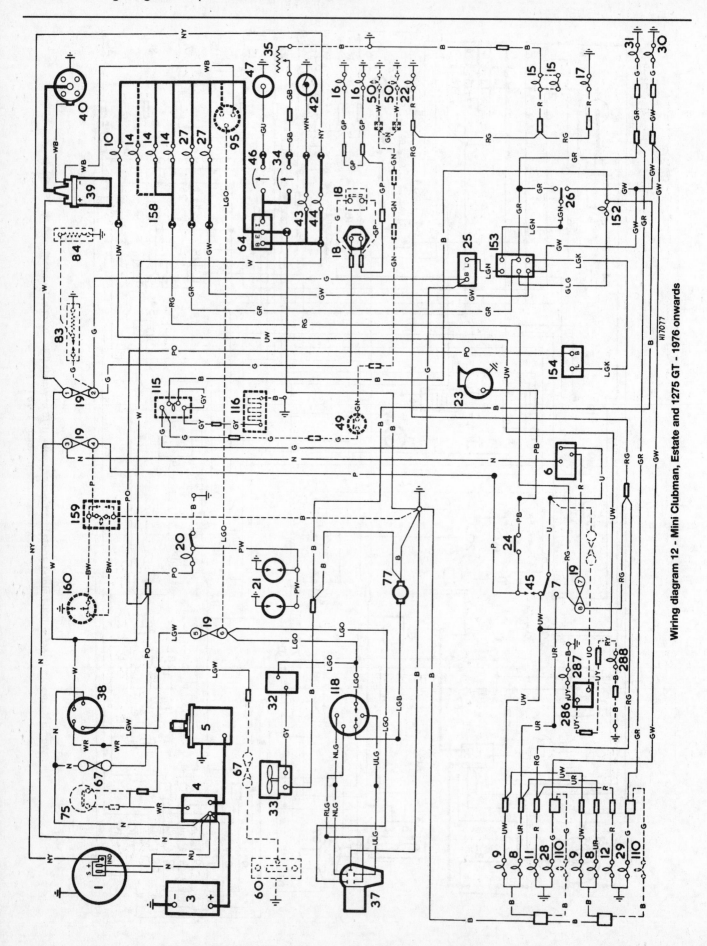

Wiring diagram 12 - Mini Clubman, Estate and 1275 GT - 1976 onwards

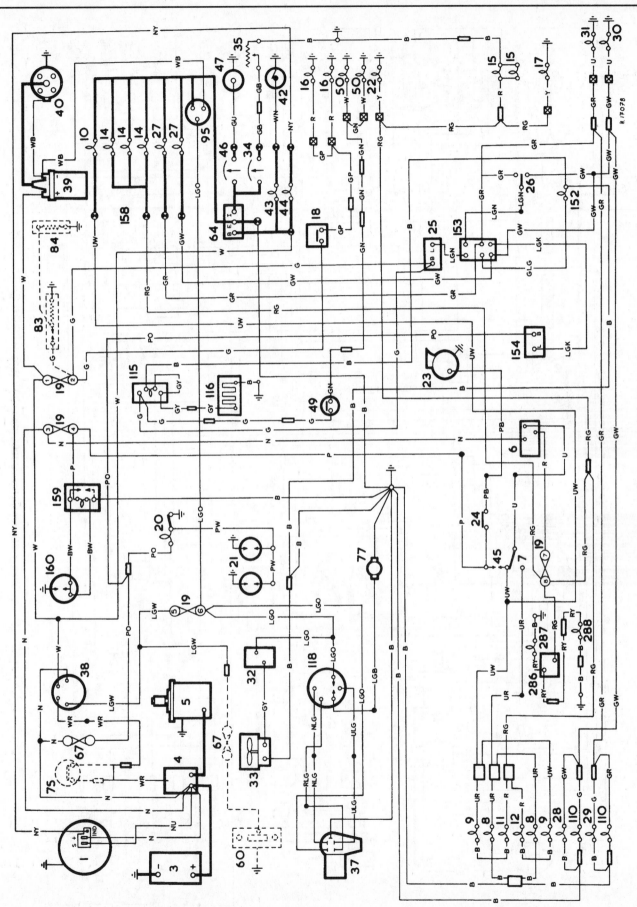

Wiring diagram 13 - Mini Special - 1977 to 78

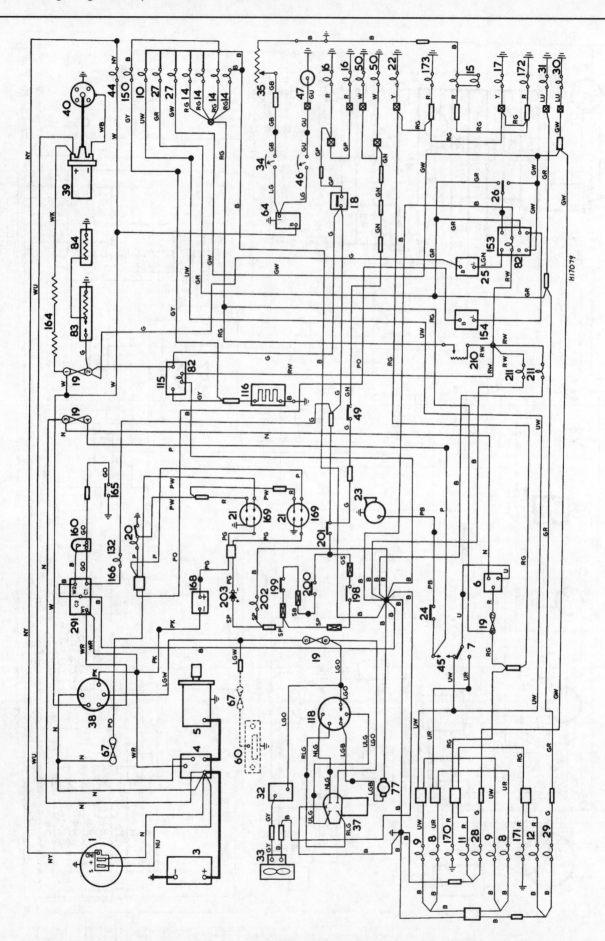

Wiring diagram 14 - Mini 1000 (Canada) - 1977 onwards

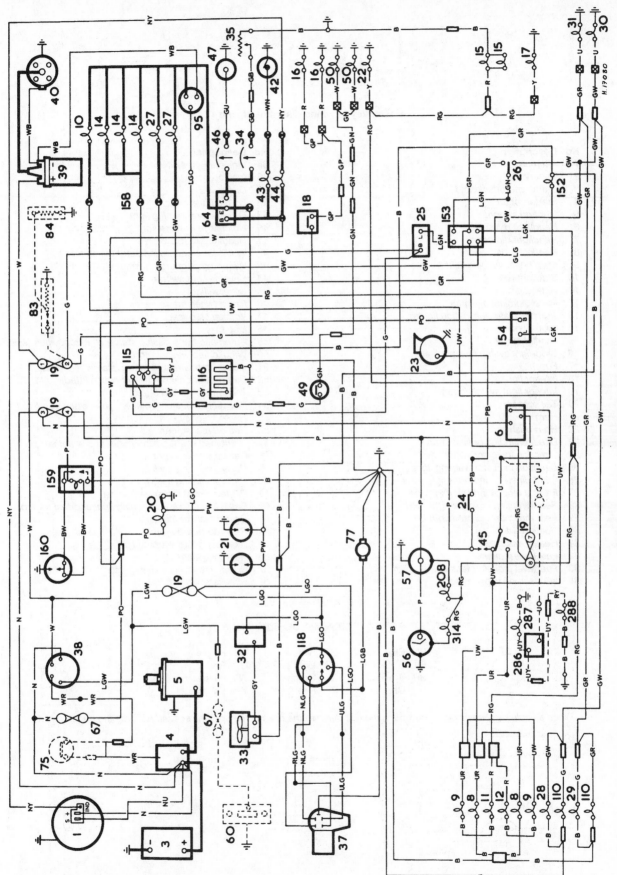

Wiring diagram 15 - Mini Special - 1979 onwards

Master key to wiring diagrams 16 and 17

No	Description	No	Description
1	Alternator	35	Ignition/start switch
2	Battery	36	Ignition coil
3	Starter motor solenoid	37	Distributor
4	Starter motor	38	Oil pressure switch
5	Lighting switch	39	Oil pressure warning light
6	Headlight dip switch	40	No charge warning light
7	Headlight dip beam	41	Headlight flash switch
8	Headlight main beam	42	Water temperature indicator (when fitted)
9	Main beam warning light	43	Water temperature transmitter (when fitted)
10	Sidelight RH	44	Reverse light switch
11	Sidelight LH	45	Reverse light
12	Panel illumination lights	46	Radio (when fitted)
13	Number plate illumination lights	47	Voltage stabiliser
14	Stop-lights	48	Line fuse
15	Tail-lights RH	49	Automatic transmission starter inhibitor switch (when fitted)
16	Stop-light switch (mechanical)	50	Windscreen washer motor
17	Fusebox	51	Induction heater and thermostat (when fitted)
18	Interior light	52	Carburettor dashpot heater (when fitted)
19	Interior light switch (door)	53	Tachometer (when fitted)
20	Tail light LH	54	Direction indicator repeater lights (when fitted)
21	Horn	55	Heated rear screen switch
22	Horn push	56	Heated rear screen
23	Direction indicator flasher unit	57	Combined windscreen washer and wiper switch
24	Direction indicator switch	58	Hazard warning light
25	Direction indicator warning light	59	Hazard warning switch
26	Front direction indicator light - RH	60	Hazard warning flasher unit
27	Front direction indicator light LH	61	Printed circuit instrument panel
28	Rear direction indicator light - RH	62	Brake low fluid level warning light and test switch
29	Rear direction indicator light LH	63	Ballast resistor (cable)
30	Heater switch	64	Rear fog-guard switch
31	Heater motor	65	Rear fog-guard warning light
32	Fuel level indicator	66	Rear fog-guard light
33	Fuel level indicator tank unit	67	Brake fluid level sensor switch
34	Windscreen wiper motor	68	Speakers (when fitted)

Cable colour code

BL	Blue	GR	Slate	PU	Purple
BK	Black	LG	Light green	R	Red
BR	Brown	O	Orange	W	White
G	Green	P	Pink	Y	Yellow

When a cable has two colour code letters, the first denotes the main colour and the second denotes the tracer colour

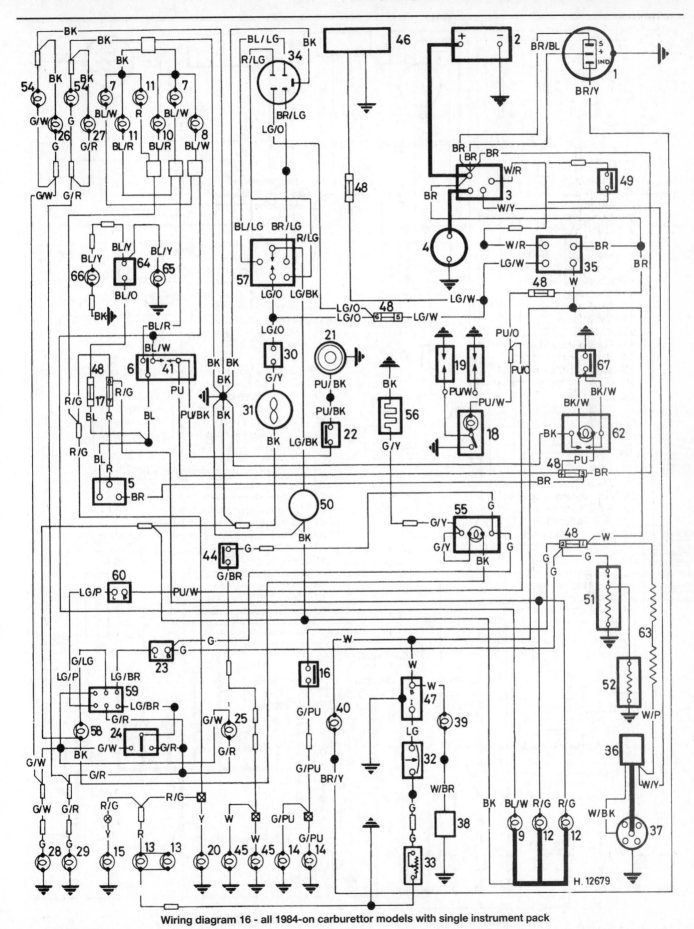

Wiring diagram 16 - all 1984-on carburettor models with single instrument pack

H. 12679

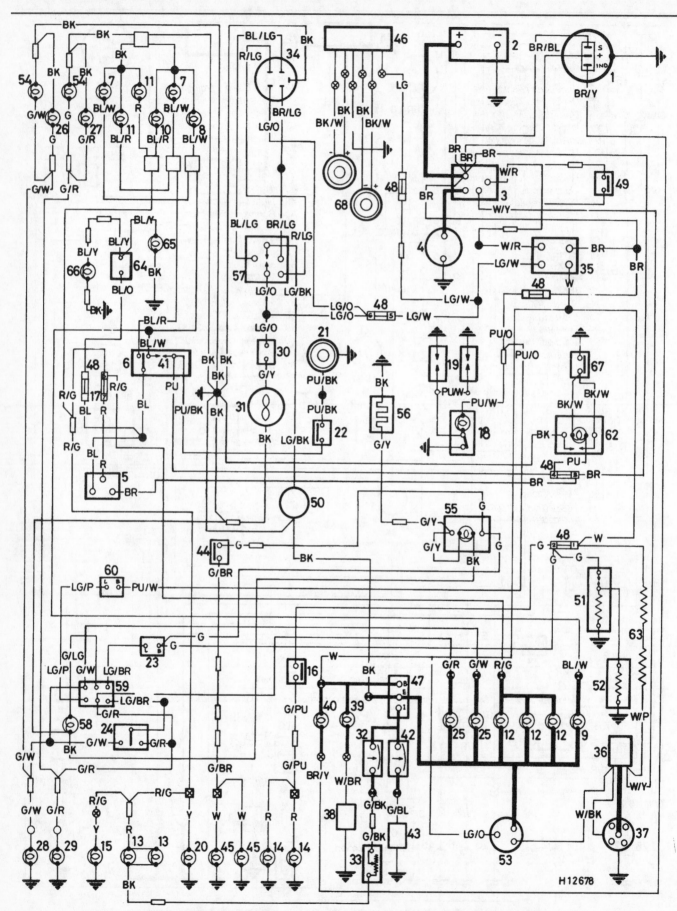

Wiring diagram 17 - all 1984-on carburettor models with multiple instrument pack

H12678

Key to wiring diagram 18

No	Description	No	Description
1	Direction indicator unit	40	Main beam warning light
2	Direction indicator switch	41	Coolant temperature gauge
3	Hazard warning switch	42	Fuel gauge
4	Hazard warning unit	43	Rear foglight warning light
5	Hazard warning light	44	Panel lights
6	RH front direction indicator	45	Heater switch
7	RH side repeater light	46	Horn switch
8	RH rear direction indicator	47	Voltage stabiliser
9	LH front direction indicator	48	Battery
10	LH side repeater light	49	Lighting switch
11	LH rear direction indicator	50	Headlight dipswitch
12	Automatic transmission starter inhibitor switch	51	Number plate illumination lights
13	Distributor	52	RH tail light
14	Ignition coil	53	LH tail light
15	Starter relay	54	Horn
16	Ignition switch	55	Windscreen wiper motor
17	Starter motor solenoid	56	Headlight flasher switch
18	Ballast resistor	57	Rear foglight switch
19	In-line fuse	58	Windscreen washer motor
20	Fuse block	59	Heated rear window element
21	Stop-light switch	60	LH front door switch
22	Dim/dip resistor	61	Wash/wipe switch
23	Heated rear window switch	62	Alternator
24	Heater motor	63	Coolant thermistor
25	Reversing light switch	64	Oil pressure switch
26	Interior light	65	Brake fluid level switch
27	RH front door switch	66	Oil pressure warning light
28	Fuel tank sender unit	67	Tachometer
29	Radio - single speaker	68	RH/single door speaker
30	Radio/cassette player	69	LH front door speaker
31	RH stop light	70	LH stop light
32	RH sidelight	71	Rear foglight
33	LH sidelight	72	Dim/dip relay
34	Headlight main beam	73	LH reversing light
35	Headlight dip beam	74	RH reversing light
36	Brake failure light test switch	75	Emission control valve switch
37	Ignition warning light	76	Heated rear window warning light
38	LH indicator warning light	77	Vacuum solenoid valve
39	RH indicator warning light		

Cable colour code

BK	Black	O	Orange
BL	Blue	P	Pink
BR	Brown	PU	Purple
G	Green	R	Red
GR	Slate	W	White
LG	Light green	Y	Yellow

When a cable has two colour code letters, the first denotes the main colour and the second the tracer

Symbols used

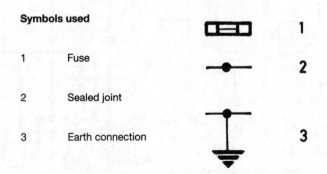

1	Fuse	1
2	Sealed joint	2
3	Earth connection	3

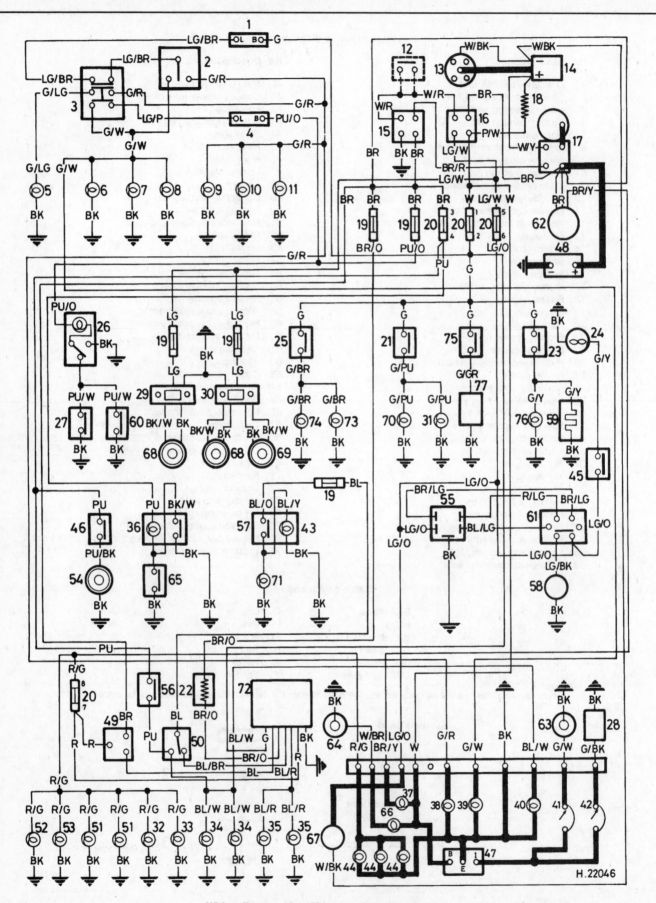

Wiring diagram 18 - 1988-on carburettor models

Key to wiring diagrams 19 to 32 inclusive

No	Description	No	Description
1	Battery	49	Fuel sender unit
2	Lighting	50	Fuel pump
3	Dip switch	51	Relay module
4	Dipped beam headlight	52	Automatic transmission starter inhibitor switch
5	Main beam headlight	53	Accelerator pedal switch
6	RH sidelight	54	Diagnostic connector
7	LH sidelight	55	Stepper motor
8	Number plate illumination light	56	Manifold PTC heater
9	RH tail light	57	Oil pressure switch
10	Brake light switch	58	Brake fluid level switch
11	LH tail light	59	Ignition/charging warning light
12	Horn	60	Oil pressure warning light
13	Horn switch	61	Brake system warning light
14	Direction indicator switch	62	Tachometer
15	RH front direction indicator light	63	Coolant temperature gauge
16	LH front direction indicator light	64	Fuel gauge
17	Heater switch	65	Main beam warning light
18	Heater motor	66	LH indicator warning light
19	Windscreen wiper motor	67	RH indicator warning light
20	Ignition switch	68	Instrument pack
21	Headlight flasher switch	69	Intake air temperature sensor
22	Rear foglight switch	70	Interior light
23	Direction indicator/hazard warning light unit	71	Radio/cassette player
24	Automatic transmission selector indicator light	72	RH speaker
25	Windscreen washer pump	73	LH speaker
26	Heated rear window switch	74	Auxiliary cooling fan relay
27	Heated rear window element	75	LH brake light
28	Hazard warning light	76	RH brake light
29	Hazard warning light switch	77	Dim-dip relay
30	Auxiliary cooling fan	78	Instrument panel illumination
31	Purge valve	79	Distributor
32	Fusible links	80	RH rear direction indicator light
33	LH side repeater light	81	LH rear direction indicator light
34	RH side repeater light	82	Voltage stabiliser
35	Driver's door interior light switch	83	Engine management ECU
36	Passenger door interior light switch	84	Lambda sensor
37	Dim-dip resistor	85	Reversing light switch
38	Auxiliary cooling fan switch	86	Rear foglight
39	Alternator	87	Fuel injector
40	Starter relay	88	Wiper column switch
41	Ignition coil	89	Starter
42	Crankshaft sensor	90	Lambda sensor relay
43	Throttle potentiometer	91	Reversing lights
44	Coolant temperature sensor	92	Direction indicator relay
45	Fuel pump relay	93	Fuse
46	Main relay	94	Line fuse
47	Manifold PTC heater relay	95	Radio fuse
48	Inertia switch		

Cable colour code

BL	Blue	O	Orange
BK	Black	P	Pink
BR	Brown	PU	Purple
G	Green	R	Red
GR	Slate	W	White
LG	Light green	Y	Yellow

When a cable has two colour code letters, the first denotes the main colour and the second denotes the tracer colour

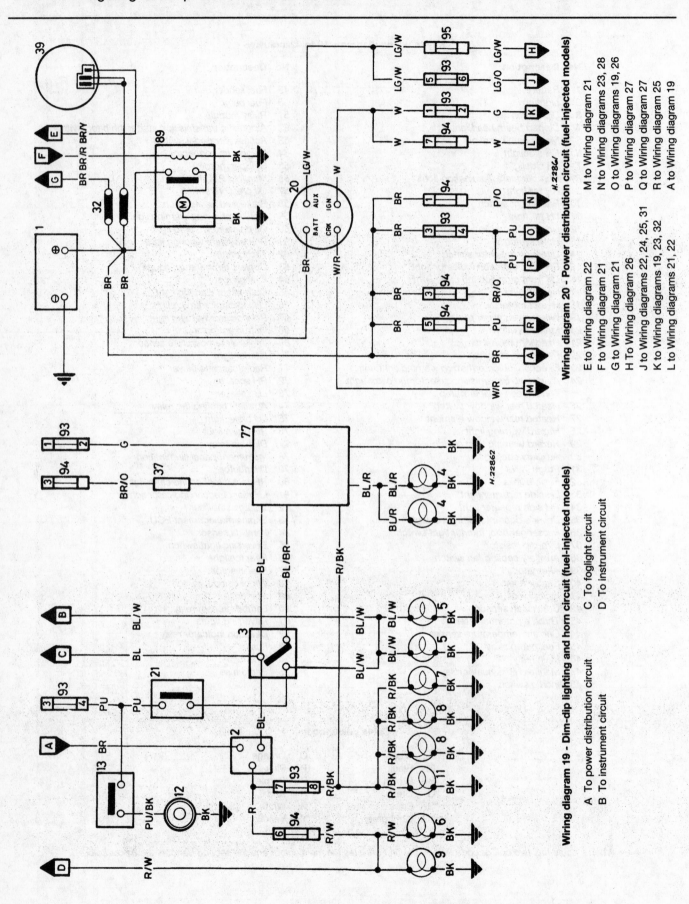

Wiring diagram 20 - Power distribution circuit (fuel-injected models)

E to Wiring diagram 22
F to Wiring diagram 21
G to Wiring diagram 21
H To Wiring diagram 26
J to Wiring diagrams 22, 24, 25, 31
K to Wiring diagrams 19, 23, 32
L to Wiring diagrams 21, 22

M to Wiring diagram 21
N to Wiring diagrams 23, 28
O to Wiring diagrams 19, 26
P to Wiring diagram 27
Q to Wiring diagram 27
R to Wiring diagram 25
A to Wiring diagram 19

Wiring diagram 19 - Dim-dip lighting and horn circuit (fuel-injected models)

A To power distribution circuit
B To instrument circuit

C To foglight circuit
D To instrument circuit

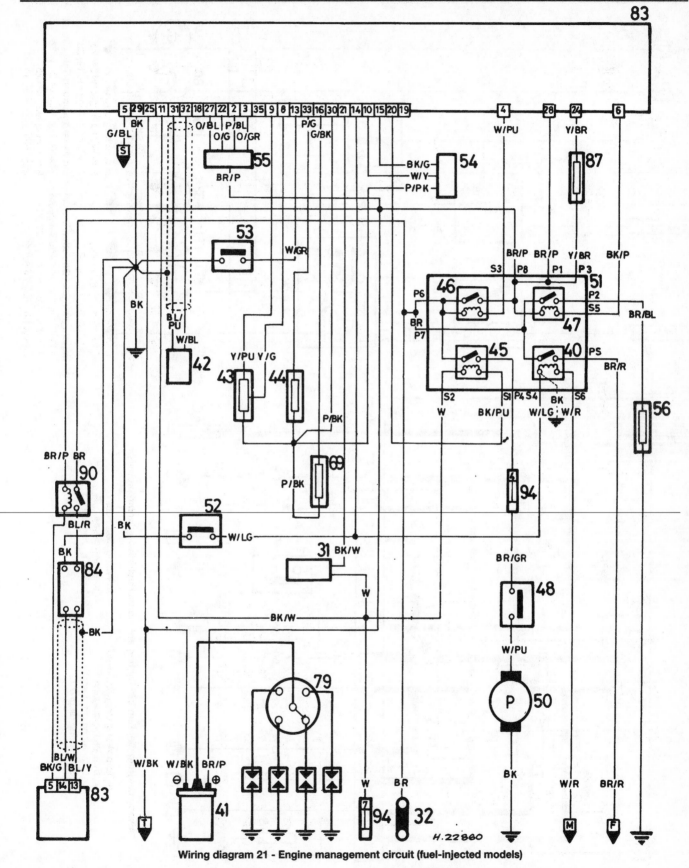

Wiring diagram 21 - Engine management circuit (fuel-injected models)

F to Wiring diagram 20   S to Wiring diagram 22
M to Wiring diagram 20   T to Wiring diagram 22

H.22860

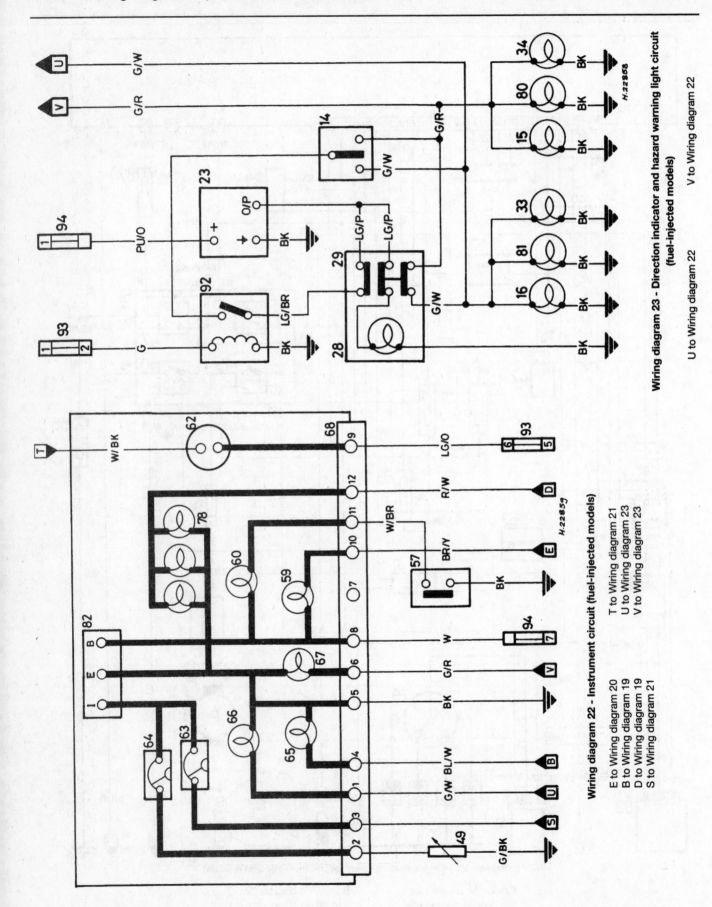

Wiring diagram 23 - Direction indicator and hazard warning light circuit (fuel-injected models)

U to Wiring diagram 22   V to Wiring diagram 22

Wiring diagram 22 - Instrument circuit (fuel-injected models)

E to Wiring diagram 20   T to Wiring diagram 21
B to Wiring diagram 19   U to Wiring diagram 23
D to Wiring diagram 19   V to Wiring diagram 23
S to Wiring diagram 21

H.22858

H.22859

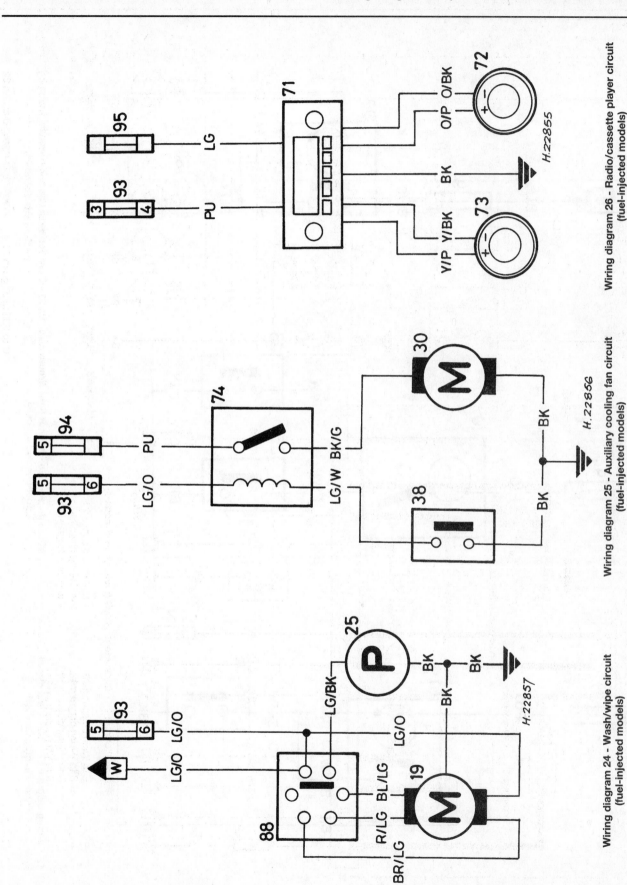

Wiring diagram 26 - Radio/cassette player circuit (fuel-injected models)

H.22855

Wiring diagram 25 - Auxiliary cooling fan circuit (fuel-injected models)

H.22856

Wiring diagram 24 - Wash/wipe circuit (fuel-injected models)

H.22857

W to Wiring diagram 30

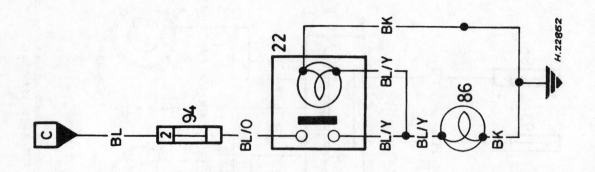

Wiring diagram 29 - Foglight circuit
(fuel-injected models)

C to Wiring diagram 19

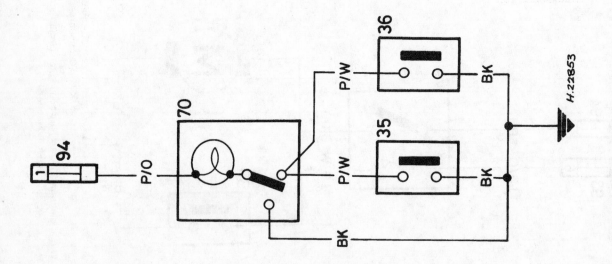

Wiring diagram 28 - Interior light circuit
(fuel-injected models)

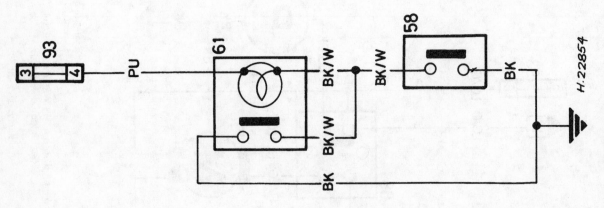

Wiring diagram 27 - Brake test circuit
(fuel-injected models)

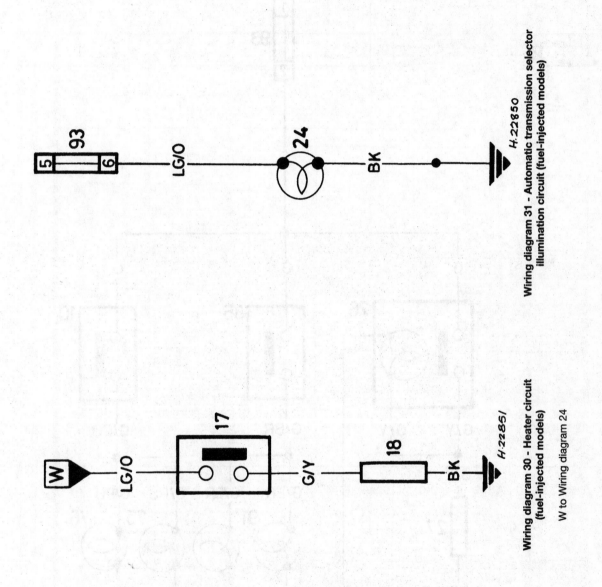

H.22850

Wiring diagram 31 – Automatic transmission selector illumination circuit (fuel-injected models)

H.22851

Wiring diagram 30 – Heater circuit (fuel-injected models)

W to Wiring diagram 24

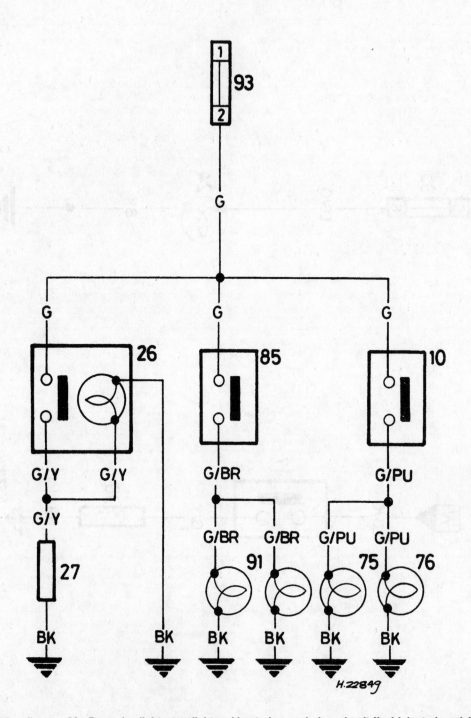

Wiring diagram 32 - Reversing light, stop-light and heated rear window circuit (fuel-injected models)

Chapter 12 Part B:
Body electrical system – October 1996 models onward

Contents

Airbag system – general information, precautions and system de-
activation 21
Airbag system components – removal and refitting 22
Anti-theft alarm system components – removal and refitting 20
Battery condition indicator, clock and oil temperature gauge –
removal and refitting 16
Bulbs (exterior lights) – renewal 5
Bulbs (interior lights) – renewal 6
Electrical fault finding – general information 2
Fuses and relays – general information 3
General information and precautions 1
Headlight adjuster motor – removal and refitting 8
Headlight beam alignment – general information 7

Horn – removal and refitting 9
Instrument panel – dismantling and reassembly 15
Instrument panel – removal and refitting 14
Loudspeakers – removal and refitting 19
Radio/cassette player – removal and refitting 18
Speedometer cable – removal and refitting 17
Switches – removal and refitting 4
Windscreen washer fluid level check .... See *Weekly Checks*
Windscreen washer pump – removal and refitting 13
Windscreen wiper arms – removal and refitting 10
Windscreen wiper motor – removal and refitting 11
Windscreen wiper wheelbox – removal and refitting 12
Wiper blade check .... See *Weekly Checks*

Degrees of difficulty

Easy, suitable for novice with little experience	Fairly easy, suitable for beginner with some experience	Fairly difficult, suitable for competent DIY mechanic	Difficult, suitable for experienced DIY mechanic	Very difficult, suitable for expert DIY or professional 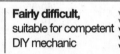

Specifications

General

System type .... 12 volt negative earth

Main fuses (passenger compartment fuseblock)

Fuse number	Rating (amp)	Circuits protected
A1	10	Right-hand headlight main beam, driving light relay
A2	10	Right-hand headlight dip beam
A3	10	Right-hand, side and tail lights
A4	10	Anti-theft alarm, instruments,
A5	Not used	
A6	Not used	
A7	Not used	
A8	15	Heater blower motor
A9	Not used	
B1	15	Driving light relay
B2	10	Rear foglight
B3	10	Headlight levelling
B4	10	Ignition auxiliaries, radio
B5	10	Airbag ECU
B6	20	Anti-theft alarm and horn
B7	15	Sunroof motor
B8	15	Wipers/washers
B9	15	Radiator auxiliary cooling fan
C1	10	Left-hand headlight main beam
C2	10	Left-hand headlight dip beam
C3	10	Left-hand, side and tail lights
C4	10	Radio, brake test switch warning light, anti-theft alarm, direction indicators, clock, hazard warning lights, interior lights
C5	Not used	
C6	15	Direction indicators, stop-lights, reversing lights
C7	10	Fuel pump
C8	10	Engine management ECU relay module (starter relay)
C9	15	Heated rear window

Line fuse

Rating (amp)	Circuits protected
15	Front foglight relay

Fusible links (engine compartment fuseblock)

Link number	Rating (amp)	Circuits protected
1	30	Passenger compartment fuseblock – fuses A9, B1, B5, B9, C4
2	30	Ignition switch, auxiliary relay
3	30	Lighting switch
4	30	Engine management relay module

Relays

Relay	Location
Auxiliary circuits	Behind facia
Direction indicator/hazard flasher	Behind facia
Direction indicators	Engine compartment, rear right-hand side
Driving lights	Engine compartment, rear right-hand side
Engine management relay module	Engine compartment, above vacuum servo unit
Front foglight	Engine compartment, rear right-hand side
Horn relay	Behind facia
Radiator auxiliary cooling fan	Engine compartment bulkhead, left-hand side
Wash/wipe delay	Behind facia

Bulbs*

	Wattage	Type
Auxiliary driving lights	55	453
Direction indicator side repeaters	5	501
Direction indicators	21	382
Headlights	60/55	472
Interior light	10	245
Number plate light	5	239
Rear foglight	21	382
Reversing lights	21	382
Sidelights	4	233
Stop/tail light	21/5	380

*Refer to a Rover dealer for details of bulbs not listed here.

Torque wrench setting

	Nm	lbf ft
Airbag unit retaining screws	7	5

1 General information and precautions

⚠️ **Warning: Before carrying out any work on the electrical system, read through the precautions given in 'Safety first!' at the beginning of this manual, and in Chapter 5A.**

1 The electrical system is of the 12 volt negative earth type. Power for the lights and all electrical accessories is supplied by a lead-acid type battery, which is charged by the alternator.

2 This Chapter covers repair and service procedures for the various electrical components not associated with the engine. Information on the battery, alternator and starter motor can be found in Chapter 5A.

3 It should be noted that, prior to working on any component in the electrical system, the battery negative terminal should first be disconnected, to prevent the possibility of electrical short-circuits and/or fires.

Caution: Before proceeding, refer to 'Disconnecting the battery' in the Reference Chapter for further information.

2 Electrical fault finding – general information

Refer to Chapter 12A, Section 2.

3 Fuses and relays – general information

Main fuses

1 The main fuses are located in a fuseblock which is mounted under the facia on the driver's side of the car. To open the fuseblock cover, use a coin to turn the cover retaining screw a quarter turn left or right and lift off the cover. The fuse positions and circuits protected are listed in the Specifications.

2 To remove a fuse, simply withdraw it from the contacts in the fuseblock; the wire within the fuse should be visible; if the fuse is blown, the wire will be broken or melted (see illustration).

3 Always renew a fuse with one of an identical rating; never use a fuse with a different rating from the original or substitute anything else. Never renew a fuse more than once without tracing the source of the trouble.

4 Persistent blowing of a particular fuse indicates a fault in the circuit(s) protected. Where more than one circuit is involved, switch on one item at a time until the fuse blows, so showing in which circuit the fault lies.

5 Besides a fault in the electrical component concerned, a blown fuse can also be caused by a short-circuit in the wiring to the component. Look for trapped or frayed wires allowing a live wire to touch vehicle metal, and for loose or damaged connectors.

3.2 To remove a fuse, withdraw it from the contacts in the fuseblock

3.7 Fusible links are located in the engine compartment fuseblock (arrowed)

4.3 Undo the screws securing the relevant steering column switch to the multifunction switch assembly

4.4 Depress the retaining tag and withdraw the relevant switch from the switch assembly

6 After renewing a fuse, refit and secure the fuseblock cover.

Fusible links

7 Additional fusible links are located in the engine compartment fuseblock **(see illustration)**. These fusible links carry a heavy current for the major vehicle circuits. Fusible links do not normally blow, but if they do, this indicates a major circuit failure or short-circuit.

Line fuses

8 A line fuse is fitted to protect an individual unit or circuit. On models covered in this Chapter Part, only one line fuse is used, to protect the front foglight relay. The fuse is located on the right-hand side of the engine compartment. To change a line fuse, hold one end of the container, press and twist off the other end.

Relays

9 A relay is an electrically-operated switch, which is used for the following reasons:
  a) A relay can switch a heavy current remotely from the circuit in which the current is flowing, allowing the use of lighter gauge wiring and switch contacts.
  b) A relay can receive more than one control input, unlike a mechanical switch.
  c) A relay can have a timer function – for example an intermittent wiper delay.

10 On later Mini models, relays are used to operate a number of circuits, mainly in the engine management and emission control systems and the lighting circuits. The engine

management system relays are contained in a sealed module mounted above the vacuum servo unit on the engine compartment bulkhead – these cannot be individually renewed and in the event of a fault in this area, the complete module must be renewed. The locations of the remaining relays are given in the Specifications.

11 If a circuit which includes a relay develops a fault, remember that the relay itself could be faulty. Testing is by substitution of a known good relay. Do not assume that relays which look similar are necessarily identical for purposes of substitution.

12 Make sure that the ignition is switched off, then pull the relay from its socket. Push the new relay firmly in to refit.

4   Switches –
removal and refitting

Note: *Disconnect the battery negative terminal (refer to 'Disconnecting the battery' in the Reference Chapter) before removing any switch and reconnect the lead after refitting the switch.*

Steering column switches

1 Remove the steering wheel as described in Chapter 10.
2 Remove the airbag rotary coupling as described in Section 22.
3 Undo the two screws securing the direction indicator/lighting switch, or the wiper/washer switch, as applicable, to the multifunction switch assembly **(see illustration).**

4 Using a small screwdriver, depress the retaining tag and withdraw the relevant switch from the switch assembly **(see illustration).**
5 Disconnect the wiring multiplugs and remove the switch **(see illustration).**
6 Refitting the switch is the reverse sequence to removal. Refit the airbag rotary coupling as described in Section 22, then refit the steering wheel as described in Chapter 10.

Horn switches

7 Using a small screwdriver, carefully prise the relevant switch from its location in the steering wheel.
8 Disconnect the two wiring connectors and remove the switch.
9 Refitting the switch is the reverse sequence to removal.

Facia rocker switches

10 Undo the two screws securing the front of the heater to the lower facia panel. Lower the front of the heater slightly for access to the rear of the switches.
11 Push the relevant switch out of the lower facia panel and disconnect the wiring multiplug.
12 Refitting is the reverse sequence to removal.

Headlight levelling switch

13 Unscrew the driver's side fresh air vent retaining collar, then turn the air vent anti-clockwise and remove it. Withdraw the air vent hose.
14 Pull off the control knob then unscrew the nut securing the switch to the facia **(see illustrations).**

4.5 Disconnect the wiring multiplugs and remove the switch

4.14a Pull off the control knob from the headlight levelling switch . . .

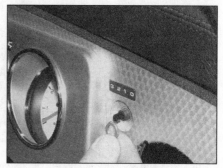

4.14b . . . then unscrew the nut securing the switch to the facia

4.15a Withdraw the switch through the fresh air vent aperture . . .

4.15b . . . and disconnect the wiring multiplug from the rear of the switch

5.1a Undo and remove the headlight outer rim securing screw . . .

15 Withdraw the switch through the fresh air vent aperture and disconnect the wiring multiplug from the rear of the switch **(see illustrations)**.
16 Refitting is the reverse sequence to removal.

Door pillar switch

17 The interior light door pillar switches are retained by a single securing screw. Undo the screw, disconnect the electrical lead and lift away the switch.

> **HAYNES HINT** *Tape the wiring to the door pillar, to prevent it falling back into the pillar. Alternatively, tie a piece of string to the wiring to retrieve it.*

18 Refitting is the reverse sequence to removal.

Stop-light switch

19 From under the facia on the driver's side, remove the heater air inlet duct.
20 Disconnect the accelerator pedal return spring from the switch mounting bracket.
21 Disconnect the two wiring connectors from the switch terminals.
22 Undo and remove the locknut and then withdraw the switch from its mounting bracket.
23 Refitting is the reverse sequence to removal. Adjust the position of the switch and

locknuts so that the stop-lights operate when the brake pedal is depressed slightly, and extinguish with the pedal released. Ensure that the switch does not prevent the brake pedal from releasing fully.

Ignition switch

24 The ignition switch is of the sealed type and can only be removed with the steering lock housing as a complete assembly. This procedure is described fully in Chapter 10, Section 24; it is not necessary to remove the steering column.

Reversing light switch

25 Firmly apply the handbrake, then jack up the front of the car and support it securely on axle stands (see *Jacking and vehicle support*).
26 Working underneath the car, disconnect the two switch wires, slacken the locknut and unscrew the switch from the gearchange remote control housing.
27 Refitting is the reverse sequence to removal.
28 Adjustment is carried out as follows. With the wires disconnected, screw the switch into the housing until slight resistance is felt.
29 Connect the wires, select reverse gear and switch on the ignition. Continue screwing the switch in until the reversing lights just come on and then screw the switch in a further half a turn.
30 Tighten the locknut and check that the reversing lights are illuminated with the gear lever in reverse and extinguished in all other

gear positions. Lower the car to the ground on completion.

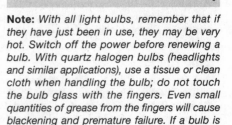

5 Bulbs (exterior lights) – renewal

Note: *With all light bulbs, remember that if they have just been in use, they may be very hot. Switch off the power before renewing a bulb. With quartz halogen bulbs (headlights and similar applications), use a tissue or clean cloth when handling the bulb; do not touch the bulb glass with the fingers. Even small quantities of grease from the fingers will cause blackening and premature failure. If a bulb is accidentally touched, clean it with methylated spirit and a clean rag.*

Headlight

1 Undo and remove the headlight outer rim securing screw and ease the bottom of the outer rim forwards, lift it up and off the retaining lugs at the top of the headlight unit **(see illustrations)**.
2 Using a screwdriver, release the headlight unit by carefully levering between the headlight body and the retaining screw on the side of the headlight **(see illustration)**. Once the side of the headlight is free, slide the unit out of the other two retaining screws.
3 Disconnect the headlight bulb wiring multiplug and pull back the rubber boot **(see illustration)**.

5.1b . . . ease the bottom of the outer rim forwards and lift it up and off the headlight retaining lugs

5.2 Release the headlight unit by levering between the headlight body and retaining screw (arrowed) then slide the unit out of the other two retaining screws

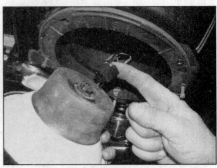

5.3 Disconnect the headlight bulb wiring multiplug

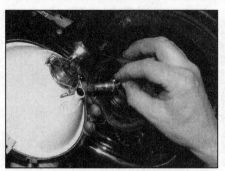

5.4 Withdraw the sidelight bulbholder from the rear of the headlight unit

5.5a Unhook the ends of the headlight bulb retaining clip . . .

5.5b . . . and lift out the bulb

5.14 Withdraw the direction indicator lens unit and disconnect the wiring connector from the rear of the bulbholder

5.18 Release the direction indicator side repeater from the front wing . . .

5.19 . . . remove the bulbholder . . .

4 Withdraw the sidelight bulbholder from the rear of the headlight and remove the headlight unit **(see illustration)**.

5 Unhook the ends of the headlight bulb retaining clip and lift out the bulb **(see illustrations)**.

6 Fit the new bulb ensuring that the larger of the three tabs on the bulb base locates in the uppermost slot in the rear of the headlight unit.

7 Secure the bulb with the retaining clip.

8 Refit the sidelight bulbholder and the rubber boot, then reconnect the headlight bulb multiplug.

9 Engage the headlight unit with two of the retaining screws, then lever the unit onto the third screw using the same procedure as for removal.

10 Locate the outer rim in position and secure with the retaining screw.

Front sidelight

11 Remove the headlight unit as described in paragraphs 1 to 4.

12 Remove the bayonet fitting type sidelight bulb from the bulbholder.

13 Fit the new bulb then refit the headlight unit as described in paragraphs 8 to 10.

Front direction indicator

14 Undo the two screws securing the lens unit to the body. Withdraw the lens unit and disconnect the wiring connector from the rear of the bulbholder **(see illustration)**.

15 Hold the lens unit and remove the bulbholder by twisting it a quarter turn anti-clockwise.

16 Remove the bayonet fitting type sidelight bulb from the bulbholder.

17 Refitting is the reverse sequence to removal.

Direction indicator side repeater

18 Push the light unit firmly to the right to release it from the front wing **(see illustration)**.

19 Withdraw the light unit and remove the bulbholder by twisting it a quarter turn anti-clockwise **(see illustration)**.

20 The push-fit bulb can now be removed from the bulbholder **(see illustration)**.

21 Refitting is the reverse of removal.

Auxiliary driving light/foglight

22 Undo the screw at the base of the light unit to release the reflector from the light unit.

23 Withdraw the reflector and disconnect the bulb wiring connector and the earth lead.

24 Disengage the spring clip from the reflector lugs and lift away the bulb.

25 Refitting is the reverse sequence to removal.

Rear combination light

26 Undo the three screws to release the two light lenses.

27 The direction indicator bulb is fitted in the top compartment, the stop/tail bulb in the centre compartment, and the reversing light bulb in the lower compartment.

28 All three bulbs have bayonet fixings; to remove push in slightly, and rotate anti-clockwise.

29 Refitting is the reverse sequence to removal, but fit the upper lens first, then slot the lower lens into it. Take care not to overtighten the lens securing screws as the lenses can easily be cracked.

High-level stop-light

30 Undo the screws and withdraw the cover from the rear of the light unit **(see illustration)**.

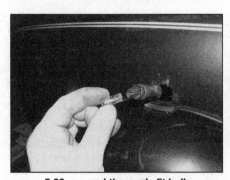

5.20 . . . and the push-fit bulb

5.30 Undo the screws and withdraw the cover from the high-level stop-light

5.31a Disengage the bulbholder and lens assembly from the light unit . . .

5.31b . . then remove the lens from the bulbholder

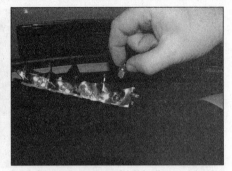

5.32 The relevant push-fit bulb can now be removed from the bulbholder

5.34 Undo the screws and remove the rear foglight lens

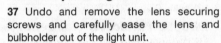

5.35 The bayonet-fit bulb can now be removed from the holder

5.38 The festoon type number plate light bulb is removed by withdrawing it from the bulbholder contacts

31 Disengage the bulbholder and lens assembly from the light unit, then remove the lens from the bulbholder **(see illustrations)**.

32 The relevant push-fit bulb can now be removed from the bulbholder **(see illustration)**.

33 Refitting is the reverse sequence to removal. When refitting the bulbholder and lens assembly to the light unit, position them horizontally by means of the slotted adjustment segment.

Rear foglight

34 Access to the bulb is gained by removing the two lens cover screws and pulling off the lens **(see illustration)**.

35 The bayonet-fit bulb can now be removed from the holder by pushing in slightly, and rotating anti-clockwise **(see illustration)**.

36 Refitting is the reverse sequence to removal.

6.7 Twist the relevant bulbholder anti-clockwise to remove it from the rear of the instrument panel

Number plate light

37 Undo and remove the lens securing screws and carefully ease the lens and bulbholder out of the light unit.

38 The festoon type bulb is removed by simply withdrawing it from the bulbholder contacts **(see illustration)**.

39 Refitting is the reverse sequence to removal.

6 Bulbs (interior lights) – renewal

Note: *With all light bulbs, remember that if they have just been in use, they may be very hot. Switch off the power before renewing a bulb.*

Interior courtesy light

1 Release the light unit by carefully prising out the end furthest from the switch, using a small screwdriver.

2 The bayonet-fit bulb can now be removed from the bulbholder by pushing in slightly, and rotating anti-clockwise.

3 Refitting is the reverse sequence to removal.

Switch illumination

4 To renew a bulb in the illuminated switches fitted to later models, insert a small screwdriver under the notch on both sides of the switch rocker. Depress the notch slightly and lever off the rocker. The bulb may be

unscrewed for renewal using the outer plastic casing of a wiring connector which is a snug fit over the bulb lens.

5 Refit the bulb and push the switch rocker back into place.

Instrument and warning lights

6 Remove the facia as described in Chapter 11B.

7 Twist the relevant bulbholder anti-clockwise to remove it from the rear of the instrument panel **(see illustration)**.

8 The bulbs are integral with the bulbholders.

9 On completion, refit the facia as described in Chapter 11B.

Facia gauge illumination

10 Remove the facia as described in Chapter 11B.

11 Withdraw the bulbholder from the rear of the relevant gauge **(see illustration)**.

6.11 Withdraw the bulbholder from the rear of the facia gauge . . .

12 Remove the push-fit bulb from the holder **(see illustration)**.

13 Fit the new bulb then refit the bulbholder.

14 Refit the facia as described in Chapter 11B.

7 Headlight beam alignment – general information

1 Accurate adjustment of the headlight beam is only possible using optical beam-setting equipment, and this work should therefore be carried out by a Rover dealer or suitably-equipped workshop.

2 Each headlight unit is equipped with a four-position vertical beam adjuster unit – this can be used to adjust the headlight beam, to compensate for the relevant load which the vehicle is carrying. The adjuster units are operated by a switch on the facia. The adjusters should be positioned as follows according to the load being carried in the vehicle:

- *Position 0: Front seats occupied (1 or 2 people), luggage compartment empty.*
- *Position 1: All seats occupied, luggage compartment empty.*
- *Position 2: All seats occupied, luggage compartment loaded.*
- *Position 3: Driver's seat occupied and luggage compartment fully loaded.*

3 Be sure to reset the adjustment if the vehicle load is altered.

8 Headlight adjuster motor – removal and refitting

Removal

1 Remove the headlight unit as described in Section 5.

2 Firmly apply the handbrake, then jack up the front of the car and support it securely on axle stands (see *Jacking and vehicle support*).

3 Working under the wheelarch, pull back the rubber boot and disconnect the wiring multiplug from the adjuster motor **(see illustration)**.

4 Rotate the adjuster motor clockwise through half a turn and release it from the rear of the headlight base **(see illustration)**.

Refitting

5 Refitting is the reverse sequence to removal.

9 Horn – removal and refitting

Removal

1 The horn is located in the engine compartment and is attached to a bracket,

which is in turn secured to the left-hand inner wing panel.

2 Disconnect the horn wiring connector, then undo the two bolts securing the horn mounting bracket to the body. Remove the horn and bracket from the engine compartment.

3 Undo and remove the nut and washer and separate the horn from the mounting bracket.

Refitting

4 Refitting is the reverse sequence to removal.

10 Windscreen wiper arms – removal and refitting

Refer to Chapter 12A, Section 10.

11 Windscreen wiper motor – removal and refitting

Refer to Chapter 12A, Section 11.

12 Windscreen wiper wheelbox – removal and refitting

Refer to Chapter 12A, Section 13.

13 Windscreen washer pump – removal and refitting

Removal

1 The washer pump and reservoir are located in the luggage compartment. The pump is clipped into the side of the reservoir.

2 Disconnect the battery negative terminal (refer to *Disconnecting the battery* in the Reference Chapter).

3 Carefully prise the wiring connector from the pump.

4 Pull the reservoir upwards from its retaining bracket. Drain the fluid into a container.

8.3 Pull back the rubber boot and disconnect the wiring multiplug from the headlight adjuster motor

6.12 . . . and remove the push-fit bulb from the bulbholder

5 Release the washer tube from the pump. The reservoir can now be removed completely.

6 Detach the pump from the reservoir.

Refitting

7 Refitting is the reverse sequence to removal, noting the following:

a) *Use a new pump seal. Fit the seal in the reservoir and lubricate it before refitting the pump.*

b) *If the washer tube is difficult to replace onto the pump, soften it by immersing it in hot water for a few minutes.*

c) *Top-up the reservoir with reference to 'Weekly Checks' and test the operation of the washers.*

14 Instrument panel – removal and refitting

Removal

1 Remove the facia as described in Chapter 11B.

2 From the rear of the facia, undo the six screws around the periphery of the instrument panel and tachometer **(see illustration)**.

3 Remove the illumination bulbholder from the tachometer, then undo the screw securing the printed circuit to the tachometer.

4 Lift up the printed circuit and withdraw the tachometer from the rear of the facia **(see illustration)**.

8.4 Rotate the adjuster motor clockwise half a turn and release it from the rear of the headlight

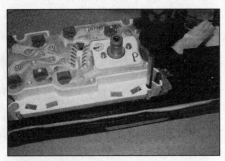

14.2 Undo the six screws securing the instrument panel and tachometer to the facia

14.4 Lift up the printed circuit and withdraw the tachometer from the rear of the facia

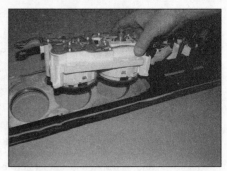

14.5 Withdraw the instrument panel from the facia

5 Withdraw the instrument panel from the facia **(see illustration)**.

Refitting

6 Refitting is the reverse sequence to removal.

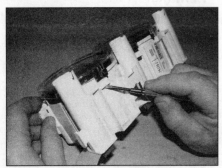

15.2a Release the legs of the instrument panel lens from the panel body . . .

---

15 Instrument panel – dismantling and reassembly

Dismantling

1 Remove the instrument panel as described in Section 14.

2 Using a small screwdriver, carefully release the legs of the instrument panel lens from the panel body. Remove the lens from the panel **(see illustrations)**.

3 Similarly, release the legs of the speedometer printed face plate and lift off the plate **(see illustrations)**.

4 Undo the two screws securing the speedometer to the rear of the instrument panel and withdraw the speedometer from the panel **(see illustrations)**.

5 Release the legs of the combined

---

fuel/temperature gauge printed face plate and lift off the plate.

6 Undo the screws securing the fuel/temperature gauge to the rear of the instrument panel and withdraw the gauge from the panel **(see illustration)**.

7 Withdraw the illumination and warning light bulbholders from the rear of the instrument panel, noting the locations of the yellow illumination bulbs to ensure correct refitting.

8 Undo the screws securing the printed circuit to the instrument panel and tachometer (if not already done), noting the locations of the longer screws.

9 Carefully release the printed circuit from the locating pegs and remove it from the rear of the panel.

Reassembly

10 Reassembly is the reverse of the dismantling sequence.

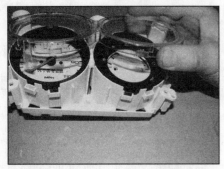

15.2b . . . and remove the lens from the panel

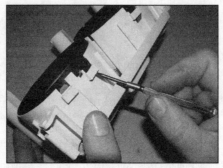

15.3a Release the legs of the speedometer printed face plate . . .

15.3b . . . and lift off the plate

15.4a Undo the two screws (arrowed) securing the speedometer to the instrument panel . . .

15.4b . . . and withdraw the speedometer from the panel

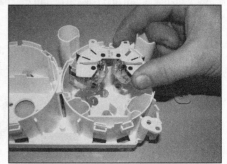

15.6 Removing the fuel/temperature gauge from the instrument panel

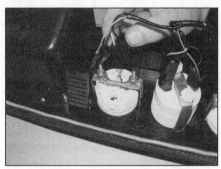

16.2 Disconnect the wiring connectors from the rear of the relevant facia gauge

16.3 Undo the two retaining nuts and lift off the retaining plate

16.4 Withdraw the gauge from the front of the facia

16 Battery condition indicator, clock and oil temperature gauge – removal and refitting

Removal

1 Remove the facia as described in Chapter 11B.

2 Disconnect the wiring connectors from the rear of the relevant gauge **(see illustration)**.

3 Undo the two retaining nuts and lift off the retaining plate **(see illustration)**.

4 Withdraw the gauge from the front of the facia **(see illustration)**.

Refitting

5 Refit the gauge using the reverse sequence to removal, then refit the facia as described in Chapter 11B.

17 Speedometer cable – removal and refitting

Removal

1 Disconnect the battery negative terminal (refer to *Disconnecting the battery* in the Reference Chapter).

2 Remove the air cleaner as described in Chapter 4C.

3 Remove the radio/cassette player as described in Section 18.

4 Working through the radio/cassette player aperture, depress the locking tab on the cable end fitting and withdraw the cable from the rear of the speedometer.

5 Pull the cable through the bulkhead grommet and into the engine compartment.

6 Firmly apply the handbrake, then jack up the front of the car and support it securely on axle stands (see *Jacking and vehicle support*).

7 Working under the car disconnect the cable from the transmission. To gain access, work through the aperture above the left-hand driveshaft.

8 Release the cable from any retaining clips or ties then remove the cable from the engine compartment.

Refitting

9 Refitting the speedometer cable is the reverse sequence to removal.

18 Radio/cassette player – removal and refitting

Removal

Note: *Once the battery has been disconnected, the radio/cassette unit cannot be re-activated until the appropriate security code has been entered. Do not remove the unit unless the appropriate code is known.*

1 Two special DIN standard removal tools, available from in-car entertainment specialists, are required for removal.

2 Disconnect the battery negative terminal (refer to *Disconnecting the battery* in the Reference Chapter).

3 Insert the removal tools into the holes on each side of the radio/cassette player front plate, and push them in until they snap into place.

4 Push the tools apart to depress the internal retaining clips, then pull the tools outwards to withdraw the radio/cassette player **(see illustration)**.

5 Disconnect the wiring connectors and the aerial lead from the rear of the unit **(see illustration)**. Release the removal tools.

Refitting

6 Reconnect the wiring connectors and the

18.4 Using the DIN removal tools to withdraw the radio/cassette player from the facia

aerial lead to the rear of the unit, then locate the unit in the facia.

7 Reconnect the battery negative terminal, then enter the appropriate code to activate the unit.

19 Loudspeakers – removal and refitting

Removal

1 Disconnect the battery negative terminal (refer to *Disconnecting the battery* in the Reference Chapter).

2 Working in the luggage compartment, disconnect the loudspeaker wiring from the underside of the speaker.

3 Undo the three nuts securing the speaker to the parcel shelf and withdraw the speaker from inside the car.

Refitting

4 Refitting is the reverse sequence to removal.

20 Anti-theft alarm system components – removal and refitting

Removal

Electronic control unit (ECU)

1 Remove the facia as described in Chapter 11B.

18.5 Disconnect the wiring connectors and the aerial lead from the rear of the radio/cassette player

2 Undo the two ECU retaining screws and disconnect the wiring multiplugs.
3 Remove the ECU from its location.

Bonnet switch

4 Open the bonnet, and undo the screw securing the switch to the front panel.
5 Lift off the switch and disconnect the wiring.

Boot switch

6 Open the boot, and disconnect the wiring from the switch.
7 Undo the switch retaining screw, and remove the switch from its bracket.

Refitting

8 Refitting is the reverse sequence to removal.

---

21 Airbag system – general information, precautions and system de-activation

General information

A driver's airbag located in the steering wheel centre pad is fitted as standard equipment on all later models. The system is armed only when the ignition is switched on, however, a reserve power source maintains a power supply to the system in the event of a break in the main electrical supply. The airbag is activated by a 'g' sensor (deceleration sensor), and controlled by an electronic control unit located under the rear seat base.

The airbag is inflated by a gas generator, which forces the bag out from its location in the steering wheel.

Precautions

⚠️ *Warning: The following precautions must be observed when working on vehicles equipped with an airbag system, to prevent the possibility of personal injury.*

General precautions

The following precautions **must** be observed when carrying out work on a vehicle equipped with an airbag:
a) *Do not disconnect the battery with the engine running.*
b) *Before carrying out any work in the vicinity of the airbag, removal of any of the airbag components, or any welding work on the vehicle, de-activate the system as described in the following sub-Section.*
c) *Do not attempt to test any of the airbag system circuits using test meters or any other test equipment.*
d) *If the airbag warning light comes on, or any fault in the system is suspected, consult a Rover dealer without delay. Do not attempt to carry out fault diagnosis, or any dismantling of the components.*

Precautions to be taken when handling an airbag

a) *Transport the airbag by itself, bag upward.*

22.6 Remove the two airbag unit retaining screws

b) *Do not put your arms around the airbag.*
c) *Carry the airbag close to the body, bag outward.*
d) *Do not drop the airbag or expose it to impacts.*
e) *Do not attempt to dismantle the airbag unit.*
f) *Do not connect any form of electrical equipment to any part of the airbag circuit.*

Precautions to be taken when storing an airbag unit

a) *Store the unit in a cupboard with the airbag upward.*
b) *Do not expose the airbag to temperatures above 80°C.*
c) *Do not expose the airbag to flames.*
d) *Do not attempt to dispose of the airbag – consult a Rover dealer.*
e) *Never refit an airbag which is known to be faulty or damaged.*

De-activation of airbag system

The system must be de-activated before carrying out any work on the airbag components or surrounding area:
a) *Switch on the ignition and check the operation of the airbag warning light on the instrument panel. The light should illuminate when the ignition is switched on, then extinguish.*
b) *Switch off the ignition.*
c) *Remove the ignition key.*
d) *Switch off all electrical equipment.*
e) *Disconnect the battery negative terminal (refer to 'Disconnecting the battery' in the Reference Section of this manual).*

22.7 Withdraw the airbag unit from the centre of the steering wheel . . .

f) *Insulate the battery negative terminal and the end of the battery negative lead to prevent any possibility of contact.*
g) *Similarly disconnect and insulate the battery positive terminal.*
h) *Wait for at least ten minutes before carrying out any further work. Wait a further ten minutes if the airbag warning light did not operate correctly.*

Activation of airbag system

To activate the system on completion of any work, proceed as follows:
a) *Ensure that there are no occupants in the vehicle, and that there are no loose objects around the vicinity of the steering wheel. Close the vehicle doors and windows.*
b) *Ensure that the ignition is switched off then reconnect the battery positive terminal, followed by the negative terminal.*
c) *Open the driver's door and switch on the ignition, without reaching across the airbag. Check that the airbag warning light illuminates briefly then extinguishes.*
d) *Switch off the ignition.*
e) *If the airbag warning light does not operate as described in paragraph c), consult a Rover dealer before driving the vehicle.*

---

22 Airbag system components – removal and refitting

⚠️ *Warning: Refer to the precautions given in Section 21 before attempting to carry out work on any of the airbag components.*

General

1 The airbag sensors are integral with the electronic control unit.
2 Any suspected faults with the airbag system should be referred to a Rover dealer – under no circumstances attempt to carry out any work other than removal and refitting of the airbag unit and/or the rotary coupling, as described in the following paragraphs.

Airbag unit

Removal

3 The airbag unit is an integral part of the steering wheel centre boss.
4 De-activate the airbag system as described in Section 21.
5 Move the steering wheel as necessary for access to the two airbag unit securing screws. The screws are located at the rear of the steering wheel boss.
6 Remove the two airbag unit retaining screws **(see illustration)**.
7 Withdraw the airbag unit from the centre of the steering wheel **(see illustration)**.
8 Disconnect the wiring connector from the rear of the airbag unit **(see illustration)**.

22.8 . . . and disconnect the wiring connector from the rear of the airbag unit

22.13a Undo the three securing screws (arrowed) . . .

22.13b . . . and withdraw the steering column upper and lower shrouds

9 If the airbag unit is to be stored for any length of time, refer to the storage precautions given in Section 21.

Refitting

10 Refitting is a reversal of removal, bearing in mind the following points:
a) *Do not strike the airbag unit, or expose it to impacts during refitting.*
b) *Tighten the airbag unit retaining screws to the specified torque.*
c) *On completion of refitting, activate the airbag system as described in Section 21.*

Airbag rotary coupling

Removal

11 Remove the airbag unit, as described previously in this Section.
12 Remove the steering wheel as described in Chapter 10.
13 Undo the three securing screws, and withdraw the steering column upper and lower shrouds **(see illustrations)**.
14 Disconnect the horn and airbag wiring multiplugs from the rear of the rotary coupling **(see illustrations)**.
15 Undo the four securing screws and lift the rotary coupling off the steering column **(see illustrations)**.

Refitting

16 Refitting is a reversal of removal, bearing in mind the following points:
a) *Ensure that the rotary coupling is centralised by aligning the marks on the rotary coupling body and the rotating centre part prior to refitting. Instructions*

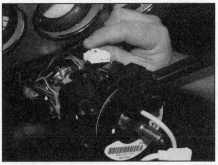

22.14a Disconnect the horn . . .

22.14b . . . and airbag wiring multiplugs from the rear of the rotary coupling

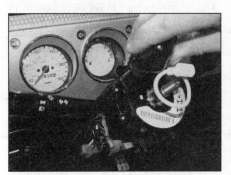

22.15a Undo the four securing screws . . .

22.15b . . . and lift the rotary coupling off the steering column

for centralising the unit are also provided on a label on the face of the unit.
b) *Ensure that the roadwheels are in the straight-ahead position before refitting the*

rotary coupling and steering wheel.
c) *Refit the steering wheel as described in Chapter 10, and refit the airbag unit as described previously in this Section.*

Wiring diagrams - October 1996-on

Diagram 1

Key to symbols

Bulb	⊗
Switch	↗
Multiple contact switch (ganged)	
Fuse/fusible link and current rating	FL2 30A
Resistor	
Variable resistor	
Variable resistor	
Wire splice or soldered joint	
Wire colour (Brown with yellow tracer)	N/Y
Connecting wires	
Item no.	2
Pump/motor	M
Gauge/meter	
Earth	
Earth and location point	E3
Diode	
Light emitting diode (LED)	
Solenoid actuator	
Heating element	

Engine compartment fusebox

Fuse	Rating	Circuits protected
FL1	30A	Passenger compartment fusebox - fuses A9, B1, B6, B9 and C4
FL2	30A	Ignition switch and auxiliary relay
FL3	30A	Light switch
FL4	30A	MEMS relay module

Passenger compartment fusebox

Fuse	Rating	Circuits protected
A1	10A	RH headlight main beam, driving light relay
A2	10A	RH headlight dipped beam
A3	10A	RH side and tail lights
A4	10A	Alarm, instrument cluster, voltage and oil temperature gauges
A5	-	Not used
A6	-	Not used
A7	-	Not used
A8	15A	Blower motor
A9	-	Not used
B1	15A	Driving light relay
B2	10A	Rear foglight relay
B3	10A	Headlight levelling
B4	10A	Radio cassette
B5	10A	Airbag control unit
B6	20A	Alarm and horn
B7	15A	Sunroof
B8	15A	Wipers and washers
B9	15A	Cooling fan
C1	10A	LH headlight main beam
C2	10A	LH headlight dipped beam
C3	10A	LH side and tail lights
C4	10A	Radio/cassette, clock, brake system warning light, direction indicator/hazard warning unit, alarm indicator light, interior light unit
C5	-	Not used
C6	15A	Direction indicator relay, stop and reversing lights
C7	10A	Inertia switch
C8	10A	MEMS relay module
C9	15A	Heated rear window

Earth locations

E1	LH side of engine compartment
E2	LH side of luggage compartment
E3	LH side of luggage compartment
E4	Beneath rear seat
E5	Behind centre of facia
E6	RH side of engine compartment
E7	RH side of engine compartment
E8	RH side of engine compartment

Wire colours

N	Brown	R	Red
U	Blue	B	Black
Y	Yellow	W	White
G	Green	P	Purple
S	Slate	K	Pink
O	Orange	LG	Light green

Key to items

1. Battery
2. Starter motor
3. Alternator
4. Ignition switch
5. Engine compartment fusebox
6. Passenger compartment fusebox
7. MEMS relay module
   a = starter relay
8. Fusible cable
9. Diode
10. Brake fluid level switch
11. Brake system warning light

H32453

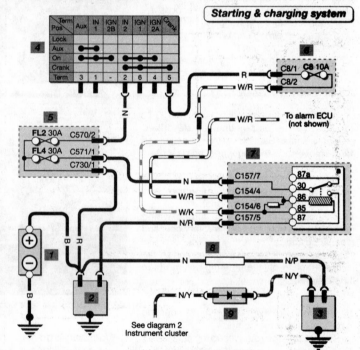

Starting & charging system

See diagram 2
Instrument cluster

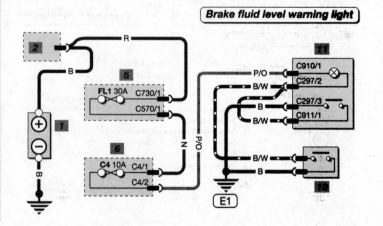

Brake fluid level warning light

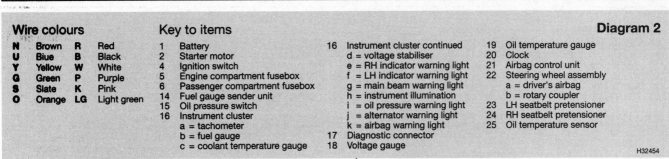

Wire colours

N	Brown	R	Red
U	Blue	B	Black
Y	Yellow	W	White
G	Green	P	Purple
S	Slate	K	Pink
O	Orange	LG	Light green

Key to items

1 Battery
2 Starter motor
4 Ignition switch
5 Engine compartment fusebox
6 Passenger compartment fusebox
14 Fuel gauge sender unit
15 Oil pressure switch
16 Instrument cluster
  a = tachometer
  b = fuel gauge
  c = coolant temperature gauge

16 Instrument cluster continued
  d = voltage stabiliser
  e = RH indicator warning light
  f = LH indicator warning light
  g = main beam warning light
  h = instrument illumination
  i = oil pressure warning light
  j = alternator warning light
  k = airbag warning light
17 Diagnostic connector
18 Voltage gauge

19 Oil temperature gauge
20 Clock
21 Airbag control unit
22 Steering wheel assembly
  a = driver's airbag
  b = rotary coupler
23 LH seatbelt pretensioner
24 RH seatbelt pretensioner
25 Oil temperature sensor

Diagram 2

H32454

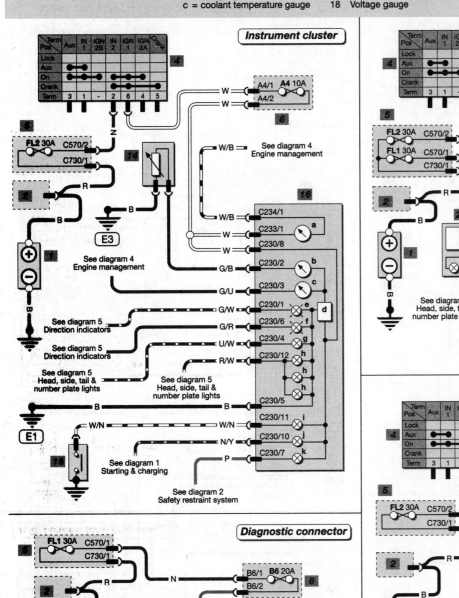

Instrument cluster

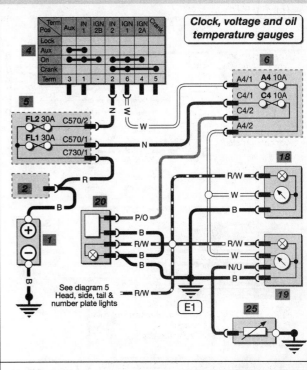

Clock, voltage and oil temperature gauges

Safety restraint system

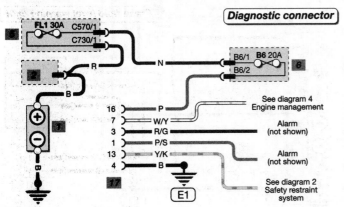

Diagnostic connector

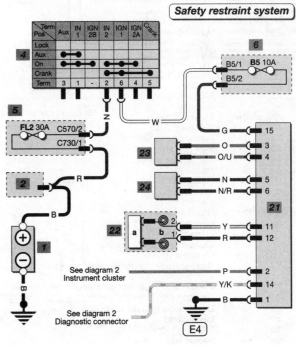

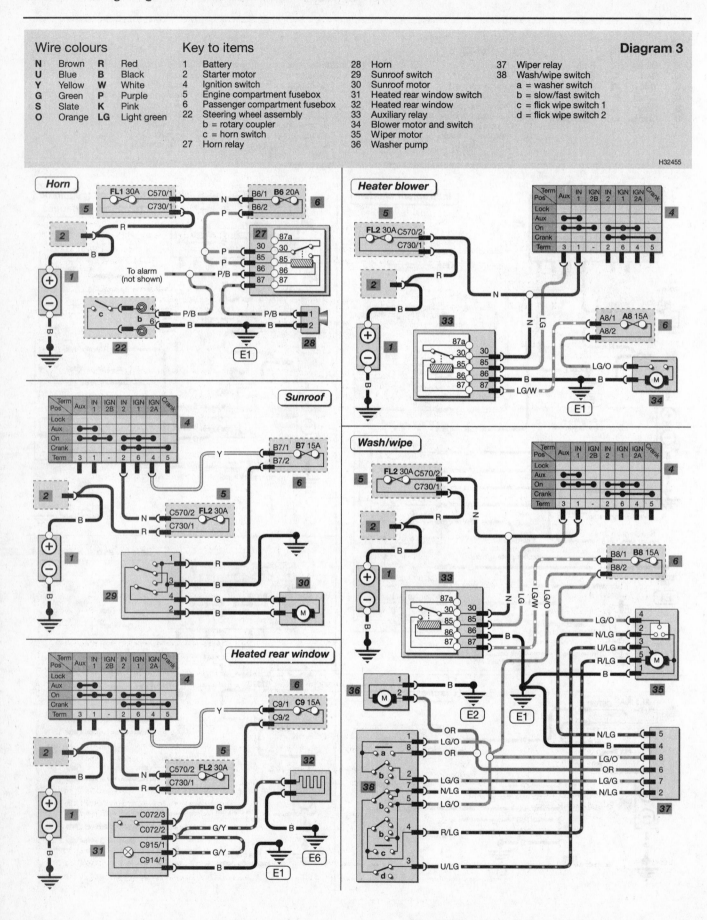

Wire colours

N	Brown	R	Red
U	Blue	B	Black
Y	Yellow	W	White
G	Green	P	Purple
S	Slate	K	Pink
O	Orange	LG	Light green

Key to items

1 Battery
2 Starter motor
4 Ignition switch
5 Engine compartment fusebox
6 Passenger compartment fusebox
22 Steering wheel assembly
   b = rotary coupler
   c = horn switch
27 Horn relay

28 Horn
29 Sunroof switch
30 Sunroof motor
31 Heated rear window switch
32 Heated rear window
33 Auxiliary relay
34 Blower motor and switch
35 Wiper motor
36 Washer pump

37 Wiper relay
38 Wash/wipe switch
   a = washer switch
   b = slow/fast switch
   c = flick wipe switch 1
   d = flick wipe switch 2

Diagram 3

H32455

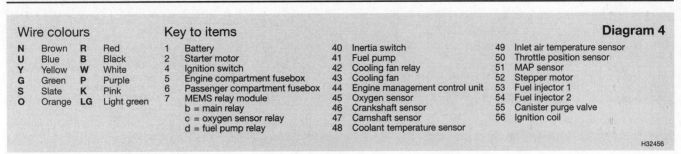

Wire colours

N	Brown	R	Red
U	Blue	B	Black
Y	Yellow	W	White
G	Green	P	Purple
S	Slate	K	Pink
O	Orange	LG	Light green

Key to items

1 Battery
2 Starter motor
4 Ignition switch
5 Engine compartment fusebox
6 Passenger compartment fusebox
7 MEMS relay module
  b = main relay
  c = oxygen sensor relay
  d = fuel pump relay

40 Inertia switch
41 Fuel pump
42 Cooling fan relay
43 Cooling fan
44 Engine management control unit
45 Oxygen sensor
46 Crankshaft sensor
47 Camshaft sensor
48 Coolant temperature sensor

49 Inlet air temperature sensor
50 Throttle position sensor
51 MAP sensor
52 Stepper motor
53 Fuel injector 1
54 Fuel injector 2
55 Canister purge valve
56 Ignition coil

Diagram 4

H32456

Engine management

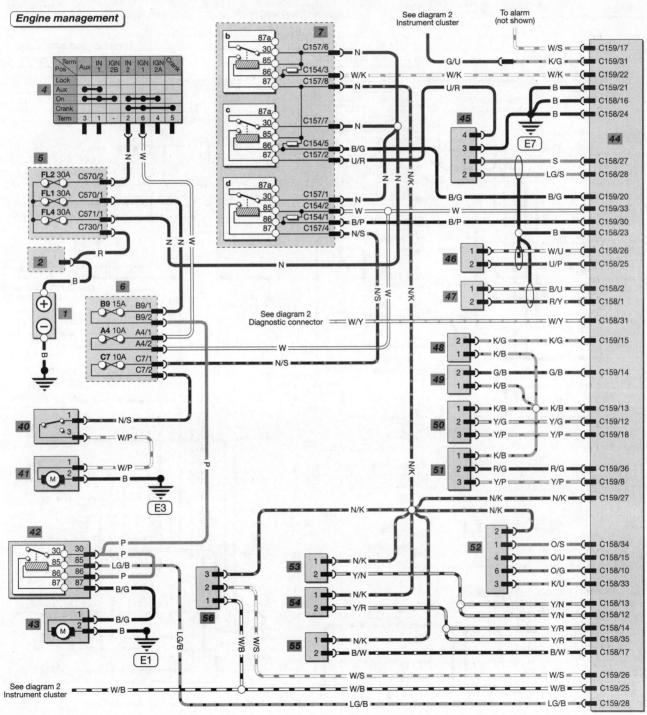

Wire colours

N	Brown	R	Red
U	Blue	B	Black
Y	Yellow	W	White
G	Green	P	Purple
S	Slate	K	Pink
O	Orange	LG	Light green

Key to items

1 Battery
2 Starter motor
4 Ignition switch
5 Engine compartment fusebox
6 Passenger compartment fusebox
60 LH headlight unit
  a = side light
  b = dip beam
  c = main beam
61 RH headlight unit
  a = side light
  b = dip beam
  c = main beam

62 LH rear light unit
  a = tail light
  b = stop light
  c = reversing light
  d = direction indicator
63 RH rear light unit
  a = tail light
  b = stop light
  c = reversing light
  d = direction indicator
64 Number plate light
65 Stop light switch
66 Reversing light switch

67 Hazard warning light switch
68 Direction indicator relay
69 Direction indicator flasher relay
70 Direction indicator switch
71 RH front direction indicator
72 RH indicator side reepeater
73 LH front direction indicator
74 LH indicator side repeater
75 Light switch
  a = side/headlight
  b = dip/main beam
  c = headlight flasher

Diagram 5

H32457

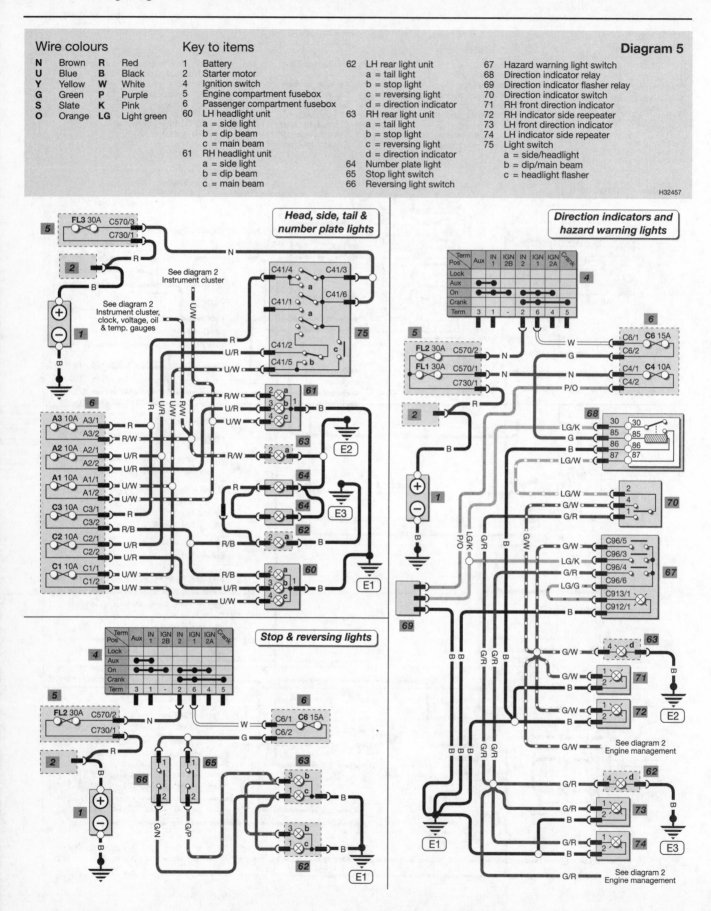

Head, side, tail & number plate lights

Stop & reversing lights

Direction indicators and hazard warning lights

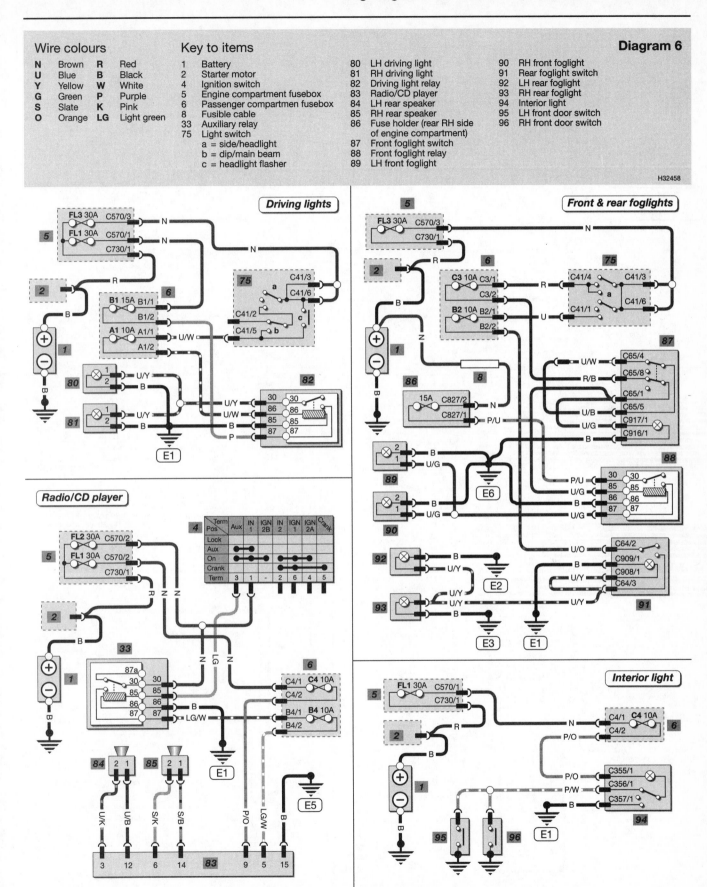

Wire colours

N	Brown	R	Red
U	Blue	B	Black
Y	Yellow	W	White
G	Green	P	Purple
S	Slate	K	Pink
O	Orange	LG	Light green

Key to items

1 Battery
2 Starter motor
4 Ignition switch
5 Engine compartment fusebox
6 Passenger compartmen fusebox
8 Fusible cable
33 Auxiliary relay
75 Light switch
  a = side/headlight
  b = dip/main beam
  c = headlight flasher

80 LH driving light
81 RH driving light
82 Driving light relay
83 Radio/CD player
84 LH rear speaker
85 RH rear speaker
86 Fuse holder (rear RH side of engine compartment)
87 Front foglight switch
88 Front foglight relay
89 LH front foglight

90 RH front foglight
91 Rear foglight switch
92 LH rear foglight
93 RH rear foglight
94 Interior light
95 LH front door switch
96 RH front door switch

Diagram 6

H32458

Notes

Dimensions and weights . . . . **REF•1**
Conversion factors . . . . **REF•2**
Buying spare parts . . . . **REF•3**
Vehicle identification . . . . **REF•3**
General repair procedures . . . . **REF•4**
Jacking and vehicle support . . . . **REF•5**

Disconnecting the battery . . . . **REF•5**
Tools and working facilities . . . . **REF•6**
MOT test checks . . . . **REF•8**
Fault finding . . . . **REF•12**
Glossary of technical terms . . . . **REF•21**
Index . . . . **REF•26**

Dimensions and weights

Note: *Due to the extensive options available, and the long production run of this vehicle, all figures are approximate. Refer to a Rover dealer for exact figures according to model and year of production.*

Dimensions

Overall length:
    Saloon . . . . 3054 mm
    Clubman Saloon . . . . 3165 mm
    Estate . . . . 3403 mm
    Van . . . . 3298 mm
    Pick-up . . . . 3314 mm
Overall width . . . . 1580 mm
Overall height . . . . 1340 mm
Wheelbase:
    Saloon . . . . 2040 mm
    Estate, Van and Pick-up . . . . 2134 mm

Weights

Kerb weight . . . . 715 kg
Maximum towing weights*:
    Saloon . . . . 404 kg
    Estate, Van and Pick-up . . . . 303 kg
Maximum towing hitch load* . . . . 45 kg
Maximum roof rack load . . . . 40 kg

Due to changes in European legislation regarding trailer towing weights, later models are not suitable for towing. Refer to a Rover dealer for specific information according to model and year of production.

Conversion factors

Length (distance)

Inches (in)	x 25.4	= Millimetres (mm)	x 0.0394	= Inches (in)
Feet (ft)	x 0.305	= Metres (m)	x 3.281	= Feet (ft)
Miles	x 1.609	= Kilometres (km)	x 0.621	= Miles

Volume (capacity)

Cubic inches (cu in; in^3)	x 16.387	= Cubic centimetres (cc; cm^3)	x 0.061	= Cubic inches (cu in; in^3)
Imperial pints (Imp pt)	x 0.568	= Litres (l)	x 1.76	= Imperial pints (Imp pt)
Imperial quarts (Imp qt)	x 1.137	= Litres (l)	x 0.88	= Imperial quarts (Imp qt)
Imperial quarts (Imp qt)	x 1.201	= US quarts (US qt)	x 0.833	= Imperial quarts (Imp qt)
US quarts (US qt)	x 0.946	= Litres (l)	x 1.057	= US quarts (US qt)
Imperial gallons (Imp gal)	x 4.546	= Litres (l)	x 0.22	= Imperial gallons (Imp gal)
Imperial gallons (Imp gal)	x 1.201	= US gallons (US gal)	x 0.833	= Imperial gallons (Imp gal)
US gallons (US gal)	x 3.785	= Litres (l)	x 0.264	= US gallons (US gal)

Mass (weight)

Ounces (oz)	x 28.35	= Grams (g)	x 0.035	= Ounces (oz)
Pounds (lb)	x 0.454	= Kilograms (kg)	x 2.205	= Pounds (lb)

Force

Ounces-force (ozf; oz)	x 0.278	= Newtons (N)	x 3.6	= Ounces-force (ozf; oz)
Pounds-force (lbf; lb)	x 4.448	= Newtons (N)	x 0.225	= Pounds-force (lbf; lb)
Newtons (N)	x 0.1	= Kilograms-force (kgf; kg)	x 9.81	= Newtons (N)

Pressure

Pounds-force per square inch (psi; lbf/in^2; lb/in^2)	x 0.070	= Kilograms-force per square centimetre (kgf/cm^2; kg/cm^2)	x 14.223	= Pounds-force per square inch (psi; lbf/in^2; lb/in^2)
Pounds-force per square inch (psi; lbf/in^2; lb/in^2)	x 0.068	= Atmospheres (atm)	x 14.696	= Pounds-force per square inch (psi; lbf/in^2; lb/in^2)
Pounds-force per square inch (psi; lbf/in^2; lb/in^2)	x 0.069	= Bars	x 14.5	= Pounds-force per square inch (psi; lbf/in^2; lb/in^2)
Pounds-force per square inch (psi; lbf/in^2; lb/in^2)	x 6.895	= Kilopascals (kPa)	x 0.145	= Pounds-force per square inch (psi; lbf/in^2; lb/in^2)
Kilopascals (kPa)	x 0.01	= Kilograms-force per square centimetre (kgf/cm^2; kg/cm^2)	x 98.1	= Kilopascals (kPa)
Millibar (mbar)	x 100	= Pascals (Pa)	x 0.01	= Millibar (mbar)
Millibar (mbar)	x 0.0145	= Pounds-force per square inch (psi; lbf/in^2; lb/in^2)	x 68.947	= Millibar (mbar)
Millibar (mbar)	x 0.75	= Millimetres of mercury (mmHg)	x 1.333	= Millibar (mbar)
Millibar (mbar)	x 0.401	= Inches of water (inH$_2$O)	x 2.491	= Millibar (mbar)
Millimetres of mercury (mmHg)	x 0.535	= Inches of water (inH$_2$O)	x 1.868	= Millimetres of mercury (mmHg)
Inches of water (inH$_2$O)	x 0.036	= Pounds-force per square inch (psi; lbf/in^2; lb/in^2)	x 27.68	= Inches of water (inH$_2$O)

Torque (moment of force)

Pounds-force inches (lbf in; lb in)	x 1.152	= Kilograms-force centimetre (kgf cm; kg cm)	x 0.868	= Pounds-force inches (lbf in; lb in)
Pounds-force inches (lbf in; lb in)	x 0.113	= Newton metres (Nm)	x 8.85	= Pounds-force inches (lbf in; lb in)
Pounds-force inches (lbf in; lb in)	x 0.083	= Pounds-force feet (lbf ft; lb ft)	x 12	= Pounds-force inches (lbf in; lb in)
Pounds-force feet (lbf ft; lb ft)	x 0.138	= Kilograms-force metres (kgf m; kg m)	x 7.233	= Pounds-force feet (lbf ft; lb ft)
Pounds-force feet (lbf ft; lb ft)	x 1.356	= Newton metres (Nm)	x 0.738	= Pounds-force feet (lbf ft; lb ft)
Newton metres (Nm)	x 0.102	= Kilograms-force metres (kgf m; kg m)	x 9.804	= Newton metres (Nm)

Power

Horsepower (hp)	x 745.7	= Watts (W)	x 0.0013	= Horsepower (hp)

Velocity (speed)

Miles per hour (miles/hr; mph)	x 1.609	= Kilometres per hour (km/hr; kph)	x 0.621	= Miles per hour (miles/hr; mph)

Fuel consumption*

Miles per gallon, Imperial (mpg)	x 0.354	= Kilometres per litre (km/l)	x 2.825	= Miles per gallon, Imperial (mpg)
Miles per gallon, US (mpg)	x 0.425	= Kilometres per litre (km/l)	x 2.352	= Miles per gallon, US (mpg)

Temperature

Degrees Fahrenheit = (°C x 1.8) + 32   Degrees Celsius (Degrees Centigrade; °C) = (°F - 32) x 0.56

It is common practice to convert from miles per gallon (mpg) to litres/100 kilometres (l/100km), where mpg x l/100 km = 282

Buying spare parts

Spare parts are available from many sources, including maker's appointed garages, accessory shops, and motor factors. To be sure of obtaining the correct parts, it will sometimes be necessary to quote the vehicle identification number. If possible, it can also be useful to take the old parts along for positive identification. Items such as starter motors and alternators may be available under a service exchange scheme - any parts returned should always be clean.

Our advice regarding spare part sources is as follows.

Officially-appointed garages

This is the best source of parts which are peculiar to your car, and which are not otherwise generally available (eg badges, interior trim, certain body panels, etc). It is also the only place at which you should buy parts if the vehicle is still under warranty.

Accessory shops

These are very good places to buy materials and components needed for the maintenance of your car (oil, air and fuel filters, spark plugs, light bulbs, drivebelts, oils and greases, brake pads, touch-up paint, etc). Components of this nature sold by a reputable shop are of the same standard as those used by the car manufacturer.

Besides components, these shops also sell tools and general accessories, usually have convenient opening hours, charge lower prices, and can often be found not far from home. Some accessory shops have parts counters where the components needed for almost any repair job can be purchased or ordered.

Motor factors

Good factors will stock all the more important components which wear out comparatively quickly, and can sometimes supply individual components needed for the overhaul of a larger assembly (eg brake seals and hydraulic parts, bearing shells, pistons, valves, alternator brushes). They may also handle work such as cylinder block reboring, crankshaft regrinding and balancing, etc.

Tyre and exhaust specialists

These outlets may be independent, or members of a local or national chain. They frequently offer competitive prices when compared with a main dealer or local garage, but it will pay to obtain several quotes before making a decision. When researching prices, also ask what extras may be added - for instance, fitting a new valve and balancing the wheel are both commonly charged on top of the price of a new tyre.

Other sources

Beware of parts or materials obtained from market stalls, car boot sales or similar outlets. Such items are not invariably sub-standard, but there is little chance of compensation if they do prove unsatisfactory. In the case of safety-critical components such as brake pads, there is the risk not only of financial loss but also of an accident causing injury or death.

Second-hand components or assemblies obtained from a car breaker can be a good buy in some circumstances, but this sort of purchase is best made by the experienced DIY mechanic.

Vehicle Identification

Modifications are a continuing and unpublished process in vehicle manufacture, quite apart from major model changes. Spare parts manuals and lists are compiled upon a numerical basis, the individual vehicle numbers being essential to correct identification of the component required.

When ordering spare parts it is essential to provide the full details of your car. It will be necessary to quote the commission and car numbers on early models, or the vehicle identification (VIN) number on later models.

When ordering parts for the engine, transmission unit or body it will also be necessary to supply these numbers.

The *commission number* (early models) is stamped on a plate fixed to the bonnet locking platform.

The *car number* (early models) is located on a plate mounted adjacent to the commission number.

The *vehicle identification number* (later models) is stamped on a plate attached to the right-hand inner wing valance. On later models it is also etched into the windscreen and rear window glass.

The *engine number* is stamped on the cylinder block or on a metal plate fixed to the right-hand side of the cylinder block.

The *transmission casing assembly number* is stamped on a facing provided on the casting just below the starter motor.

The *body number* is stamped on a metal plate fixed to the bonnet locking platform.

Whenever servicing, repair or overhaul work is carried out on the car or its components, observe the following procedures and instructions. This will assist in carrying out the operation efficiently and to a professional standard of workmanship.

Joint mating faces and gaskets

When separating components at their mating faces, never insert screwdrivers or similar implements into the joint between the faces in order to prise them apart. This can cause severe damage which results in oil leaks, coolant leaks, etc upon reassembly. Separation is usually achieved by tapping along the joint with a soft-faced hammer in order to break the seal. However, note that this method may not be suitable where dowels are used for component location.

Where a gasket is used between the mating faces of two components, a new one must be fitted on reassembly; fit it dry unless otherwise stated in the repair procedure. Make sure that the mating faces are clean and dry, with all traces of old gasket removed. When cleaning a joint face, use a tool which is unlikely to score or damage the face, and remove any burrs or nicks with an oilstone or fine file.

Make sure that tapped holes are cleaned with a pipe cleaner, and keep them free of jointing compound, if this is being used, unless specifically instructed otherwise.

Ensure that all orifices, channels or pipes are clear, and blow through them, preferably using compressed air.

Oil seals

Oil seals can be removed by levering them out with a wide flat-bladed screwdriver or similar implement. Alternatively, a number of self-tapping screws may be screwed into the seal, and these used as a purchase for pliers or some similar device in order to pull the seal free.

Whenever an oil seal is removed from its working location, either individually or as part of an assembly, it should be renewed.

The very fine sealing lip of the seal is easily damaged, and will not seal if the surface it contacts is not completely clean and free from scratches, nicks or grooves. If the original sealing surface of the component cannot be restored, and the manufacturer has not made provision for slight relocation of the seal relative to the sealing surface, the component should be renewed.

Protect the lips of the seal from any surface which may damage them in the course of fitting. Use tape or a conical sleeve where possible. Lubricate the seal lips with oil before fitting and, on dual-lipped seals, fill the space between the lips with grease.

Unless otherwise stated, oil seals must be fitted with their sealing lips toward the lubricant to be sealed.

Use a tubular drift or block of wood of the appropriate size to install the seal and, if the seal housing is shouldered, drive the seal down to the shoulder. If the seal housing is unshouldered, the seal should be fitted with its face flush with the housing top face (unless otherwise instructed).

Screw threads and fastenings

Seized nuts, bolts and screws are quite a common occurrence where corrosion has set in, and the use of penetrating oil or releasing fluid will often overcome this problem if the offending item is soaked for a while before attempting to release it. The use of an impact driver may also provide a means of releasing such stubborn fastening devices, when used in conjunction with the appropriate screwdriver bit or socket. If none of these methods works, it may be necessary to resort to the careful application of heat, or the use of a hacksaw or nut splitter device.

Studs are usually removed by locking two nuts together on the threaded part, and then using a spanner on the lower nut to unscrew the stud. Studs or bolts which have broken off below the surface of the component in which they are mounted can sometimes be removed using a stud extractor. Always ensure that a blind tapped hole is completely free from oil, grease, water or other fluid before installing the bolt or stud. Failure to do this could cause the housing to crack due to the hydraulic action of the bolt or stud as it is screwed in.

When tightening a castellated nut to accept a split pin, tighten the nut to the specified torque, where applicable, and then tighten further to the next split pin hole. Never slacken the nut to align the split pin hole, unless stated in the repair procedure.

When checking or retightening a nut or bolt to a specified torque setting, slacken the nut or bolt by a quarter of a turn, and then retighten to the specified setting. However, this should not be attempted where angular tightening has been used.

For some screw fastenings, notably cylinder head bolts or nuts, torque wrench settings are no longer specified for the latter stages of tightening, "angle-tightening" being called up instead. Typically, a fairly low torque wrench setting will be applied to the bolts/nuts in the correct sequence, followed by one or more stages of tightening through specified angles.

Locknuts, locktabs and washers

Any fastening which will rotate against a component or housing during tightening should always have a washer between it and the relevant component or housing.

Spring or split washers should always be renewed when they are used to lock a critical component such as a big-end bearing retaining bolt or nut. Locktabs which are folded over to retain a nut or bolt should always be renewed.

Self-locking nuts can be re-used in non-critical areas, providing resistance can be felt when the locking portion passes over the bolt or stud thread. However, it should be noted that self-locking stiffnuts tend to lose their effectiveness after long periods of use, and should then be renewed as a matter of course.

Split pins must always be replaced with new ones of the correct size for the hole.

When thread-locking compound is found on the threads of a fastener which is to be re-used, it should be cleaned off with a wire brush and solvent, and fresh compound applied on reassembly.

Special tools

Some repair procedures in this manual entail the use of special tools such as a press, two or three-legged pullers, spring compressors, etc. Wherever possible, suitable readily-available alternatives to the manufacturer's special tools are described, and are shown in use. In some instances, where no alternative is possible, it has been necessary to resort to the use of a manufacturer's tool, and this has been done for reasons of safety as well as the efficient completion of the repair operation. Unless you are highly-skilled and have a thorough understanding of the procedures described, never attempt to bypass the use of any special tool when the procedure described specifies its use. Not only is there a very great risk of personal injury, but expensive damage could be caused to the components involved.

Environmental considerations

When disposing of used engine oil, brake fluid, antifreeze, etc, give due consideration to any detrimental environmental effects. Do not, for instance, pour any of the above liquids down drains into the general sewage system, or onto the ground to soak away. Many local council refuse tips provide a facility for waste oil disposal, as do some garages. If none of these facilities are available, consult your local Environmental Health Department, or the National Rivers Authority, for further advice.

With the universal tightening-up of legislation regarding the emission of environmentally-harmful substances from motor vehicles, most vehicles have tamperproof devices fitted to the main adjustment points of the fuel system. These devices are primarily designed to prevent unqualified persons from adjusting the fuel/air mixture, with the chance of a consequent increase in toxic emissions. If such devices are found during servicing or overhaul, they should, wherever possible, be renewed or refitted in accordance with the manufacturer's requirements or current legislation.

Note: It is antisocial and illegal to dump oil down the drain. To find the location of your local oil recycling bank, call this number free.

The jack supplied with the vehicle tool kit should only be used for changing the roadwheels – see *Wheel changing* at the front of this manual. When carrying out any other kind of work, raise the vehicle using a hydraulic (or trolley) jack, and always supplement the jack with axle stands.

The reinforced side members of the front and rear subframes should be used as jacking points for raising one side of the car at the front or rear **(see illustration)**. A beam may be placed transversely under the front and rear subframe side members, with the jack head positioned centrally under it, if it is wished to raise the complete front or rear of the car. Take care not to damage the exhaust system or any pipes or hoses if this method is being used. The side-members of the subframes should also be used as axle stand support points. **Do not** jack the vehicle under the transmission or under any of the steering or suspension components.

⚠ *Warning: Never work under, around, or near a raised vehicle, unless it is adequately supported in at least two places.*

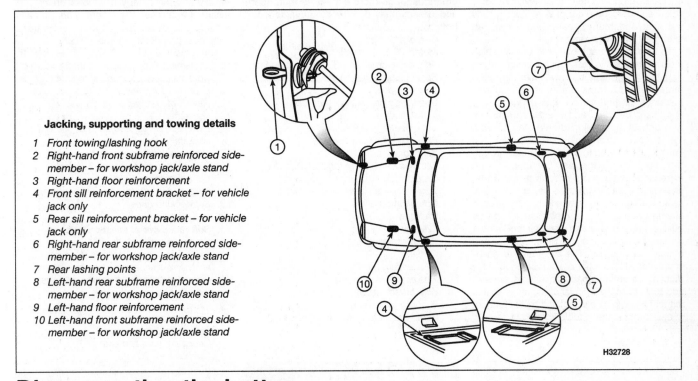

Jacking, supporting and towing details

1 *Front towing/lashing hook*
2 *Right-hand front subframe reinforced side-member – for workshop jack/axle stand*
3 *Right-hand floor reinforcement*
4 *Front sill reinforcement bracket – for vehicle jack only*
5 *Rear sill reinforcement bracket – for vehicle jack only*
6 *Right-hand rear subframe reinforced side-member – for workshop jack/axle stand*
7 *Rear lashing points*
8 *Left-hand rear subframe reinforced side-member – for workshop jack/axle stand*
9 *Left-hand floor reinforcement*
10 *Left-hand front subframe reinforced side-member – for workshop jack/axle stand*

H32728

Disconnecting the battery

Numerous systems fitted to the vehicle require battery power to be available at all times, either to ensure their continued operation (such as the clock) or to maintain control unit memories which would be erased if the battery were to be disconnected. Whenever the battery is to be disconnected therefore, first note the following, to ensure that there are no unforeseen consequences of this action:

a) *On later models, depending on type and specification, the anti-theft alarm system may be of the type which is automatically activated when the vehicle battery is disconnected and/or reconnected. To prevent the alarm sounding on models so equipped, always ensure that the alarm is disabled by means of the handset before disconnecting the battery. Refer to the driver's handbook supplied with the car for detailed information on alarm operation.*

b) *If a security-coded audio unit is fitted, and the unit and/or the battery is disconnected, the unit will not function again on reconnection until the correct security code is entered. Details of this procedure, which varies according to the unit fitted, are given in the vehicle audio*

system operating instructions. Ensure you have the correct code before you disconnect the battery. If you do not have the code or details of the correct procedure, but can supply proof of ownership and a legitimate reason for wanting this information, a Rover dealer may be able to help.

c) *On fuel injection engines, the engine management electronic control unit is of the self-learning type, meaning that as it operates it also monitors and stores the settings which give optimum engine performance under all operating conditions. When the battery is disconnected, some of these settings may be lost and the ECU reverts to the base settings programmed into its memory at the factory. On restarting, this may lead to the engine running/idling roughly for a short while, until the ECU has relearned the optimum settings. This process is best accomplished by taking the vehicle on a road test (for approximately 15 minutes), covering all engine speeds and loads, concentrating mainly in the 2500 to 3500 rpm region.*

d) *On all later models, when reconnecting the battery after disconnection, switch on the ignition and wait 10 seconds to allow the electronic vehicle systems to stabilise and re-initialise.*

Devices known as memory-savers (or code-savers) can be used to avoid some of the above problems. Precise details vary according to the device used. Typically, it is plugged into the cigarette lighter, and is connected by its own wires to a spare battery; the vehicles own battery is then disconnected from the electrical system, leaving the memory-saver to pass sufficient current to maintain audio unit security codes and any other memory values, and also to run permanently-live circuits such as the clock.

⚠ *Warning: Some of these devices allow a considerable amount of current to pass, which can mean that many of the vehicles systems are still operational when the main battery is disconnected. If a memory saver is used, ensure that the circuit concerned is actually dead before carrying out any work on it!*

Tools and working facilities

Introduction

A selection of good tools is a fundamental requirement for anyone contemplating the maintenance and repair of a motor vehicle. For the owner who does not possess any, their purchase will prove a considerable expense, offsetting some of the savings made by doing-it-yourself. However, provided that the tools purchased meet the relevant national safety standards and are of good quality, they will last for many years and prove an extremely worthwhile investment.

To help the average owner to decide which tools are needed to carry out the various tasks detailed in this manual, we have compiled three lists of tools under the following headings: *Maintenance and minor repair*, *Repair and overhaul*, and *Special*. Newcomers to practical mechanics should start off with the *Maintenance and minor repair* tool kit, and confine themselves to the simpler jobs around the vehicle. Then, as confidence and experience grow, more difficult tasks can be undertaken, with extra tools being purchased as, and when, they are needed. In this way, a *Maintenance and minor repair* tool kit can be built up into a *Repair and overhaul* tool kit over a considerable period of time, without any major cash outlays. The experienced do-it-yourselfer will have a tool kit good enough for most repair and overhaul procedures, and will add tools from the *Special* category when it is felt that the expense is justified by the amount of use to which these tools will be put.

Maintenance and minor repair tool kit

The tools given in this list should be considered as a minimum requirement if routine maintenance, servicing and minor repair operations are to be undertaken. We recommend the purchase of combination spanners (ring one end, open-ended the other); although more expensive than open-ended ones, they do give the advantages of both types of spanner.

☐ *Combination spanners:*
  Metric - 8 to 19 mm inclusive
☐ *Adjustable spanner - 35 mm jaw (approx.)*
☐ *Spark plug spanner (with rubber insert) - petrol models*
☐ *Spark plug gap adjustment tool - petrol models*
☐ *Set of feeler gauges*
☐ *Brake bleed nipple spanner*
☐ *Screwdrivers:*
  Flat blade - 100 mm long x 6 mm dia
  Cross blade - 100 mm long x 6 mm dia
  Torx - various sizes (not all vehicles)
☐ *Combination pliers*
☐ *Hacksaw (junior)*
☐ *Tyre pump*
☐ *Tyre pressure gauge*
☐ *Oil can*
☐ *Oil filter removal tool*
☐ *Fine emery cloth*
☐ *Wire brush (small)*
☐ *Funnel (medium size)*
☐ *Sump drain plug key (not all vehicles)*

Repair and overhaul tool kit

These tools are virtually essential for anyone undertaking any major repairs to a motor vehicle, and are additional to those given in the *Maintenance and minor repair* list. Included in this list is a comprehensive set of sockets. Although these are expensive, they will be found invaluable as they are so versatile - particularly if various drives are included in the set. We recommend the half-inch square-drive type, as this can be used with most proprietary torque wrenches.

The tools in this list will sometimes need to be supplemented by tools from the *Special* list:

☐ *Sockets (or box spanners) to cover range in previous list (including Torx sockets)*
☐ *Reversible ratchet drive (for use with sockets)*
☐ *Extension piece, 250 mm (for use with sockets)*
☐ *Universal joint (for use with sockets)*
☐ *Flexible handle or sliding T "breaker bar" (for use with sockets)*
☐ *Torque wrench (for use with sockets)*
☐ *Self-locking grips*
☐ *Ball pein hammer*
☐ *Soft-faced mallet (plastic or rubber)*
☐ *Screwdrivers:*
  Flat blade - long & sturdy, short (chubby), and narrow (electrician's) types
  Cross blade - long & sturdy, and short (chubby) types
☐ *Pliers:*
  Long-nosed
  Side cutters (electrician's)
  Circlip (internal and external)
☐ *Cold chisel - 25 mm*
☐ *Scriber*
☐ *Scraper*
☐ *Centre-punch*
☐ *Pin punch*
☐ *Hacksaw*
☐ *Brake hose clamp*
☐ *Brake/clutch bleeding kit*
☐ *Selection of twist drills*
☐ *Steel rule/straight-edge*
☐ *Allen keys (inc. splined/Torx type)*
☐ *Selection of files*
☐ *Wire brush*
☐ *Axle stands*
☐ *Jack (strong trolley or hydraulic type)*
☐ *Light with extension lead*
☐ *Universal electrical multi-meter*

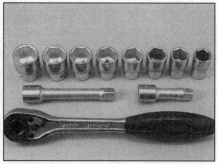

Sockets and reversible ratchet drive

Brake bleeding kit

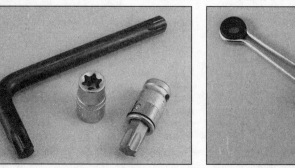

Torx key, socket and bit

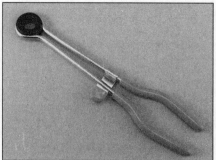

Hose clamp

Angular-tightening gauge

Special tools

The tools in this list are those which are not used regularly, are expensive to buy, or which need to be used in accordance with their manufacturers' instructions. Unless relatively difficult mechanical jobs are undertaken frequently, it will not be economic to buy many of these tools. Where this is the case, you could consider clubbing together with friends (or joining a motorists' club) to make a joint purchase, or borrowing the tools against a deposit from a local garage or tool hire specialist. It is worth noting that many of the larger DIY superstores now carry a large range of special tools for hire at modest rates.

The following list contains only those tools and instruments freely available to the public, and not those special tools produced by the vehicle manufacturer specifically for its dealer network. You will find occasional references to these manufacturers' special tools in the text of this manual. Generally, an alternative method of doing the job without the vehicle manufacturers' special tool is given. However, sometimes there is no alternative to using them. Where this is the case and the relevant tool cannot be bought or borrowed, you will have to entrust the work to a dealer.

☐ Angular-tightening gauge
☐ Valve spring compressor
☐ Valve grinding tool
☐ Piston ring compressor
☐ Piston ring removal/installation tool
☐ Cylinder bore hone
☐ Balljoint separator
☐ Coil spring compressors (where applicable)
☐ Two/three-legged hub and bearing puller
☐ Impact screwdriver
☐ Micrometer and/or vernier calipers
☐ Dial gauge
☐ Stroboscopic timing light
☐ Dwell angle meter/tachometer
☐ Fault code reader
☐ Cylinder compression gauge
☐ Hand-operated vacuum pump and gauge
☐ Clutch plate alignment set
☐ Brake shoe steady spring cup removal tool
☐ Bush and bearing removal/installation set
☐ Stud extractors
☐ Tap and die set
☐ Lifting tackle
☐ Trolley jack

Buying tools

Reputable motor accessory shops and superstores often offer excellent quality tools at discount prices, so it pays to shop around.

Remember, you don't have to buy the most expensive items on the shelf, but it is always advisable to steer clear of the very cheap tools. Beware of 'bargains' offered on market stalls or at car boot sales. There are plenty of good tools around at reasonable prices, but always aim to purchase items which meet the relevant national safety standards. If in doubt, ask the proprietor or manager of the shop for advice before making a purchase.

Care and maintenance of tools

Having purchased a reasonable tool kit, it is necessary to keep the tools in a clean and serviceable condition. After use, always wipe off any dirt, grease and metal particles using a clean, dry cloth, before putting the tools away. Never leave them lying around after they have been used. A simple tool rack on the garage or workshop wall for items such as screwdrivers and pliers is a good idea. Store all normal spanners and sockets in a metal box. Any measuring instruments, gauges, meters, etc, must be carefully stored where they cannot be damaged or become rusty.

Take a little care when tools are used. Hammer heads inevitably become marked, and screwdrivers lose the keen edge on their blades from time to time. A little timely attention with emery cloth or a file will soon restore items like this to a good finish.

Working facilities

Not to be forgotten when discussing tools is the workshop itself. If anything more than routine maintenance is to be carried out, a suitable working area becomes essential.

It is appreciated that many an owner-mechanic is forced by circumstances to remove an engine or similar item without the benefit of a garage or workshop. Having done this, any repairs should always be done under the cover of a roof.

Wherever possible, any dismantling should be done on a clean, flat workbench or table at a suitable working height.

Any workbench needs a vice; one with a jaw opening of 100 mm is suitable for most jobs. As mentioned previously, some clean dry storage space is also required for tools, as well as for any lubricants, cleaning fluids, touch-up paints etc, which become necessary.

Another item which may be required, and which has a much more general usage, is an electric drill with a chuck capacity of at least 8 mm. This, together with a good range of twist drills, is virtually essential for fitting accessories.

Last, but not least, always keep a supply of old newspapers and clean, lint-free rags available, and try to keep any working area as clean as possible.

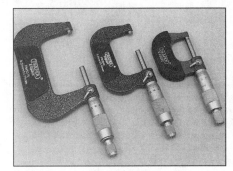
Micrometers

Dial test indicator ("dial gauge")

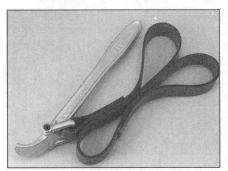
Strap wrench

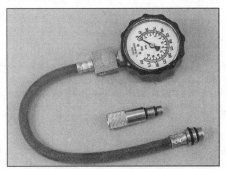
Compression tester

Fault code reader

This is a guide to getting your vehicle through the MOT test. Obviously it will not be possible to examine the vehicle to the same standard as the professional MOT tester. However, working through the following checks will enable you to identify any problem areas before submitting the vehicle for the test.

Where a testable component is in borderline condition, the tester has discretion in deciding whether to pass or fail it. The basis of such discretion is whether the tester would be happy for a close relative or friend to use the vehicle with the component in that condition. If the vehicle presented is clean and evidently well cared for, the tester may be more inclined to pass a borderline component than if the vehicle is scruffy and apparently neglected.

It has only been possible to summarise the test requirements here, based on the regulations in force at the time of printing. Test standards are becoming increasingly stringent, although there are some exemptions for older vehicles.

An assistant will be needed to help carry out some of these checks.

The checks have been sub-divided into four categories, as follows:

1 Checks carried out **FROM THE DRIVER'S SEAT**

2 Checks carried out **WITH THE VEHICLE ON THE GROUND**

3 Checks carried out **WITH THE VEHICLE RAISED AND THE WHEELS FREE TO TURN**

4 Checks carried out on **YOUR VEHICLE'S EXHAUST EMISSION SYSTEM**

---

1 Checks carried out **FROM THE DRIVER'S SEAT**

Handbrake

☐ Test the operation of the handbrake. Excessive travel (too many clicks) indicates incorrect brake or cable adjustment.

☐ Check that the handbrake cannot be released by tapping the lever sideways. Check the security of the lever mountings.

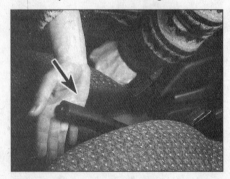

Footbrake

☐ Depress the brake pedal and check that it does not creep down to the floor, indicating a master cylinder fault. Release the pedal, wait a few seconds, then depress it again. If the pedal travels nearly to the floor before firm resistance is felt, brake adjustment or repair is necessary. If the pedal feels spongy, there is air in the hydraulic system which must be removed by bleeding.

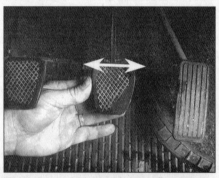

☐ Check that the brake pedal is secure and in good condition. Check also for signs of fluid leaks on the pedal, floor or carpets, which would indicate failed seals in the brake master cylinder.

☐ Check the servo unit (when applicable) by operating the brake pedal several times, then keeping the pedal depressed and starting the engine. As the engine starts, the pedal will move down slightly. If not, the vacuum hose or the servo itself may be faulty.

Steering wheel and column

☐ Examine the steering wheel for fractures or looseness of the hub, spokes or rim.

☐ Move the steering wheel from side to side and then up and down. Check that the steering wheel is not loose on the column, indicating wear or a loose retaining nut. Continue moving the steering wheel as before, but also turn it slightly from left to right.

☐ Check that the steering wheel is not loose on the column, and that there is no abnormal

movement of the steering wheel, indicating wear in the column support bearings or couplings.

Windscreen, mirrors and sunvisor

☐ The windscreen must be free of cracks or other significant damage within the driver's field of view. (Small stone chips are acceptable.) Rear view mirrors must be secure, intact, and capable of being adjusted.

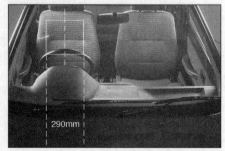

☐ The driver's sunvisor must be capable of being stored in the "up" position.

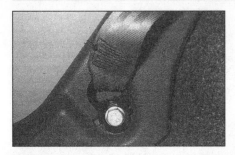

Seat belts and seats

Note: *The following checks are applicable to all seat belts, front and rear.*

☐ Examine the webbing of all the belts (including rear belts if fitted) for cuts, serious fraying or deterioration. Fasten and unfasten each belt to check the buckles. If applicable, check the retracting mechanism. Check the security of all seat belt mountings accessible from inside the vehicle.

☐ Seat belts with pre-tensioners, once activated, have a "flag" or similar showing on the seat belt stalk. This, in itself, is not a reason for test failure.

☐ The front seats themselves must be securely attached and the backrests must lock in the upright position.

Doors

☐ Both front doors must be able to be opened and closed from outside and inside, and must latch securely when closed.

2 Checks carried out WITH THE VEHICLE ON THE GROUND

Vehicle identification

☐ Number plates must be in good condition, secure and legible, with letters and numbers correctly spaced – spacing at (A) should be at least twice that at (B).

☐ The VIN plate and/or homologation plate must be legible.

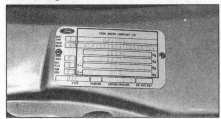

Electrical equipment

☐ Switch on the ignition and check the operation of the horn.

☐ Check the windscreen washers and wipers, examining the wiper blades; renew damaged or perished blades. Also check the operation of the stop-lights.

☐ Check the operation of the sidelights and number plate lights. The lenses and reflectors must be secure, clean and undamaged.

☐ Check the operation and alignment of the headlights. The headlight reflectors must not be tarnished and the lenses must be undamaged.

☐ Switch on the ignition and check the operation of the direction indicators (including the instrument panel tell-tale) and the hazard warning lights. Operation of the sidelights and stop-lights must not affect the indicators - if it does, the cause is usually a bad earth at the rear light cluster.

☐ Check the operation of the rear foglight(s), including the warning light on the instrument panel or in the switch.

☐ The ABS warning light must illuminate in accordance with the manufacturers' design. For most vehicles, the ABS warning light should illuminate when the ignition is switched on, and (if the system is operating properly) extinguish after a few seconds. Refer to the owner's handbook.

Footbrake

☐ Examine the master cylinder, brake pipes and servo unit for leaks, loose mountings, corrosion or other damage.

☐ The fluid reservoir must be secure and the fluid level must be between the upper (**A**) and lower (**B**) markings.

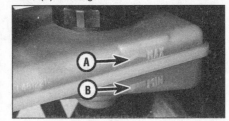

☐ Inspect both front brake flexible hoses for cracks or deterioration of the rubber. Turn the steering from lock to lock, and ensure that the hoses do not contact the wheel, tyre, or any part of the steering or suspension mechanism. With the brake pedal firmly depressed, check the hoses for bulges or leaks under pressure.

Steering and suspension

☐ Have your assistant turn the steering wheel from side to side slightly, up to the point where the steering gear just begins to transmit this movement to the roadwheels. Check for excessive free play between the steering wheel and the steering gear, indicating wear or insecurity of the steering column joints, the column-to-steering gear coupling, or the steering gear itself.

☐ Have your assistant turn the steering wheel more vigorously in each direction, so that the roadwheels just begin to turn. As this is done, examine all the steering joints, linkages, fittings and attachments. Renew any component that shows signs of wear or damage. On vehicles with power steering, check the security and condition of the steering pump, drivebelt and hoses.

☐ Check that the vehicle is standing level, and at approximately the correct ride height.

Shock absorbers

☐ Depress each corner of the vehicle in turn, then release it. The vehicle should rise and then settle in its normal position. If the vehicle continues to rise and fall, the shock absorber is defective. A shock absorber which has seized will also cause the vehicle to fail.

Exhaust system

☐ Start the engine. With your assistant holding a rag over the tailpipe, check the entire system for leaks. Repair or renew leaking sections.

3 Checks carried out **WITH THE VEHICLE RAISED AND THE WHEELS FREE TO TURN**

Jack up the front and rear of the vehicle, and securely support it on axle stands. Position the stands clear of the suspension assemblies. Ensure that the wheels are clear of the ground and that the steering can be turned from lock to lock.

Steering mechanism

☐ Have your assistant turn the steering from lock to lock. Check that the steering turns smoothly, and that no part of the steering mechanism, including a wheel or tyre, fouls any brake hose or pipe or any part of the body structure.

☐ Examine the steering rack rubber gaiters for damage or insecurity of the retaining clips. If power steering is fitted, check for signs of damage or leakage of the fluid hoses, pipes or connections. Also check for excessive stiffness or binding of the steering, a missing split pin or locking device, or severe corrosion of the body structure within 30 cm of any steering component attachment point.

Front and rear suspension and wheel bearings

☐ Starting at the front right-hand side, grasp the roadwheel at the 3 o'clock and 9 o'clock positions and rock gently but firmly. Check for free play or insecurity at the wheel bearings, suspension balljoints, or suspension mountings, pivots and attachments.

☐ Now grasp the wheel at the 12 o'clock and 6 o'clock positions and repeat the previous inspection. Spin the wheel, and check for roughness or tightness of the front wheel bearing.

☐ If excess free play is suspected at a component pivot point, this can be confirmed by using a large screwdriver or similar tool and levering between the mounting and the component attachment. This will confirm whether the wear is in the pivot bush, its retaining bolt, or in the mounting itself (the bolt holes can often become elongated).

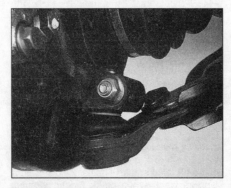

☐ Carry out all the above checks at the other front wheel, and then at both rear wheels.

Springs and shock absorbers

☐ Examine the suspension struts (when applicable) for serious fluid leakage, corrosion, or damage to the casing. Also check the security of the mounting points.

☐ If coil springs are fitted, check that the spring ends locate in their seats, and that the spring is not corroded, cracked or broken.

☐ If leaf springs are fitted, check that all leaves are intact, that the axle is securely attached to each spring, and that there is no deterioration of the spring eye mountings, bushes, and shackles.

☐ The same general checks apply to vehicles fitted with other suspension types, such as torsion bars, hydraulic displacer units, etc. Ensure that all mountings and attachments are secure, that there are no signs of excessive wear, corrosion or damage, and (on hydraulic types) that there are no fluid leaks or damaged pipes.

☐ Inspect the shock absorbers for signs of serious fluid leakage. Check for wear of the mounting bushes or attachments, or damage to the body of the unit.

Driveshafts (fwd vehicles only)

☐ Rotate each front wheel in turn and inspect the constant velocity joint gaiters for splits or damage. Also check that each driveshaft is straight and undamaged.

Braking system

☐ If possible without dismantling, check brake pad wear and disc condition. Ensure that the friction lining material has not worn excessively, (A) and that the discs are not fractured, pitted, scored or badly worn (B).

☐ Examine all the rigid brake pipes underneath the vehicle, and the flexible hose(s) at the rear. Look for corrosion, chafing or insecurity of the pipes, and for signs of bulging under pressure, chafing, splits or deterioration of the flexible hoses.

☐ Look for signs of fluid leaks at the brake calipers or on the brake backplates. Repair or renew leaking components.

☐ Slowly spin each wheel, while your assistant depresses and releases the footbrake. Ensure that each brake is operating and does not bind when the pedal is released.

☐ Examine the handbrake mechanism, checking for frayed or broken cables, excessive corrosion, or wear or insecurity of the linkage. Check that the mechanism works on each relevant wheel, and releases fully, without binding.

☐ It is not possible to test brake efficiency without special equipment, but a road test can be carried out later to check that the vehicle pulls up in a straight line.

Fuel and exhaust systems

☐ Inspect the fuel tank (including the filler cap), fuel pipes, hoses and unions. All components must be secure and free from leaks.

☐ Examine the exhaust system over its entire length, checking for any damaged, broken or missing mountings, security of the retaining clamps and rust or corrosion.

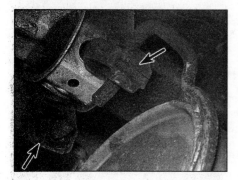

Wheels and tyres

☐ Examine the sidewalls and tread area of each tyre in turn. Check for cuts, tears, lumps, bulges, separation of the tread, and exposure of the ply or cord due to wear or damage. Check that the tyre bead is correctly seated on the wheel rim, that the valve is sound and properly seated, and that the wheel is not distorted or damaged.

☐ Check that the tyres are of the correct size for the vehicle, that they are of the same size and type on each axle, and that the pressures are correct.

☐ Check the tyre tread depth. The legal minimum at the time of writing is 1.6 mm over at least three-quarters of the tread width. Abnormal tread wear may indicate incorrect front wheel alignment.

Body corrosion

☐ Check the condition of the entire vehicle structure for signs of corrosion in load-bearing areas. (These include chassis box sections, side sills, cross-members, pillars, and all suspension, steering, braking system and seat belt mountings and anchorages.) Any corrosion which has seriously reduced the thickness of a load-bearing area is likely to cause the vehicle to fail. In this case professional repairs are likely to be needed.

☐ Damage or corrosion which causes sharp or otherwise dangerous edges to be exposed will also cause the vehicle to fail.

4 Checks carried out on
YOUR VEHICLE'S EXHAUST EMISSION SYSTEM

Petrol models

☐ Have the engine at normal operating temperature, and make sure that it is in good tune (ignition system in good order, air filter element clean, etc).

☐ Before any measurements are carried out, raise the engine speed to around 2500 rpm, and hold it at this speed for 20 seconds. Allow the engine speed to return to idle, and watch for smoke emissions from the exhaust tailpipe. If the idle speed is obviously much too high, or if dense blue or clearly-visible black smoke comes from the tailpipe for more than 5 seconds, the vehicle will fail. As a rule of thumb, blue smoke signifies oil being burnt (engine wear) while black smoke signifies unburnt fuel (dirty air cleaner element, or other carburettor or fuel system fault).

☐ An exhaust gas analyser capable of measuring carbon monoxide (CO) and hydrocarbons (HC) is now needed. If such an instrument cannot be hired or borrowed, a local garage may agree to perform the check for a small fee.

CO emissions (mixture)

☐ At the time of writing, for vehicles first used between 1st August 1975 and 31st July 1986 (P to C registration), the CO level must not exceed 4.5% by volume. For vehicles first used between 1st August 1986 and 31st July 1992 (D to J registration), the CO level must not exceed 3.5% by volume. Vehicles first

used after 1st August 1992 (K registration) must conform to the manufacturer's specification. The MOT tester has access to a DOT database or emissions handbook, which lists the CO and HC limits for each make and model of vehicle. The CO level is measured with the engine at idle speed, and at "fast idle". The following limits are given as a general guide:

> At idle speed -
> CO level no more than 0.5%
> At "fast idle" (2500 to 3000 rpm) -
> CO level no more than 0.3%
> (Minimum oil temperature 60°C)

☐ If the CO level cannot be reduced far enough to pass the test (and the fuel and ignition systems are otherwise in good condition) then the carburettor is badly worn, or there is some problem in the fuel injection system or catalytic converter (as applicable).

HC emissions

☐ With the CO within limits, HC emissions for vehicles first used between 1st August 1975 and 31st July 1992 (P to J registration) must not exceed 1200 ppm. Vehicles first used after 1st August 1992 (K registration) must conform to the manufacturer's specification. The MOT tester has access to a DOT database or emissions handbook, which lists the CO and HC limits for each make and model of vehicle. The HC level is measured with the engine at "fast idle". The following is given as a general guide:

> At "fast idle" (2500 to 3000 rpm) -
> HC level no more than 200 ppm
> (Minimum oil temperature 60°C)

☐ Excessive HC emissions are caused by incomplete combustion, the causes of which can include oil being burnt, mechanical wear and ignition/fuel system malfunction.

Diesel models

☐ The only emission test applicable to Diesel engines is the measuring of exhaust smoke density. The test involves accelerating the engine several times to its maximum unloaded speed.

Note: *It is of the utmost importance that the engine timing belt is in good condition before the test is carried out.*

☐ The limits for Diesel engine exhaust smoke, introduced in September 1995 are:
Vehicles first used before 1st August 1979:
> Exempt from metered smoke testing, but must not emit "dense blue or clearly visible black smoke for a period of more than 5 seconds at idle" or "dense blue or clearly visible black smoke during acceleration which would obscure the view of other road users".
Non-turbocharged vehicles first used after
> *1st August 1979:* 2.5m⁻¹
Turbocharged vehicles first used after
> *1st August 1979:* 3.0m⁻¹

☐ Excessive smoke can be caused by a dirty air cleaner element. Otherwise, professional advice may be needed to find the cause.

Engine

- ☐ Engine fails to rotate when attempting to start
- ☐ Engine rotates, but will not start
- ☐ Engine difficult to start when cold
- ☐ Engine difficult to start when hot
- ☐ Starter motor noisy or excessively-rough in engagement
- ☐ Engine starts, but stops immediately
- ☐ Engine idles erratically
- ☐ Engine misfires at idle speed
- ☐ Engine misfires throughout the driving speed range
- ☐ Engine hesitates on acceleration
- ☐ Engine stalls
- ☐ Engine lacks power
- ☐ Engine backfires
- ☐ Oil pressure warning light illuminated with engine running
- ☐ Engine runs-on after switching off
- ☐ Engine noises

Cooling system

- ☐ Overheating
- ☐ Overcooling
- ☐ External coolant leakage
- ☐ Internal coolant leakage
- ☐ Corrosion

Fuel and exhaust systems

- ☐ Excessive fuel consumption
- ☐ Fuel leakage and/or fuel odour
- ☐ Excessive noise or fumes from exhaust system

Clutch

- ☐ Pedal travels to floor – no pressure or very little resistance
- ☐ Clutch fails to disengage (unable to select gears)
- ☐ Clutch slips (engine speed increases, with no increase in vehicle speed)
- ☐ Judder as clutch is engaged
- ☐ Noise when depressing or releasing clutch pedal

Manual gearbox

- ☐ Noisy in neutral with engine running
- ☐ Noisy in one particular gear
- ☐ Difficulty engaging gears
- ☐ Jumps out of gear
- ☐ Vibration
- ☐ Lubricant leaks

Automatic transmission

- ☐ Fluid leakage
- ☐ General gear selection problems
- ☐ Transmission will not downshift (kickdown) with accelerator pedal fully depressed
- ☐ Engine will not start in any gear, or starts in gears other than Park or Neutral
- ☐ Transmission slips, shifts roughly, is noisy, or has no drive in forward or reverse gears

Driveshafts

- ☐ Clicking or knocking noise on turns (at slow speed on full-lock)
- ☐ Vibration when accelerating or decelerating

Braking system

- ☐ Vehicle pulls to one side under braking
- ☐ Noise (grinding or high-pitched squeal) when brakes applied
- ☐ Excessive brake pedal travel
- ☐ Brake pedal feels spongy when depressed
- ☐ Excessive brake pedal effort required to stop vehicle
- ☐ Judder felt through brake pedal or steering wheel when braking
- ☐ Brakes binding
- ☐ Rear wheels locking under normal braking

Suspension and steering systems

- ☐ Vehicle pulls to one side
- ☐ Wheel wobble and vibration
- ☐ Excessive pitching and/or rolling around corners, or during braking
- ☐ Wandering or general instability
- ☐ Excessively-stiff steering
- ☐ Excessive play in steering
- ☐ Tyre wear excessive

Electrical system

- ☐ Battery will not hold a charge for more than a few days
- ☐ Ignition/no-charge warning light remains illuminated with engine running
- ☐ Ignition/no-charge warning light fails to come on
- ☐ Lights inoperative
- ☐ Instrument readings inaccurate or erratic
- ☐ Horn inoperative, or unsatisfactory in operation
- ☐ Windscreen wipers inoperative, or unsatisfactory in operation
- ☐ Windscreen washers inoperative, or unsatisfactory in operation

Introduction

The vehicle owner who does his or her own maintenance according to the recommended service schedules should not have to use this section of the manual very often. Modern component reliability is such that, provided those items subject to wear or deterioration are inspected or renewed at the specified intervals, sudden failure is comparatively rare. Faults do not usually just happen as a result of sudden failure, but develop over a period of time. Major mechanical failures in particular are usually preceded by characteristic symptoms over hundreds or even thousands of miles. Those components which do occasionally fail without warning are often small and easily carried in the vehicle.

With any fault-finding, the first step is to decide where to begin investigations. Sometimes this is obvious, but on other occasions, a little detective work will be necessary. The owner who makes half a dozen haphazard adjustments or replacements may be successful in curing a fault (or its symptoms), but will be none the wiser if the fault recurs, and ultimately may have spent more time and money than was necessary. A calm and logical approach will be found to be more satisfactory in the long run. Always take into account any warning signs or abnormalities that may have been noticed in the period preceding the fault – power loss, high or low gauge readings,

unusual smells, etc – and remember that failure of components such as fuses or spark plugs may only be pointers to some underlying fault.

The pages which follow provide an easy-reference guide to the more common problems which may occur during the operation of the vehicle. These problems and their possible causes are grouped under headings denoting various components or systems, such as Engine, Cooling system, etc. The Chapter which deals with the problem is shown in brackets, but in some instances it will be necessary to refer to the specific Chapter Part, depending on model or system, as applicable. Some problems may be more obvious, such as loose or disconnected wiring, and in these instances a Chapter reference may not be given as the problem can be simply overcome by dealing with the fault as it stands. Whatever the problem, certain basic principles apply. These are as follows:

Verify the fault. This is simply a matter of being sure that you know what the symptoms are before starting work. This is particularly important if you are investigating a fault for someone else, who may not have described it very accurately.

Don't overlook the obvious. For example, if the vehicle wont start, is there petrol in the tank? (Don't take anyone else's word on this particular point, and dot trust the fuel gauge either!) If an electrical fault is indicated, look for loose or broken wires before digging out the test gear.

Cure the disease, not the symptom. Substituting a flat battery with a fully-charged one will get you off the hard shoulder, but if the underlying cause is not attended to, the new battery will go the same way. Similarly, changing oil-fouled spark plugs (petrol models)

for a new set will get you moving again, but remember that the reason for the fouling (if it wasn't simply an incorrect grade of plug) will have to be established and corrected.

Don't take anything for granted. Particularly, don't forget that a new component may itself be defective (especially if its been rattling around in the boot for months), and don't leave components out of a fault diagnosis sequence just because they are new or recently-fitted. When you do finally diagnose a difficult fault, you'll probably realise that all the evidence was there from the start.

Engine

Engine fails to rotate when attempting to start

- [ ] Battery terminal connections loose or corroded (Weekly checks).
- [ ] Battery discharged or faulty (Chapter 5).
- [ ] Broken, loose or disconnected wiring in the starting circuit (Chapter 5).
- [ ] Defective starter solenoid or switch (Chapter 5).
- [ ] Defective starter motor (Chapter 5).
- [ ] Starter pinion or flywheel ring gear teeth loose or broken (Chapters 2 and 5).
- [ ] Engine earth strap broken or disconnected (Chapter 5).
- [ ] Automatic transmission selector not in N, or inhibitor switch faulty (Chapter 7).
- [ ] Anti-theft alarm system armed (later models).

Engine rotates, but will not start

- [ ] Fuel tank empty.
- [ ] Battery discharged (engine rotates slowly) (Chapter 5).
- [ ] Battery terminal connections loose or corroded (Weekly checks).
- [ ] Ignition components damp or damaged (Chapter 1).
- [ ] Worn or incorrectly adjusted contact breaker points (Chapter 5).
- [ ] Broken, loose or disconnected wiring in the ignition circuit (Chapter 1).
- [ ] Worn, faulty or incorrectly-gapped spark plugs (Chapter 1).
- [ ] Choke mechanism incorrectly adjusted, worn or sticking – carburettor models (Chapter 4).
- [ ] Fuel injection system fault – fuel injection models (Chapter 4).
- [ ] Major mechanical failure (eg camshaft drive) (Chapter 2).

Engine difficult to start when cold

- [ ] Battery discharged (Chapter 5).
- [ ] Battery terminal connections loose or corroded (Chapter 1).
- [ ] Worn, faulty or incorrectly-gapped spark plugs (Chapter 1).
- [ ] Worn or incorrectly adjusted contact breaker points (Chapter 5).
- [ ] Choke mechanism incorrectly adjusted, worn or sticking – carburettor models (Chapter 4).
- [ ] Fuel injection/engine management system fault (Chapters 4 and 5).
- [ ] Other ignition system fault (Chapters 1 and 5).
- [ ] Low cylinder compressions (Chapter 2).

Engine difficult to start when hot

- [ ] Air filter element dirty or clogged (Chapter 1).
- [ ] Choke mechanism incorrectly adjusted, worn or sticking – carburettor models (Chapter 4).
- [ ] Fuel injection/engine management system fault (Chapters 4 and 5).
- [ ] Worn or incorrectly adjusted contact breaker points (Chapter 5).
- [ ] Uneven or low cylinder compressions (Chapter 2).

Starter motor noisy or excessively-rough in engagement

- [ ] Starter pinion or flywheel ring gear teeth loose or broken (Chapter 2).
- [ ] Starter motor mounting bolts loose or missing (Chapter 5).
- [ ] Starter motor internal components worn or damaged (Chapter 5).

Engine starts, but stops immediately

- [ ] Loose or faulty electrical connections in the ignition circuit (Chapters 1 and 5).
- [ ] Vacuum leak at the carburettor/throttle body or inlet manifold (Chapter 4).
- [ ] Worn or incorrectly adjusted contact breaker points (Chapter 5).
- [ ] Ballasted ignition system fault (Chapter 5).
- [ ] Blocked injector/fuel injection system fault – fuel injection models (Chapter 4).

Engine idles erratically

- [ ] Air filter element clogged (Chapter 1).
- [ ] Vacuum leak at the carburettor/throttle body, inlet manifold or associated hoses (Chapter 4).
- [ ] Worn, faulty or incorrectly-gapped spark plugs (Chapter 1).
- [ ] Worn or incorrectly adjusted contact breaker points (Chapter 5).
- [ ] Uneven or low cylinder compressions (Chapter 2).
- [ ] Camshaft lobes worn (Chapter 2).
- [ ] Incorrect idle speed and mixture adjustment – carburettor models (Chapter 4).
- [ ] Blocked injector/fuel injection system fault – fuel injection models (Chapter 4).
- [ ] Incorrect valve clearances (Chapter 2A).
- [ ] Broken valve spring(s) (Chapter 2).
- [ ] Burnt, sticking or leaking valves (Chapter 2).
- [ ] Worn valve stems or guides (Chapter 2).
- [ ] Worn or damaged pistons, piston rings and bores (Chapter 2).

Engine misfires at idle speed

- [ ] Worn, faulty or incorrectly-gapped spark plugs (Chapter 1).
- [ ] Faulty spark plug HT leads (Chapter 1).
- [ ] Worn or incorrectly adjusted contact breaker points (Chapter 5).
- [ ] Incorrect idle speed and mixture adjustment – carburettor models (Chapter 4).
- [ ] Vacuum leak at the carburettor/throttle body, inlet manifold or associated hoses (Chapter 4).
- [ ] Blocked injector/fuel injection system fault – fuel injection models (Chapter 5).
- [ ] Distributor cap cracked or tracking internally (Chapter 1).
- [ ] Incorrect valve clearances (Chapter 2).
- [ ] Uneven or low cylinder compressions (Chapter 2).
- [ ] Disconnected, leaking, or perished crankcase ventilation hoses (Chapters 1 and 4).

Engine (continued)

Engine misfires throughout the driving speed range

- [ ] Fuel filter choked – fuel injection models (Chapter 1).
- [ ] Incorrect idle speed and mixture adjustment – carburettor models (Chapter 4).
- [ ] Incorrect ignition timing (Chapter 5).
- [ ] Choke mechanism incorrectly adjusted, worn or sticking – carburettor models (Chapter 4).
- [ ] Worn or incorrectly adjusted contact breaker points (Chapter 5).
- [ ] Fuel pump faulty, or delivery pressure low (Chapter 4).
- [ ] Fuel tank vent blocked, or fuel pipes restricted (Chapter 4).
- [ ] Carburettor float chamber flooding (float height incorrect) – carburettor models (Chapter 4).
- [ ] Vacuum leak at the carburettor/throttle body, inlet manifold or associated hoses (Chapter 4).
- [ ] Worn, faulty or incorrectly-gapped spark plugs (Chapter 1).
- [ ] Faulty spark plug HT leads (Chapter 1).
- [ ] Distributor cap cracked or tracking internally (where applicable) (Chapter 1).
- [ ] Faulty ignition coil or ignition module (Chapter 5).
- [ ] Incorrect valve clearances (Chapter 2).
- [ ] Uneven or low cylinder compressions (Chapter 2).
- [ ] Blocked injector/fuel injection system fault – fuel injection models (Chapter 4).

Engine hesitates on acceleration

- [ ] Worn, faulty or incorrectly-gapped spark plugs (Chapter 1).
- [ ] Vacuum leak at the carburettor/throttle body, inlet manifold or associated hoses (Chapter 4).
- [ ] Incorrect idle speed and mixture adjustment – carburettor models (Chapter 4).
- [ ] Choke mechanism incorrectly adjusted, worn or sticking – carburettor models (Chapter 4).
- [ ] Worn or incorrectly adjusted contact breaker points (Chapter 5).
- [ ] Blocked injector/fuel injection system fault – fuel injection models (Chapter 4).

Engine stalls

- [ ] Vacuum leak at the carburettor/throttle body, inlet manifold or associated hoses (Chapter 4).
- [ ] Incorrect idle speed and mixture adjustment – carburettor models (Chapter 4).
- [ ] Choke mechanism incorrectly adjusted, worn or sticking – carburettor models (Chapter 4).
- [ ] Carburettor float chamber flooding (float height incorrect) – carburettor models (Chapter 4).
- [ ] Fuel filter choked – fuel injection models (Chapter 1).
- [ ] Fuel pump faulty, or delivery pressure low (Chapter 4).
- [ ] Fuel tank vent blocked, or fuel pipes restricted (Chapter 4).
- [ ] Blocked injector/fuel injection system fault – fuel injection models (Chapter 4).

Engine lacks power

- [ ] Timing chain incorrectly fitted (Chapter 2).
- [ ] Incorrect idle speed and mixture adjustment – carburettor models (Chapter 4).
- [ ] Incorrect ignition timing (Chapter 5).
- [ ] Fuel filter choked – fuel injection models (Chapter 1).
- [ ] Fuel pump faulty, or delivery pressure low (Chapter 4).
- [ ] Incorrect valve clearances (Chapter 2).
- [ ] Uneven or low cylinder compressions (Chapter 2).
- [ ] Worn, faulty or incorrectly-gapped spark plugs (Chapter 1).
- [ ] Vacuum leak at the carburettor/throttle body, inlet manifold or associated hoses (Chapter 4).
- [ ] Blocked injector/fuel injection system fault – fuel injection models (Chapter 4).
- [ ] Brakes binding (Chapters 1 and 9).
- [ ] Clutch slipping (Chapter 6).

Engine backfires

- [ ] Timing chain incorrectly fitted (Chapter 2).
- [ ] Vacuum leak at the carburettor/throttle body, inlet manifold or associated hoses (Chapter 4).
- [ ] Incorrect ignition timing (Chapter 5).
- [ ] Blocked carburettor jet(s) or internal passages – carburettor models (Chapter 4).
- [ ] Blocked injector/fuel injection system fault – fuel injection models (Chapter 4).

Oil pressure warning light illuminated with engine running

- [ ] Low oil level, or incorrect oil grade (Chapter 1).
- [ ] Worn engine bearings and/or oil pump (Chapter 2).
- [ ] High engine operating temperature (Chapter 3).
- [ ] Oil pressure relief valve defective (Chapter 2).
- [ ] Oil pick-up strainer clogged (Chapter 2).

Engine runs-on after switching off

- [ ] Excessive carbon build-up in engine (Chapter 2).
- [ ] Incorrectly adjusted idle speed (Chapter 4).
- [ ] Incorrect ignition timing (Chapter 5).
- [ ] High engine operating temperature (Chapter 3).
- [ ] Fuel injection/engine management system fault (Chapters 4 and 5).

Engine noises

Pre-ignition (pinking) or knocking during acceleration or under load

- [ ] Ignition timing incorrect/ignition system fault (Chapter 5).
- [ ] Incorrect grade of spark plug (Chapter 1).
- [ ] Incorrect grade of fuel (Chapter 1).
- [ ] Vacuum leak at the carburettor/throttle body, inlet manifold or associated hoses (Chapter 4).
- [ ] Excessive carbon build-up in engine (Chapter 2).
- [ ] Blocked injector/Fuel injection/engine management system fault (Chapters 4 and 5).

Whistling or wheezing noises

- [ ] Leaking inlet manifold or carburettor/throttle body gasket (Chapter 4).
- [ ] Leaking exhaust manifold gasket or pipe-to-manifold joint (Chapter 4).
- [ ] Leaking vacuum hose (Chapters 4 and 9).
- [ ] Blowing cylinder head gasket (Chapter 2).

Tapping or rattling noises

- [ ] Incorrect valve clearances (Chapter 2).
- [ ] Worn timing chain tensioner, valve gear or camshaft (Chapter 2).
- [ ] Ancillary component fault (water pump, dynamo, alternator, etc) (Chapters 3, 5, etc).

Knocking or thumping noises

- [ ] Worn big-end bearings (regular heavy knocking, perhaps less under load) (Chapter 2).
- [ ] Worn main bearings (rumbling and knocking, perhaps worsening under load) (Chapter 2).
- [ ] Piston slap (most noticeable when cold) (Chapter 2).
- [ ] Ancillary component fault (water pump, dynamo, alternator, etc) (Chapters 3, 5, etc).

Cooling system

Overheating

☐ Insufficient coolant in system (Weekly checks).
☐ Thermostat faulty (Chapter 3).
☐ Radiator core blocked, or grille restricted (Chapter 3).
☐ Electric cooling fan or thermoswitch faulty – later models (Chapter 3).
☐ Pressure cap faulty (Chapter 3).
☐ Blown cylinder head gasket (Chapter 2).
☐ Ignition timing incorrect/ignition system fault (Chapter 5).
☐ Inaccurate temperature gauge sender unit (Chapter 3).
☐ Airlock in cooling system (Chapter 1).

Overcooling

☐ Thermostat faulty (Chapter 3).
☐ Inaccurate temperature gauge sender unit (Chapter 3).

External coolant leakage

☐ Deteriorated or damaged hoses or hose clips (Chapter 1).
☐ Radiator core or heater matrix leaking (Chapter 3).
☐ Pressure cap faulty (Chapter 3).
☐ Water pump seal leaking (Chapter 3).
☐ Boiling due to overheating (Chapter 3).
☐ Core plug leaking (Chapter 2).

Internal coolant leakage

☐ Leaking cylinder head gasket (Chapter 2).
☐ Cracked cylinder head or cylinder bore (Chapter 2).

Corrosion

☐ Infrequent draining and flushing (Chapter 1).
☐ Incorrect coolant mixture or inappropriate coolant type (Chapter 1).

Fuel and exhaust systems

Excessive fuel consumption

☐ Air filter element dirty or clogged (Chapter 1).
☐ Incorrect idle speed and mixture adjustment – carburettor models (Chapter 4).
☐ Choke cable incorrectly adjusted, or choke sticking – carburettor models (Chapter 4).
☐ Fuel injection system fault – fuel injection models (Chapter)4.
☐ Ignition timing incorrect/ignition system fault (Chapter 5).
☐ Tyres under-inflated (Weekly checks).

Fuel leakage and/or fuel odour

☐ Damaged or corroded fuel tank, pipes or connections (Chapter 4).
☐ Carburettor float chamber flooding (float height incorrect) – carburettor models (Chapter 4).

Excessive noise or fumes from exhaust system

☐ Leaking exhaust system or manifold joints (Chapters 1 and 4).
☐ Leaking, corroded or damaged silencers or pipe (Chapters 1 and 4).
☐ Broken mountings causing body or suspension contact (Chapter1 and 4).

Clutch

Pedal travels to floor (no pressure or very little resistance)

☐ Air in clutch hydraulic system (Chapter 6).
☐ Faulty clutch master cylinder (Chapter 6).
☐ Faulty clutch slave cylinder (Chapter 6).
☐ Incorrect clutch return stop adjustment (Chapter 1).
☐ Incorrect clutch throw-out stop adjustment (Chapter 6).
☐ Broken clutch release bearing (Chapter 6).
☐ Broken diaphragm spring in clutch pressure plate (Chapter 6).

Clutch fails to disengage (unable to select gears)

☐ Incorrect clutch return stop adjustment (Chapter 1).
☐ Incorrect clutch throw-out stop adjustment (Chapter 6).
☐ Clutch disc sticking on primary gear splines (Chapter 6).
☐ Clutch disc sticking to flywheel or pressure plate (Chapter 6).
☐ Faulty pressure plate assembly (Chapter 6).
☐ Clutch release mechanism worn or incorrectly assembled (Chapter 6).

Clutch slips (engine speed increases, with no increase in vehicle speed)

☐ Incorrect clutch return stop adjustment (Chapter 1).
☐ Clutch disc linings excessively worn (Chapter 6).
☐ Clutch disc linings contaminated with oil or grease (Chapter 6).
☐ Faulty pressure plate or weak diaphragm spring (Chapter 6).

Judder as clutch is engaged

☐ Worn or loose engine or transmission mountings (Chapter 2A).
☐ Clutch disc linings contaminated with oil or grease (Chapter 6).
☐ Clutch disc linings excessively worn (Chapter 6).
☐ Faulty or distorted pressure plate or diaphragm spring (Chapter 6).
☐ Clutch disc hub or primary gear splines worn (Chapter 6).

Noise when depressing or releasing clutch pedal

☐ Worn clutch release bearing (Chapter 6).
☐ Worn or dry clutch pedal bushes (Chapter 6).
☐ Faulty pressure plate assembly (Chapter 6).
☐ Pressure plate diaphragm spring broken (Chapter 6).

Manual transmission

Noisy in neutral with engine running

☐ Transfer gear bearings worn (noise apparent with clutch pedal released, but not when depressed) (Chapter 7A).*
☐ Clutch release bearing worn (noise apparent with clutch pedal depressed, possibly less when released) (Chapter 6).

Noisy in one particular gear

☐ Worn, damaged or chipped gear teeth (Chapter 7A).*

Difficulty engaging gears

☐ Clutch fault (Chapter 6).
☐ Worn or damaged gear linkage (Chapter 7A).
☐ Worn synchroniser units (Chapter 7A).*

Jumps out of gear

☐ Worn or damaged gear linkage (Chapter 7A).
☐ Incorrectly-adjusted gear linkage (Chapter 7A).
☐ Worn synchroniser units (Chapter 7A).*
☐ Worn selector forks (Chapter 7A).*

Vibration

☐ Lack of oil (Chapter 1).
☐ Worn bearings (Chapter 7A).*

Lubricant leaks

☐ Leaking differential output (driveshaft) oil seal (Chapter 7A).
☐ Leaking housing joint (Chapter 2 or 7A).*

Although the corrective action necessary to remedy the symptoms described is beyond the scope of the home mechanic, the above information should be helpful in isolating the cause of the condition, so that the owner can communicate clearly with a professional mechanic.

Automatic transmission

Note: *Due to the complexity of the automatic transmission, it is difficult for the home mechanic to properly diagnose and service this unit. For problems other than the following, the vehicle should be taken to a dealer service department or automatic transmission specialist. Do not be too hasty in removing the transmission if a fault is suspected, as most of the testing is carried out with the unit still fitted.*

Fluid leakage

☐ To determine the source of a leak, first remove all built-up dirt and grime from the transmission housing and surrounding areas using a degreasing agent, or by steam-cleaning. Drive the vehicle at low speed, so airflow will not blow the leak far from its source. Raise and support the vehicle, and determine where the leak is coming from. The following are common areas of leakage:
a) *Leaking differential output (driveshaft) oil seal (Chapter 7B).*
b) *Leaking housing joint (Chapter 2 or 7B).*
c) *Leaking selector transverse rod oil seal (Chapter 7B).*

General gear selection problems

☐ Chapter 7B deals with checking and adjusting the selector cable on automatic transmissions. The following are common problems which may be caused by a poorly-adjusted cable:
a) *Engine starting in gears other than Neutral.*
b) *Indicator panel indicating a gear other than the one actually being used.*
c) *Vehicle moves when in Park or Neutral.*
d) *Poor gear shift quality or erratic gear changes.*

Transmission will not downshift (kickdown) with accelerator pedal fully depressed

☐ Low engine/transmission oil level (Chapter 1).
☐ Incorrect selector cable adjustment (Chapter 7B).

Engine will not start in any gear, or starts in gears other than Neutral

☐ Incorrect starter/inhibitor switch adjustment (Chapter 7B).
☐ Incorrect selector cable adjustment (Chapter 7B).

Transmission slips, shifts roughly, is noisy, or has no drive in forward or reverse gears

☐ There are many probable causes for the above problems, which can really only be accurately diagnosed using pressure gauges in conjunction with a step-by step diagnostic procedure. Problems of this nature must, therefore, be referred to a dealer or automatic transmission specialist.

Driveshafts

Clicking or knocking noise on turns (at slow speed on full-lock)

☐ Lack of constant velocity joint lubricant, possibly due to damaged gaiters (Chapter 8).
☐ Worn outer constant velocity joint (Chapter 8).

Vibration when accelerating or decelerating

☐ Worn inner constant velocity joint (Chapter 8).
☐ Bent or distorted driveshaft (Chapter 8).

Braking system

Note: *Before assuming that a brake problem exists, make sure that the tyres are in good condition and correctly inflated, that the front wheel alignment is correct, and that the vehicle is not loaded with weight in an unequal manner.*

Vehicle pulls to one side under braking

☐ Worn, defective, damaged or contaminated brake shoes/pads on one side (Chapters 1 and 9).
☐ Seized or partially-seized front wheel cylinder piston or brake caliper piston (Chapters 1 and 9).
☐ A mixture of brake shoe/ pad lining materials fitted between sides (Chapters 1 and 9).
☐ Brake backplate or caliper mounting bolts loose (Chapter 9).
☐ Worn or damaged steering or suspension components (Chapters 1 and 10).

Noise (grinding or high-pitched squeal) when brakes applied

☐ Brake shoe or pad friction lining material worn down to metal backing (Chapters 1 and 9).
☐ Excessive corrosion of brake drum or disc. (May be apparent after the vehicle has been standing for some time (Chapters 1 and 9).

Excessive brake pedal travel

☐ Incorrect drum brake adjustment (Chapter 1).
☐ Faulty master cylinder (Chapter 9).
☐ Air in hydraulic system (Chapter 9).
☐ Faulty vacuum servo unit – where fitted (Chapter 9).

Brake pedal feels spongy when depressed

☐ Air in hydraulic system (Chapter 9).
☐ Deteriorated flexible rubber brake hoses (Chapters 1 and 9).
☐ Master cylinder mounting nuts loose (Chapter 9).
☐ Faulty master cylinder (Chapter 9).

Excessive brake pedal effort required to stop vehicle

☐ Faulty vacuum servo unit – where fitted (Chapter 9).
☐ Disconnected, damaged or insecure brake servo vacuum hose (Chapter 9).
☐ Primary or secondary hydraulic circuit failure (Chapter 9).
☐ Seized wheel cylinder or brake caliper piston(s) (Chapter 9).
☐ Brake shoes or pads incorrectly fitted (Chapters 1 and 9).
☐ Incorrect grade of brake shoes or pads fitted (Chapters 1 and 9).
☐ Brake shoe linings or pads contaminated (Chapters 1 and 9).

Judder felt through brake pedal or steering wheel when braking

☐ Excessive run-out or distortion of drums/discs (Chapters 1 and 9).
☐ Brake shoe or pad linings worn (Chapters 1 and 9).
☐ Brake backplate or caliper mounting bolts loose (Chapter 9).
☐ Wear in suspension or steering components or mountings (Chapters 1 and 10).

Brakes binding

☐ Incorrect drum brake adjustment (Chapter 1).
☐ Seized wheel cylinder or brake caliper piston(s) (Chapter 9).
☐ Incorrectly-adjusted handbrake mechanism (Chapter 9).
☐ Seized handbrake cable moving sectors (Chapter 9).
☐ Faulty master cylinder (Chapter 9).

Rear wheels locking under normal braking

☐ Rear brake shoe linings contaminated (Chapters 1 and 9).
☐ Faulty brake pressure regulating valve or reducing valve (Chapter 9).

Suspension and steering systems

Note: *Before diagnosing suspension or steering faults, be sure that the trouble is not due to incorrect tyre pressures, mixtures of tyre types, or binding brakes.*

Vehicle pulls to one side

- ☐ Defective tyre (Weekly checks).
- ☐ Excessive wear in suspension or steering components (Chapters 1 and 10).
- ☐ Incorrect front wheel alignment (Chapter 10).
- ☐ Worn or broken subframe mountings (Chapter 10).
- ☐ Accident damage to steering or suspension components (Chapter 1).

Wheel wobble and vibration

- ☐ Front roadwheels out of balance (vibration felt mainly through the steering wheel) (Chapters 1 and 10).
- ☐ Rear roadwheels out of balance (vibration felt throughout the vehicle) (Chapters 1 and 10).
- ☐ Roadwheels damaged or distorted (Chapters 1 and 10).
- ☐ Defective tyre (Weekly checks).
- ☐ Worn steering or suspension joints, bushes or components (Chapters 1 and 10).
- ☐ Wheel nuts loose (Chapters 1 and 10).

Excessive pitching and/or rolling around corners, or during braking

- ☐ Defective shock absorbers – rubber cone suspension models (Chapter 10).
- ☐ Incorrect vehicle ride height – Hydrolastic suspension models (Chapter 10).
- ☐ Worn or damaged suspension component or mounting (Chapter 10).

Wandering or general instability

- ☐ Incorrect front wheel alignment (Chapter 10).
- ☐ Worn steering or suspension joints, bushes or components (Chapters 1 and 10).
- ☐ Roadwheels out of balance (Chapters 1 and 10).
- ☐ Defective tyre (Weekly checks).
- ☐ Wheel nuts loose (Chapters 1 and 10).
- ☐ Defective shock absorbers – rubber cone suspension models (Chapter 10).
- ☐ Incorrect vehicle ride height – Hydrolastic suspension models (Chapter 10).

Excessively-stiff steering

- ☐ Lack of steering gear lubricant (Chapter 10).
- ☐ Seized tie-rod or suspension balljoint (Chapters 1 and 10).
- ☐ Incorrect front wheel alignment (Chapter 10).
- ☐ Steering rack or column bent or damaged (Chapter 10).

Excessive play in steering

- ☐ Worn steering tie-rod balljoints (Chapters 1 and 10).
- ☐ Loose steering column clamp bolt (Chapter 10).
- ☐ Worn rack-and-pinion steering gear (Chapter 10).
- ☐ Worn steering or suspension joints, bushes or components (Chapters 1 and 10).

Tyre wear excessive

Tyres worn on inside or outside edges

- ☐ Tyres under-inflated (wear on both edges) (Weekly checks).
- ☐ Incorrect camber or castor angles (wear on one edge only) (Chapter 10).
- ☐ Worn steering or suspension joints, bushes or components (Chapters 1 and 10).
- ☐ Worn or broken subframe mountings (Chapter 10).
- ☐ Incorrect vehicle ride height – Hydrolastic suspension models (Chapter 10).
- ☐ Excessively-hard cornering.
- ☐ Accident damage.

Tyre treads exhibit feathered edges

- ☐ Incorrect toe setting (Chapter 10).

Tyres worn in centre of tread

- ☐ Tyres over-inflated (Weekly checks).

Tyres worn on inside and outside edges

- ☐ Tyres under-inflated (Weekly checks).

Tyres worn unevenly

- ☐ Tyres/wheels out of balance (Chapter 1).
- ☐ Excessive wheel or tyre run-out (Chapter 1).
- ☐ Defective tyre (Weekly checks).
- ☐ Defective shock absorbers – rubber cone suspension models (Chapter 10).

Electrical system

Note: *For problems associated with the starting system, refer to the faults listed under Engine earlier in this Section.*

Battery will not hold a charge for more than a few days

- ☐ Battery defective internally (Chapter 5).
- ☐ Battery terminal connections loose or corroded (Weekly checks).
- ☐ Auxiliary drivebelt worn or incorrectly adjusted (Chapter 1).
- ☐ Dynamo/alternator not charging at correct output (Chapter 5).
- ☐ Alternator or voltage regulator faulty (Chapter 5).
- ☐ Short-circuit causing continual battery drain (Chapters 5 and 12).

Ignition/no-charge warning light remains illuminated with engine running

- ☐ Auxiliary drivebelt broken, worn, or incorrectly adjusted (Chapter 1).
- ☐ Dynamo/alternator brushes worn, sticking, or dirty (Chapter 5).
- ☐ Dynamo/alternator brush springs weak or broken (Chapter 5).
- ☐ Internal fault in alternator or voltage regulator (Chapter 5).
- ☐ Broken, disconnected, or loose wiring in charging circuit (Chapter 5).

Ignition/no-charge warning light fails to come on

- ☐ Warning light bulb blown (Chapter 12).
- ☐ Broken, disconnected, or loose wiring in warning light circuit (Chapter 12).
- ☐ Alternator faulty (Chapter 5).

Lights inoperative

- ☐ Bulb blown (Chapter 12).
- ☐ Corrosion of bulb or bulbholder contacts (Chapter 12).
- ☐ Blown fuse (Chapter 12).
- ☐ Faulty relay (Chapter 12).
- ☐ Broken, loose, or disconnected wiring (Chapter 12).
- ☐ Faulty switch (Chapter 12).

Instrument readings inaccurate or erratic

Instrument readings increase with engine speed

- ☐ Faulty voltage regulator (Chapter 12).

Fuel or temperature gauges give no reading

- ☐ Faulty gauge sender unit (Chapters 3 or 4).
- ☐ Wiring open-circuit (Chapter 12).
- ☐ Faulty gauge (Chapter 12).

Fuel or temperature gauges give continuous maximum reading

- ☐ Faulty gauge sender unit (Chapters 3 or 4).
- ☐ Wiring short-circuit (Chapter 12).
- ☐ Faulty gauge (Chapter 12).

Horn inoperative, or unsatisfactory in operation

Horn operates all the time

- ☐ Horn push either earthed or stuck down (Chapter 12).
- ☐ Horn cable-to-horn push earthed (Chapter 12).

Horn fails to operate

- ☐ Blown fuse (Chapter 12).
- ☐ Cable or cable connections loose, broken or disconnected (Chapter 12).
- ☐ Faulty horn (Chapter 12).

Horn emits intermittent or unsatisfactory sound

- ☐ Cable connections loose (Chapter 12).
- ☐ Horn mountings loose (Chapter 12).
- ☐ Faulty horn (Chapter 12).

Windscreen wipers inoperative, or unsatisfactory in operation

Wipers fail to operate, or operate very slowly

- ☐ Wiper blades stuck to screen, or linkage seized or binding.
- ☐ Blown fuse (Chapter 12).
- ☐ Cable or cable connections loose, broken or disconnected (Chapter 12).
- ☐ Faulty relay (Chapter 12).
- ☐ Faulty wiper motor (Chapter 12).

Wiper blades sweep over too large or too small an area of the glass

- ☐ Wiper arms incorrectly positioned on spindles.
- ☐ Excessive wear of wiper linkage (Chapter 12).
- ☐ Wiper motor or linkage mountings loose or insecure (Chapter 12).

Wiper blades fail to clean the glass effectively

- ☐ Wiper blade rubbers worn or perished (Weekly checks).
- ☐ Wiper arm tension springs broken, or arm pivots seized (Chapter 12).
- ☐ Insufficient windscreen washer additive to adequately remove road film (Weekly checks).

Windscreen washers inoperative, or unsatisfactory in operation

One or more washer jets inoperative

- ☐ Blocked washer jet (Chapter 12).
- ☐ Disconnected, kinked or restricted fluid hose (Chapter 12).
- ☐ Insufficient fluid in washer reservoir (Weekly checks).

Washer pump fails to operate

- ☐ Broken or disconnected wiring or connections (Chapter 12).
- ☐ Blown fuse (Chapter 12).
- ☐ Faulty washer switch (Chapter 12).
- ☐ Faulty washer pump (Chapter 12).

Washer pump runs for some time before fluid is emitted from jets

- ☐ Faulty one-way valve in fluid supply hose (Chapter 12).

A

ABS (Anti-lock brake system) A system, usually electronically controlled, that senses incipient wheel lockup during braking and relieves hydraulic pressure at wheels that are about to skid.

Air bag An inflatable bag hidden in the steering wheel (driver's side) or the dash or glovebox (passenger side). In a head-on collision, the bags inflate, preventing the driver and front passenger from being thrown forward into the steering wheel or windscreen.

Air cleaner A metal or plastic housing, containing a filter element, which removes dust and dirt from the air being drawn into the engine.

Air filter element The actual filter in an air cleaner system, usually manufactured from pleated paper and requiring renewal at regular intervals.

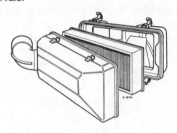

Air filter

Allen key A hexagonal wrench which fits into a recessed hexagonal hole.

Alligator clip A long-nosed spring-loaded metal clip with meshing teeth. Used to make temporary electrical connections.

Alternator A component in the electrical system which converts mechanical energy from a drivebelt into electrical energy to charge the battery and to operate the starting system, ignition system and electrical accessories.

Alternator (exploded view)

Ampere (amp) A unit of measurement for the flow of electric current. One amp is the amount of current produced by one volt acting through a resistance of one ohm.

Anaerobic sealer A substance used to prevent bolts and screws from loosening. Anaerobic means that it does not require oxygen for activation. The Loctite brand is widely used.

Antifreeze A substance (usually ethylene glycol) mixed with water, and added to a vehicle's cooling system, to prevent freezing of the coolant in winter. Antifreeze also contains chemicals to inhibit corrosion and the formation of rust and other deposits that

would tend to clog the radiator and coolant passages and reduce cooling efficiency.

Anti-seize compound A coating that reduces the risk of seizing on fasteners that are subjected to high temperatures, such as exhaust manifold bolts and nuts.

Anti-seize compound

Asbestos A natural fibrous mineral with great heat resistance, commonly used in the composition of brake friction materials. Asbestos is a health hazard and the dust created by brake systems should never be inhaled or ingested.

Axle A shaft on which a wheel revolves, or which revolves with a wheel. Also, a solid beam that connects the two wheels at one end of the vehicle. An axle which also transmits power to the wheels is known as a live axle.

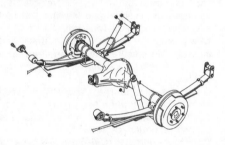

Axle assembly

Axleshaft A single rotating shaft, on either side of the differential, which delivers power from the final drive assembly to the drive wheels. Also called a driveshaft or a halfshaft.

B

Ball bearing An anti-friction bearing consisting of a hardened inner and outer race with hardened steel balls between two races.

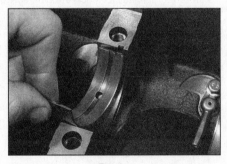

Bearing

Bearing The curved surface on a shaft or in a bore, or the part assembled into either, that permits relative motion between them with minimum wear and friction.

Big-end bearing The bearing in the end of the connecting rod that's attached to the crankshaft.

Bleed nipple A valve on a brake wheel cylinder, caliper or other hydraulic component that is opened to purge the hydraulic system of air. Also called a bleed screw.

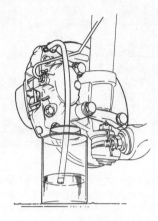

Brake bleeding

Brake bleeding Procedure for removing air from lines of a hydraulic brake system.

Brake disc The component of a disc brake that rotates with the wheels.

Brake drum The component of a drum brake that rotates with the wheels.

Brake linings The friction material which contacts the brake disc or drum to retard the vehicle's speed. The linings are bonded or riveted to the brake pads or shoes.

Brake pads The replaceable friction pads that pinch the brake disc when the brakes are applied. Brake pads consist of a friction material bonded or riveted to a rigid backing plate.

Brake shoe The crescent-shaped carrier to which the brake linings are mounted and which forces the lining against the rotating drum during braking.

Braking systems For more information on braking systems, consult the *Haynes Automotive Brake Manual*.

Breaker bar A long socket wrench handle providing greater leverage.

Bulkhead The insulated partition between the engine and the passenger compartment.

C

Caliper The non-rotating part of a disc-brake assembly that straddles the disc and carries the brake pads. The caliper also contains the hydraulic components that cause the pads to pinch the disc when the brakes are applied. A caliper is also a measuring tool that can be set to measure inside or outside dimensions of an object.

Camshaft A rotating shaft on which a series of cam lobes operate the valve mechanisms. The camshaft may be driven by gears, by sprockets and chain or by sprockets and a belt.

Canister A container in an evaporative emission control system; contains activated charcoal granules to trap vapours from the fuel system.

Canister

Carburettor A device which mixes fuel with air in the proper proportions to provide a desired power output from a spark ignition internal combustion engine.

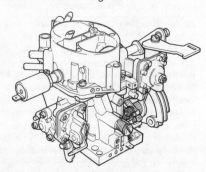

Carburettor

Castellated Resembling the parapets along the top of a castle wall. For example, a castellated balljoint stud nut.

Castellated nut

Castor In wheel alignment, the backward or forward tilt of the steering axis. Castor is positive when the steering axis is inclined rearward at the top.

Catalytic converter A silencer-like device in the exhaust system which converts certain pollutants in the exhaust gases into less harmful substances.

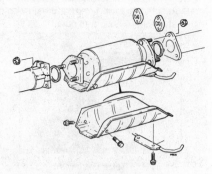

Catalytic converter

Circlip A ring-shaped clip used to prevent endwise movement of cylindrical parts and shafts. An internal circlip is installed in a groove in a housing; an external circlip fits into a groove on the outside of a cylindrical piece such as a shaft.

Clearance The amount of space between two parts. For example, between a piston and a cylinder, between a bearing and a journal, etc.

Coil spring A spiral of elastic steel found in various sizes throughout a vehicle, for example as a springing medium in the suspension and in the valve train.

Compression Reduction in volume, and increase in pressure and temperature, of a gas, caused by squeezing it into a smaller space.

Compression ratio The relationship between cylinder volume when the piston is at top dead centre and cylinder volume when the piston is at bottom dead centre.

Constant velocity (CV) joint A type of universal joint that cancels out vibrations caused by driving power being transmitted through an angle.

Core plug A disc or cup-shaped metal device inserted in a hole in a casting through which core was removed when the casting was formed. Also known as a freeze plug or expansion plug.

Crankcase The lower part of the engine block in which the crankshaft rotates.

Crankshaft The main rotating member, or shaft, running the length of the crankcase, with offset "throws" to which the connecting rods are attached.

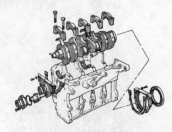

Crankshaft assembly

Crocodile clip See Alligator clip

D

Diagnostic code Code numbers obtained by accessing the diagnostic mode of an engine management computer. This code can be used to determine the area in the system where a malfunction may be located.

Disc brake A brake design incorporating a rotating disc onto which brake pads are squeezed. The resulting friction converts the energy of a moving vehicle into heat.

Double-overhead cam (DOHC) An engine that uses two overhead camshafts, usually one for the intake valves and one for the exhaust valves.

Drivebelt(s) The belt(s) used to drive accessories such as the alternator, water pump, power steering pump, air conditioning compressor, etc. off the crankshaft pulley.

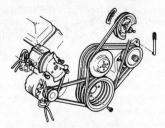

Accessory drivebelts

Driveshaft Any shaft used to transmit motion. Commonly used when referring to the axleshafts on a front wheel drive vehicle.

Driveshaft

Drum brake A type of brake using a drum-shaped metal cylinder attached to the inner surface of the wheel. When the brake pedal is pressed, curved brake shoes with friction linings press against the inside of the drum to slow or stop the vehicle.

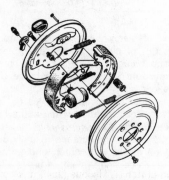

Drum brake assembly

E

EGR valve A valve used to introduce exhaust gases into the intake air stream.

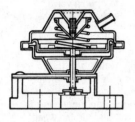

EGR valve

Electronic control unit (ECU) A computer which controls (for instance) ignition and fuel injection systems, or an anti-lock braking system. For more information refer to the *Haynes Automotive Electrical and Electronic Systems Manual.*

Electronic Fuel Injection (EFI) A computer controlled fuel system that distributes fuel through an injector located in each intake port of the engine.

Emergency brake A braking system, independent of the main hydraulic system, that can be used to slow or stop the vehicle if the primary brakes fail, or to hold the vehicle stationary even though the brake pedal isn't depressed. It usually consists of a hand lever that actuates either front or rear brakes mechanically through a series of cables and linkages. Also known as a handbrake or parking brake.

Endfloat The amount of lengthwise movement between two parts. As applied to a crankshaft, the distance that the crankshaft can move forward and back in the cylinder block.

Engine management system (EMS) A computer controlled system which manages the fuel injection and the ignition systems in an integrated fashion.

Exhaust manifold A part with several passages through which exhaust gases leave the engine combustion chambers and enter the exhaust pipe.

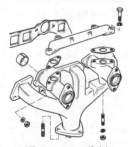

Exhaust manifold

F

Fan clutch A viscous (fluid) drive coupling device which permits variable engine fan speeds in relation to engine speeds.

Feeler blade A thin strip or blade of hardened steel, ground to an exact thickness, used to check or measure clearances between parts.

Feeler blade

Firing order The order in which the engine cylinders fire, or deliver their power strokes, beginning with the number one cylinder.

Flywheel A heavy spinning wheel in which energy is absorbed and stored by means of momentum. On cars, the flywheel is attached to the crankshaft to smooth out firing impulses.

Free play The amount of travel before any action takes place. The "looseness" in a linkage, or an assembly of parts, between the initial application of force and actual movement. For example, the distance the brake pedal moves before the pistons in the master cylinder are actuated.

Fuse An electrical device which protects a circuit against accidental overload. The typical fuse contains a soft piece of metal which is calibrated to melt at a predetermined current flow (expressed as amps) and break the circuit.

Fusible link A circuit protection device consisting of a conductor surrounded by heat-resistant insulation. The conductor is smaller than the wire it protects, so it acts as the weakest link in the circuit. Unlike a blown fuse, a failed fusible link must frequently be cut from the wire for replacement.

G

Gap The distance the spark must travel in jumping from the centre electrode to the side

Adjusting spark plug gap

electrode in a spark plug. Also refers to the spacing between the points in a contact breaker assembly in a conventional points-type ignition, or to the distance between the reluctor or rotor and the pickup coil in an electronic ignition.

Gasket Any thin, soft material - usually cork, cardboard, asbestos or soft metal - installed between two metal surfaces to ensure a good seal. For instance, the cylinder head gasket seals the joint between the block and the cylinder head.

Gasket

Gauge An instrument panel display used to monitor engine conditions. A gauge with a movable pointer on a dial or a fixed scale is an analogue gauge. A gauge with a numerical readout is called a digital gauge.

H

Halfshaft A rotating shaft that transmits power from the final drive unit to a drive wheel, usually when referring to a live rear axle.

Harmonic balancer A device designed to reduce torsion or twisting vibration in the crankshaft. May be incorporated in the crankshaft pulley. Also known as a vibration damper.

Hone An abrasive tool for correcting small irregularities or differences in diameter in an engine cylinder, brake cylinder, etc.

Hydraulic tappet A tappet that utilises hydraulic pressure from the engine's lubrication system to maintain zero clearance (constant contact with both camshaft and valve stem). Automatically adjusts to variation in valve stem length. Hydraulic tappets also reduce valve noise.

I

Ignition timing The moment at which the spark plug fires, usually expressed in the number of crankshaft degrees before the piston reaches the top of its stroke.

Inlet manifold A tube or housing with passages through which flows the air-fuel mixture (carburettor vehicles and vehicles with throttle body injection) or air only (port fuel-injected vehicles) to the port openings in the cylinder head.

J

Jump start Starting the engine of a vehicle with a discharged or weak battery by attaching jump leads from the weak battery to a charged or helper battery.

L

Load Sensing Proportioning Valve (LSPV) A brake hydraulic system control valve that works like a proportioning valve, but also takes into consideration the amount of weight carried by the rear axle.

Locknut A nut used to lock an adjustment nut, or other threaded component, in place. For example, a locknut is employed to keep the adjusting nut on the rocker arm in position.

Lockwasher A form of washer designed to prevent an attaching nut from working loose.

M

MacPherson strut A type of front suspension system devised by Earle MacPherson at Ford of England. In its original form, a simple lateral link with the anti-roll bar creates the lower control arm. A long strut - an integral coil spring and shock absorber - is mounted between the body and the steering knuckle. Many modern so-called MacPherson strut systems use a conventional lower A-arm and don't rely on the anti-roll bar for location.

Multimeter An electrical test instrument with the capability to measure voltage, current and resistance.

N

NOx Oxides of Nitrogen. A common toxic pollutant emitted by petrol and diesel engines at higher temperatures.

O

Ohm The unit of electrical resistance. One volt applied to a resistance of one ohm will produce a current of one amp.

Ohmmeter An instrument for measuring electrical resistance.

O-ring A type of sealing ring made of a special rubber-like material; in use, the O-ring is compressed into a groove to provide the sealing action.

O-ring

Overhead cam (ohc) engine An engine with the camshaft(s) located on top of the cylinder head(s).

Overhead valve (ohv) engine An engine with the valves located in the cylinder head, but with the camshaft located in the engine block.

Oxygen sensor A device installed in the engine exhaust manifold, which senses the oxygen content in the exhaust and converts this information into an electric current. Also called a Lambda sensor.

P

Phillips screw A type of screw head having a cross instead of a slot for a corresponding type of screwdriver.

Plastigage A thin strip of plastic thread, available in different sizes, used for measuring clearances. For example, a strip of Plastigage is laid across a bearing journal. The parts are assembled and dismantled; the width of the crushed strip indicates the clearance between journal and bearing.

Plastigage

Propeller shaft The long hollow tube with universal joints at both ends that carries power from the transmission to the differential on front-engined rear wheel drive vehicles.

Proportioning valve A hydraulic control valve which limits the amount of pressure to the rear brakes during panic stops to prevent wheel lock-up.

R

Rack-and-pinion steering A steering system with a pinion gear on the end of the steering shaft that mates with a rack (think of a geared wheel opened up and laid flat). When the steering wheel is turned, the pinion turns, moving the rack to the left or right. This movement is transmitted through the track rods to the steering arms at the wheels.

Radiator A liquid-to-air heat transfer device designed to reduce the temperature of the coolant in an internal combustion engine cooling system.

Refrigerant Any substance used as a heat transfer agent in an air-conditioning system. R-12 has been the principle refrigerant for many years; recently, however, manufacturers have begun using R-134a, a non-CFC substance that is considered less harmful to the ozone in the upper atmosphere.

Rocker arm A lever arm that rocks on a shaft or pivots on a stud. In an overhead valve engine, the rocker arm converts the upward movement of the pushrod into a downward movement to open a valve.

Rotor In a distributor, the rotating device inside the cap that connects the centre electrode and the outer terminals as it turns, distributing the high voltage from the coil secondary winding to the proper spark plug. Also, that part of an alternator which rotates inside the stator. Also, the rotating assembly of a turbocharger, including the compressor wheel, shaft and turbine wheel.

Runout The amount of wobble (in-and-out movement) of a gear or wheel as it's rotated. The amount a shaft rotates "out-of-true." The out-of-round condition of a rotating part.

S

Sealant A liquid or paste used to prevent leakage at a joint. Sometimes used in conjunction with a gasket.

Sealed beam lamp An older headlight design which integrates the reflector, lens and filaments into a hermetically-sealed one-piece unit. When a filament burns out or the lens cracks, the entire unit is simply replaced.

Serpentine drivebelt A single, long, wide accessory drivebelt that's used on some newer vehicles to drive all the accessories, instead of a series of smaller, shorter belts. Serpentine drivebelts are usually tensioned by an automatic tensioner.

Serpentine drivebelt

Shim Thin spacer, commonly used to adjust the clearance or relative positions between two parts. For example, shims inserted into or under bucket tappets control valve clearances. Clearance is adjusted by changing the thickness of the shim.

Slide hammer A special puller that screws into or hooks onto a component such as a shaft or bearing; a heavy sliding handle on the shaft bottoms against the end of the shaft to knock the component free.

Sprocket A tooth or projection on the periphery of a wheel, shaped to engage with a chain or drivebelt. Commonly used to refer to the sprocket wheel itself.

Starter inhibitor switch On vehicles with an automatic transmission, a switch that prevents starting if the vehicle is not in Neutral or Park.

Strut See MacPherson strut.

T

Tappet A cylindrical component which transmits motion from the cam to the valve stem, either directly or via a pushrod and rocker arm. Also called a cam follower.

Thermostat A heat-controlled valve that regulates the flow of coolant between the cylinder block and the radiator, so maintaining optimum engine operating temperature. A thermostat is also used in some air cleaners in which the temperature is regulated.

Thrust bearing The bearing in the clutch assembly that is moved in to the release levers by clutch pedal action to disengage the clutch. Also referred to as a release bearing.

Timing belt A toothed belt which drives the camshaft. Serious engine damage may result if it breaks in service.

Timing chain A chain which drives the camshaft.

Toe-in The amount the front wheels are closer together at the front than at the rear. On rear wheel drive vehicles, a slight amount of toe-in is usually specified to keep the front wheels running parallel on the road by offsetting other forces that tend to spread the wheels apart.

Toe-out The amount the front wheels are closer together at the rear than at the front. On front wheel drive vehicles, a slight amount of toe-out is usually specified.

Tools For full information on choosing and using tools, refer to the *Haynes Automotive Tools Manual.*

Tracer A stripe of a second colour applied to a wire insulator to distinguish that wire from another one with the same colour insulator.

Tune-up A process of accurate and careful adjustments and parts replacement to obtain the best possible engine performance.

Turbocharger A centrifugal device, driven by exhaust gases, that pressurises the intake air. Normally used to increase the power output from a given engine displacement, but can also be used primarily to reduce exhaust emissions (as on VW's "Umwelt" Diesel engine).

U

Universal joint or U-joint A double-pivoted connection for transmitting power from a driving to a driven shaft through an angle. A U-joint consists of two Y-shaped yokes and a cross-shaped member called the spider.

V

Valve A device through which the flow of liquid, gas, vacuum, or loose material in bulk may be started, stopped, or regulated by a movable part that opens, shuts, or partially obstructs one or more ports or passageways. A valve is also the movable part of such a device.

Valve clearance The clearance between the valve tip (the end of the valve stem) and the rocker arm or tappet. The valve clearance is measured when the valve is closed.

Vernier caliper A precision measuring instrument that measures inside and outside dimensions. Not quite as accurate as a micrometer, but more convenient.

Viscosity The thickness of a liquid or its resistance to flow.

Volt A unit for expressing electrical "pressure" in a circuit. One volt that will produce a current of one ampere through a resistance of one ohm.

W

Welding Various processes used to join metal items by heating the areas to be joined to a molten state and fusing them together. For more information refer to the *Haynes Automotive Welding Manual.*

Wiring diagram A drawing portraying the components and wires in a vehicle's electrical system, using standardised symbols. For more information refer to the *Haynes Automotive Electrical and Electronic Systems Manual.*

Note: *References throughout this index are in the form "Chapter number"•"page number"*

A

Accelerator cable
carburettor engines – 4A•4
multi-point fuel injection engines – 4C•3
single-point fuel injection engines – 4B•3
Accelerator pedal
carburettor engines – 4A•5
multi-point fuel injection engines – 4C•3
single-point fuel injection engines – 4B•4
Accelerator pedal switch – 4B•8
Air cleaner assembly
carburettor engines – 4A•3
multi-point fuel injection engines – 4C•2
single-point fuel injection engines – 4B•3
Air cleaner element renewal – 1•17
Air control valve – 4C•6
Air manifold – 4D•8
Air pump – 4D•7, 4D•8
drivebelt check and renewal – 1•11
Air temperature control
single-point fuel injection engines – 4B•3
single-point fuel injection engines – 4B•3
Air temperature sensor
multi-point fuel injection engines – 4C•7
single-point fuel injection engines – 4B•8
Air vent assembly – 3•12
Airbag system – 12B•10
Alternator – 5A•6
Antifreeze – 3•2
Anti-run-on valve – 4A•18
Anti-theft alarm system components – 12A•17, 12B•9
Automatic transmission – 2C•4, 2C•10, 7B•1 *et seq*, REF•17
Auxiliary cooling fan – 3•7
Auxiliary drivebelt check and renewal – 1•10
Auxiliary driving light – 12A•8

B

Ballasted ignition system – 5B•4
Battery – 0•5, 0•15, 5A•3
Battery condition indicator – 12B•9
Big-end bearings – 2C•18, 2C•21
Bleeding
brakes – 9•2
clutch – 6•2
Body electrical system – October 1996 models onward – 12B•1 *et seq*
Body electrical system – pre-October 1996 models – 12A•1 *et seq*
Bodywork and fittings – October 1996 models onward – 11B•1 *et seq*
Bodywork and fittings – pre-October 1996 models – 11A•1 *et seq*
Bodywork, paint and exterior trim check – 1•17
Bonnet – 11A•8
check and lubrication – 1•17
lock
October 1996 models onward – 11B•3
pre-October 1996 model – 11A•8
switch (anti-theft alarm system)
October 1996 models onward – 12B•10
pre-October 1996 models – 12A•17
Boot
check and lubrication – 1•17
lid – 11A•8
lock – 11A•9
switch (anti-theft alarm system)
October 1996 models onward – 12B•10
pre-October 1996 models – 12A•17

Braking system – 1•17, 9•1 *et seq*, REF•9, REF•10
drum – 1•7
handbrake – 1•8
fault finding – REF•18
fluid – 0•14, 0•18, 1•21
wear check – 1•14, 1•15
Brushes – 5A•4, 5A•6
Bulbs (exterior lights)
October 1996 models onward – 12B•4
pre-October 1996 models – 12A•7
Bulbs (interior lights)
October 1996 models onward – 12B•6
pre-October 1996 models – 12A•9
Bumpers
October 1996 models onward – 11B•4
pre-October 1996 model – 11A•12

C

Cables
accelerator
carburettor engines – 4A•4
multi-point fuel injection engines – 4C•3
single-point fuel injection engines – 4B•3
bonnet lock release – 11A•8, 11B•3
choke – 4A•5
gear selector – 7B•2, 7B•5
handbrake – 9•9
heater – 3•8
speedometer
October 1996 models onward – 12B•9
pre-October 1996 models – 12A•16
Calipers – 9•8
Camshaft and tappets – 2C•13
Camshaft position sensor – 4C•7
Capacitor – 5B•8
Carburettor – 4A•8, 4A•9
dashpot oil – 0•18
Carpets – 11A•2
Cassette player – 12B•9
Catalytic converter – 4D•3, 4D•8, 4D•9
Centre console – 11A•11
Changing the wheel – 0•9
Charcoal canister – 4D•6
Charging – 5A•3
alternator – 5A•6
dynamo – 5A•4
Check valve – 4D•7, 4D•8
Choke cable – 4A•5
Clock – 12B•9
Clutch – 1•17, 6•1 *et seq*
check – 1•12
fault finding – REF•16
fluid – 0•14, 0•18
return stop adjustment – 1•16
Coil – 5B•14
Companion box – 11B•6
Compression test
October 1996 models onward – 2B•3
pre-October 1996 models – 2A•3
Condenser – 5B•8
Cone spring
front – 10•8
rear – 10•11
Connecting rods – 2C•15, 2C•21
Console – 11A•11

Constant velocity joint – 8•3, 8•4
Contact breaker ignition system – 5B•3, 5B•4, 5B•6, 5B•8
Control box – 1•16, 5A•5
Conversion factors – REF•2
Coolant – 0•13, 0•18, 1•20
 temperature sensor
  multi-point fuel injection engines – 4C•7
  single-point fuel injection engines – 4B•8
Cooling, heating and ventilation systems – 3•1 *et seq*
 fault finding – REF•15
Crankcase emission control – 4D•1, 4D•5
Crankshaft – 2C•16, 2C•20
Crankshaft oil seals
 October 1996 models onward – 2B•10
 pre-October 1996 models – 2A•11
Crankshaft position sensor
 distributor ignition system – 5B•15
 distributorless ignition system – 5C•3
Crankshaft pulley
 October 1996 models onward – 2B•5
 pre-October 1996 models – 2A•5
Cut-out adjustment – 5A•5
Cylinder block/crankcase – 2C•17
Cylinder head – 2C•11
 carburettor engines
  pre-October 1996 models – 2A•8
 fuel injection engines
  October 1996 models onward – 2B•8
  pre-October 1996 models – 2A•10

D

Depressurisation (fuel system)
 multi-point fuel injection engines – 4C•3
 single-point fuel injection engines – 4B•4
Dim-dip lighting system components – 12A•11
Dimensions and weights – REF•1
Direction indicator
 October 1996 models onward – 12B•5
 pre-October 1996 models – 12A•8
DIS module – 5C•2
Disc brake
 caliper – 9•8
 pads – 9•7
Disconnecting the battery – REF•5
Discs – 9•8
Distributor – 5B•9, 5B•10
 check – 1•18
 driveshaft
  pre-October 1996 models – 2A•14
 lubrication – 1•16
Distributor ignition system – 5B•1 *et seq*
Distributorless ignition system – 5C•1 *et seq*
Diverter valve – 4D•7, 4D•8
Doors – REF•9
 exterior handle
  October 1996 models onward – 11B•3
  pre-October 1996 model – 11A•7
 glass
  October 1996 models onward – 11B•2
  pre-October 1996 model – 11A•6
 hinge – 11A•5
 interior trim panel
  October 1996 models onward – 11B•2
  pre-October 1996 model – 11A•4
 lock
  October 1996 models onward – 11B•3
  pre-October 1996 model – 11A•6, 11A•9

 lubrication – 1•17
 pillar switch
  October 1996 models onward – 12B•4
  pre-October 1996 models – 12A•6
 striker plate – 11A•8
 window – 11A•10
Drivebelt check and renewal – 1•10, 1•11
Driveshaft flange oil seals – 7A•4
Driveshafts – 8•1, REF•10
 gaiter check – 1•14
 fault finding – REF•17
Driving light
 October 1996 models onward – 12B•5
 pre-October 1996 models – 12A•8
Drum brake – 9•4
 adjustment – 1•7
 shoes – 9•5
 wheel cylinder – 9•6
Dynamo – 5A•4
 check and lubrication – 1•16

E

ECU
 anti-theft alarm system
  pre-October 1996 models – 12A•17
  October 1996 models onward – 12B•9
 engine management
  multi-point fuel injection engines – 4C•7
  single-point fuel injection engines – 4B•7
Electrical equipment – 1•17, REF•9
Electrical systems – 0•16
 fault finding – 12A•3, REF•20
Electronic ignition system – 5B•4, 5B•5, 5B•6
Emission control equipment check – 1•19
Emission system – REF•11
Engine
 fault finding – 0•7, REF•13, REF•14
  distributor ignition system – 5B•5
  distributorless ignition system – 5C•2
Engine in-car repair procedures – October 1996 models onward – 2B•1 *et seq*
Engine in-car repair procedures – pre-October 1996 models – 2A•1 *et seq*
Engine management ECU
 multi-point fuel injection engines – 4C•7
 single-point fuel injection engines – 4B•7
Engine oil – 0•12, 0•18
 filter renewal – 1•12
Engine removal and overhaul procedures – 2C•1 *et seq*
Evaporative emission control – 4D•1, 4D•5
Exhaust and emission control systems – 4D•1 *et seq*
Exhaust manifold – 4D•4
Exhaust system – 4D•1, 4D•2, 4D•3, REF•10, REF•11
 check – 1•9

F

Facia gauge illumination – 12B•6
Facia
 October 1996 models onward – 11B•3
 pre-October 1996 model – 11A•10
 switches
  October 1996 models onward – 12B•3
  pre-October 1996 models – 12A•5
 top rail cover
  October 1996 models onward – 11B•4
  pre-October 1996 model – 11A•10

Fan – 3•7
Fault finding – REF•12 et seq
  automatic transmission – REF•17
  braking system – REF•18
  clutch – REF•16
  cooling system – REF•15
  ignition system
    distributor ignition system – 5B•5
    distributorless ignition system – 5C•2
  driveshafts – REF•17
  electrical system – REF•20
  engine – 0•7, REF•13, REF•14
  fuel and exhaust systems – REF•15
    carburettor engines – 4A•9, 4A•13
  manual gearbox – REF•16
  suspension and steering systems – REF•19
Filter
  air – 1•17
    carburettor engines – 4A•3
    multi-point fuel injection engines – 4C•2
    single-point fuel injection engines – 4B•3
  fuel – 1•21
  oil – 1•12
  vacuum servo unit – 9•18
Flywheel – 6•5, 6•6, 6•8, 6•9
Foglight
  October 1996 models onward – 12B•5, 12B•6
  pre-October 1996 models – 12A•9
Footbrake – REF•8
Footwell light – 12A•9
Fresh air vent assembly – 3•12
Fuel and temperature gauge – 12A•15
Fuel cut-off inertia switch
  multi-point fuel injection engines – 4C•8
  single-point fuel injection engines – 4B•8
Fuel filter renewal – 1•21
Fuel gauge sender unit
  carburettor engines – 4A•6
  multi-point fuel injection engines – 4C•4
  single-point fuel injection engines – 4B•5
Fuel hoses – 1•15
Fuel injector(s)
  single-point fuel injection engines – 4B•6
  multi-point fuel injection engines – 4C•5
Fuel pressure regulator
  multi-point fuel injection engines – 4C•6
  single-point fuel injection engines – 4B•7
Fuel pump
  carburettor engines – 4A•5, 4A•6
  multi-point fuel injection engines – 4C•4
  single-point fuel injection engines – 4B•5
Fuel system – carburettor engines – 4A•1 et seq, REF•11, REF•15
Fuel system – multi-point fuel injection engines – 4C•1 et seq, REF•11, REF•15
Fuel system – single-point fuel injection engines – 4B•1 et seq, REF•11, REF•15
Fuel system components, checks and lubrication – 1•16
Fuel tank breather – 4D•7
Fuel tank
  carburettor engines – 4A•7
  multi-point fuel injection engines – 4C•4
  single-point fuel injection engines – 4B•5
Fuses and relays
  October 1996 models onward – 12B•2
  pre-October 1996 models – 12A•4

G

Gaiters
  driveshaft – 8•4
    check – 1•14
  steering rack – 10•17
Gear lever – 7A•1
  remote control housing – 7A•2
Gear selector
  automatic transmission
    cable – 7B•2, 7B•5
    lever housing – 7B•5
General repair procedures – REF•4
Glass
  door
    October 1996 models onward – 11B•2
    pre-October 1996 model – 11A•6, 11A•10
  quarterlight – 11A•10
  rear – 11A•10
  side screen – 11A•10
Glossary of technical terms – REF•21 et seq
Glovebox light – 12A•10
Governor control rod – 7B•3
Grille panel
  October 1996 models onward – 11B•4
  pre-October 1996 model – 11A•11
Gulp valve – 4D•7, 4D•8

H

Handbrake – REF•8
  cable – 9•9
  check and adjustment – 1•8
  lever – 9•11
Handle – 11A•7, 11B•3
Headlight
  adjuster motor – 12B•7
  beam alignment check – 1•12
    October 1996 models onward – 12B•7
    pre-October 1996 models – 12A•10
  bulb– 12A•7, 12B•4
  levelling switch – 12B•3
Heat shields – 4D•4
Heater assembly – 3•9
Heater water valve – 3•8
  control cable – 3•8
Helper spring – 10•12
High-level stop-light – 12B•5
Hinge door – 11A•5
Horn – 12A•11, 12B•7
  switches – 12B•3
Hoses – 1•15, 3•2, 9•4
HT lead check – 1•18
Hub bearings
  check – 1•9
  front – 10•4
  rear – 10•11
Hydraulic pipes and hoses – 9•4
Hydrolastic suspension system – 10•3
  displacer unit – 10•9, 10•11

I

Idle air control valve – 4C•6
Idle speed and mixture adjustment – 4A•15, 4A•17
Idler gear endfloat adjustment – 7A•4
Ignition coil – 5B•14

Ignition switch
October 1996 models onward – 12B•4
pre-October 1996 models – 12A•6
Ignition timing
distributor ignition system – 5B•15, 5B•16
distributorless ignition system – 5C•3
Inertia switch
multi-point fuel injection engines – 4C•8
single-point fuel injection engines – 4B•8
Inhibitor switch – 5B•16
Injector housing – 4B•6
Injectors
multi-point fuel injection engines – 4C•5
single-point fuel injection engines – 4B•6
Inlet air temperature sensor
multi-point fuel injection engines – 4C•7
single-point fuel injection engines – 4B•8
Inlet manifold
carburettor engines – 4A•18
multi-point fuel injection engines – 4C•8
PTC heater – 4B•8
single-point fuel injection engines – 4B•9
Instrument and warning lights
October 1996 models onward – 12B•6
pre-October 1996 models – 12A•10
Instrument panel
October 1996 models onward – 12B•7, 12B•8
pre-October 1996 models – 12A•14, 12A•15
Interior courtesy light
October 1996 models onward – 12B•6
pre-October 1996 models – 12A•9
Introduction to the Mini – 0•6

J

Jacking and vehicle support – REF•5
Jump starting – 0•8

L

Lambda sensor – 4D•8
Line fuses – 12A•5, 12B•3
Locks
bonnet – 11A•8, 11B•3
boot lid – 11A•9
door
October 1996 models onward – 11B•3
pre-October 1996 models – 11A•6, 11A•9
Loudspeakers – 12B•9
Lower suspension arm – 10•7
Lubricants and fluids – 0•18

M

Main bearings – 2C•18, 2C•20
Maintenance schedule – 1•3
Manifold absolute pressure (MAP) sensor
multi-point fuel injection engines – 4C•7
single-point fuel injection engines – 4B•7
Manifold PTC heater – 4B•8
Manifolds
carburettor engines – 4A•18
multi-point fuel injection engines – 4C•8
single-point fuel injection engines – 4B•9
Manual transmission – 2C•4, 2C•6, 2C•7, 7A•1 *et seq*, REF•16
Master cylinder
brakes – 9•11, 9•13, 9•14, 9•15
clutch – 6•4
Mirrors – REF•8

Misfire
distributor ignition system – 5B•5
distributorless ignition system – 5C•2
Mixture adjustment – 4A•15, 4A•17
MOT test checks – REF•8 *et seq*
Mountings
October 1996 models onward – 2B•12
pre-October 1996 models – 2A•13

N

Number plate light
October 1996 models onward – 12B•6
pre-October 1996 models – 12A•9

O

Oil
carburettor dashpot – 0•18
engine/transmission – 0•12, 0•18, 1•12
Oil cooler – 2A•16
Oil filter housing and delivery pipe – 2A•15
Oil pressure relief valve
October 1996 models onward – 2B•13
pre-October 1996 models – 2A•15
Oil pressure switch – 2B•13
Oil pump – 2C•14
Oil seals – REF•4
automatic transmission – 7B•5
crankshaft
October 1996 models onward – 2B•10
pre-October 1996 models – 2A•11
manual transmission – 7A•4
primary gear
October 1996 models onward – 2B•10
pre-October 1996 models – 2A•11
timing cover
October 1996 models onward – 2B•10
pre-October 1996 models – 2A•11
Oil temperature gauge – 12B•9
Oil temperature sensor – 2B•14
Open-circuit – 12A•3

P

Pads – 9•7
Pedals
accelerator
carburettor engines – 4A•5
multi-point fuel injection engines – 4C•3
single-point fuel injection engines – 4B•4, 4B•8
brake – 9•18
clutch – 6•5
Piston rings – 2C•19
Piston/connecting rod assemblies – 2C•15, 2C•21
Plastic components – 11A•3
Points – 5B•3, 5B•4, 5B•6, 5B•8
Pressure check
fuel system
multi-point fuel injection engines – 4C•3
single-point fuel injection engines – 4B•4
Pressure differential warning actuator – 9•17
Pressure regulating valve – 9•16
Pressure regulator
multi-point fuel injection engines – 4C•6
single-point fuel injection engines – 4B•7
Primary gear endfloat adjustment – 7A•4

Primary gear oil seal
  October 1996 models onward – 2B•10
  pre-October 1996 models – 2A•11
Printed circuit & voltage stabiliser – 12A•16
PTC heater – 4B•9
Puncture repair – 0•9
Purge control valve – 4D•7

Q

Quarterlight glass – 11A•10

R

Radiator
  front-mounted – 3•4
  side-mounted – 3•3
Radio – 12A•16, 12B•9
Radius arm – 1•9, 10•12
Rear combination light – 12B•5
Rear quarter companion box – 11B•6
Relays
  lambda sensor – 4D•8
  module
    multi-point fuel injection engines – 4C•8
    single-point fuel injection engines – 4B•8
  October 1996 models onward – 12B•2
  pre-October 1996 models – 12A•4
  PTC heater – 4B•9
Release bearing – 6•11
Reluctor ring
  distributor ignition system – 5B•15
  distributorless ignition system – 5C•3
Reversing light – 12A•9
Reversing light switch
  automatic transmission – 7B•2
  manual transmission
    October 1996 models onward – 12B•4
    pre-October 1996 models – 12A•6
Rocker cover
  October 1996 models onward – 2B•3
  pre-October 1996 models – 2A•4
Rocker shaft assembly
  October 1996 models onward – 2B•8
  pre-October 1996 models – 2A•7
Rotor arm and HT lead check – 1•18
Routine maintenance – bodywork and underframe – 11A•1
Routine maintenance – upholstery and carpets – 11A•2
Routine maintenance and servicing – 1•1 *et seq*
Rubber cone spring
  front – 10•8
  rear – 10•11
Rubber gaiter
  driveshaft – 8•4
  steering rack – 10•17

S

Safety first! – 0•5, 0•14
Screen washer fluid – 0•15
Seat belts
  check – 1•12
  October 1996 models onward – 11B•5
Seats
  check – 1•12
  October 1996 models onward – 11B•5
Selector shaft oil seal – 7A•5
Servicing specifications – 1•2
Servo unit – 9•17

Shock absorbers – REF•9, REF•10
  front – 10•9
  rear – 10•12
Shoes – 9•5
Short-circuit – 12A•4
Side screen window – 11A•10
Sidelight
  October 1996 models onward – 12B•5
  pre-October 1996 models – 12A•8
Silencer – 4D•3
Single stalk multifunction switch – 12A•5
Slave cylinder – 6•3, 6•4
Solenoid valve – 5B•16
Spare parts – REF•3
Spark plug renewal – 1•19
Speedometer cable
  October 1996 models onward – 12B•9
  pre-October 1996 models – 12A•16
Springs – REF•10
Starter inhibitor switch – 7B•1
Starter motor – 5A•7, 5A•8
Starter solenoid – 5A•8
Starting and charging systems – 5A•1 *et seq*
Start-up after overhaul and reassembly – 2C•22
Steering – 1•17, REF•9, REF•10
  lubrication – 1•14
  angles – 10•18
  check – 1•8
Steering column – 10•15, 10•16, 10•17, REF•8
  switches
    October 1996 models onward – 12B•3
    pre-October 1996 models – 12A•5
Steering gear – 10•17, 10•18
Steering wheel – 10•15, REF•8
Stepper motor – 4B•7
Stop-light
  pre-October 1996 models – 12A•6, 12A•8
  October 1996 models onward – 12B•4, 12B•5
Subframe mountings
  front – 10•10
  rear – 10•13
Sunroof components
  October 1996 models onward – 11B•5
  pre-October 1996 model – 11A•12
Suspension and steering – 1•17, REF•9, REF•10, 10•1 *et seq*
  arm mountings check – 1•9
  check – 1•8
  fault finding – REF•19
  lubrication – 1•14
Switches
  accelerator pedal – 4B•8
  auxiliary cooling fan – 3•7
  bonnet anti-theft alarm system
    October 1996 models onward – 12B•10
    pre-October 1996 models – 12A•17
  boot anti-theft alarm system
    October 1996 models onward – 12B•10
    pre-October 1996 models – 12A•17
  door pillar
    October 1996 models onward – 12B•4
    pre-October 1996 models – 12A•6
  facia
    October 1996 models onward – 12B•3
    pre-October 1996 models – 12A•5
  fuel cut-off
    multi-point fuel injection engines – 4C•8
    single-point fuel injection engines – 4B•8
  headlight levelling – 12B•3

horn – 12B•3
ignition
  October 1996 models onward – 12B•4
  pre-October 1996 models – 12A•6
illumination
  October 1996 models onward – 12B•6
  pre-October 1996 models – 12A•10
oil pressure
  October 1996 models onward – 2B•13
  pre-October 1996 models – 12A•5
reversing light (automatic transmission) – 7B•2
reversing light (manual transmission)
  October 1996 models onward – 12B•4
  pre-October 1996 models – 12A•6
starter inhibitor – 7B•1
steering column
  October 1996 models onward – 12B•3
  pre-October 1996 models – 12A•5
stop-light
  October 1996 models onward – 12B•4
  pre-October 1996 models – 12A•6
Swivel hub – 10•3
balljoints – 10•6
check – 1•9

T

Tachometer – 12A•16
Tail light
  pre-October 1996 models – 12A•8
  October 1996 models onward – 12B•5
Tailgate – 11A•9
Tappets – 2C•13
Temperature gauge
  October 1996 models onward – 12B•9
  pre-October 1996 models – 12A•15
Temperature sensor
  multi-point fuel injection engines – 4C•7
  October 1996 models onward – 2B•14
  single-point fuel injection engines – 4B•8
Thermac switch – 4B•3
Thermostat – 3•5
Throttle body
  multi-point fuel injection engines – 4C•5
  single-point fuel injection engines – 4B•5
Throttle potentiometer
  multi-point fuel injection engines – 4C•6
  single-point fuel injection engines – 4B•7
Throw-out stop – 6•2
Tie-bar – 10•7
  October 1996 models onward – 2B•12
  pre-October 1996 models – 2A•14
Tie-rod outer balljoint – 10•17
Timing chain, tensioner and sprockets
  October 1996 models onward – 2B•6
  pre-October 1996 models – 2A•6
Timing cover oil seal
  October 1996 models onward – 2B•10
  pre-October 1996 models – 2A•11
Timing
  distributor ignition system – 5B•15, 5B•16
  distributorless ignition system – 5C•3
Tools and working facilities – REF•4, REF•6 *et seq*
Top Dead Centre (TDC) for number one piston location
  October 1996 models onward – 2B•4
  pre-October 1996 models – 2A•4
Torque converter – 2A•12

Transfer gears
  automatic transmission – 7B•5
  manual transmission – 7A•3, 7A•4
Transmission – 2C•4, 2C•6, 2C•7, 2C•10
  mountings
    October 1996 models onward – 2B•12
    pre-October 1996 models – 2A•13
  oil – 0•12, 0•18
Transmission-controlled ignition advance – 5B•16
Trim – 11A•12
  October 1996 models onward – 11B•2, 11B•6
  pre-October 1996 model – 11A•4
Twin stalk multifunction switch – 12A•5
Tyres – 0•17, REF•11
  pressures – 0•18

U

Underbody and fuel/brake line check – 1•9
Underbonnet check for fluid leaks and hose condition – 1•15
Underbonnet check points – 0•11
Unleaded petrol
  carburettor engines – 4A•8
  multi-point fuel injection engines – 4C•4
  single-point fuel injection engines – 4B•5
Upper suspension arm – 10•8

V

Vacuum hoses – 1•15
Vacuum servo unit – 9•17
  air filter – 9•18
Vacuum valve – 4D•6
Valve clearances
  October 1996 models onward – 2B•4
  pre-October 1996 models – 2A•5
Valves – 2C•13
Vehicle identification – REF•3, REF•9
Voltage regulator adjustment – 5A•5
Voltage stabiliser – 12A•16

W

Warning lights – 12A•10
Washer pump
  October 1996 models onward – 12B•7
  pre-October 1996 models – 12A•13
Water pump
  front-mounted radiator – 3•7
  side-mounted radiator – 3•6
Weekly checks – 0•11 *et seq*
Weights – REF•1
Wheels – REF•11
  alignment and steering angles – 10•18
  bearings – REF•10
  changing – 0•9
Wheel cylinders – 9•6
Wheelarch extensions – 11B•4
Windscreen – 11A•9, REF•8
Wiper arms – 12A•12
Wiper blades – 0•16
Wiper motor – 12A•12
Wiper wheelbox – 12A•13
Wiring diagrams
  October 1996 models onward – 12B•12 et seq
  pre-October 1996 models – 12A•17 *et seq*
Wooden facia – 11A•10

Haynes Manuals – The Complete UK Car List

Title	Book No.
ALFA ROMEO Alfasud/Sprint (74 - 88) up to F *	0292
Alfa Romeo Alfetta (73 - 87) up to E *	0531
AUDI 80, 90 & Coupe Petrol (79 - Nov 88) up to F	0605
Audi 80, 90 & Coupe Petrol (Oct 86 - 90) D to H	1491
Audi 100 & 200 Petrol (Oct 82 - 90) up to H	0907
Audi 100 & A6 Petrol & Diesel (May 91 - May 97) H to P	3504
Audi A3 Petrol & Diesel (96 - May 03) P to 03	4253
Audi A4 Petrol & Diesel (95 - 00) M to X	3575
Audi A4 Petrol & Diesel (01 - 04) X to 54	4609
AUSTIN A35 & A40 (56 - 67) up to F *	0118
Austin/MG/Rover Maestro 1.3 & 1.6 Petrol (83 - 95) up to M	0922
Austin/MG Metro (80 - May 90) up to G	0718
Austin/Rover Montego 1.3 & 1.6 Petrol (84 - 94) A to L	1066
Austin/MG/Rover Montego 2.0 Petrol (84 - 95) A to M	1067
Mini (59 - 69) up to H *	0527
Mini (69 - 01) up to X	0646
Austin/Rover 2.0 litre Diesel Engine (86 - 93) C to L	1857
Austin Healey 100/6 & 3000 (56 - 68) up to G *	0049
BEDFORD CF Petrol (69 - 87) up to E	0163
Bedford/Vauxhall Rascal & Suzuki Supercarry (86 - Oct 94) C to M	3015
BMW 316, 320 & 320i (4-cyl) (75 - Feb 83) up to Y *	0276
BMW 320, 320i, 323i & 325i (6-cyl) (Oct 77 - Sept 87) up to E	0815
BMW 3- & 5-Series Petrol (81 - 91) up to J	1948
BMW 3-Series Petrol (Apr 91 - 99) H to V	3210
BMW 3-Series Petrol (Sept 98 - 03) S to 53	4067
BMW 520i & 525e (Oct 81 - June 88) up to E	1560
BMW 525, 528 & 528i (73 - Sept 81) up to X *	0632
BMW 5-Series 6-cyl Petrol (April 96 - Aug 03) N to 03	4151
BMW 1500, 1502, 1600, 1602, 2000 & 2002 (59 - 77) up to S *	0240
CHRYSLER PT Cruiser Petrol (00 - 03) W to 53	4058
CITROËN 2CV, Ami & Dyane (67 - 90) up to H	0196
Citroën AX Petrol & Diesel (87 - 97) D to P	3014
Citroën Berlingo & Peugeot Partner Petrol & Diesel (96 - 05) P to 55	4281
Citroën BX Petrol (83 - 94) A to L	0908
Citroën C15 Van Petrol & Diesel (89 - Oct 98) F to S	3509
Citroën C3 Petrol & Diesel (02 - 05) 51 to 05	4197
Citroen C5 Petrol & Diesel (01-08) Y to 08	4745
Citroën CX Petrol (75 - 88) up to F	0528
Citroën Saxo Petrol & Diesel (96 - 04) N to 54	3506
Citroën Visa Petrol (79 - 88) up to F	0620
Citroën Xantia Petrol & Diesel (93 - 01) K to Y	3082
Citroën XM Petrol & Diesel (89 - 00) G to X	3451
Citroën Xsara Petrol & Diesel (97 - Sept 00) R to W	3751
Citroën Xsara Picasso Petrol & Diesel (00 - 02) W to 52	3944
Citroen Xsara Picasso (03-08)	4784
Citroën ZX Diesel (91 - 98) J to S	1922
Citroën ZX Petrol (91 - 98) H to S	1881
Citroën 1.7 & 1.9 litre Diesel Engine (84 - 96) A to N	1379
FIAT 126 (73 - 87) up to E *	0305
Fiat 500 (57 - 73) up to M *	0090
Fiat Bravo & Brava Petrol (95 - 00) N to W	3572
Fiat Cinquecento (93 - 98) K to R	3501
Fiat Panda (81 - 95) up to M	0793
Fiat Punto Petrol & Diesel (94 - Oct 99) L to V	3251
Fiat Punto Petrol (Oct 99 - July 03) V to 03	4066
Fiat Punto Petrol (03-07) 03 to 07	4746
Fiat Regata Petrol (84 - 88) A to F	1167
Fiat Tipo Petrol (88 - 91) E to J	1625
Fiat Uno Petrol (83 - 95) up to M	0923
Fiat X1/9 (74 - 89) up to G *	0273
FORD Anglia (59 - 68) up to G *	0001

Title	Book No.
Ford Capri II (& III) 1.6 & 2.0 (74 - 87) up to E *	0283
Ford Capri II (& III) 2.8 & 3.0 V6 (74 - 87) up to E	1309
Ford Cortina Mk I & Corsair 1500 ('62 - '66) up to D*	0214
Ford Cortina Mk III 1300 & 1600 (70 - 76) up to P *0070
Ford Escort Mk I 1100 & 1300 (68 - 74) up to N *	0171
Ford Escort Mk I Mexico, RS 1600 & RS 2000 (70 - 74) up to N *	0139
Ford Escort Mk II Mexico, RS 1800 & RS 2000 (75 - 80) up to W *	0735
Ford Escort (75 - Aug 80) up to V *	0280
Ford Escort Petrol (Sept 80 - Sept 90) up to H	0686
Ford Escort & Orion Petrol (Sept 90 - 00) H to X	1737
Ford Escort & Orion Diesel (Sept 90 - 00) H to X	4081
Ford Fiesta (76 - Aug 83) up to Y	0334
Ford Fiesta Petrol (Aug 83 - Feb 89) A to F	1030
Ford Fiesta Petrol (Feb 89 - Oct 95) F to N	1595
Ford Fiesta Petrol & Diesel (Oct 95 - Mar 02) N to 02	3397
Ford Fiesta Petrol & Diesel (Apr 02 - 07) 02 to 57	4170
Ford Focus Petrol & Diesel (98 - 01) S to Y	3759
Ford Focus Petrol & Diesel (Oct 01 - 05) 51 to 05	4167
Ford Galaxy Petrol & Diesel (95 - Aug 00) M to W	3984
Ford Granada Petrol (Sept 77 - Feb 85) up to B *	0481
Ford Granada & Scorpio Petrol (Mar 85 - 94) B to M	1245
Ford Ka (96 - 02) P to 52	3570
Ford Mondeo Petrol (93 - Sept 00) K to X	1923
Ford Mondeo Petrol & Diesel (Oct 00 - Jul 03) X to 03	3990
Ford Mondeo Petrol & Diesel (July 03 - 07) 03 to 56	4619
Ford Mondeo Diesel (93 - 96) L to N	3465
Ford Orion Petrol (83 - Sept 90) up to H	1009
Ford Sierra 4-cyl Petrol (82 - 93) up to K	0903
Ford Sierra V6 Petrol (82 - 91) up to J	0904
Ford Transit Petrol (Mk 2) (78 - Jan 86) up to C	0719
Ford Transit Petrol (Mk 3) (Feb 86 - 89) C to G	1468
Ford Transit Diesel (Feb 86 - 99) C to T	3019
Ford Transit Diesel (00-06)	4775
Ford 1.6 & 1.8 litre Diesel Engine (84 - 96) A to N	1172
Ford 2.1, 2.3 & 2.5 litre Diesel Engine (77 - 90) up to H	1606
FREIGHT ROVER Sherpa Petrol (74 - 87) up to E	0463
HILLMAN Avenger (70 - 82) up to Y	0037
Hillman Imp (63 - 76) up to R *	0022
HONDA Civic (Feb 84 - Oct 87) A to E	1226
Honda Civic (Nov 91 - 96) J to N	3199
Honda Civic Petrol (Mar 95 - 00) M to X	4050
Honda Civic Petrol & Diesel (01 - 05) X to 55	4611
Honda CR-V Petrol & Diesel (01-06)	4747
Honda Jazz (01 - Feb 08) 51 - 57	4735
HYUNDAI Pony (85 - 94) C to M	3398
JAGUAR E Type (61 - 72) up to L *	0140
Jaguar MkI & II, 240 & 340 (55 - 69) up to H *	0098
Jaguar XJ6, XJ & Sovereign; Daimler Sovereign (68 - Oct 86) up to D	0242
Jaguar XJ6 & Sovereign (Oct 86 - Sept 94) D to M	3261
Jaguar XJ12, XJS & Sovereign; Daimler Double Six (72 - 88) up to F	0478
JEEP Cherokee Petrol (93 - 96) K to N	1943
LADA 1200, 1300, 1500 & 1600 (74 - 91) up to J	0413
Lada Samara (87 - 91) D to J	1610
LAND ROVER 90, 110 & Defender Diesel (83 - 07) up to 56	3017
Land Rover Discovery Petrol & Diesel (89 - 98) G to S	3016
Land Rover Discovery Diesel (Nov 98 - Jul 04) S to 04	4606
Land Rover Freelander Petrol & Diesel (97 - Sept 03) R to 53	3929
Land Rover Freelander Petrol & Diesel (Oct 03 - Oct 06) 53 to 56	4623

Title	Book No.
Land Rover Series IIA & III Diesel (58 - 85) up to C	0529
Land Rover Series II, IIA & III 4-cyl Petrol (58 - 85) up to C	0314
MAZDA 323 (Mar 81 - Oct 89) up to G	1608
Mazda 323 (Oct 89 - 98) G to R	3455
Mazda 626 (May 83 - Sept 87) up to E	0929
Mazda B1600, B1800 & B2000 Pick-up Petrol (72 - 88) up to F	0267
Mazda RX-7 (79 - 85) up to C *	0460
MERCEDES-BENZ 190, 190E & 190D Petrol & Diesel (83 - 93) A to L	3450
Mercedes-Benz 200D, 240D, 240TD, 300D & 300TD 123 Series Diesel (Oct 76 - 85)	1114
Mercedes-Benz 250 & 280 (68 - 72) up to L *	0346
Mercedes-Benz 250 & 280 123 Series Petrol (Oct 76 - 84) up to B *	0677
Mercedes-Benz 124 Series Petrol & Diesel (85 - Aug 93) C to K	3253
Mercedes-Benz A-Class Petrol & Diesel (98-04) S to 54	4748
Mercedes-Benz C-Class Petrol & Diesel (93 - Aug 00) L to W	3511
Mercedes-Benz C-Class (00-06)	4780
MGA (55 - 62) *	0475
MGB (62 - 80) up to W	0111
MG Midget & Austin-Healey Sprite (58 - 80) up to W *	0265
MINI Petrol (July 01 - 05) Y to 05	4273
MITSUBISHI Shogun & L200 Pick-Ups Petrol (83 - 94) up to M	1944
MORRIS Ital 1.3 (80 - 84) up to B	0705
Morris Minor 1000 (56 - 71) up to K	0024
NISSAN Almera Petrol (95 - Feb 00) N to V	4053
Nissan Almera & Tino Petrol (Feb 00 - 07) V to 56	4612
Nissan Bluebird (May 84 - Mar 86) A to C	1223
Nissan Bluebird Petrol (Mar 86 - 90) C to H	1473
Nissan Cherry (Sept 82 - 86) up to D	1031
Nissan Micra (83 - Jan 93) up to K	0931
Nissan Micra (93 - 02) K to 52	3254
Nissan Micra Petrol (03-07) 52 to 57	4734
Nissan Primera Petrol (90 - Aug 99) H to T	1851
Nissan Stanza (82 - 86) up to D	0824
Nissan Sunny Petrol (May 82 - Oct 86) up to D	0895
Nissan Sunny Petrol (Oct 86 - Mar 91) D to H	1378
Nissan Sunny Petrol (Apr 91 - 95) H to N	3219
OPEL Ascona & Manta (B Series) (Sept 75 - 88) up to F *	0316
Opel Ascona Petrol (81 - 88)	3215
Opel Astra Petrol (Oct 91 - Feb 98)	3156
Opel Corsa Petrol (83 - Mar 93)	3160
Opel Corsa Petrol (Mar 93 - 97)	3159
Opel Kadett Petrol (Nov 79 - Oct 84) up to B	0634
Opel Kadett Petrol (Oct 84 - Oct 91)	3196
Opel Omega & Senator Petrol (Nov 86 - 94)	3157
Opel Rekord Petrol (Feb 78 - Oct 86) up to D	0543
Opel Vectra Petrol (Oct 88 - Oct 95)	3158
PEUGEOT 106 Petrol & Diesel (91 - 04) J to 53	1882
Peugeot 205 Petrol (83 - 97) A to P	0932
Peugeot 206 Petrol & Diesel (98 - 01) S to X	3757
Peugeot 206 Petrol & Diesel (02 - 06) 51 to 06	4613
Peugeot 306 Petrol & Diesel (93 - 02) K to 02	3073
Peugeot 307 Petrol & Diesel (01 - 04) Y to 54	4147
Peugeot 309 Petrol (86 - 93) C to K	1266
Peugeot 405 Petrol (88 - 97) E to P	1559
Peugeot 405 Diesel (88 - 97) E to P	3198
Peugeot 406 Petrol & Diesel (96 - Mar 99) N to T	3394
Peugeot 406 Petrol & Diesel (Mar 99 - 02) T to 52	3982

* Classic reprint

Title	Book No.
Peugeot 505 Petrol (79 - 89) up to G	0762
Peugeot 1.7/1.8 & 1.9 litre Diesel Engine (82 - 96) up to N	0950
Peugeot 2.0, 2.1, 2.3 & 2.5 litre Diesel Engines (74 - 90) up to H	1607
PORSCHE 911 (65 - 85) up to C	0264
Porsche 924 & 924 Turbo (76 - 85) up to C	0397
PROTON (89 - 97) F to P	3255
RANGE ROVER V8 Petrol (70 - Oct 92) up to K	0606
RELIANT Robin & Kitten (73 - 83) up to A *	0436
RENAULT 4 (61 - 86) up to D *	0072
Renault 5 Petrol (Feb 85 - 96) B to N	1219
Renault 9 & 11 Petrol (82 - 89) up to F	0822
Renault 18 Petrol (79 - 86) up to D	0598
Renault 19 Petrol (89 - 96) F to N	1646
Renault 19 Diesel (89 - 96) F to N	1946
Renault 21 Petrol (86 - 94) C to M	1397
Renault 25 Petrol & Diesel (84 - 92) B to K	1228
Renault Clio Petrol (91 - May 98) H to R	1853
Renault Clio Diesel (91 - June 96) H to N	3031
Renault Clio Petrol & Diesel (May 98 - May 01) R to Y	3906
Renault Clio Petrol & Diesel (June '01 - '05) Y to 55	4168
Renault Espace Petrol & Diesel (85 - 96) C to N	3197
Renault Laguna Petrol & Diesel (94 - 00) L to W	3252
Renault Laguna Petrol & Diesel (Feb 01 - Feb 05) X to 54	4283
Renault Mégane & Scénic Petrol & Diesel (96 - 99) N to T	3395
Renault Mégane & Scénic Petrol & Diesel (Apr 99 - 02) T to 52	3916
Renault Megane Petrol & Diesel (Oct 02 - 05) 52 to 55	4284
Renault Scenic Petrol & Diesel (Sept 03 - 06) 53 to 06	4297
ROVER 213 & 216 (84 - 89) A to G	1116
Rover 214 & 414 Petrol (89 - 96) G to N	1689
Rover 216 & 416 Petrol (89 - 96) G to N	1830
Rover 211, 214, 216, 218 & 220 Petrol & Diesel (Dec 95 - 99) N to V	3399
Rover 25 & MG ZR Petrol & Diesel (Oct 99 - 04) V to 54	4145
Rover 414, 416 & 420 Petrol & Diesel (May 95 - 98) M to R	3453
Rover 45 / MG ZS Petrol & Diesel (99 - 05) V to 55	4384
Rover 618, 620 & 623 Petrol & Diesel (93 - 97) K to P	3257
Rover 75 / MG ZT Petrol & Diesel (99 - 06) S to 06	4292
Rover 820, 825 & 827 Petrol (86 - 95) D to N	1380
Rover 3500 (76 - 87) up to E *	0365
Rover Metro, 111 & 114 Petrol (May 90 - 98) G to S	1711
SAAB 95 & 96 (66 - 76) up to R *	0198
Saab 90, 99 & 900 (79 - Oct 93) up to L	0765
Saab 900 (Oct 93 - 98) L to R	3512
Saab 9000 (4-cyl) (85 - 98) C to S	1686
Saab 9-3 Petrol & Diesel (98 - Aug 02) R to 02	4614
Saab 9-3 Petrol & Diesel (02-07) 52 to 57	4749
Saab 9-5 4-cyl Petrol (97 - 04) R to 54	4156
SEAT Ibiza & Cordoba Petrol & Diesel (Oct 93 - Oct 99) L to V	3571
Seat Ibiza & Malaga Petrol (85 - 92) B to K	1609
SKODA Estelle (77 - 89) up to G	0604
Skoda Fabia Petrol & Diesel (00 - 06) W to 06	4376
Skoda Favorit (89 - 96) F to N	1801
Skoda Felicia Petrol & Diesel (95 - 01) M to X	3505
Skoda Octavia Petrol & Diesel (98 - Apr 04) R to 04	4285
SUBARU 1600 & 1800 (Nov 79 - 90) up to H *	0995

Title	Book No.
SUNBEAM Alpine, Rapier & H120 (67 - 74) up to N *	0051
SUZUKI SJ Series, Samurai & Vitara (4-cyl) Petrol (82 - 97) up to P	1942
Suzuki Supercarry & Bedford/Vauxhall Rascal (86 - Oct 94) C to M	3015
TALBOT Alpine, Solara, Minx & Rapier (75 - 86) up to D	0337
Talbot Horizon Petrol (78 - 86) up to D	0473
Talbot Samba (82 - 86) up to D	0823
TOYOTA Avensis Petrol (98 - Jan 03) R to 52	4264
Toyota Carina E Petrol (May 92 - 97) J to P	3256
Toyota Corolla (80 - 85) up to C	0683
Toyota Corolla (Sept 83 - Sept 87) A to E	1024
Toyota Corolla (Sept 87 - Aug 92) E to K	1683
Toyota Corolla Petrol (Aug 92 - 97) K to P	3259
Toyota Corolla Petrol (July 97 - Feb 02) P to 51	4286
Toyota Hi-Ace & Hi-Lux Petrol (69 - Oct 83) up to A	0304
Toyota RAV4 Petrol & Diesel (94-06) L to 55	4750
Toyota Yaris Petrol (99 - 05) T to 05	4265
TRIUMPH GT6 & Vitesse (62 - 74) up to N *	0112
Triumph Herald (59 - 71) up to K *	0010
Triumph Spitfire (62 - 81) up to X	0113
Triumph Stag (70 - 78) up to T *	0441
Triumph TR2, TR3, TR3A, TR4 & TR4A (52 - 67) up to F *	0028
Triumph TR5 & 6 (67 - 75) up to P *	0031
Triumph TR7 (75 - 82) up to Y *	0322
VAUXHALL Astra Petrol (80 - Oct 84) up to B	0635
Vauxhall Astra & Belmont Petrol (Oct 84 - Oct 91) B to J	1136
Vauxhall Astra Petrol (Oct 91 - Feb 98) J to R	1832
Vauxhall/Opel Astra & Zafira Petrol (Feb 98 - Apr 04) R to 04	3758
Vauxhall/Opel Astra & Zafira Diesel (Feb 98 - Apr 04) R to 04	3797
Vauxhall/Opel Astra Petrol (04 - 08)	4732
Vauxhall/Opel Astra Diesel (04 - 08)	4733
Vauxhall/Opel Calibra (90 - 98) G to S	3502
Vauxhall Carlton Petrol (Oct 78 - Oct 86) up to D	0480
Vauxhall Carlton & Senator Petrol (Nov 86 - 94) D to L	1469
Vauxhall Cavalier Petrol (81 - Oct 88) up to F	0812
Vauxhall Cavalier Petrol (Oct 88 - 95) F to N	1570
Vauxhall Chevette (75 - 84) up to B	0285
Vauxhall/Opel Corsa Diesel (Mar 93 - Oct 00) K to X	4087
Vauxhall Corsa Petrol (Mar 93 - 97) K to R	1985
Vauxhall/Opel Corsa Petrol (Apr 97 - Oct 00) P to X	3921
Vauxhall/Opel Corsa Petrol & Diesel (Oct 00 - Sept 03) X to 53	4079
Vauxhall/Opel Corsa Petrol & Diesel (Oct 03 - Aug 06) 53 to 06	4617
Vauxhall/Opel Frontera Petrol & Diesel (91 - Sept 98) J to S	3454
Vauxhall Nova Petrol (83 - 93) up to K	0909
Vauxhall/Opel Omega Petrol (94 - 99) L to T	3510
Vauxhall/Opel Vectra Petrol & Diesel (95 - Feb 99) N to S	3396
Vauxhall/Opel Vectra Petrol & Diesel (Mar 99 - May 02) T to 02	3930
Vauxhall/Opel Vectra Petrol & Diesel (June 02 - Sept 05) 02 to 55	4618
Vauxhall/Opel 1.5, 1.6 & 1.7 litre Diesel Engine (82 - 96) up to N	1222
VW 411 & 412 (68 - 75) up to P *	0091
VW Beetle 1200 (54 - 77) up to S	0036
VW Beetle 1300 & 1500 (65 - 75) up to P	0039

Title	Book No.
VW 1302 & 1302S (70 - 72) up to L *	0110
VW Beetle 1303, 1303S & GT (72 - 75) up to P	0159
VW Beetle Petrol & Diesel (Apr 99 - 07) T to 57	3798
VW Golf & Jetta Mk 1 Petrol 1.1 & 1.3 (74 - 84) up to A	0716
VW Golf, Jetta & Scirocco Mk 1 Petrol 1.5, 1.6 & 1.8 (74 - 84) up to A	0726
VW Golf & Jetta Mk 1 Diesel (78 - 84) up to A	0451
VW Golf & Jetta Mk 2 Petrol (Mar 84 - Feb 92) A to J	1081
VW Golf & Vento Petrol & Diesel (Feb 92 - Mar 98) J to R	3097
VW Golf & Bora Petrol & Diesel (April 98 - 00) R to X	3727
VW Golf & Bora 4-cyl Petrol & Diesel (01 - 03) X to 53	4169
VW Golf & Jetta Petrol & Diesel (04 - 07) 53 to 07	4610
VW LT Petrol Vans & Light Trucks (76 - 87) up to E	0637
VW Passat & Santana Petrol (Sept 81 - May 88) up to E	0814
VW Passat 4-cyl Petrol & Diesel (May 88 - 96) E to P	3498
VW Passat 4-cyl Petrol & Diesel (Dec 96 - Nov 00) P to X	3917
VW Passat Petrol & Diesel (Dec 00 - May 05) X to 05	4279
VW Polo & Derby (76 - Jan 82) up to X	0335
VW Polo (82 - Oct 90) up to H	0813
VW Polo Petrol (Nov 90 - Aug 94) H to L	3245
VW Polo Hatchback Petrol & Diesel (94 - 99) M to S	3500
VW Polo Hatchback Petrol (00 - Jan 02) V to 51	4150
VW Polo Petrol & Diesel (02 - May 05) 51 to 05	4608
VW Scirocco (82 - 90) up to H *	1224
VW Transporter 1600 (68 - 79) up to V	0082
VW Transporter 1700, 1800 & 2000 (72 - 79) up to V *	0226
VW Transporter (air-cooled) Petrol (79 - 82) up to Y *	0638
VW Transporter (water-cooled) Petrol (82 - 90) up to H	3452
VW Type 3 (63 - 73) up to M *	0084
VOLVO 120 & 130 Series (& P1800) (61 - 73) up to M *	0203
Volvo 142, 144 & 145 (66 - 74) up to N *	0129
Volvo 240 Series Petrol (74 - 93) up to K	0270
Volvo 262, 264 & 260/265 (75 - 85) up to C *	0400
Volvo 340, 343, 345 & 360 (76 - 91) up to J	0715
Volvo 440, 460 & 480 Petrol (87 - 97) D to P	1691
Volvo 740 & 760 Petrol (82 - 91) up to J	1258
Volvo 850 Petrol (92 - 96) J to P	3260
Volvo 940 petrol (90 - 98) H to R	3249
Volvo S40 & V40 Petrol (96 - Mar 04) N to 04	3569
Volvo S40 & V50 Petrol & Diesel (Mar 04 - Jun 07) 04 to 07	4731
Volvo S60 Petrol & Diesel (01-08)	4793
Volvo S70, V70 & C70 Petrol (96 - 99) P to V	3573
Volvo V70 / S80 Petrol & Diesel (98 - 05) S to 55	4263

DIY MANUAL SERIES

Title	Book No.
The Haynes Air Conditioning Manual	4192
The Haynes Car Electrical Systems Manual	4251
The Haynes Manual on Bodywork	4198
The Haynes Manual on Brakes	4178
The Haynes Manual on Carburettors	4177
The Haynes Manual on Diesel Engines	4174
The Haynes Manual on Engine Management	4199
The Haynes Manual on Fault Codes	4175
The Haynes Manual on Practical Electrical Systems	4267
The Haynes Manual on Small Engines	4250
The Haynes Manual on Welding	4176

* Classic reprint

Preserving Our Motoring Heritage

> The Model J Duesenberg Derham Tourster. Only eight of these magnificent cars were ever built – this is the only example to be found outside the United States of America

Almost every car you've ever loved, loathed or desired is gathered under one roof at the Haynes Motor Museum. Over 300 immaculately presented cars and motorbikes represent every aspect of our motoring heritage, from elegant reminders of bygone days, such as the superb Model J Duesenberg to curiosities like the bug-eyed BMW Isetta. There are also many old friends and flames. Perhaps you remember the 1959 Ford Popular that you did your courting in? The magnificent 'Red Collection' is a spectacle of classic sports cars including AC, Alfa Romeo, Austin Healey, Ferrari, Lamborghini, Maserati, MG, Riley, Porsche and Triumph.

A Perfect Day Out

Each and every vehicle at the Haynes Motor Museum has played its part in the history and culture of Motoring. Today, they make a wonderful spectacle and a great day out for all the family. Bring the kids, bring Mum and Dad, but above all bring your camera to capture those golden memories for ever. You will also find an impressive array of motoring memorabilia, a comfortable 70 seat video cinema and one of the most extensive transport book shops in Britain. The Pit Stop Cafe serves everything from a cup of tea to wholesome, home-made meals or, if you prefer, you can enjoy the large picnic area nestled in the beautiful rural surroundings of Somerset.

> John Haynes O.B.E., Founder and Chairman of the museum at the wheel of a Haynes Light 12.

> Graham Hill's Lola Cosworth Formula 1 car next to a 1934 Riley Sports.

The Museum is situated on the A359 Yeovil to Frome road at Sparkford, just off the A303 in Somerset. It is about 40 miles south of Bristol, and 25 minutes drive from the M5 intersection at Taunton.

Open 9.30am - 5.30pm (10.00am - 4.00pm Winter) 7 days a week, *except Christmas Day, Boxing Day and New Years Day*

Special rates available for schools, coach parties and outings Charitable Trust No. 292048